EXPLORING MICROSOFT® EXCEL FOR WINDOWS™ 95

VERSION 7.0

Robert T. Grauer / *Maryann Barber*

University of Miami

Prentice Hall, Upper Saddle River, New Jersey 07458

Library of Congress Cataloging-in-Publication Data

Grauer, Robert T. [date]
  Exploring Microsoft Excel for Windows 95 Version 7.0 / Robert T. Grauer,
  Maryann Barber.
    p. cm.
  Includes index.
  ISBN 0-13-503401-9
    1. Microsoft Excel. 2. Business—Computer programs.
  3. Electronic spreadsheets. I. Barber, Maryann M. II. Title.
HF5548.4.M523G72 1996
005.369—dc20   95-12937
                                                          CIP

Acquisitions editor: Carolyn Henderson
Editorial/production supervisor: Greg Hubit Bookworks
Interior and cover design: Suzanne Behnke
Manufacturing buyer: Paul Smolenski
Managing editor: Nicholas Radhuber
Editorial assistant: Audrey Regan
Production coordinator: Renée Pelletier

©1996 by Prentice Hall, Inc.
A Simon & Schuster Company
Upper Saddle River, New Jersey 07458

Printed in the United States of America
10 9 8 7 6 5 4 3 2

ISBN 0-13-503401-9

Prentice Hall International (UK) Limited, *London*
Prentice Hall of Australia Pty. Limited, *Sydney*
Prentice Hall of Canada Inc., *Toronto*
Prentice Hall Hispanoamericano, S.A., *Mexico*
Prentice Hall of India Private Limited, *New Delhi*
Prentice Hall of Japan, Inc., *Tokyo*
Simon & Schuster Asia Pte. Ltd., *Singapore*
Editora Prentice Hall do Brasil, Ltda., *Rio de Janeiro*

CONTENTS

2

Gaining Proficiency: Copying, Formatting, and Isolating Assumptions   41

3

Spreadsheets in Decision Making: What If?   87

4

Graphs and Charts: Delivering a Message   139

5

List and Data Management: Converting Data to Information 197

6

Consolidating Data: 3-D Workbooks and File Linking 251

7

Automating Repetitive Tasks: Macros and Visual Basic   295

Prerequisites: Essentials of Windows 95®

PREFACE

Exploring Microsoft Excel for Windows 95 Version 7.0 is one of several books in the *Exploring Windows 95* series. Other series titles include: *Exploring Windows 95 and Essential Computing Concepts, Exploring Microsoft Word Version 7.0, Exploring Microsoft PowerPoint Version 7.0, Exploring Microsoft Access Version 7.0, Exploring Microsoft Office 95* (a combination of selected chapters from the individual books), *Exploring Lotus 95, Exploring WordPerfect 95,* and *Exploring the Internet.* Each book in the series is suitable on a stand-alone basis for any course that teaches a specific application. Alternatively, several modules can be packaged together for a single course that teaches multiple applications.

The *Exploring Windows* series is different from other texts, both in its scope as well as in the way in which material is presented. Students learn by doing. Concepts are stressed and memorization is minimized. Shortcuts and other important information are consistently highlighted in the many tips that appear throughout the series. Every chapter contains an average of three guided exercises to be completed at the computer.

Each book in the *Exploring Windows* series is accompanied by a comprehensive Instructor's Resource Manual with tests, transparency masters, and student/instructor resource disks. (The Instructor's Resource Manual for the entire series is available on CD-ROM.) Instructors can also use the Prentice Hall Computerized Online Testing System to prepare customized tests for their courses and may obtain Interactive Multimedia courseware as a further supplement. The *Exploring Windows* series is part of the Prentice Hall custom binding program.

What's New

Exploring Microsoft Excel for Windows 95 Version 7.0 is a revision of our existing text, *Exploring Excel 5.0.* In addition to updating the book to reflect changes in the new release, we also sought to add topics that were previously omitted. Chapter 2 has been expanded to include a financial forecast that teaches the development of a spreadsheet model. Chapter 3 now includes Scenario Manager and the Goal Seek command. Chapter 6 is entirely new and focuses on three-dimensional workbooks and file linking. Chapter 7 introduces macros and Visual Basic. Three appendices have also been added. Appendix A focuses on spreadsheet validation, Appendix B covers the Solver add-in, and Appendix C introduces Data Mapping.

We believe, however, that our most significant improvement is the expanded end-of-chapter material, which provides a wide variety of student assignments. Every chapter contains *15 multiple-choice questions* (with answers) so that students can test themselves quickly and objectively. Every chapter has *four conceptual problems* that do not require participation at the computer. Every chapter also has *four computer-based practice exercises* to build student proficiency. And finally, every chapter ends with *four case studies* in which the student is given little guidance in the means of solution. This unique *15-four-by-four-by-four* format provides substantial opportunity for students to master the material while simultaneously giving instructors considerable flexibility in student assignments.

FEATURES AND BENEFITS

Exploring Microsoft Excel Version 7.0 is written for the computer novice and assumes no previous knowledge about Windows 95. A detailed supplement introduces the reader to the operating system and emphasizes the file operations he or she will need.

An introductory section on the Microsoft Office emphasizes the benefits of the common user interface. Although the text assumes no previous knowledge, individuals already acquainted with another Office application can take advantage of what they already know.

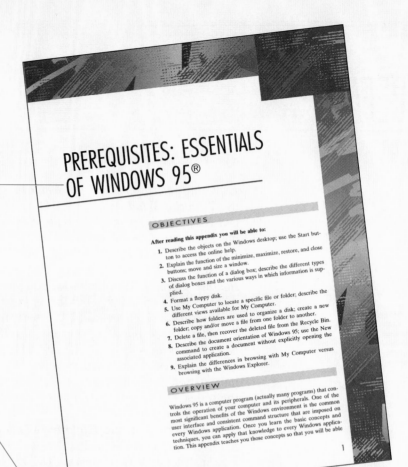

PREREQUISITES: ESSENTIALS OF WINDOWS 95®

OBJECTIVES

After reading this appendix you will be able to:

1. Describe the objects on the Windows desktop; use the Start button to access the online help.
2. Explain the function of the minimize, maximize, restore, and close buttons; move and size a window.
3. Discuss the function of a dialog box; describe the different types of dialog boxes and the various ways in which information is supplied.
4. Format a floppy disk.
5. Use My Computer to locate a specific file or folder; describe the different views available for My Computer.
6. Describe how folders are used to organize a disk; create a new folder; copy and/or move a file from one folder to another.
7. Delete a file, then recover the deleted file from the Recycle Bin.
8. Describe the document orientation of Windows 95; use the New command to create a document without explicitly opening the associated application.
9. Explain the differences in browsing with My Computer versus browsing with the Windows Explorer.

OVERVIEW

Windows 95 is a computer program (actually many programs) that controls the operation of your computer and its peripherals. One of the most significant benefits of the Windows environment is the common user interface and consistent command structure that are imposed on every Windows application. Once you learn the basic concepts and techniques, you can apply that knowledge to every Windows application. This appendix teaches you those concepts so that you will be able

1

---

into a single document. And finally, we include a hands-on exercise that lets you sit down at the computer and apply what you have learned.

TRY THE COLLEGE BOOKSTORE

Any machine you buy will come with Windows 95, but that is only the beginning since you must also obtain the application software you intend to run. Many first-time buyers are surprised that they have to pay extra for software, so you had better allow for software in your budget. Some hardware vendors will bundle (at no additional cost) Microsoft Office as an inducement to buy from them. If you have already purchased your system and you need software, the best place to buy Microsoft Office is the college bookstore, where it can be obtained at a substantial educational discount.

MICROSOFT OFFICE FOR WINDOWS 95

All Office applications share the common user interface for Windows 95 with which you may already be familiar. (If you are new to Windows 95, then read the appendix on the "Essentials of Windows 95," which appears at the end of this book.) Figure 1 displays a screen from each application in the Microsoft Office—Word, Excel, PowerPoint, and Access, in Figures 1a, 1b, 1c, and 1d, respectively. Look closely at Figure 1, and realize that each screen contains both an application window and a document window, and that each document window has been maximized within the application window. The title bars of the application and document windows have been merged into a single title bar that appears at the top of the application window. The title bar displays the application (e.g., Microsoft Word in Figure 1a) as well as the name of the document (Letter to My Instructor in Figure 1a) on which you are working.

All four screens in Figure 1 are similar in appearance despite the fact that the applications accomplish very different tasks. Each application window has an identifying icon, a menu bar, a title bar, and a minimize, maximize or restore, and a close button. Each document window has its own identifying icon, and its own minimize, maximize or restore, and close button. The Windows 95 taskbar appears at the bottom of each application window and shows the open applications. The status bar appears above the taskbar and displays information relevant to the window or selected object.

Each application in Microsoft Office uses a consistent command structure in which the same basic menus are found in all applications. The File, Edit, View, Insert, Tools, Window, and Help menus are present in all four applications. The same commands are found in the same menus. The Save, Open, Print, and Exit commands, for example, are contained in the File menu. The Cut, Copy, Paste, and Undo commands are found in the Edit menu.

The means for accessing the pull-down menus are consistent from one application to the next. Click the menu name on the menu bar, or press the Alt key plus the underlined letter of the menu name; for example, press Alt+F to pull down the File menu. If you already know some keyboard shortcuts in one application, there is a good chance that the shortcuts will work in another application. Ctrl+Home and Ctrl+End, for example, move to the beginning and end of a document, respectively. Ctrl+B, Ctrl+I, and Ctrl+U boldface, italicize, and underline text. Ctrl+X (the "X" is supposed to remind you of a pair of scissors), Ctrl+C, and Ctrl+V will cut, copy, and paste, respectively. You may not know what these

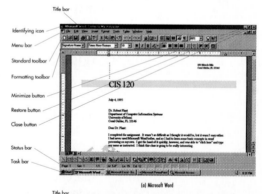

(a) Microsoft Word

(b) Microsoft Excel

FIGURE 1 The Common User Interface

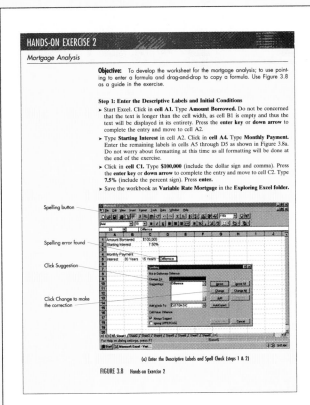

Mortgage Analysis

Objective: To develop the worksheet for the mortgage analysis; to use pointing to enter a formula and drag-and-drop to copy a formula. Use Figure 3.8 as a guide in the exercise.

Step 1: Enter the Descriptive Labels and Initial Conditions

➤ Start Excel. Click in **cell A1.** Type **Amount Borrowed.** Do not be concerned that the text is longer than the cell width, as cell B1 is empty and thus the text will be displayed in its entirety. Press the **enter key** or **down arrow** to complete the entry and move to cell A2.

➤ Type **Starting Interest** in cell A2. Click in **cell A4.** Type **Monthly Payment.** Enter the remaining labels in cells A5 through D5 as shown in Figure 3.8a. Do not worry about formatting at this time as all formatting will be done at the end of the exercise.

➤ Click in **cell C1.** Type **$100,000** (include the dollar sign and comma). Press the **enter key** or **down arrow** to complete the entry and move to cell C2. Type **7.5%** (include the percent sign). Press **enter.**

➤ Save the workbook as **Variable Rate Mortgage** in the **Exploring Excel folder.**

Spelling button

Spelling error found

Click Suggestion

Click Change to make the correction

(a) Enter the Descriptive Labels and Spell Check (steps 1 & 2)

FIGURE 3.8   Hands-on Exercise 2

RESET THE TIPWIZARD

The TipWizard will not repeat a suggestion (from an earlier session) unless you reset it at the start of the new session. This is especially important in a laboratory situation where you are sharing a computer with many other students. Pull down the Tools menu, click Options, and click the General tab. Click the check box to Reset TipWizard, then click OK. Click the TipWizard button on the Standard toolbar to open (close) the TipWizard toolbar to view suggestions. You can view the suggestions as they occur, or you can wait until the end of the session to view all of the suggestions at one time.

Step 2: The Spell Check

➤ Click in **cell A1** to begin the spell check at the beginning of the worksheet.

➤ Click the **Spelling button** on the Standard toolbar to initiate the spell check as shown in Figure 3.8a. Make corrections, as necessary, just as you would in Microsoft Word.

➤ Save the workbook.

Step 3: Copy the Column of Interest Rates (the Fill Handle)

➤ Click in **cell A6.** Type **=C2** to reference the starting interest rate in cell C2.

➤ Click in **cell A7.** Type the formula **=A6+.01** to compute the interest rate in this cell, which is one percent more than the interest rate in row 6. Press **enter.**

➤ Click in **cell A7.** Point to the **fill handle** in the lower corner of cell A7. The mouse pointer changes to a thin crosshair.

➤ Drag the **fill handle** over cells **A8** through **A11.** A border appears, indicating the destination range as in Figure 3.8b. Release the mouse to complete the copy operation. The formula and associated percentage format in cell A7 have been copied to cells A8 through A11.

➤ Click in **cell C2.** Type **5%.** The entries in cells A6 through A11 change automatically. Click the **Undo button** on the Standard toolbar to return to the 7.5% interest rate.

➤ Save the workbook.

THE EDIT CLEAR COMMAND

The Edit Clear command erases the contents of a cell and/or its formatting. Select the cell or cells to erase, pull down the Edit menu, click the Clear command, then click All, Formats, Contents, or Notes from the cascaded menu. Pressing the Del key is equivalent to executing the Edit Clear Contents command; that is, it clears the contents of a cell but not the formatting.

A total of 27 in-depth tutorials (hands-on exercises) guide the reader at the computer. Each tutorial is illustrated with large, full-color, screen captures that are clear and easy to read. Each tutorial is accompanied by numerous tips that present different ways to accomplish a given task, but in a logical and relaxed fashion.

Object Linking and Embedding is stressed throughout the series, beginning in the introductory section on Microsoft Office, where the reader is shown the power of this all-important technology. Examples of OLE appear throughout the book and are distinguished by an OLE icon.

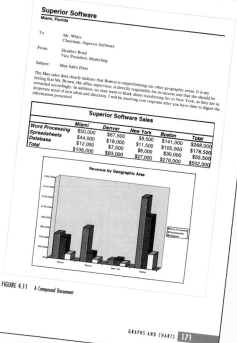

OBJECT LINKING AND EMBEDDING

One of the primary advantages of the Windows environment is the ability to create a *compound document* that contains data *(objects)* from multiple applications. The memo in Figure 4.11 is an example of a compound document. The memo was created in Microsoft Word (the *client application*), and it contains objects (a worksheet and a chart) that were developed in Microsoft Excel (the *server application*). *Object Linking and Embedding* (*OLE,* pronounced "oh-lay") is the means by which you create the compound document.

FIGURE 4.11   A Compound Document

1. Figure 2.14 contains a worksheet that was used to calculate the difference between the Asking Price and Selling Price on various real estate listings that were sold during June, as well as the commission paid to the real estate agency as a result of selling those listings. Complete the worksheet, following the steps outlined below:

   a. Open the partially completed *Chapter 2 Practice 1* workbook on the data disk, then save the workbook as *Finished Chapter 2 Practice 1*.

   b. Click cell E5 and enter the formula to calculate the difference between the asking price and the selling price for the property belonging to Mr. Landry.

   c. Click cell F5 and enter the formula to calculate the commission paid to the agency as a result of selling the property. (Pay close attention to the difference between relative and absolute cell references.)

   d. Select cells E5:F5 and copy the formulas to E6:F11 to calculate the difference and commission for the rest of the properties.

   e. Click cell C13 and enter the formula to calculate the total asking price, which is the sum of the asking prices for the individual listings in cells C5:C11.

   f. Copy the formula in C13 to the range D13:F13 to calculate the other totals.

   g. Select the range C5:F13 and format the numbers so that they display with dollar signs and commas, and no decimal places (e.g., $450,000).

   h. Click cell B15 and format the number as a percentage.

   i. Click cell A1 and center the title across the width of the worksheet. With the cell still selected, select cells A3:F4 as well and change the font to 12 point Arial bold italic.

   j. Select cells A4:F4 and create a bottom border to separate the headings from the data.

   k. Select cells F5:F11 and shade the commissions.

   l. Print the worksheet.

	A	B	C	D	E	F
1	Coaches Realty - Sales for June					
2						
3			Asking	Selling		
4	Customer	Address	Price	Price	Difference	Commission
5	Landry	122 West 75 Terr.	450000	350000		
6	Spurrier	4567 S.W. 95 Street	750000	648500		
7	Shula	123 Alamo Road	350000	275000		
8	Lombardi	9000 Brickell Place	275000	250000		
9	Johnson	5596 Powerline Road	189000	189000		
10	Erickson	8900 N.W. 89 Street	456000	390000		
11	Bowden	75 Maynada Blvd.	300000	265000		
12						
13		Totals:				
14						
15	Commission %:	0.035				

FIGURE 2.14   Spreadsheet for Practice Exercise 1

2. The Sales Invoice: Use Figure 2.15 as the basis for a sales invoice that you will create and submit to your instructor. Your spreadsheet should follow the general format shown in the figure with respect to including a uniform discount for each item. Your spreadsheet should also include the sales tax. The discount percentage and sales tax percentage should be entered in a separate area so that they can be easily modified.

Use your imagination and sell any product at any price. You must, however, include at least four items in your invoice. Formatting is important, but you need not follow our format exactly. See how creative you can be, then submit your completed invoice to your instructor for inclusion in a class contest for the best invoice. Be sure your name appears somewhere on the worksheet as a sales associate. If you are really ambitious, you might include an object from the ClipArt Gallery.

	A	B	C	D	E	F
1			Bargain Basement Shopping			
2						
3	Item	Quantity	List Price	Discount	Your Price	Total
4	Hayes 28.8 Fax/Modem	2	$169.00	$33.80	$135.20	$270.40
5	Sony 4X CD-ROM	6	$329.00	$65.80	$263.20	$1,579.20
6	Seagate 1Gb Hard Drive	4	$338.00	$67.60	$270.40	$1,081.60
7	Iomega Zip Drive	10	$199.00	$39.80	$159.20	$1,592.00
8						
9	Subtotal					$4,523.20
10	Tax					$294.01
11	Amount Due					$4,817.21
12						
13	Discount Percentage	20%				
14	Sales Tax Percentage	6.50%				
15	Sales Associate	Serena Cruz				

FIGURE 2.15   Spreadsheet for Practice Exercise 2

3. The Probability Expert: How much would you bet *against* two people in your class having the same birthday? Don't be too hasty, for the odds of two classmates sharing the same birthday (month and day) are much higher than you would expect. For example, there is a fifty percent chance (.5063) in a class of 23 students that two people will have been born on the same day, as shown in the spreadsheet in Figure 2.16. The probability jumps to seventy percent (.7053) in a class of 30, and to ninety percent (.9025) in a class of 41. Don't take our word for it, but try the experiment in your class.

You need a basic knowledge of probability to create the spreadsheet. In essence you calculate the probability of individuals not having the same birthday, then subtract this number from one, to obtain the probability of the event coming true. In a group of two people, for example, the probability of not being born on the same day is 365/366; i.e., the second person can be born on any of 365 days and still have a different birthday. The probability of two people having the same birthday becomes 1 − 365/366.

The probability for different birthdays in a group of three is (365/366)*(364/366); the probability of not having different birthdays—that is, of two people having the same birthday, is one minus this number. Each row in the spreadsheet is calculated from the previous row. It's not as hard as it looks, and the results are quite interesting!

At the end of every chapter are abundant and thought-provoking exercises that review and extend the material in different ways. There are objective multiple-choice questions, conceptual problems that do not require interaction with the computer, guided computer exercises, and less structured case studies that encourage the reader to further exploration and independent study.

CASE STUDIES

The Financial Consultant

A friend of yours is in the process of buying a home and has asked you to compare the payments and total interest on a 15- and a 30-year loan. You want to do as professional a job as possible and have decided to analyze the loans in Excel, then incorporate the results into a memo written in Microsoft Word. As of now, the principal is $150,000, but it is very likely that your friend will change his mind several times, and so you want to use the OLE capability within Windows to dynamically link the worksheet to the word processing document. Your memo should include a letterhead that takes advantage of the formatting capabilities within Word; a graphic logo would be a nice touch.

Compensation Analysis

A corporation typically uses several different measures of compensation in an effort to pay its employees fairly. Most organizations closely monitor an employee's salary history, keeping both the present and previous salary in order to compute various statistics, including:

- The percent salary increase, which is computed by taking the difference between the present and previous salary, and dividing by the previous salary.
- The months between increase, which is the elapsed time between the date the present salary took effect, and the date of the previous salary. (Assume 30 days per month for ease of calculation.)
- The annualized rate of increase, which is the percent salary increase divided by the months between increase; for example, a 5% raise after 6 months is equivalent to an annualized increase of 10%; a 5% raise after two years is equivalent to an annual increase of 2.5%.

Use the data in the *Compensation Analysis* workbook on the data disk to compute salary statistics for the employees who have had a salary increase; employees who have not received an increase should have a suitable indication in the cell. Compute the average, minimum, and maximum value for each measure of compensation for those employees who have received an increase.

The Automobile Dealership

The purchase of a car usually entails extensive bargaining between the dealer and the consumer. The dealer has an asking price but typically settles for less. The commission paid to a salesperson depends on how close the selling price is to the asking price. Exotic Motors has the following compensation policy for its sales staff:

- A 3% commission on the actual selling price for cars sold at 95% or more of the asking price.
- A 2% commission on the actual selling price for cars sold at 90% or more (but less than 95%) of the asking price.
- A 1% commission on the actual selling price for cars sold at less than 90% of the asking price. The dealer will not go below 85% of his asking price.

Advanced topics are covered in the later chapters. Chapter 5 focuses on list management, Chapter 6 addresses three-dimensional workbooks and file linking, while Chapter 7 introduces macros and Visual Basic.

Additional topics of an advanced nature are presented in the appendices. Appendix A discusses the spreadsheet audit, Appendix B covers the Solver add-in (a widely used optimization tool), and Appendix C presents the data-mapping application.

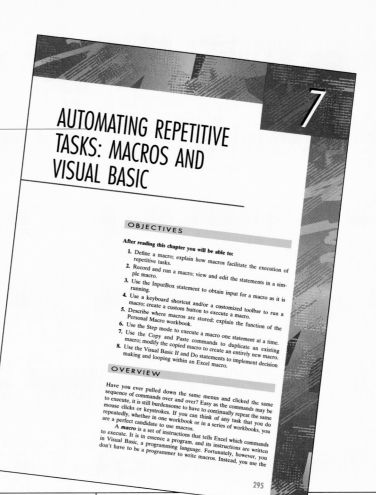

7

AUTOMATING REPETITIVE TASKS: MACROS AND VISUAL BASIC

OBJECTIVES

After reading this chapter you will be able to:

1. Define a macro; explain how macros facilitate the execution of repetitive tasks.
2. Record and run a macro; view and edit the statements in a simple macro.
3. Use the InputBox statement to obtain input for a macro as it is running.
4. Use a keyboard shortcut and/or a customized toolbar to run a macro; create a custom button to execute a macro.
5. Describe where macros are stored; explain the function of the Personal Macro workbook.
6. Use the Step mode to execute a macro one statement at a time.
7. Use the Copy and Paste commands to duplicate an existing macro; modify the copied macro to create an entirely new macro.
8. Use the Visual Basic If and Do statements to implement decision making and looping within an Excel macro.

OVERVIEW

Have you ever pulled down the same menus and clicked the same sequence of commands over and over? Easy as the commands may be to execute, it is still burdensome to have to continually repeat the same mouse clicks or keystrokes. If you can think of any task that you do repeatedly, whether in one workbook or in a series of workbooks, you are a perfect candidate to use macros.

A **macro** is a set of instructions that tells Excel which commands to execute. It is in essence a program, and its instructions are written in Visual Basic, a programming language. Fortunately, however, you don't have to be a programmer to write macros. Instead, you use the

295

State	Electoral Votes	Winner	Bush	Clinton	Perot
Alabama	9	Bush	804,283	690,080	183,109
Alaska	3	Bush	102,000	78,294	73,481
Arizona	8	Bush	572,086	543,050	253,741
Arkansas	6	Clinton	337,324	505,823	99,132
California	54	Clinton	3,630,574	5,121,325	2,296,006
Colorado	8	Clinton	562,850	629,681	366,010
Connecticut	8	Clinton	578,313	682,318	348,771
Delaware	3	Clinton	102,313	126,055	59,213
Florida	25	Bush	2,173,310	2,072,798	1,053,067
Georgia	13	Clinton	995,252	1,008,966	309,657
Hawaii	4	Clinton	136,822	179,310	53,003
Idaho	4	Bush	202,645	137,013	130,395
Illinois	22	Clinton	1,734,096	2,453,350	840,515
Indiana	12	Bush	989,375	848,420	455,934
Iowa	7	Clinton	504,891	586,353	253,468
Kansas	6	Bush	449,951	390,434	312,358
Kentucky	8	Clinton	617,178	665,104	203,944
Louisiana	9	Clinton	733,386	815,971	211,478
Maine	4	Clinton	206,504	263,420	206,820
Maryland	10	Clinton	707,094	988,571	281,414
Massachusetts	12	Clinton	805,039	1,318,639	630,731
Michigan	18	Clinton	1,554,940	1,871,182	824,813
Minnesota	10	Clinton	747,841	1,020,997	562,506
Mississippi	7	Bush	487,793	400,258	85,626
Missouri	11	Clinton	811,159	1,053,873	518,741
Montana	3	Clinton	144,207	154,507	107,225
Nebraska	5	Bush	344,346	217,344	174,687
Nevada	4	Clinton	175,828	189,148	132,580
New Hampshire	4	Clinton	202,484	209,040	121,337
New Jersey	15	Clinton	1,356,865	1,436,206	521,829
New Mexico	5	Clinton	212,824	261,617	91,895
New York	33	Clinton	2,346,649	3,444,450	1,090,721
North Carolina	14	Bush	1,134,661	1,114,042	357,864
North Dakota	3	Bush	136,244	99,168	71,084
Ohio	21	Clinton	1,894,310	1,984,942	1,036,426
Oklahoma	8	Bush	592,929	473,066	319,878
Oregon	7	Clinton	475,757	621,314	354,091
Pennsylvania	23	Clinton	1,791,841	2,239,164	902,667
Rhode Island	4	Clinton	131,605	213,302	105,051
South Carolina	8	Bush	577,507	479,514	138,872
South Dakota	3	Bush	136,718	124,888	73,295
Tennessee	11	Clinton	841,300	933,521	199,968
Texas	32	Bush	2,496,071	2,281,815	1,354,781
Utah	5	Bush	322,632	183,429	203,400
Vermont	3	Clinton	88,122	133,592	65,991
Virginia	13	Bush	1,150,517	1,038,650	348,639
Washington	11	Clinton	731,235	993,039	541,801
West Virginia	5	Clinton	241,974	331,001	108,829
Wisconsin	11	Clinton	930,855	1,041,066	544,479
Wyoming	3	Bush	79,347	68,160	51,263
Total	535		39,083,847	44,717,270	19,632,586
Electoral Vote totals					
Clinton	370				
Bush	168				

(a) Worksheet Data

FIGURE C.1   Data Mapping

(b) 1992 Election Results

(c) Strategy for 1996

FIGURE C.1   Data Mapping (continued)

CREATING A MAP

The exercise that follows shortly illustrates the basic commands in the Data Mapping application and gives you an appreciation for its overall capability. Creating a map is easy provided you have a basic proficiency with Microsoft Excel. In essence, you do the following:

1. Select the cell range(s) containing the data for the map. (At least one column of the data must be recognizable as geographic names that are present in one of the available maps.)

Acknowledgments

We want to thank the many individuals who helped bring this project to fruition. We are especially grateful to our editors at Prentice Hall, Carolyn Henderson and P. J. Boardman, without whom the series would not have been possible. Cecil Yarbrough and Susan Hoffman did an outstanding job in checking the manuscript and proofs for technical accuracy. Suzanne Behnke created the innovative and attractive design. Gretchen Marx of Saint Joseph College and Carlotta Eaton of Radford University produced an outstanding set of Instructor Manuals. Dave Moles created the Instructor's CD-ROM. Phyllis Bregman put us online. Greg Hubit was in charge of production. Nancy Evans and Deborah Emry, our marketing managers at Prentice Hall, developed the innovative campaigns that helped make the series a success. We also want to acknowledge our reviewers who, through their comments and constructive criticism, greatly improved the *Exploring Windows* series.

Lynne Band, Middlesex Community College
Stuart P. Brian, Holy Family College
Carl M. Briggs, Indiana University School of Business
Kimberly Chambers, Scottsdale Community College
Alok Charturvedi, Purdue University
Jerry Chin, Southwest Missouri State University
Dean Combellick, Scottsdale Community College
Cody Copeland, Johnson County Community College
Larry S. Corman, Fort Lewis College
Janis Cox, Tri-County Technical College
Martin Crossland, Southwest Missouri State University
Paul E. Daurelle, Western Piedmont Community College
David Douglas, University of Arkansas
Carlotta Eaton, Radford University
Raymond Frost, Central Connecticut State University
James Gips, Boston College
Vernon Griffin, Austin Community College
Michael Hassett, Fort Hays State University
Wanda D. Heller, Seminole Community College
Bonnie Homan, San Francisco State University
Ernie Ivey, Polk Community College
Mike Kelly, Community College of Rhode Island
Jane King, Everett Community College

John Lesson, University of Central Florida
David B. Meinert, Southwest Missouri State University
Alan Moltz, Naugatuck Valley Technical Community College
Kim Montney, Kellogg Community College
Kevin Pauli, University of Nebraska
Mary McKenry Percival, University of Miami
Delores Pusins, Hillsborough Community College
Gale E. Rand, College Misericordia
Judith Rice, Santa Fe Community College
David Rinehard, Lansing Community College
Marilyn Salas, Scottsdale Community College
John Shepherd, Duquesne University
Helen Stoloff, Hudson Valley Community College
Mike Thomas, Indiana University School of Business
Suzanne Tomlinson, Iowa State University
Karen Tracey, Central Connecticut State University
Sally Visci, Lorain County Community College
David Weiner, University of San Francisco
Connie Wells, Georgia State University
Wallace John Whistance-Smith, Ryerson Polytechnic University
Jack Zeller, Kirkwood Community College

A final word of thanks to the unnamed students at the University of Miami who make it all worthwhile. And most of all, thanks to you, our readers, for choosing this book. Please feel free to contact us with any comments and suggestions.

Robert T. Grauer
RGRAUER@UMIAMI.MIAMI.EDU
http://www.bus.miami.edu/~rgrauer

Maryann Barber
MBARBER@UMIAMI.MIAMI.EDU
http://www.bus.miami.edu/~mbarber

MICROSOFT OFFICE FOR WINDOWS 95: FOUR APPLICATIONS IN ONE

OVERVIEW

Word processing, spreadsheets, and data management have always been significant microcomputer applications. The early days of the PC saw these applications emerge from different vendors with radically different user interfaces. WordPerfect, Lotus, and dBASE, for example, were dominant applications in their respective areas, and each was developed by a different company. The applications were totally dissimilar, and knowledge of one application did not help in learning another.

The widespread acceptance of Windows 3.1 promoted the concept of a common user interface, which required all applications to follow a consistent set of conventions. This meant that all applications worked essentially the same way, and it provided a sense of familiarity when you learned a new application, since every application presented the same user interface. The development of a suite of applications from a single vendor extended this concept by imposing additional similarities on all applications within the suite.

This introduction will acquaint you with the *Microsoft Office for Windows 95* and its four major applications—Word, Excel, Power-Point, and Access. Our primary purpose is to emphasize the similarities between these applications and to help you extend your knowledge from one application to the next. You will find the same commands in the same menus. You will also recognize familiar toolbars and will be able to take advantage of similar keyboard shortcuts. Our goal is to show you how much you already know and to get you up and running as quickly as possible.

The introduction also introduces you to Schedule+, and to shared applications and utilities such as the ClipArt Gallery and WordArt, which are included within Microsoft Office. We discuss the Office Shortcut Bar and describe how to start an application and open a new or existing document. We introduce you to Object Linking and Embedding, which enables you to combine data from multiple applications into a single document. And finally, we include a hands-on exercise that lets you sit down at the computer and apply what you have learned.

TRY THE COLLEGE BOOKSTORE

Any machine you buy will come with Windows 95, but that is only the beginning since you must also obtain the application software you intend to run. Many first-time buyers are surprised that they have to pay extra for software, so you had better allow for software in your budget. Some hardware vendors will bundle (at no additional cost) Microsoft Office as an inducement to buy from them. If you have already purchased your system and you need software, the best place to buy Microsoft Office is the college bookstore, where it can be obtained at a substantial educational discount.

MICROSOFT OFFICE FOR WINDOWS 95

All Office applications share the common user interface for Windows 95 with which you may already be familiar. (If you are new to Windows 95, then read the appendix on the "Essentials of Windows 95," which appears at the end of this book.) Figure 1 displays a screen from each application in the Microsoft Office—Word, Excel, PowerPoint, and Access, in Figures 1a, 1b, 1c, and 1d, respectively. Look closely at Figure 1, and realize that each screen contains both an application window and a document window, and that each document window has been maximized within the application window. The title bars of the application and document windows have been merged into a single title bar that appears at the top of the application window. The title bar displays the application (e.g., Microsoft Word in Figure 1a) as well as the name of the document (Letter to My Instructor in Figure 1a) on which you are working.

All four screens in Figure 1 are similar in appearance despite the fact that the applications accomplish very different tasks. Each application window has an identifying icon, a menu bar, a title bar, and a minimize, maximize or restore, and a close button. Each document window has its own identifying icon, and its own minimize, maximize or restore, and close button. The Windows 95 taskbar appears at the bottom of each application window and shows the open applications. The status bar appears above the taskbar and displays information relevant to the window or selected object.

Each application in Microsoft Office uses a consistent command structure in which the same basic menus are found in all applications. The File, Edit, View, Insert, Tools, Window, and Help menus are present in all four applications. The same commands are found in the same menus. The Save, Open, Print, and Exit commands, for example, are contained in the File menu. The Cut, Copy, Paste, and Undo commands are found in the Edit menu.

The means for accessing the pull-down menus are consistent from one application to the next. Click the menu name on the menu bar, or press the Alt key plus the underlined letter of the menu name; for example, press Alt+F to pull down the File menu. If you already know some keyboard shortcuts in one application, there is a good chance that the shortcuts will work in another application. Ctrl+Home and Ctrl+End, for example, move to the beginning and end of a document, respectively. Ctrl+B, Ctrl+I, and Ctrl+U boldface, italicize, and underline text. Ctrl+X (the "X" is supposed to remind you of a pair of scissors), Ctrl+C, and Ctrl+V will cut, copy, and paste, respectively. You may not know what these

Title bar

Identifying icon

Menu bar

Standard toolbar

Formatting toolbar

Minimize button

Restore button

Close button

Status bar

Task bar

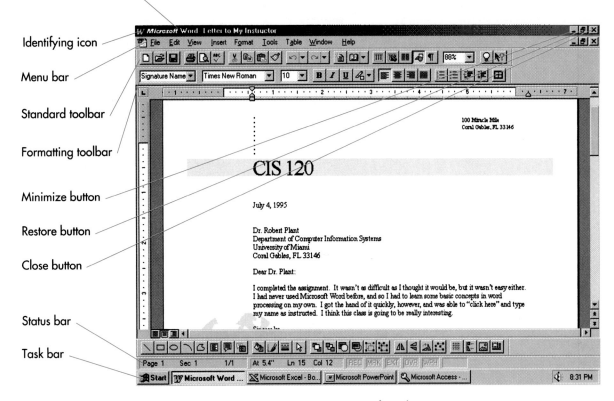

(a) Microsoft Word

Title bar

Identifying icon

Menu bar

Standard toolbar

Formatting toolbar

Minimize button

Restore button

Close button

Status bar

Task bar

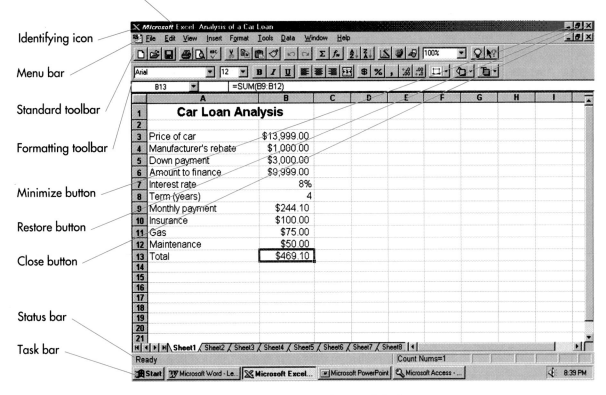

(b) Microsoft Excel

FIGURE 1   The Common User Interface

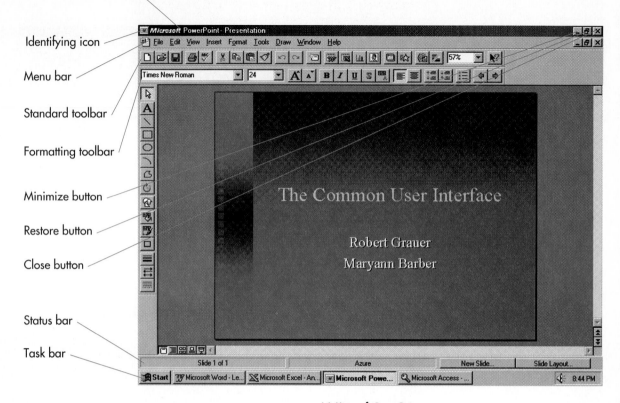

Title bar

Identifying icon

Menu bar

Standard toolbar

Formatting toolbar

Minimize button

Restore button

Close button

Status bar

Task bar

(c) Microsoft PowerPoint

The Common User Interface

Robert Grauer

Maryann Barber

Title bar

Identifying icon

Menu bar

Toolbar

Minimize button

Restore button

Close button

Status bar

Task bar

Field Properties

(d) Microsoft Access

FIGURE 1   The Common User Interface (continued)

commands do now, but once you learn how they work in one application, you will intuitively know how they work in the others.

All four applications use consistent (and often identical) dialog boxes. The dialog boxes to open and close a file, for example, are identical in every application. All four applications also share a common dictionary. The AutoCorrect feature (to correct common spelling mistakes) works identically in all four applications. The help feature also functions identically.

There are, of course, differences between the applications. Each application has its own unique menus and associated toolbars. Nevertheless, the Standard and Formatting toolbars in all applications contain many of the same tools (especially the first several tools on the left of each toolbar). The **Standard toolbar** contains buttons for basic commands such as Open, Save, or Print. It also contains buttons to cut, copy, and paste, and all of these buttons are identical in all four applications. The **Formatting toolbar** provides access to common formatting operations such as boldface, italics, or underlining, or changing the font or point size, and again, these buttons are identical in all four applications. ToolTips are present in all applications. Suffice it to say, therefore, that once you know one Office application, you have a tremendous head start in learning another.

MICROSOFT OFFICE VERSUS OFFICE PROFESSIONAL

Microsoft distributes two versions of the Office Suite: Standard Office and Office Professional. Both versions include Word, Excel, and PowerPoint. The Office Professional also has Microsoft Access. The difference is important when you are shopping and comparing prices from different sources. Be sure to purchase the version that is appropriate for your needs.

Online Help

Each application in the Microsoft Office has the extensive **online help** facility as shown in Figure 2. Help is available at any time, and is accessed from the application's Help menu. (The Help screens in Figure 2 pertain to Microsoft Office, as opposed to a specific application, and were accessed through the Answer Wizard button on the Office Shortcut Bar.)

The **Contents tab** in Figure 2a is similar to the table of contents in an ordinary book. The major topics are represented by books, each of which can be opened to display additional topics. Each open book displays one or more topics, which may be viewed and/or printed to provide the indicated information.

The **Index tab** in Figure 2b is analogous to the index of an ordinary book. Type the first several letters of the topic to look up, such as "he" in Figure 2b. Help then returns all of the topics beginning with the letters you entered. Select the topic you want, then display the topic for immediate viewing, or print it for later reference.

The **Answer Wizard** in Figure 2c lets you ask questions in your own words, then it returns the relevant help topics. The Help screen in Figure 2d was accessed from the selections provided by the Answer Wizard, and it, in turn, will lead you to new features in the individual applications.

Office Shortcut Bar

The **Microsoft Office Shortcut Bar** provides immediate access to each application within Microsoft Office. It consists of a row of buttons and can be placed anywhere

Subtopics

Major topics

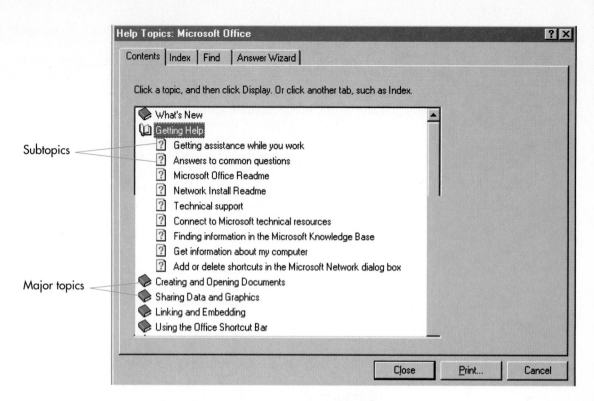

(a) Contents Tab

Type initial letters of
the topic to look up

Select the
desired topic

Click Display

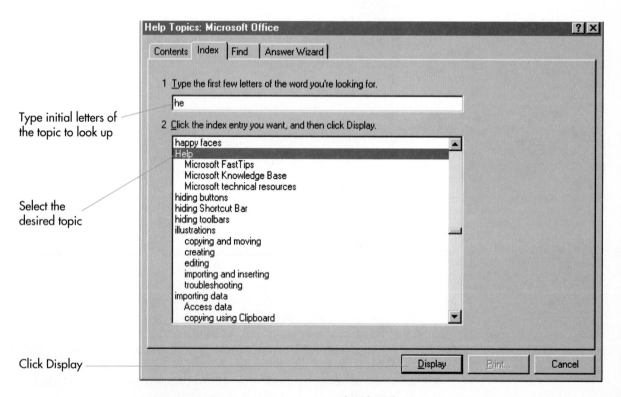

(b) Index Tab

FIGURE 2   Online Help

Type in your question ————

List of related topics ————

Double click to see the
information on the topic ————

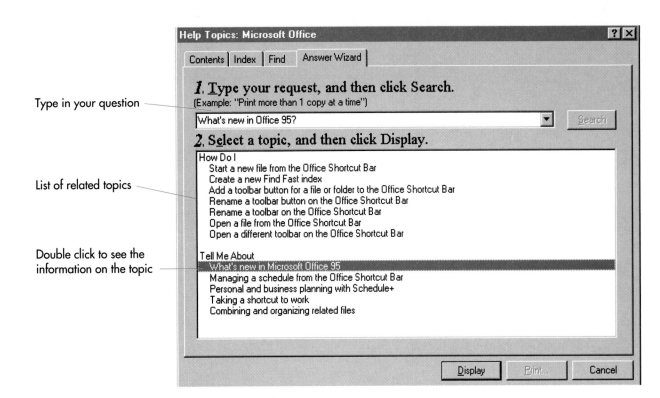

(c) Answer Wizard

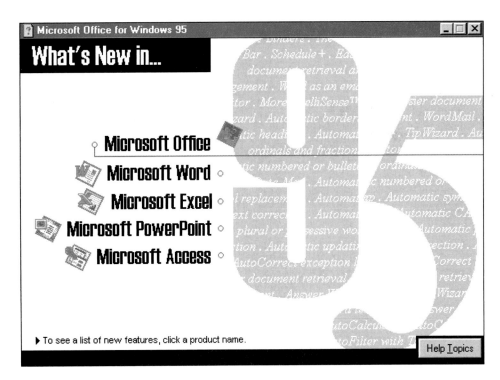

(d) What's New in Office 95?

FIGURE 2   Online Help (continued)

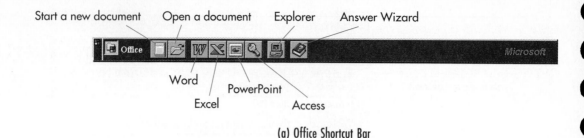

Start a new document   Open a document   Explorer   Answer Wizard

Word

Excel

PowerPoint

Access

(a) Office Shortcut Bar

Buttons to be displayed
on the Shortcut Bar

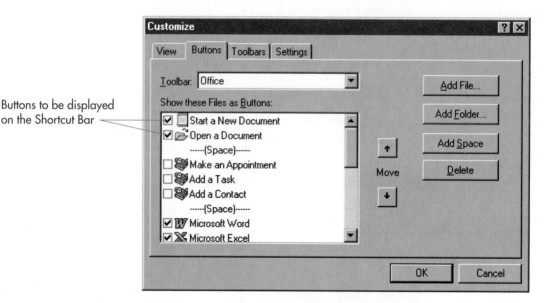

(b) Customize Dialog Box

FIGURE 3 Office Shortcut Bar

on the screen. The Shortcut Bar is anchored by default on the right side of the desktop, but you can position it along any edge, or have it "float" in the middle of the desktop. You can even hide it from view when it is not in use.

Figure 3a displays the Shortcut Bar as it appears on our desktop. The buttons that are displayed (and the order in which they appear) are established through the Customize dialog box in Figure 3b. (We show you how to customize the Shortcut Bar in the hands-on exercise that follows shortly.) Our Shortcut Bar contains a button for each Office application, a button for the Windows Explorer, and a button to access help.

Docucentric Orientation

Our Shortcut Bar contains two additional buttons: to open an existing document and to start a new document. These buttons are very useful and take advantage of the "docucentric" orientation of Microsoft Office, which lets you think in terms of a document rather than the associated application. You can still open a document in traditional fashion, by starting the application (e.g., clicking its button on the Shortcut Bar), then using the File Open command to open the document. It's easier, however, to locate the document, then double click its icon, which automatically loads the associated program.

Consider, for example, the Open dialog box in Figure 4a, which is displayed by clicking the Open a Document button on the Shortcut Bar. The Open dialog

Details button

Selected folder

Double click document name to open it

List of files in the folder

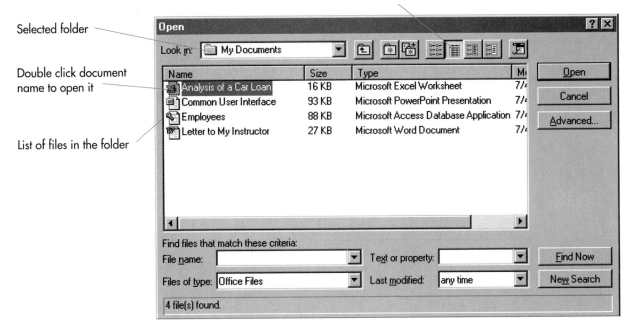

(a) Open an Existing Document

Details button

Letters & Faxes tab

Double click template name to open it

Preview of template

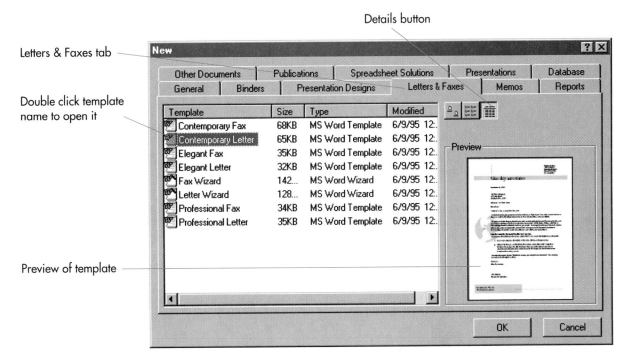

(b) Start a New Document

FIGURE 4   Document Orientation

box is common to all Office applications, and it works identically in each application. The My Documents folder is selected in Figure 4a, and it contains four documents of various file types. The documents are displayed in the Details view, which shows the document name, size, file type, and date and time the document was last modified. To open any document—for example, "Analysis of a Car

Loan"—just double click its name or icon. The associated application (Microsoft Excel in this example) will be started automatically; and it, in turn, will open the selected workbook.

The "docucentric" orientation also applies to new documents. Click the Start a New Document button on the Office Shortcut Bar, and you display the New dialog box in Figure 4b. Click the tab corresponding to the type of document you want to create, such as Letters & Faxes in Figure 4b. Change to the Preview view, then click (select) various templates so that you can choose the one most appropriate for your purpose. Double click the desired template to start the application, which opens the template and enables you to create the document.

CHANGE THE VIEW

The toolbar in the Open dialog box displays the documents within the selected folder in one of several views. Click the Details button to switch to the Details view and see the date and time the file was last modified, as well as its size and type. Click the List button to display an icon representing the associated application, enabling you to see many more files than in the Details view. The Preview button lets you see a document before you open it. The Properties button displays information about the document, including the number of revisions.

LEARNING BY DOING

Learning is best accomplished by doing, and so we come now to the first of many hands-on exercises that appear throughout the book. The exercises enable you to apply the concepts you have learned, then extend those concepts to further exploration on your own. This exercise focuses on the Office Shortcut Bar and assumes a basic knowledge of the Windows 95 desktop and associated mouse operations. (See the supplement on "Essentials of Windows 95" at the end of the book if you need to brush up on this material.)

The exercise has you display the Office Shortcut Bar, then customize its appearance. It also guides you in creating a new document based on an existing template that is accessed through the Start a New Document button. At the end of the exercise you will have created a letter to introduce yourself to your instructor. We are confident you will be able to do the exercise, even if you have never used Microsoft Word, because of your knowledge of the common user interface. Should you get stuck (and you won't), try the online help facility that functions identically in every Windows application.

HANDS-ON EXERCISE 1

Introduction to Microsoft Office

Objective: To load and customize the Microsoft Office Shortcut Bar; to create and print a Word document. Use Figure 5 as a guide in the exercise.

STEP 1: Welcome to Windows 95

➤ Turn on the computer and all of its peripherals. The floppy drive should be empty prior to starting your machine. This ensures that the system starts by reading files from the hard disk (which contains the Windows files), as opposed to a floppy disk (which does not).

➤ Your system will take a minute or so to get started, after which you should see the desktop in Figure 5a. Do not be concerned if the appearance of your desktop is different from ours.

➤ If you are new to Windows 95 and you want a quick introduction, click the **What's New** or **Windows Tour command buttons.** Follow the instructions in the boxed tip to display the dialog box if it does not appear on the system.

➤ Click the **Close button** to close the Welcome window and continue with the exercise.

TAKE THE WINDOWS 95 TOUR

Windows 95 greets you with a Welcome window that contains a command button to take you on a 10-minute tour of Windows 95. Click the command button and enjoy the show. You might also try the What's New command button for a quick overview of changes from Windows 3.1. If you do not see the Welcome window when you start Windows 95, click the Start button, click Run, type C:\WINDOWS\WELCOME in the Open text box, and press enter.

Click to take the
Windows tour

Click to see Whats New
in Windows 95

Click to close the
Welcome window

Click the Start button to
display the Programs menu

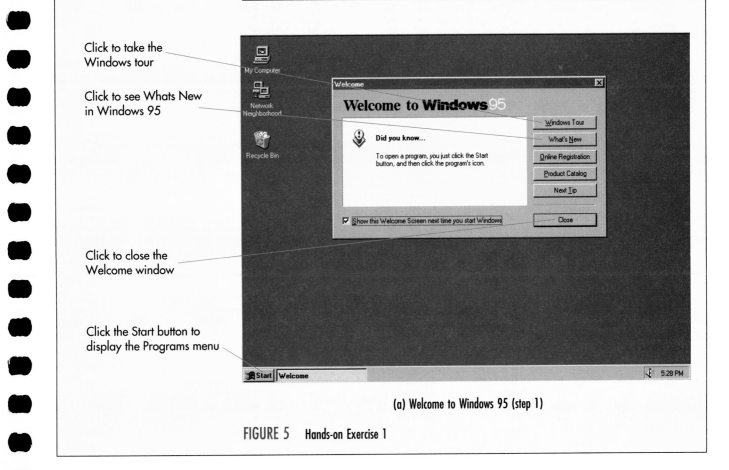

(a) Welcome to Windows 95 (step 1)

FIGURE 5   Hands-on Exercise 1

STEP 2: The Office Shortcut Bar

➤ We don't know why, but Microsoft does not make it easy to display the Office Shortcut bar. Click the **Start button,** click (or point to) the **Find command,** then click **Files or Folders** to display the Find Folders dialog box.

➤ Enter **Msoffice.exe** (the file you are searching for) in the Named Text box. Click the **down arrow** in the Look in list box, then enter **My Computer** to search all drives on your system.

➤ Click the **Find Now button** to initiate the search, which should display the program within the dialog box. Double click the icon for **Msoffice.exe** from within the Find dialog box to start the program and display the Office shortcut bar.

➤ You can position the Shortcut bar anywhere on the desktop. Just point to an empty area on the bar, then click and drag to a new location.

MODIFY THE START MENU

You can add your favorite program to the Start menu so that you can execute it with a click of the button. Locate the program using Explorer or the Find command, then click and drag the icon for the program to the Start button on the taskbar. The next time you click the Start button you will see a (shortcut) icon corresponding to the program you dragged to the Start button.

STEP 3: Customize the Shortcut Bar

➤ Do not be concerned if your Shortcut Bar is different from Figure 5b since its appearance or content is easily changed.

➤ Point to an empty area of the Shortcut Bar, then click the **right mouse button** to display a Shortcut menu. Click **Customize** to display the Customize dialog box.

➤ If necessary, click the **View tab,** then check (or clear) the various option buttons according to the options you prefer. The settings do not take effect until you click the **OK command button** to close the dialog box.

➤ Clear the check box to Use the Standard Toolbar color, then click the **Change Color command button** to display the Color dialog box in Figure 5b.

➤ Click (select) a color, then click **OK** to accept the color change and close the Color dialog box. Click **OK** a second time to close the Customize dialog box and implement the changes.

AUTO HIDE THE SHORTCUT BAR

The Auto Hide option hides the Shortcut Bar between uses, giving you additional space on the desktop when you are in another application. Point to an empty space on the Shortcut Bar, click the right mouse button to display a menu, then check the Auto Hide command. (Clicking the command a second time removes the check and toggles the command off). To use the Shortcut Bar when it's hidden, point to the edge of the screen where the Shortcut Bar is docked, and the bar will appear. Click the appropriate button on the Shortcut Bar, then move the mouse back into the window containing your document to return to work.

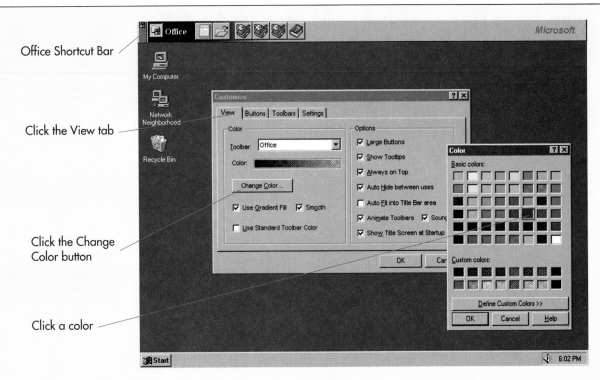

Office Shortcut Bar

Click the View tab

Click the Change
Color button

Click a color

(b) Customize the Toolbar (step 3)

FIGURE 5   Hands-on Exercise 1 (continued)

STEP 4: Add/Remove Buttons

➤ Point to an empty area of the Shortcut Bar, then click the **right mouse button** to display a shortcut menu. Click **Customize** to display the Customize dialog box, then click the **Buttons tab** to display the dialog box in Figure 5c.

➤ Check (clear) the buttons you wish to display or hide. The effects of checking (or clearing) a button are visible immediately, without having to exit the dialog box; for example, checking the button for Microsoft Word displays the associated button immediately on the Shortcut Bar.

➤ Click **OK** to close the Customize dialog box.

ADD THE EXPLORER

The Windows Explorer is the primary means of file management within Windows 95, and thus, it is convenient to have it readily available. To add the Explorer to the Shortcut Bar, right click the Shortcut Bar, click the Customize command, click the Buttons tab, then scroll until you can check the box to add the Windows Explorer. Click OK to close the Customize dialog box. The Explorer has been added to the Shortcut Bar and is now a mouse click away.

Click to select buttons to
be displayed on Shortcut Bar

Clear check box to remove
buttons from Shortcut Bar

(c) Add/Remove Buttons (step 4)

FIGURE 5   Hands-on Exercise 1 (continued)

STEP 5: Start a New Document

➤ Click the **Start a New Document button** to display the New dialog box in Figure 5d. Click the **Letters & Faxes tab** as shown in Figure 5d.

➤ Click the **Details button** to change the view within the New dialog box. Click and drag the border separating the Template and Size columns so that you can read the title of the template.

➤ Select (click) the **Contemporary Letter template** as shown in Figure 5d. The preview for the selected document appears in the right of the dialog box. Click the **OK command button** to open the template.

ONLINE HELP

Online help is available for Microsoft Office just as it is for any other Windows application. Click the Answer Wizard button on the Office Shortcut Bar to display the dialog box containing Help Topics for Microsoft Office. The help facility is intuitive and easy to use and functions identically in every Windows application. The help displays are task specific and fit in a single screen to keep you from having to scroll through large amounts of information.

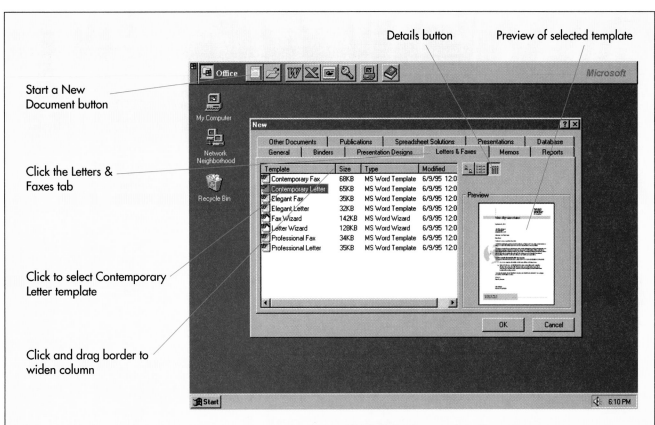

Start a New Document button

Details button

Preview of selected template

Click the Letters & Faxes tab

Click to select Contemporary Letter template

Click and drag border to widen column

(d) Start a New Document (step 5)

FIGURE 5   Hands-on Exercise 1 (continued)

STEP 6: Click Here

➤ You should see the contemporary letter template open as a Word document as shown in Figure 5e. Do not be concerned if the appearance of your screen is different from ours.

➤ Follow the indicated instructions within the template, but do not enter the company name or the body of the letter at this time. Simply click where indicated at various points in the letter, then enter the appropriate text:

• Click on the message **[Click here and type return address]** as shown in Figure 5e. Type your street address (which replaces the existing text), press **enter,** then type your city, state, and zip code.

THE AUTOMATIC SPELL CHECK

A red wavy line under an entry indicates that the underlined word is misspelled or that the word is spelled correctly but not found in the Office dictionary. In either event, point to the underlined word, then click the right mouse button to display a shortcut menu. Select (click) the corrected spelling from the list of suggestions. You can also click the Add command to add the word to an auxiliary dictionary or the Ignore command to accept the word as it is.

Click here and type
your return address

Click here and type
recipient's address

Click here and type
recipient's name

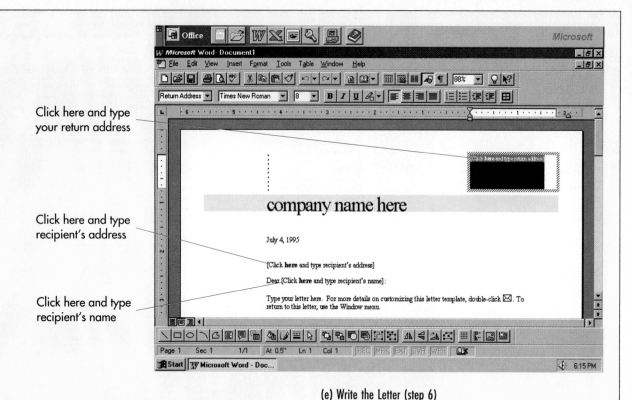

(e) Write the Letter (step 6)

FIGURE 5   Hands-on Exercise 1 (continued)

- Click beneath the date on the message **[Click here and type recipient's address]** and type your instructor's name and address. Press **enter** at the end of each line of the address.
- Click beneath your professor's address on the message **[Click here and type recipient's name]** and enter an appropriate salutation.

STEP 7: Select-then-do

➤ Click and drag to select the text "Company Name Here" as shown in Figure 5f. Type the name of your course, which replaces the selected text.

➤ You have just taken advantage of the select-then-do methodology in which you select the text to which a command is to apply, then you execute the command:

- The most basic way to select text is by dragging the mouse; that is, click at the beginning of the selection, press and hold the left mouse button as you move to the end of the selection, then release the mouse.
- To delete and replace text in one operation, select the text to be replaced, then just type the new text (as you did to replace the entry "Company Name Here").
- To boldface or italicize text, select the text, then click the Bold or Italic button on the Formatting toolbar.
- To left, center, right align, or justify text, select the text, then click the appropriate button on the Formatting toolbar.
- Selected text is affected by any subsequent operation. The text continues to be selected until you click elsewhere in the document.

Undo button

Click and drag to select "company name here"; then type your course name

Click and drag to select the paragraph; then enter your note

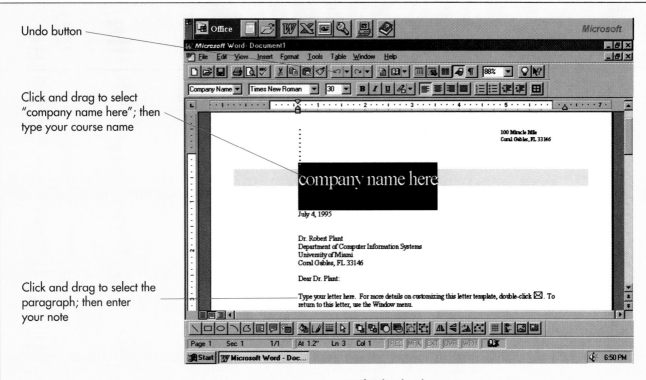

(f) Select-then-do (step 7)

FIGURE 5   Hands-on Exercise 1 (continued)

➤ Click and drag to select the paragraph beginning "Type your letter here", then enter a note to your instructor. Type just as you would on a typewriter with one exception; do *not* press the enter key at the end of a line because Word will automatically wrap text from one line to the next. Press the **enter key** at the end of the paragraph.

➤ Click the **Undo button** to reverse the last command or whenever something happens in your document that differs from what you expected.

---

100 LEVELS OF UNDO

The Undo command is present in Microsoft Word as it is in every other Office application. Incredible as it sounds, however, Word enables you to undo the last 100 changes to a document. Click the arrow next to the Undo button to produce a reverse-order list of your previous actions, then click the action you want to undo, which also undoes all of the preceding commands in the list. Undoing the fifth command in the list, for example, will also undo the preceding four commands.

STEP 8: Complete the Letter

➤ If necessary, click the **down arrow** on the vertical scroll bar to bring the signature portion of the document into view as shown in Figure 5g.

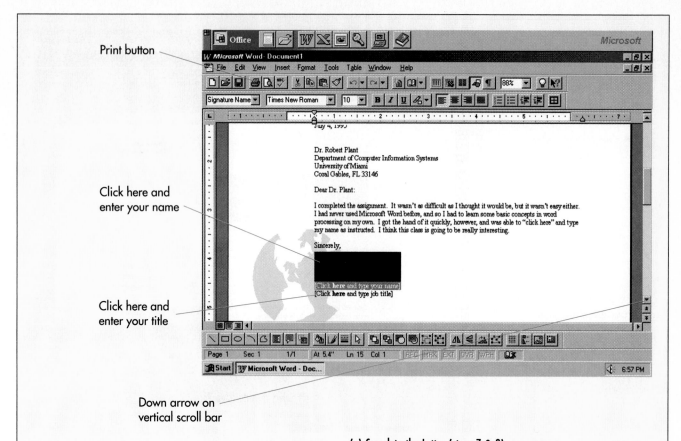

Print button

Click here and
enter your name

Click here and
enter your title

Down arrow on
vertical scroll bar

(g) Complete the Letter (steps 7 & 8)

FIGURE 5   Hands-on Exercise 1 (continued)

➤ Click at the indicated position to enter your name. Click beneath your name to enter your title.

➤ Pull down the **File menu,** click the **Print command,** and click **OK** (or click the **Print button** on the Standard toolbar) to print the document. Submit it to your instructor.

➤ Pull down the **File menu** and click **Exit** to close Microsoft Word, which displays a dialog box asking whether you want to save the document:

• Click **Yes** if you want to save the document, which in turn displays a second dialog box in which you specify the drive and folder to contain the document, as well as a name for the document. The procedure to save a document is discussed in detail in Chapter 1.

• Click **No** if you do not want to save the document. (You will not need this document again.)

➤ Congratulations on a job well done.

SHARED APPLICATIONS AND UTILITIES

Microsoft Office includes a fifth application, Schedule+, as well as several smaller applications and shared utilities. ***Schedule+*** can be started from the Office Short-cut Bar or from the submenu for Microsoft Office, which is accessed through the Programs command on the Start button. Figure 6a displays one screen from Schedule+, providing some indication of what the application can do.

Scheduled appointments

Tabs indicate
other functions

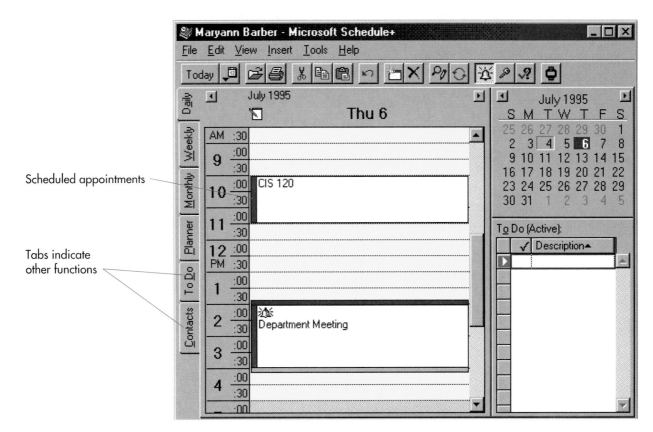

(a) Microsoft Schedule+

Selected clip art image

Selected category

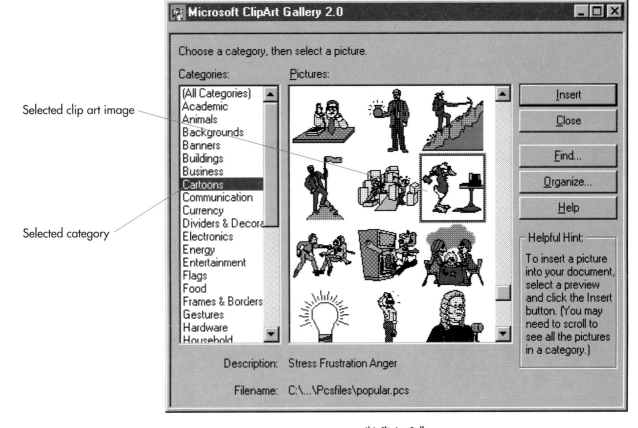

(b) ClipArt Gallery

FIGURE 6   Shared Applications

Enter your text here

Shape of text

Rotate the text

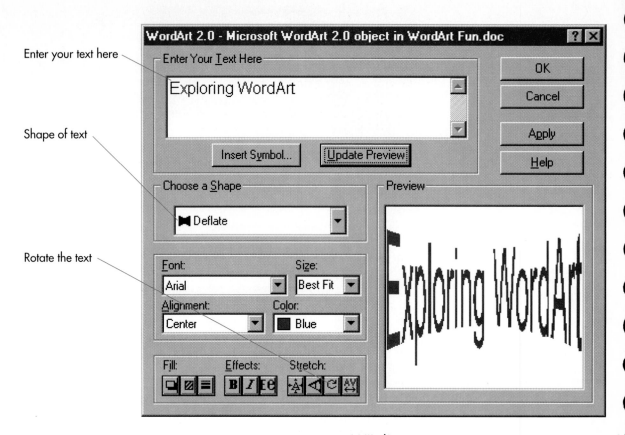

(c) WordArt

Information on
your system

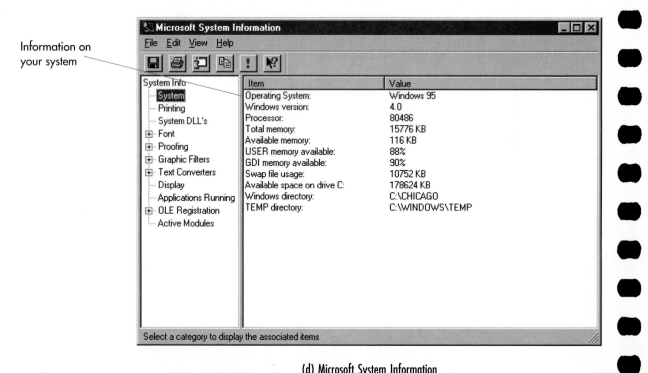

(d) Microsoft System Information

FIGURE 6   Shared Applications (continued)

In essence, Schedule+ is a personal information manager that helps you schedule (and keep) appointments. It will display your schedule on a daily, weekly, or monthly basis. It will beep to remind you of appointments. It will also maintain a list of important phone numbers and contacts. Schedule+ is beyond the scope of our text, but it is an easy application to learn since it follows the common user interface and has a detailed help facility.

The other applications (or applets as they are sometimes known) are easy to miss because they do not appear as buttons on the Shortcut Bar. Nor do they appear as options on any menu. Instead, these applications are loaded from within one of the major applications, typically through the Insert Object command. Two of the more popular applications, the *ClipArt Gallery* and *WordArt,* are illustrated in Figures 6b and 6c, respectively.

The ClipArt Gallery contains more than 1,100 clip art images in 26 different categories. Select a category such as Cartoons, select an image such as the duck smashing a computer, then click the Insert command button to insert the clip art into a document. Once an object is inserted into a document (regardless of whether it is a Word document, an Excel worksheet, a PowerPoint presentation, or an Access form or report), it can be moved and sized like any other Windows object.

WordArt enables you to create special effects with text. It lets you rotate and/or flip text, shade it, slant it, arch it, or even print it upside down. WordArt is intuitively easy to use. In essence, you enter the text in the dialog box of Figure 6c, choose a shape from the drop-down list box, then choose a font and point size. You can boldface or italicize the text or add special effects such as stretching or shadows.

The *System Information Utility* in Figure 6d is accessed from any major application by pulling down the Help menu, clicking the About button, then clicking the System Info command button. The utility provides detailed information about all aspects of your system. The information may prove to be invaluable should problems arise on your system and you need to supply technical details to support personnel.

THE OTHER SHARED APPLICATIONS

Microsoft Office includes several additional applications whose functions can be inferred from their names. The Equation Editor, Organization Chart, Data Map, and Graph utilities are accessed through the Insert Object command. All of these applications are straightforward and easy to use as they follow the common user interface and provide online help.

OBJECT LINKING AND EMBEDDING

The applications in Microsoft Office are thoroughly integrated with one another. They look alike and they work in consistent fashion. Equally important, they share information through a technology known as *Object Linking and Embedding* (OLE), which enables you to create a *compound document* containing data (objects) from multiple applications.

The compound document in Figure 7 was created in Word, and it contains objects (a worksheet and a chart) that were created in Excel. The letterhead uses a logo that was taken from the ClipArt Gallery, while the name and address of the recipient were drawn from an Access database. The various objects were inserted into the compound document through linking or embedding, which are

Office of Residential Living

University of Miami • **P.O. Box 243984** • **Coral Gables, FL 33124**

September 25, 1995

Mr. Jeffrey Redmond, President
Dynamic Dining Services
4329 Palmetto Lane
Miami, FL 33157

Dear Jeff,

As per our earlier conversation, occupancy is up in all of the dorms for the 1995 - 1996 school year. I have enclosed a spreadsheet and chart that show our occupancy rates for the 1992 - 1995 school years. Please realize, however, that the 1995 figures are projections, as the Fall 1995 numbers are still incomplete. The final 1995 numbers should be confirmed within the next two weeks. I hope that this helps with your planning. If you need further information, please contact me at the above address.

Dorm Occupancy				
	1992	1993	1994	1995
Beatty	330	285	270	310
Broward	620	580	520	565
Graham	450	397	352	393
Rawlings	435	375	326	372
Tolbert	615	554	524	581

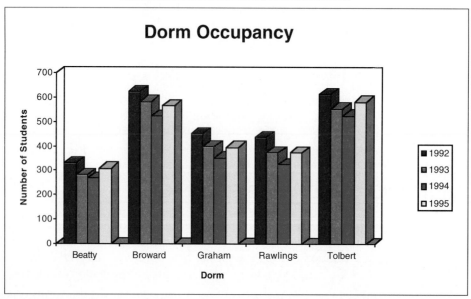

FIGURE 7   A Compound Document

actually two very different techniques. Both operations, however, are much more sophisticated than simply pasting an object, because with either linking or embedding, you can edit the object by using the tools of the original application.

The difference between linking and embedding depends on whether the object is stored within the compound document (*embedding*) or in its own file (*linking*). An *embedded object* is stored in the compound document, which in turn becomes the only user (client) of that object. A *linked object* is stored in its own file, and the compound document is one of many potential clients of that object. The compound document does not contain the linked object per se, but only a representation of the object as well as a pointer (link) to the file containing the object. The advantage of linking is that the document is updated automatically if the object changes.

The choice between linking and embedding depends on how the object will be used. Linking is preferable if the object is likely to change and the compound document requires the latest version. Linking should also be used when the same object is placed in many documents so that any change to the object has to be made in only one place. Embedding should be used if you need to take the object with you—for example, if you intend to edit the document on a different computer.

OBJECT LINKING AND EMBEDDING

Object Linking and Embedding (OLE) enables you to create a compound document containing objects (data) from multiple Windows applications. OLE is one of the major benefits of working in the Windows environment, but it would be impossible to illustrate all of the techniques in a single exercise. Accordingly, we have created the icon at the left to help you identify the many examples of object linking and embedding that appear throughout the Exploring Windows series.

SUMMARY

The common user interface requires every Windows application to follow a consistent set of conventions and ensures that all applications work basically the same way. The development of a suite of applications from a single vendor extends this concept by imposing additional similarities on all applications within the suite.

Microsoft distributes two versions of the Office Suite: Standard Office and Office Professional. Both versions include Word, Excel, and PowerPoint. The Office Professional also has Microsoft Access. Both versions also include a fifth application, Schedule+, as well as several smaller applications and shared utilities.

The Microsoft Office Shortcut Bar provides immediate access to each application in Microsoft Office. The Shortcut Bar is fully customizable with respect to the buttons it displays, its appearance, and its position on the desktop. The Open a Document and Start a New Document buttons enable you to think in terms of a document rather than the associated application.

Object Linking and Embedding (OLE) enables you to create a compound document containing data (objects) from multiple applications. Linking and embedding are different operations. The difference between the two depends on whether the object is stored within the compound document (embedding) or in its own file (linking).

Answer Wizard
ClipArt Gallery
Compound document
Common user interface
Contents tab
Embedding
Formatting toolbar
Index tab
Linking

Microsoft Access
Microsoft Excel
Microsoft Office
  Professional
Microsoft PowerPoint
Microsoft Standard
  Office
Microsoft Word
Object Linking and
  Embedding (OLE)

Microsoft Office
  Shortcut Bar
Online help
Schedule+
Standard toolbar
System Information
  Utility
WordArt

INTRODUCTION TO MICROSOFT EXCEL: WHAT IS A SPREADSHEET?

OBJECTIVES

After reading this chapter you will be able to:

1. Describe a spreadsheet and suggest several potential applications; explain how the rows and columns of a spreadsheet are identified, and how its cells are labeled.

2. Distinguish between a formula and a constant; explain the use of a predefined function within a formula.

3. Open an Excel workbook; add and delete rows and columns of a worksheet; save and print the modified worksheet.

4. Distinguish between a pull-down menu, a shortcut menu, and a toolbar.

5. Describe the three-dimensional nature of an Excel workbook; distinguish between a workbook and a worksheet.

6. Print a worksheet two ways: to show the computed values or the cell formulas.

7. Use the Page Setup command to print a worksheet with or without gridlines and/or row and column headings; preview a worksheet before printing.

OVERVIEW

This chapter provides a broad-based introduction to spreadsheets in general, and to Microsoft Excel in particular. The spreadsheet is the microcomputer application that is most widely used by managers and executives. Our intent is to show the wide diversity of business and other uses to which the spreadsheet model can be applied. For one example, we draw an analogy between the spreadsheet and the accountant's ledger. For a second example, we create an instructor's grade book.

The chapter covers the fundamentals of spreadsheets as implemented in Excel, which uses the term worksheet rather than spreadsheet. It discusses how the rows and columns of an Excel worksheet are labeled, the difference between a formula and a constant, and the ability of a worksheet to recalculate itself after a change is made. We also distinguish between a worksheet and a workbook.

The hands-on exercises in the chapter enable you to apply all of the material at the computer, and are indispensable to the learn-by-doing philosophy we follow throughout the text. As you do the exercises, you may recognize many commands from other Windows applications, all of which share a common user interface and consistent command structure. Excel will be even easier to learn if you already know another application in Microsoft Office.

INTRODUCTION TO SPREADSHEETS

A ***spreadsheet*** is the computerized equivalent of an accountant's ledger. As with the ledger, it consists of a grid of rows and columns that enables you to organize data in a readily understandable format. Figures 1.1a and 1.1b show the same information displayed in ledger and spreadsheet format, respectively.

"What is the big deal?" you might ask. The big deal is that after you change an entry (or entries), the spreadsheet will, automatically and almost instantly, recompute all of the formulas. Consider, for example, the profit projection spreadsheet shown in Figure 1.1b. As the spreadsheet is presently constructed, the unit price is $20 and the projected sales are 1,200 units, producing gross sales of $24,000 ($20/unit × 1,200 units). The projected expenses are $19,200, which yields a profit of $4,800 ($24,000 − $19,200). If the unit price is increased to $22 per unit, the spreadsheet recomputes every formula, adjusting the values of gross sales and net profit. The modified spreadsheet of Figure 1.1c appears automatically.

With a calculator and bottle of correction fluid or a good eraser, the same changes could also be made to the ledger. But imagine for a moment a ledger with hundreds of entries, many of which depend on the entry you wish to change. You can appreciate the time required to make all the necessary changes to the ledger by hand. The same spreadsheet, with hundreds of entries, will be recomputed automatically by the computer. And the computer will not make mistakes. Herein lies the advantage of a spreadsheet—the ability to make changes, and to have the com-

						Initials Date		
						Prepared by: Approved by:		
		1	2	3	4	5	6	
1	UNIT PRICE		20					1
2	UNIT SALES		1,200					2
3	GROSS PROFIT		24,000					3
4								4
5	EXPENSES							5
6	PRODUCTION		10,000					6
7	DISTRIBUTION		1,200					7
8	MARKETING		5,000					8
9	OVERHEAD		3,000					9
10	TOTAL EXPENSES		19,200					10
11								11
12	NET PROFIT		4,800					12

(a) The Accountant's Ledger

FIGURE 1.1 The Accountant's Ledger

Unit price is increased to $22

Formulas recompute automatically

	A	B
1	Profit Projection	
2		
3	Unit Price	$20
4	Unit Sales	1,200
5	Gross Sales	$24,000
6		
7	Expenses	
8	Production	$10,000
9	Distribution	$1,200
10	Marketing	$5,000
11	Overhead	$3,000
12	Total Expenses	$19,200
13		
14	Net Profit	$4,800

(b) Original Spreadsheet

	A	B
1	Profit Projection	
2		
3	Unit Price	$22
4	Unit Sales	1,200
5	Gross Sales	$26,400
6		
7	Expenses	
8	Production	$10,000
9	Distribution	$1,200
10	Marketing	$5,000
11	Overhead	$3,000
12	Total Expenses	$19,200
13		
14	Net Profit	$7,200

(c) Modified Spreadsheet

FIGURE 1.1   The Accountant's Ledger (continued)

puter carry out the recalculation faster and more accurately than could be accomplished manually.

The Professor's Grade Book

A second example of a spreadsheet, one with which you can easily identify, is that of a professor's grade book. The grades are recorded by hand in a notebook, which is nothing more than a different kind of accountant's ledger. Figure 1.2 contains both manual and spreadsheet versions of a grade book.

Figure 1.2a shows a handwritten grade book as it has been done since the days of the little red schoolhouse. For the sake of simplicity, only five students are shown, each with three grades. The professor has computed class averages for each exam, as well as a semester average for every student, in which the final counts *twice* as much as either test; for example, Adams's average is equal to $(100+90+81+81)/4 = 88$.

Figure 1.2b shows the grade book as it might appear in a spreadsheet, and is essentially unchanged from Figure 1.2a. Walker's grade on the final exam in Figure 1.2b is 90, giving him a semester average of 85 and producing a class average on the final of 75.2 as well. Now consider Figure 1.2c, in which the grade on Walker's final has been changed to 100, causing Walker's semester average to change from 85 to 90, and the class average on the final to go from 75.2 to 77.2. As with the profit projection, a change to any entry within the grade book automatically recalculates all other dependent formulas as well. Hence, when Walker's final exam was regraded, all dependent formulas (the class average for the final as well as Walker's semester average) were recomputed.

As simple as the idea of a spreadsheet may seem, it provided the first major reason for managers to have a personal computer on their desks. Essentially, anything that can be done with a pencil, a pad of paper, and a calculator can be done faster and far more accurately with a spreadsheet.

Final counts twice so average is
computed as (100 + 90 + 81 + 81)/4

	TEST 1	TEST 2	FINAL	AVERAGE
ADAMS	100	90	81	88
BAKER	90	76	87	85
GLASSMAN	90	78	78	81
MOLDOF	60	60	40	50
WALKER	80	80	90	85
CLASS AVERAGE	84.0	76.8	75.2	
NOTE: FINAL COUNTS DOUBLE				

(a) The Professor's Grade Book

	A	B	C	D	E
1	Student	Test 1	Test 2	Final	Average
2					
3	Adams	100	90	81	88.0
4	Baker	90	76	87	85.0
5	Glassman	90	78	78	81.0
6	Moldof	60	60	40	50.0
7	Walker	80	80	90	85.0
8					
9	Class Average	84.0	76.8	75.2	

(b) Original Grades

Grade on Walker's
final is changed to 100

	A	B	C	D	E
1	Student	Test 1	Test 2	Final	Average
2					
3	Adams	100	90	81	88.0
4	Baker	90	76	87	85.0
5	Glassman	90	78	78	81.0
6	Moldof	60	60	40	50.0
7	Walker	80	80	100	90.0
8					
9	Class Average	84.0	76.8	77.2	

Formulas recompute automatically

(c) Modified Spreadsheet

FIGURE 1.2 The Professor's Grade Book

Row and Column Headings

A spreadsheet is divided into rows and columns, with each row and column assigned a heading. Rows are given numeric headings ranging from 1 to 16,384 (the maximum number of rows allowed). Columns are assigned alphabetic headings from column A to Z, then continue from AA to AZ and then from BA to BZ and so on, until the last of 256 columns (column IV) is reached.

The intersection of a row and column forms a *cell,* with the number of cells in a spreadsheet equal to the number of rows times the number of columns. The professor's grade book in Figure 1.2, for example, has 5 columns labeled A through E, 9 rows numbered from 1 to 9, and a total of 45 cells. Each cell has a unique *cell reference;* for example, the cell at the intersection of column A and row 9 is known as cell A9. The column heading always precedes the row heading in the cell reference.

Formulas and Constants

Figure 1.3 shows an alternate view of the spreadsheet for the professor's grade book that displays the *cell contents* rather than the computed *values.* This figure displays the actual entries (formulas and constants) that were entered into the individual cells, which enable the spreadsheet to recalculate formulas whenever any entry changes.

A *constant* is an entry that does not change; that is, it may be a number, such as a student's grade on an exam, or it may be descriptive text (a label), such as a student's name. A *formula* is a combination of numeric constants, cell references, arithmetic operators, and/or functions (described below) that displays the result of a calculation. Every cell in a spreadsheet contains either a formula or a constant.

A formula always begins with an equal sign; a constant does not. Consider, for example, the formula in cell E3, =(B3+C3+2*D3)/4, which computes Adams's semester average. The formula is built in accordance with the professor's rules for computing a student's semester average, which counts the final twice as much as either exam. Excel uses symbols +, −, *, /, and ^ to indicate addition, subtraction, multiplication, division, and exponentiation, respectively, and follows the normal rules of arithmetic precedence. Any expression in parentheses is evaluated first, then within an expression exponentiation is performed first, followed by multiplication or division in left to right order, then finally addition or subtraction, also in left-to-right order.

The formula in cell E3 takes the grade on the first exam (in cell B3), plus the grade on the second exam (in cell C3), plus two times the grade on the final (in cell D3), and divides the result by four. Because we entered a formula for the semester average (rather than a constant), should any of the exam grades change, the semester average (a formula whose results depend on the individual exam grades) will also change. This, in essence, is the basic principle behind the spreadsheet and explains why, when one number changes, various other numbers throughout the spreadsheet change as well.

A formula may also include a *function,* or predefined computational task, such as the *AVERAGE function* in cells B9, C9, and D9. The function in cell B9, for example, =AVERAGE(B3:B7), is interpreted to mean the average of all cells starting at cell B3 and ending at cell B7 and is equivalent to the formula =(B3+B4+B5+B6+B7)/5. You can appreciate that functions are often easier to use than the corresponding formulas, especially with larger spreadsheets (and classes with many students).

Constant (entry that does not change)

Formula (displays the result of a calculation)

Function (predefined computational task)

	A	B	C	D	E
1	Student	Test 1	Test 2	Final	Average
2					
3	Adams	100	90	81	=(B3+C3+2*D3)/4
4	Baker	90	76	87	=(B4+C4+2*D4)/4
5	Glassman	90	78	78	=(B5+C5+2*D5)/4
6	Moldof	60	60	40	=(B6+C6+2*D6)/4
7	Walker	80	80	90	=(B7+C7+2*D7)/4
8					
9	Class Average	=AVERAGE(B3:B7)	=AVERAGE(C3:C7)	=AVERAGE(D3:D7)	

FIGURE 1.3   The Professor's Grade Book (cell formulas)

Figure 1.4 displays the professor's grade book as it is implemented in Microsoft Excel. Microsoft Excel is a Windows application, and thus shares the common user interface with which you are already familiar. You should recognize, therefore, that the desktop in Figure 1.4 has two open windows—an application window for Microsoft Excel and a document window for the workbook, which is currently open.

Each window has its own Minimize, Maximize (or Restore), and Close buttons. Both windows have been maximized and thus the title bars have been merged into a single title bar that appears at the top of the application window. The title bar reflects the application (Microsoft Excel) as well as the name of the workbook (Grade Book) on which you are working. A menu bar appears immediately below the title bar. Two toolbars, which are discussed in depth on page 8, appear below the menu bar. The TipWizard appears immediately under the toolbars and offers suggestions to enable you to work more efficiently. Vertical and horizontal scroll bars appear at the right and bottom of the document window. The Windows 95 taskbar appears at the bottom of the screen and shows the open applications.

The terminology is important, and we distinguish here between spreadsheet, worksheet, and workbook. Excel refers to a spreadsheet as a *worksheet*. Spreadsheet is a generic term; *workbook* and *worksheet* are unique to Excel. An Excel *workbook* contains one or more worksheets. The professor's grades for this class are contained in the CIS120 worksheet within the Grade Book workbook. This workbook also contains additional worksheets (CIS223 and CIS316) as indicated by the worksheet tabs at the bottom of the window. These worksheets contain the professor's grades for other courses that he or she is teaching this semester. (See practice problem 1 at the end of the chapter.)

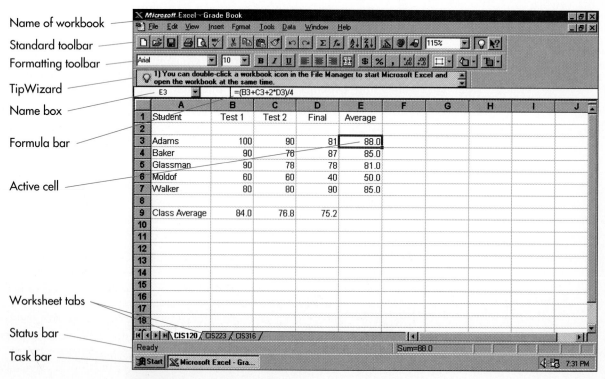

FIGURE 1.4 Professor's Grade Book

Figure 1.4 resembles the grade book shown earlier, but it includes several other elements that enable you to create and/or edit the worksheet. The heavy border around cell E3 indicates that it (cell E3) is the *active cell.* Any entry made at this time is made into the active cell, and any commands that are executed affect the contents of the active cell. The active cell can be changed by clicking a different cell, or by using the arrow keys to move to a different cell.

The displayed value in cell E3 is 88.0, but as indicated earlier, the cell contains a formula to compute the semester average rather than the number itself. The contents of the active cell, $=(B3+C3+2*D3)/4$, are displayed in the *formula bar* near the top of the worksheet. The cell reference for the active cell, cell E3 in Figure 1.4, appears in the *Name box* at the left of the formula bar.

The *status bar* at the bottom of the worksheet keeps you informed of what is happening as you work within Excel. It displays information about a selected command or an operation in progress. It also shows the status of the keyboard toggle switches, such as the Caps Lock key or the Ins key, neither of which has been toggled on in the figure.

THE EXCEL WORKBOOK

An Excel workbook is the electronic equivalent of the three-ring binder. A workbook contains one or more worksheets (or chart sheets), each of which is identified by a *tab* at the bottom of the workbook. The worksheets in a workbook are normally related to one another; for example, each worksheet may contain the sales for a specific division within a company. The advantage of a workbook is that all of its worksheets are stored in a single file, which is accessed as a unit.

Toolbars

Excel provides several different ways to accomplish the same task. Commands may be accessed from a pull-down menu, from a shortcut menu (which is displayed by pointing to an object and clicking the right mouse button), and/or through keyboard equivalents. Commands can also be executed from one of many *toolbars* that appear immediately below the menu bar. The Standard and Formatting toolbars are displayed by default. (All toolbars can be displayed or hidden by using the View menu as described on page 25 later in the chapter.)

The *Standard toolbar* contains buttons corresponding to the most basic commands in Excel—for example, opening and closing a workbook, printing a workbook, and so on. The icon on the button is intended to be indicative of its function (e.g., a printer to indicate the Print command). You can also point to the button to display a *ToolTip* showing the name of the button. The *Formatting toolbar* appears under the Standard toolbar, and provides access to common formatting operations such as boldface, italics, or underlining. The easiest way to master the toolbars is to view the buttons in groups according to their general function, as shown in Figure 1.5.

The toolbars may appear overwhelming at first, but there is absolutely no need to memorize what the individual buttons do. That will come with time. Indeed, if you use another office application such as Microsoft Word, you may already recognize many of the buttons on the Standard and Formatting toolbars. Most individuals start by using the pull-down menus, then look for shortcuts along the way.

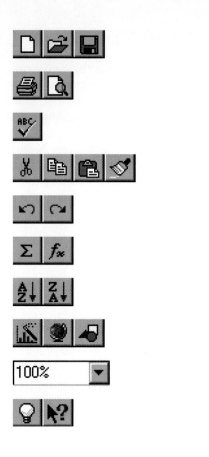

Opens a new workbook; opens an existing workbook; saves the workbook to disk

Prints the workbook; previews the workbook prior to printing

Checks spelling

Cuts or copies the selection to the clipboard; pastes the clipboard contents; copies the format of the selected cells

Undoes or redoes the previously executed command

Sums the suggested range; displays the Function Wizard dialog box

Performs an ascending or descending sort

Creates a chart; creates a map; toggles the Drawing toolbar on and off

Changes the zoom percentage

Displays the TipWizard; accesses online help

(a) The Standard Toolbar

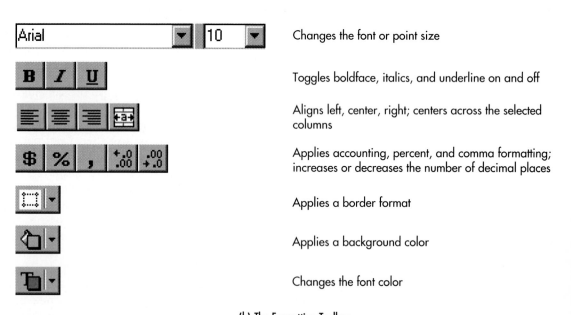

Changes the font or point size

Toggles boldface, italics, and underline on and off

Aligns left, center, right; centers across the selected columns

Applies accounting, percent, and comma formatting; increases or decreases the number of decimal places

Applies a border format

Applies a background color

Changes the font color

(b) The Formatting Toolbar

FIGURE 1.5   Toolbars

Entering Data

Data is entered into a worksheet by selecting a cell, then typing the constant or formula that is to go into that cell. The entry is displayed in the formula bar at the top of the window as it is being typed. The entry is completed by pressing the enter key, which moves the active cell to the cell immediately below the current cell, or by pressing any of the arrow keys to move to the next cell in the indicated direction. Pressing the right arrow key, for example, completes the entry and moves the active cell to the next cell in the same row. You can also complete the entry by clicking in a new cell, or by clicking the green check that appears to the left of the formula bar as data is entered.

To replace an existing entry, select the cell by clicking in the cell, or by using the keyboard to move to the cell. Type the corrected entry (as though you were entering it for the first time), then complete the entry as described above.

THE FILE MENU

The *File menu* is a critically important menu in virtually every Windows application. It contains the *Save command* to save a workbook to disk, and the *Open command* to subsequently retrieve (open) the workbook at a later time. The File Menu also contains the *Print command* to print a workbook, the *Close command* to close the current workbook but continue working in Excel, and the *Exit command* to quit Excel altogether.

The *Save command* copies the workbook that is currently being edited (the workbook in memory) to disk. The Save As dialog box appears the first time a workbook is saved so that you can specify the filename and other required information. All subsequent executions of the Save command save the workbook under the assigned name, replacing the previously saved version with the new version.

The Save As dialog box requires a filename (e.g., My First Spreadsheet in Figure 1.6a), which can be up to 255 characters in length. The filename may contain spaces and commas. The dialog box also requires the drive (and folder) in which the file is to be saved, as well as the file type that determines which application the file is associated with. (Long-time DOS users will remember the three-character extension at the end of a filename such as XLS to indicate an Excel workbook. The extension is generally hidden in Windows 95, according to options that are set through the View menu in My Computer. See page 30 in the Windows appendix.)

The Open command brings a copy of a previously saved workbook into memory, enabling you to edit the workbook. The Open command displays the Open dialog box in which you specify the file to retrieve. You indicate the drive (and optionally the folder) that contains the file, as well as the type of file you want to retrieve. Excel will then list all files of that type on the designated drive (and folder), enabling you to open the file you want.

Drive/Folder in which
file is to be saved

Click to select
Details view

Filename

File type

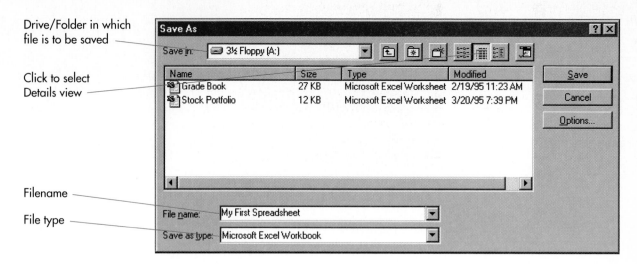

(a) Save As Dialog Box

Drive/Folder containing
the file

Click to select
Details view

File to be retrieved

File type

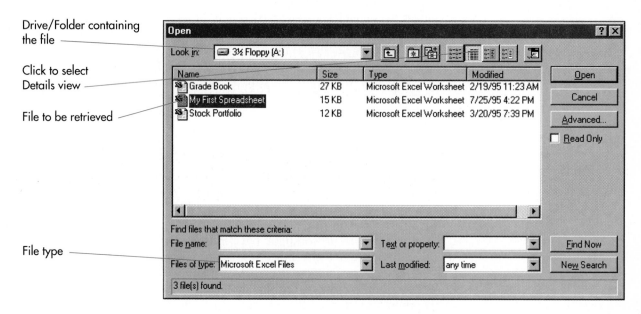

(b) File Open Dialog Box

FIGURE 1.6   The Save and Open Commands

The Save and Open commands work in conjunction with one another. The Save As dialog box in Figure 1.6a, for example, saves the file *My First Spreadsheet* onto the disk in drive A. The Open dialog box in Figure 1.6b brings that file back into memory so that you can work with the file, after which you can save the revised file for use at a later time.

The Save As and Open dialog boxes share a common toolbar that enables you to display the files on a specific drive (or folder) in different ways. The Details view is selected in both dialog boxes and displays the file size as well as the date and time a file was last modified. The drop-down arrow on the Look-in box enables you to display files on a different drive or folder.

THE SAVE AS COMMAND

The *Save As command* saves a workbook under a different name, and is useful when you want to retain a copy of the original workbook. The Save As command provides you with two copies of a workbook. The original workbook is kept on disk under its original name. A copy of the workbook is saved on disk under a new name and remains in memory. All subsequent editing is done on the new (renamed) workbook.

LEARNING BY DOING

We come now to the first of two hands-on exercises in this chapter that implement our learn-by-doing philosophy. The exercise shows you how to start Microsoft Excel and open the professor's grade book from the *data disk* that is referenced throughout the text. You can obtain a copy of the data disk from your instructor, or you can download the files on the data disk as described in the exercise. The data disk contains a series of Excel workbooks that are used in various exercises throughout the text. It can also be used to store the workbooks you create (or you can store the workbooks on a hard disk if you have access to your own computer).

HANDS-ON EXERCISE 1

Introduction to Microsoft Excel

Objectives: To start Microsoft Excel; to open, modify, and print an existing worksheet. Use Figure 1.7 as a guide in the exercise.

Step 1: Welcome to Windows 95

➤ Turn on the computer and all of its peripherals. The floppy drive should be empty prior to starting your machine. This ensures that the system starts by reading from the hard disk, which contains the Windows files, as opposed to a floppy disk, which does not.

➤ Your system will take a minute or so to get started, after which you should see the desktop in Figure 1.7a. Do not be concerned if the appearance of your desktop is different from ours.

➤ If you are new to Windows 95 and you want a quick introduction, click the **What's New** or **Windows Tour command buttons.** (Follow the instructions in the boxed tip to display the dialog box if it does not appear on your system.)

➤ Click the **Close button** to close the Welcome window and continue with the exercise.

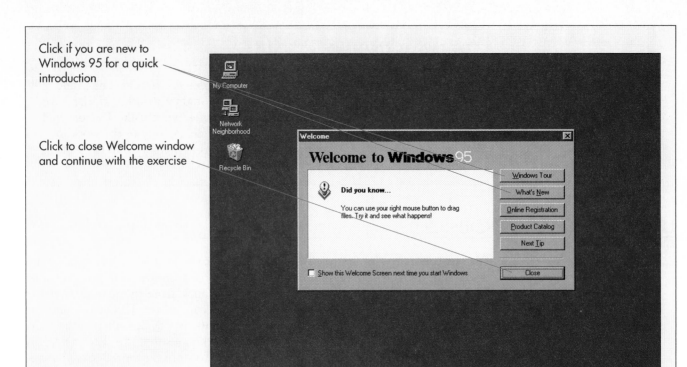

Click if you are new to Windows 95 for a quick introduction

Click to close Welcome window and continue with the exercise

Click to display the Start menu

(a) Welcome to Windows 95 (step 1)

FIGURE 1.7   Hands-on Exercise 1

TAKE THE WINDOWS 95 TOUR (REQUIRES CD-ROM INSTALLATION)

Windows 95 greets you with a Welcome window that contains a command button to take you on a 10-minute tour of Windows 95. Click the command button and enjoy the show. You might also try the What's New command button for a quick overview of changes from Windows 3.1. If you do not see the Welcome window when you start Windows 95, click the Start button, click Run, type C:\WINDOWS\WELCOME in the Open *text box,* and press enter.

STEP 2: Install the Data Disk

➤ Your instructor will make the files referenced on the data disk available to you in different ways. For example:

• The files may be on a network drive, in which case you can use the Windows Explorer to copy the files from the network to a floppy disk.

• There may be an actual "data disk" that you are to check out from the lab in order to use the Copy Disk command to duplicate the disk.

➤ Alternatively, you can download the data disk from the lab at school, or from home if you have access to the Internet and World Wide Web. Ask your instructor for any additional instructions that pertain to your school.

STEP 3: Start Microsoft Excel

➤ Click the **Start button** to display the Start menu. Click (or point to) the **Programs menu,** then click **Microsoft Excel** to start the program.

➤ If necessary, click the **Maximize button** in the application window so that Excel takes the entire desktop as shown in Figure 1.7b. Click the **Maximize button** in the document window (if necessary) so that the document window is as large as possible.

POINT AND SLIDE

Click the Start button, then slowly slide the mouse pointer over the various menu options. Notice that each time you point to a submenu, its items are displayed. Point to (don't click) the Programs menu, then click the Microsoft Excel item to start the program. In other words, you don't have to click a submenu—you can just point and slide!

STEP 4: Open the Workbook

➤ Pull down the **File menu** and click **Open** (or click the **Open button** on the Standard toolbar). You should see a dialog box similar to the one in Figure 1.7b.

➤ Click the **Details button** to change to the Details view. Click and drag the vertical border between two columns to increase (or decrease) the size of a column.

➤ Click the **drop-down arrow** on the Look In list box. Click the appropriate drive, drive C or drive A, depending on the location of your data. Double click the **Exploring Excel folder** to make it the active folder (the folder from which you will retrieve and into which you will save the workbook).

➤ Click the **down scroll arrow** if you need to scroll in order to click **Grade Book** to select the professor's grade book. Click the **Open command button** to open the workbook and begin the exercise.

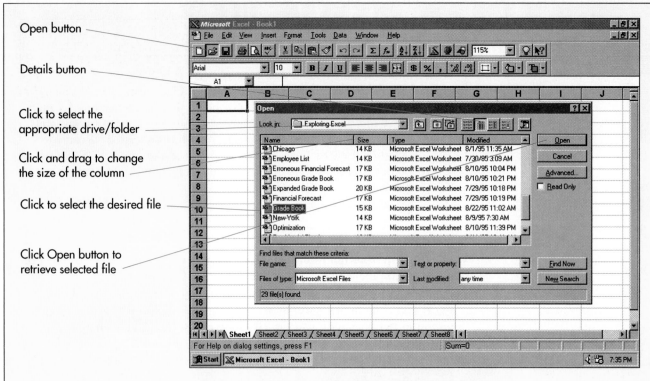

Open button

Details button

Click to select the appropriate drive/folder

Click and drag to change the size of the column

Click to select the desired file

Click Open button to retrieve selected file

(b) Open the Grade Book (steps 3 & 4)

FIGURE 1.7   Hands-on Exercise 1 (continued)

A VERY USEFUL TOOLBAR

The Open and Save As dialog boxes share a common toolbar with several very useful buttons. Click the Details button to switch to the Details view and see the date and time the file was last modified as well as its size. Click the List button to display an icon for each file, enabling you to see many more files at the same time than in the Details view. The Preview button lets you see a workbook before you open it. The Properties button displays information about the workbook, including the number of revisions.

STEP 5: The Active Cell and Formula Bar

➤ You should see the workbook in Figure 1.7c. Click in **cell B3,** the cell containing Adams's grade on the first test. Cell B3 is now the active cell and is surrounded by a heavy border. The Name box indicates that cell B3 is the active cell, and its contents are displayed in the formula bar.

➤ Click in **cell B4** (or press the **down arrow key**) to make it the active cell. The Name box indicates cell B4 while the formula bar indicates a grade of 90.

➤ Click in **cell E3,** the cell containing the formula to compute Adams's semester average; the worksheet displays the computed average of 88.0, but the formula bar displays the formula, =(B3+C3+2*D3)/4, to compute that average based on the test grades.

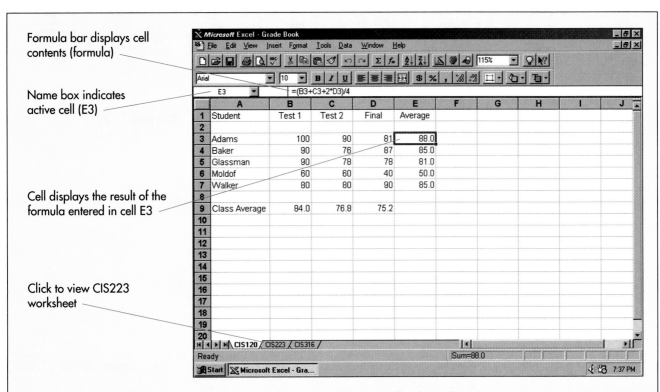

Formula bar displays cell contents (formula)

Name box indicates active cell (E3)

Cell displays the result of the formula entered in cell E3

Click to view CIS223 worksheet

(c) The Active Cell and Formula Bar (step 5)

FIGURE 1.7   Hands-on Exercise 1 (continued)

➤ Continue to change the active cell (with the mouse or arrow keys) and notice how the display in the Name box and formula bar change to reflect the active cell.

THE ANSWER WIZARD

The Answer Wizard enables you to request help by posing a question in English. Pull down the Help menu and click the Answer Wizard command. Type your question in the text box, for example, "How do I get help?", then click the Search command button. The wizard will return a list of help topics that answer your question together with a list of related topics that may be of interest to you.

STEP 6: View the Other Worksheets

➤ Click the **CIS223 tab** to view a different worksheet within the same workbook. This worksheet contains the grades for a different class.

➤ Click the **CIS316 tab** to view this worksheet. Click the **CIS120 tab** to return to this worksheet and continue with the exercise.

STEP 7: Experiment (What If?)

➤ Click in **cell C4,** the cell containing Baker's grade on the second test. Enter a corrected value of **86** (instead of the previous entry of 76). Press **enter** (or click in another cell).

➤ The effects of this change ripple through the worksheet, automatically changing the computed value for Baker's average in cell E4 to 87.5. The class average on the second test in cell C9 changes to 78.8.

➤ Change Walker's grade on the final from 90 to **100.** Press **enter** (or click in another cell). Walker's average in cell E7 changes to 90.0, while the class average in cell D9 changes to 77.2.

➤ Your worksheet should match Figure 1.7d.

THE UNDO COMMAND

The *Undo command* reverses the effect of the most recent operation and is invaluable at any time, but especially when you are learning. Pull down the Edit menu and click Undo (or click the Undo button on the Standard toolbar) to cancel the effects of the preceding command. Use the Undo command whenever something happens to your worksheet that is different from what you intended.

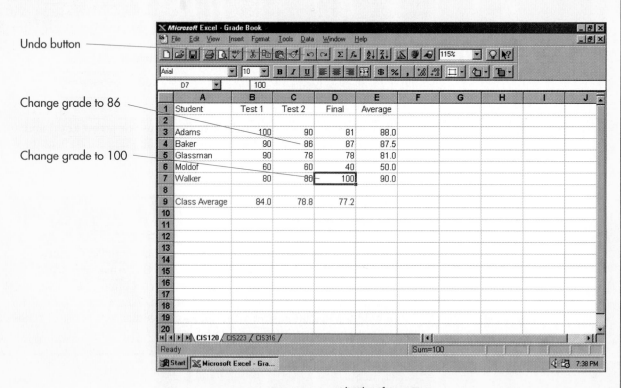

(d) What If (step 7)

FIGURE 1.7   Hands-on Exercise 1 (continued)

STEP 8: Print the Worksheet

➤ Pull down the **File menu** and click **Save** (or click the **Save button** on the Standard toolbar).

➤ Pull down the **File menu.** Click **Print** to produce a dialog box requesting information about the Print command as shown in Figure 1.7e. Click **OK** to accept the default options (you need to print only the selected worksheet).

Print button

Save button

Click OK to print the worksheet

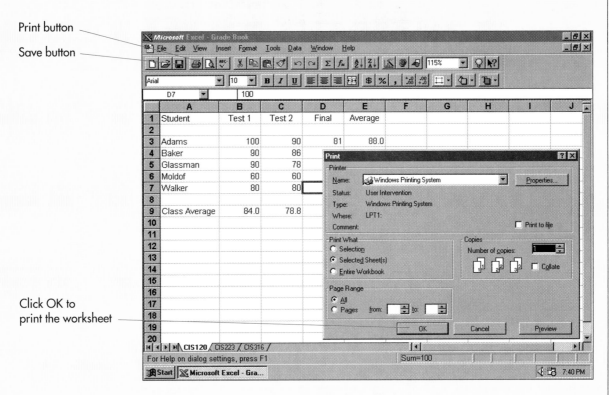

(e) Print the Workbook (step 8)

FIGURE 1.7   Hands-on Exercise 1 (continued)

ABOUT MICROSOFT EXCEL

Pull down the Help menu and click About Microsoft Excel to display the specific release number as well as other licensing information, including the product serial number. This help screen also contains two very useful command buttons, System Info and Technical Support. The first button displays information about the hardware installed on your system, including the amount of memory and available space on the hard drive. The Technical Support button provides the telephone numbers to call for technical assistance.

STEP 9: Close the Workbook

➤ Pull down the **File menu.** Click **Close** to close the workbook but leave Excel open.

➤ Pull down the **File menu** a second time. Click **Exit** if you do not want to continue with the next exercise at this time.

We trust that you completed the hands-on exercise without difficulty and that you are more confident in your ability than when you first began. The exercise was not complicated, but it did accomplish several objectives and set the stage for a second exercise, which follows shortly.

Consider now Figure 1.8, which contains a modified version of the professor's grade book. Figure 1.8a shows the grade book at the end of the first hands-on exercise and reflects the changes made to the grades for Baker and Walker. Figure 1.8b shows the worksheet as it will appear at the end of the second exercise. Several changes bear mention:

1. One student has dropped the class and two other students have been added. Moldof appeared in the original worksheet in Figure 1.8a, but has somehow managed to withdraw; Coulter and Courier did not appear in the original grade book but have been added to the worksheet in Figure 1.8b.
2. A new column containing the students' majors has been added.

The implementation of these changes is accomplished through a combination of the Insert and Delete commands that enable you to add or remove rows or columns as necessary.

Insert and Delete Commands

The *Insert command* adds row(s) or column(s) to an existing worksheet. The *Delete command* removes existing row(s) or column(s). Both commands auto-

	A	B	C	D	E
1	Student	Test 1	Test 2	Final	Average
2					
3	Adams	100	90	81	88.0
4	Baker	90	86	87	87.5
5	Glassman	90	78	78	81.0
6	Moldof	60	60	40	50.0
7	Walker	80	80	100	90.0
8					
9	Class Average	84.0	78.8	77.2	

(a) After Hands-on Exercise 1

A new column has been added (Major)

Two new students have been added

Moldof has been deleted

	A	B	C	D	E	F
1	Student	Major	Test 1	Test 2	Final	Average
2						
3	Adams	CIS	100	90	81	88.0
4	Baker	MKT	90	86	87	87.5
5	Coulter	ACC	85	95	100	95.0
6	Courier	FIN	75	75	85	80.0
7	Glassman	CIS	90	78	78	81.0
8	Walker	CIS	80	80	100	90.0
9						

(b) After Hands-on Exercise 2

FIGURE 1.8   The Modified Grade Book

matically adjust the cell references in existing formulas to account for the insertion or deletion of rows and columns within the worksheet.

Figure 1.9 displays the cell formulas in the professor's grade book and corresponds to the worksheets in Figure 1.8. The "before" and "after" worksheets reflect the insertion of a new column containing the students' majors, the addition of two new students, Coulter and Courier, and the deletion of an existing student, Moldof.

Let us consider the formula to compute Adams's semester average, which is contained in cell E3 of the original grade book, but in cell F3 in the modified grade book. The formula in Figure 1.9a referenced cells B3, C3, and D3 (the grades on test 1, test 2, and the final). The corresponding formula in Figure 1.9b reflects the fact that a new column has been inserted, and references cells C3, D3, and E3. The change in the formula is made automatically by Excel, without any action on the part of the user other than to insert the new column. The formulas for all other students have been adjusted in similar fashion.

Some students (all students below Baker) have had a further adjustment to reflect the addition of the new students through insertion of new rows in the worksheet. Glassman, for example, appeared in row 5 of the original worksheet, but appears in row 7 of the revised worksheet. Hence the formula to compute Glassman's semester average now references the grades in row 7, rather than in row 5 as in the original worksheet.

Finally, the formulas to compute the class averages have also been adjusted. These formulas appeared in row 9 of Figure 1.9a and averaged the grades in rows 3 through 7. The revised worksheet has a net increase of one student, which automatically moves these formulas to row 10, where the formulas are adjusted to average the grades in rows 3 through 8.

Formula references grades in B3, C3, and D3 —

Function references grades in rows 3–7 —

	A	B	C	D	E
1	Student	Test1	Test2	Final	Average
2					
3	Adams	100	90	81	=(B3+C3+2*D3)/4
4	Baker	90	86	87	=(B4+C4+2*D4)/4
5	Glassman	90	78	78	=(B5+C5+2*D5)/4
6	Moldof	60	60	40	=(B6+C6+2*D6)/4
7	Walker	80	80	100	=(B7+C7+2*D7)/4
8					
9	Class Average	=AVERAGE(B3:B7)	=AVERAGE(C3:C7)	=AVERAGE(D3:D7)	

(a) Before

	A	B	C	D	E	F
1	Student	Major	Test1	Test2	Final	Average
2						
3	Adams	CIS	100	90	81	=(C3+D3+2*E3)/4
4	Baker	MKT	90	86	87	=(C4+D4+2*E4)/4
5	Coulter	ACC	85	95	100	=(C5+D5+2*E5)/4
6	Courier	FIN	75	75	85	=(C6+D6+2*E6)/4
7	Glassman	CIS	90	78	78	=(C7+D7+2*E7)/4
8	Walker	CIS	80	80	100	=(C8+D8+2*E8)/4
9						
10	Class Average		=AVERAGE(C3:C8)	=AVERAGE(D3:D8)	=AVERAGE(E3:E8)	

Function changes to reference grades in rows 3–8 (due to addition of 2 new students and deletion of 1)

Formula changes to reference grades in C3, D3, and E3 due to addition of new column

(b) After

FIGURE 1.9   The Insert and Delete Commands

THE PAGE SETUP COMMAND

The Print command was used at the end of the first hands-on exercise to print the completed workbook. The **Page Setup command** gives you complete control of the printed worksheet as illustrated in Figure 1.10. Many of the options may not appear important now, but you will appreciate them as you develop larger and more complicated worksheets later in the text.

The Page tab in Figure 1.10a determines the orientation and scaling of the printed page. **Portrait orientation** (8½ × 11) prints vertically down the page. **Landscape orientation** (11 × 8½) prints horizontally across the page and is used

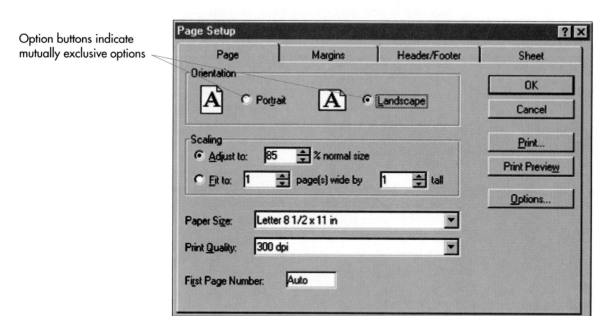

(a) The Page Tab

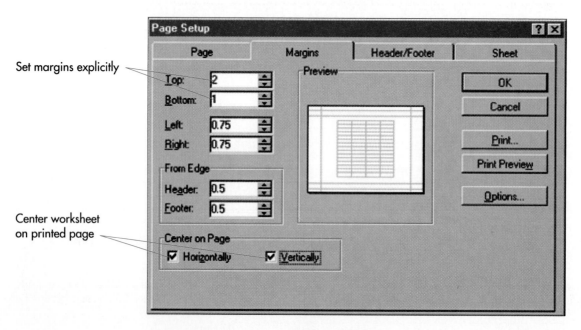

(b) The Margins Tab

FIGURE 1.10   The Page Setup Command

when the worksheet is too wide to fit on a portrait page. The option buttons indicate mutually exclusive items, one of which *must* be selected; that is, a worksheet must be printed in either portrait or landscape orientation. Option buttons are also used to choose the scaling factor. You can reduce (enlarge) the output by a designated scaling factor, or you can force the output to fit on a specified number of pages. The latter option is typically used to force a worksheet to fit on a single page.

Click to select a preformatted header

Click to select a preformatted footer

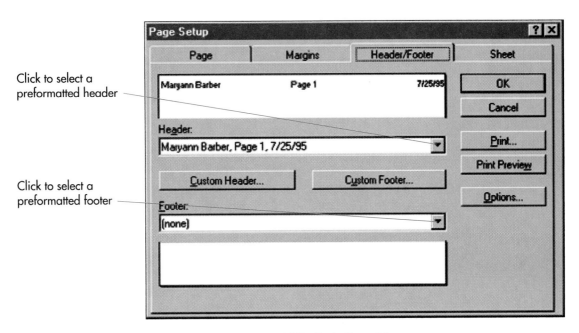

(c) The Header/Footer Tab

Help button

Print row/column headings

Print gridlines

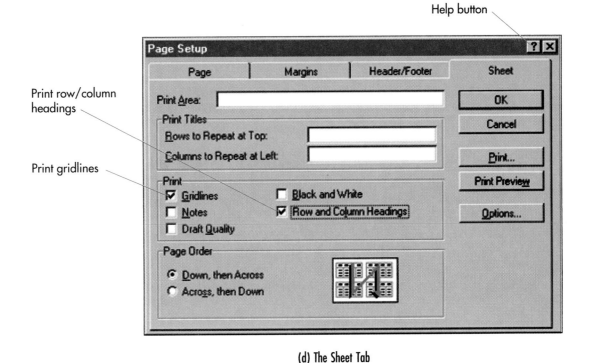

(d) The Sheet Tab

FIGURE 1.10   The Page Setup Command (continued)

The Margins tab in Figure 1.10b not only controls the margins, but will also center the worksheet horizontally and/or vertically. Check boxes are associated with the centering options and indicate that multiple options can be chosen; for example, horizontally and vertically are both selected. The Margins tab also determines the distance of the header and footer from the edge of the page.

The Header/Footer tab in Figure 1.10c lets you create a header (and/or footer) that appears at the top (and/or bottom) of every page. The pull-down list boxes let you choose from several preformatted entries, or alternatively, you can click the appropriate command button to customize either entry.

The Sheet tab in Figure 1.10d offers several additional options. The Gridlines option prints lines to separate the cells within the worksheet. The Row and Column Headings option displays the column letters and row numbers. Both options should be selected for most worksheets. Information about the additional entries can be obtained by clicking the Help button.

THE PRINT PREVIEW COMMAND

The **Print Preview command** displays the worksheet as it will appear when printed. The command is invaluable and will save you considerable time as you don't have to rely on trial and error to obtain the perfect printout. The Print Preview command can be executed from the File menu, via the Print Preview button on the Standard toolbar, or from the Print Preview command button within the Page Setup command.

HANDS-ON EXERCISE 2

Modifying a Worksheet

Objective: To open an existing workbook; to insert and delete rows and columns in a worksheet; to print cell formulas and displayed values; to use the Page Setup command to modify the appearance of a printed workbook. Use Figure 1.11 as a guide in doing the exercise.

STEP 1: Open the Workbook

➤ Open the grade book as you did in the previous exercise. Pull down the **File menu** and click **Open** (or click the **Open button** on the Standard toolbar) to display the Open dialog box.

➤ Click the **drop-down arrow** on the Look In list box. Click the appropriate drive, drive C or drive A, depending on the location of your data. Double click the **Exploring Excel folder** to make it the active folder (the folder in which you will save the workbook).

➤ Click the **down scroll arrow** until you can select (click) the **Grade Book** workbook. Click the **Open command button** to open the workbook and begin the exercise.

STEP 2: The Save As Command

➤ Pull down the **File menu.** Click **Save As** to display the dialog box shown in Figure 1.11a.

➤ Enter **Finished Grade Book** as the name of the new workbook. (A filename may contain up to 255 characters. Spaces and commas are allowed in the filename.)

➤ Click the **Save button.** Press the **Esc key** or click the **Close button** if you see a Properties dialog box.

➤ There are now two identical copies of the file on disk: "Grade Book," which is the completed workbook from the previous exercise, and "Finished Grade Book," which you just created. The title bar shows the latter name, which is the workbook currently in memory.

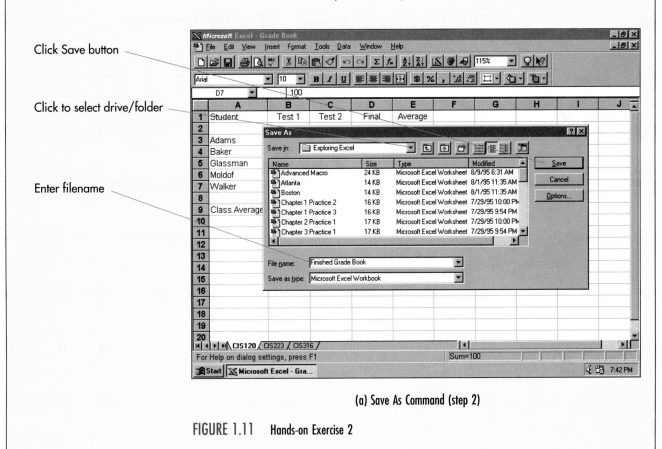

Click Save button

Click to select drive/folder

Enter filename

(a) Save As Command (step 2)

FIGURE 1.11   Hands-on Exercise 2

FILE PROPERTIES

Excel automatically stores summary information and other properties for each workbook you create, and prompts for that information when the workbook is saved initially. The information is interesting, but is typically not used by beginners, and hence we suggest you suppress the prompt for this information. Pull down the Tools menu, click Options, click the General tab, then clear the box to Prompt for File Properties. You can view (edit) the properties of any workbook by clicking the Properties command in the File menu.

STEP 3: Delete a Row

➤ Click any cell in **row 6** (the row you will delete). Pull down the **Edit menu.** Click **Delete** to display the dialog box in Figure 1.11b. Click **Entire Row.** Click **OK** to delete row 6.

➤ Moldof has disappeared from the grade book, and the class averages (now in row 8) have been updated automatically to reflect the fact that Moldof is gone.

Undo button

Click any cell in row 6

Select Entire Row

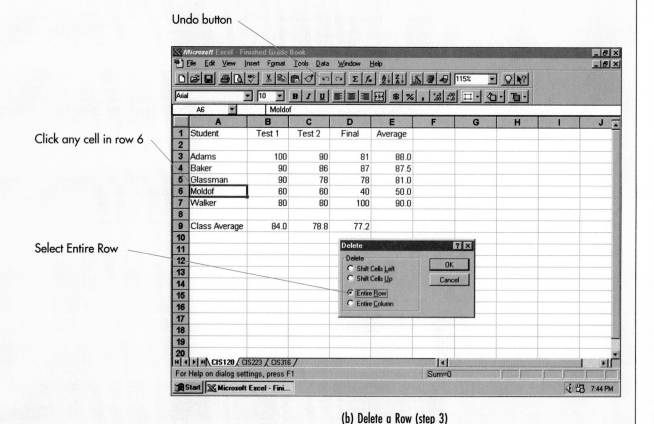

(b) Delete a Row (step 3)

FIGURE 1.11   Hands-on Exercise 2 (continued)

ERASING VERSUS DELETING

The Edit Delete command deletes the selected cell, row, or column from the worksheet. It is very different from the Edit Clear command, which erases the contents (and/or formatting) of the selected cells, but does not delete the cells from the worksheet. The Edit Delete command causes Excel to adjust cell references throughout the worksheet. The Edit Clear command does not adjust cell references as no cells are moved.

STEP 4: The Undo Command

➤ Pull down the **Edit menu** and click **Undo Delete** (or click the **Undo button** on the Standard toolbar) to reverse the last command and put Moldof back in the worksheet.

➤ Click any cell in **row 6,** and this time delete the entire row for good.

MISSING TOOLBARS

The Standard and Formatting toolbars are displayed by default, but either or both can be hidden from view. To display (or hide) a toolbar, point to any toolbar, click the right mouse button to display the Toolbar shortcut menu, then click the individual toolbars on or off as appropriate. If you do not see any toolbars at all, pull down the View menu, click Toolbars to display a dialog box listing the available toolbars, check the toolbars you want displayed, and click OK.

STEP 5: Insert a Row

➤ Click any cell in **row 5** (the row containing Glassman's grades).

➤ Pull down the **Insert menu.** Click **Rows** to add a new row above the current row. Row 5 is now blank (it is the newly inserted row), and Glassman (who was in row 5) is now in row 6.

➤ Enter the data for the new student in row 5 as shown in Figure 1.11c:

- Click in **cell A5.** Type **Coulter.** Press the **right arrow key** or click in **cell B5.**
- Type **85.** Press the **right arrow key** or click in **cell C5.**
- Type **95.** Press the **right arrow key** or click in **cell D5.**
- Type **100.** Press the **right arrow key** or click in **cell E5.**
- Enter the formula to compute the semester average, **=(B5+C5+2*D5)/4.** Be sure to begin the formula with an equal sign. Press **enter.**
- Click the **Save button** on the Standard toolbar, or pull down the **File menu** and click **Save** to save the changes made to this point.

Save button —

Enter the formula for the new student —

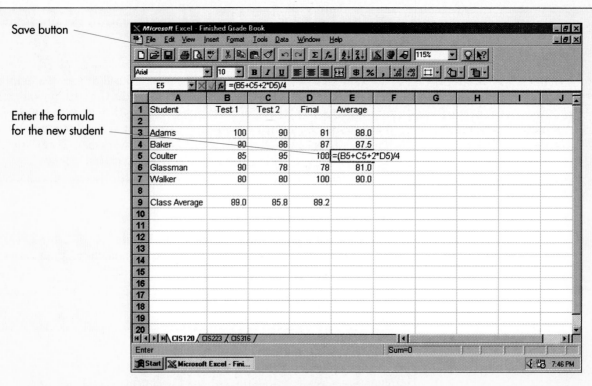

(c) Insert a Row (step 5)

FIGURE 1.11   Hands-on Exercise 2 (continued)

INSERTING (DELETING) ROWS AND COLUMNS

The fastest way to insert or delete a row is to point to the row number, then click the right mouse button to simultaneously select the row and display a shortcut menu. Click Insert to add a row above the selected row, or click Delete to delete the selected row. Use a similar technique to insert or delete a column, by pointing to the column heading, then clicking the right mouse button to display a shortcut menu from which you can select the appropriate command.

STEP 6: Insert a Second Row

➤ Point to the row heading for **row 6** (which now contains Glassman's grades), then click the **right mouse button** to select the row and display a shortcut menu. Click **Insert** to insert a new row 6, which moves Glassman to row 7.

➤ Click in **cell A6.** Type **C,** the first letter in "Courier," which also happens to be the first letter in "Coulter," a previous entry in column A. If the Auto-Complete feature is on (see boxed tip), Coulter's name will be automatically inserted in cell A6 with "oulter" selected. Type **ourier** (the remaining letters in "Courier," which replace "oulter."

➤ Enter Courier's grades in the appropriate cells (75, 75, and 85 in cells B6, C6, and D6, respectively).

➤ Click in **cell E6.** Enter the formula to compute the semester average, **=(B6+C6+2*D6)/4.** Press **enter.**

➤ Save the workbook.

AUTOCOMPLETE

The *AutoComplete* feature is Excel's way of trying to speed data entry. As soon as you begin typing a label into a cell, Excel searches for and (automatically) displays any other label in that column that matches the letters you typed. It's handy if you want to repeat a label, but it can be distracting if you want to enter a different label that just happens to begin with the same letter. To turn the feature on (off), pull down the Tools menu, click Options, then click the Edit tab. Check (clear) the box to enable the AutoComplete feature.

STEP 7: Insert a Column

➤ Point to the column heading for column B, then click the **right mouse button** to display a shortcut menu as shown in Figure 1.11d. Click **Insert** to insert a new column, which becomes the new column B. All existing columns have been moved to the right.

(d) Insert a Column (step 7)

FIGURE 1.11   Hands-on Exercise 2 (continued)

➤ Click in **cell B1.** Type **Major.**

➤ Click in **cell B3.** Enter **CIS** as Adams's major. Press the **down arrow** to move automatically to the major for the next student.

➤ Type **MKT** in cell B4. Press the **down arrow.** Type **ACC** in cell B5. Press the **down arrow.** Type **FIN** in cell B6.

➤ Press the **down arrow** to move to cell B7. Type **C** (AutoComplete will automatically enter "IS" to complete the entry). Press the **down arrow** to move to cell B8. Type **C** (the AutoComplete feature again enters "IS"), then press **enter** to complete the entry.

➤ Save the workbook.

SHORTCUT MENUS

Shortcut menus provide an alternate way to execute commands. Point to any object in a worksheet—a cell, a row or column heading, a worksheet tab, or a toolbar—then click the right mouse button to display a shortcut menu with commands appropriate to the object. Click the left mouse button to select a command from the shortcut menu, or press the Esc key (or click outside the menu) to close the shortcut menu without executing a command.

STEP 8: Display the Cell Formulas

➤ Pull down the **Tools menu.** Click **Options** to display the Options dialog box. Click the **View tab.** Check the box for **Formulas.** Click **OK.**

➤ The worksheet should display the cell formulas as shown in Figure 1.11e. If necessary, click the **right scroll arrow** on the horizontal scroll bar until column F, the column containing the formulas to compute the semester averages, comes into view.

➤ If necessary (i.e., if the formulas are not completely visible), double click the border between the column headings for columns F and G. This increases the width of column F to accommodate the widest entry in that column.

DISPLAY CELL FORMULAS

A worksheet should always be printed twice, once to show the computed results, and once to show the cell formulas. The fastest way to toggle (switch) between cell formulas and displayed values is to use the Ctrl+` keyboard shortcut. (The ` is on the same key as the ~ at the upper left of the keyboard.) Press Ctrl+` and you switch from displayed values to cell formulas. Press Ctrl+` a second time and you are back to the displayed values.

If necessary, click right scroll arrow to see column F

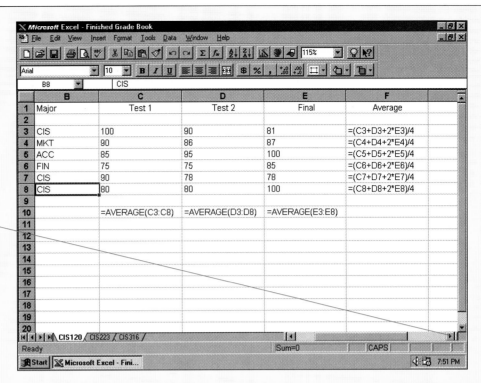

	B	C	D	E	F
1	Major	Test 1	Test 2	Final	Average
2					
3	CIS	100	90	81	=(C3+D3+2*E3)/4
4	MKT	90	86	87	=(C4+D4+2*E4)/4
5	ACC	85	95	100	=(C5+D5+2*E5)/4
6	FIN	75	75	85	=(C6+D6+2*E6)/4
7	CIS	90	78	78	=(C7+D7+2*E7)/4
8	CIS	80	80	100	=(C8+D8+2*E8)/4
9					
10		=AVERAGE(C3:C8)	=AVERAGE(D3:D8)	=AVERAGE(E3:E8)	

(e) Display the Cell Formulas (step 8)

FIGURE 1.11   Hands-on Exercise 2 (continued)

STEP 9: The Page Setup Command

➤ Pull down the **File menu.** Click the **Page Setup command** to display the Page Setup dialog box as shown in Figure 1.11f.

- Click the **Page tab.** Click the **Landscape option button.** Click the option button to **Fit to 1 page.**
- Click the **Margins tab.** Check the box to center the worksheet horizontally.
- Click the **Header/Footer tab.** Click the **drop-down arrow** on the Header list box. Scroll to the top of the list and click **(none)** to remove the header. Click the **drop-down arrow** on the Footer list box. Scroll to the top of the list and click **(none)** to remove the footer.
- Click the **Sheet tab.** Check the boxes to print Row and Column Headings and Gridlines.

➤ Click **OK** to exit the Page Setup dialog box. Save the workbook.

Print Preview button ───

Click Landscape ───

Click Fit to 1 page ───

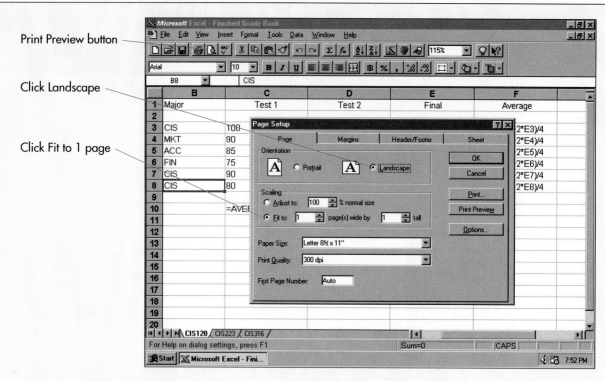

(f) The Page Setup Command (step 9)

FIGURE 1.11   Hands-on Exercise 2 (continued)

KEYBOARD SHORTCUTS—THE DIALOG BOX

Press Tab or Shift+Tab to move forward (backward) between fields in a dialog box, or press the Alt key plus the underlined letter to move directly to an option. Use the space bar to toggle check boxes on or off and the up (down) arrow keys to move between options in a list box. Press enter to activate the highlighted command button and Esc to exit the dialog box without accepting the changes.

STEP 10: The Print Preview Command

➤ Pull down the **File menu** and click **Print Preview** (or click the **Print Preview button** on the Standard toolbar). Your monitor should match the display in Figure 1.11g.

➤ Click the **Print command button** to display the Print dialog box, then click **OK** to print the worksheet.

➤ Press **Ctrl+`** to switch to displayed values rather than cell formulas. Click the **Print button** on the Standard toolbar to print the worksheet without displaying the Print dialog box.

➤ Save the workbook.

➤ Pull down the **File menu.** Click **Exit** to leave Excel.

Click Print command button

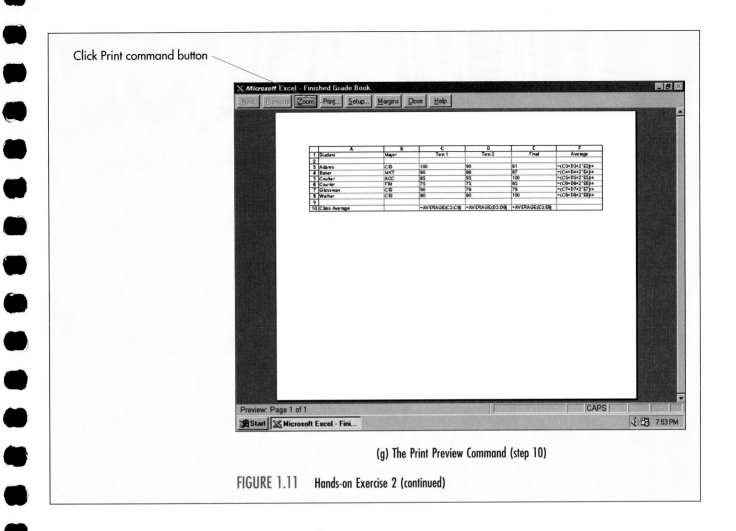

(g) The Print Preview Command (step 10)

FIGURE 1.11   Hands-on Exercise 2 (continued)

SUMMARY

A spreadsheet is the computerized equivalent of an accountant's ledger. It is divided into rows and columns, with each row and column assigned a heading. The intersection of a row and column forms a cell.

Spreadsheet is a generic term. Workbook and worksheet are Excel specific. An Excel workbook contains one or more worksheets.

Every cell in a worksheet (spreadsheet) contains either a formula or a constant. A formula begins with an equal sign, a constant does not. A constant is an entry that does not change and may be numeric or descriptive text. A formula is a combination of numeric constants, cell references, arithmetic operators, and/or functions that produces a new value from existing values.

The Insert and Delete commands add or remove rows or columns from a worksheet. The Open command brings a workbook from disk into memory. The Save command copies the workbook in memory to disk.

The Page Setup command provides complete control over the printed page, enabling you to print a worksheet with or without gridlines or row and column headings. The Page Setup command also controls margins, headers and footers, centering, and orientation. The Print Preview command shows the worksheet as it will print and should be used prior to printing.

A worksheet should always be printed twice, once with displayed values and once with cell formulas. The latter is an important tool in checking the accuracy of a worksheet, which is far more important than its appearance.

Active cell	Formula	Save command
AutoComplete	Formula bar	Shortcut menu
AVERAGE function	Function	Spreadsheet
Cell	Insert command	Standard toolbar
Cell contents	Landscape orientation	Status bar
Cell reference	Name box	Text box
Close command	Open command	Toolbar
Constant	Page Setup command	ToolTips
Delete command	Portrait orientation	Undo command
Exit command	Print command	Value
File menu	Print Preview command	Workbook
Formatting toolbar	Save As command	Worksheet

MULTIPLE CHOICE

1. Which of the following is true?
   (a) A worksheet contains one or more workbooks
   (b) A workbook contains one or more worksheets
   (c) A spreadsheet contains one or more worksheets
   (d) A worksheet contains one or more spreadsheets

2. A worksheet is superior to manual calculation because:
   (a) The worksheet computes its entries faster
   (b) The worksheet computes its results more accurately
   (c) The worksheet recalculates its results whenever cell contents are changed
   (d) All of the above

3. The cell at the intersection of the second column and third row has the cell reference:
   (a) B3
   (b) 3B
   (c) C2
   (d) 2C

4. A right-handed person will normally:
   (a) Click the right and left mouse button to access a pull-down menu and shortcut menu, respectively
   (b) Click the left and right mouse button to access a pull-down menu and shortcut menu, respectively
   (c) Click the left mouse button to access both a pull-down menu and a shortcut menu
   (d) Click the right mouse button to access both a pull-down menu and a shortcut menu

5. What is the effect of typing F5+F6 into a cell without a beginning equal sign?
   (a) The entry is equivalent to the formula =F5+F6
   (b) The cell will display the contents of cell F5 plus cell F6
   (c) The entry will be treated as a text entry and display F5+F6 in the cell
   (d) The entry will be rejected by Excel, which will signal an error message

6. The Open command:
   (a) Brings a workbook from disk into memory
   (b) Brings a workbook from disk into memory, then erases the workbook on disk
   (c) Stores the workbook in memory on disk
   (d) Stores the workbook in memory on disk, then erases the workbook from memory

7. The Save command:
   (a) Brings a workbook from disk into memory
   (b) Brings a workbook from disk into memory, then erases the workbook on disk
   (c) Stores the workbook in memory on disk
   (d) Stores the workbook in memory on disk, then erases the workbook from memory

8. How do you open an Excel workbook?
   (a) Pull down the File menu and click the Open command
   (b) Click the Open button on the Standard toolbar
   (c) Either (a) or (b)
   (d) Neither (a) nor (b)

9. In the absence of parentheses, the order of operation is:
   (a) Exponentiation, addition or subtraction, multiplication or division
   (b) Addition or subtraction, multiplication or division, exponentiation
   (c) Multiplication or division, exponentiation, addition or subtraction
   (d) Exponentiation, multiplication or division, addition or subtraction

10. Given that cells A1, A2, and A3 contain the values 10, 20, and 40, respectively, what value will be displayed in a cell containing the cell formula =A1/A2*A3+1?
    (a) 1.125
    (b) 21
    (c) 20.125
    (d) Impossible to determine

11. The entry =AVERAGE(A4:A6):
    (a) Is invalid because the cells are not contiguous
    (b) Computes the average of cells A4 and A6
    (c) Computes the average of cells A4, A5, and A6
    (d) None of the above

12. Which of the following was suggested with respect to printing a workbook?
    (a) Print the displayed values only
    (b) Print the cell formulas only
    (c) Print both the displayed values and cell formulas
    (d) Print neither the displayed values nor the cell formulas

13. Which of the following is true regarding a printed worksheet?
  (a) It may be printed with or without the row and column headings
  (b) It may be printed with or without the gridlines
  (c) Both (a) and (b) above
  (d) Neither (a) nor (b)

14. Which options are mutually exclusive in the Page Setup menu?
  (a) Portrait and landscape orientation
  (b) Cell gridlines and row and column headings
  (c) Headers and footers
  (d) Left and right margins

15. Which of the following is controlled by the Page Setup command?
  (a) Headers and footers
  (b) Margins
  (c) Orientation
  (d) All of the above

ANSWERS

1. b	**6.** a	**11.** c
2. d	**7.** c	**12.** c
3. a	**8.** c	**13.** c
4. b	**9.** d	**14.** a
5. c	**10.** b	**15.** d

EXPLORING EXCEL 7.0

1. Use Figure 1.12 to identify the elements of a Microsoft Excel screen by matching each element with the appropriate number.

____ Formatting toolbar ____ Standard toolbar
____ Active cell ____ Contains the Open command
____ Contains the Delete command ____ Name box
____ Help button ____ Formula bar
____ Tip Wizard button ____ Contains the Print command

2. Troubleshooting: The informational messages in Figure 1.13 appeared (or could have appeared) in response to various commands issued during the chapter.

  a. The message in Figure 1.13a is produced when the user exits Excel, but only under a specific circumstance. When will that message be produced? When would "No" be an appropriate response to this message?

  b. The message in Figure 1.13b appeared in response to a File Print command. What is the most likely corrective action?

  c. The message in Figure 1.13c appeared in response to a File Open command. What corrective action needs to be taken?

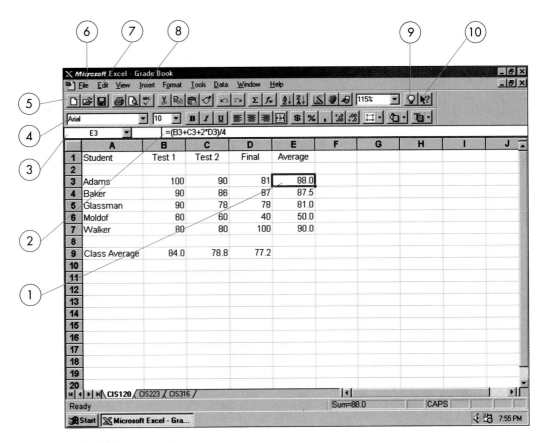

FIGURE 1.12   Screen for Problem 1

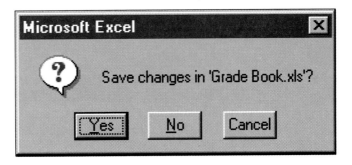

(a) Informational Message 1

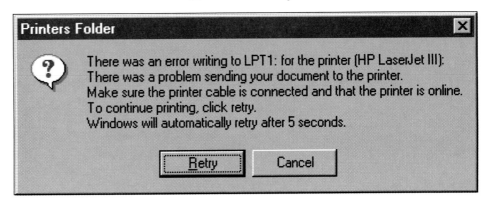

(b) Informational Message 2

FIGURE 1.13   Informational Messages for Problem 2

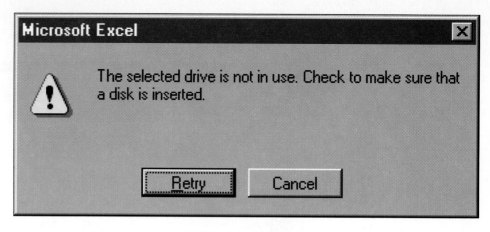

(c) Informational Message 3

FIGURE 1.13   Informational Messages for Problem 2 (continued)

3. Figure 1.14 contains a simple worksheet showing the earnings for Widgets of America, before and after taxes. The cell values in cells B6, B7, and B9 may be produced in several ways, two of which are shown below. For example:

	Method 1	**Method 2**
Cell B6	=10000−4000	=B3−B4
Cell B7	=.30*6000	=.30*B6
Cell B9	=6000−1800	=B6−B7

Which is the better method and why?

	A	B
1	Widgets of America	
2		
3	Revenue	10000
4	Expenses	4000
5		
6	Earnings before taxes	6000
7	Taxes	1800
8		
9	Earnings after taxes	4200

FIGURE 1.14   Spreadsheet for Problem 3

4. Answer the following with respect to Figure 1.15, which depicts the use of a worksheet in a simplified calculation for income tax. (Assume that all cells in column C contain a formula rather than a constant.)

   a. What is the active cell? What are the contents of the active cell?

   b. Assume that the income in cell B2 changes to $125,000. What other numbers will change automatically?

   c. Assume that an additional deduction for local income taxes of $3,000 is entered between rows 9 and 10. Which formula (if any) has to be explicitly changed to accommodate the new deduction?

   d. Which formula(s) will change automatically after the formula(s) in part c is (are) changed to accommodate the new deduction?

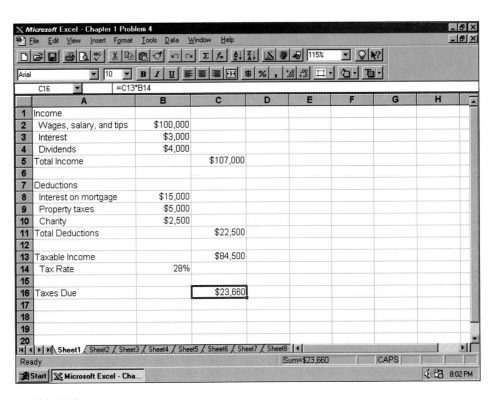

FIGURE 1.15   Screen for Problem 4

PRACTICE WITH EXCEL 7.0

1. Your professor is very impressed with the way you did the hands-on exercises in the chapter and has hired you as his grading assistant to handle all of his classes this semester. He would like you to take the Finished Grade Book that you used in the chapter, and save it as *Chapter 1 Practice 1*. Make the following changes in the new workbook:

   a. Click the worksheet tab for CIS120 to move to this worksheet. Add Milgrom as a new student majoring in Finance with grades of 88, 80, and 84, respectively. Delete Baker. Be sure that the class averages adjust automatically for the insertion and deletion of these students.

   b. Click the worksheet tab for CIS223. Enter the formulas to compute the class averages on all tests as well as each student's semester average. All tests count equally.

   c. Click the worksheet tab for CIS316 to move to this worksheet. Insert a new column for the Final, then enter the following grades for the students in this class (Bippen, 90; Freeman, 75; Manni, 84; Peck, 93; Tanney, 87).

   d. Enter the formulas to compute the semester average for each student in the class. (Tests 1, 2, and 3 each count 20%. The final counts 40%.)

   e. Enter the formulas to compute the class average on each test and the final.

   f. Enter the label *Grading Assistant* followed by your name on each worksheet. Print the entire workbook and submit all three pages of the printout to your instructor as proof that you did this exercise.

2. The worksheet in Figure 1.16 displays the last week's sales from the Exotic Gardens Nurseries. There are four different locations, each of which divides its sales into three general areas.

a. Open the partially completed *Chapter 1 Practice 2* workbook on the data disk. Save the workbook as *Finished Chapter 1 Practice 2*.

b. Enter the appropriate formulas in row 5 of the worksheet to compute the total sales for each location. Use the SUM function to compute the total for each location; for example, type =SUM(B2:B4) in cell B5 (as opposed to =B2+B3+B4) to compute the total sales for the Las Olas location.

c. Insert a new row 4 for a new category of product. Type *Insecticides* in cell A4, and enter $1,000 for each store in this category. The total sales for each store should adjust automatically to include the additional business.

d. Enter the appropriate formulas in column F of the worksheet to compute the total sales for each category.

e. Delete column D, the column containing the sales for the Galleria location. Check to be sure that the totals for each product adjust automatically.

f. Add your name somewhere in the worksheet as the bookkeeper.

g. Print the completed worksheet two times, to show both displayed values and cell formulas. Submit both pages to your instructor.

	A	B	C		E	F
1		Las Olas	Coral Gables	Galleria	Miracle Mile	Total
2	Indoor Plants	1,500	3,000	4,500	800	
3	Accessories	350	725	1,200	128	
4	Landscaping	3,750	7,300	12,000	1,500	
5	Total					
6						
7						
8						

FIGURE 1.16   Spreadsheet for Practice Exercise 2

3. Formatting is not covered until Chapter 2, but we think you are ready to try your hand at basic formatting now. Most formatting operations are done in the context of select-then-do. You select the cell or cells you want to format, then you execute the appropriate formatting command, most easily by clicking the appropriate button on the Formatting toolbar. The function of each button should be apparent from its icon, but you can simply point to a button to display a ToolTip that is indicative of the button's function.

Open the unformatted version of the *Chapter 1 Practice 3* workbook on the data disk, and save it as *Finished Chapter 1 Practice 3*. Add a new row 6 and enter data for Hume Hall as shown in Figure 1.17. Format the

Residential Colleges

	Freshmen	Sophomores	Juniors	Seniors	Graduates	Totals
Broward Hall	176	143	77	29	13	438
Graham Hall	375	112	37	23	7	554
Hume Hall	212	108	45	43	12	420
Jennings Hall	89	54	23	46	23	235
Rawlings Hall	75	167	93	145	43	523
Tolbert Hall	172	102	26	17	22	339
Totals	1099	686	301	303	120	2509

FIGURE 1.17   Spreadsheet for Practice Exercise 3

remainder of the worksheet so that it matches the completed worksheet in Figure 1.17. Add your name in bold italics somewhere in the worksheet as the Residence Hall Coordinator, then print the completed worksheet and submit it to your instructor.

4. Create a worksheet that shows your income and expenses for a typical semester according to the format in Figure 1.18. Enter your budget rather than ours by entering your name in cell A1.

   a. Enter at least five different expenses in consecutive rows, beginning in A6, and enter the corresponding amounts in column B.

   b. Enter the text *Total Expenses* in the row immediately below your last expense item and then enter the formula to compute the total in the corresponding cells in columns B through E.

   c. Skip one blank row and then enter the text *What's Left For Fun* in column A and the formula to compute how much money you have left at the end of the month in columns B through E.

   d. Insert a new row 8. Add an additional expense that you left out, entering the text in A8 and the amount in cells B8 through E8. Do the formulas for total expenses reflect the additional expense? If not, change the formulas so they adjust automatically.

   e. Save the workbook as *Chapter 1 Practice 4*. Center the worksheet horizontally, then print the worksheet two ways, to show cell formulas and displayed values. Submit both printed pages to your instructor.

	A	B	C	D	E
1	Maryann Barber's Budget				
2		Sept	Oct	Nov	Dec
3	Monthly Income	$ 1,000	$ 1,000	$ 1,000	$ 1,400
4					
5	Monthly Expenses				
6	Food	$ 250	$ 250	$ 250	$ 250
7	Rent	$ 350	$ 350	$ 350	$ 350
8	Utilities	$ 100	$ 100	$ 125	$ 140
9	Phone	$ 30	$ 30	$ 30	$ 20
10	Gas	$ 40	$ 40	$ 40	$ 75
11	Total Expenses	$ 770	$ 770	$ 795	$ 835
12					
13	What's left for fun	$ 230	$ 230	$ 205	$ 565

FIGURE 1.18   Spreadsheet for Practice Exercise 4

CASE STUDIES

Buying a Computer

You have decided to buy a PC and have settled on a minimum configuration consisting of an entry-level Pentium, with 8MB of RAM, a quad-speed CD-ROM, and a 500MB hard disk. You would like a modem if it fits into the budget, and you need a printer. You also need Windows 95 and Microsoft Office 95. You can spend up to $2500 and hope, that at today's prices, you can find a system that goes beyond your minimum requirements; for example, a system with a faster processor and 16MB of RAM. We suggest you shop around and look for educational discounts on software to save money.

Create a spreadsheet based on real data that presents several alternatives. Show different configurations from the same vendor and/or comparable systems from different vendors. Include the vendor's telephone number with its estimate. Bring the spreadsheet to class together with the supporting documentation in the form of printed advertisements.

Portfolio Management

A spreadsheet is an ideal vehicle to track the progress of your investments. You need to maintain the name of the company, the number of shares purchased, the date of the purchase, and the purchase price. You can then enter the current price and see immediately the potential gain or loss on each investment as well as the current value of the portfolio. Retrieve the *Stock Portfolio* workbook from the data disk, enter the closing prices of the listed investments, and compute the current value of the portfolio.

Accuracy Counts

The *Underbid* workbook on the data disk was the last assignment completed by your predecessor prior to his unfortunate dismissal. The worksheet contains a significant error, which caused your company to underbid a contract and assume a subsequent loss of $100,000. As you look for the error, don't be distracted by the attractive formatting. The shading, lines, and other touches are nice, but accuracy is more important than anything else. Write a memo to your instructor describing the nature of the error. Include suggestions in the memo on how to avoid mistakes of this nature in the future.

Planning for Disaster

This case has nothing to do with spreadsheets per se, but it is perhaps the most important case of all, as it deals with the question of backup. Do you have a backup strategy? Do you even know what a backup strategy is? Now is a good time to learn, because sooner or later you will wish you had one. You will erase a file, be unable to read from a floppy disk, or worse yet, suffer a hardware failure in which you are unable to access the hard drive. The problem always seems to occur the night before an assignment is due. The ultimate disaster is the disappearance of your computer, by theft or natural disaster (e.g., Hurricane Andrew, the floods in the Midwest, or the Los Angeles earthquake). Describe in 250 words or less the backup strategy you plan to implement in conjunction with your work in this class.

GAINING PROFICIENCY: COPYING, FORMATTING, AND ISOLATING ASSUMPTIONS

OBJECTIVES

After reading this chapter you will be able to:

1. Explain the importance of isolating assumptions within a worksheet.
2. Define a cell range; select and deselect ranges within a worksheet.
3. Copy and/or move cells within a worksheet; differentiate between relative, absolute, and mixed addresses.
4. Format a worksheet to include boldface, italics, shading, and borders; change the font and/or alignment of a selected entry.
5. Change the width of a column; explain what happens if a column is too narrow to display the computed result.
6. Describe in general terms the steps to build a worksheet for a financial forecast.
7. Define the TipWizard and explain how it can make you more proficient in Excel; explain the need to reset the TipWizard.

OVERVIEW

This chapter continues the grade book example of Chapter 1. It is perhaps the most important chapter in the entire text as it describes the basic commands to create a worksheet. We begin with the definition of a cell range and the commands to build a worksheet without regard to its appearance. We focus on the Copy command and the difference between relative and absolute addresses. We stress the importance of isolating the assumptions within a worksheet so that alternative strategies may be easily evaluated.

The second half of the chapter presents formatting commands to improve the appearance of a worksheet after it has been created. You will be pleased with the dramatic impact you can achieve with a few simple commands, but we emphasize that accuracy in a worksheet is much more important than appearance.

The hands-on exercises are absolutely critical if you are to master the material. As you do the exercises, you will realize that there are many different ways to accomplish the same task. Our approach is to present the most basic way first and the shortcuts later. You will like the shortcuts better, but you may not remember them and hence you need to understand the underlying concepts. You can always find the necessary command from the appropriate menu, and if you don't know which menu, you can always look to online help.

A BETTER GRADE BOOK

Figure 2.1 contains a much improved version of the professor's grade book over the one from the previous chapter. The most obvious difference is in the appearance of the worksheet, as a variety of formatting commands have been used to make it more attractive. The exam scores and semester averages are centered under the appropriate headings. Boldface and italics are used for emphasis. Shading and borders are used to highlight different areas of the worksheet. The title has been centered over the worksheet and is set in a larger typeface.

The most *significant* differences, however, are that the weight of each exam is indicated within the worksheet, and that the formulas to compute the students' semester averages reference these cells in their calculations. The professor can change the contents of the cells containing the exam weights and see immediately the effect on the student averages.

The isolation of cells whose values are subject to change is one of the most important concepts in the development of a spreadsheet. This technique lets the professor explore alternative grading strategies. He may notice, for example, that the class did significantly better on the final than on either of the first two exams. He may then decide to give the class a break and increase the weight of the final relative to the other tests. But before he says anything to the class, he wants to know the effect of increasing the weight of the final to 60%. What if he decides that the final should count 70%? The effect of these changes can be seen immediately by entering the new exam weights in the appropriate cells at the bottom of the worksheet.

Title is centered and in a larger typeface

Boldface, italics, shading, and borders are used for emphasis

Exam scores are centered

Exam weights are used to calculate the students' semester averages

	A	B	C	D	E
1	*CIS 120 - Spring 1996*				
2					
3	*Student*	*Test 1*	*Test 2*	*Final*	*Average*
4	Costa, Frank	70	80	90	82.5
5	Ford, Judd	70	65	80	73.8
6	Grauer, Jessica	90	80	98	91.5
7	Howard, Lauren	80	78	98	88.5
8	Krein, Darren	85	70	95	86.3
9	Moldof, Adam	75	75	80	77.5
10					
11	*Class Averages*	*78.3*	*74.7*	*90.2*	
12					
13	*Exam Weights*	*25%*	*25%*	*50%*	

FIGURE 2.1   A Better Grade Book

CELL RANGES

Every command in Excel operates on a rectangular group of cells known as a **range**. A range may be as small as a single cell or as large as the entire worksheet. It may consist of a row or part of a row, a column or part of a column, or multiple rows and/or columns. The cells within a range are specified by indicating the diagonally opposite corners, typically the upper-left and lower-right corners of the rectangle. Many different ranges could be selected in conjunction with the worksheet of Figure 2.1. The exam weights, for example, are found in the range B13:D13. The semester averages are found in the range E4:E9. The student data is contained in the range A4:E9.

The easiest way to select a range is to click and drag—click at the beginning of the range, then press and hold the left mouse button as you drag the mouse to the end of the range where you release the mouse. Once selected, the range is highlighted and its cells will be affected by any subsequent command. The range remains selected until another range is defined or until you click another cell anywhere on the worksheet.

COPY COMMAND

The **Copy command** duplicates the contents of a cell, or range of cells, and saves you from having to enter the contents of every cell individually. It is much easier, for example, to enter the formula to compute the class average once (for test 1), then copy it to obtain the average for the remaining tests, rather than explicitly entering the formula for every test.

Figure 2.2 illustrates how the Copy command can be used to duplicate the formula to compute the class average. The cell(s) that you are copying from, cell B11, is called the **source range.** The cells that you are copying to, cells C11 and D11, are the **destination** (or target) **range**. The formula is not copied exactly, but is adjusted as it is copied, to compute the average for the pertinent test.

The formula to compute the average on the first test was entered in cell B11 as =AVERAGE(B4:B9). The range in the formula references the cell seven rows above the cell containing the formula (i.e., cell B4 is seven rows above cell B11) as well as the cell two rows above the formula (i.e., cell B9). When the formula in cell B11 is copied to C11, it is adjusted so that the cells referenced in the new formula are in the same relative position as those in the original formula; that is,

Absolute reference   Relative reference

	A	B	C	D	E
1			CIS 120 - Spring 1996		
2					
3	Student	Test 1	Test 2	Final	Average
4	Costa, Frank	70	80	90	=$B$13*B4+$C$13*C4+$D$13*D4
5	Ford, Judd	70	65	80	=$B$13*B5+$C$13*C5+$D$13*D5
6	Grauer, Jessica	90	80	98	=$B$13*B6+$C$13*C6+$D$13*D6
7	Howard, Lauren	80	78	98	=$B$13*B7+$C$13*C7+$D$13*D7
8	Krein, Darren	85	70	95	=$B$13*B8+$C$13*C8+$D$13*D8
9	Moldof, Adam	75	75	80	=$B$13*B9+$C$13*C9+$D$13*D9
10					
11	Class Averages	=AVERAGE(B4:B9)	=AVERAGE(C4:C9)	=AVERAGE(D4:D9)	
12					
13	Exam Weights	25%	25%	50%	

Source range (B11)   Destination range (C11:D11)

FIGURE 2.2   The Copy Command

seven and two rows above the formula itself. Thus, the formula in cell C11 becomes =AVERAGE(C4:C9). In similar fashion, the formula in cell D11 becomes =AVERAGE(D4:D9).

Figure 2.2 also illustrates how the Copy command is used to copy the formula for a student's semester average, from cell E4 (the source range) to cells E5 through E9 (the destination range). This is slightly more complicated than the previous example because the formula is based on a student's grades, which vary from one student to the next, and on the exam weights, which do not. The cells referring to the student's grades should adjust as the formula is copied, but the addresses referencing the exam weights should not.

The distinction between cell references that remain constant versus cell addresses that change is made by means of a dollar sign. An **absolute reference** remains constant throughout the copy operation and is specified with a dollar sign in front of the column and row designation, for example, $B$13. A **relative reference**, on the other hand, adjusts during a copy operation and is specified without dollar signs; for example, B4. (A **mixed reference** uses a single dollar sign to make the column absolute and the row relative; for example, $A5. Alternatively, you can make the column relative and the row absolute as in A$5. Mixed references are not discussed further.)

Consider, for example, the formula to compute a student's semester average as it appears in cell E4 of Figure 2.2:

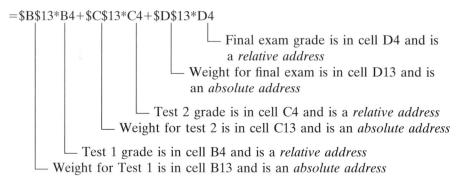

=$B$13*B4+$C$13*C4+$D$13*D4

    Final exam grade is in cell D4 and is a *relative address*

    Weight for final exam is in cell D13 and is an *absolute address*

    Test 2 grade is in cell C4 and is a *relative address*

    Weight for test 2 is in cell C13 and is an *absolute address*

    Test 1 grade is in cell B4 and is a *relative address*

    Weight for Test 1 is in cell B13 and is an *absolute address*

The formula in cell E4 uses a combination of relative and absolute addresses to compute the student's semester average. Relative addresses are used for the exam grades (found in cells B4, C4, and D4) and change automatically when the formula is copied to the other rows. Absolute addresses are used for the exam weights (found in cells B13, C13, and D13) and remain constant from student to student.

The copy operation is implemented by using the Windows **clipboard** and a combination of the **Copy** and **Paste commands** from the Edit menu. The contents of the source range are copied to the clipboard, from where they are pasted to the destination range. The contents of the clipboard are replaced with each subsequent Copy command but are unaffected by the Paste command. Thus, you can execute the Paste command several times in succession to paste the contents of the clipboard to multiple locations.

MOVE OPERATION

The **move operation** is not used in the grade book, but its presentation is essential for the sake of completeness. The move operation transfers the contents of a cell (or range of cells) from one location to another. After the move is completed, the cells where the move originated (that is, the source range) are empty. This is in contrast to the Copy command, where the entries remain in the source range and are duplicated in the destination range.

A simple move operation is depicted in Figure 2.3a, in which the contents of cell A3 are moved to cell C3, with the formula in cell C3 unchanged after the move. In other words, the move operation simply picks up the contents of cell A3 (a formula that adds the values in cells A1 and A2) and puts it down in cell C3. The source range, cell A3, is empty after the move operation has been executed.

Figure 2.3b depicts a situation where the formula itself remains in the same cell, but one of the values it references is moved to a new location; that is, the entry in A1 is moved to C1. The formula in cell A3 is adjusted to follow the moved entry to its new location; that is, the formula is now =C1+A2.

The situation is different in Figure 2.3c as the contents of all three cells—A1, A2, and A3—are moved. After the move has taken place, cells C1 and C2 contain the 5 and the 2, respectively, with the formula in cell C3 adjusted to reflect the movement of the contents of cells A1 and A2. Once again the source range (A1:A3) is empty after the move is completed.

Figure 2.3d contains an additional formula in cell B1, which is *dependent* on cell A3, which in turn is moved to cell C3. The formula in cell C3 is unchanged

Source range is empty after move

	A	B	C
1	5		
2	2		
3	=A1+A2		

	A	B	C
1	5		
2	2		
3			=A1+A2

(a) Example 1 (only cell A3 is moved)

Cell reference is adjusted to follow moved entry

	A	B	C
1	5		
2	2		
3	=A1+A2		

	A	B	C
1			5
2	2		
3	=C1+A2		

(b) Example 2 (only cell A1 is moved)

Both cell references adjust to follow moved entries

	A	B	C
1	5		
2	2		
3	=A1+A2		

	A	B	C
1			5
2			2
3			=C1+C2

(c) Example 3 (all three cells in column A are moved)

Cell reference adjusts to follow moved entry

Moved formula is unchanged

	A	B	C
1	5	=A3*4	
2	2		
3	=A1+A2		

	A	B	C
1	5	=C3*4	
2	2		
3			=A1+A2

(d) Example 4 (dependent cells)

Cell reference adjusts to follow moved entry

	A	B	C
1	5	=$A$3*4	
2	2		
3	=$A$1+$A$2		

	A	B	C
1		=$C$3*4	5
2			2
3			=$C$1+$C$2

Both cell references adjust to follow moved entries

(e) Example 5 (absolute cell addresses)

FIGURE 2.3   The Move Command

after the move because *only* the formula was moved, *not* the values it referenced. The formula in cell B1 changes (even though the contents of cell B1 were not moved) because cell B1 refers to an entry (cell A3) that was moved to a new location (cell C3).

Figure 2.3e shows that the specification of an absolute reference has no meaning in a move operation, because absolute references are adjusted as necessary to reflect a move. Moving a formula that contains an absolute reference does not adjust the formula. Moving a value that is specified as an absolute reference, however, adjusts the formula to follow the cell to its new location. Thus all of the absolute references in Figure 2.3e are changed to reflect the entries that were moved.

The move operation is a convenient way to improve the appearance of a worksheet after it has been developed. It is subtle in its operation, and we suggest you think twice before moving cell entries because of the complexities involved.

The move operation is implemented by using the Windows clipboard and a combination of the **Cut** and **Paste commands** from the Edit menu. The contents of the source range are transferred to the clipboard, from which they are pasted to the destination range. (Executing a Paste command after a Cut command empties the clipboard. This is different from pasting after a Copy command, which does not affect the contents of the clipboard.)

THE TIPWIZARD

The **TipWizard** greets you with a *tip of the day* every time you start Excel, but that is only one of its capabilities. The true purpose of the TipWizard is to introduce you to new features by suggesting more efficient ways to accomplish the tasks you are doing.

The TipWizard monitors your work and offers advice throughout a session. The TipWizard button on the Standard toolbar "lights up" whenever there is a suggestion. (Click the button to display the TipWizard; click the button a second time to close it.) You can read the suggestions as they occur and/or review them at the end of a session. You needn't always follow the advice of the TipWizard (at first you may not even understand all of its suggestions), but over time it will make you much more proficient.

The TipWizard will not repeat a tip from one session to the next unless it is specifically reset as described in step one of the following exercise. This is especially important in a laboratory situation when you are sharing the same computer with other students.

LEARNING BY DOING

As we have already indicated, there are many different ways to accomplish the same task. You can execute commands using a pull-down menu, a shortcut menu, a toolbar, or the keyboard. In the exercise that follows we emphasize pull-down menus (the most basic technique) but suggest various shortcuts as appropriate. We also direct you to reset the TipWizard so that Excel can monitor your actions and offer additional suggestions.

Realize, however, that while the shortcuts are interesting, it is far more important to focus on the underlying concepts in the exercise, rather than specific key strokes or mouse clicks. The professor's grade book was developed to emphasize the difference between relative and absolute cell references. The grade book also illustrates the importance of isolating assumptions so that alternative strategies (e.g., different exam weights) can be considered.

Creating a Worksheet

Objective: To create a formula containing relative and absolute references; to use the Copy command within a worksheet. Use Figure 2.4 as a guide.

STEP 1: Start Excel

➤ Start Microsoft Excel as described in the previous chapter. If necessary, click the **TipWizard button** on the Standard toolbar to display the tip of the day as shown in Figure 2.4a. Do not be concerned if your tip is different from ours.

➤ Pull down the **Tools menu,** click **Options,** then click the **General tab** to display the dialog box in Figure 2.4a.

➤ Click the check box to **Reset TipWizard.** Click **OK.** The contents of the Tip-Wizard box change to indicate that you have reset the TipWizard and that the tips may repeat.

➤ Click the **TipWizard button** to close the TipWizard box.

TipWizard button

Tip of the day

Reset the TipWizard

(a) Reset the TipWizard (step 1)

FIGURE 2.4   Hands-on Exercise 1

STEP 2: Enter the Column Headings

➤ Click in **cell A1.** Enter the title of the worksheet, **CIS120 - Spring 1996** as in Figure 2.4b.

➤ Press the **down arrow key** twice to move to cell A3. Type **Student.**

Save button

Click to select drive/folder

Enter filename

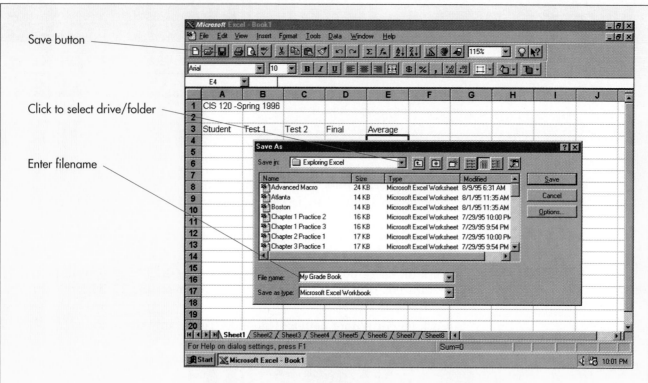

(b) Dialog Box for the Save Command (step 3)

FIGURE 2.4   Hands-on Exercise 1 (continued)

➤ Press the **right arrow key** to move to cell B3. Type **Test 1.**
➤ Press the **right arrow key** to move to cell C3. Type **Test 2.**
➤ Press the **right arrow key** to move to cell D3. Type **Final.**
➤ Press the **right arrow key** to move to cell E3. Type **Average.** Press **enter.**

STEP 3: Save the Workbook

➤ Pull down the **File menu** and click **Save** (or click the **Save button** on the Standard toolbar).

➤ Click the **drop-down arrow** on the Save In list box. Click the appropriate drive, drive C or drive A, depending on whether or not you installed the data disk.

LONG FILENAMES

Windows 95 allows filenames of up to 255 characters (spaces and commas are permitted). Anyone using Windows 95 for the first time will take descriptive names such as *My Grade Book* for granted, but veterans of MS-DOS and Windows 3.1 will appreciate the improvement over the earlier 8.3 naming convention (an eight-character name followed by a three-letter extension to indicate the file type).

➤ Double click the **Exploring Excel folder** to make it the active folder (the folder in which you will save the document).

➤ Click and drag **Book1** (the default entry) in the File name text box. Type **My Grade Book** as the name of the workbook. Click **Save** or press the **enter key.**

➤ The title bar changes to reflect the name of the workbook.

STEP 4: Enter Student Data and Literal Information

➤ Click in **cell A4** and type **Costa, Frank.** Move across row 4 and enter Frank's grades on the two tests and the final. Use Figure 2.4c as a guide.

- Do *not* enter Frank's average in cell E4 as that will be entered as a formula in step 6.

- Do *not* be concerned that you cannot see Frank's entire name because the default width of column A is not wide enough to display the entire name.

➤ Enter the names and grades for the other students in rows 5 through 9. Do *not* enter their averages.

➤ Complete the entries in column A by typing **Class Averages** and **Exam Weights** in cells **A11** and **A13,** respectively.

➤ Click the **Save button** on the Standard toolbar to save the workbook.

Enter exam weights in B13:D13

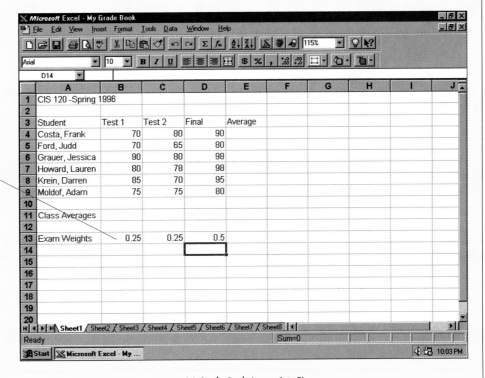

(c) Grade Book (steps 4 & 5)

FIGURE 2.4   Hands-on Exercise 1 (continued)

STEP 5: Enter Exam Weights

➤ Click in **cell B13** and enter **.25,** the weight for the first exam.

➤ Press the **right arrow key** to move to cell C13 and enter **.25,** the weight for the second exam.

➤ Press the **right arrow key** to move to cell D13 and enter **.5,** the weight for the final. Press **enter.** Do *not* be concerned that the exam weights do not appear as percentages; they will be formatted in the second exercise later in the chapter.

➤ The worksheet should match Figure 2.4c except that column A is too narrow to display the entire name of each student.

STEP 6: Compute the Semester Average

➤ Click in **cell E4** and type the formula **=$B$13*B4+$C$13*C4+$D$13*D4** to compute the semester average for the first student. Press the **enter key** when you have completed the formula.

➤ Check that the displayed value in cell E4 is 82.5, which indicates you entered the formula correctly.

➤ Save the workbook.

CORRECTING MISTAKES

The fastest way to change the contents of an existing cell is to double click in the cell in order to make the changes directly in the cell rather than on the formula bar. Use the mouse or arrow keys to position the insertion point at the point of correction. Press the Ins key to toggle between insert and overtype and/or use the Backspace or Del key to erase a character. Press the Home and End keys to move to the first and last characters in the cell, respectively.

STEP 7: Copy the Semester Average

➤ Click in **cell E4.** Pull down the **Edit menu** as in Figure 2.4d. Click **Copy.** A moving border will surround cell E4, indicating that its contents have been copied to the clipboard.

➤ Click **cell E5.** Drag the mouse over cells **E5** through **E9** to select the destination range as in Figure 2.4e.

Enter formula to calculate semester average

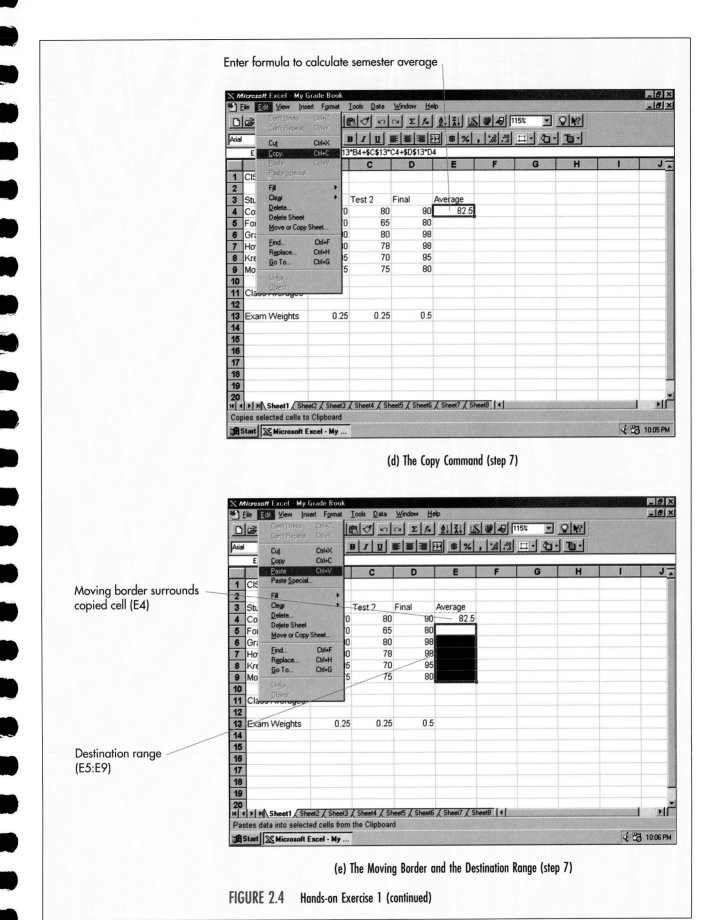

(d) The Copy Command (step 7)

Moving border surrounds copied cell (E4)

Destination range (E5:E9)

(e) The Moving Border and the Destination Range (step 7)

FIGURE 2.4   Hands-on Exercise 1 (continued)

➤ Pull down the **Edit menu** and click **Paste** to copy the contents of the clipboard to the destination range. You should see the semester averages for the other students in cells E5 through E9.

➤ Press **Esc** to remove the moving border around cell E4. Click anywhere in the worksheet to deselect cells E5 through E9.

➤ Click in **cell E5** and look at the formula. The cells that reference the grades have changed to B5, C5, and D5. The cells that reference the exam weights—$B$13, $C$13, and $D$13—are the same as in cell E4.

➤ Save the workbook.

CUT, COPY AND PASTE

Ctrl+X (the X is supposed to remind you of a pair of scissors), Ctrl+C, and Ctrl+V are keyboard equivalents to cut, copy, and paste, respectively, and apply to Excel, Word, PowerPoint and Access, as well as Windows applications in general. (The keystrokes are easier to remember when you realize that the operative letters, X, C, and V, are next to each other at the bottom-left side of the keyboard.) Alternatively, you can use the Cut, Copy, and Paste buttons on the Standard toolbar, which are also found on the Standard toolbar in the other Office applications.

STEP 8: Compute Class Averages

➤ Click in **cell B11** and type the formula **=AVERAGE(B4:B9)** to compute the class average on the first test. Press the **enter key** when you have completed the formula.

➤ Point to **cell B11,** then click the **right mouse button** to display the shortcut menu in Figure 2.4f. Click **Copy,** which produces the moving border around cell B11.

➤ Click **cell C11.** Drag the mouse over cells **C11** and **D11,** the destination range for the Copy command.

➤ Click the **Paste button** on the Standard toolbar (or press Ctrl+V) to paste the contents of the clipboard to the destination range.

➤ Press **Esc** to remove the moving border. Click anywhere in the worksheet to deselect cells C11 through D11.

DEFINING A RANGE WITH A KEYBOARD

To define a range with the keyboard, move to the first cell in the range, that is, the cell in the upper-left corner. Press and hold the Shift key as you use the arrow keys to extend the selection over the remaining cells in the range.

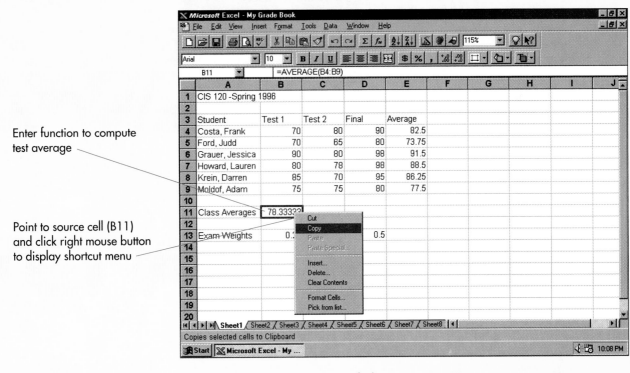

Enter function to compute
test average

Point to source cell (B11)
and click right mouse button
to display shortcut menu

(f) Shortcut Menu (step 8)

FIGURE 2.4   Hands-on Exercise 1 (continued)

STEP 9: What If? Change Exam Weights

➤ Change the entries in cells B13 and C13 to **.20** and the entry in cell D13 to **.60.** The semester average for every student changes automatically; for example, Costa and Moldof change to 84 and 78, respectively.

➤ The professor decides this does not make a significant difference and goes back to the original weights; reenter .25, .25, and .50 in cells B13, C13, and D13, respectively.

➤ Click the **Save button** on the Standard toolbar to save the workbook.

STEP 10: Review the TipWizard

➤ Click the **TipWizard button** on the Standard toolbar to display the TipWizard dialog box.

➤ Read the displayed tip, then click the **up arrow** to read the previous tip. Continue in this fashion until you have read all of the suggested tips.

➤ Close the workbook. Exit Excel if you are not ready to begin the next exercise at this time.

FORMATTING

In this chapter the professor's grade book is developed in two stages, as shown in Figure 2.5. The exercise just completed created the grade book, but paid no attention to its appearance. It had you enter the data for every student, develop the formulas to compute the semester average for every student based on the exam weights at the bottom of the worksheet, and finally, develop the formulas to compute the class averages for each exam.

Figure 2.5a shows the grade book as it exists at the end of the first hands-on exercise. Figure 2.5b shows the grade book at the end of the second exercise after it has been formatted. The differences between the two are due entirely to formatting. Consider:

- The exam weights are formatted as percentages in Figure 2.5b, as opposed to decimals in Figure 2.5a. The class and semester averages are displayed with a single decimal point in Figure 2.5b.
- Boldface and italics are used for emphasis, as are shading and borders.
- Exam grades and computed averages are centered under their respective headings.
- The worksheet title is set in larger type and centered across all five columns.
- The width of column A has been increased so that the students' names are completely visible.

	A	B	C	D	E
1	CIS 120 - Spring 1996				
2					
3	Student	Test 1	Test 2	Final	Average
4	Costa, F	70	80	90	82.5
5	Ford, Jud	70	65	80	73.75
6	Grauer, J	90	80	98	91.5
7	Howard,	80	78	98	88.5
8	Krein, Da	85	70	95	86.25
9	Moldof, A	75	75	80	77.5
10					
11	Class Av	78.333	74.667	90.167	
12					
13	Exam We	0.25	0.25	0.5	

(a) At the End of Hands-on Exercise 1

Title is centered across the worksheet and set in larger typeface

Column A is wider

Boldface, italics, shading, and borders used for emphasis

Grades are centered in column

Results are displayed with 1 decimal place

Exam weights are formatted as %

	A	B	C	D	E
1	*CIS 120 - Spring 1996*				
2					
3	*Student*	*Test 1*	*Test 2*	*Final*	*Average*
4	Costa, Frank	70	80	90	82.5
5	Ford, Judd	70	65	80	73.8
6	Grauer, Jessica	90	80	98	91.5
7	Howard, Lauren	80	78	98	88.5
8	Krein, Darren	85	70	95	86.3
9	Moldof, Adam	75	75	80	77.5
10					
11	*Class Averages*	78.3	74.7	90.2	
12					
13	*Exam Weights*	25%	25%	50%	

(b) At the End of Hands-on Exercise 2

FIGURE 2.5 Developing the Grade Book

Column Widths

A column is often too narrow to display the contents of one or more cells in that column. When this happens, the display depends on whether the cell contains a text or numeric entry, and if it is a text entry, on whether or not the adjacent cell is empty.

The student names in Figure 2.5a, for example, are partially hidden because column A is too narrow to display the entire name. Cells A4 through A9 contain the complete names of each student, but because the adjacent cells in column B contain data, the displayed entries in column A are truncated (cut off) at the cell width. The situation is different for the worksheet title in cell A1. This time the adjacent cell (cell B1) is empty, so that the contents of cell A1 overflow into that cell and are completely visible.

Numbers are treated differently from text and do not depend on the contents of the adjacent cell. Excel displays a series of number signs (######) when a cell containing a numeric entry is too narrow to display the entry in its current format. You may be able to correct the problem by changing the format of the number (e.g., display the number with fewer decimal places). Alternatively, you can increase the *column width* by using the *Column command* in the Format menu.

Row Heights

The *row height* changes automatically as the font size is increased. Row 1 in Figure 2.5b, for example, has a greater height than the other rows to accommodate the larger font size in the title of the worksheet. The row height can also be changed manually through the *Row command* in the Format menu.

FORMAT CELLS COMMAND

The *Format Cells command* controls the formatting for numbers, alignment, fonts, borders, and patterns (color). Execution of the command produces a tabbed dialog box in which you choose the particular formatting category, then enter the desired options. (Almost every formatting option can also be specified from the Formatting toolbar.)

All formatting is done within the context of *select-then-do.* You select the cells to which the formatting is to apply, then you execute the Format Cells command or click the appropriate button on the Formatting toolbar.

FORMATS VERSUS VALUES

Changing the format of a number changes the way the number is displayed but does *not* change its value. If, for example, you entered 1.2345 into a cell but displayed the number as 1.23, the actual value (1.2345) would be used in all calculations involving that cell.

Numeric Formats

General format is the default format for numeric entries and displays a number according to the way it was originally entered. Numbers are shown as integers (e.g., 123), decimal fractions (e.g., 1.23), or in scientific notation (e.g., 1.23E+10) if the number is larger than the width of the cell or if it exceeds 11 digits. You can also display any number in one of several formats as shown in Figure 2.6a:

- **Number format,** which displays a number with or without the 1000 separator (e.g., a comma) and with any number of decimal places.
- **Currency format,** which displays a number with the 1000 separator, an optional dollar sign (which is placed immediately to the left of the number), and negative values preceded by a minus sign or shown in red.
- **Accounting format,** which displays a number with the 1000 separator, an optional dollar sign (at the left of the cell that vertically aligns the dollar signs within a column), negative values in parentheses, and zero values as hyphens.
- **Date format,** which displays the date in different ways, such as March 4, 1994, 3/4/94, or 4-Mar-94.
- **Time format,** which displays the time in different formats, such as 10:50 PM or the equivalent 22:50 (24-hour time).
- **Percentage format,** whereby the number is multiplied by 100 for display purposes only, a percent sign is included, and any number of decimal places can be specified.
- **Fraction format,** which displays a number as a fraction, and is appropriate when there is no exact decimal equivalent, for example, ⅓.
- **Scientific format,** which displays a number as a decimal fraction followed by a whole number exponent of 10; for example, the number 12345 would appear as 1.2345E+04. The exponent, +04 in the example, is the number of places the decimal point is moved to the left (or right if the exponent is negative). Very small numbers have negative exponents; for example, the entry .0000012 would be displayed as 1.2E−06. Scientific notation is used only with very large or very small numbers.
- **Text format,** which left aligns the entry and is useful for numerical values that are treated as text, such as zip codes.

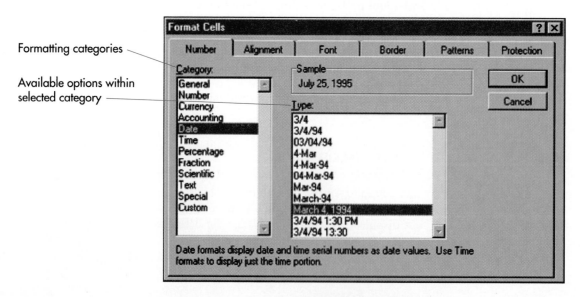

Formatting categories

Available options within selected category

(a) The Number Tab

FIGURE 2.6 The Format Cells Command

- *Special format,* which displays a number with editing characters, such as hyphens in a social security number or parentheses around the area code of a telephone number.
- *Custom format,* which allows you to develop your own formats.

DATES VERSUS FRACTIONS

A fraction may be entered into a cell by preceding the fraction with an equal sign, for example, =1/3. The fraction is converted to its decimal equivalent and displayed in that format in the worksheet. Omission of the equal sign causes Excel to treat the entry as a date; that is, 1/3 will be stored as January 3 (of the current year).

Alignment

The contents of a cell (whether text or numeric) may be aligned horizontally and/or vertically as indicated by the dialog box of Figure 2.6b. The options for horizontal *alignment* include left (the default for text), center, right (the default for numbers), and justify. You can also center an entry across a range of selected cells, as in the grade book of Figure 2.5b, which centered the title that was entered in cell A1 across columns A through E. The Fill option duplicates the characters in the cell across the entire width of that cell.

Vertical alignment is important only if the row height is changed and the characters are smaller than the height of the row. Entries may be vertically aligned at the top, center, or bottom (the default) of a cell.

It is also possible to wrap the text within a cell to emulate the word wrap of a word processor. And finally, you can achieve some very interesting effects by choosing from one of the four orientations within the alignment window.

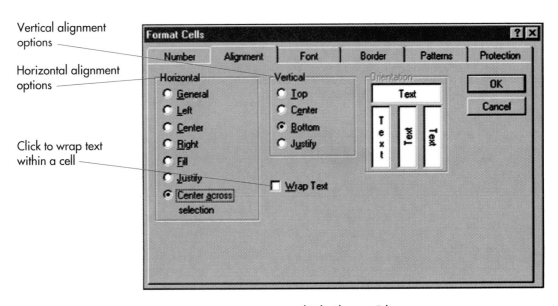

Vertical alignment options

Horizontal alignment options

Click to wrap text within a cell

(b) The Alignment Tab

FIGURE 2.6   The Format Cells Command (continued)

Fonts

You can use the same fonts (typefaces) in Excel as you can in any other Windows application. Windows itself includes a limited number of fonts (Arial, Times New Roman, Courier New, Symbol, and Wingdings) to provide variety in creating documents. Additional fonts can be obtained from Microsoft and/or other vendors. All fonts are WYSIWYG (What You See Is What You Get), meaning that the worksheet you see on the monitor will match the worksheet produced by the printer.

Any entry in a worksheet may be displayed in any font, style, or point size as indicated by the dialog box of Figure 2.6c. The example shows Arial, Bold Italic, and 14 points, and corresponds to the selection for the worksheet title in the improved grade book. Special effects, such as subscripts or superscripts, are also possible. You can even select a different color, but you will need a color printer to see the effect on the printed page. The Preview box shows the text as it will appear in the worksheet.

USE RESTRAINT

More is not better, especially in the case of too many typefaces and styles, which produce cluttered worksheets that impress no one. Limit yourself to a maximum of two typefaces per worksheet, but choose multiple sizes and/or styles within those typefaces. Use boldface or italics for emphasis, but do so in moderation, because if you emphasize too many elements, the effect is lost.

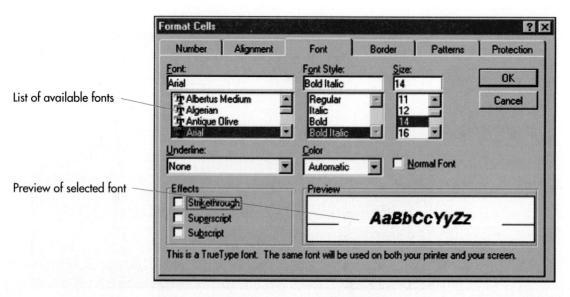

(c) The Font Tab

FIGURE 2.6   The Format Cells Command (continued)

Borders, Patterns, and Shading

The **Border tab** in Figure 2.6d enables you to create a border around a cell (or cells) for additional emphasis. You can outline the entire selection, or you can choose the specific side or sides; for example, thicker lines on the bottom and right sides produce a drop shadow, which is very effective. You can also specify a different color for the border, but you will need a color printer to see the effect on the printed output.

The **Patterns tab** in Figure 2.6e lets you choose a different color in which to shade the cell and further emphasize its contents. The Pattern drop-down list box lets you select an alternate pattern, such as dots or slanted lines.

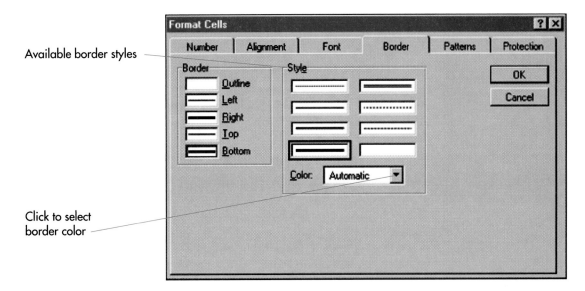

(d) The Border Tab

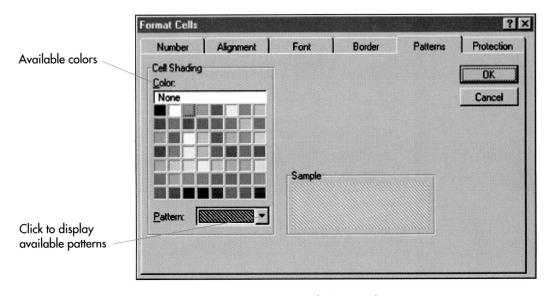

(e) The Patterns Tab

FIGURE 2.6   The Format Cells Command (continued)

Objective: To format a worksheet using both pull-down menus and the Formatting toolbar; to use boldface, italics, shading, and borders; to change the font and/or alignment of a selected entry; to change the width of a column; to print the cell contents as well as the computed values. Use Figure 2.7 as a guide in the exercise.

STEP 1: Fonts

➤ Open **My Grade Book** from the previous exercise. Pull down the **Tools menu,** click **Options,** click the **General Tab,** then check the box to **Reset TipWizard.** Click **OK.**

➤ Click in **cell A1** to select the cell containing the title of the worksheet.

➤ Pull down the **Format menu.** Click **Cells.** If necessary, click the **Font tab.** Click **Arial** from the Font list box, **Bold Italic** from the Font Style box, and **14** from the Size box. Click **OK.**

CHANGE THE DEFAULT FILE LOCATION

The *default file location* is the folder Excel uses to open (save) a workbook unless it is otherwise instructed. To change the default location, pull down the Tools menu, click Options, and click the General tab. Type the name of the new folder (e.g., C:\Exploring Excel) in the Default File Location text box, then click OK. The next time you access the Open or Save commands from the File menu, the Look In text box will reflect the change.

STEP 2: Alignment

➤ Click and drag to select cells **A1** through **E1,** which represents the width of the entire worksheet.

➤ Pull down the **Format menu** a second time. Click **Cells.** Click the **Alignment tab.** Click the **Center Across Selection option button** as in Figure 2.7a. Click **OK** to center the entry in cell A1 over the selected range (cells A1 through E1).

➤ If necessary, click the **TipWizard button** to open the TipWizard toolbar. The TipWizard suggests that you click the **Center Across Selection button** on the Formatting toolbar as a more efficient way to center text.

➤ Click and drag over cells **B3** through **E13.** Click the **Centering button** on the Formatting toolbar.

Center across selection button

Center button

Select A1:E1

Click here to center across
selected columns

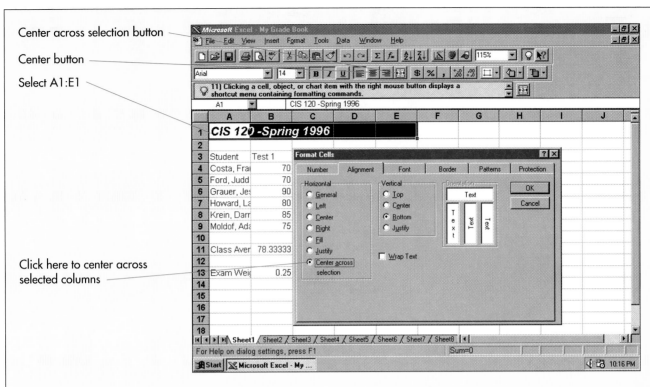

(a) Center across Columns (step 2)

FIGURE 2.7   Hands-on Exercise 2

QUIT WITHOUT SAVING

There will be times when you do not want to save the changes to a workbook—for example, when you have edited it beyond recognition and wish
you had never started. The Undo command, useful as it is, reverses only
the most recent operation and is of no use if you need to cancel all
changes. Pull down the File menu and click the Close command, then
click No in response to the message asking whether to save the changes.
Pull down the File menu, click the file's name at the bottom of the menu
to reopen the file, then begin all over.

STEP 3: Increase the Width of Column A

➤ Click in **cell A4.** Drag the mouse over cells **A4** through **A13.**

➤ Pull down the **Format menu,** click **Column,** then click **AutoFit Selection** as
shown in Figure 2.7b. The width of the selected cells increases to accommodate the longest entry in the selected range.

➤ Save the workbook.

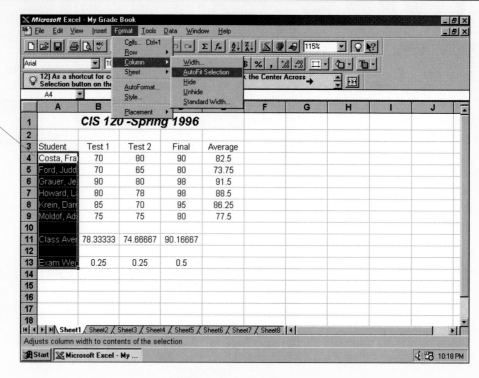

Select A4:A13

(b) Changing Column Widths (step 3)

FIGURE 2.7   Hands-on Exercise 2 (continued)

COLUMN WIDTHS AND ROW HEIGHTS

Drag the border between column headings to change the column width; for example, to increase (decrease) the width of column A, drag the border between column headings A and B to the right (left). Double click the right boundary of a column heading to change the column width to accommodate the widest entry in that column. Use the same techniques to change the row heights.

STEP 4: Format the Exam Weights

➤ Click and drag to select cells **B13** through **D13.** Point to the selected cells and click the **right mouse button** to display the shortcut menu in Figure 2.7c. Click **Format Cells** to produce the Format Cells dialog box.

➤ If necessary, click the **Number tab.** Click **Percentage** in the Category list box. Click the **down arrow** in the Decimal Places box to reduce the number of decimals to zero, then click **OK.** The exam weights are displayed with percent signs and no decimal places.

➤ Click the **Undo button** on the Standard toolbar to cancel the formatting command.

➤ Click the **% button** on the Formatting toolbar to reformat the exam weights as percentages.

Undo button

% button

Select B13:D13

Click right mouse button to
display shortcut menu

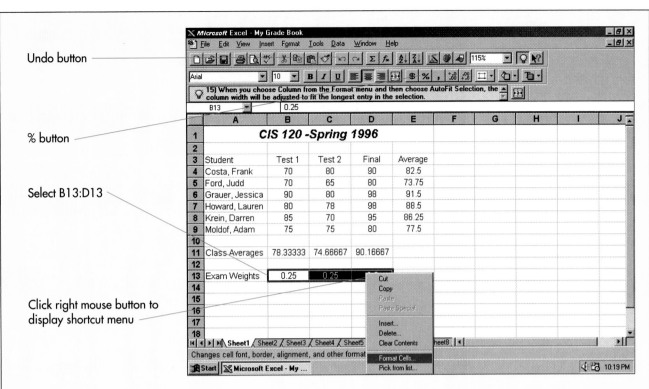

(c) Format Exam Weights (step 4)

FIGURE 2.7   Hands-on Exercise 2 (continued)

AUTOMATIC FORMATTING

Excel converts any number entered with a beginning dollar sign to currency format, and any number entered with an ending percent sign to percentage format. The automatic formatting enables you to save a step by typing $100,000 or 7.5% directly into a cell, rather than entering 100000 or .075 and having to format the number. The formatting is applied to the cell and affects any subsequent numbers in that cell.

STEP 5: Noncontiguous Ranges

➤ Select cells **B11** through **D11,** the cells that contain the class averages for the three exams.

➤ Press *and* hold the **Ctrl key** as you click and drag to select cells **E4** through **E9.** Release the **Ctrl key.**

➤ You will see two noncontiguous (nonadjacent) ranges highlighted, cells B11:D11 and cells E4:E9 as in Figure 2.7d. Format the selected cells using either the Formatting toolbar or the Format menu:

  • To use the Formatting toolbar, click the appropriate button to increase or decrease the number of decimal places to one.

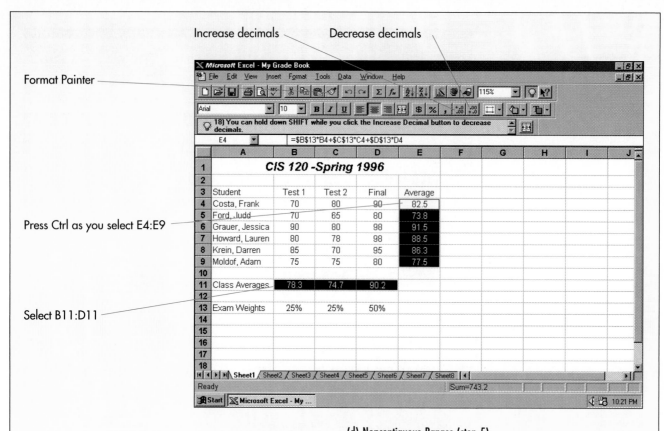

Increase decimals   Decrease decimals

Format Painter

Press Ctrl as you select E4:E9

Select B11:D11

(d) Noncontiguous Ranges (step 5)

FIGURE 2.7   Hands-on Exercise 2 (continued)

- To use the Format menu, pull down the **Format menu,** click **Cells,** click the **Number tab,** then click **Number** in the Category list box. Click the **down arrow** in the Decimal Places text box to reduce the decimal places to one. Click **OK.**

THE FORMAT PAINTER

The *Format Painter* copies the formatting of the selected cell to other cells in the worksheet. Click the cell whose formatting you want to copy, then double click the Format Painter button on the Standard toolbar. The mouse pointer changes to a paintbrush to indicate that you can copy the current formatting; just click and drag the paintbrush over the additional cells that you want to assume the identical formatting as the original cell. Repeat the painting process as often as necessary, then click the Format Painter button a second time to return to normal editing.

STEP 6: Borders

➤ Click and drag to select cells **A3** through **E3.** Press *and* hold the **Ctrl key** as you click and drag to select the range **A11:E11.** Continue to press the **Ctrl key** as you click and drag to select cells **A13:E13.**

➤ Pull down the **Format menu** and click **Cells** (or click the **right mouse button** to produce a shortcut menu, then click **Format Cells**). Click the **Border tab** to access the dialog box in Figure 2.7e.

➤ Choose a line width from the Style section. Click the **Top** and **Bottom** boxes in the Border section. Click **OK** to exit the dialog box and return to the worksheet.

SELECTING NONCONTIGUOUS RANGES

Dragging the mouse to select a range always produces some type of rectangle; that is, a single cell, a row or column, or a group of rows and columns. You can, however, select *noncontiguous* (nonadjacent) *ranges* by selecting the first range in the normal fashion, then pressing and holding the Ctrl key as you select the additional range(s). This is especially useful when the same command is to be applied to multiple ranges within a worksheet.

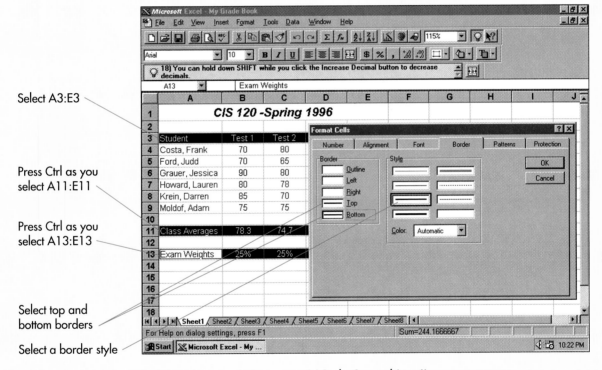

Select A3:E3

Press Ctrl as you select A11:E11

Press Ctrl as you select A13:E13

Select top and bottom borders

Select a border style

(e) Border Command (step 6)

FIGURE 2.7   Hands-on Exercise 2 (continued)

STEP 7: Color

➤ Check that all three ranges are still selected (A3:E3, A11:E11, *and* A13:E13).

➤ Click the **down arrow** on the **Color button** on the Formatting toolbar. Click light gray (or whatever color appeals to you) as shown in Figure 2.7f.

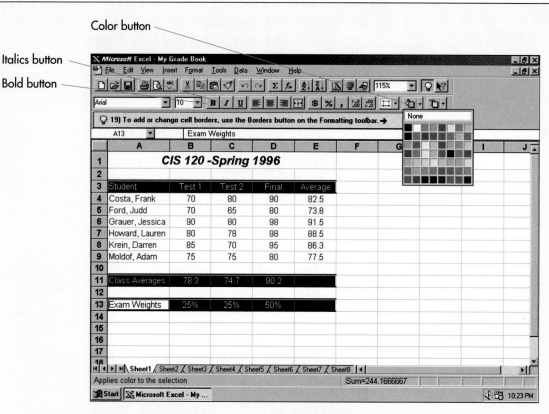

Color button

Italics button

Bold button

(f) Patterns (step 7)

FIGURE 2.7 Hands-on Exercise 2 (continued)

➤ Click the **boldface** and **italics buttons** on the Formatting toolbar. Click outside the selected cells to see the effects of the formatting change.

➤ Save the workbook.

DESELECTING A RANGE

The effects of a formatting change are often difficult to see when the selected cells are highlighted. Thus, you may need to deselect the range by clicking elsewhere in the worksheet to see the results of a formatting command.

STEP 8: Enter Your Name and Social Security Number

➤ Click in **cell A15.** Type **Grading Assistant.** Press the **down arrow key.** Type your name, press the **down arrow key,** and enter your social security number *without* the hyphens. Press **enter.**

➤ Point to **cell A17,** then click the **right mouse button** to display a shortcut menu. Click **Format Cells** to display the dialog box in Figure 2.7g.

➤ Click the **Number tab,** click **Special** in the Category list box, then click **Social Security Number** in the Type list box. Click **OK.** Hyphens have been inserted into your social security number.

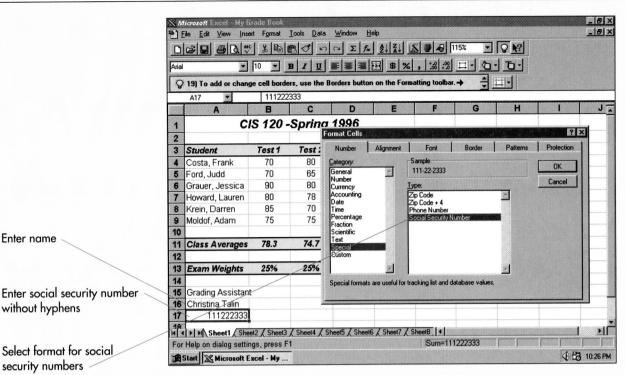

Enter name

Enter social security number without hyphens

Select format for social security numbers

(g) Add Your Name and Social Security Number (step 8)

FIGURE 2.7   Hands-on Exercise 2 (continued)

STEP 9: The Page Setup Command

➤ Pull down the **File menu.** Click **Page Setup** to display the Page Setup dialog box.

- Click the **Margins tab.** Check the box to center the worksheet Horizontally.

- Click the **Sheet tab.** Check the boxes to print Row and Column Headings and Gridlines.

- Click the **Header/Footer tab.** Click the **drop-down arrow** on the Header list box. Scroll to the top of the list and click **(none)** to remove the header. Click the **drop-down arrow** on the Footer list box. Scroll to the top of the list and click **(none)** to remove the footer.

- Click **OK** to exit the Page Setup dialog box.

➤ Click the **Print Preview button** to preview the worksheet before printing:

- If you are satisfied with the appearance of the worksheet, click the **Print button** within the Preview window, then click **OK** to print the worksheet.

- If you are not satisfied with the appearance of the worksheet, click the **Setup button** within the Preview window to make the necessary changes, after which you can print the worksheet.

➤ Save the workbook.

STEP 10: Print the Cell Formulas

➤ Pull down the **Tools menu,** click **Options,** click the **View tab,** check the box for **Formulas,** then click **OK** (or use the keyboard shortcut **Ctrl+`**). The worksheet should display the cell formulas.

➤ If necessary, click the arrow to the right of the horizontal scroll box so that column E, the column containing the cell formulas, comes into view.

➤ Double click the border between the column headings for columns E and F to increase the width of column E to accommodate the widest entry in the column.

➤ Pull down the **File menu.** Click the **Page Setup** command to display the Page Setup dialog box.

- Click the **Page tab.** Click the **Landscape orientation button.**
- Click the option button to **Fit to 1 page.** Click **OK** to exit the Page Setup dialog box.

➤ Click the **Print Preview button** to preview the worksheet before printing. It should match the display in Figure 2.7h:

- If you are satisfied with the appearance of the worksheet, click the **Print button** within the Preview window, then click **OK** to print the worksheet.
- If you are not satisfied with the appearance of the worksheet, click the **Setup button** within the Preview window to make the necessary changes, after which you can print the worksheet.

➤ Pull down the **File menu.** Click **Close.** Click **No** if prompted to save changes.

➤ Exit Excel if you do not want to continue with the next exercise at this time.

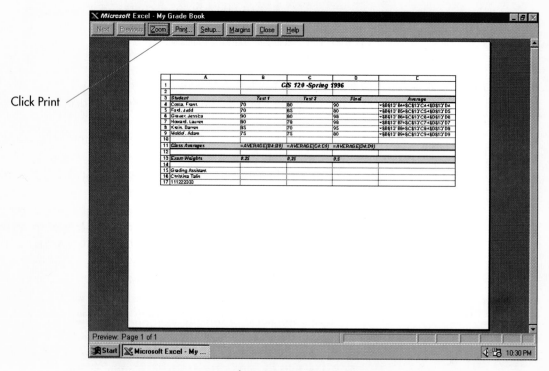

Click Print

(h) Print Preview Command (step 10)

FIGURE 2.7   Hands-on Exercise 2 (continued)

A FINANCIAL FORECAST

Financial forecasting is one of the most common business applications of spreadsheets. Figure 2.8 depicts one such illustration, in which the income and expenses of Get Rich Quick Enterprises are projected over a five-year period. The displayed values are shown in Figure 2.8a, and the cell formulas are shown in Figure 2.8b.

Income in any given year is equal to the number of units sold times the unit price. The projected income in 1996, for example, is $300,000 based on sales of 100,000 units at a price of $3.00 per unit. The variable costs for the same year are estimated at $150,000 (100,000 units times $1.50 per unit). The production facility costs an additional $50,000, and administrative expenses add another $25,000.

100,000 units at $3.00 per unit

100,000 units at $1.50 per unit

Assumptions and initial conditions are isolated and are used in developing formulas

	A	B	C	D	E	F
1	Get Rich Quick Enterprises					
2		1996	1997	1998	1999	2000
3	Income					
4	Units Sold	100,000	110,000	121,000	133,100	146,410
5	Unit Price	$3.00	$3.15	$3.31	$3.47	$3.65
6	Gross Revenue	$300,000	$346,500	$400,208	$462,240	$533,887
7						
8	Fixed costs					
9	Production facility	$50,000	$54,000	$58,320	$62,986	$68,024
10	Administration	$25,000	$26,250	$27,563	$28,941	$30,388
11	Variable cost					
12	Unit mfg cost	$1.50	$1.65	$1.82	$2.00	$2.20
13	Variable mfg cost	$150,000	$181,500	$219,615	$265,734	$321,538
14						
15	Earnings before taxes	$75,000	$84,750	$94,710	$104,579	$113,936
16						
17	Initial conditions			Annual increase		
18	First year sales	100,000		10%		
19	Selling price	$3.00		5%		
20	Unit mfg cost	$1.50		10%		
21	Production facility	$50,000		8%		
22	Administration	$25,000		5%		
23	First year of forecast	1996				

(a) Displayed Values

	A	B	C	D	E	F
1	Get Rich Quick Enterprises					
2		=B23	=B2+1	=C2+1	=D2+1	=E2+1
3	Income					
4	Units Sold	=B18	=B4+B4*$D$18	=C4+C4*$D$18	=D4+D4*$D$18	=E4+E4*$D$18
5	Unit Price	=B19	=B5+B5*$D$19	=C5+C5*$D$19	=D5+D5*$D$19	=E5+E5*$D$19
6	Gross Revenue	=B4*B5	=C4*C5	=D4*D5	=E4*E5	=F4*F5
7						
8	Fixed costs					
9	Production facility	=B21	=B9+B9*$D$21	=C9+C9*$D$21	=D9+D9*$D$21	=E9+E9*$D$21
10	Administration	=B22	=B10+B10*$D$22	=C10+C10*$D$22	=D10+D10*$D$22	=E10+E10*$D$22
11	Variable cost					
12	Unit mfg cost	=B20	=B12+B12*$D$20	=C12+C12*$D$20	=D12+D12*$D$20	=E12+E12*$D$20
13	Variable mfg cost	=B4*B12	=C4*C12	=D4*D12	=E4*E12	=F4*F12
14						
15	Earnings before taxes	=B6-(B9+B10+B13)	=C6-(C9+C10+C13)	=D6-(D9+D10+D13)	=E6-(E9+E10+E13)	=F6-(F9+F10+F13)
16						
17	Initial conditions			Annual increase		
18	First year sales	100,000		10%		
19	Selling price	$3.00		5%		
20	Unit mfg cost	$1.50		10%		
21	Production facility	$50,000		8%		
22	Administration	$25,000		5%		
23	First year of forecast	1996				

(b) Cell Formulas

FIGURE 2.8 The Financial Forecast

Subtracting the total expenses from the estimated income yields a net income before taxes of $75,000.

The estimated income and expenses for each succeeding year are based on an assumed percentage increase over the previous year. The projected rates of increase as well as the initial conditions are shown at the bottom of the worksheet. We cannot overemphasize the importance of isolating **assumptions** and **initial conditions** in this manner, and further, that all entries in the body of the spreadsheet be developed as formulas that reference these cells. The entry in cell B4, for example, is *not* the constant 100,000, but rather a reference to cell B18, which contains the value 100,000.

The distinction may seem trivial, but most assuredly it is not, as two important objectives are achieved. The user sees at a glance which factors affect the results of the spreadsheet (i.e., the cost and earnings projections), and further, the user can easily change any of those values to see their effect on the overall forecast. Assume, for example, that the first-year forecast changes to 80,000 units and that this number will increase at 8 percent a year (rather than 10). The only changes in the worksheet are to the entries in cells B18 and D18, because the projected sales are calculated using the values in these cells.

Once you appreciate the necessity of isolating the assumptions and initial conditions, you can design the actual spreadsheet. Ask yourself why you are building the spreadsheet in the first place and what you hope to accomplish. (The financial forecast in this example is intended to answer questions regarding projected rates of growth, and more important, how changes in the assumptions and initial conditions will affect the income, expenses, and earnings in later years.) By clarifying what you hope to accomplish, you facilitate the creation of the spreadsheet, which is done in five general stages:

1. Enter the row and column headings, and the values for the initial conditions and the assumed rates of change.
2. Develop the formulas for the first year of the forecast based on the initial conditions at the bottom of the spreadsheet.
3. Develop the formulas for the second year based on the values in year one and the assumed rates of change.
4. Copy the formulas for year two to the remaining years of the forecast.
5. Format the spreadsheet, then print the completed forecast.

Perhaps the most critical step is the development of the formulas for the second year (1997 in Figure 2.8), which are based on the results of 1996 and the assumptions about how these results will change for the next year. The units sold in 1997, for example, are equal to the sales in 1996 (cell B4) plus the estimated increase (B4*$D$18); that is,

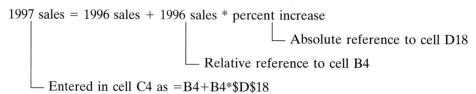

1997 sales = 1996 sales + 1996 sales * percent increase
└─ Absolute reference to cell D18
└─ Relative reference to cell B4
└─ Entered in cell C4 as =B4+B4*$D$18

The formula to compute the sales for 1997 uses both absolute and relative references, so that it will be copied properly to the other columns for the remaining years in the forecast. An absolute reference ($D$18) is used for the cell containing the percent increase in sales, because this reference should remain the same when the formula is copied. A relative reference (B4) is used for the sales from the previous year, because this reference should change when the formula is copied. Many of the other formulas in column C are also based on percentage increases from column B, and are developed in similar fashion, as shown in Figure 2.8b.

The formulas for year two (1997) are parallel to those in the remaining years of the forecast (1998 through 2000), and so they can be copied directly to obtain the finished worksheet.

HANDS-ON EXERCISE 3

A Financial Forecast

Objective: Develop a spreadsheet for a financial forecast based on the principles of absolute and relative addresses, and the importance of isolating assumptions and initial conditions. Use Figure 2.9 as a guide in the exercise.

STEP 1: Enter the Formulas for Year One

➤ Start Excel and reset the TipWizard. Pull down the **Tools menu,** click **Options,** click the **General tab,** then click the check box to **Reset TipWizard.** Click **OK.**

➤ Open the **Financial Forecast** workbook in the **Exploring Excel folder** to display the workbook in Figure 2.9a. (Cells B4 through B15 will be empty on your worksheet.)

➤ Save the workbook as **Finished Financial Forecast.**

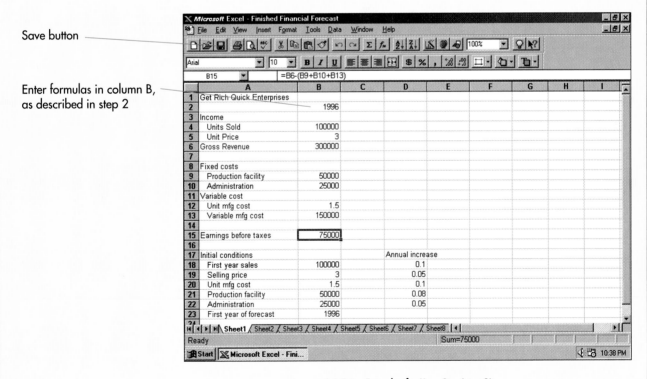

Save button

Enter formulas in column B, as described in step 2

(a) Enter Formulas for Year One (step 2)

FIGURE 2.9   Hands-on Exercise 3

STEP 2: Enter the Formulas for Year One

➤ Click in **cell B2.** Type **=B23** and press **enter.** This is very different from entering 1996 in cell B2 as described in the boxed tip on isolating assumptions.

➤ Enter the remaining formulas for year one:
  - Click in **cell B4.** Type **=B18.**
  - Click in **cell B5.** Type **=B19.**
  - Click in **cell B6.** Type **=B4*B5.**
  - Click in **cell B9.** Type **=B21.**
  - Click in **cell B10.** Type **=B22.**
  - Click in **cell B12.** Type **=B20.**
  - Click in **cell B13.** Type **=B4*B12.**
  - Click in **cell B15.** Type **=B6−(B9+B10+B13).**

➤ The cell contents for year one (1996) are complete. The displayed values in this column should match the numbers shown in Figure 2.9a.

➤ Save the workbook.

ISOLATE ASSUMPTIONS

The formulas in a worksheet should be based on cell references rather than specific values; for example, B17 or $B$17 rather than 100,000. The cells containing these values should be clearly labeled and set apart from the rest of the worksheet. You can then vary the inputs (assumptions) to the worksheet and immediately see the effect. The chance for error is also minimized because you are changing the contents of a single cell, rather than changing multiple formulas.

STEP 3: Enter the Formulas for Year Two

➤ Click in **cell C2.** Type **=B2+1,** which is the formula to determine the second year of the forecast.

➤ Click in **cell C4.** Type **=B4+B4*$D$18.** This formula computes the sales for year two as a function of the sales in year one and the assumed rate of increase.

➤ Enter the remaining formulas for year two:
  - Click in **cell C5.** Type **=B5+B5*$D$19.**
  - Click in **cell C6.** Type **=C4*C5.**
  - Click in **cell C9.** Type **=B9+B9*$D$21.**
  - Click in **cell C10.** Type **=B10+B10*$D$22.**
  - Click in **cell C12.** Type **=B12+B12*$D$20**
  - Click in **cell C13.** Type **=C4*C12.**
  - Click in **cell C15.** Type **=C6−(C9+C10+C13).**

➤ The cell contents for the second year (1997) are complete. The displayed values in this column should match the numbers shown in Figure 2.9b.

➤ Save the workbook.

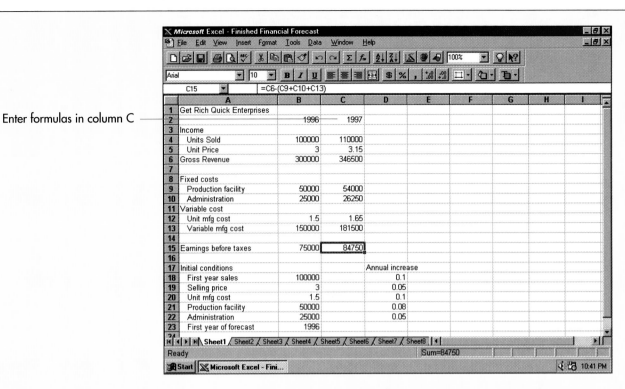

Enter formulas in column C

(b) Enter Formulas for Year Two (step 3)

FIGURE 2.9   Hands-on Exercise 3 (continued)

STEP 4: Copy the Formulas to the Remaining Years

➤ Click and drag to select cells **C2** through **C15** (the cells containing the formulas for year two). Click the **Copy button** on the Standard toolbar. A moving border will surround these cells to indicate that their contents have been copied to the clipboard.

➤ Click and drag to select cells **D2** through **F15** (the cells that will contain the formulas for years three to five). Point to the selection and click the **right mouse button** to display the shortcut menu in Figure 2.9c.

➤ Click **Paste** to paste the contents of the clipboard into the selected cells. The displayed values for the last three years of the forecast should be visible in the worksheet. (You should see earnings before taxes of 113936.384 for the year 2000.)

➤ Press **Esc** to remove the moving border. Save the workbook.

THE HELP BUTTON

Click the Help button on the Standard toolbar (the mouse pointer changes to include a large question mark), then click any other toolbar button to display a help screen with information about that button. Double click the Help button to open online help, which functions identically in every Office application. Click the Answer Wizard tab, for example, and you can ask a question in your own words.

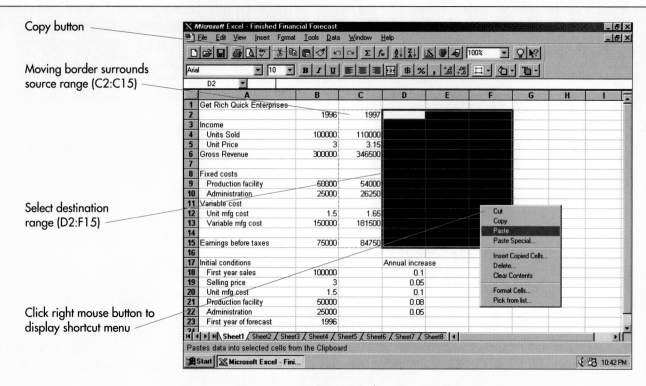

Copy button

Moving border surrounds source range (C2:C15)

Select destination range (D2:F15)

Click right mouse button to display shortcut menu

(c) Copy Formulas to Remaining Years (step 4)

FIGURE 2.9   Hands-on Exercise 3 (continued)

STEP 5: Format the Spreadsheet

➤ The hard part is done, and you are ready to format the worksheet. The specifics of the formatting operation are left to you, but Figure 2.9d is provided to guide you to the completed result.

➤ Formatting is done within the context of select-then-do; that is, you select the cell(s) to which you want the formatting to apply, then you execute the appropriate formatting command.

➤ Remember to press and hold the Ctrl key if you want to select noncontiguous cells prior to executing a formatting command as described in the tip on page 65.

THE FORMATTING TOOLBAR

The *Formatting toolbar* is the fastest way to implement most formatting operations. There are buttons for boldface, italics, and underlining, alignment (including centering across columns), currency, percent, and comma formats, as well as buttons to increase or decrease the number of decimal places. There are also several list boxes, which enable you to choose the font, point size, and font color, as well as the type of border and shading.

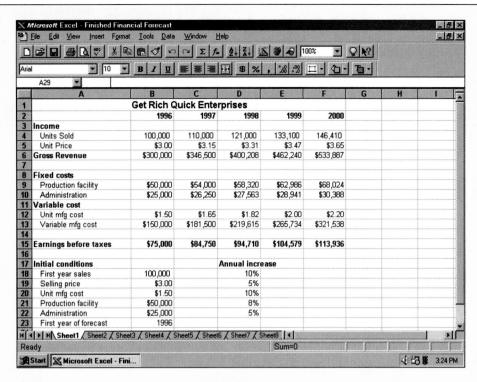

(d) The Completed Spreadsheet (step 5)

FIGURE 2.9   Hands-on Exercise 3 (continued)

STEP 6: Print the Completed Spreadsheet

➤ Add your name somewhere in the worksheet to prove to your instructor that you did the exercise.

➤ Print the completed spreadsheet twice, once to show the displayed values and once to show the cell formulas. Submit both printouts to your instructor.

➤ Review the suggestions of the TipWizard. Exit Excel.

➤ Congratulations on a job well done!

SUMMARY

All worksheet commands operate on a cell or group of cells known as a range. A range is selected by dragging the mouse to highlight the range. The range remains selected until another range is defined or you click another cell in the worksheet. Noncontiguous (nonadjacent) ranges may be selected in conjunction with the Ctrl key.

The formulas in a cell or range of cells may be copied or moved anywhere within a worksheet. An absolute reference remains constant throughout a copy operation, whereas a relative address is adjusted for the new location. Absolute and relative references have no meaning in a move operation. The copy and move operations are implemented through the Copy and Paste commands, and the Cut and Paste commands, respectively.

Formatting is done within the context of select-then-do; that is, select the cell or range of cells, then execute the appropriate command. The Format Cells command controls the formatting for Numbers, Alignment, Fonts, Borders, and Patterns (colors). The Formatting toolbar simplifies the formatting process.

A spreadsheet is first and foremost a tool for decision making, and as such, the subject of continual what-if speculation. It is critical, therefore, that the initial conditions and assumptions be isolated and clearly visible, and further that all formulas in the body of the spreadsheet be developed using these cells.

The TipWizard suggests more efficient ways to accomplish the tasks you are doing. The TipWizard will not repeat a tip from one session to the next unless it is specifically reset at the beginning of a session.

KEY WORDS AND CONCEPTS

Absolute reference	Date format	Percentage format
Accounting format	Destination range	Range
Alignment	Format cells command	Relative reference
Assumptions	Format menu	Row command
Automatic formatting	Format Painter	Row height
Border tab	Formatting toolbar	Scientific format
Cell formulas	Fraction format	Select-then-do
Clipboard	General format	Source range
Column command	Initial conditions	Special format
Column width	Move operation	Text format
Copy command	Noncontiguous range	Time format
Currency format	Number format	TipWizard
Custom format	Paste command	
Cut command	Patterns tab	

MULTIPLE CHOICE

1. Cell F6 contains the formula =AVERAGE(B6:D6). What will be the contents of cell F7 if the entry in cell F6 is *copied* to cell F7?
   (a) =AVERAGE(B6:D6)
   (b) =AVERAGE(B7:D7)
   (c) =AVERAGE($B$6:$D$6)
   (d) =AVERAGE($B$7:$D$7)

2. Cell F6 contains the formula =AVERAGE(B6:D6). What will be the contents of cell F7 if the entry in cell F6 is *moved* to cell F7?
   (a) =AVERAGE(B6:D6)
   (b) =AVERAGE(B7:D7)
   (c) =AVERAGE($B$6:$D$6)
   (d) =AVERAGE($B$7:$D$7)

3. A formula containing the entry =$A$4 is copied to a cell one column over and two rows down. How will the entry appear in its new location?
   (a) Both the row and column will change
   (b) Neither the row nor column will change
   (c) The row will change but the column will remain the same
   (d) The column will change but the row will remain the same

4. Which commands are necessary to implement a move?
   (a) Cut and Paste commands
   (b) Move command from the Edit menu
   (c) Either (a) or (b)
   (d) Neither (a) nor (b)

5. A cell range may consist of:
   (a) A single cell
   (b) A row or set of rows
   (c) A column or set of columns
   (d) All of the above

6. Which command will take a cell, or group of cells, and duplicate them elsewhere in the worksheet, without changing the original cell references?
   (a) Copy command, provided relative addresses were specified
   (b) Copy command, provided absolute addresses were specified
   (c) Move command, provided relative addresses were specified
   (d) Move command, provided absolute addresses were specified

7. The contents of cell B4 consist of the formula =B2*B3, yet the displayed value in cell B4 is a series of pound signs. What is the most likely explanation for this?
   (a) Cells B2 and B3 contain text entries rather than numeric entries and so the formula in cell B4 cannot be evaluated
   (b) Cell B4 is too narrow to display the computed result
   (c) Both (a) and (b)
   (d) Neither (a) nor (b)

8. The Formatting toolbar contains buttons to
   (a) Change to percent format
   (b) Increase or decrease the number of decimal places
   (c) Center an entry across columns
   (d) All of the above

9. Given that the percentage format is in effect, and that the number .056 has been entered into the active cell, how will the contents of the cell appear?
   (a) .056
   (b) 5.6%
   (c) .056%
   (d) 56%

10. Which of the following entries is equivalent to the decimal number .2?
    (a) 1/5
    (b) =1/5
    (c) Both (a) and (b)
    (d) Neither (a) nor (b)

11. What is the effect of two successive Undo commands, one right after the other?
    (a) The situation is not possible because the Undo command is not available in Microsoft Excel
    (b) The situation is not possible because the Undo command cannot be executed twice in a row
    (c) The Undo commands cancel each other out; that is, the worksheet is as it was prior to the first Undo command
    (d) The last two commands prior to the first Undo command are reversed

12. Which of the following fonts are included in Windows?
    (a) Arial and Times New Roman
    (b) Courier New
    (c) Wingdings and Symbol
    (d) All of the above

13. A numerical entry may be
    (a) Displayed in boldface and/or italics
    (b) Left, centered, or right aligned in a cell
    (c) Displayed in any TrueType font in any available point size
    (d) All of the above

14. Which of the following best describes the formula to compute the sales in the second year of the financial forecast?
    (a) It contains a relative reference to the assumed rate of increase and an absolute reference to the sales from the previous year
    (b) It contains an absolute reference to the assumed rate of increase and a relative reference to the sales from the previous year
    (c) It contains absolute references to both the assumed rate of increase and the sales from the previous year
    (d) It contains relative references to both the assumed rate of increase and the sales from the previous year

15. The estimated sales for the first year of a financial forecast are contained in cell B3. The sales for year two are assumed to be 10% higher than the first year, with the rate of increase (10%) stored in cell C23 at the bottom of the spreadsheet. Which of the following is the best way to enter the projected sales for year two, assuming that this formula is to be copied to the remaining years of the forecast?.
    (a) =B3+B3*.10
    (b) =B3+B3*C23
    (c) =B3+B3*$C$23
    (d) All of the above are equivalent entries

ANSWERS

1. b	**6.** b	**11.** c
2. a	**7.** b	**12.** d
3. b	**8.** d	**13.** d
4. a	**9.** b	**14.** b
5. d	**10.** b	**15.** c

EXPLORING EXCEL 7.0

1. Use Figure 2.10 to match each action with its result; a given action may be used more than once or not at all.

Action

a. Click at 8, then click at 15

b. Click at 6, then click at 15

c. Click at 7, drag to 3, click at 16

d. Click at 4, drag to 2, click at 16

e. Click at 5, drag to 1, click at 20

f. Click at 12, drag to 10, click at 19

g. Click at 12, then click at 13

h. Click at 11, drag to 9, click at 14

Result

_____ Format the exam weights as percentages

_____ Copy the formula to calculate the semester average for Frank Costa to the clipboard

_____ Change the font size of the worksheet title

_____ Paste the formula to calculate the semester average for the remaining students

_____ Create a bottom border that separates the column titles from the students' names and grades

_____ Copy the formula to calculate the average for Test 1 to the clipboard

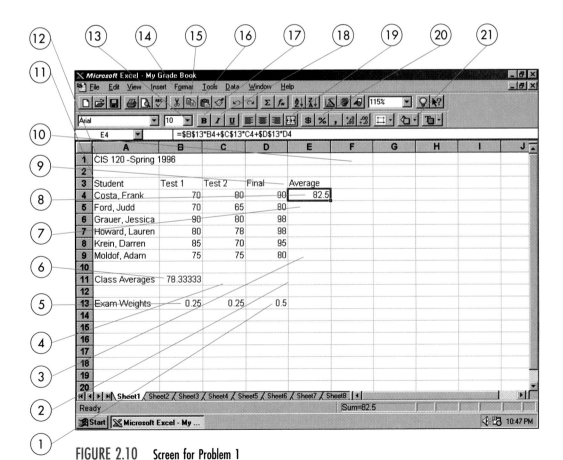

FIGURE 2.10   Screen for Problem 1

Action		Result
i. Click at 8, drag to 3, click at 21	_____	Apply boldface and italic formatting to the worksheet title
j. Click at 12, click at 17, click at 18	_____	Paste the formula to calculate the test average for Test 2 and the final
	_____	Shade the student averages a light gray
	_____	Center the worksheet title over the width of the worksheet

2. Figure 2.11 contains a worksheet depicting simplified payroll calculations for gross pay, withholding tax, social security tax (FICA), and net pay.

   a. What formula should be entered in cell E3 to compute an individual's gross pay? (An individual receives time and a half for overtime.)

   b. What formula should be entered in cell F3 to compute the withholding tax?

   c. What formula should be entered in cell G3 to compute the social security tax?

   d. What formula should be entered in cell H3 to compute the net pay?

   e. What formula should be entered in cell E10 to compute the total gross pay for the company? What formulas should be entered in cells F10 through H10 to compute the remaining totals?

	A	B	C	D	E	F	G	H
1	Employee	Hourly	Regular	Overtime	Gross	Withholding	Social Security	Net
2	Name	Wage	Hours	Hours	Pay	Tax	Tax	Pay
3	Adams	$8.00	40	3	$356.00	$99.68	$23.14	$233.18
4	Hall	$6.25	40	0	$250.00	$70.00	$16.25	$163.75
5	Costo	$9.50	25	0	$237.50	$66.50	$15.44	$155.56
6	Lee	$4.50	40	5	$213.75	$59.85	$13.89	$140.01
7	Arnold	$6.25	35	0	$218.75	$61.25	$14.22	$143.28
8	Vedo	$5.50	40	2	$236.50	$66.22	$15.37	$154.91
9								
10			Totals		$1,512.50	$423.50	$98.31	$990.69
11								
12	Assumptions:							
13	Withholding Tax:		28.0%					
14	Social Security Tax:		6.5%					

FIGURE 2.11 Spreadsheet for Problem 2

3. Relative versus Absolute Addressing: Figure 2.12 contains two versions of a worksheet in which sales, costs, and profits are to be projected over a five-year horizon. The worksheets are only partially completed, and the intent in both is to copy the entries from year 2 (cells C2 through C4) to the remainder of the worksheet. As you can see, the first worksheet uses only relative references and the second uses only absolute references. Both worksheets are in error.

   a. Show the erroneous formulas that will result when column C is copied to columns D, E, and F for both worksheets.

   b. What are the correct formulas for column C so that the formulas will copy correctly?

	A	B	C	D	E	F
1		Year 1	Year 2	Year 3	Year 4	Year 5
2	Sales	1000	=B2+B2*C7			
3	Cost	800	=B3+B3*C8			
4	Profit	200	=C2-C3			
5						
6	Assumptions:					
7	Annual Sales Increase		10%			
8	Annual Cost Increase		8%			

(a) Error 1 (relative cell addresses)

	A	B	C	D	E	F
1		Year 1	Year 2	Year 3	Year 4	Year 5
2	Sales	1000	=$B$2+$B$2*$C$7			
3	Cost	800	=$B$3+$B$3*$C$8			
4	Profit	200	=$C$2-$C$3			
5						
6	Assumptions:					
7	Annual Sales Increase		10%			
8	Annual Cost Increase		8%			

(b) Error 2 (absolute cell addresses)

FIGURE 2.12   Spreadsheets for Problem 3

4. The spreadsheet is an invaluable tool in decision making, but what if the spreadsheet contains an error? Unfortunately, it is all too easy to get caught up in the appearance of an attractively formatted spreadsheet without paying attention to its underlying accuracy.

Figure 2.13 contains a modified (and erroneous) version of the financial forecast in which the initial selling price has been revised downward to $2.25. The lower selling price is *not* to be considered an error as it reflects the results of a more recent marketing survey. Look carefully at the displayed values in Figure 2.13 and see if you can detect the underlying error(s) in the revised spreadsheet. Should you recommend the project based on the revised selling price?

	A	B	C	D	E	F
1	Get Rich Quick Enterprises					
2		1996	1997	1998	1999	2000
3	Income					
4	Units Sold	100,000	110,000	121,000	133,100	146,410
5	Unit Price	$2.25	$2.36	$2.48	$2.60	$2.73
6	Gross Revenue	$225,000	$259,875	$300,156	$346,680	$400,415
7						
8	Fixed costs					
9	Production facility	$50,000	$54,000	$54,000	$54,000	$54,000
10	Administration	$25,000	$26,250	$27,563	$28,941	$30,388
11	Variable cost					
12	Unit mfg cost	$1.50	$1.65	$1.82	$2.00	$2.20
13	Variable mfg cost	$150,000	$181,500	$219,615	$265,734	$321,538
14						
15	Earnings before taxes	$25,000	$24,375	$26,541	$26,946	$24,877
16						
17	Initial conditions			Annual increase		
18	First year sales	100,000		10%		
19	Selling price	$2.25		5%		
20	Unit mfg cost	$1.50		10%		
21	Production facility	$50,000		8%		
22	Administration	$25,000		5%		
23	First year of forecast	1996				

FIGURE 2.13   Spreadsheet for Problem 4

PRACTICE WITH EXCEL 7.0

1. Figure 2.14 contains a worksheet that was used to calculate the difference between the Asking Price and Selling Price on various real estate listings that were sold during June, as well as the commission paid to the real estate agency as a result of selling those listings. Complete the worksheet, following the steps outlined below:

   a. Open the partially completed *Chapter 2 Practice 1* workbook on the data disk, then save the workbook as *Finished Chapter 2 Practice 1*.

   b. Click cell E5 and enter the formula to calculate the difference between the asking price and the selling price for the property belonging to Mr. Landry.

   c. Click cell F5 and enter the formula to calculate the commission paid to the agency as a result of selling the property. (Pay close attention to the difference between relative and absolute cell references.)

   d. Select cells E5:F5 and copy the formulas to E6:F11 to calculate the difference and commission for the rest of the properties.

   e. Click cell C13 and enter the formula to calculate the total asking price, which is the sum of the asking prices for the individual listings in cells C5:C11.

   f. Copy the formula in C13 to the range D13:F13 to calculate the other totals.

   g. Select the range C5:F13 and format the numbers so that they display with dollar signs and commas, and no decimal places (e.g., $450,000).

   h. Click cell B15 and format the number as a percentage.

   i. Click cell A1 and center the title across the width of the worksheet. With the cell still selected, select cells A3:F4 as well and change the font to 12 point Arial bold italic.

   j. Select cells A4:F4 and create a bottom border to separate the headings from the data.

   k. Select cells F5:F11 and shade the commissions.

   l. Print the worksheet.

	A	B	C	D	E	F
1	Coaches Realty - Sales for June					
2						
3			Asking	Selling		
4	Customer	Address	Price	Price	Difference	Commission
5	Landry	122 West 75 Terr.	450000	350000		
6	Spurrier	4567 S.W. 95 Street	750000	648500		
7	Shula	123 Alamo Road	350000	275000		
8	Lombardi	9000 Brickell Place	275000	250000		
9	Johnson	5596 Powerline Road	189000	189000		
10	Erickson	8900 N.W. 89 Street	456000	390000		
11	Bowden	75 Maynada Blvd.	300000	265000		
12						
13		Totals:				
14						
15	Commission %:	0.035				

FIGURE 2.14   Spreadsheet for Practice Exercise 1

2. The Sales Invoice: Use Figure 2.15 as the basis for a sales invoice that you will create and submit to your instructor. Your spreadsheet should follow the general format shown in the figure with respect to including a uniform discount for each item. Your spreadsheet should also include the sales tax. The discount percentage and sales tax percentage should be entered in a separate area so that they can be easily modified.

Use your imagination and sell any product at any price. You must, however, include at least four items in your invoice. Formatting is important, but you need not follow our format exactly. See how creative you can be, then submit your completed invoice to your instructor for inclusion in a class contest for the best invoice. Be sure your name appears somewhere on the worksheet as a sales associate. If you are really ambitious, you might include an object from the ClipArt Gallery.

	A	B	C	D	E	F
1		**Bargain Basement Shopping**					
2						
3	*Item*	*Quantity*	*List Price*	*Discount*	*Your Price*	*Total*
4	Hayes 28.8 Fax/Modem	2	$169.00	$33.80	$135.20	$270.40
5	Sony 4X CD-ROM	6	$329.00	$65.80	$263.20	$1,579.20
6	Seagate 1Gb Hard Drive	4	$338.00	$67.60	$270.40	$1,081.60
7	Iomega Zip Drive	10	$199.00	$39.80	$159.20	$1,592.00
8						
9	*Subtotal*					$4,523.20
10	*Tax*					$294.01
11	*Amount Due*					$4,817.21
12						
13	*Discount Percentage*	20%				
14	*Sales Tax Percentage*	6.50%				
15	*Sales Associate*	Serena Cruz				

FIGURE 2.15 Spreadsheet for Practice Exercise 2

3. The Probability Expert: How much would you bet *against* two people in your class having the same birthday? Don't be too hasty, for the odds of two classmates sharing the same birthday (month and day) are much higher than you would expect. For example, there is a fifty percent chance (.5063) in a class of 23 students that two people will have been born on the same day, as shown in the spreadsheet in Figure 2.16. The probability jumps to seventy percent (.7053) in a class of 30, and to ninety percent (.9025) in a class of 41. Don't take our word for it, but try the experiment in your class.

You need a basic knowledge of probability to create the spreadsheet. In essence you calculate the probability of individuals not having the same birthday, then subtract this number from one, to obtain the probability of the event coming true. In a group of two people, for example, the probability of not being born on the same day is 365/366; i.e., the second person can be born on any of 365 days and still have a different birthday. The probability of two people having the same birthday becomes 1 − 365/366.

The probability for different birthdays in a group of three is (365/366)*(364/366); the probability of not having different birthdays—that is, of two people having the same birthday, is one minus this number. Each row in the spreadsheet is calculated from the previous row. It's not as hard as it looks, and the results are quite interesting!

	A	B	C
1	The Birthday Problem		
2	Number of People	Probability of Different Birthdays	Probability of the Same Birthday
3	2	99.73%	0.27%
4	3	99.18%	0.82%
5	4	98.37%	1.63%
6	5	97.29%	2.71%
7	6	95.96%	4.04%
8	7	94.39%	5.61%
9	8	92.59%	7.41%
10	9	90.56%	9.44%
11	10	88.34%	11.66%
	.	.	.
24	23	49.37%	50.63%
	.	.	.
42	41	9.75%	90.25%
	.	.	.
51	50	2.99%	97.01%

FIGURE 2.16   Spreadsheet for Practice Exercise 3

4. Help for Your Sibling: Develop the multiplication table for a younger sibling shown in Figure 2.17. Creating the row and column headings is easy in that you can enter the numbers manually, or you can use online help to learn about the AutoFill feature. The hard part is creating the formulas in the body of the worksheet (we don't want you to enter the numbers manually). The trick is to use mixed references for the formula in cell B4, then copy that single cell to the remainder of the table.

Add your name to the worksheet and submit it to your instructor. Remember, this worksheet is for a younger sibling, and so formatting is important. Print the cell formulas as well so that you can see how the mixed reference changes throughout the worksheet. Submit the complete assignment (title page, displayed values, and cell formulas) to your instructor. Using mixed references correctly is challenging, but once you arrive at the correct solution, you will have learned a lot about mixed references.

	A	B	C	D	E	F	G	H	I	J	K	L	M
1	A Multiplication Table for My Younger Sister												
2													
3		1	2	3	4	5	6	7	8	9	10	11	12
4	1	1	2	3	4	5	6	7	8	9	10	11	12
5	2	2	4	6	8	10	12	14	16	18	20	22	24
6	3	3	6	9	12	15	18	21	24	27	30	33	36
7	4	4	8	12	16	20	24	28	32	36	40	44	48
8	5	5	10	15	20	25	30	35	40	45	50	55	60
9	6	6	12	18	24	30	36	42	48	54	60	66	72
10	7	7	14	21	28	35	42	49	56	63	70	77	84
11	8	8	16	24	32	40	48	56	64	72	80	88	96
12	9	9	18	27	36	45	54	63	72	81	90	99	108
13	10	10	20	30	40	50	60	70	80	90	100	110	120
14	11	11	22	33	44	55	66	77	88	99	110	121	132
15	12	12	24	36	48	60	72	84	96	108	120	132	144

FIGURE 2.17   Spreadsheet for Practice Exercise 4

CASE STUDIES

Establishing a Budget

You want to join a sorority, and you really would like a car. Convince your parents that you can afford both by developing a detailed budget for your four years at school. Your worksheet should include all sources of income (scholarships, loans, summer jobs, work-study, etc.) as well as all expenses (tuition, books, room and board, and entertainment). Make the budget as realistic as possible by building in projected increases over the four-year period.

Be sure to isolate the assumptions and initial conditions so that your spreadsheet is amenable to change. Print the spreadsheet twice, once to show displayed values, and once to show the cell formulas. Submit both pages to your instructor together with a cover page for your assignment.

The Entrepreneur

You have developed the perfect product and are seeking venture capital to go into immediate production. Your investors are asking for a projected income statement for the first four years of operation. The sales of your product are estimated at $200,000 the first year and are projected to grow at 10 percent annually. The cost of goods sold is 60 percent of the sales amount, which is expected to remain constant. You also have to pay a 10 percent sales commission, which is also expected to remain constant.

Develop a financial forecast that will show the projected profits before and after taxes (assuming a tax rate of 36 percent). Your worksheet should be completely flexible and capable of accommodating a change in any of the initial conditions or projected rates of increase, *without* having to edit or recopy any of the formulas.

Break-even Analysis

Widgets of America has developed the perfect product and is ready to go into production, pending a review of a five-year break-even analysis. The manufacturing cost in the first year is $1.00 per unit and is estimated to increase at 5% annually. The projected selling price is $2.00 per unit and can increase at 10% annually. Overhead expenses are fixed at $100,000 per year over the life of the project. The advertising budget is $50,000 in the first year but will decrease 15% a year as the product gains acceptance. How many units have to be sold each year for the company to break even, given the current cost estimates and projected rates of increase?

As in the previous case, your worksheet should be completely flexible and capable of accommodating a change in any of the initial conditions or projected rates of increase or decrease. Be sure to isolate all of the assumptions (i.e., the initial conditions and rates of increase) in one area of the worksheet, and then reference these cells as absolute references when building the formulas.

The Corporate Balance Sheet

A balance sheet is a snapshot of a firm's condition at a given point in time. One part of the balance sheet shows the firm's assets and includes items such as cash on hand, accounts receivable, and inventory. It also includes the value of fixed assets, such as the land and/or buildings owned by the firm. The other part of the balance sheet shows the firm's liabilities and includes accounts payable, accrued wages, and debt. It also includes owner's equity and retained earnings.

The best place to see examples of a real balance sheet is in an annual report, which is easily obtained from any public corporation. Obtain a copy of the annual report, find the balance sheet, then recreate the balance sheet for your instructor. Formatting and accuracy are important so do the best job you can. Include your name somewhere on the balance sheet as the financial auditor.

SPREADSHEETS IN DECISION MAKING: WHAT IF?

3

OBJECTIVES

After reading this chapter you will be able to:

1. Describe the use of spreadsheets in decision making; explain how the Goal Seek command and Scenario Manager facilitate the decision making process.
2. List the arguments of the PMT function and describe its use in financial decisions.
3. Use the Function Wizard to select a function, identify the function arguments, then enter the function into a worksheet.
4. Use the fill handle to copy a cell range to a range of adjacent cells; use the AutoFill capability to enter a series into a worksheet.
5. Use pointing to create a formula; explain the advantage of pointing over explicitly typing cell references.
6. Use the AVERAGE, MAX, MIN, and COUNT functions in a worksheet.
7. Use the IF function to implement a decision; explain the VLOOKUP function and how it is used in a worksheet.
8. Describe the additional measures needed to print large worksheets; explain how freezing panes may help in the development of a large worksheet.

OVERVIEW

Excel is a truly fascinating program, but it is only a means to an end. A spreadsheet is first and foremost a tool for decision making, and the objective of this chapter is to show you just how valuable that tool can be. We begin by presenting two worksheets that we think will be truly useful to you. The first evaluates the purchase of a car and helps you determine just how much car you can afford. The second will be of interest when you are looking for a mortgage to buy a home.

The chapter continues to develop your knowledge of Excel with emphasis on the predefined functions that are built into the program. We consider financial functions such as the PMT function to determine the monthly payment on a loan. We introduce the MAX, MIN, COUNT, and COUNTA statistical functions. We also present the IF and VLOOKUP functions that provide decision making within a worksheet.

The chapter also discusses two important commands that facilitate the decision-making process. The Goal Seek command lets you enter the desired end result (such as the monthly payment on a car loan) and from that, determines the input (e.g., the price of the car) to produce that result. The Scenario Manager enables you to specify multiple sets of assumptions and input conditions (scenarios), then see at a glance the results of any given scenario.

The examples in this chapter review the important concepts of relative and absolute cell references, as well as the need to isolate the assumptions and initial conditions in a worksheet. The hands-on exercises introduce new techniques in the form of powerful shortcuts that will make you more proficient in Excel. We show you how to use the fill handle to copy cells within a worksheet and how to use the AutoFill capability to enter a data series. We also explain how to enter formulas by pointing to cells within a worksheet, as opposed to having to explicitly type the cell references.

ANALYSIS OF A CAR LOAN

Figure 3.1 shows how a worksheet might be applied to the purchase of a car. In essence, you need to know the monthly payment, which depends on the price of the car, the down payment, and the terms of the loan. In other words:

- Can you afford the monthly payment on the car of your choice?
- What if you settle for a less expensive car and receive a manufacturer's rebate?
- What if you work next summer to earn money for a down payment?
- What if you extend the life of the loan and receive a more favorable interest rate?

The answers to these and other questions determine whether you can afford a car, and if so, which car, and how you will pay for it. The decision is made easier by developing the worksheet in Figure 3.1, and then by changing the various parameters as indicated.

Figure 3.1a contains the *template*, or "empty" worksheet, in which the text entries and formulas have already been entered, the formatting has already been applied, but no specific data has been input. The template requires that you enter the price of the car, the manufacturer's rebate, the down payment, the interest rate, and the length of the loan. The worksheet uses these parameters to compute the monthly payment. (Implicit in this discussion is the existence of a PMT function within the worksheet program, which is explained in the next section.)

The availability of the worksheet lets you consider several alternatives, and therein lies its true value. You quickly realize that the purchase of a $14,999 car as shown in Figure 3.1b is prohibitive because the monthly payment is almost $500. Settling for a less expensive car, coming up with a substantial down payment, and obtaining a manufacturer's rebate in Figure 3.1c helps considerably, but the $317 monthly payment is still too steep. Extending the loan to a fourth year at a lower interest rate in Figure 3.1d reduces the monthly payment to (a more affordable) $244.

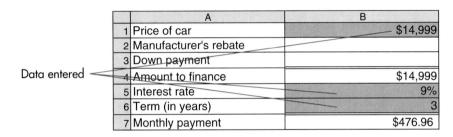

	A	B
1	Price of car	
2	Manufacturer's rebate	
3	Down payment	
4	Amount to finance	=B1-(B2+B3)
5	Interest rate	
6	Term (in years)	
7	Monthly payment	=PMT(B5/12,B6*12,-B4)

No specific data has been input

(a) The Template

	A	B
1	Price of car	$14,999
2	Manufacturer's rebate	
3	Down payment	
4	Amount to finance	$14,999
5	Interest rate	9%
6	Term (in years)	3
7	Monthly payment	$476.96

Data entered

(b) Initial Parameters

	A	B
1	Price of car	$13,999
2	Manufacturer's rebate	$1,000
3	Down payment	$3,000
4	Amount to finance	$9,999
5	Interest rate	9%
6	Term (in years)	3
7	Monthly payment	$317.97

Less expensive car

Rebate

Down payment made

(c) Less Expensive Car with Down Payment and Rebate

	A	B
1	Price of car	$13,999
2	Manufacturer's rebate	$1,000
3	Down payment	$3,000
4	Amount to finance	$9,999
5	Interest rate	8%
6	Term (in years)	4
7	Monthly payment	$244.10

Lower interest rate

Longer term

(d) Longer Term and Better Interest Rate

FIGURE 3.1   Spreadsheets in Decision Making

PMT Function

A *function* is a predefined formula that accepts one or more *arguments* as input, performs the indicated calculation, then returns another value as output. Excel has more than 100 different functions in various categories. Financial functions, such as the PMT function we are about to study, are especially important in business.

The *PMT function* requires three arguments (the interest rate per period, the number of periods, and the amount of the loan) from which it computes the associated payment on a loan. The arguments are placed in parentheses and are separated by commas. Consider, for example, the PMT function as it might apply to Figure 3.1b:

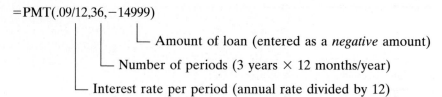

=PMT(.09/12,36,−14999)
— Amount of loan (entered as a *negative* amount)
— Number of periods (3 years × 12 months/year)
— Interest rate per period (annual rate divided by 12)

Instead of using specific values, however, the arguments in the PMT function are supplied as cell references, so that the computed payment can be based on values supplied by the user elsewhere in the worksheet. Thus, the PMT function is entered as =PMT(B5/12,B6*12,−B4) to reflect the terms of a specific loan whose arguments are in cells B4, B5, and B6. (The principal is entered as a negative amount because the money is lent to you and represents an outflow of cash from the bank.)

The Goal Seek Command

The analysis in Figure 3.1 enabled us to reduce the projected monthly payment from $476 to a more affordable $244. What if, however, we can afford a payment of only $200, and we want to know how much money to borrow in order to keep the payment to the specified amount. The *Goal Seek command* is designed to solve this type of problem as it enables you to set an end result (e.g., the monthly payment) in order to determine the input (the price of the car) to produce that result. Only one parameter (e.g., the price of the car *or* the interest rate) can be varied at a time.

Figure 3.2 extends our earlier analysis to illustrate the Goal Seek command. You create the spreadsheet as usual, then you pull down the Tools menu, and select the Goal Seek command to display the dialog box in Figure 3.2a. Enter the address of the cell containing the dependent formula (the monthly payment in cell B7) and the desired value of this cell ($200). Indicate the cell whose contents will change (the price of the car in cell B1), then click OK to execute the command. The Goal Seek command then varies the price of the car until the monthly payment returns the desired value of $200. (Not every problem has a solution, however, in which case Excel will return a message indicating that a solution cannot be found.)

In this example the Goal Seek command is able to find a solution and returns a purchase price of $12,192 as shown in Figure 3.2b. You now have all the information you need. Find a car that sells for $12,192 (or less), hold the other parameters to the values shown in the figure, and your monthly payment will be (at most) $200.

The analyses in Figures 3.1 and 3.2 illustrate how a worksheet is used in the decision-making process. An individual defines a problem, then develops a worksheet that includes all of the associated parameters. He or she can then plug in specific numbers, changing one or more of the variables until a decision can be reached.

LIMITATIONS OF THE GOAL SEEK COMMAND

The Goal Seek command, powerful as it is, is limited to a single variable; that is, you set the desired result but are limited to changing the value of a single input variable. Excel does, however, provide a more powerful tool known as Solver, which can vary multiple input variables. This is a much more complex analysis and is beyond the scope of the present discussion.

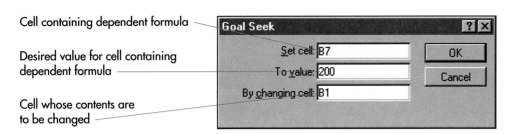

Cell containing dependent formula

Desired value for cell containing dependent formula

Cell whose contents are to be changed

(a) Set the Maximum Payment

Required purchase price for a $200 monthly payment

	A	B
1	Price of car	$12,192
2	Manufacturer's rebate	$1,000
3	Down payment	$3,000
4	Amount to finance	$8,192
5	Interest rate	8%
6	Term (in years)	4
7	Monthly payment	$200.00

(b) Solution

FIGURE 3.2   The Goal Seek Command

HANDS-ON EXERCISE 1

Analysis of a Car Loan

Objective: To create a spreadsheet that will analyze a car loan; to illustrate the PMT function and the Goal Seek command. Use Figure 3.3 as a guide.

Step 1: Enter the Descriptive Labels

➤ Start Excel. If necessary, click the **New button** on the Standard toolbar to open a new workbook.

➤ Click in **cell A1,** type the label **Price of car,** then press the **enter key** or **down arrow** to complete the entry and move automatically to cell A2.

➤ Enter the remaining labels for column A as shown in Figure 3.3a.

THE SPELL CHECK

Anyone familiar with a word processor takes the spell check for granted, but did you know the same capability exists within Excel? Click the Spelling button on the Standard toolbar to initiate the spell check, then implement corrections just as you do in Microsoft Word. All of the applications in Microsoft Office share the same custom dictionary, so that any words you add to the custom dictionary in one application are automatically recognized in the other applications.

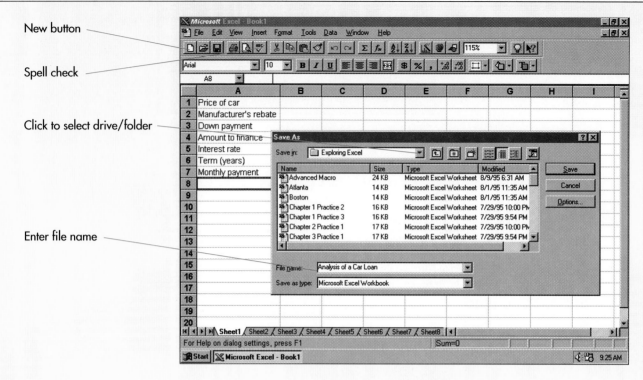

New button

Spell check

Click to select drive/folder

Enter file name

(a) Enter the Descriptive Labels (step 1)

FIGURE 3.3   Hands-on Exercise 1

➤ Click and drag the column border between columns A and B to increase the width of column A to accommodate its widest entry.

➤ Save the workbook as **Analysis of a Car Loan** in the **Exploring Excel folder** as shown in Figure 3.3a.

Step 2: Enter the PMT Function and Its Parameters

➤ Enter **14999** in cell B1 as shown in Figure 3.3b.

➤ Click in **cell B4.** Enter **=B1−(B2+B3),** which calculates the amount to finance (i.e., the principal of the loan).

➤ Enter **9%** and **3** in cells B5 and B6 as shown in Figure 3.3b.

➤ Click in **cell B7.** Enter **=PMT(B5/12,B6*12,−B4)** as the payment function. The arguments in the PMT function are the interest rate per period, the number of periods, and the principal, and correspond to the parameters of the loan.

THE FORMATTING IS IN THE CELL

Once a number format has been assigned to a cell, either by including the format as you entered a number or through execution of a formatting command, the formatting remains in the cell. Thus, to change the contents in a formatted cell, all you need to do is enter the new number without the formatting. Entering 5000, for example, in a cell that was previously formatted as currency will display the number as $5,000.

Enter formulas in column B

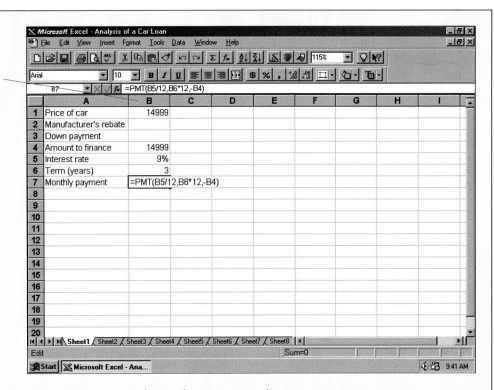

(b) Enter the PMT Function and Its Parameters (step 2)

FIGURE 3.3   Hands-on Exercise 1 (continued)

➤ Click and drag to select cells **B1** through **B4.** Format these cells in **currency format** with no decimals. You should see $476.96 as the displayed value in cell B7.

➤ Save the workbook.

Step 3: What If?

➤ Click in **cell B1** and change the price of the car to **$13,999.** The monthly payment drops to $445.16.

➤ Click in **cell B2** and enter a manufacturer's rebate of **$1,000.** Click in **cell B3** and enter a down payment of **$3,000.** The monthly payment drops to $317.97.

➤ Change the interest rate to **8%** and the term of the loan to **4** years. The payment drops to $244.10.

Step 4: The Goal Seek Command

➤ Click in **cell B7,** the cell containing the formula for the monthly payment. This is the cell whose value we want to set to a fixed amount.

➤ Pull down the **Tools menu.** Click **Goal Seek** to display the dialog box in Figure 3.3c.

➤ Click in the **To value** text box. Type **200** (the desired value of the monthly payment).

➤ Click in the **By changing cell** text box. Type **B1,** the cell containing the price of the car. This is the cell whose value will be determined.

➤ Click **OK.**

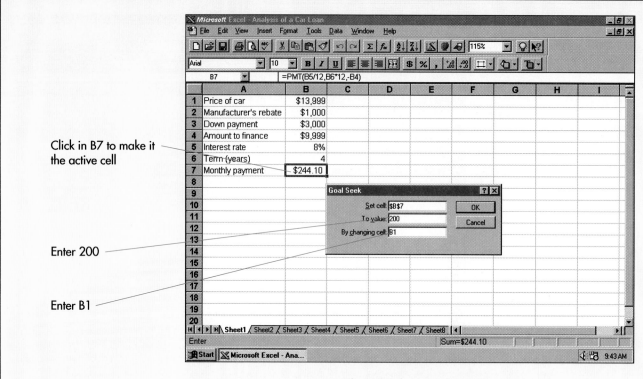

Click in B7 to make it
the active cell

Enter 200

Enter B1

(c) The Goal Seek Command (step 4)

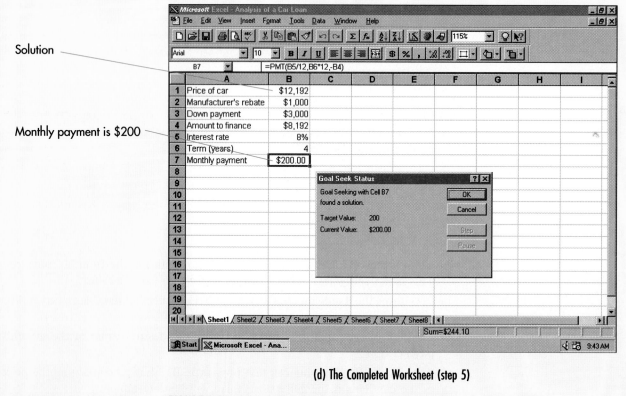

Solution

Monthly payment is $200

(d) The Completed Worksheet (step 5)

FIGURE 3.3   Hands-on Exercise 1 (continued)

Step 5: The Goal Seek Command (continued)

- The Goal Seek command returns a successful solution as indicated by the dialog box in Figure 3.3d. The worksheet changes to display $12,192 and $200 in cells B1 and B7, respectively, corresponding to the parameters in the Goal Seek command:
  - Click **OK** to accept the solution and close the Goal Seek dialog box, *or*
  - Click **Cancel** if you don't like the solution and want to return to the original values.
- Save the workbook. Close the workbook. Exit Excel if you do not want to continue with the next exercise at this time.

HOME MORTGAGES

The PMT function is used in our next example in conjunction with the purchase of a home. The example also reviews the concept of relative and absolute addresses from Chapter 2. In addition, it introduces several other techniques to make you more proficient in Excel.

The spreadsheet in Figure 3.4 illustrates a variable rate mortgage, which will be developed over the next several pages. The user enters the amount he or she wishes to borrow and a starting interest rate, and the spreadsheet displays the associated monthly payment. The spreadsheet enables the user to see the monthly payment at varying interest rates, and to contrast the amount of the payment for a 15- and a 30-year mortgage.

Most first-time buyers opt for the longer term, but they would do well to consider a 15-year mortgage. Note, for example, that the difference in monthly payments for a $100,000 mortgage at 7.5% is only $227.80 (the difference between $927.01 for a 15-year mortgage versus $699.21 for the 30-year mortgage). This is a significant amount of money, but when viewed as a percentage of the total cost of a home (property taxes, maintenance, and so on), it becomes less significant, and it results in significant savings in reducing the amount of interest you will pay over the life of the mortgage.

Figure 3.5 expands the spreadsheet to show the total interest over the life of the loan for both the 15- and the 30-year mortgage. The total interest on a $100,000 loan at 7.5% is $151,717 for a 30-year mortgage, but only $66,862 for a 15-year mortgage. In other words, you will pay back the $100,000 in principal plus another $151,717 in interest if you select the longer term. This is more than twice the interest for the 15-year mortgage.

Difference between a 30-year and a 15-year mortgage at 7.5%

	A	B	C	D
1	Amount Borrowed		$100,000	
2	Starting Interest		7.50%	
3				
4		Monthly Payment		
5	Interest	30 Years	15 Years	Difference
6	7.50%	$699.21	$927.01	$227.80
7	8.50%	$768.91	$984.74	$215.83
8	9.50%	$840.85	$1,044.22	$203.37
9	10.50%	$914.74	$1,105.40	$190.66
10	11.50%	$990.29	$1,168.19	$177.90
11	12.50%	$1,067.26	$1,232.52	$165.26

FIGURE 3.4 Variable Rate Mortgages

Less interest is paid on a
15-year loan ($66,862 vs
$151,717 on a 30-year loan)

	A	B	C	D	E
1	Amount Borrowed			$100,000	
2	Starting Interest			7.50%	
3					
4		30 Years		15 Years	
5	Interest	Monthly Payment	Total Interest	Monthly Payment	Total Interest
6	7.50%	$699.21	$151,717	$927.01	$66,862
7	8.50%	$768.91	$176,809	$984.74	$77,253
8	9.50%	$840.85	$202,708	$1,044.22	$87,960
9	10.50%	$914.74	$229,306	$1,105.40	$98,972
10	11.50%	$990.29	$256,505	$1,168.19	$110,274
11	12.50%	$1,067.26	$284,213	$1,232.52	$121,854

(a) Total Interest

	A	B	C	D
1		Amortization Schedule		
2				
3	Principal		$100,000	
4	Annual Interest		7.50%	
5	Term (in years)		30	
6	Monthly Payment		$699.21	
7				
8	Month	Toward Interest	Toward Principal	Balance
9				$100,000.00
10	1	$625.00	$74.21	$99,925.79
11	2	$624.54	$74.68	$99,851.11
12	3	$624.07	$75.15	$99,775.96
13	4	$623.60	$75.61	$99,700.35
14	5	$623.13	$76.09	$99,624.26
15	6	$622.65	$76.56	$99,547.70
·	·	·	·	·
65	56	$594.67	$104.55	$95,042.20
66	57	$594.01	$105.20	$94,937.00
67	58	$593.36	$105.86	$94,831.14
68	59	$592.69	$106.52	$94,724.62
69	60	$592.03	$107.19	$94,617.44

Less than $6,000 of the
principal has been paid off

5 years (60 months)

(b) Amortization Schedule

FIGURE 3.5   15- vs 30-Year Mortgage

If, like most people, you move before you pay off the mortgage, you will discover that almost all of the early payments in the 30-year loan go to interest rather than principal. The amortization schedule in Figure 3.5b shows that if you were to move at the end of five years (60 months), less than $6,000 (of the $44,952 you paid during those five years) goes toward the principal. (A 15-year mortgage, however, would pay off almost $22,000 during the same five-year period. The latter number is not shown, but can be displayed by changing the term of the mortgage in cell C5.)

Our objective is not to convince you of the merits of one loan over another, but to show you how useful a worksheet can be in the decision-making process. If you do eventually buy a home, and you select a 15-year mortgage, think of us.

Relative versus Absolute Addresses

Figure 3.6 displays the cell formulas for the mortgage analysis. All of the formulas are based on the amount borrowed and the starting interest, in cells C1 and C2, respectively. You can vary either or both of these parameters, and the worksheet will automatically recalculate the monthly payments.

The similarity in the formulas from one row to the next implies that the copy operation will be essential to the development of the worksheet. You must, however, remember the distinction between a *relative* and an *absolute reference*—that is, a cell reference that changes during a copy operation (relative) versus one that does not (absolute). Consider the PMT function as it appears in cell B6:

=PMT(A6/12,30*12,−$C$1)

- The amount of the loan, −$C$1, is an absolute reference that remains constant
- Number of periods (30 years*12 months/year)
- The interest rate, A6/12, is a relative reference that changes

The entry A6/12 (which is the first argument in the formula in cell B6) is interpreted to mean "divide the contents of the cell one column to the left by 12." Thus, when the PMT function in cell B6 is copied to cell B7, it (the copied formula) is adjusted to maintain this relationship and will contain the entry A7/12. The Copy command does not duplicate a relative address exactly, but adjusts it from row to row (or column to column) to maintain the relative relationship. The cell reference for the amount of the loan should not change when the formula is copied, and hence it is specified as an absolute address.

ISOLATE ASSUMPTIONS

The formulas in a worksheet should be based on cell references rather than specific values—for example, C1 or $C$1 rather than $100,000. The cells containing these values should be clearly labeled and set apart from the rest of the worksheet. You can then vary the inputs (assumptions) to the worksheet and immediately see the effect. The chance for error is also minimized because you are changing the contents of a single cell, rather than changing multiple formulas.

Relative reference (adjusts during copy operation)

Absolute reference (doesn't adjust during copy operation)

	A	B	C	D
1	Amount Borrowed		$100,000	
2	Starting Interest		7.50%	
3				
4		Monthly Payment		
5	Interest	30 Years	15 Years	Difference
6	=C2	=PMT(A6/12,30*12,-$C$1)	=PMT(A6/12,15*12,-$C$1)	=C6-B6
7	=A6+0.01	=PMT(A7/12,30*12,-$C$1)	=PMT(A7/12,15*12,-$C$1)	=C7-B7
8	=A7+0.01	=PMT(A8/12,30*12,-$C$1)	=PMT(A8/12,15*12,-$C$1)	=C8-B8
9	=A8+0.01	=PMT(A9/12,30*12,-$C$1)	=PMT(A9/12,15*12,-$C$1)	=C9-B9
10	=A9+0.01	=PMT(A10/12,30*12,-$C$1)	=PMT(A10/12,15*12,-$C$1)	=C10-B10
11	=A10+0.01	=PMT(A11/12,30*12,-$C$1)	=PMT(A11/12,15*12,-$C$1)	=C11-B11

FIGURE 3.6   Cell Formulas

You already know enough about Excel to develop the worksheet for the mortgage analysis. Excel is so powerful, however, and offers so many shortcuts, that we would be remiss not to show you alternative techniques. This section introduces the fill handle as a shortcut for copying cells, and pointing as a more accurate way to enter cell formulas. It also presents the Function Wizard, which helps you to enter the arguments in a function correctly.

The Fill Handle

The *fill handle* is a tiny black square that appears in the lower-right corner of the selected cells—it is the fastest way to copy a cell (or range of cells) to an *adjacent* cell (or range of cells). The process is quite easy, and you get to practice in the exercise (see Figure 3.8b) that follows shortly. In essence, you:

- Select the cell or cells to be copied.
- Point to the fill handle for the selected cell(s), which changes the mouse pointer to a thin crosshair.
- Click and drag the fill handle over the destination range. A border appears to outline the destination range.
- Release the mouse to complete the copy operation.

Pointing

A cell address is entered into a formula by typing the reference explicitly (as we have done throughout the text) or by pointing. If you type the address, it is all too easy to make a mistake, such as typing A40 when you really mean A41. *Pointing* is more accurate, since you use the mouse or arrow keys to select the cell directly as you build the formula. The process is much easier than it sounds, and you get to practice in the hands-on exercise (see Figure 3.8d). In essence, you:

- Select (click) the cell to contain the formula.
- Type an equal sign to begin entering the formula. The status bar indicates that you are in the *Enter mode,* which means that the formula bar is active and the formula can be entered.
- Click the cell you want to reference in the formula (or use the arrow keys to move to the cell). A moving border appears around the cell, and the cell reference is displayed in both the cell and formula bar. The status bar indicates the *Point mode.*
- Type any arithmetic operator to place the cell reference in the formula and return to the Enter mode.
- Continue pointing to additional cells and entering arithmetic operators until you complete the formula. Press the enter key to complete the formula.

As with everything else, the more you practice, the easier it is. The hands-on exercises will give you ample opportunity to practice everything that you have learned.

The Function Wizard

The *Function Wizard* helps you to select the appropriate function, then helps you enter the correct arguments for that function. The functions in Excel are grouped into categories, as shown in the open list box in Figure 3.7a. Select the function

Select function category

Select function name

Click Next to continue

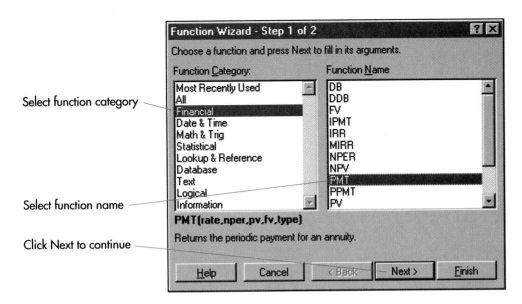

(a) Step 1

Computed value
of function

Computed value of the
individual argument

Text box for
individual argument

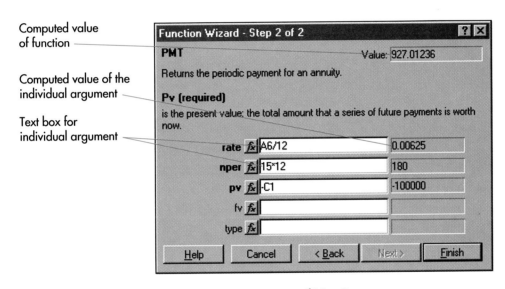

(b) Step 2

FIGURE 3.7   The Function Wizard

category you want, then choose the desired function from within that category. Click the Next command button to produce the dialog box in Figure 3.7b, in which you specify the arguments for the function.

The Function Wizard displays a text box for each argument, a description of each argument (as the text box is selected), and an indication of whether or not the argument is required. (Only the first three arguments are required in the PMT function.) Enter the value, cell reference, or formula for each argument by clicking in the text box and typing the entry, or by clicking the appropriate cell(s) in the worksheet.

Excel displays the calculated value for each argument immediately to the right of the argument. It also shows the computed value for the function as a whole at the top of the dialog box. All you need to do is click the Finish button to insert the function into the worksheet. The Function Wizard is illustrated in step 5 of the following exercise.

Mortgage Analysis

Objective: To develop the worksheet for the mortgage analysis; to use pointing to enter a formula and drag-and-drop to copy a formula. Use Figure 3.8 as a guide in the exercise.

Step 1: Enter the Descriptive Labels and Initial Conditions

➤ Start Excel. Click in **cell A1.** Type **Amount Borrowed.** Do not be concerned that the text is longer than the cell width, as cell B1 is empty and thus the text will be displayed in its entirety. Press the **enter key** or **down arrow** to complete the entry and move to cell A2.

➤ Type **Starting Interest** in cell A2. Click in **cell A4.** Type **Monthly Payment.** Enter the remaining labels in cells A5 through D5 as shown in Figure 3.8a. Do not worry about formatting at this time as all formatting will be done at the end of the exercise.

➤ Click in **cell C1.** Type **$100,000** (include the dollar sign and comma). Press the **enter key** or **down arrow** to complete the entry and move to cell C2. Type **7.5%** (include the percent sign). Press **enter.**

➤ Save the workbook as **Variable Rate Mortgage** in the **Exploring Excel folder.**

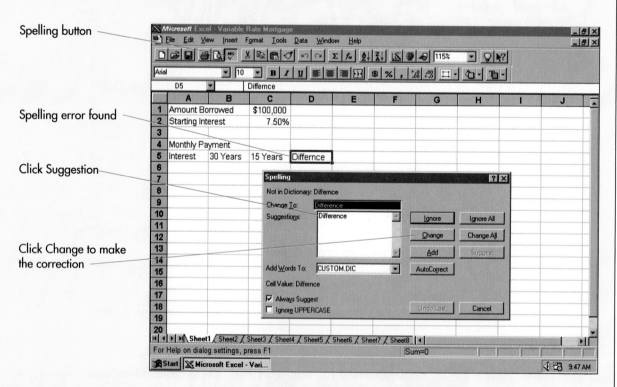

Spelling button

Spelling error found

Click Suggestion

Click Change to make the correction

(a) Enter the Descriptive Labels and Spell Check (steps 1 & 2)

FIGURE 3.8   Hands-on Exercise 2

Step 2: The Spell Check

➤ Click in **cell A1** to begin the spell check at the beginning of the worksheet.

➤ Click the **Spelling button** on the Standard toolbar to initiate the spell check as shown in Figure 3.8a. Make corrections, as necessary, just as you would in Microsoft Word.

➤ Save the workbook.

Step 3: Copy the Column of Interest Rates (the Fill Handle)

➤ Click in **cell A6.** Type **=C2** to reference the starting interest rate in cell C2.

➤ Click in **cell A7.** Type the formula **=A6+.01** to compute the interest rate in this cell, which is one percent more than the interest rate in row 6. Press **enter.**

➤ Click in **cell A7.** Point to the **fill handle** in the lower corner of cell A7. The mouse pointer changes to a thin crosshair.

➤ Drag the **fill handle** over cells **A8** through **A11.** A border appears, indicating the destination range as in Figure 3.8b. Release the mouse to complete the copy operation. The formula and associated percentage format in cell A7 have been copied to cells A8 through A11.

➤ Click in **cell C2.** Type **5%.** The entries in cells A6 through A11 change automatically. Click the **Undo button** on the Standard toolbar to return to the 7.5% interest rate.

➤ Save the workbook.

Undo button

Point to fill handle and
drag over A8:A11

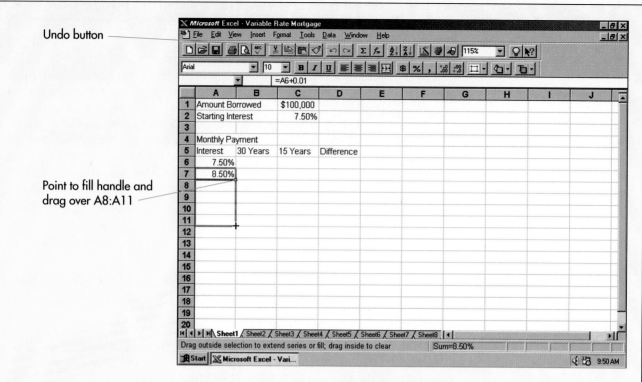

(b) The Fill Handle (step 3)

FIGURE 3.8   Hands-on Exercise 2 (continued)

Step 4: Determine the 30-Year Payments

➤ Click in **cell B6.** Type the formula **=PMT(A6/12,30*12,−$C$1).** Press the **enter key.** Cell B6 should display $699.21.

➤ Click in **cell B6.** Point to the **fill handle** in the bottom-right corner of cell B6. The mouse pointer changes to a thin crosshair. Drag the **fill handle** over cells **B7** through **B11.** A border appears to indicate the destination range. Release the mouse to complete the copy operation.

➤ The PMT function in cell B6 has been copied to cells B7 through B11. The payment amounts are visible in cells B7 through B10, but cell B11 displays a series of pound signs, meaning that the cell (column) is too narrow to display the computed results in the selected format.

THE OPTIMAL (BEST FIT) COLUMN WIDTH

The appearance of pound signs within a cell indicates that the cell width (column width) is insufficient to display the computed results in the selected format. Double click the right border of the column heading to change the column width to accommodate the widest entry in that column. For example, to increase the width of column B, double click the border between the column headings for columns B and C.

➤ Check that cell B11 is still selected. Pull down the **Format menu,** click **Column,** then click **AutoFit Selection** from the cascaded menu. Cell B11 should display $1,067.26.

➤ Save the workbook.

Step 5: The Function Wizard

➤ Click in **cell C6.** Pull down the **Insert menu** and click **Function** (or click the **Function Wizard button** on the Standard toolbar) to display step 1 of the Function Wizard.

➤ Click **Financial** in the Function Category list box. Click **PMT** in the Function Name list box. Click the **Next command button** to display the dialog box in Figure 3.8c.

➤ Click the text box for **rate.** Type **A6/12.** The Function Wizard displays the computed value of .00625.

➤ Click the text box for the number of periods **(nper).** Type **15*12,** corresponding to 15 years and 12 months per year.

➤ Click the text box for the present value **(pv).** Type **−$C$1.** Be sure to include the minus sign in front of the absolute reference.

➤ Check that the computed values on your monitor match those in Figure 3.8c. Make corrections as necessary. Click the **Finish command button** to insert the function into the worksheet. Cell C6 should display $927.01.

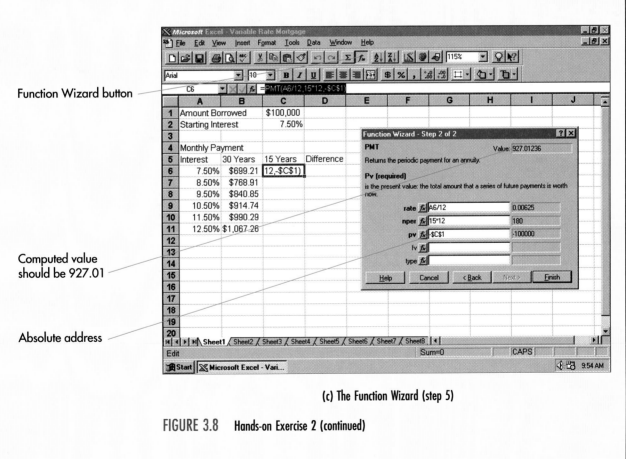

(c) The Function Wizard (step 5)

FIGURE 3.8   Hands-on Exercise 2 (continued)

Step 6: Copy the 15-Year Payments

➤ Check that cell C6 is still selected. Point to the **fill handle** in the lower-right corner of cell C6. The mouse pointer changes to a thin crosshair.

➤ Drag the **fill handle** to copy the PMT function to cells **C7** through **C11.** Adjust the width of these cells so that you can see the displayed values.

➤ Cell C11 should display $1,232.52 if you have done this step correctly. Save the workbook.

MORE ABOUT THE FILL HANDLE

Use the fill handle as a shortcut for the Edit Clear command. To clear the contents of a cell, drag the fill handle to the top of the cell (the cell will be shaded in gray) and release the mouse. To clear the contents *and* the format, press and hold the Ctrl key as you drag the fill handle to the top of the cell. You can apply the same technique to a cell range by selecting the range, then dragging the fill handle to the top (or left) of the range.

Step 7: Compute the Monthly Difference (Pointing)

➤ Click in **cell D6.** Type = to begin the formula. Press the **left arrow key** (or click in **cell C6**), which produces the moving border around the entry in cell C6. The status bar indicates the point mode as shown in Figure 3.8d.

➤ Press the **minus sign,** then press the **left arrow key** twice (or click in **cell B6**).

➤ Press **enter** to complete the formula. Cell D6 should display $227.80.

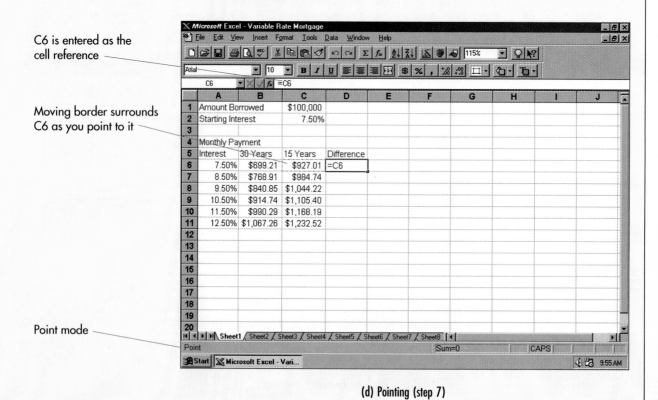

(d) Pointing (step 7)

FIGURE 3.8   Hands-on Exercise 2 (continued)

➤ Use the **fill handle** to copy the contents of cell D6 to cells **D7** through **D11.** If you have done the step correctly, cell D11 will display $165.26 as shown in Figure 3.8e.

➤ Save the workbook.

Step 8: The Finishing Touches

➤ Type **Financial consultant:** in cell A13. Enter **your name** in cell C13.

➤ Add formatting as necessary, using Figure 3.8e as a guide:

• Click **cell A4.** Drag the mouse over cells **A4** through **D4.** Click the **Center Across Columns button** on the Formatting toolbar to center the entry in cell A4.

• Center the column headings in row 5. Add boldface and/or italics to the text and/or numbers as you see fit.

➤ Save the workbook.

Step 9: Print the Worksheet

➤ Pull down the **File menu** and click **Print Preview** (or click the **Print Preview button** on the Standard toolbar).

➤ Click the **Setup command button** to display the Page Setup dialog box.

• Click the **Margins tab.** Check the box to center the worksheet Horizontally.

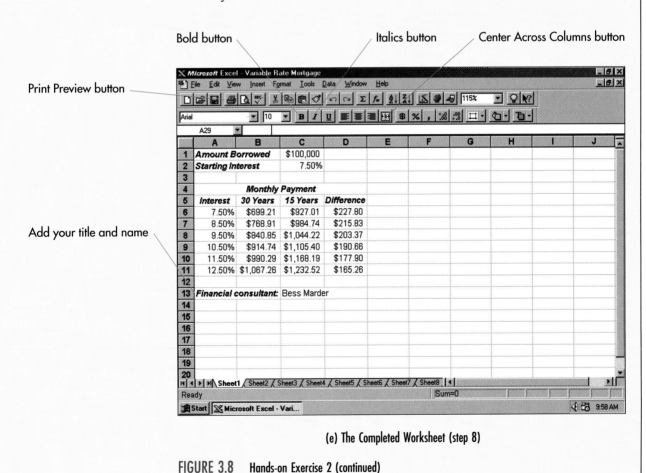

(e) The Completed Worksheet (step 8)

FIGURE 3.8   Hands-on Exercise 2 (continued)

- Click the **Sheet tab.** Check the boxes to include Row and Column Headings and Gridlines.
- Click **OK** to exit the Page Setup dialog box.
➤ Click the **Print command button** to display the Print dialog box, then click **OK** to print the worksheet.
➤ Press **Ctrl+`** to display the cell formulas. (The left quotation mark is on the same key as the ~.) Widen the cells as necessary to see the complete cell formulas.
➤ Click the **Print button** on the Standard toolbar to print the cell formulas.
➤ Close the workbook. Click **No** when asked whether you want to save the changes, or else you will save the workbook with the settings to print the cell formulas rather than the displayed values.
➤ Exit Excel if you do not want to continue with the next exercise at this time.

THE GRADE BOOK REVISITED

Financial functions are only one of several categories of functions that are included in Excel. Our next example presents an expanded version of the professor's grade book. It introduces several new functions and shows how those functions can aid in the professor's determination of a student's grade. The worksheet shown in Figure 3.9 illustrates several additional features. Consider:

Statistical functions: The AVERAGE, MAX, and MIN functions are used to compute the statistics on each test for the class as a whole. The range on each test is computed by subtracting the minimum value from the maximum value.

	A	B	C	D	E	F	G	H	I	J
1					Professor's Grade Book					
2										
3	Name	Student ID	Test 1	Test 2	Test 3	Test 4	Test Avg	Homework	Semester Avg	Grade
4	Adams, John	011-12-2333	80	71	70	84	77.8	Poor	77.8	C
5	Barber, Maryann	444-55-6666	96	98	97	90	94.2	OK	97.2	A
6	Boone, Dan	777-88-9999	78	81	70	78	77.0	OK	80.0	B
7	Borow, Jeff	123-45-6789	65	65	65	60	63.0	OK	66.0	D
8	Brown, James	999-99-9999	92	95	79	80	85.2	OK	88.2	B
9	Carson, Kit	888-88-8888	90	90	90	70	82.0	OK	85.0	B
10	Coulter, Sara	100-00-0000	60	50	40	79	61.6	OK	64.6	D
11	Fegin, Richard	222-22-2222	75	70	65	95	80.0	OK	83.0	B
12	Ford, Judd	200-00-0000	90	90	80	90	88.0	Poor	88.0	B
13	Glassman, Kris	444-44-4444	82	78	62	77	75.2	OK	78.2	C
14	Goodman, Neil	555-55-5555	92	88	65	78	80.2	OK	83.2	B
15	Milgrom, Marion	666-66-6666	94	92	86	84	88.0	OK	91.0	A
16	Moldof, Adam	300-00-0000	92	78	65	84	80.6	OK	83.6	B
17	Smith, Adam	777-77-7777	60	50	65	80	67.0	Poor	67.0	D
18										
19	Average		81.9	78.3	71.4	80.6	HW Bonus:	3	Grading Criteria	
20	Highest Grade		96	98	97	95			(No Curve)	
21	Lowest Grade		60	50	40	60				F
22	Range		36	48	57	35			60	D
23									70	C
24	Exam Weights		20%	20%	20%	40%			80	B
25									90	A

Statistical functions   IF function   Table Lookup function

FIGURE 3.9   The Expanded Grade Book

IF function: The IF function conditionally adds a homework bonus of three points to the semester average, prior to determining the letter grade. The bonus is awarded to those students whose homework is "OK." Students whose homework is not "OK" do not receive the bonus.

VLOOKUP function: The expanded grade book converts a student's semester average to a letter grade, in accordance with the table shown in the lower-right portion of the worksheet. A student with an average of 60 to 69 will receive a D, 70 to 79 a C, and so on. Any student with an average less than 60 receives an F.

Scenario Manager: The table for grading criteria indicates that grades (in this worksheet) are determined without a curve. The professor also has the capability to enter an alternative set of criteria (scenario) in which he or she assigns grades based on a curve.

Statistical Functions

The *MAX, MIN,* and *AVERAGE* functions return the highest, lowest, and average values, respectively, from an argument list. The list may include individual cell references, ranges, numeric values, functions, or mathematical expressions (formulas). The *statistical functions* are illustrated in the worksheet of Figure 3.10.

The first example, =AVERAGE(A1:A3), computes the average for cells A1 through A3 by adding the values in the indicated range (70, 80, and 90), then dividing the result by three, to obtain an average of 80. Additional arguments in the form of values and/or cell addresses can be specified within the parentheses; for example, the function =AVERAGE(A1:A3,200), computes the average of cells A1, A2, and A3, and the number 200.

Cells that are empty or cells that contain text values are *not* included in the computation. Thus, since cell A4 is empty, the function =AVERAGE(A1:A4)

Function	Value
=AVERAGE(A1:A3)	80
=AVERAGE(A1:A3,200)	110
=AVERAGE(A1:A4)	80
=AVERAGE(A1:A3,A5)	80
=MAX(A1:A3)	90
=MAX(A1:A3,200)	200
=MAX(A1:A4)	90
=MAX(A1:A3,A5)	90
=MIN(A1:A3)	70
=MIN(A1:A3,200)	70
=MIN(A1:A4)	70
=MIN(A1:A3,A5)	70
=COUNT(A1:A3)	3
=COUNT(A1:A3,200)	4
=COUNT(A1:A4)	3
=COUNT(A1:A3,A5)	3
=COUNTA(A1:A3)	3
=COUNTA(A1:A3,200)	4
=COUNTA(A1:A4)	3
=COUNTA(A1:A3,A5)	4

Empty and/or text values are not included in the computation

	A
1	70
2	80
3	90
4	
5	Study hard

Empty cell

Text value

The spreadsheet

Empty and/or text values are not included in the computation (COUNT)

Empty cells are not included in the computation (COUNTA)

Text values are included in the computation (COUNTA)

Illustrative functions

FIGURE 3.10   Statistical Functions with a Text Entry

also returns an average of 80 (240/3). In similar fashion, the function =AVERAGE(A1:A3,A5) includes only three values in its computation (cells A1, A2, and A3), because the text entry in cell A5 is excluded. The results of the MIN and MAX functions are obtained in a comparable way, as indicated in Figure 3.10. As with the AVERAGE function, empty cells and text entries are not included in the computation.

The COUNT and COUNTA functions each tally the number of entries in the argument list and are subtly different. The **COUNT function** returns the number of cells containing a numeric entry, including formulas that evaluate to numeric results. The **COUNTA function** includes cells with text as well as numeric values. In Figure 3.10, the functions =COUNT(A1:A3) and =COUNTA(A1:A3) both return a value of 3 as do the two functions =COUNT(A1:A4) and =COUNTA(A1:A4). (Cell A4 is empty and is excluded from the latter computations.) The function =COUNT(A1:A3,A5) also returns a value of 3 because it does not include the text entry in cell A5. However, the function =COUNTA(A1:A3,A5) returns a value of 4 because it includes the text entry in cell A5.

Arithmetic Expressions versus Functions

Many worksheet calculations, such as an average or a sum, can be performed in two ways. You can enter a formula such as =(A1+A2+A3)/3, or you can use the equivalent function =AVERAGE(A1:A3). *The use of functions is generally preferable* as shown in Figure 3.11.

The two worksheets in Figure 3.11a may appear equivalent, but the SUM function is superior to the arithmetic expression. This is true despite the fact that the entries in cell A5 of both worksheets return a value of 100.

Consider what happens if a new row is inserted between existing rows 2 and 3, with the entry in the new cell equal to 25. The **SUM function** adjusts automatically to include the new value (returning a sum of 125) because the SUM function was defined originally for the cell range *A1 through A4.* The new row is inserted within these cells, moving the entry in cell A4 to cell A5, and changing the range to include cell A5.

No such accommodation is made in the arithmetic expression, which was defined to include four *specific* cells rather than a range of cells. The addition of the new row modifies the cell references (since the values in cells A3 and A4 have been moved to cells A4 and A5), and does not include the new row in the adjusted expression.

Similar reasoning holds for deleting a row. Figure 3.11c deletes row two from the *original* worksheets, which moves the entry in cell A4 to cell A3. The SUM function adjusts automatically to =SUM(A1:A3) and returns the value 80. The formula, however, returns an error (to indicate an illegal cell reference) because it is still attempting to add the entries in four cells, one of which no longer exists. In summary, a function expands and contracts to adjust for insertions or deletions, and should be used wherever possible.

#REF!—ILLEGAL CELL REFERENCE

The #REF! error occurs when you refer to a cell that is not valid. The error is displayed whenever Excel is unable to evaluate a formula because of an illegal cell reference. The most common cause of the error is deleting the row, column, or cell that contained the original cell reference.

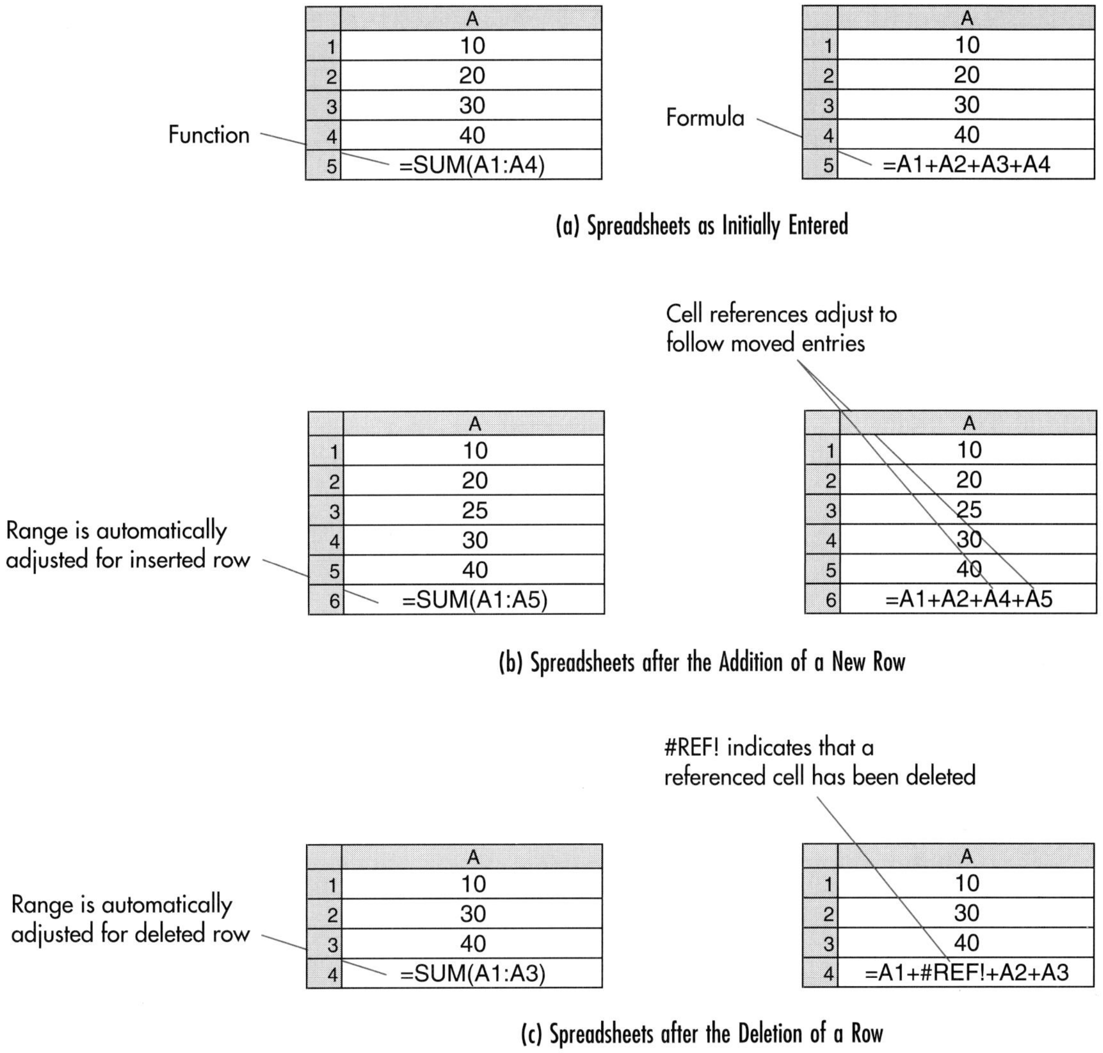

(a) Spreadsheets as Initially Entered

(b) Spreadsheets after the Addition of a New Row

(c) Spreadsheets after the Deletion of a Row

FIGURE 3.11 Arithmetic Expressions vs. Functions

IF Function

The **_IF function_** enables decision making to be implemented within a worksheet—for example, a conditional bonus for students whose homework is satisfactory. Students with inferior homework do not get this bonus.

The IF function has three arguments: a condition that is evaluated as true or false, the value to be returned if the condition is true, and the value to be returned if the condition is false. Consider:

=IF(condition,value-if-true,value-if-false)

Value returned for a false condition

Value returned for a true condition

Condition is either true or false

The IF function returns either the second or third argument, depending on the result of the condition; that is, if the condition is true, the function returns the second argument, whereas if the condition is false, the function returns the third argument.

The condition uses one of the six *relational operators* in Figure 3.12a to perform *logical tests*. The IF function is illustrated in the worksheet in Figure 3.12b, which is used to create the examples in Figure 3.12c. In every instance the condition is evaluated, then the second or third argument is returned, depending on whether the condition is true or false. The arguments may be numeric (1000 or 2000), a cell reference to display the contents of the specific cell (B1 or B2), a formula (=B1+10 or =B1−10), a function (MAX(B1:B2) or MIN(B1:B2)), or a text entry enclosed in quotation marks ("Go" or "Hold").

Operator	Description
=	Equal to
<>	Not equal to
<	Less than
>	Greater than
<=	Less than or equal to
>=	Greater than or equal to

(a) Relational Operators

	A	B	C
1	10	15	April
2	10	30	May

(b) The Spreadsheet

IF Function	Evaluation	Result
=IF(A1=A2,1000,2000)	10 is equal to 10: TRUE	1000
=IF(A1<>A2,1000,2000)	10 is not equal to 10: FALSE	2000
=IF(A1<>A2,B1,B2)	10 is not equal to 10:FALSE	30
=IF(A1<B2,MAX(B1:B2),MIN(B1:B2)	10 is less than 30: TRUE	30
=IF(A1<A2,B1+10,B1-10)	10 is less than 10:FALSE	5
=IF(A1=A2,C1,C2)	10 is equal to 10: TRUE	April
=IF(SUM(A1:A2)>20,"Go","Hold")	10+10 is greater than 20:FALSE	Hold

(c) Examples

FIGURE 3.12   The IF Function

The IF function is used in the grade book of Figure 3.9 to award a bonus for homework. Students whose homework is "OK" receive the bonus, whereas other students do not. The IF function to implement this logic for the first student is entered in cell H4 as follows:

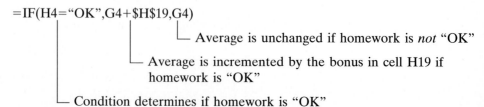

=IF(H4="OK",G4+$H$19,G4)

└ Average is unchanged if homework is *not* "OK"

└ Average is incremented by the bonus in cell H19 if homework is "OK"

└ Condition determines if homework is "OK"

The IF function compares the value in cell H4 (the homework grade) to the literal "OK." If the condition is true (the homework is "OK"), the bonus in cell H19 is added to the student's test average in cell G4. If, however, the condition is false (the homework is not "OK"), the average is unchanged.

The bonus is specified as a cell address rather than a specific value so that the number of bonus points can be easily changed; that is, the professor can make a single change to the worksheet by increasing (decreasing) the bonus in cell H19 and see immediately the effect on every student without having to edit or retype any other formula. An absolute (rather than a relative) reference is used to reference the homework bonus so that when the IF function is copied to the other rows in the column, the address will remain constant. A relative reference, however, was used for the student's homework and semester averages, in cells H4 and G4, because these addresses change from one student to the next.

VLOOKUP Function

Consider, for a moment, how the professor assigns letter grades to students at the end of the semester. He or she computes a test average for each student and conditionally awards the bonus for homework. The professor then determines a letter grade according to a predetermined scale; for example, 90 or above is an A, 80 to 89 is a B, and so on.

The **VLOOKUP** (vertical lookup) *function* duplicates this process within a worksheet, by assigning an entry to a cell based on a numeric value contained in another cell. In other words, just as the professor knows where on the grading scale a student's numerical average will fall, the VLOOKUP function determines where within a specified table (the grading criteria) a numeric value (a student's average) is found, and retrieves the corresponding entry (the letter grade).

The VLOOKUP function requires three arguments: the numeric value to look up, the range of cells containing the table in which the value is to be looked up, and the column-number within the table that contains the result. These concepts are illustrated in Figure 3.13, which was taken from the expanded grade book in Figure 3.9. The table in Figure 3.13 extends over two columns (I and J), and five rows (21 through 25); that is, the table is located in the range I21:J25. The **breakpoints** or matching values (the lowest numeric value for each grade) are contained in column I (the first column in the table) and are in ascending order. The corresponding letter grades are found in column J.

= VLOOKUP(I4,$I$21:$J$25,2)

	A	B	G	H	I	J
1			Professor's Grade Book			
2						
3	Name		Test Avg	Homework	Semester Avg	Grade
4	Adams, John		77.8	Poor	77.8	C
18						
19	Average		HW Bonus:	3	Grading Criteria	
20	Highest Grade				(No Curve)	
21	Lowest Grade					F
22	Range				60	D
23					70	C
24	Exam Weights				80	B
25					90	A

Breakpoints (in ascending order)

Grades are in column 2 of the table

FIGURE 3.13   Table Lookup Function

The VLOOKUP function in cell J4 determines the letter grade (for John Adams) based on the computed average in cell I4. Consider:

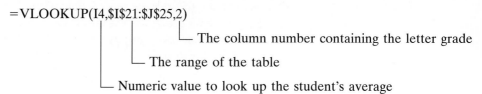

=VLOOKUP(I4,$I$21:$J$25,2)

└─ The column number containing the letter grade

└─ The range of the table

└─ Numeric value to look up the student's average

The first argument is the value to look up, which in this example is Adams's computed average, found in cell I4. A relative reference is used so that the address will adjust when the formula is copied to the other rows in the worksheet.

The second argument is the range of the table, found in cells I21 through J25, as explained earlier. Absolute references are specified so that the addresses will not change when the function is copied to determine the letter grades for the other students. The first column in the table (column I in this example) contains the breakpoints, which must be in ascending order.

The third argument indicates the column containing the value to be returned (the letter grades). To determine the letter grade for Adams (whose computed average is 77.8), the VLOOKUP function searches cells I21 through I25 for the largest value less than or equal to 77.8 (the computed average in cell I4). The lookup function finds the number 70 in cell I23. It then retrieves the corresponding letter grade from the second column in that row (cell J23). Adams, with an average of 77.8, is assigned a grade of C.

Scrolling

A large worksheet, such as the extended grade book, can seldom be seen on the monitor in its entirety; that is, only a portion of the worksheet is in view at any given time. The specific rows and columns that are displayed are determined by an operation called *scrolling,* which shows different parts of a worksheet at different times. Scrolling enables you to see any portion of the worksheet at the expense of not seeing another portion. The worksheet in Figure 3.14a, for example, displays column J containing the students' grades, but not columns A and B, which contain the students' names and social security numbers. In similar fashion, you can see rows 21 through 25 that display the grading criteria, but you cannot see the column headings, which identify the data in those columns.

Scrolling comes about automatically as the active cell changes and may take place in both horizontal and vertical directions. Clicking the right arrow on the horizontal scroll bar (or pressing the right arrow key when the active cell is already in the rightmost column of the screen) causes the entire screen to move one column to the right. In similar fashion, clicking the down arrow in the vertical scroll bar (or pressing the down arrow key when the active cell is in the bottom row of the screen) causes the entire screen to move down one row.

Freezing Panes

Scrolling brings distant portions of a large worksheet into view, but it also moves the descriptive headings for existing rows and/or columns off the screen. You can, however, retain these headings by freezing panes as shown in Figure 3.14b. The grades and grading criteria are visible as in the previous figure, but so too are the student names at the left of the worksheet and the column headings at the top.

Can't see columns A–B
or rows 1–9

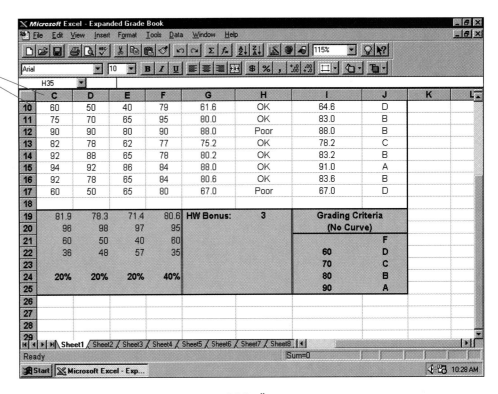

(a) Scrolling

Column A remains on the
screen as B–D scroll off

Rows 1–3 remain on the
screen as rows 4–9
scroll off

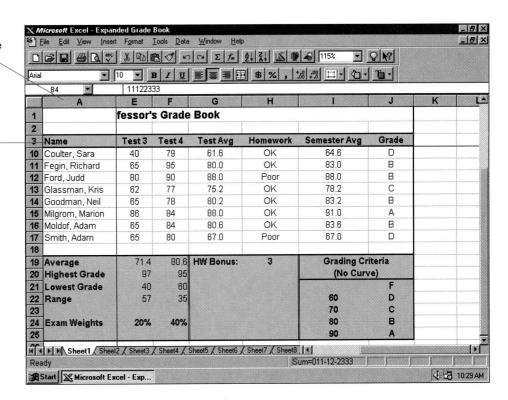

(b) Freezing Panes

FIGURE 3.14   Large Spreadsheets

Look closely at Figure 3.12b and you will see that columns B through D (social security number, test 1, and test 2) are missing, as are rows 4 through 9 (the first six students). You will also notice a horizontal line under row 3, and a vertical line after column A, to indicate that these rows and columns have been frozen. Scrolling still takes place as you move beyond the rightmost column or below the bottom row, but you will always see column A and rows 1, 2, and 3 displayed on the monitor.

The *Freeze Panes command,* in the Window menu, displays the desired row or column headings regardless of the scrolling in effect. It is especially helpful when viewing or entering data in a large worksheet. The rows and/or columns that are frozen are the ones above and to the left of the active cell when the command is issued. You may still access (and edit) cells in the frozen area by clicking the desired cell. The *Unfreeze command,* also in the Window menu, returns to normal scrolling.

SCROLLING: THE MOUSE VERSUS THE KEYBOARD

You can use either the mouse or the keyboard to scroll within the worksheet, but there is one critical difference. Scrolling with the keyboard also changes the active cell. Scrolling with the mouse does not.

Scenario Manager

The *Scenario Manager* enables you to evaluate multiple sets of initial conditions and assumptions (scenarios). Each *scenario* represents a different set of what-if conditions that you want to consider in assessing the outcome of a spreadsheet model. You could, for example, look at optimistic, most likely, and pessimistic assumptions in a financial forecast. Our professor will use the Scenario Manager to evaluate his semester grades with and without a curve.

Figure 3.15 illustrates the use of the Scenario Manager in conjunction with the expanded grade book. Each scenario is stored under its own name, such as "Curve" and "No Curve" as shown in Figure 3.15a. Each scenario is comprised of a set of cells whose values vary from scenario to scenario, as well as the values for those cells. Figure 3.15b shows the scenario when no curve is in effect and contains the values for the homework bonus and the breakpoints for the grade distribution table. Figure 3.15c displays a different scenario in which the professor increases the homework bonus and introduces a curve in computing the grades for the class.

Once the individual scenarios have been defined, you can display the worksheet under any scenario by clicking the Show button in the Scenario Manager dialog box. The professor can consider the outcome (the grades assigned to individual students) under the different scenarios and arrive at the best possible decision (the grading criteria to use).

AutoFill

The *AutoFill capability* is a wonderful shortcut and the fastest way to enter certain series into adjacent cells. In essence, you enter the first value(s) of a series, then drag the fill handle to the adjacent cells that are to contain the remaining values in that series. Excel creates the series for you based on the initial value(s) you supply. If, for example, you wanted the months of the year to appear in 12 successive cells, you would enter January (or Jan) in the first cell, then drag the

Available scenarios

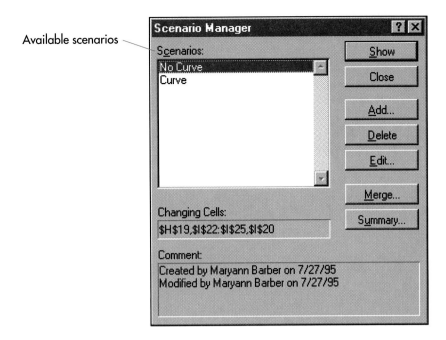

(a) Existing Scenarios

Homework bonus

Breakpoints

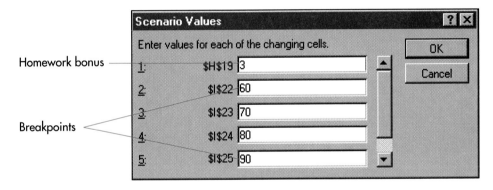

(b) Scenario Values (No Curve)

Homework bonus

Breakpoints

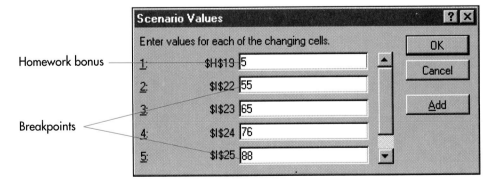

(c) Scenario Values (Curve)

FIGURE 3.15   Scenario Manager

fill handle over the next 11 cells in the direction you want to fill. Excel will enter the remaining months of the year in those cells.

Excel "guesses" at the type of series you want and fills the cells accordingly. You can type Monday (rather than January), and Excel will return the days of the week. You can enter a text and numeric combination, such as Quarter 1 or 1st Quarter, and Excel will extend the series appropriately. You can also create a numeric series by entering the first two numbers in that series; for example, to enter the years 1990 through 1999, type 1990 and 1991 in the first two cells, select both of these cells, and drag the fill handle in the appropriate direction over the destination range.

HANDS-ON EXERCISE 3

The Expanded Grade Book

Objective: To develop the expanded grade book; to use statistical (AVERAGE, MAX, and MIN) and logical (IF and VLOOKUP) functions; to demonstrate scrolling and the Freeze Panes command; to illustrate the AutoFill capability and the Scenario Manager. Use Figure 3.16 as a guide in the exercise.

Step 1: Open the Extended Grade Book

➤ Pull down the **File menu** and click **Open** (or click the **Open button** on the Standard toolbar) to display the Open dialog box.

➤ Click the **drop-down arrow** on the Look In list box. Click the appropriate drive, drive C or drive A, depending on the location of your data. Double click the **Exploring Excel folder** to make it the active folder (the folder from which you will retrieve the workbook).

➤ Double click **Expanded Grade Book** to open the workbook.

➤ Pull down the **File menu** and save the workbook as **Finished Expanded Grade Book** so that you can always return to the original workbook if necessary.

MISSING SCROLL BARS

The horizontal and vertical scroll bars are essential, especially with larger worksheets that cannot be seen in their entirety. If either scroll bar is missing, it is because a previous user elected to hide it. Pull down the Tools menu, click Options, and click the View tab. Click the check boxes to display the horizontal and vertical scroll bars, then click the OK command button to exit the dialog box and return to the worksheet.

Step 2: The AutoFill Capability

➤ Click in **cell C3,** the cell containing the label Test 1. Point to the **fill handle** in the lower-right corner, as shown in Figure 3.16a. The mouse pointer changes to a thin crosshair.

➤ Click and drag the **fill handle** over cells **D3, E3,** and **F3,** then release the mouse. Cells D3, E3, and F3 now contain the labels Test 2, Test 3, and Test 4, respectively.

Point to the fill handle, then drag over D3:F3

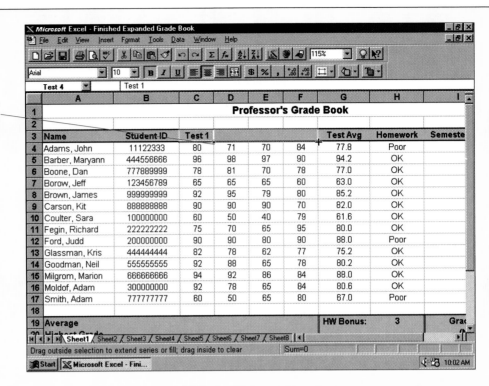

(a) The AutoFill Command (step 2)

FIGURE 3.16   Hands-on Exercise 3

CREATE A CUSTOM SERIES

A custom series is very helpful if you repeatedly enter the same lists of data. Pull down the Tools menu, click Options, then click the Custom Lists tab. Click New List in the Custom Lists box to position the insertion point in the List Entries box. Enter the items in the series (e.g., Tom, Dick, and Harry), using a comma or the enter key to separate one item from the next. Click the Add button. Click OK. The next time you type Tom, Dick, or Harry in a cell and drag the fill handle, you will see the series Tom, Dick, and Harry repeated through the entire range.

Step 3: Format the Social Security Numbers

➤ Click and drag to select cells **B4** through **B17,** the cells containing the unformatted social security numbers.

➤ Point to the selected cells and click the **right mouse button** to display a shortcut menu. Click the **Format Cells command,** click the **Number tab,** then click **Special** in the Category list box.

➤ Click **Social Security Number** in the Type box, then click **OK** to accept the formatting and close the Format Cells dialog box. The social security numbers are displayed with hyphens.

➤ Save the workbook.

Step 4: Scrolling and Freezing Panes

➤ Press **Ctrl+Home** to move to cell A1. Click the **right arrow** on the horizontal scroll bar until column A scrolls off the screen. Cell A1 is still the active cell, as can be seen in the Name box, because scrolling with the mouse does not change the active cell.

➤ Press **Ctrl+Home.** Press the **right arrow key** until column A scrolls off the screen. The active cell changes as you scroll with the keyboard.

➤ Press **Ctrl+Home** to return to cell A1. Click the **down arrow** on the vertical scroll bar (or press the **down arrow key** until row 1 scrolls off the screen). Note whether the active cell changes or not.

➤ Press **Ctrl+Home** again, then click in **cell B4.** Pull down the **Window menu.** Click **Freeze Panes** as shown in Figure 3.16b. You will see a line to the right

---

KEYBOARD SHORTCUTS: MOVING WITHIN A WORKSHEET

Press PgUp or PgDn to scroll an entire screen in the indicated direction. Press Ctrl+Home or Ctrl+End to move to the beginning and end of a worksheet—that is, to cell A1 and to the cell in the lower-right corner, respectively. If these keys do not work, it is because the transition navigation keys (i.e., Lotus 1-2-3 conventions) are in effect. Pull down the Tools menu, click Options, and click the Transition tab. Clear the check in the Transition Navigation Keys check box, then click OK.

Click in B4 to make it the active cell (rows 1–3 and column A will be frozen)

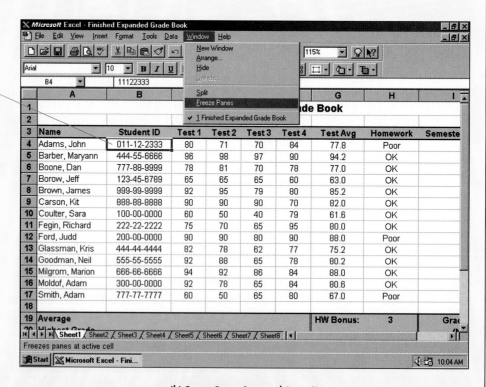

(b) Freeze Panes Command (step 4)

FIGURE 3.16   Hands-on Exercise 3 (continued)

of column A and below row 3; that is, column A and rows 1 through 3 will always be visible regardless of scrolling.

➤ Click the **right arrow** on the horizontal scroll bar (or press the **right arrow key**) repeatedly until column J is visible. Note that column A is visible (frozen), but that one or more columns are not shown.

➤ Click the **down arrow** on the vertical scroll bar (or press the **down arrow key**) repeatedly until row 25 is visible. Note that rows one through three are visible (frozen), but that one or more rows are not shown.

Step 5: The IF Function

➤ Scroll to the top of the worksheet, then scroll until Column I is visible on the screen. Click in **cell I4.**

➤ Click the **Function Wizard button** on the Standard toolbar. Click **Logical** in the Function Category list box. Click **IF** in the Function Name list box, then click the **Next command button** to move to step 2 of the Function Wizard and display the dialog box in Figure 3.16c.

➤ Enter the arguments for the IF function as shown in the figure. You can enter the arguments directly, or you can use pointing as follows:

- Click the **logical_test** text box. Click **cell H4** in the worksheet. (You may need to move the dialog box to access cell H4. Click and drag the title bar of the dialog box to move it out of the way.) Type =**"OK"** to complete the logical test.

- Click the **value_if_true** text box. Click **cell G4** in the worksheet, type a **plus sign,** click **cell H19** in the worksheet (scrolling if necessary), and finally press the **F4 key** (see boxed tip) to convert the reference to cell H19 to an absolute reference ($H$19).

Function Wizard button

Computed value of function

Enter arguments

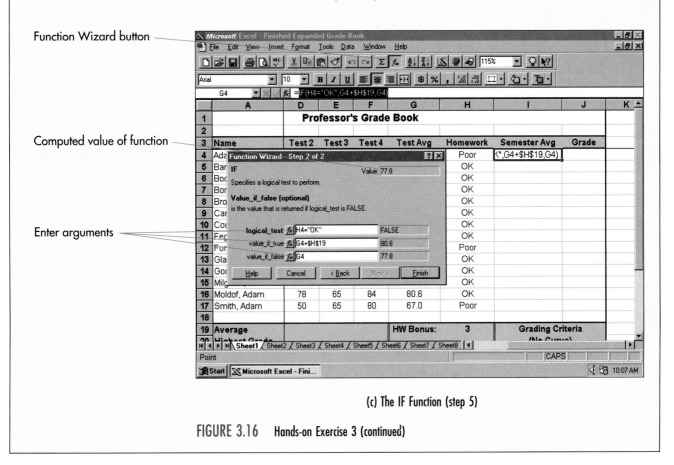

(c) The IF Function (step 5)

FIGURE 3.16   Hands-on Exercise 3 (continued)

- Click the **value_if_false** text box. Click **cell G4** in the worksheet, scrolling if necessary.
- ➤ Check that the dialog box on your worksheet matches the one in Figure 3.16c. Make corrections as necessary. Click the **Finish command button** to insert the function into your worksheet.
- ➤ Save the workbook.

THE F4 KEY

The F4 key cycles through relative, absolute, and mixed addresses. Click on any reference within the formula bar; for example, click on A1 in the formula =A1+A2. Press the F4 key once, and it changes to an absolute reference. Press the F4 key a second time, and it becomes a mixed reference, A$1; press it again, and it is a different mixed reference, $A1. Press the F4 key a fourth time, and it returns to the original relative address, A1.

Step 6: The VLOOKUP Function

- ➤ Click in **cell J4.**
- ➤ Click the **Function Wizard button** on the Standard toolbar. Click **Lookup & Reference** in the Function Category list box. Scroll in the Function name list box until you can select **VLOOKUP.** Click the **Next command button** to move to step 2 of the Function Wizard and display the dialog box in Figure 3.16d.
- ➤ Enter the arguments for the VLOOKUP function as shown in the figure. You can enter the arguments directly, or you can use pointing as follows:
  - Click the **lookup_value** text box. Click **cell I4** in the worksheet.
  - Click the **table_array** text box. Click **cell I21** and drag to cell **J25** (scrolling if necessary). Press the **F4 key** to convert to an absolute reference.
  - Click the **col_index_num** text box. Type **2.**
- ➤ Check that the dialog box on your worksheet matches the one in Figure 3.16d. Make corrections as necessary. Click the **Finish command button** to insert the function into your worksheet.
- ➤ Save the workbook.

Step 7: Copy the IF and VLOOKUP Functions (the Fill Handle)

- ➤ If necessary, scroll to the top of the worksheet. Select cells **I4** and **J4** as in Figure 3.16e.
- ➤ Point to the **fill handle** in the lower-right corner of the selected range. The mouse pointer changes to a thin crosshair.
- ➤ Drag the **fill handle** over cells **I5** through **J17.** A border appears, indicating the destination range as shown in Figure 3.16e. Release the mouse to complete the copy operation. If you have done everything correctly, Adam Smith should have a grade of D based on a semester average of 67. Format the semester averages in column I to one decimal place.
- ➤ Save the workbook.

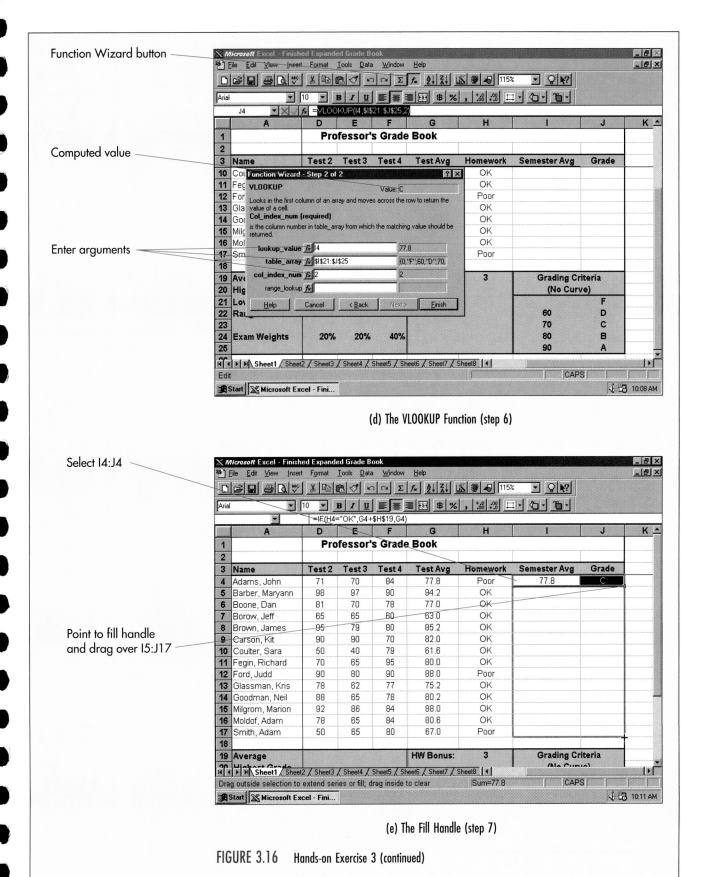

Function Wizard button

Computed value

Enter arguments

(d) The VLOOKUP Function (step 6)

Select I4:J4

Point to fill handle
and drag over I5:J17

(e) The Fill Handle (step 7)

FIGURE 3.16   Hands-on Exercise 3 (continued)

Step 8: Statistical Functions

➤ Click in **cell C19.** Type **=AVERAGE(C4:C17).** Press **enter.** Cell C19 should display 81.857. Format the average to one decimal place.

➤ Click in **cell C20.** Type **=MAX(C4:C17).** Press **enter.** Cell C20 should display a value of 96.

➤ Click in **cell C21.** Type **=MIN(C4:C17).** Press **enter.** Cell C21 should display a value of 60.

➤ Click in **cell C22.** Type **=C20-C21.** Press **enter.** Cell C22 should display 36.

#NAME? AND OTHER ERRORS

Excel displays an error value when it is unable to calculate the formula in a cell. Misspelling a function name (e.g., using AVG instead of AVERAGE) results in #NAME?, which is perplexing at first, but easily corrected once you know the meaning of the error. All error values begin with a pound sign (#). Pull down the Help menu, click Microsoft Excel Help topics, click the Index tab, then enter # for a list of the error values. Click the desired error value, then click the Display button for an explanation.

Step 9: Copy the Statistical Functions (Shortcut Menu)

➤ Select cells **C19** through **C22** as shown in Figure 3.16f. Click the **right mouse button** to display the shortcut menu shown in the figure. Click **Copy.** A moving border appears around the selected cells.

➤ Drag the mouse over cells **D19** through **F19.** Click the **Paste button** on the Standard toolbar to complete the copy operation, then press **Esc** to remove the moving border. If you have done everything correctly, cells F19, F20, F21, and F22 will display 80.6, 95, 60, and 35, respectively.

➤ Save the workbook.

SEE THE WHOLE WORKSHEET

Press Ctrl+Home to move to the beginning of the worksheet. Press the F8 key to enter the extended selection mode (EXT will appear on the status bar), then press Ctrl+End to move to the end of the worksheet and simultaneously select the entire worksheet. Pull down the View menu, click Zoom, then click the Fit Selection option button. Click OK to close the dialog box. The magnification shrinks to display the entire worksheet on the screen; how well you can read the display depends on the size of your monitor and the size of the worksheet.

Step 10: Create the No Curve Scenario

➤ Click in **cell H19.** Pull down the **Tools menu.** Click **Scenarios** to display the Scenario Manager dialog box. Click the **Add command button** to display the Add Scenario dialog box in Figure 3.16g.

Click the right mouse button
to display the shortcut menu

Select C19:C22

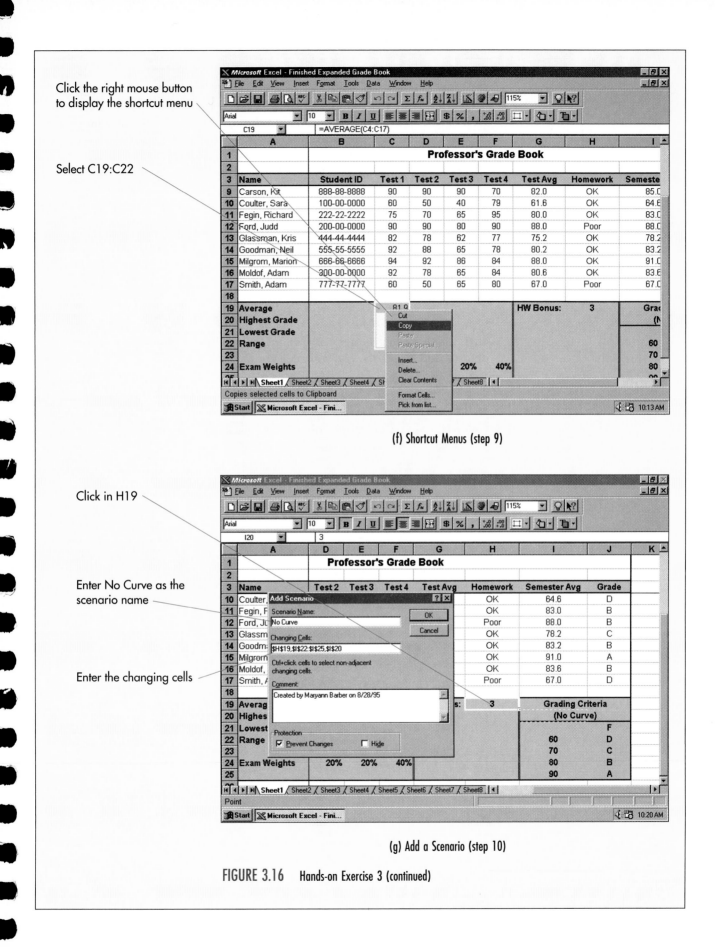

(f) Shortcut Menus (step 9)

Click in H19

Enter No Curve as the
scenario name

Enter the changing cells

(g) Add a Scenario (step 10)

FIGURE 3.16   Hands-on Exercise 3 (continued)

➤ Type **No Curve** in the Scenario Name text box.

➤ Click in the **Changing Cells text box** to the right of $H$19. Cell H19 (the active cell) is already entered as the first cell in the scenario. Type a **comma,** then click and drag to select cells **I22** through **I25** (the cells containing the breakpoints for the grade distribution table). Scroll to these cells if necessary.

➤ Type another **comma,** then click in **cell I20.** The Add Scenarios dialog box should match the display in Figure 3.16g. Click **OK.**

➤ You should see the Scenario Values dialog box with the values of this scenario (No Curve) already entered. Only the first five cells are displayed, and you must scroll to see the others.

➤ Click **OK** to complete the No Curve scenario and close the Scenario Values dialog box.

Step 11: Add the Curve Scenario

➤ The Scenario Manager dialog box should still be open. Click the **Add button** to add a second scenario and display the Add Scenario dialog box.

➤ Type **Curve** in the Scenario Name text box. The changing cells are already entered and match the changing cells in the No Curve scenario. Click **OK.**

➤ Enter **5** as the new value for cell H19 (the bonus for homework). Press the **Tab key** to move to the text box for the next cell. Enter 55, 65, 76, and 88 as the values for cells I22 through I25, respectively.

➤ Enter **(Curve)** as the value for cell I20. Click **OK** to complete the scenario and close the Scenario Values dialog box.

INCLUDE THE SCENARIO NAME

A scenario is composed of one or more changing cells whose values you want to consider in evaluating the outcome of a spreadsheet model. We find it useful to include an additional cell within the scenario that contains the name of the scenario itself, so that the scenario name appears within the worksheet when the worksheet is printed.

Step 12: View the Scenarios

➤ The Scenario Manager dialog box should still be open as shown in Figure 3.16h. (If necessary, pull down the **Tools menu** and click the **Scenarios command** to reopen the Scenario Manager.) There should be two scenarios listed, No Curve and Curve, corresponding to the scenarios that were just created.

➤ Select the **Curve** scenario, then click the **Show button** to display the grade book under this scenario. Some, but not all, of the grades will change under the easier criteria. Ford, for example, goes from a B to an A.

➤ Select the **No Curve** scenario. Click the **Show button** to display the grades under the initial set of assumptions. Click the **Close button** and review the changes. Ford goes from an A back to a B.

➤ Show the grades under the **Curve** scenario a second time, then click the **Close button** to exit the Scenario Manager.

➤ Save the workbook.

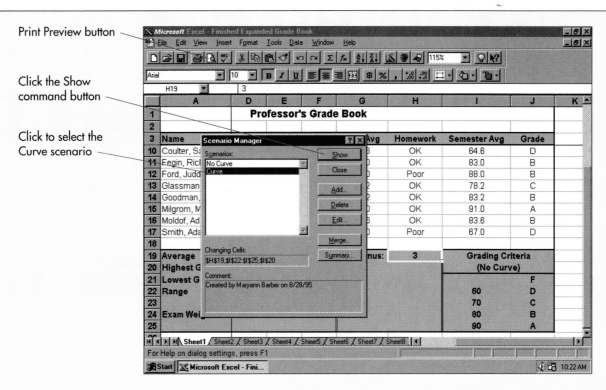

Print Preview button

Click the Show command button

Click to select the Curve scenario

(h) View the Scenarios (step 12)

FIGURE 3.16   Hands-on Exercise 3 (continued)

THE SCENARIO MANAGER LIST BOX

The Scenario Manager List Box enables you to select a scenario directly from a toolbar. Point to any toolbar, click the right mouse button to display a shortcut menu, then click Customize to display the Customize dialog box. Select Utility in the Categories list box, then click and drag the Scenario list box to an empty space on the toolbar. Click Close to close the dialog box and return to the workbook. Click the down arrow on the Scenario list box, which now appears on the toolbar, to choose from the scenarios that have been defined within the current workbook.

Step 13: Print the Worksheet

➤ Add your name and title (**Grading Assistant**) in cells G26 and G27. Save the workbook.

➤ Pull down the **File menu.** Click **Page Setup** to display the Page Setup dialog box:

• Click the **Page tab.** Click the **Landscape option button.** Click the option button to **Fit to 1 page.**

• Click the **Margins tab.** Check the box to center the worksheet Horizontally on the page.

• Click the **Header/Footer tab.** Click the **down arrow** on both the Header and Footer list boxes and select **none** for both of these items.

- Click the **Sheet tab.** Check the boxes for **Row and Column Headings** and for **Gridlines.**

➤ Click the **Print Preview button** to display the completed spreadsheet, which should match the screen in Figure 3.16i. Click the **Print command button** and click **OK** to print the workbook. Submit it to your instructor as proof that you did the exercise.

➤ Save the workbook. Exit Excel.

MAKE IT FIT

The Page Setup command offers different ways to make a large worksheet fit on one page. Click the Print Preview button on the Standard toolbar to view the worksheet prior to printing. Click the Margins command button to display (hide) sizing handles for the page margins and column widths, then drag any handle to adjust the margin or column width. You can also click the Setup command button from the Print Preview screen to display the Page Setup dialog box. Use the Page tab to change to landscape printing and/or to select the scaling option to Fit to 1 page.

Click the Print command button

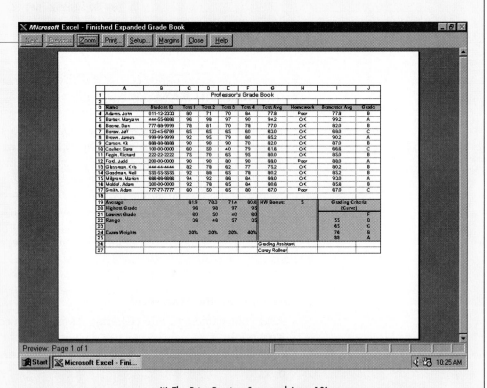

(i) The Print Preview Command (step 13)

FIGURE 3.16   Hands-on Exercise 3 (continued)

Excel contains several different categories of built-in functions. The PMT function computes the periodic payment for a loan based on three arguments (the interest rate per period, the number of periods, and the amount of the loan). The PMT function was used in the analysis of a car loan and in the comparison of 15- and 30-year mortgages.

Statistical functions were also discussed. The AVERAGE, MAX, and MIN functions return the average, highest, and lowest values in the argument list. The COUNT function returns the number of cells with numeric entries. The COUNTA function displays the number of cells with numeric and/or text entries.

The IF and VLOOKUP functions implement decision making within a worksheet. The IF function has three arguments: a logical test, which is evaluated as true or false; a value if the test is true; and a value if the test is false. The VLOOKUP (table lookup) function also has three arguments: the numeric value to look up, the range of cells containing the table, and the column number within the table that contains the result.

The hands-on exercises introduced several techniques to make you more proficient. The fill handle is used to copy a cell or group of cells to a range of adjacent cells. Pointing is a more accurate way to enter a cell reference into a formula as it uses the mouse or arrow keys to select the cell as you build the formula. The Function Wizard helps you choose the appropriate function, then enter the arguments in the proper sequence. The AutoFill capability creates a series based on the initial value(s) you supply.

Scrolling enables you to view any portion of a large worksheet but moves the labels for existing rows and/or columns off the screen. The Freeze Panes command keeps the row and/or column headings on the screen while scrolling in a large worksheet.

A spreadsheet is first and foremost a tool for decision making, and thus Excel includes several commands to aid in that process. The Goal Seek command lets you enter the desired end result of a spreadsheet model (such as the monthly payment on a car loan) and determines the input (the price of the car) to produce that result. The Scenario Manager enables you to specify multiple sets of assumptions (scenarios), and see at a glance the results of any scenario.

KEY WORDS AND CONCEPTS

=AVERAGE	AutoFill capability	Pointing
=COUNT	AutoFit Selection	Relational operator
=COUNTA	Breakpoint	Relative reference
=IF	Custom series	Scenario
=MAX	Edit Clear command	Scenario Manager
=MIN	Enter mode	Scrolling
=PMT	Fill handle	Spell check
=SUM	Freeze Panes command	Statistical functions
=VLOOKUP	Function	Template
Absolute reference	Function Wizard	Unfreeze command
Arguments	Goal Seek command	
Assumptions	Logical test	

MULTIPLE CHOICE

1. Which of the following options may be used to print a large worksheet?
   (a) Landscape orientation
   (b) Scaling
   (c) Reduced margins
   (d) All of the above

2. If the results of a formula contain more characters than can be displayed according to the present format and cell width,
   (a) The extra characters will be truncated under all circumstances
   (b) All of the characters will be displayed if the cell to the right is empty
   (c) A series of asterisks will be displayed
   (d) A series of pound signs will be displayed

3. Which cell—A1, A2, or A3—will contain the amount of the loan, given the function =PMT(A1,A2,A3)?
   (a) A1
   (b) A2
   (c) A3
   (d) Impossible to determine

4. Which of the following will compute the average of the values in cells D2, D3, and D4?
   (a) The function =AVERAGE(D2:D4)
   (b) The function =AVERAGE(D2,D4)
   (c) Both (a) and (b)
   (d) Neither (a) nor (b)

5. The function =IF(A1>A2,A1+A2,A1*A2) returns
   (a) The product of cells A1 and A2 if cell A1 is greater than A2
   (b) The sum of cells A1 and A2 if cell A1 is less than A2
   (c) Both (a) and (b)
   (d) Neither (a) nor (b)

6. Which of the following is the preferred way to sum the values contained in cells A1 to A4?
   (a) =SUM(A1:A4)
   (b) =A1+A2+A3+A4
   (c) Either (a) or (b) is equally good
   (d) Neither (a) nor (b) is correct

7. Which of the following will return the highest and lowest arguments from a list of arguments?
   (a) HIGH/LOW
   (b) LARGEST/SMALLEST
   (c) MAX/MIN
   (d) All of the above

8. Which of the following is a *required* technique to develop the worksheet for the mortgage analysis?
   (a) Pointing
   (b) Copying with the fill handle
   (c) Both (a) and (b)
   (d) Neither (a) nor (b)

9. Given that cells B6, C6, and D6 contain the numbers 10, 20, and 30, respectively, what value will be returned by the function =IF(B6>10,C6*2,D6*3)?
   (a) 10
   (b) 40
   (c) 60
   (d) 90

10. Which of the following is not an input to the Goal Seek command?
    (a) The cell containing the end result
    (b) The desired value of the end result
    (c) The cell whose value will change to reach the end result
    (d) The value of the input cell that is required to reach the end result

11. Each scenario in the Scenario Manager:
    (a) Is stored in a separate worksheet
    (b) Contains the value of a single assumption or input condition
    (c) Both (a) and (b)
    (d) Neither (a) nor (b)

12. Which function will return the number of nonempty cells in the range A2 through A6, including in the result cells that contain text as well as numeric entries?
    (a) =COUNT(A2:A6)
    (b) =COUNTA(A2:A6)
    (c) =COUNT(A2,A6)
    (d) =COUNTA(A2,A6)

13. What happens if you select a range, then press the right (alternate) mouse button?
    (a) The range will be deselected
    (b) Nothing; that is, the button has no effect
    (c) The Edit and Format menus will be displayed in their entirety
    (d) A shortcut menu with commands from both the Edit and Format menus will be displayed

14. The worksheet displayed in the monitor shows columns A and B, skips columns D, E, and F, then displays columns G, H, I, J, and K. What is the most likely explanation for the missing columns?
    (a) The columns were previously deleted
    (b) The columns are empty and thus are automatically hidden from view
    (c) Either (a) or (b) is a satisfactory explanation
    (d) Neither (a) nor (b) is a likely reason

15. Given the function =VLOOKUP(C6,D12:F18,3)
    (a) The entries in cells D12 through D18 are in ascending order
    (b) The entries in cells D12 through D18 are in descending order
    (c) The entries in cells F12 through F18 are in ascending order
    (d) The entries in cells F12 through F18 are in descending order

Exploring Excel 7.0

1. Use Figure 3.17 to match each action with its result; a given action may be used more than once or not at all.

Action	**Result**
a. Click at 10, type =AVERAGE(, then click at 6, drag to 8, and press enter	_____ Freeze column A and rows 1, 2, and 3 on the screen for scrolling
b. Click at 7, then click at 16	_____ Use the AutoFill feature to enter the column titles for Test 2, Test 3, and Test 4
c. Click at 12	_____ Increase the number of decimal places for the test averages
d. Click at 13	_____ Use the Function Wizard to enter the IF function for the semester averages in column I
e. Click at 14	
f. Click in the lower-right corner of 9, then drag to 11	_____ Preview the worksheet prior to printing
g. Click at 10, drag to 4, then click at 18	_____ Save the workbook
	_____ Enter the formula to compute the range for the scores on Test 1
h. Click at 19, click at 17	_____ Format the social security number with hyphens
i. Click at 7, drag to 5, click at 15	_____ Enter the function to compute the test average for John Adams
j. Click at 1, type =, click at 3, type −, click at 2, then press enter	_____ Spell check the worksheet

2. Consider the two worksheets shown in Figure 3.18 and the entries, =AVERAGE(A1:A4) versus =(A1+A2+A3+A4)/4, both of which calculate the average of cells A1 through A4. Assume that a new row is inserted in the worksheet between existing rows 2 and 3, with the entry in the new cell equal to 100.

   a. What value will be returned by the AVERAGE function in worksheet 1 after the new row has been inserted?

   b. What value will be returned by the formula in worksheet 2 after the new row has been inserted?

   c. In which cell will the AVERAGE function itself be located after the new row has been inserted?

   Return to the original problem, but this time delete row 2.

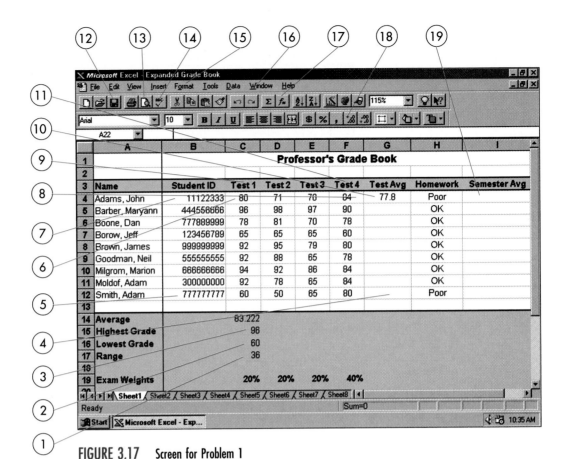

FIGURE 3.17   Screen for Problem 1

d. What value will be returned by the AVERAGE function in worksheet 1 after the row has been deleted?

e. What will be returned by the formula in worksheet 2 after the row has been deleted?

	A
1	10
2	20
3	30
4	40
5	=AVERAGE(A1:A4)

(a) Worksheet 1

	A
1	10
2	20
3	30
4	40
5	=(A1+A2+A3+A4)/4

(b) Worksheet 2

FIGURE 3.18   Spreadsheets for Problem 2

3. Answer the following with respect to Figure 3.19. (Cell B5 is empty.) What value will be returned by the worksheet functions?

a. =IF(A1=0,A2,A3)

b. =SUM(A1:A5)

c. =MAX(A1:A5,B1:B5)

d. =MIN(A1:A3,5,A5)

e. =AVERAGE(B1:B4)

f. =AVERAGE(B1:B5)

	A	B
1	10	60
2	20	70
3	30	80
4	40	90
5	50	

FIGURE 3.19   Spreadsheet for Problem 3

   g. =MIN(10,MAX(A2:A4))
   h. =MAX(10,MIN(A2:A4))
   i. =COUNTA(A1:A5)
   j. =COUNTA(B1:B5)
   k. =COUNT(A1:A5)
   l. =COUNT(B1:B5)
   m. =VLOOKUP(15,A1:B5,2)
   n. =VLOOKUP(20,A1:B5,2)

4. The spreadsheet in Figure 3.20 illustrates the use of the PMT function to compute the amortization schedule on a loan. The mortgagee is trying to pay off the note in less time than the indicated 15 years, and so he pays an additional amount every month toward the principal.

   a. What formula should be entered in cell C6 to compute the monthly payment?

   b. What formula should be entered in cell B10? (The amount of each payment that goes toward interest is the interest rate per period times the unpaid balance of the loan.)

	A	B	C	D	E
1			Amortization Schedule		
2					
3	Principal		$100,000		
4	Annual Interest		7.50%		
5	Term (in years)		15		
	Extra principal		$100		
6	Monthly Payment		$927.01		
7					
8	Month	Toward Interest	Toward Principal	Extra Payment	Balance
9					$100,000.00
10	1	$625.00	$302.01	$100.00	$99,597.99
11	2	$622.49	$304.52	$100.00	$99,193.46
12	3	$619.96	$307.05	$100.00	$98,786.41
13	4	$617.42	$309.60	$100.00	$98,376.81
14	5	$614.86	$312.16	$100.00	$97,964.65
15	6	$612.28	$314.73	$100.00	$97,549.92
65	56	$460.69	$466.32	$100.00	$73,144.11
66	57	$457.15	$469.86	$100.00	$72,574.25
67	58	$453.59	$473.42	$100.00	$72,000.83
68	59	$450.01	$477.01	$100.00	$71,423.82
69	60	$446.40	$480.61	$100.00	$70,843.21

FIGURE 3.20   Spreadsheet for Problem 4

c. What formula should be entered in cell C10? (The amount of each payment that goes toward principal is the monthly payment minus the amount that goes toward interest.)

d. What formula should be entered in cell E10 to compute the new balance?

e. The mortgagee wants to pay off the loan even faster and has as his goal a balance of $50,000 at the end of five years. Explain how to use the Goal Seek command to determine the amount of extra principal needed each month (beginning in the first month) to reach the stated goal.

PRACTICE WITH EXCEL 7.0

1. Startup Airlines: The partially completed spreadsheet in Figure 3.21 is used by a new airline to calculate the fuel requirements and associated cost for its available flights. The airline has only two types of planes, B27s and DC-9s. The fuel needed for any given flight depends on the aircraft and number of flying hours; for example, a five-hour flight in a DC-9 can be expected to use 40,000 gallons. In addition, the plane must carry an additional 10% of the required fuel to maintain a holding pattern (4,000 gallons in this example) and an additional 20% as reserve (8,000 gallons in this example).

Retrieve the partially completed *Chapter 3 Practice 1* from the data disk and save it as *Finished Chapter 3 Practice 1*. Compute the fuel necessary for the listed flights based on a fuel price of $1.00 per gallon. Your worksheet should be completely flexible and amenable to change; that is, the hourly fuel requirements, price per gallon, holding and reserve percentages are all subject to change at a moment's notice.

After completing the cell formulas, format the spreadsheet as you see fit. Add your name somewhere in the worksheet, then print the completed worksheet and cell formulas, and submit the assignment to your instructor.

	A	B	C	D	E	F	G	H
1	Fuel Estimates							
2								
3	Plane	Flight	Flying Hours	Flying Fuel	Reserve Fuel	Holding Fuel	Total Fuel Needed	Estimated Fuel Cost
4	Boeing-727	MIA-JFK	2.75					
5	DC-9	MIA-ATL	1.25					
6	Boeing-727	MIA-IAH	2.25					
7	Boeing-727	MIA-LAX	5.5					
8	DC-9	MIA-MSY	1.5					
9		Totals						
10								
11	Fuel Facts:							
12	Gallons per hour: Boeing-727				10000			
13	Gallons per hour: DC-9				8000			
14	Fuel cost per gallon				1			
15								
16	% of Flying Fuel required for:							
17	Reserve Fuel				0.2			
18	Holding Fuel				0.1			

FIGURE 3.21   Spreadsheet for Practice Exercise 1

2. A partially completed version of the worksheet in Figure 3.22 can be found on the data disk as *Chapter 3 Practice 2*. Retrieve the workbook from the data disk and complete it so that it is identical to the worksheet in Figure 3.22. In completing the spreadsheet you need to understand the discount policy, which states that a discount is given if the total sale is equal to or greater than the discount threshold. (The amount of the discount is equal to the total sale multiplied by the discount percentage, which is contained in the assumption area at the bottom of the worksheet.) If the total sale is less than the discount threshold, no discount is given.

Complete the worksheet in Figure 3.22, then create two additional scenarios for different selling strategies. In one scenario lower the discount threshold and discount percentage to $3000 and 12%, respectively. Increase these values in a second scenario to $10,000 and 20%. Add your name somewhere in the worksheet, then print all three scenarios (the two you created plus the original set of numbers) and submit the completed assignment.

	A	B	C	D	E	F	G	H	I
1				Hot Spot Software Distributors					
2				Miami, Florida					
3									
4	Customer Name	Program	Current Price	Units Sold	Total Sale	Amount of Discount	Discounted Total	Sales Tax	Amount Due
5	AAA Software Sales	Windows 95	$62.99	23	$1,448.77	$0.00	$1,448.77	$94.17	$1,542.94
6	CompuSoft, Inc.	Microsoft Office 95	$335.99	45	$15,119.55	$2,267.93	$12,851.62	$835.36	$13,686.97
7	Kings Bay Software	Adobe Photoshop	$398.99	10	$3,989.90	$0.00	$3,989.90	$259.34	$4,249.24
8	MicroSales, Inc	Corel Draw	$300.99	30	$9,029.70	$1,354.46	$7,675.25	$498.89	$8,174.14
9	PC and Me Software	Microsoft Office 95	$335.99	17	$5,711.83	$0.00	$5,711.83	$371.27	$6,083.10
10	Personal Software Sales	Corel Draw	$300.99	25	$7,524.75	$1,128.71	$6,396.04	$415.74	$6,811.78
11	Service Software	Adobe Photoshop	$398.99	35	$13,964.65	$2,094.70	$11,869.95	$771.55	$12,641.50
12	Software and More	Windows 95	$62.99	25	$1,574.75	$0.00	$1,574.75	$102.36	$1,677.11
13	Software To Go	Windows 95	$62.99	35	$2,204.65	$0.00	$2,204.65	$143.30	$2,347.95
14	Unique Software Sales	Microsoft Office 95	$335.99	50	$16,799.50	$2,519.93	$14,279.58	$928.17	$15,207.75
15									
16	Discount Threshold	$6,000.00					Number of customers		10
17	Discount Percentage	15.0%					Highest current price		$398.99
18	Sales Tax	6.5%					Fewest units sold		10
19							Average Discount		$936.57
20							Total Amount Due		$72,422.48

FIGURE 3.22   Spreadsheet for Practice Exercise 2

3. Object Linking and Embedding: Figure 3.23 extends the analysis of a car loan to include monthly expenditures for gas, insurance, and maintenance. It also includes an IF function in cell B13 that compares the total monthly cost to $500 (the maximum you can afford), and prints "Yes" or "No" depending on the answer. And finally, it uses the Insert Object command to insert a picture of the car from the Microsoft ClipArt Gallery.

Enter parameters for the car of your dreams, together with realistic terms for a car loan in today's economy. Add your name somewhere in the worksheet, insert a clip art object, then print the completed worksheet and submit it to your instructor.

4. Scenario Summary: The report in Figure 3.24 illustrates the summary capability within Scenario Manager and is based on the completed financial forecast from Chapter 2. Return to the Finished Financial Forecast that you created in the third hands-on exercise, then add the Optimistic and Pessimistic scenarios as shown in Figure 3.24.

The changing cells in both scenarios are cells B18 and B19, which contain the first-year sales and selling price, and cells D18 and D19 containing the projected increase in these values. [Note, however, that the summary

	A	B
1	Price of car	$13,999
2	Manufacturer's rebate	$1,000
3	Down payment	$3,000
4	Amount to finance	$9,999
5	Interest rate	8%
6	Term (in years)	4
7	Monthly payment	$244.10
8	Insurance	$100.00
9	Gas	$75.00
10	Maintenance	$50.00
11	Total	$469.10
12		
13	Can I afford it?	Yes
14		
15		
16		
17		
18		
19		
20		
21		

FIGURE 3.23   Spreadsheet for Practice Exercise 3

table uses descriptive names rather than cell references (e.g., FirstYearSales instead of cell B18) because the Insert Name command was used to assign a descriptive name to the associated cell reference. This should be done prior to using the Scenario Manager. (Use online help to learn how to name a formula or reference.)]

The Scenario Summary is created by clicking the Summary command button within Scenario Manager, then choosing the Scenario Summary option button from the available report types. To create the summary, you will need to specify the result cells (cells B15 through F15 in the financial forecast) whose values will be displayed in the summary table shown in the figure.

Create one additional scenario (with any values you like) that identifies you by name, then print the scenario summary and submit it to your instructor.

Scenario Summary		Current Values:	Optimistic	Pessimistic
Changing Cells:				
	FirstYearSales	$100,000	$150,000	$75,000
	SellingPrice	$3.00	$4.50	$2.50
	SalesIncrease	10%	15%	8%
	PriceIncrease	5%	8%	5%
Result Cells:				
	EarningsYear1	$75,000	$375,000	$0
	EarningsYear2	$84,750	$473,475	-$1,275
	EarningsYear3	$94,710	$595,298	-$3,542
	EarningsYear4	$104,579	$745,818	-$7,126
	EarningsYear5	$113,936	$931,591	-$12,434
Notes: Current Values column represents values of changing cells at time Scenario Summary Report was created. Changing cells for each scenario are highlighted in gray.				

FIGURE 3.24   Spreadsheet for Practice Exercise 4

The Financial Consultant

A friend of yours is in the process of buying a home and has asked you to compare the payments and total interest on a 15- and a 30-year loan. You want to do as professional a job as possible and have decided to analyze the loans in Excel, then incorporate the results into a memo written in Microsoft Word. As of now, the principal is $150,000, but it is very likely that your friend will change his mind several times, and so you want to use the OLE capability within Windows to dynamically link the worksheet to the word processing document. Your memo should include a letterhead that takes advantage of the formatting capabilities within Word; a graphic logo would be a nice touch.

Compensation Analysis

A corporation typically uses several different measures of compensation in an effort to pay its employees fairly. Most organizations closely monitor an employee's salary history, keeping both the present and previous salary in order to compute various statistics, including:

- The percent salary increase, which is computed by taking the difference between the present and previous salary, and dividing by the previous salary.
- The months between increase, which is the elapsed time between the date the present salary took effect and the date of the previous salary. (Assume 30 days per month for ease of calculation.)
- The annualized rate of increase, which is the percent salary increase divided by the months between increase; for example, a 5% raise after 6 months is equivalent to an annualized increase of 10%; a 5% raise after two years is equivalent to an annual increase of 2.5%.

Use the data in the *Compensation Analysis* workbook on the data disk to compute salary statistics for the employees who have had a salary increase; employees who have not received an increase should have a suitable indication in the cell. Compute the average, minimum, and maximum value for each measure of compensation for those employees who have received an increase.

The Automobile Dealership

The purchase of a car usually entails extensive bargaining between the dealer and the consumer. The dealer has an asking price but typically settles for less. The commission paid to a salesperson depends on how close the selling price is to the asking price. Exotic Motors has the following compensation policy for its sales staff:

- A 3% commission on the actual selling price for cars sold at 95% or more of the asking price.
- A 2% commission on the actual selling price for cars sold at 90% or more (but less than 95%) of the asking price
- A 1% commission on the actual selling price for cars sold at less than 90% of the asking price. The dealer will not go below 85% of his asking price.

The dealer's asking price is based on the dealer's cost plus a 20% markup; for example, the asking price on a car that cost the dealer $20,000 would be $24,000. Develop a worksheet to be used by the dealer that shows his profit (the selling price minus the cost of the car minus the salesperson's commission) on every sale. The worksheet should be completely flexible and allow the dealer to vary the markup or commission percentages without having to edit or recopy any of the formulas. Use the data in the *Exotic Motors* workbook to test your worksheet.

The Lottery

Many states raise money through lotteries that advertise prizes of several million dollars. In reality, however, the actual value of the prize is considerably less than the advertised value, although the winners almost certainly do not care. One state, for example, recently offered a twenty million dollar prize that was to be distributed in twenty annual payments of one million dollars each. How much was the prize actually worth, assuming a long-term interest rate of seven percent? What is the value of the prize if the interest rate decreases to six percent? If it increases to eight percent?

GRAPHS AND CHARTS: DELIVERING A MESSAGE

OBJECTIVES

After reading this chapter you will be able to:

1. Distinguish between the different types of charts, stating the advantages and disadvantages of each.
2. Distinguish between a chart embedded in a worksheet and one in a separate chart sheet; explain how many charts can be associated with the same worksheet.
3. Use the ChartWizard to create and/or modify a chart.
4. Enhance a chart by using arrows and text.
5. Differentiate between data series specified in rows and data series specified in columns.
6. Describe how a chart can be statistically accurate yet totally misleading.
7. Create a compound document consisting of a word processing memo, a worksheet, and a chart.

OVERVIEW

Business has always known that the graphic representation of data is an attractive, easy-to-understand way to convey information. Indeed, business graphics has become one of the most exciting Windows applications, whereby charts (graphs) are easily created from a worksheet, with just a few simple keystrokes or mouse clicks.

The chapter begins by emphasizing the importance of determining the message to be conveyed by a chart. It describes the different types of charts available within Excel and how to choose among them. It explains how to create a chart by using the ChartWizard, how to embed a chart within a worksheet, and how to create a chart in a separate chart sheet. It also describes how to enhance a chart with arrows and additional text.

The second half of the chapter explains how one chart can plot multiple sets of data, and how several charts can be based on the same worksheet. It also describes how to create a compound document, in which a chart and its associated worksheet are dynamically linked to a memo created by a word processor. All told, we think you will find this to be one of the most enjoyable chapters in the text.

CHART TYPES

A *chart* is a graphic representation of data in a worksheet. The chart is based on descriptive entries called *category labels,* and on numeric values called *data points.* The data points are grouped into one or more *data series* that appear in row(s) or column(s) on the worksheet. In every chart there is exactly one data point, in each data series, for each value of the category label.

The worksheet in Figure 4.1 will be used throughout the chapter as the basis for the charts we will create. Your manager believes that the sales data can be understood more easily from charts than from the strict numerical presentation of a worksheet. You have been given the assignment of analyzing the data in the worksheet and are developing a series of charts to convey that information.

	A	B	C	D	E	F
1		Superior Software Sales				
2						
3		Miami	Denver	New York	Boston	Total
4	Word Processing	$50,000	$67,500	$9,500	$141,000	$268,000
5	Spreadsheets	$44,000	$18,000	$11,500	$105,000	$178,500
6	Database	$12,000	$7,500	$6,000	$30,000	$55,500
7	Total	$106,000	$93,000	$27,000	$276,000	$502,000

FIGURE 4.1   Superior Software

The sales data in the worksheet can be presented several ways—for example, by city, by product, or by a combination of the two. Ask yourself which type of chart is best suited to answer the following questions:

- What percentage of total revenue comes from each city? from each product?
- What is the dollar revenue produced by each city? by each product?
- What is the rank of each city with respect to sales?
- How much revenue does each product contribute in each city?

In every instance realize that a chart exists only to deliver a message, and that you cannot create an effective chart unless you are sure of what that message is. The next several pages discuss the different types of business charts, each of which is best suited to a particular type of message.

KEEP IT SIMPLE

Keep it simple. This rule applies to both your message and the means of conveying that message. Excel makes it almost too easy to change fonts, styles, type sizes, and colors, but such changes will often detract from, rather than enhance, a chart. More is not necessarily better, and you do not have to use the features just because they are there. Remember that a chart must ultimately succeed on the basis of content, and content alone.

Pie Charts

A *pie chart* is the most effective way to display proportional relationships. It is the type of chart to select whenever words like *percentage* or *market share* appear in the message to be delivered. The pie, or complete circle, denotes the total amount. Each slice of the pie corresponds to its respective percentage of the total.

The pie chart in Figure 4.2a divides the pie representing total sales into four slices, one for each city. The size of each slice is proportional to the percentage of total sales in that city. The chart depicts a single data series, which appears in cells B7 through E7 on the associated worksheet. The data series has four data points corresponding to the total sales in each city.

To create the pie chart, Excel computes the total sales ($502,000 in our example), calculates the percentage contributed by each city, and draws each slice of the pie in proportion to its computed percentage. Boston's sales of $276,000 account for 55 percent of the total, and so this slice of the pie is allotted 55 percent of the area of the circle.

An *exploded pie chart,* as shown in Figure 4.2b, separates one or more slices of the pie for emphasis. Another way to achieve emphasis in a chart is to choose a title that reflects the message you are trying to deliver. The title in Figure 4.2a, for example, *Revenue by Geographic Area*, is neutral and leaves the reader to develop his or her own conclusion about the relative contribution of each area. By contrast, the title in Figure 4.2b, *New York Accounts for Only 5% of Revenue,* is more suggestive and emphasizes the problems in this office. Alternatively, the title could be changed to *Boston Exceeds 50% of Total Revenue* if the intent were to emphasize the contribution of Boston.

Three-dimensional pie charts may be created in exploded or nonexploded format as shown in Figures 4.2c and 4.2d, respectively. Excel also enables you to add arrows and text for emphasis.

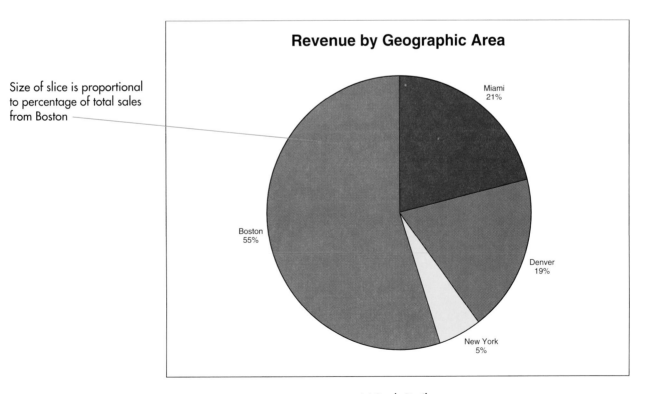

Size of slice is proportional to percentage of total sales from Boston

(a) Simple Pie Chart

FIGURE 4.2   Pie Charts

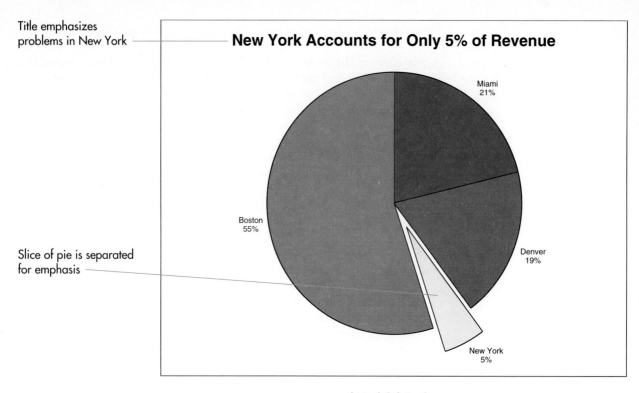

Title emphasizes
problems in New York

Slice of pie is separated
for emphasis

New York Accounts for Only 5% of Revenue

Miami
21%

Denver
19%

New York
5%

Boston
55%

(b) Exploded Pie Chart

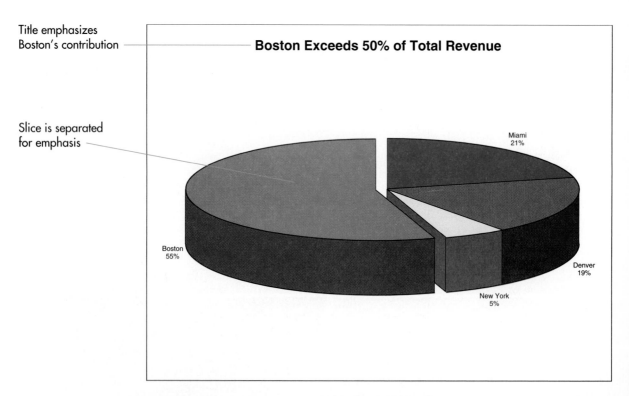

Title emphasizes
Boston's contribution

Slice is separated
for emphasis

Boston Exceeds 50% of Total Revenue

Miami
21%

Denver
19%

New York
5%

Boston
55%

(c) Three-dimensional Pie Chart

FIGURE 4.2   Pie Charts (continued)

Arrows and text added for emphasis

Boston Exceeds 50% of Total Revenue

Boston's revenues are more than 10 times those of New York

Miami
21%

Denver
19%

New York
5%

Boston
55%

(d) Enhanced Pie Chart

FIGURE 4.2   Pie Charts (continued)

A pie chart is easiest to read when the number of slices is limited (not more than six or seven), and when small categories (percentages less than five) are grouped into a single category called "Other."

EXPLODED PIE CHARTS

Click and drag wedges out of a pie chart to convert an ordinary pie chart to an exploded pie chart. For best results pull the wedge out only slightly from the main body of the pie.

Column and Bar Charts

A *column chart* is used when there is a need to show actual numbers rather than percentages. The column chart in Figure 4.3a plots the same data series as the earlier pie chart, but displays it differently. The category labels (Miami, Denver, New York, and Boston) are shown along the *X* (horizontal) *axis.* The data points (monthly sales) are plotted along the *Y* (vertical) *axis,* with the height of each column reflecting the value of the data point.

A column chart can be given a horizontal orientation and converted to a *bar chart* as in Figure 4.3b. Some individuals prefer the bar chart over the corresponding column chart because the longer horizontal bars accentuate the difference between the cities. Bar charts are also preferable when the descriptive labels are long to eliminate the crowding that can occur along the horizontal axis of a

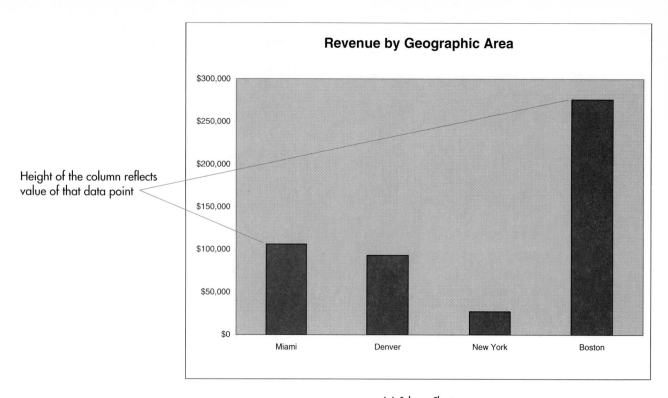

Height of the column reflects value of that data point

Revenue by Geographic Area

(a) Column Chart

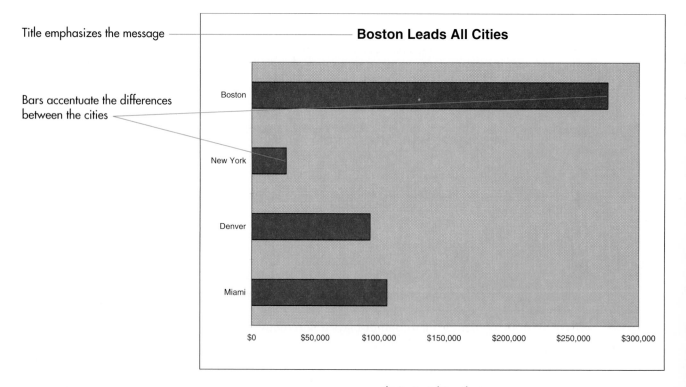

Title emphasizes the message

Boston Leads All Cities

Bars accentuate the differences between the cities

(b) Horizontal Bar Chart

FIGURE 4.3   Column/Bar Charts

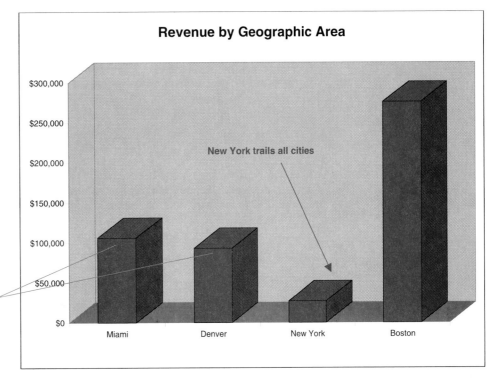

(c) Three-dimensional Column Chart

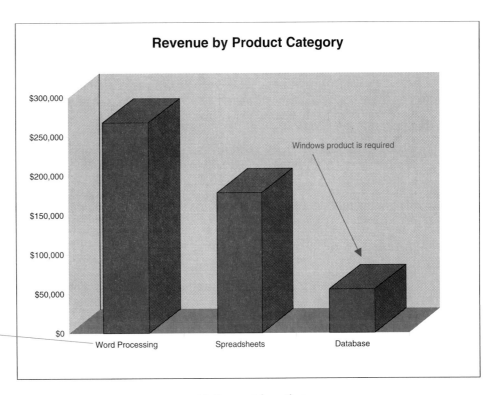

(d) Alternate Column Chart

FIGURE 4.3   Column/Bar Charts (continued)

column chart. As with the pie chart, a title can be developed to lead the reader and further emphasize the message, as with *Boston Leads All Cities* in Figure 4.3b.

A three-dimensional effect can produce added interest as shown in Figures 4.3c and 4.3d. Figure 4.3d plots a different set of numbers than we have seen so far (the sales for each application, rather than the sales for each city). The choice between the charts in Figures 4.3c and 4.3d depends on the message you want to convey—whether you want to emphasize the contribution of each city or each product. The title can be developed to emphasize the message. Arrows and text can be added to either chart to enhance the message.

As with a pie chart, column and bar charts are easiest to read when the number of categories is relatively small (seven or fewer). Otherwise the columns (bars) are plotted so close together that labeling becomes impossible.

CREATING A CHART

There are two ways to create a chart in Excel. You can embed the chart in a worksheet, or you can create the chart in a separate *chart sheet.* Figure 4.4a displays an embedded column chart. Figure 4.4b shows a pie chart in its own chart sheet. Both techniques are valid. The choice between the two depends on your personal preference.

Regardless of where it is kept (embedded in a worksheet or in its own chart sheet), a chart is linked to the worksheet on which it is based. The charts in Figure 4.4 plot the same data series (the total sales for each city). Change any of these data points on the worksheet, and both charts will be updated automatically to reflect the new data.

Both charts are part of the same workbook (Software Sales) as indicated in the title bar of each figure. The tabs within the workbook have been renamed to indicate the contents of the associated sheet. Additional charts may be created and embedded in the worksheet and/or placed on their own chart sheets. And, as previously stated, if you change the worksheet, the chart (or charts) based upon it will also change.

Study the column chart in Figure 4.4a to see how it corresponds to the worksheet on which it is based. The descriptive names on the X axis are known as *category labels* and match the entries in cells B3 through E3. The quantitative values (data points) are plotted on the Y axis and match the total sales in cells B7 through E7. Even the numeric format matches; that is, the currency format used in the worksheet appears automatically on the scale of the Y axis.

The *sizing handles* on the embedded chart indicate it is currently selected and can be sized, moved, or deleted the same way as any other Windows object:

- To size the selected chart, point to a sizing handle (the mouse pointer changes to a double arrow), then drag the handle in the desired direction.
- To move the selected chart, point to the chart (the mouse pointer is a single arrow), then drag the chart to its new location.
- To copy the selected chart, click the Copy button to copy the chart to the clipboard, click in the workbook where you want the copied chart to go, then click the Paste button to paste the chart at that location.
- To delete the selected chart, press the Del key.

The same operations apply to any of the objects within the chart (e.g., its title), as will be discussed in the section on enhancing a chart.

Workbook name

Sizing handles

Data points are plotted on the
Y axis and reflect entries in
B7:E7

Descriptive names (category
labels) match entries in B3:E3

Tabs renamed to reflect
content of sheet

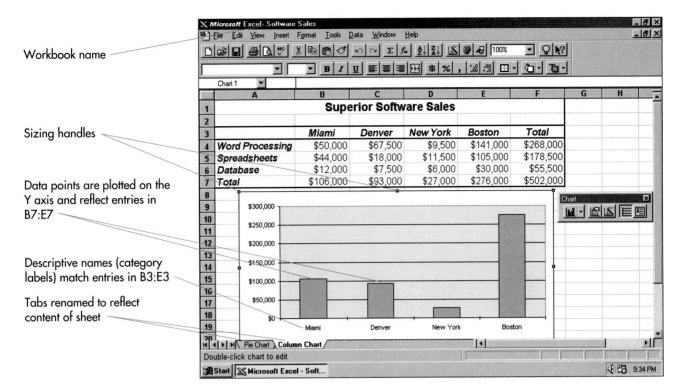

(a) Embedded Chart

Workbook name

Selected sheet

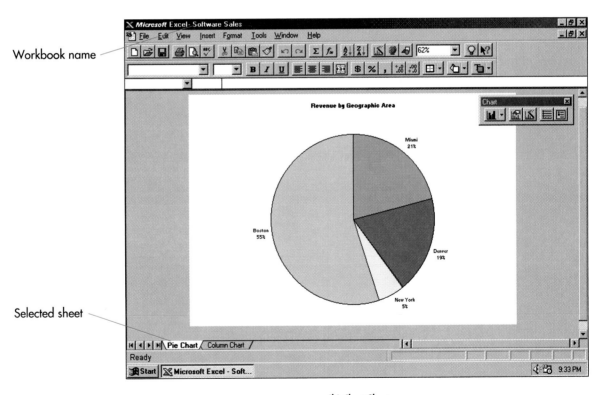

(b) Chart Sheet

FIGURE 4.4   Creating a Chart

The ChartWizard

The **ChartWizard** is the easiest way to create a chart. Just select the cells that contain the data, click the ChartWizard button on the Standard toolbar, and let the Wizard do the rest. The process is illustrated in Figure 4.5, which shows how the Wizard creates a column chart to plot total sales by geographic area.

The steps in Figure 4.5 appear automatically, one after the other, as you click the Next command button to move from one step to the next. You can retrace your steps at any time by pressing the Back command button, access the online help facility with the Help command button, or negate the process with the Cancel command button.

Step 1, shown in Figure 4.5a, confirms the range of selected cells, $B$3:$E$3 (containing the city names) and $B$7:$E$7 (containing the total sales for each city). Step 2 asks you to choose one of the available chart types, and step 3 has you choose the specific format for the type of chart you selected. Step 4 shows you a preview of the completed chart. (The distinction between data series in rows versus columns is explained after the hands-on exercise.) Step 5 enables you to add a title and a legend. It's that simple, and the entire process takes but a few minutes.

Selected cells from which chart is created

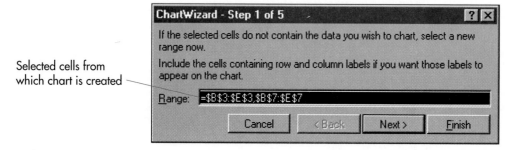

(a) Step 1—Define the Range

Selected chart type

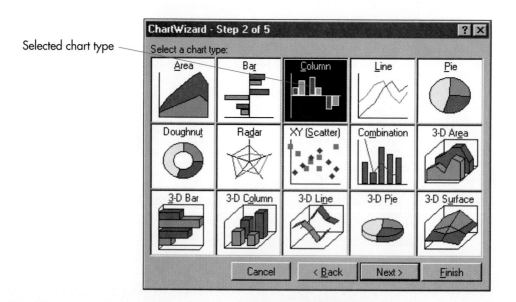

(b) Step 2—Select the Chart Type

FIGURE 4.5   The ChartWizard

Selected format

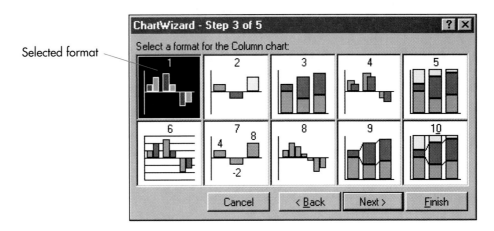

(c) Step 3—Select the Format for the Column Chart

Preview of chart

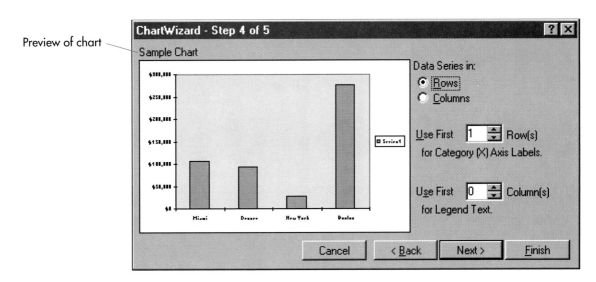

(d) Step 4—Preview the Chart

Specify whether a legend is to be displayed

Enter a title for the chart

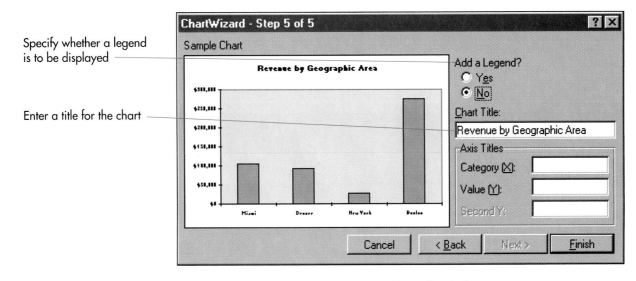

(e) Step 5—Add Legends and Titles

FIGURE 4.5   The ChartWizard (continued)

Enhancing a Chart

A chart can be enhanced in several ways. You can change the chart type, add (remove) a legend, and/or add (remove) gridlines. You can select any part of the chart (e.g., the title) and change its formatting. You can also add arrows and text.

Figure 4.6 displays an enhanced version of the column chart that was created by using the ChartWizard in Figure 4.5. The chart type has been changed to a *three-dimensional column chart,* and gridlines have been added. Both changes were accomplished by using buttons on the *Chart toolbar.*

A text box and an arrow have been added by using the corresponding tools on the *Drawing toolbar.* A *text box* is a block of text that is added to a chart (or worksheet) for emphasis. You can format all or part of the text by selecting it and choosing a different font or point size. You can also apply boldface or italics. Text wraps within the box as it is entered.

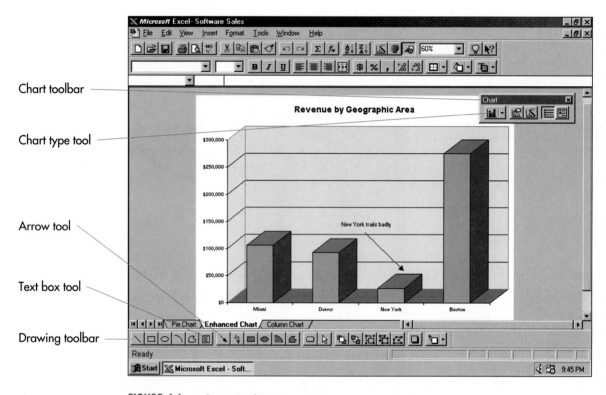

FIGURE 4.6   Enhancing a Chart

HANDS-ON EXERCISE 1

The ChartWizard

Objective: To create and modify a chart by using the ChartWizard; to embed a chart within a worksheet; to enhance a chart to include arrows and text. Use Figure 4.7 as a guide in the exercise.

STEP 1: Open the Software Sales Workbook

➤ Start Excel. Open the **Software Sales** workbook in the **Exploring Excel folder.** Save the workbook as **Finished Software Sales.**

➤ Pull down the **Tools menu**, click **Options**, click the **General tab**, check the box to **Reset TipWizard**, and click **OK.**

STEP 2: Start the ChartWizard

➤ Drag the mouse over **cells B3** through **E3** to select the category labels (the names of the cities) as shown in Figure 4.7a.

➤ Press and hold the **Ctrl key** as you drag the mouse over **cells B7** through **E7** to select the data series (the cells containing the total sales for the individual cities).

➤ Check that both ranges **B3:E3** and **B7:E7** are selected.

➤ Click the button for the **ChartWizard.** A moving border will appear around the selected ranges, and the mouse pointer changes to a tiny crosshair with a tiny bar chart.

➤ Click below **cell A7**, then drag the mouse to define the area to hold the chart as shown in Figure 4.7a. Release the mouse.

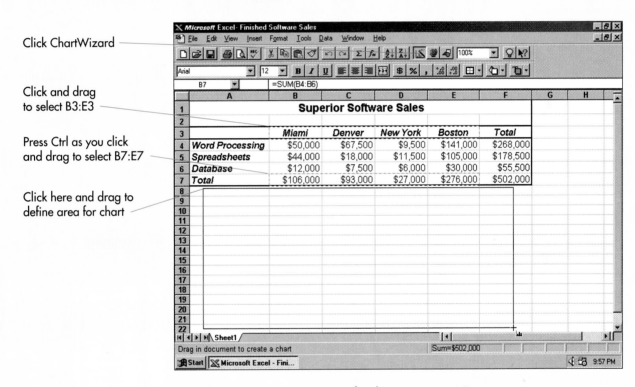

(a) Define the Data Range (step 2)

FIGURE 4.7 Hands-on Exercise 1

STEP 3: The ChartWizard (continued)

➤ You should see the dialog box for step 1 of the ChartWizard as shown in Figure 4.7b. If the range is correct (i.e., the ChartWizard displays $B$3:$E$3 and $B$7:$E$7), click the **Next command button.** If the range is incorrect, click **Cancel** and begin again, or click in the text box and enter the correct range.

➤ If necessary, click the icon for a **column chart** (the default). Click the **Next command button.**

➤ If necessary, click the column chart format in **box number 6** (the default). Click the **Next command button.**

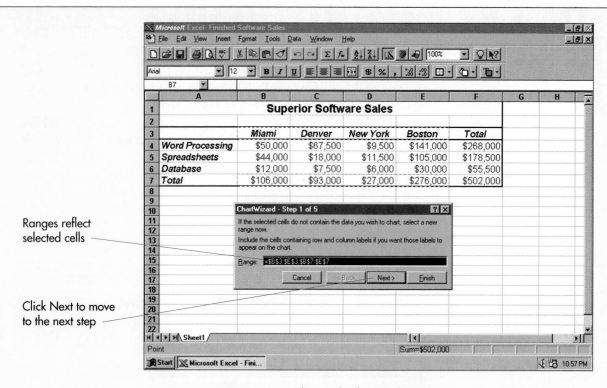

Ranges reflect
selected cells

Click Next to move
to the next step

(b) Start the ChartWizard (step 3)

FIGURE 4.7   Hands-on Exercise 1 (continued)

➤ View the sample chart shown in step 4 of the ChartWizard:

- If you are satisfied with your chart (do not be concerned about the legend at this time), click the **Next command button.**
- If you are not satisfied, click the **Back command button** to return to the previous step, where you can change the chart type.

STEP 4: The ChartWizard (continued)

➤ Complete the chart in step 5 of the ChartWizard as shown in Figure 4.7c:

- Click the **No option button** to suppress the legend.
- Click in the text box to add the title. Type **Revenue by Geographic Area.**
- Click the **Finish command button** to exit the ChartWizard and place the chart on the worksheet.

➤ Save the workbook.

STEP 5: The Column Chart

➤ You should see the chart in Figure 4.7d.

- The sizing handles indicate that the chart is selected and will be affected by subsequent commands.
- The Chart toolbar is automatically displayed when the chart is selected.

➤ Press the **Del key.** The chart (and Chart toolbar) disappears from the worksheet. Click the **Undo button** on the Standard toolbar to cancel the last command. The chart is back in the worksheet, and the Chart toolbar is redisplayed.

➤ Click anywhere outside the chart to deselect it.

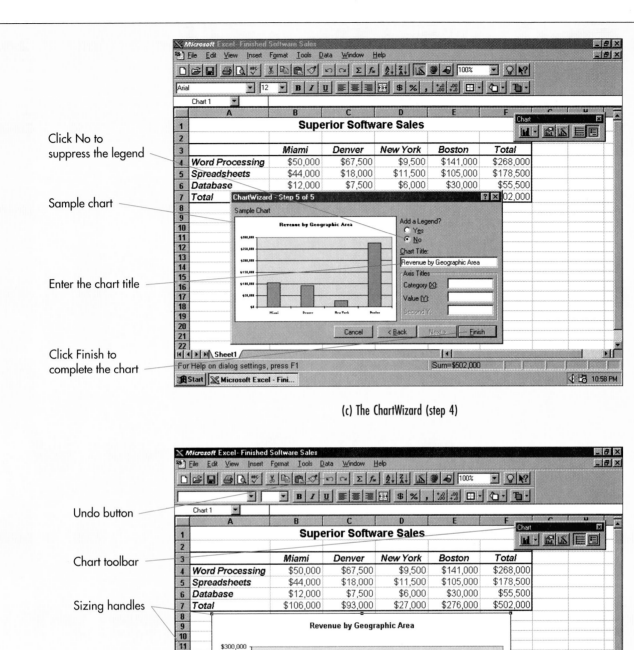

Click No to
suppress the legend

Sample chart

Enter the chart title

Click Finish to
complete the chart

(c) The ChartWizard (step 4)

Undo button

Chart toolbar

Sizing handles

(d) The Embedded Chart (step 5)

FIGURE 4.7   Hands-on Exercise 1 (continued)

FLOATING TOOLBARS

Any toolbar can be docked along the edge of the application window, or it can be displayed as a floating toolbar within the application window. To move a docked toolbar, drag the toolbar background. To move a floating toolbar, drag its title bar. To size a floating toolbar, drag any border in the direction you want to go. Double click the background of any toolbar to toggle between a floating toolbar and a docked (fixed) toolbar.

STEP 6: Change the Worksheet

➤ Click in **cell B4.** Change the entry to **$300,000.** Press the **enter key.** The totals in cells F4, B7, and F7 change automatically to reflect the increased sales for word processing in the Miami office.

➤ The column for Miami also changes in the chart and is now larger than the column for Boston.

➤ Click the **Undo button** on the Standard toolbar to return to the initial value of $50,000.

➤ The worksheet and chart are restored to their original values.

THE FORMAT OBJECT COMMAND

Dress up an embedded chart by changing its border to include color or a different line thickness or style. Select the chart, pull down the Format menu, then click Object to produce the Format Object dialog box. Click the Patterns tab, which displays check boxes, to choose a shadow effect and rounded corners. You can also specify a different border style, thickness (weight), or color as well as a background color and/or pattern for the entire chart. Click OK to exit the dialog box.

STEP 7: Modify the Chart

➤ Double click anywhere in the chart to select it for editing. The chart is enclosed in a hashed line as shown in Figure 4.7e.

➤ Pull down the **Format menu.** Click **Chart Type** to display the dialog box in Figure 4.7e.

➤ Click the box containing a **Pie chart.** Click the **3-D option button.** Click **OK.** You will see a three-dimensional pie chart, but the slices are not yet labeled.

➤ Pull down the **Format menu** a second time. Click **AutoFormat** to display a dialog box with various pie charts. Click format **number 7,** which will label the slices of the pie with percentages and the city names.

➤ Click **OK** to close the AutoFormat dialog box. The completed pie chart is shown in Figure 4.7f.

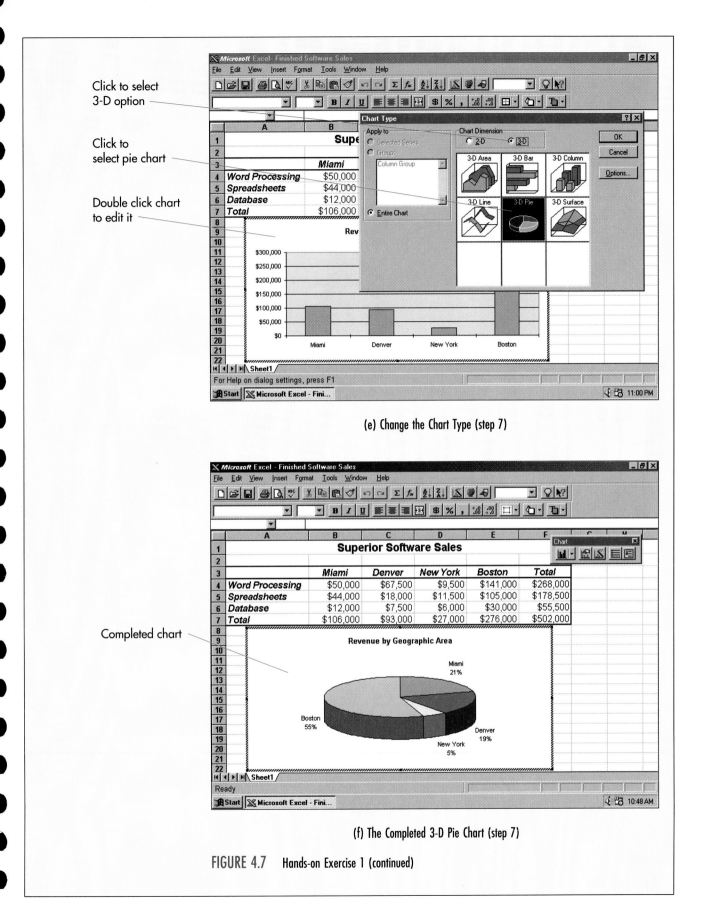

Click to select
3-D option

Click to
select pie chart

Double click chart
to edit it

(e) Change the Chart Type (step 7)

Completed chart

(f) The Completed 3-D Pie Chart (step 7)

FIGURE 4.7   Hands-on Exercise 1 (continued)

EMBEDDED CHARTS

An embedded chart is treated as an object that can be moved, sized, copied, or deleted just as any other Windows object. To move an embedded chart, click anywhere in the chart to select the chart, then drag it to a new location in the worksheet. To size the chart, select it, then drag any of the eight sizing handles in the desired direction. To delete the chart, select it, then press the Del key. To copy the chart, select it, click the Copy button on the Standard toolbar to copy the chart to the clipboard, click where you want the copied chart, then click the Paste button.

STEP 8: Create a Second Chart

➤ Click outside the chart to deselect the chart. Drag the mouse over **cells A4** through **A6** to select the category labels as shown in Figure 4.7g.

➤ Press and hold the **Ctrl key** as you drag the mouse over **cells F4** through **F6** to select the data series (the total sales for the product categories).

➤ Pull down the **Insert menu.** Click **Chart.** Click **As New Sheet.**

Click and drag to select A4:A6 (category labels)

Press Ctrl key as you click and drag to select F4:F6 (data series)

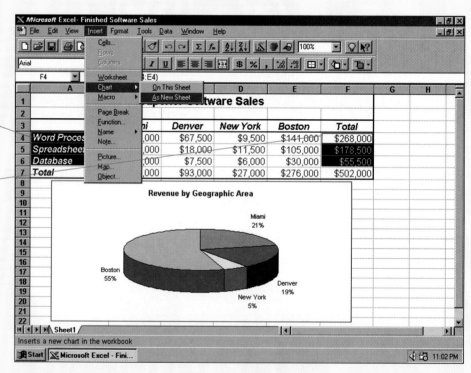

(g) Insert Chart Command (step 8)

FIGURE 4.7   Hands-on Exercise 1 (continued)

STEP 9: The ChartWizard

➤ You should see step 1 of the ChartWizard with the ranges A4:A6 and F4:F6 displayed in the text box.

  • Click the **Next command button** if the range is correct, or

- Click the **Cancel command button** if the range is incorrect, or click in the text box to enter the correct range.

➤ Click the icon for a **3-D Column chart.** Click the **Next command button.**

➤ Click the column chart format in **box number 1.** Click the **Next command button.**

➤ View the sample chart shown in step 4 of the ChartWizard:

- If you are satisfied, click the **Next command button** to move to step 5 of the ChartWizard.

- If you are not satisfied, click the **Back command button** to return to the previous step, where you can change the chart format.

➤ Complete the chart in step 5 of the ChartWizard:

- Click the **No option button** to suppress the legend.

- Click in the text box to add the title. Type **Revenue by Product Category.**

- Click the **Finish command button.**

➤ You should see the chart in Figure 4.7h, but without the text box and arrow. Save the workbook.

STEP 10: Workbook Tabs

➤ The 3-D column chart has been created in the chart sheet labeled Chart1. Click the **Sheet1 tab** to return to the worksheet and embedded chart from the first part of the exercise.

➤ Click the **Chart1 tab** to return to the chart sheet containing the 3-D column chart.

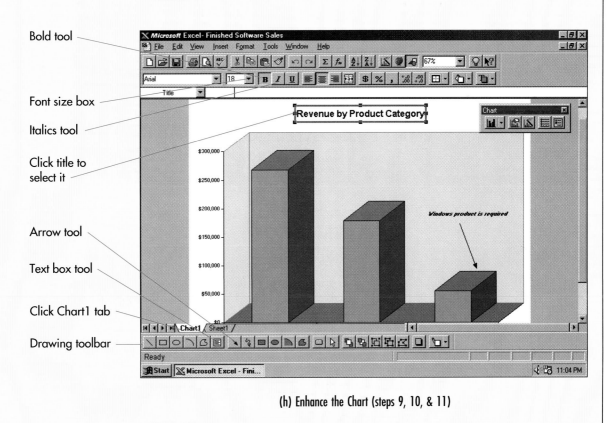

(h) Enhance the Chart (steps 9, 10, & 11)

FIGURE 4.7   Hands-on Exercise 1 (continued)

THE EXCEL WORKBOOK

The Excel workbook is the electronic equivalent of the three-ring binder. A workbook contains one or more worksheets and/or chart sheets, each of which is identified by a tab at the bottom of the workbook. The various sheets in a workbook are typically related to one another. One worksheet, for example, may contain data for several charts, each of which appears on a separate chart sheet in the workbook. The advantage of a workbook is that all of its sheets are stored in a single file, which is accessed as a unit.

STEP 11: Enhance the Chart

➤ Point to any visible toolbar. Click the **right mouse button** to display the Toolbar shortcut menu. Click **Drawing** to display the Drawing toolbar, which will be used to enhance the chart. (If necessary, click and drag the toolbar to dock it along an edge of the window.)

➤ Click the **black arrow button** on the Drawing toolbar. The mouse pointer changes to a thin crosshair. Click in the chart where you want the arrow to begin, drag the mouse to extend the arrow, then release the mouse to complete the arrow as shown in Figure 4.7h.

➤ Click the **text box button** on the Drawing toolbar. The mouse pointer changes to a thin crosshair. Click in the chart where you want the text box to begin, drag the mouse to extend the box, then release the mouse.

➤ Click the **Bold** and **Italic buttons** on the Formatting toolbar. Type **Windows product is required** as shown in Figure 4.7h. Click outside the text box to complete the entry.

➤ Click the title of the chart. You will see sizing handles around the title to indicate it has been selected.

➤ Click the **arrow** on the Font Size box on the Formatting toolbar. Click **18** to increase the size of the title.

➤ Use the text tool to add your name somewhere in the chart so that your instructor will know the assignment is from you. Save the workbook.

ENHANCEMENT TIPS

Arrows and text boxes are the basis of many chart enhancements. To draw an arrow that is perfectly horizontal, vertical, or at a forty-five degree angle, press and hold the Shift key as you drag the mouse to create the line. To change the appearance of the shaft or arrowhead, double click the arrow to display the Format Object dialog box, make your changes, then click OK. To resize a text box so that it fits the text exactly, select the text box, pull down the Format menu, and click Selected Object. Click the Alignment tab, check the Automatic Size box, and click OK. Move or size an arrow or text box just as you would any other Windows object.

STEP 12: Format the Data Series

➤ Click any of the columns to select the data series. (All three columns will be selected. However, clicking a column after the data series has been selected selects only that column and deselects the others.) Be sure that all three columns are selected as shown in Figure 4.7i.

➤ Point to any column and click the **right mouse button** to display the shortcut menu in Figure 4.7i. Click **Format Data Series** to display a dialog box, click the **Patterns tab,** select (click) a different color, then click **OK** to accept the change and close the dialog box.

➤ Point to the **X axis** (scrolling if necessary), click the **right mouse button** to display a shortcut menu, then click the **Format Axis command.** Experiment with different formatting options for the X axis, then close the dialog box.

➤ Save the workbook.

Click column to select the data series

Point to any column and click right mouse button to display shortcut menu

(i) Format the Data Series (step 12)

FIGURE 4.7   Hands-on Exercise 1 (continued)

STEP 13: Print the Workbook

➤ Pull down the **File menu** and click **Print** to display the dialog box in Figure 4.7j. Click the option button to print the **Entire Workbook.** Click **OK.**

➤ Click the **TipWizard button** to open the TipWizard box. Click the **up arrow** on the tip box to review the suggestions made by the TipWizard during the exercise. Close the TipWizard.

➤ Close the workbook. Exit Excel if you do not want to continue with the next exercise at this time.

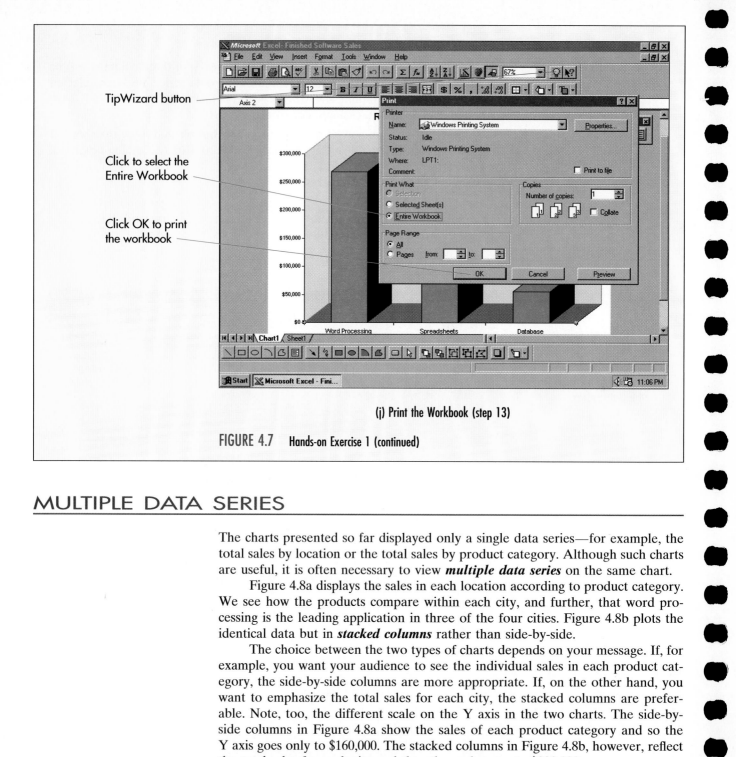

TipWizard button

Click to select the
Entire Workbook

Click OK to print
the workbook

(j) Print the Workbook (step 13)

FIGURE 4.7   Hands-on Exercise 1 (continued)

MULTIPLE DATA SERIES

The charts presented so far displayed only a single data series—for example, the total sales by location or the total sales by product category. Although such charts are useful, it is often necessary to view **multiple data series** on the same chart.

Figure 4.8a displays the sales in each location according to product category. We see how the products compare within each city, and further, that word processing is the leading application in three of the four cities. Figure 4.8b plots the identical data but in **stacked columns** rather than side-by-side.

The choice between the two types of charts depends on your message. If, for example, you want your audience to see the individual sales in each product category, the side-by-side columns are more appropriate. If, on the other hand, you want to emphasize the total sales for each city, the stacked columns are preferable. Note, too, the different scale on the Y axis in the two charts. The side-by-side columns in Figure 4.8a show the sales of each product category and so the Y axis goes only to $160,000. The stacked columns in Figure 4.8b, however, reflect the total sales for each city and thus the scale goes to $300,000.

The biggest difference is that the stacked column explicitly totals the sales for each city while the side-by-side column does not. The advantage of the stacked column is that the city totals are clearly shown and can be easily compared, and further the relative contributions of each product category within each city are apparent. The disadvantage is that the segments within each column do not start at the same point, making it difficult to determine the actual sales for the individual product categories or to compare the product categories among cities.

Realize, too, that for a stacked column chart to make sense, its numbers must be additive. This is true in Figure 4.8b, where the stacked columns consist of three

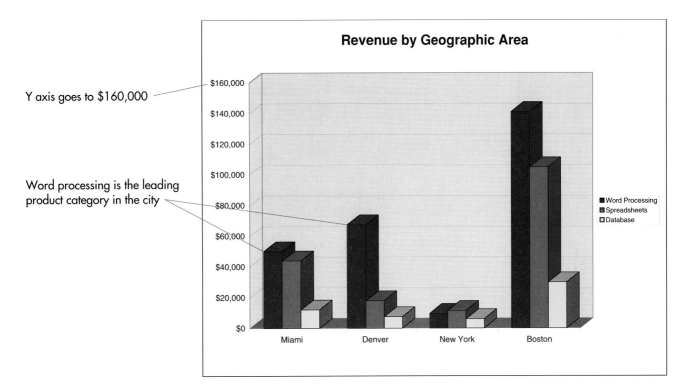

Y axis goes to $160,000

Word processing is the leading product category in the city

(a) Side-by-Side Column Chart

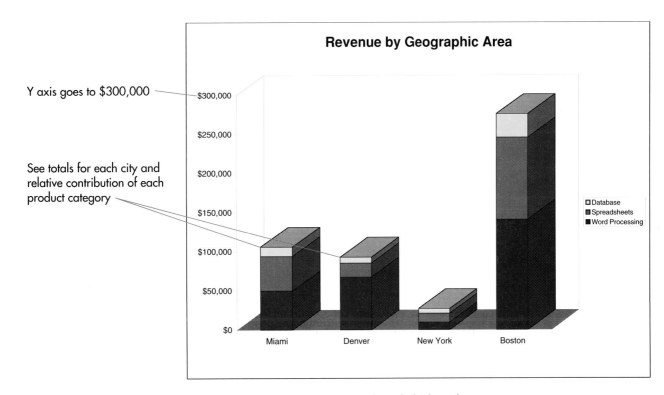

Y axis goes to $300,000

See totals for each city and relative contribution of each product category

(b) Stacked Column Chart

FIGURE 4.8   Column Charts

components, each of which is measured in dollars, and which can be logically added together to produce a total. You shouldn't, however, automatically convert a side-by-side column chart to its stacked column equivalent. It would not make sense, for example, to convert a column chart that plots unit sales and dollar sales side-by-side, into a stacked column chart that adds the two, because units and dollars represent different physical concepts and are not additive.

Rows versus Columns

Figure 4.9 illustrates a critical concept associated with multiple data series—whether the data series are in rows or columns. Figure 4.9a displays the worksheet with multiple data series selected. (Column A and Row 3 are included in the selection to provide the category labels and legend.) Figure 4.9b contains the chart when the data series are in rows (B4:E4, B5:E5, and B6:E6). Figure 4.9c displays the chart based on data series in columns (B4:B6, C4:C6, D4:D6, and E4:E6).

Both charts plot a total of twelve data points (three product categories for each of four locations), but they group the data differently. Figure 4.9b displays the data by city; that is, the sales of three product categories are shown for each of four cities. Figure 4.9c is the reverse and groups the data by product category; this time the sales in the four cities are shown for each of the three product categories. The choice between the two depends on your message and whether you want to emphasize revenue by city or by product category. It sounds complicated, but it's not, and Excel will create either chart for you according to your specifications.

- If the data series are in rows (Figure 4.9b), the Wizard will:
  - Use the first row (cells B3 through E3) in the selected range for the category labels on the X axis
  - Use the first column (cells A4 through A6) for the legend text
- If the data series are in columns (Figure 4.9c), the Wizard will:
  - Use the first column (cells A4 through A6) in the selected range for the category labels on the X axis
  - Use the first row (cells B3 through E3) for the legend text

Stated another way, the data series in Figure 4.9b are in rows. Thus, there are three data series (B4:E4, B5:E5, and B6:E6), one for each product category. The first data series plots the word processing sales in Miami, Denver, New York, and Boston; the second series plots the spreadsheet sales for each city, and so on.

The data series in Figure 4.9c are in columns. This time there are four data series (B4:B6, C4:C6, D4:D6, and E4:E6), one for each city. The first series plots the Miami sales for word processing, spreadsheets, and database; the second series plots the Denver sales for each software category, and so on.

A3:E6 is selected

	A	B	C	D	E	F
1		Superior Software Sales				
2						
3		*Miami*	*Denver*	*New York*	*Boston*	*Total*
4	*Word Processing*	$50,000	$67,500	$9,500	$141,000	$268,000
5	*Spreadsheets*	$44,000	$18,000	$11,500	$105,000	$178,500
6	*Database*	$12,000	$7,500	$6,000	$30,000	$55,500
7	*Total*	$106,000	$93,000	$27,000	$276,000	$502,000

(a) The Worksheet

FIGURE 4.9   Multiple Data Series

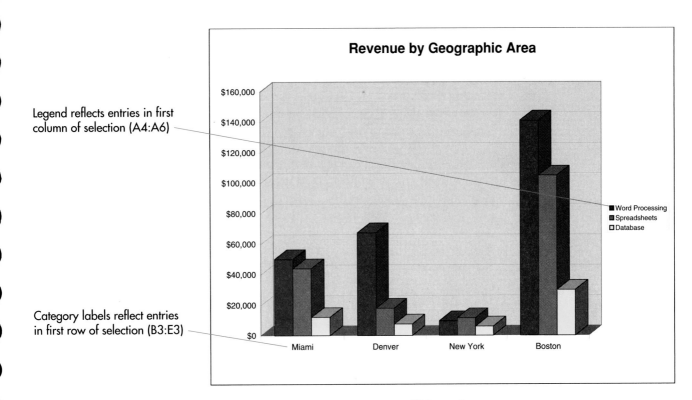

Legend reflects entries in first column of selection (A4:A6)

Category labels reflect entries in first row of selection (B3:E3)

(b) Data in Rows

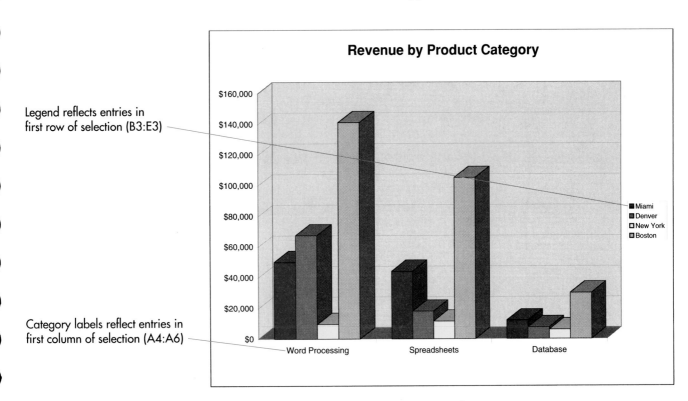

Legend reflects entries in first row of selection (B3:E3)

Category labels reflect entries in first column of selection (A4:A6)

(c) Data in Columns

FIGURE 4.9   Multiple Data Series (continued)

Default Selections

Excel makes a default determination as to whether the data is in rows or columns by assuming that you want fewer data series than categories. Thus, if the selected cells contain fewer rows than columns (or if the number of rows and columns are equal), it assumes the data series are in rows. If, on the other hand, there are fewer columns than rows, it will assume the data series are in columns.

Be sure to include the text for both the category labels and legend in your selection so that Excel can create these elements for you. And remember, you can subsequently override any default selection by using the ChartWizard to edit the *default chart.*

HANDS-ON EXERCISE 2

Multiple Data Series

Objective: To plot multiple data series in the same chart; to differentiate between data series in rows and columns; to create and save multiple charts associated with the same worksheet. Use Figure 4.10 as a guide in doing the exercise.

STEP 1: Rename the Workbook Tabs

➤ Open the **Finished Software Sales workbook** from the previous exercise. Reset the TipWizard as you have been doing throughout the text so that you will see all of the tips the Wizard has to offer.

➤ Point to the workbook tab labeled **Sheet1** as shown in Figure 4.10a. Click the **right mouse button** to display a shortcut menu with commands pertaining to the worksheet tab.

➤ Click **Rename** to display the Rename Sheet dialog box in Figure 4.10a. Type **Sales Data.** Click **OK.**

➤ Point to the tab labeled **Chart1** (which contains the three-dimensional column chart created in the previous exercise). Click the **right mouse button** to display a shortcut menu.

➤ Click **Rename** to display the Rename Sheet dialog box in Figure 4.10a. Type **Revenue by Product Category.** Click **OK.**

➤ Save the workbook.

THE RIGHT MOUSE BUTTON

Point to a cell (or group of selected cells), a chart or worksheet tab, a toolbar, or chart (or a selected object on the chart), then click the right mouse button to display a shortcut menu. All shortcut menus are context sensitive and display commands appropriate for the selected object. Right clicking a toolbar, for example, enables you to display (hide) additional toolbars. Right clicking a sheet tab enables you to rename, move, copy, or delete the sheet. Right clicking a chart displays commands that enable you to edit the chart.

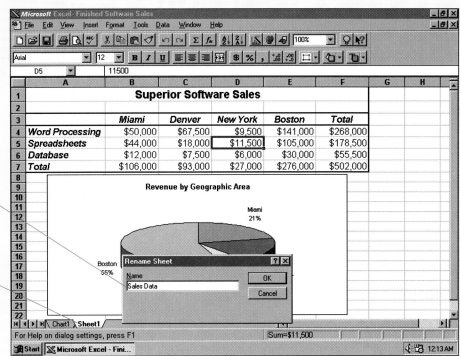

Enter new name for sheet

Point to Sheet1 tab and click right mouse button to display shortcut menu

(a) Rename the Worksheet Tab (step 1)

FIGURE 4.10   Hands-on Exercise 2

STEP 2: Multiple Data Series

➤ Click the **Sales Data tab,** then click and drag to select **cells A3** through **E6** as shown in Figure 4.10b.

➤ Pull down the **Insert menu.** Click **Chart.** Click **As New Sheet** to bring up step 1 of the ChartWizard as shown in Figure 4.10b.

➤ Click the **Finish command button** to skip the remaining steps in the ChartWizard and create the default chart with no additional input from you.

➤ The new chart is in its own chart sheet labeled Chart1 (The tab may reflect a higher number, depending on how many charts you have created this session.)

➤ Save the workbook.

THE F11 KEY

The F11 key is the fastest way to create a chart in its own sheet. Select the data series, including the legends and category labels, then press the F11 key to create the chart according to the default format built into Excel. After the chart has been created, you can use the menu bar, Chart toolbar, or shortcut menus to choose a different chart type and/or customize the formatting.

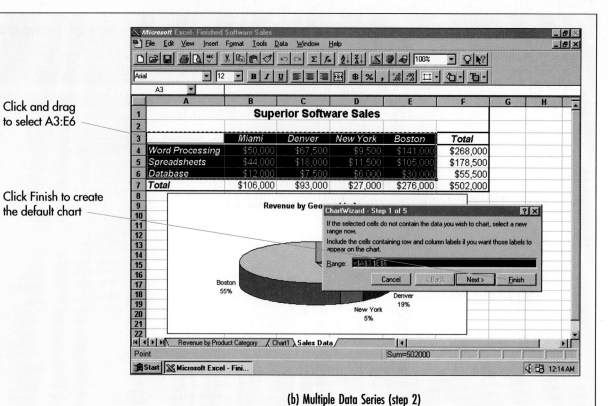

Click and drag
to select A3:E6

Click Finish to create
the default chart

(b) Multiple Data Series (step 2)

FIGURE 4.10   Hands-on Exercise 2 (continued)

STEP 3: Insert the Title

➤ Click the tab for the newly created chart sheet. Pull down the **Insert menu.**
Click **Titles** to bring up the Titles dialog box. Click the **check box** next to
Chart Title. Click **OK.**

➤ Type the title of the chart, **Revenue by Geographic Area.** Press the **enter key.**
The title should still be selected, enabling you to change its font and/or the
point size.

➤ Click the **arrow** on the Font Size box on the Formatting toolbar as shown in
Figure 4.10c. Click **18** to increase the size of the title. Click outside the title
to deselect it.

➤ Save the workbook.

STEP 4: Change the Chart Type

➤ Pull down the **Format menu** and click **AutoFormat.** (You can also point to
the chart and click the **right mouse button,** then select AutoFormat from the
shortcut menu.)

➤ Click the **down arrow** on the Galleries list box to scroll through the available
chart types. Click **3-D Column** to produce the dialog box in Figure 4.10d.

➤ Click **Format 1.** Click **OK.** The chart changes to a three-dimensional column
chart.

➤ Point to the tab containing this chart, click the **right mouse button** to display
a shortcut menu, then click the **Rename command.** Enter **Revenue by Area**
as the new name. Click **OK.**

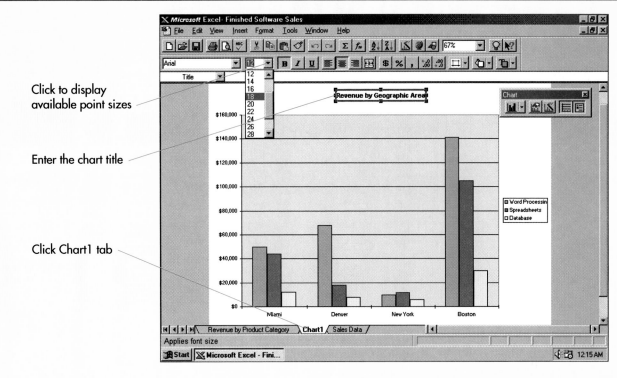

Click to display
available point sizes

Enter the chart title

Click Chart1 tab

(c) Add the Title (step 3)

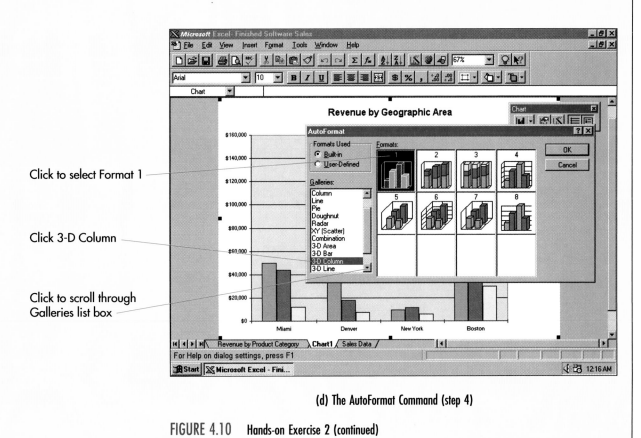

Click to select Format 1

Click 3-D Column

Click to scroll through
Galleries list box

(d) The AutoFormat Command (step 4)

FIGURE 4.10   Hands-on Exercise 2 (continued)

STEP 5: Copying Sheets

➤ Point to the tab named **Revenue by Area.** Click the **right mouse button.** Click **Move** or **Copy** to display the dialog box in Figure 4.10e.

➤ Click **Sales Data** in the Before Sheet list box. Click the check box to **Create a Copy.** Click **OK** to create a duplicate worksheet called Revenue by Area (2) and insert it before (to the left of) the Sales Data worksheet.

➤ Rename the copied sheet **Revenue by Product.** Save the workbook.

MOVING AND COPYING A CHART SHEET

The fastest way to move or copy a chart sheet is to drag its tab. To move a sheet, point to its tab, then click and drag the tab to its new position. To copy a sheet, press and hold the Ctrl key as you drag the tab to the desired position for the second sheet. Rename the copied sheet (or any other sheet) by pointing to its tab and clicking the right mouse button to produce a shortcut menu. Click Rename, then enter the new name in the resulting dialog box.

Click Sales Data to insert duplicated sheet to the left of it (i.e., before it)

Click to select option to create a copy

Rename tab, then point to tab and click right mouse button to display a shortcut menu

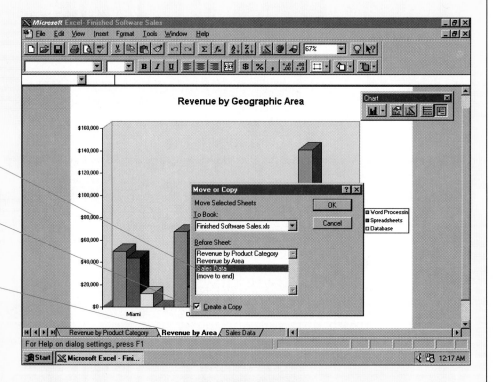

(e) Copy the Chart Sheet (step 5)

FIGURE 4.10   Hands-on Exercise 2 (continued)

STEP 6: Change the Data Series

➤ Click the **Revenue by Product tab** to make it the active sheet. Click anywhere in the chart to select it.

➤ Click the **ChartWizard button** on the Chart toolbar. The Sales Data sheet is displayed on the screen, and you will see a dialog box indicating step 1 of 2 in ChartWizard.

➤ Click the **Next command button** to redisplay the Revenue by Product chart and produce the dialog box in Figure 4.10f.

➤ Click the **Columns option button** to change the data series to columns; this will display the data by product category rather than location. Click **OK.**

➤ The orientation of the chart changes so that the applications appear as the category labels on the X axis. The legend contains the names of the cities. This was done automatically by the ChartWizard in conjunction with the options shown in Figure 4.10f.

➤ Click anywhere in the title of the chart to select the title. Drag the mouse over **Geographic Area** to select this text. Type **Product Category.** Click outside the title to deselect it.

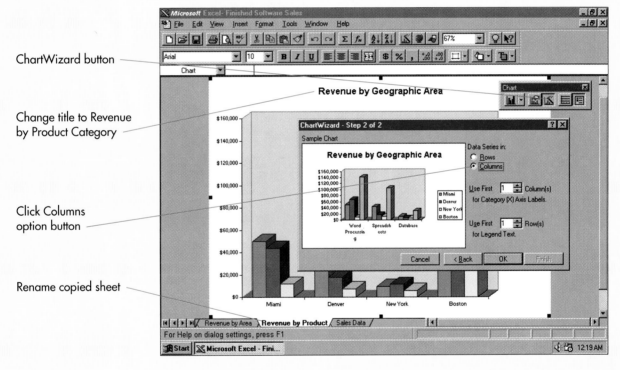

ChartWizard button

Change title to Revenue by Product Category

Click Columns option button

Rename copied sheet

(f) Change the Data Series (step 6)

FIGURE 4.10   Hands-on Exercise 2 (continued)

STEP 7: The Stacked Column Chart

➤ Pull down the **Format menu** and click **AutoFormat.** (You can also point to the chart and click the **right mouse button,** then select AutoFormat from the shortcut menu.)

➤ Click **Format 2** in the Formats area. Click **OK.** The chart changes to a stacked bar chart as shown in Figure 4.10g.

➤ Save the workbook a final time.

THE HORIZONTAL SCROLL BAR

The horizontal scroll bar contains four scrolling buttons to scroll through the worksheet tabs in a workbook. Click ◄ or ► to scroll one tab to the left or right. Click |◄ or ►| to scroll to the first or last tab in the workbook. Once the desired tab is visible, click the tab to select it. Five tabs are visible simultaneously (the default workbook has 16 worksheets); you can, however, drag the tab split box to change the number of tabs that can be seen at one time.

Save button

Stacked columns

Tab split box

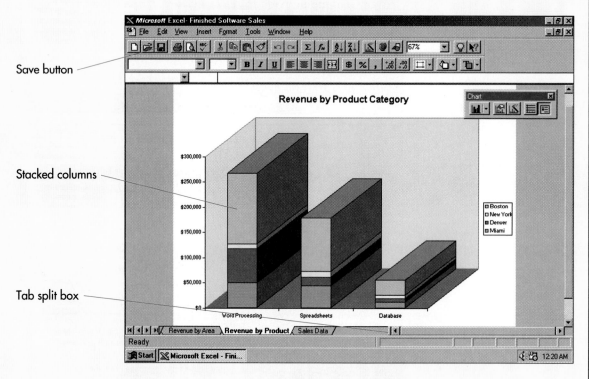

(g) Stacked Column Chart (step 7)

FIGURE 4.10   Hands-on Exercise 2 (continued)

STEP 8: Print the Completed Workbook

➤ Pull down the **File menu,** click the **Print command,** then click the option button to print the **Entire Workbook.** (Clicking the Print button on the Standard toolbar prints only the selected sheet, as opposed to the entire workbook.)

➤ Click **OK** to print the workbook, and submit it to your instructor as proof that you completed the exercise.

➤ Close the workbook. Exit Excel if you do not want to continue with the next exercise at this time.

OBJECT LINKING AND EMBEDDING

One of the primary advantages of the Windows environment is the ability to create a ***compound document*** that contains data ***(objects)*** from multiple applications. The memo in Figure 4.11 is an example of a compound document. The memo was created in Microsoft Word (the ***client application***), and it contains objects (a worksheet and a chart) that were developed in Microsoft Excel (the ***server application***). ***Object Linking and Embedding*** (***OLE,*** pronounced "oh-lay") is the means by which you create the compound document.

Superior Software
Miami, Florida

To: Mr. White
          Chairman, Superior Software

From: Heather Bond
          Vice President, Marketing

Subject: May Sales Data

The May sales data clearly indicate that Boston is outperforming our other geographic areas. It is my feeling that Ms. Brown, the office supervisor, is directly responsible for its success and that she should be rewarded accordingly. In addition, we may want to think about transferring her to New York, as they are in desperate need of new ideas and direction. I will be awaiting your response after you have time to digest the information presented.

Superior Software Sales					
	Miami	Denver	New York	Boston	Total
Word Processing	$50,000	$67,500	$9,500	$141,000	$268,000
Spreadsheets	$44,000	$18,000	$11,500	$105,000	$178,500
Database	$12,000	$7,500	$6,000	$30,000	$55,500
Total	$106,000	$93,000	$27,000	$276,000	$502,000

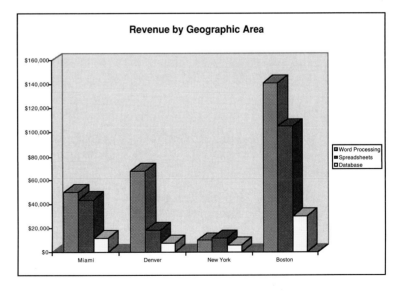

FIGURE 4.11   A Compound Document

The essential difference between linking and embedding is whether the object is stored within the compound document *(embedding)* or in its own file *(linking).* An *embedded object* is stored in the compound document, which in turn becomes the only client for that object. A *linked object* is stored in its own file, and the compound document is one of many potential clients for that object. The compound document does not contain the linked object per se, but only a representation of the object as well as a pointer (link) to the file containing the object. The advantage of linking is that any document that is linked to the object is updated automatically if the object is changed.

The choice between linking and embedding depends on how the object will be used. Linking is preferable if the object is likely to change and the compound document requires the latest version. Linking should also be used when the same object is placed in many documents, so that any change to the object has to be made in only one place. Embedding should be used if you need to take the object with you—for example, if you intend to edit the compound document on a different computer.

The following exercise uses linking to create a Word document containing an Excel worksheet and chart. As you do the exercise, both applications (Word and Excel) will be open, and it will be necessary to switch back and forth between the two. This in turn demonstrates the *multitasking* capability within Windows 95 and the use of the Windows 95 taskbar to switch between the open applications.

OBJECT LINKING AND EMBEDDING

Object Linking and Embedding (OLE) enables you to create a compound document containing objects (data) from multiple Windows applications. In actuality, there are two distinct techniques, linking and embedding, and each can be implemented in different ways. OLE is one of the major benefits of working in the Windows environment, but it would be impossible to illustrate all of the techniques in a single exercise. Accordingly, we have created the icon at the left to help you identify the many examples of object linking and embedding that appear throughout the Exploring Windows series.

HANDS-ON EXERCISE 3

Object Linking and Embedding

Objective: To create a compound document consisting of a memo, worksheet, and chart. Use Figure 4.12 as a guide in the exercise.

STEP 1: Open the Software Memo
➤ Click the **Start button** on the taskbar to display the Start menu.
➤ Click (or point to) the **Programs menu,** then click **Microsoft Word** to start the program.
➤ Word is now active, and the taskbar contains a button for Microsoft Word. It may (or may not) contain a button for Microsoft Excel, depending on whether or not you closed Excel at the end of the previous exercise.
➤ If necessary, click the **Maximize button** in the application window so that Word takes the entire desktop as shown in Figure 4.12a. (The Open dialog

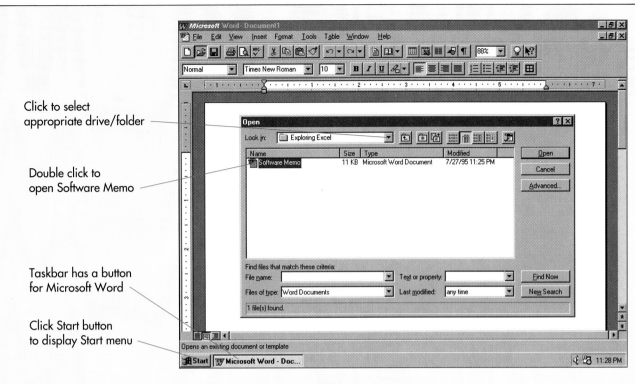

Click to select
appropriate drive/folder

Double click to
open Software Memo

Taskbar has a button
for Microsoft Word

Click Start button
to display Start menu

(a) Open the Software Sales Document (step 1)

FIGURE 4.12   Hands-on Exercise 3

box is not yet visible.) Click the **Maximize button** in the document window
(if necessary) so that the document window is as large as possible.

➤ Pull down the **File menu** and click **Open** (or click the **Open button** on the
Standard toolbar).

- Click the **drop-down arrow** on the Look In list box. Click the appropriate
drive, drive C or drive A, depending on the location of your data.

- Double click the **Exploring Excel folder** (we placed the Word memo in the
Excel folder) to open the folder. Double click the **Software Memo** to open
the document.

- Save the document as **Finished Software Memo.**

➤ Pull down the **View menu.** Click **Page Layout** to change to the Page Layout
view. Pull down the **View menu.** Click **Zoom.** Click **Page Width.**

THE MICROSOFT TOOLBAR

The Microsoft toolbar contains a button for each application in Microsoft
Office and provides a quick and easy way to launch any of these applications. To display the toolbar, point to any visible toolbar, then click the
right mouse button to produce a shortcut menu containing the available
toolbars. Click (check) Microsoft to display the toolbar and close the
menu. Click and drag the newly displayed toolbar to position it as desired.

STEP 2: Copy the Worksheet

➤ Open (or return to) the **Finished Software Sales workbook** from the previous exercise.

  • If you did not close Microsoft Excel at the end of the previous exercise, you will see its button on the taskbar. Click the **Microsoft Excel button** to return to the Finished Software Sales workbook.

  • If you closed Microsoft Excel, click the **Start button** to start Excel, then open the Finished Software Sales workbook.

➤ The taskbar should now contain a button for both Microsoft Word and Microsoft Excel. Click either button to move back and forth between the open applications. End by clicking the Microsoft Excel button so that you see the Finished Software Sales workbook.

➤ Click the tab for **Sales Data.** Click and drag to select **A1** through **F7** to select the entire worksheet as shown in Figure 4.12b.

➤ Point to the selected area and click the **right mouse button** to display the shortcut menu. Click **Copy.** A moving border appears around the entire worksheet, indicating that it has been copied to the clipboard.

THE WINDOWS 95 TASKBAR

Multitasking, the ability to run multiple applications at the same time, is one of the primary advantages of the Windows environment. Each button on the taskbar appears automatically when its application or folder is opened, and disappears upon closing. (The buttons are resized automatically according to the number of open windows.) You can customize the taskbar by right clicking an empty area to display a shortcut menu, then clicking the Properties command. You can resize the taskbar by pointing to the inside edge and then dragging when you see the double-headed arrow. You can also move the taskbar to the left or right edge of the desktop, or to the top of the desktop, by dragging a blank area of the taskbar to the desired position.

STEP 3: Create the Link

➤ Click the **Microsoft Word button** on the taskbar to return to the memo as shown in Figure 4.12c. Press **Ctrl+End** to move to the end of the memo, which is where you will insert the Excel worksheet.

➤ Pull down the **Edit menu.** Click **Paste Special** to display the dialog box in Figure 4.12c.

➤ Click **Microsoft Excel 5.0 Worksheet Object** in the As list. Click the **Paste Link option button.** Click **OK** to insert the worksheet into the document.

➤ Press the **enter key** twice (to create a blank line between the worksheet and the chart that will be added in step 5).

➤ Pull down the **File menu** and click **Save** (or click the **Save button** on the Standard toolbar) to save the memo.

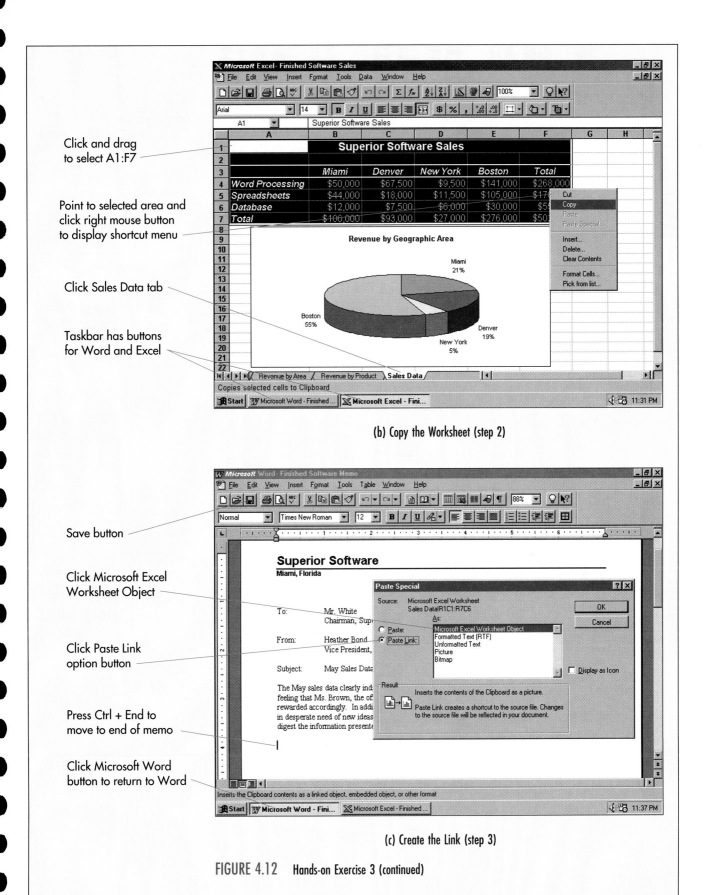

Click and drag to select A1:F7

Point to selected area and click right mouse button to display shortcut menu

Click Sales Data tab

Taskbar has buttons for Word and Excel

(b) Copy the Worksheet (step 2)

Save button

Click Microsoft Excel Worksheet Object

Click Paste Link option button

Press Ctrl + End to move to end of memo

Click Microsoft Word button to return to Word

(c) Create the Link (step 3)

FIGURE 4.12   Hands-on Exercise 3 (continued)

THE COMMON USER INTERFACE

The common user interface provides a sense of familiarity from one Windows application to the next. Even if you have never used Microsoft Word, you will recognize many of the elements present in Excel. The applications share a common menu structure with consistent ways to execute commands from those menus. The Standard and Formatting toolbars are present in both applications. Many keyboard shortcuts are also common, such as Ctrl+Home and Ctrl+End to move to the beginning and end of a document.

STEP 4: Copy the Chart

➤ Click the **Microsoft Excel button** on the taskbar to return to the worksheet. Click outside the selected area (cells A1 through F7) to deselect the cells.

➤ Click the **Revenue by Area tab** to select the chart sheet. Point just inside the border of the chart, then click the left mouse button to select the chart. Be sure you have selected the entire chart and that you see the same sizing handles as in Figure 4.12d.

➤ Pull down the **Edit menu** and click **Copy** (or click the **Copy button** on the Standard toolbar).

STEP 5: Add the Chart

➤ Click the **Microsoft Word button** on the taskbar to return to the memo. If necessary, press **Ctrl+End** to move to the end of the Word document.

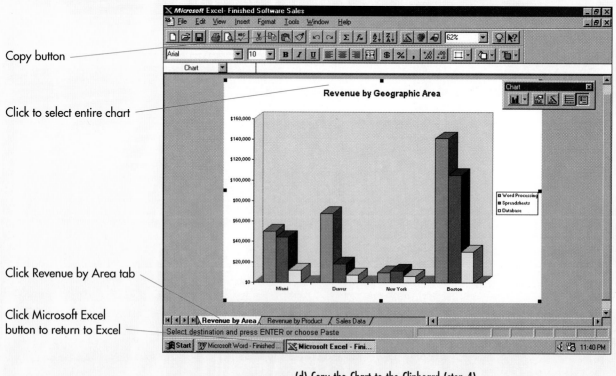

(d) Copy the Chart to the Clipboard (step 4)

FIGURE 4.12   Hands-on Exercise 3 (continued)

➤ Pull down the **Edit menu.** Click **Paste Special.** Click the **Paste Link** option button. If necessary, click **Microsoft Excel 5.0 Chart Object.** Click **OK** to insert the chart into the document.

➤ Click on the chart to select it and display the sizing handles. Click and drag a corner sizing handle inward to make the chart smaller.

➤ Click the **up** or **down arrow** on the vertical scroll bar so that you will be able to see the worksheet and the chart as shown in Figure 4.12e. (Do not be concerned if you do not see all of the chart.)

LINKING VERSUS EMBEDDING

The *Paste Special command* will link or embed an object, depending on whether the *Paste Link command* or *Paste command* option button is checked. Linking stores a pointer to the file containing the object together with a reference to the server application, and changes to the object are automatically reflected in all compound documents that are linked to the object. Embedding stores a copy of the object with a reference to the server application, but changes to the copy of the object within the compound document are not reflected in the original object. With both linking and embedding, however, you can double click the object in the compound document to edit the object, using the tools of the server application.

Sales for word processing in New York are $9,500

Click the Microsoft Word button to return to Word

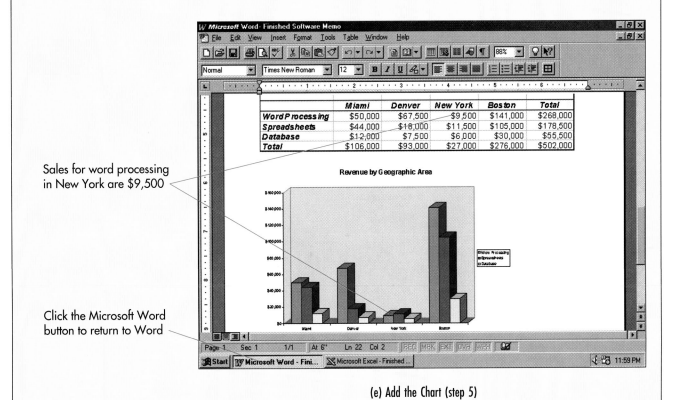

(e) Add the Chart (step 5)

FIGURE 4.12   Hands-on Exercise 3 (continued)

➤ Look carefully at the worksheet and chart in the document. The sales for word processing in New York are currently $9,500, and the chart reflects this amount. Save the memo.

➤ Point to the **Microsoft Excel button** on the taskbar and click the **right mouse button** to display a shortcut menu. Click **Close** to close Excel. Click **Yes** if prompted whether to save the changes to the Finished Software Sales workbook.

➤ The Microsoft Excel button disappears from the taskbar, indicating that Excel has been closed. Word is now the only open application.

STEP 6: Modify the Worksheet

➤ Click anywhere in the worksheet to select the worksheet and display the sizing handles as shown in Figure 4.12f. (We suggest you do not move or size the object until step 8 in the exercise.)

➤ The status bar indicates that you can double click to edit the worksheet. Double click anywhere within the worksheet to reopen Excel in order to change the data.

➤ The system pauses as it loads Excel and reopens the Finished Software Sales workbook. If necessary, click the **Maximize button** to maximize the Excel window.

➤ Click the **Sales Data tab** within the workbook. Click in **cell D4.** Type **$200,000.** Press **enter.** You may need to widen the column in order to display the larger number.

➤ Click the **Revenue by Area tab** to select the chart sheet. The chart has been modified automatically and reflects the increased sales for New York.

Click worksheet to select it; double click to edit it

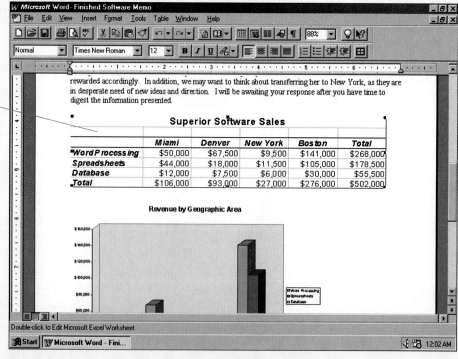

(f) Modify the Worksheet (step 6)

FIGURE 4.12   Hands-on Exercise 3 (continued)

ALT+TAB STILL WORKS

Alt+Tab was a treasured shortcut in Windows 3.1 that enabled users to switch back and forth between open applications. The shortcut also works in Windows 95. Press and hold the Alt key while you press and release the Tab key repeatedly to cycle through the open applications, whose icons are displayed in a small rectangular window in the middle of the screen. Release the Alt key when you have selected the icon for the application you want.

STEP 7: Update the Links

➤ Use the taskbar to return to Microsoft Word and the Software Memo. The links for the worksheet and chart may (or may not) be updated automatically, according to the options that are set in Microsoft Word.

- Point to the worksheet, click the **right mouse button** to display the shortcut menu, then click the **Update Link command.** The New York word processing sales should be $200,000.

- Point to the chart, click the **right mouse button** to display the shortcut menu in Figure 4.12g, then click the **Update Link command.**

➤ Save the Word document.

New York sales are updated to $200,000

Point to chart and click right mouse button to display shortcut menu

Microsoft Excel is reopened

Click Microsoft Word button to return to Word

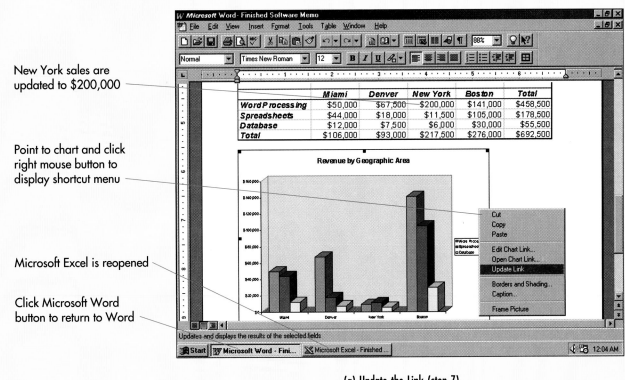

(g) Update the Link (step 7)

FIGURE 4.12   Hands-on Exercise 3 (continued)

STEP 8: The Completed Memo

➤ Pull down the **View menu.** Click **Zoom.** Click **Whole Page.** Click **OK.** You should see the completed memo as shown in Figure 4.12h.

➤ Point to the chart, then click the **right mouse button** to display the shortcut menu. Click **Frame Picture** to place the chart in a frame, which facilitates moving the chart within a document. Frame the worksheet in similar fashion.

➤ Click and drag the worksheet and chart until you are satisfied with the appearance of the completed memo. Save the memo a final time.

➤ Print the memo. Exit Word. Exit Excel. (Save the changes to Finished Software Sales.) Congratulations on a job well done.

THE FORMAT FRAME COMMAND

All objects should be placed into a frame, a special type of (invisible) container in Microsoft Word that facilitates positioning an object within a Word document. An unframed object is treated as an ordinary paragraph, and movement is restricted to one of three positions (left, center, or right). A second limitation is that text cannot be wrapped around an unframed object. A framed object, however, can be precisely positioned by right clicking the object, selecting the Format Frame command, then entering the information about the object's desired position.

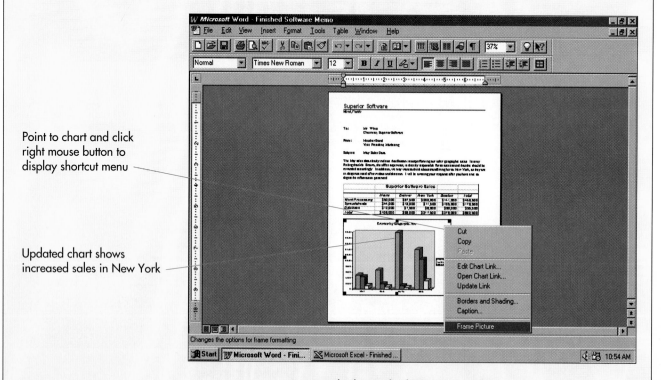

Point to chart and click right mouse button to display shortcut menu

Updated chart shows increased sales in New York

(h) The Completed Document (step 8)

FIGURE 4.12   Hands-on Exercise 3 (continued)

ADDITIONAL CHART TYPES

Excel offers a total of 15 **chart types,** each with several formats. The chart types are displayed in the ChartWizard (see Figure 4.5b) and are listed here for convenience. The chart types are Area, Bar, Column, Line, Pie, Doughnut, Radar, XY (scatter), Combination, 3-D Area, 3-D Bar, 3-D Column, 3-D Line, 3-D Pie, and 3-D Surface.

It is not possible to cover every type of chart, and so we concentrate on the most common. We have already presented the bar, column, and pie charts and continue with the line and combination charts. We use a different example, the worksheet in Figure 4.13a, which plots financial data for the National Widgets Corporation in Figures 4.13b and 4.13c. Both charts were created through the ChartWizard, then modified as necessary using the techniques from the previous exercises.

	A	B	C	D	E	F
1	National Widgets Financial Data					
2						
3		*1992*	*1993*	*1994*	*1995*	*1996*
4	*Revenue*	$50,000,000	$60,000,000	$70,000,000	$80,000,000	$90,000,000
5	*Profit*	$10,000,000	$8,000,000	$6,000,000	$4,000,000	$2,000,000
6	*Stock Price*	$40	$35	$36	$31	$24

(a) The Worksheet

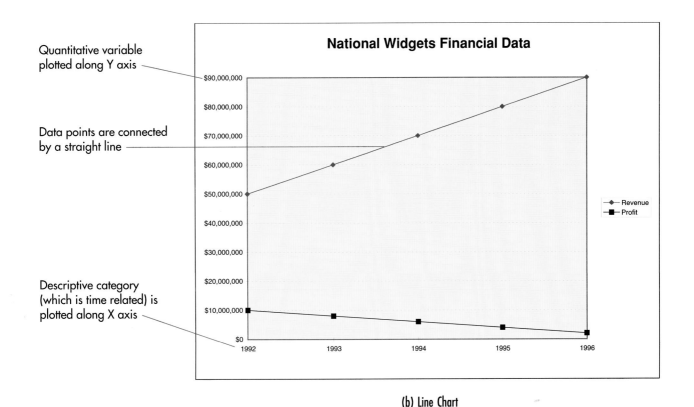

(b) Line Chart

FIGURE 4.13   National Widgets Financial Data

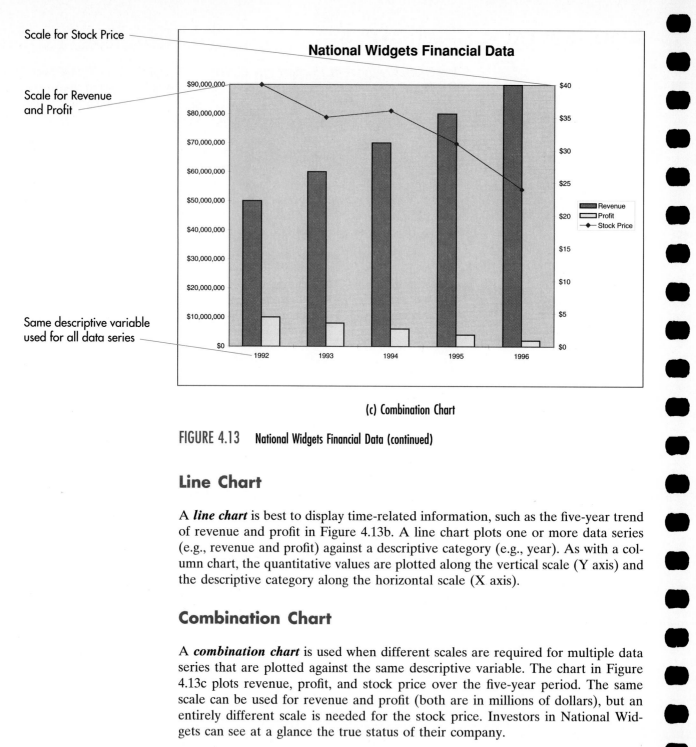

Scale for Stock Price

Scale for Revenue and Profit

Same descriptive variable used for all data series

National Widgets Financial Data

(c) Combination Chart

FIGURE 4.13   National Widgets Financial Data (continued)

Line Chart

A *line chart* is best to display time-related information, such as the five-year trend of revenue and profit in Figure 4.13b. A line chart plots one or more data series (e.g., revenue and profit) against a descriptive category (e.g., year). As with a column chart, the quantitative values are plotted along the vertical scale (Y axis) and the descriptive category along the horizontal scale (X axis).

Combination Chart

A *combination chart* is used when different scales are required for multiple data series that are plotted against the same descriptive variable. The chart in Figure 4.13c plots revenue, profit, and stock price over the five-year period. The same scale can be used for revenue and profit (both are in millions of dollars), but an entirely different scale is needed for the stock price. Investors in National Widgets can see at a glance the true status of their company.

USE AND ABUSE OF CHARTS

The hands-on exercises in the chapter demonstrate how easily numbers in a worksheet can be converted to their graphic equivalent. *The numbers can, however, just as easily be converted into erroneous or misleading charts, a fact that is often overlooked.* Indeed, some individuals are so delighted just to obtain the charts, that they accept the data without question. Accordingly, we present two examples of statistically accurate yet entirely misleading graphical data, drawn from charts submitted by our students in response to homework assignments.

> Lying graphics cheapen the graphical art everywhere ... When a chart on television lies, it lies millions of times over; when a *New York Times* chart lies, it lies 900,000 times over to a great many important and influential readers. The lies are told about the major issues of public policy—the government budget, medical care, prices, and fuel economy standards, for example. The lies are systematic and quite predictable, nearly always exaggerating the rate of recent change.
>
> **Edward Tufte**

Improper (Omitted) Labels

The difference between *unit sales* and *dollar sales* is a concept of great importance, yet one which is often missed. Consider, for example, the two pie charts in Figures 4.14a and 4.14b, both of which are intended to identify the leading salesperson, based on the underlying worksheet in Figure 4.14c. The charts yield two different answers, Jones and Smith, respectively, depending on which chart you use.

As you can see, the two charts reflect different percentages and would appear therefore to contradict each other. Both charts, however, are technically correct, as the percentages depend on whether they express unit sales or dollar sales. *Jones is the leader in terms of units, whereas Smith is the leader in terms of dollars.* The

Omitted titles can lead to erroneous conclusions

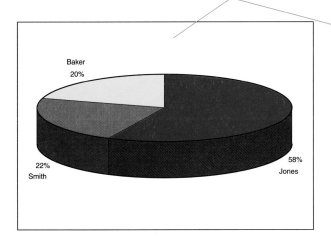

(a) Units

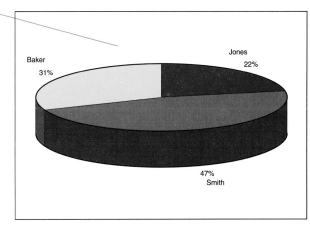

(b) Dollars

Sales Data - First Quarter							
		Jones		**Smith**		**Baker**	
	Price	Units	Dollars	Units	Dollars	Units	Dollars
Product 1	$1	200	$200	20	$20	30	$30
Product 2	$5	50	$250	30	$150	30	$150
Product 3	$20	5	$100	50	$1,000	30	$600
	Totals	255	$550	100	$1,170	90	$780

(c) Underlying Spreadsheet

FIGURE 4.14   Omitted Labels

latter is generally more significant, and hence the measure that is probably most important to the reader. Neither chart, however, was properly labeled (there is no indication of whether units or dollars are plotted), which in turn may lead to erroneous conclusions on the part of the reader.

Good practice demands that every chart have a title and that as much information be included on the chart as possible to help the reader interpret the data. Use titles for the X axis and Y axis if necessary. Add text boxes for additional explanation.

Adding Dissimilar Quantities

The conversion of a side-by-side column chart to a stacked column chart is a simple matter, requiring only a few mouse clicks. Because the procedure is so easy, however, it can be done without thought, and in situations where the stacked column chart is inappropriate.

Figures 4.15a and 4.15b display a side-by-side and a stacked column chart, respectively. One chart is appropriate and one chart is not. The side-by-side columns in Figure 4.15a indicate increasing sales in conjunction with decreasing profits. This is a realistic portrayal of the company, which is becoming less efficient because profits are decreasing as sales are increasing.

The stacked column chart in Figure 4.15b plots the identical numbers. It is deceptive, however, as it implies an optimistic trend whose stacked columns reflect a nonsensical addition. The problem is that although sales and profits are both measured in dollars, they should not be added together because the sum does not represent a meaningful concept.

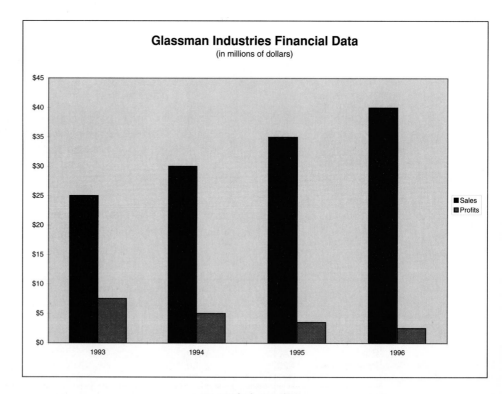

(a) Multiple Bar Chart

FIGURE 4.15   Adding Dissimilar Quantities

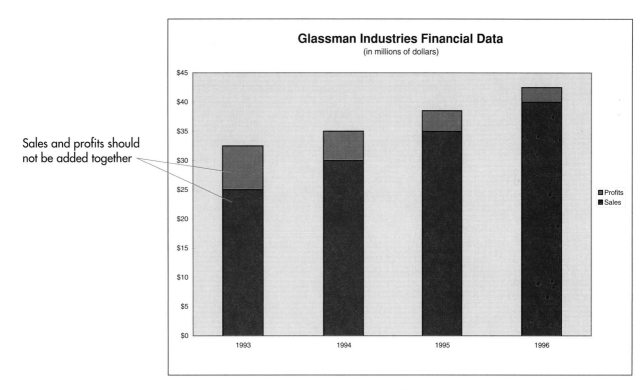

Sales and profits should not be added together

Glassman Industries Financial Data
(in millions of dollars)

(b) Stacked Bar Chart

FIGURE 4.15   Adding Dissimilar Quantities (continued)

SUMMARY

A chart is a graphic representation of data in a worksheet. The type of chart chosen depends on the message to be conveyed. A pie chart is best for proportional relationships. A column or bar chart is used to show actual numbers rather than percentages. A line chart is preferable for time-related data.

The ChartWizard is the easiest way to create a chart. Once created, a chart can be enhanced with arrows and text boxes found on the Drawing toolbar.

A chart may be embedded in a worksheet or created in a separate chart sheet. An embedded chart may be moved within a worksheet by selecting it and dragging it to its new location. An embedded chart may be sized by selecting it and dragging any of the sizing handles in the desired direction.

Multiple data series may be specified in either rows or columns. If the data is in rows, the first row is assumed to contain the category labels, and the first column is assumed to contain the legend. Conversely, if the data is in columns, the first column is assumed to contain the category labels, and the first row the legend. The ChartWizard makes it easy to switch from rows to columns and vice versa.

Object Linking and Embedding enables the creation of a compound document containing data (objects) from multiple applications. The essential difference between linking and embedding is whether the object is stored within the compound document (embedding) or in its own file (linking). An embedded object is stored in the compound document, which in turn becomes the only user (client) of that object. A linked object is stored in its own file, and the compound document is one of many potential clients of that object.

Bar chart
Category label
Chart
Chart sheet
Chart toolbar
Chart type
ChartWizard
Client application
Column chart
Combination chart
Common user interface
Compound document
Data point
Data series
Default chart
Docked toolbar

Drawing toolbar
Embedded chart
Embedded object
Embedding
Exploded pie chart
Floating toolbar
Legend
Line chart
Linked object
Linking
Multiple data series
Multitasking
Object
Object Linking and
  Embedding (OLE)
Paste command

Paste Link command
Paste Special command
Pie chart
Server application
Sheet tab
Sizing handles
Stacked columns
Taskbar
Text box
Three-dimensional
  column chart
Three-dimensional pie
  chart
X axis
Y axis

MULTIPLE CHOICE

1. Which type of chart is best to portray proportion or market share?
   (a) Pie chart
   (b) Line
   (c) Column chart
   (d) Combination chart

2. Which type of chart is typically used to display time-related data?
   (a) Pie chart
   (b) Line chart
   (c) Column chart
   (d) Combination chart

3. Which of the following chart types is *not* suitable to display multiple data series?
   (a) Pie chart
   (b) Horizontal bar chart
   (c) Column chart
   (d) All of the above are equally suitable

4. Which of the following is best to display additive information from multiple data series?
   (a) A column chart with the data series stacked one on top of another
   (b) A column chart with the data series side by side
   (c) Both (a) and (b) are equally appropriate
   (d) Neither (a) nor (b) is appropriate

5. A workbook must contain:
   (a) A separate chart sheet for every worksheet
   (b) A separate worksheet for every chart sheet
   (c) Both (a) and (b)
   (d) Neither (a) nor (b)

6. Which of the following is true regarding an embedded chart?
   (a) It can be moved elsewhere within the worksheet
   (b) It can be made larger or smaller
   (c) Both (a) and (b)
   (d) Neither (a) nor (b)

7. Which of the following will produce a shortcut menu?
   (a) Pointing to a workbook tab and clicking the right mouse button
   (b) Pointing to an embedded chart and clicking the right mouse button
   (c) Pointing to a selected cell range and clicking the right mouse button
   (d) All of the above

8. Which of the following is done *prior* to invoking the ChartWizard?
   (a) The data series are selected
   (b) The location of the embedded chart within the worksheet is specified
   (c) Both (a) and (b)
   (d) Neither (a) nor (b)

9. Which of the following will display sizing handles when selected?
   (a) An embedded chart
   (b) The title of a chart
   (c) A text box or arrow
   (d) All of the above

10. How do you switch between open applications?
    (a) Click the appropriate button on the taskbar
    (b) Use Alt+Tab to cycle through the applications
    (c) Both (a) and (b)
    (d) Neither (a) nor (b)

11. Which of the following is true regarding the compound document (the memo containing the worksheet and chart) that was created in the chapter?
    (a) The compound document contains more than one object
    (b) Excel is the server application and Word for Windows is the client application
    (c) Both (a) and (b)
    (d) Neither (a) nor (b)

12. In order to represent multiple data series on the same chart:
    (a) The data series must be in rows and the rows must be adjacent to one another on the worksheet
    (b) The data series must be in columns and the columns must be adjacent to one another on the worksheet
    (c) The data series may be in rows or columns so long as they are adjacent to one another
    (d) The data series may be in rows or columns with no requirement to be next to one another

13. If multiple data series are selected and rows are specified:
   (a) The first row will be used for the category (X axis) labels
   (b) The first column will be used for the legend
   (c) Both (a) and (b)
   (d) Neither (a) nor (b)

14. If multiple data series are selected and columns are specified:
   (a) The first column will be used for the category (X axis) labels
   (b) The first row will be used for the legend
   (c) Both (a) and (b)
   (d) Neither (a) nor (b)

15. Which of the following is true about the scale on the Y axis in a column chart that plots multiple data series side-by-side versus one that stacks the values one on top of another?
   (a) The scale for the stacked columns will contain larger values than if the columns are plotted side-by-side
   (b) The scale for the side-by-side columns will contain larger values than if the columns are stacked
   (c) The values on the scale will be the same regardless of whether the columns are stacked or side-by-side
   (d) The values on the scale will be different but it is not possible to tell which chart will contain the higher values

ANSWERS

1. a	**6.** c	**11.** c
2. b	**7.** d	**12.** d
3. a	**8.** a	**13.** c
4. a	**9.** d	**14.** c
5. d	**10.** c	**15.** a

EXPLORING EXCEL 7.0

1. Use Figure 4.16 to match each action with its result; a given action may be used more than once or not at all.

Action	Result
a. Click at 1	_____ Switch to the Sales Data sheet
b. Click at 2	_____ Create gridlines on the chart
c. Click right mouse button at 3	_____ Change the font used for the chart title
d. Click at 4	_____ Rename the current sheet
e. Click at 5	_____ Place an arrow on the chart
f. Click at 6	_____ Change the chart type
g. Click at 7	_____ Create a new chart on its own sheet

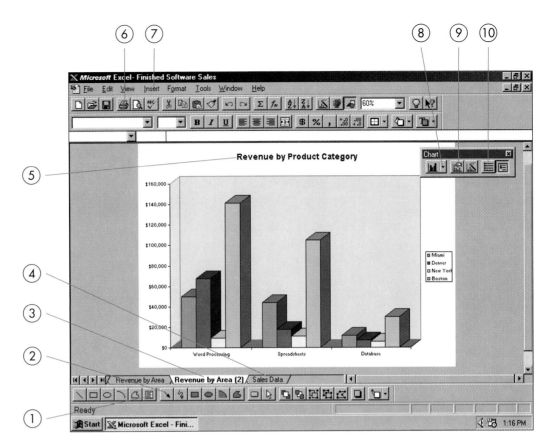

FIGURE 4.16   Screen for Problem 1

h. Click at 8 _____ Print the chart

i. Click at 9 _____ Place a text box on the chart

j. Click at 10 _____ Change the data series from columns to rows

2. The value of a chart is aptly demonstrated by writing a verbal equivalent to a graphic analysis. Accordingly, write the corresponding written description of the information contained in Figure 4.8a. Can you better appreciate the effectiveness of the graphic presentation?

3. The worksheet of Figure 4.17c is the basis for the two charts of Figures 4.17a and 4.17b. Although the charts may at first glance appear to be satisfactory, each reflects a fundamental error. Discuss the problems associated with each chart.

4. Answer the following with respect to the worksheet and embedded chart of Figure 4.18:

   a. Are the data series in rows or columns? How many data series are there?

   b. Which cells contain the category labels? Which cells contain the legends?

   c. Which toolbars in the figure are docked? Which are floating?

   d. How do you change the size of an embedded chart? How do you move an embedded chart? How do you delete it?

   e. What is the difference between clicking and double clicking the embedded chart? Was the chart in Figure 4.18 clicked or double clicked?

   f. What is the easiest way to reverse the way the data is plotted (i.e., switch rows to columns or vice versa)? (Hint: look at the floating toolbar and ToolTip.)

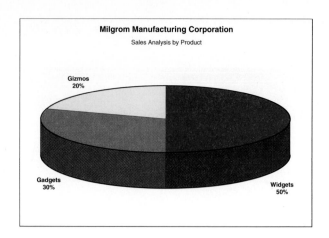

(a) Error 1

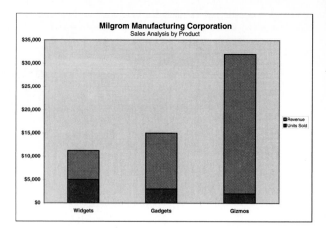

(b) Error 2

Milgrom Manufacturing Corporation Sales Analysis by Product			
	Unit Price	*Units Sold*	*Revenue*
Widgets	$1.25	5000	$6,250
Gadgets	$4.00	3000	$12,000
Gizmos	$14.99	2000	$29,980

(c) The Worksheet

FIGURE 4.17 Spreadsheet and Graphs for Problem 3

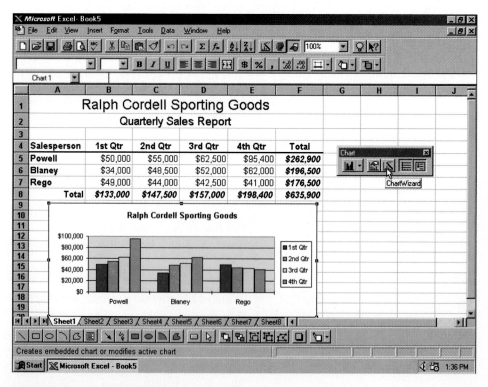

FIGURE 4.18 Screen for Problem 4

PRACTICE WITH EXCEL 7.0

1. The worksheet in Figure 4.19 is to be used as the basis of several charts that analyze the sales data for the chain of four Michael Moldof clothing boutiques. The worksheet is found on the data disk in the *Chapter 4 Practice 1 workbook*. Use the worksheet to develop the following charts:

   a. A pie chart showing the percentage of total sales attributed to each store.
   b. A column chart showing the total sales for each store.
   c. A stacked column chart showing total sales for each store, broken down by clothing category.
   d. A stacked column chart showing total dollars for each clothing category, broken down by store.
   e. Create each chart in its own chart sheet. Rename the various chart sheets to reflect the charts they contain.
   f. Title each chart appropriately and enhance each chart as you see fit.
   g. Print the entire workbook (the worksheet and all four chart sheets).
   h. Add a title page with your name and date, then submit the completed assignment to your instructor.

	A	B	C	D	E	F
1	Michael Moldof Men's Boutique					
2	January Sales					
3						
4		Store 1	Store 2	Store 3	Store 4	Total
5	Slacks	$25,000	$28,750	$21,500	$9,400	$84,650
6	Shirts	$43,000	$49,450	$36,900	$46,000	$175,350
7	Underwear	$18,000	$20,700	$15,500	$21,000	$75,200
8	Accessories	$7,000	$8,050	$8,000	$4,000	$27,050
9						
10	Total	$93,000	$106,950	$81,900	$80,400	$362,250

FIGURE 4.19   Spreadsheet for Practice Exercise 1

2. The worksheet in Figure 4.20 is to be used by the corporate marketing manager in a presentation in which she describes sales over the past four years. The manager has placed the worksheet on the data disk (in the *Chapter 4 Practice 2 workbook*) and would like you, her student intern, to do all of the following:

   a. Format the worksheet attractively so that it can be used as part of the presentation. Include your name somewhere in the worksheet.
   b. Create any chart(s) you think appropriate to emphasize the successful performance enjoyed by the London office.
   c. Use the same data and chart type(s) as in part (a) but modify the title (and/or callouts) to emphasize the disappointing performance of the Paris office.
   d. Print the worksheet together with all charts and submit them to your instructor. Be sure to title all charts appropriately and to use the text and arrow tools to add the required emphasis.

	A	B	C	D	E	F
1	Unique Boutiques					
2	Sales for 1992- 1995					
3						
4	Store	1992	1993	1994	1995	Totals
5	Miami	1500000	2750000	3000000	3250000	10500000
6	London	4300000	5500000	6700000	13000000	29500000
7	Paris	2200000	1800000	1400000	1000000	6400000
8	Rome	2000000	3000000	4000000	5000000	14000000
9	Totals	10000000	13050000	15100000	22250000	60400000

FIGURE 4.20   Spreadsheet for Practice Exercise 2

3. The worksheet in Figure 4.21 is to be used as the basis for several charts depicting information on hotel capacities. Each of the charts is to be created in its own chart sheet within the *Chapter 4 Practice 3 workbook* on the data disk. We describe the message we want to convey, but it is up to you to determine the appropriate chart and associated data range(s). Accordingly, you are to create a chart that:

   a. Compares the total capacity of the individual hotels to one another.

   b. Shows the percent of total capacity for each hotel.

   c. Compares the number of standard and deluxe rooms for all hotels, with the number of standard and deluxe rooms side-by-side for each hotel.

   d. Compares the standard and deluxe room rates for all hotels, with the two different rates side-by-side for each hotel.

   e. Add your name to the worksheet as the Hotel Manager, then print the complete workbook, which will consist of the original worksheet plus the four chart sheets you created.

	A	B	C	D	E	F
1		**Hotel Capacities and Room Rates**				
2						
3	Hotel	No. of Standard Rooms	Standard Rate	No. of Deluxe Rooms	Deluxe Rate	Total Number of Rooms
4	Holiday Inn	300	100	100	150	400
5	Hyatt	225	120	50	175	275
6	Ramada Inn	150	115	35	190	185
7	Sheraton	175	95	25	150	200
8	Marriott	325	100	100	175	425
9	Hilton	250	80	45	120	295
10	Best Western	150	75	25	125	175
11	Days Inn	100	50	15	100	115

FIGURE 4.21   Spreadsheet for Practice Exercise 3

4. Object Linking and Embedding: The compound document in Figure 4.22 contains a memo and combination chart. (The worksheet is contained in the *Chapter 4 Practice 4 workbook*. The text of the memo is in the *Chapter 4 Practice 4 Memo,* which exists as a Word document in the Exploring Excel folder on the data disk.) You are to complete the compound document and submit it to your instructor by completing the following steps:

   a. Create a letterhead for the memo containing your name, address, phone number, and any other information you deem appropriate.

   b. Create the combination chart that appears in the memo.

   c. Link the chart to the memo.

   d. Print the compound document and submit it to your instructor.

Steven Stocks

Financial Investments   •   100 Century Tower   •   New York, NY 10020

To: Carlos Rosell

From: Steven Stocks

Subject: Status Report on National Widgets

I have uncovered some information that I feel is important to the overall health of your investment portfolio. The graph below clearly shows that while revenues for National Widgets have steadily increased since 1992, profits have steadily decreased. In addition, the stock price is continuing to decline. Although at one time I felt that a turnaround was imminent, I am no longer so optimistic and am advising you to cut your losses and sell your National Widgets stock as soon as possible.

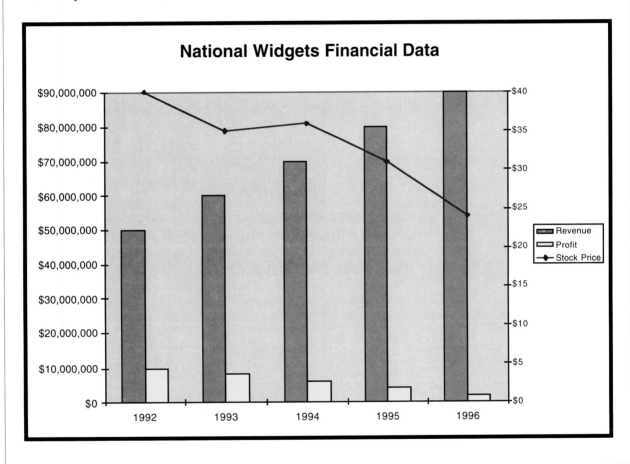

FIGURE 4.22   Compound Document for Practice Exercise 4

University Enrollments

Your assistantship next semester has placed you in the Provost's office, where you are to help create a presentation for the Board of Trustees. The Provost is expected to make recommendations to the Board regarding the expansion of some programs and the reduction of others. You are expected to help the Provost by developing a series of charts to illustrate enrollment trends. The Provost has created the *Student Enrollments workbook* on the data disk, which contains summary data over the last several years.

The Federal Budget

Deficit reduction or not, the federal government spends billions more than it takes in; for example, in fiscal year 1993, government expenditures totaled $1,408 billion versus income of only $1,154 billion, leaving a deficit of $254 billion. Thirty-one percent of the income came from Social Security and Medicare taxes, 36% from personal income taxes, 8% from corporate income taxes, and 7% from excise, estate, and other miscellaneous taxes. The remaining 18% was borrowed.

Social Security and Medicare accounted for 35% of the expenditures, and the defense budget another 24%. Social programs including Medicaid and aid to dependent children totaled 17%. Community development (consisting of agricultural, educational, environmental, economic, and space programs) totaled 8% of the budget. Interest on the national debt amounted to 14%. The cost of law enforcement and government itself accounted for the final 2%.

Use the information contained within this problem to create the appropriate charts to reflect the distribution of income and expenditures. Do some independent research and obtain data on the budget, the deficit, and the national debt for the years 1945, 1967, and 1980. The numbers may surprise you; for example, how does the interest expense for the current year compare to the total budget in 1967 (at the height of the Viet Nam War)? To the total budget in 1945 (at the end of World War II)? Create charts to reflect your findings, then write your representative in Congress. We are in trouble!

The Annual Report

Corporate America spends a small fortune to produce its annual reports, which are readily available to the public at large. Choose any company and obtain a copy of its most recent annual report. Use your imagination on how best to obtain the data. You might try a stock broker, the 800 directory, or even the Internet.

Consolidate the information in the company's report to produce a two-page document of your own. Your report should include a description of the company's progress in the last year, a worksheet with any data you deem relevant, and at least two charts in support of the worksheet or written material. Formatting is important, and you are expected to use Microsoft Word in addition to the worksheet to present the information in an attractive manner.

Computer Mapping

Your boss has asked you to look into computer mapping in an effort to better analyze sales data for your organization. She suggested you use the online help facility to explore the Data Map feature within Excel, which enables you to create color-coded maps from columns of numerical data. You mentioned this assignment to a colleague who suggested that you open the *Mapstats workbook* that is installed with Excel to see the sample maps and demographic data included with Excel. (You will need to use the Windows 95 Find command to locate the workbook, as it is not in our Exploring Excel folder). You have two days to learn what computer mapping can do, at which time you are to report to your boss to discuss the potential for computer mapping. She expects at least a three-page written report with real examples.

5

LIST AND DATA MANAGEMENT: CONVERTING DATA TO INFORMATION

OBJECTIVES

After reading this chapter you will be able to:

1. Create a list within Excel; explain the importance of proper planning and design prior to creating the list.
2. Add, edit, and delete records in an existing list; explain the significance of data validation.
3. Distinguish between data and information; describe how one is converted to the other.
4. Describe the TODAY function and explain the use of date arithmetic.
5. Use the Sort command; distinguish between an ascending and a descending sort, and among primary, secondary, and tertiary keys.
6. Use the DSUM, DAVERAGE, DMAX, DMIN, and DCOUNT functions.
7. Use the AutoFilter and Advanced Filter commands to display a subset of a list.
8. Use the Subtotals command to summarize data in a list.
9. Create a pivot table and explain how it provides flexibility in data analysis.

OVERVIEW

All businesses maintain data in the form of lists. Companies have lists of their employees. Magazines and newspapers keep lists of their subscribers. Political candidates monitor voter lists, and so on. This chapter presents the fundamentals of list management as it is implemented in Excel. We begin with the definition of basic terms, such as field and record, then cover the commands to create a list, to add a new record, or to modify or delete an existing record.

The second half of the chapter distinguishes between data and information and describes how one is converted to the other. We introduce the AutoFilter and Advanced Filter commands that display selected records in a list. We use the Sort command to rearrange the list. We discuss database functions and the associated criteria range. We also introduce date functions and date arithmetic. The chapter ends with a discussion of subtotals and pivot tables, two powerful capabilities associated with lists.

All of this is accomplished using Excel, and although it may eventually be necessary for you to use a dedicated database program (e.g., Microsoft Access), you will be pleased with what you can do. The chapter contains three hands-on exercises, each of which focuses on a different aspect of data management.

LIST AND DATA MANAGEMENT

Imagine, if you will, that you are the personnel director of a medium-sized company with offices in several cities, and that you manually maintain employee data for the company. Accordingly, you have recorded the specifics of every individual's employment (name, salary, location, title, and so on) in a manila folder, and you have stored the entire set of folders in a file cabinet. You have written the name of each employee on the label of his or her folder and have arranged the folders alphabetically in the filing cabinet.

The manual system just described illustrates the basics of data management terminology. The set of manila folders corresponds to a *file.* Each individual folder is known as a *record.* Each data item (fact) within a folder is called a *field.* The folders are arranged alphabetically in the file cabinet (according to the employee name on the label) to simplify the retrieval of any given folder. Likewise, the records in a computer-based system are also in sequence according to a specific field known as a *key.*

Excel maintains data in the form of a list. A *list* is an area in the worksheet that contains rows of similar data. A list can be used as a simple *database,* where the rows correspond to records and the columns correspond to fields. The first row contains the column labels or *field names,* which identify the data that will be entered in that column (field). Each additional row in the list contains a record. Each column represents a field. Each cell in the worksheet contains a value for a specific field in a specific record. Every record (row) contains the same fields (columns) in the same order as every other record.

Figure 5.1 contains an employee list with 13 records. There are four fields in every record—name, location, title, and salary. The field names should be meaningful and must be unique. (A field name may contain up to 255 characters, but you should keep them as short as possible so that a column does not become too wide and thus difficult to work with.) The arrangement of the fields within a record is consistent from record to record. The employee name was chosen as the key, and thus the records are in alphabetical order.

Normal business operations require that you make repeated trips to the filing cabinet to maintain the accuracy of the data. You will have to add a folder whenever a new employee is hired. In similar fashion, you will have to remove the folder of any employee who leaves the company, or modify the data in the folder of any employee who receives a raise, changes location, and so on.

Changes of this nature (additions, deletions, and modifications) are known as *file maintenance* and constitute a critical activity within any system. Indeed, without adequate file maintenance, the data in a system quickly becomes obsolete and the information useless. Imagine, if you will, the consequences of producing a payroll based on data that is six months old.

	A	B	C	D
1	Name	Location	Title	Salary
2	Adams	Atlanta	Trainee	$19,500
3	Adamson	Chicago	Manager	$52,000
4	Brown	Atlanta	Trainee	$18,500
5	Charles	Boston	Account Rep	$40,000
6	Coulter	Atlanta	Manager	$100,000
7	Frank	Miami	Manager	$75,000
8	James	Chicago	Account Rep	$42,500
9	Johnson	Chicag	Account Rep	$47,500
10	Manin	Boston	Accout Rep	$49,500
11	Marder	Chicago	Account Rep	$38,500
12	Milgrom	Boston	Manager	$57,500
13	Rubin	Boston	Account Rep	$45,000
14	Smith	Atlanta	Account Rep	$65,000

FIGURE 5.1   The Employee List

Nor is it sufficient simply to add (edit or delete) a record without adequate checks on the validity of the data. Look carefully at the entries in Figure 5.1 and ask yourself if a computer-generated report listing employees in the Chicago office will include Johnson. Will a report listing account reps include Manin? The answer to both questions is *no* because the data for these employees was entered incorrectly. Chicago is misspelled in Johnson's record (the "o" was omitted). Account rep is misspelled in Manin's title. *You* know that Johnson works in Chicago, but the computer does not, because it searches for the correct spelling. It also will omit Manin from a listing of account reps because of the misspelled title.

GARBAGE IN, GARBAGE OUT (GIGO)

A computer does exactly what you tell it to do, which is not necessarily what you want it to do. It is absolutely critical, therefore, that you validate the data that goes into a system, or else the associated information will not be correct. No system, no matter how sophisticated, can produce valid output from invalid input. In other words, garbage in—garbage out.

IMPLEMENTATION IN EXCEL

Creating a list is easy because there is little to do other than enter the data. You choose the area in the worksheet that will contain the list, then you enter the field names in the first row of the designated area. Each field name should be a unique text entry. The data for the individual records should be entered in the rows immediately below the row of field names.

Once a list has been created, you can edit any field, in any record, just as you would change the entries in an ordinary worksheet. The **Insert Rows command** lets you add new rows (records) to the list. The **Insert Columns command** lets you add additional columns (fields). The **Delete command** in the Edit menu enables you to delete a row or column. You can also use shortcut menus to execute commands more quickly. And finally, you can also format the entries within a list, just as you format the entries in any other worksheet.

LIST SIZE AND LOCATION

A list can appear anywhere within a worksheet and can theoretically be as large as an entire worksheet (16,384 rows by 256 columns). Practically, the list will be much smaller, giving rise to the following guideline for its placement: leave at least one blank column and one blank row between the list and the other entries in the worksheet. Excel will then be able to find the boundaries of the list automatically whenever a cell within the list is selected. It simply searches for the first blank row above and below the selected cell, and for the first blank column to the left and right of the selected cell.

Data Form Command

A *data form* provides an easy way to add, edit, and delete records in a list. The *Form command* in the Data menu displays a dialog box based on the fields in the list and contains the command buttons shown in Figure 5.2. Every record in the list contains the same fields in the same order (e.g., Name, Location, Title, and Salary in Figure 5.2), and the fields are displayed in this order within the dialog box. You do not have to enter a value for every field; that is, you may leave a field blank if the data is unknown.

Next to each field name is a text box into which data can be entered for a new record, or edited for an existing record. The scroll bar to the right of the data is used to scroll through the records in the list. The functions of the various command buttons are explained briefly:

New — Adds a record to the end of a list, then lets you enter data in that record. The formulas for computed fields, if any, are automatically copied to the new record.

Delete — Permanently removes the currently displayed record. The remaining records move up one row.

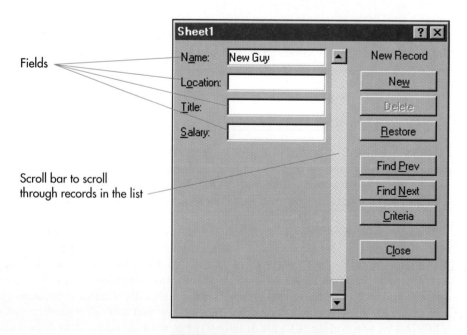

Fields

Scroll bar to scroll through records in the list

FIGURE 5.2 The Data Form Command

Restore — Cancels any changes made to the current record. (You must press the Restore button before pressing the enter key or scrolling to a new record.)

Find Prev — Displays the previous record (or the previous record that matches the existing criteria when criteria are defined).

Find Next — Displays the next record (or the next record that matches the existing criteria when criteria are defined).

Criteria — Displays a dialog box in which you specify the criteria for the Find Prev and/or Find Next command buttons to limit the displayed records to those that match the criteria.

Close — Closes the data form and returns to the worksheet.

Note, too, the What's This button (the question mark) on the title bar of the Data Form, which provides access to online help. Click the What's This button, then click any of the command buttons for an explanation. As indicated, the Data Form command provides an easy way to add, edit, and delete records in a list. It is not required, however, and you can use the Insert and Delete commands within the Edit menu as an alternate means of data entry.

Sort Command

The **Sort command** arranges the records in a list according to the value of one or more fields within that list. You can sort the list in **ascending** (low-to-high) or **descending** (high-to-low) **sequence.** (Putting a list in alphabetical order is considered an ascending sort.) You can also sort on more than one field at a time; for example, by location and then alphabetically by last name within each location. The field(s) on which you sort the list is (are) known as the key(s).

The records in Figure 5.3a are listed alphabetically (in ascending sequence according to employee name). Adams comes before Adamson, who comes before Brown, and so on. Figure 5.3b displays the identical records but in descending sequence by employee salary. The employee with the highest salary is listed first, and the employee with the lowest salary is last.

Figure 5.3c sorts the employees on two keys—by location, and by descending salary within location. Location is the more important, or **primary key.** Salary is the less important, or **secondary key.** The Sort command groups employees according to like values of the primary key (location), then within the like values of the primary key arranges them in descending sequence (ascending could have been chosen just as easily) according to the secondary key (salary). Excel provides a maximum of three keys—primary, secondary, and **tertiary.**

CHOOSE A CUSTOM SORT SEQUENCE

Alphabetic fields are normally arranged in strict alphabetical order. You can, however, choose a custom sort sequence such as the days of the week or the months of the year. Pull down the Data menu, click Sort, click the Options command button, then click the arrow on the drop-down list box to choose a sequence other than the alphabetic. You can also create your own sequence. Pull down the Tools menu, click Options, click the Custom Lists tab, then enter the items in desired sequence in the List Entries Box. Click Add to create the sequence, then close the dialog box.

	A	B	C	D
1	Name	Location	Title	Salary
2	Adams	Atlanta	Trainee	$19,500
3	Adamson	Chicago	Manager	$52,000
4	Brown	Atlanta	Trainee	$18,500
5	Charles	Boston	Account Rep	$40,000
6	Coulter	Atlanta	Manager	$100,000
7	Frank	Miami	Manager	$75,000
8	James	Chicago	Account Rep	$42,500
9	Johnson	Chicago	Account Rep	$47,500
10	Manin	Boston	Account Rep	$49,500
11	Marder	Chicago	Account Rep	$38,500
12	Milgrom	Boston	Manager	$57,500
13	Rubin	Boston	Account Rep	$45,000
14	Smith	Atlanta	Account Rep	$65,000

Records are listed in ascending sequence by employee name

(a) Ascending Sequence (by name)

	A	B	C	D
1	Name	Location	Title	Salary
2	Coulter	Atlanta	Manager	$100,000
3	Frank	Miami	Manager	$75,000
4	Smith	Atlanta	Account Rep	$65,000
5	Milgrom	Boston	Manager	$57,500
6	Adamson	Chicago	Manager	$52,000
7	Manin	Boston	Account Rep	$49,500
8	Johnson	Chicago	Account Rep	$47,500
9	Rubin	Boston	Account Rep	$45,000
10	James	Chicago	Account Rep	$42,500
11	Charles	Boston	Account Rep	$40,000
12	Marder	Chicago	Account Rep	$38,500
13	Adams	Atlanta	Trainee	$19,500
14	Brown	Atlanta	Trainee	$18,500

Records are listed in descending sequence by salary

(b) Descending Sequence (by salary)

	A	B	C	D
1	Name	Location	Title	Salary
2	Coulter	Atlanta	Manager	$100,000
3	Smith	Atlanta	Account Rep	$65,000
4	Adams	Atlanta	Trainee	$19,500
5	Brown	Atlanta	Trainee	$18,500
6	Milgrom	Boston	Manager	$57,500
7	Manin	Boston	Account Rep	$49,500
8	Rubin	Boston	Account Rep	$45,000
9	Charles	Boston	Account Rep	$40,000
10	Adamson	Chicago	Manager	$52,000
11	Johnson	Chicago	Account Rep	$47,500
12	James	Chicago	Account Rep	$42,500
13	Marder	Chicago	Account Rep	$38,500
14	Frank	Miami	Manager	$75,000

Location is the primary key (ascending sequence)

Salary is the secondary key (descending sequence)

(c) Primary and Secondary Keys

FIGURE 5.3   The Sort Command

DATE ARITHMETIC

A date is stored internally as an integer number corresponding to the number of days in this century. January 1, 1900 is stored as the number 1; January 2, 1900 as the number 2; and so on. July 29, 1995 corresponds to the number 34909 as can

Displays the current date

Always displays
same date

Age is calculated

	A	B	C	D
1		Cell Formulas	Date Format	Number Format
2	Today's Date	=TODAY()	7/29/95	34909
3	Birth Date	3/16/77	3/16/77	28200
4				
5	Elapsed Time (days)	=B2-B3		6709
6	Age (years)	=B5/365		18.4
7				
8		=IF(B6>=21,"Legal","Minor")		Minor

FIGURE 5.4   Date Arithmetic

be seen in Figure 5.4. The fact that dates are stored as integer numbers enables you to compute the number of elapsed days between two dates through simple subtraction. Age, for example, can be computed by subtracting a person's date of birth from today's date, and dividing the result by 365 (or more accurately by 365¼ to adjust for leap years).

The calculation of an individual's age requires the integer value of the current date, which is stored in the *TODAY() function.* Thus, whenever the worksheet is retrieved, the TODAY function will reflect the new date, and the calculated value of age will adjust automatically.

A specific date, such as March 16, 1977, is entered by typing the date in conventional fashion as 3/16/77. (Entering 00 for year, as in 1/21/00, signifies the year 2000.) Once entered, the date can be displayed in one of many formats. Note, too, the IF function in Figure 5.4, which examines the computed age, then displays an appropriate message indicating whether the individual is of legal age or still under the age of 21.

BIRTH DATE VERSUS AGE

An individual's age and birth date provide equivalent information, as one is calculated from the other. It might seem easier, therefore, to enter the age directly into the list and avoid the calculation, but this would be a mistake. A person's age changes continually, whereas the birth date remains constant. Thus, the date, and not the age, should be stored, so that the data in the list remains current. Similar reasoning applies to an employee's hire date and the length of service.

HANDS-ON EXERCISE 1

Creating and Maintaining a List

Objective: To add, edit, and delete records in an employee list; to introduce the Data Form and Data Sort commands; to use the spell check to validate data. Use Figure 5.5 as a guide in the exercise.

STEP 1: Open the Employee Workbook

➤ Start Excel. Open the **Employee List** workbook in the **Exploring Excel folder** as shown in Figure 5.5a.

Select a cell within the list

Click the New button to enter data for a new record

Click Close to return to worksheet

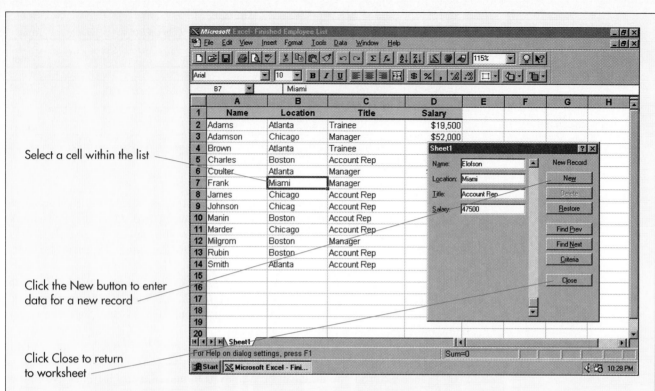

(a) The Data Form Command (step 2)

FIGURE 5.5   Hands-on Exercise 1

➤ Save the workbook as **Finished Employee List** so that you can always return to the original workbook.

➤ Reset the TipWizard.

EMPHASIZE THE COLUMN LABELS (FIELD NAMES)

Use a different font, alignment, style (boldface and/or italics), pattern, or border to distinguish the first row containing the field names from the remaining rows (records) in a list. This ensures that Excel will recognize the first row as a header row, enabling you to sort the list simply by selecting a cell in the list, then clicking the Ascending or Descending sort buttons on the Standard toolbar.

STEP 2: Add a Record (The Data Form Command)

➤ Click a single cell anywhere within the employee list (**cells A1** through **D14**). Pull down the **Data menu.** Click **Form** to display a dialog box with data for the first record in the list (Adams). Click the **New command button** to clear the text boxes and begin entering a new record.

➤ Enter the data for **Elofson** as shown in Figure 5.5a, using the Tab key to move from field to field within the data form. Click the **Close command button** after entering the salary. Elofson has been added to the list and appears in row 15.

➤ Save the workbook.

PRESS TAB, NOT ENTER

Press the Tab key to move to the next field within a data form. Press Shift+Tab to move to the previous field. Press the enter key only after the last field has been entered to move to the first field in the next record.

STEP 3: Add a Record (The Insert Rows Command)

➤ Click the **row heading** for **row 8.** Pull down the **Insert menu.** Click **Rows** as shown in Figure 5.5b.

➤ Add the data for **Gillenson,** who works in **Miami** as an **Account Rep** with a salary of **$55,000.**

➤ Save the workbook.

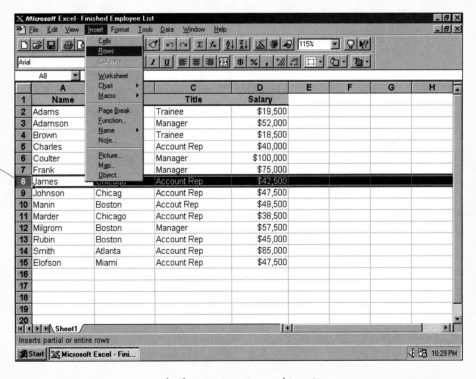

Click row heading
to select row 8

(b) The Insert Rows Command (step 3)

FIGURE 5.5   Hands-on Exercise 1 (continued)

THE FREEZE PANES COMMAND

The Freeze Panes command is useful with large lists as it prevents the column labels (field names) from scrolling off the screen. Click in the first column (field) of the first record. Pull down the Window menu, then click the Freeze Panes command. A horizontal line will appear under the field names to indicate that the command is in effect.

STEP 4: The Spell Check

➤ Select **cells B2:C16** as in Figure 5.5c. Pull down the **Tools menu** and click **Spelling** (or click the **Spelling button** on the Standard toolbar).

➤ Chicago is misspelled in cell B10 and flagged accordingly. Click the **Change command button** to accept the suggested correction and continue checking the document.

➤ Account is misspelled in cell C11 and flagged accordingly. Click **Account** in the Suggestions list box, then click the **Change command button** to correct the misspelling.

➤ Excel will indicate that it has finished checking the selected cells. Click **OK** to return to the worksheet.

➤ Save the workbook.

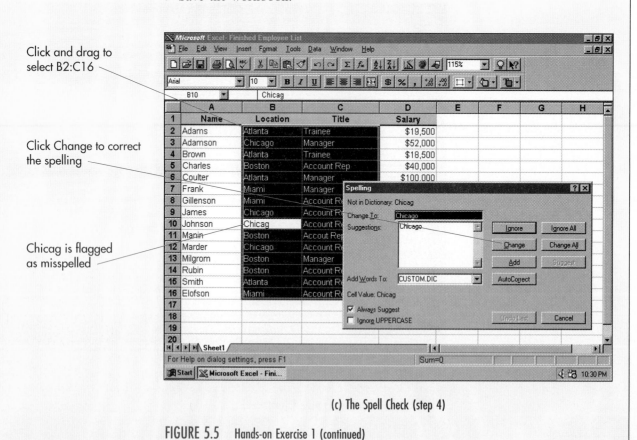

Click and drag to select B2:C16

Click Change to correct the spelling

Chicag is flagged as misspelled

(c) The Spell Check (step 4)

FIGURE 5.5   Hands-on Exercise 1 (continued)

CREATE YOUR OWN SHORTHAND

The AutoCorrect feature is common to all Office applications and corrects mistakes as they are made according to entries in a predefined list. Type "teh", for example, and it is corrected automatically to "the" as soon as you press the space bar. You can use the feature to create your own shorthand by having it expand abbreviations such as "cis" for "Computer Information Systems". Pull down the Tools menu, click AutoCorrect, type the abbreviation in the Replace text box and the expanded entry in the With text box. Click the Add command button, then click OK to exit the dialog box and return to the document. The next time you type cis in a spreadsheet, it will automatically be expanded to Computer Information Systems.

STEP 5: Sort the List

➤ Click a single cell anywhere in the employee list (**cells A1** through **D16**). Pull down the **Data menu.** Click **Sort** to display the dialog box in Figure 5.5d.

• Click the **drop-down arrow** in the Sort By list box. Click **Location** as the primary key.

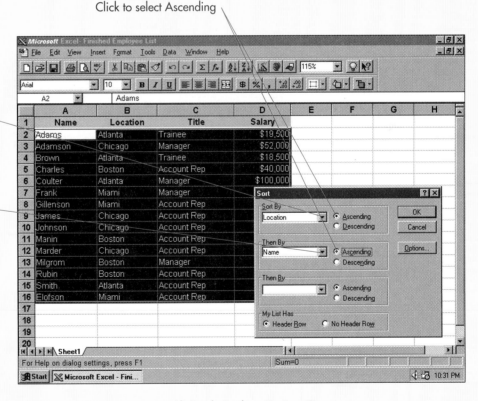

Click to select Ascending

Click to select field name for primary key

Click to select field name for secondary key

(d) Sort the Employee List (step 5)

FIGURE 5.5   Hands-on Exercise 1 (continued)

- Click the **drop-down arrow** in the first Then By list box. Click **Name** as the secondary key.
- Be Sure the **Header Row option button** is checked (so that the field names are not mixed in with the records in the list).
- Check that the **Ascending option button** is selected for both the primary and secondary keys.
- Click **OK** to sort the list and return to the worksheet.

➤ The employees are listed by location and alphabetically within location.

➤ Save the workbook.

USE THE SORT BUTTONS

Use the Sort Ascending or Sort Descending buttons on the Standard toolbar to sort on one or more keys. To sort on a single key, click any cell in the column containing the key, then click the appropriate button, depending on whether you want an ascending or a descending sort. You can also sort on multiple keys, by clicking either button multiple times, but the trick is to do it in the right order. Sort on the least significant field first, then work your way up to the most significant. For example, to sort a list by location, and name within location, sort by name first (the secondary key), then sort by location (the primary key).

STEP 6: Delete a Record

➤ A record may be deleted by using the Edit Delete command or the Data Form command; both methods will be illustrated to delete the record for Frank, which is currently in row 15.

➤ To delete a record by using the Edit Delete command:
- Click the **row heading** in **row 15** (containing the record for Frank, which is slated for deletion).
- Pull down the **Edit menu.** Click **Delete.** Frank has been deleted.

➤ Click the **Undo button** on the Standard toolbar. The record for Frank has been restored.

➤ To delete a record by using the Data Form command:
- Click a single cell within the employee list.
- Pull down the **Data menu.** Click **Form** to display the data form.
- Click the **down arrow** in the scroll bar until you come to the record for Frank.
- Click the **Delete command button.**
- Click **OK** in response to the warning message shown in Figure 5.5e. (The record cannot be undeleted as it could with the Edit Delete command.)
- Click **Close** to close the Data Form.

➤ Save the workbook.

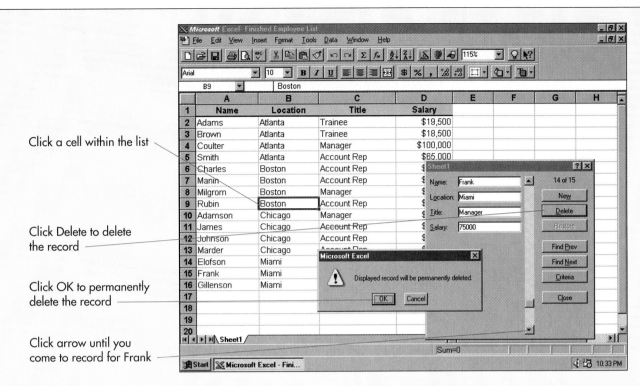

Click a cell within the list

Click Delete to delete
the record

Click OK to permanently
delete the record

Click arrow until you
come to record for Frank

(e) Delete a Record (step 6)

FIGURE 5.5   Hands-on Exercise 1 (continued)

STEP 7: Insert a Field

➤ Click the **column heading** in **column D.** Click the **right mouse button** to display a shortcut menu. Click **Insert.** The employee salaries have been moved to column E.

➤ Click **cell D1.** Type **Hire Date** and press **enter.** Adjust the column width if necessary.

STEP 8: Enter the Hire Dates

➤ Dates may be entered in several different formats. Do not be concerned if Excel displays the date in a different format from the way you entered it.

- Type **11/24/93** in cell D2. Press the **down arrow key.**
- Type **Nov 24, 1993** in cell D3. Type a **comma** after the day, but do not type a period after the month. Press the **down arrow key** to move to cell D4.
- Type **=Date(93,11,24)** in cell D4. Press the **down arrow key.**
- Type **11-24-93** in cell D5.

➤ For ease of data entry, assume that the next several employees were hired on the same day, 3/16/92.

- Click in **cell D6.** Type **3/16/92.** Press **enter.**
- Click in **cell D6.** Click the **Copy button** on the Standard toolbar, which produces a moving border around cell D6. Drag the mouse over **cells D7** through **D10.** Click the **Paste button** on the Standard toolbar to complete the copy operation.
- Press **Esc** to remove the moving border around cell D6.

➤ The last five employees were hired one year apart, beginning October 31, 1989.

- Click in **cell D11** and type **10/31/89.**
- Click in **cell D12** and type **10/31/90.**
- Select **cells D11** and **D12.**
- Drag the **fill handle** at the bottom of cell D12 over **cells D13, D14,** and **D15.** Release the mouse to complete the AutoFill operation.

➤ Save the workbook.

DATES AND THE FILL HANDLE

The AutoFill facility is the fastest way to create a series of dates. Enter the first two dates in the series, then select both cells and drag the fill handle over the remaining cells. Excel will create a series based on the increment between the first two cells; for example, if the first two dates are one month apart, the remaining dates will also be one month apart.

STEP 9: Format the Date

➤ Click in the **column heading** for **column D** to select the column of dates as in Figure 5.5f.

➤ Click the **right mouse button** to display a shortcut menu. Click **Format Cells.**

➤ Click the **Number tab** in the Format Cells dialog box. Click **Date** in the Category list box. Select (click) the date format shown in Figure 5.5f. Click **OK.**

➤ Click elsewhere in the workbook to deselect the dates. Reduce the width of column D as appropriate. Save the workbook.

DATES VERSUS FRACTIONS

A fraction is entered into a cell by preceding the fraction with an equal sign—for example, =1/4. The fraction is displayed as its decimal equivalent (.25) unless the cell is formatted to display fractions. Select the cell, pull down the Format menu, and click the Cells command. Click the Numbers tab, then choose Fraction from the Category list box. Omission of the equal sign, when entering a fraction, treats the entry as a date; that is, typing 1/4 (without the equal sign) will store the entry as a date and display it as January 4th (of the current year).

STEP 10: Exit Excel

➤ Click the **TipWizard button** to open the TipWizard box. Click the **up (down) arrow** to review the suggestions made by the TipWizard during the exercise.

➤ Close the workbook. Exit Excel if you do not want to continue with the next exercise at this time.

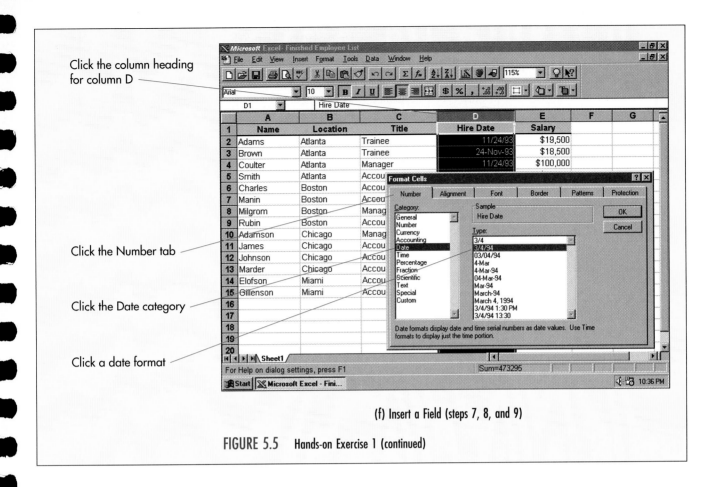

Click the column heading for column D

Click the Number tab

Click the Date category

Click a date format

(f) Insert a Field (steps 7, 8, and 9)

FIGURE 5.5   Hands-on Exercise 1 (continued)

DATA VERSUS INFORMATION

Data and information are not synonymous. *Data* refers to a fact or facts about a specific record, such as an employee's name, title, or salary. *Information,* on the other hand, is data that has been rearranged into a form perceived as useful by the recipient. A list of employees earning more than $35,000 or a total of all employee salaries are examples of information produced from data about individual employees. Put another way, data is the raw material, and information is the finished product.

Decisions in an organization are based on information rather than raw data; for example, in assessing the effects of a proposed across-the-board salary increase, management needs to know the total payroll rather than individual salary amounts. In similar fashion, decisions about next year's hiring will be influenced, at least in part, by knowing how many individuals are currently employed in each job category.

Data is converted to information through a combination of database commands and functions whose capabilities are illustrated by the reports in Figure 5.6. The reports are based on the employee list as it existed at the end of the first hands-on exercise. Each report presents the data in a different way, according to the information requirements of the end-user. As you view each report, ask yourself how it was produced; that is, what was done to the data in order to produce the information?

Figure 5.6a contains a master list of all employees, listing employees by location, and alphabetically by last name within location. The report was created by sorting the list on two keys, location and name. Location is the more important or primary key. Name is the less important or secondary key. The sorted report

Location Report

Name	Location	Title	Hire Date	Salary
Adams	Atlanta	Trainee	11/24/93	$19,500
Brown	Atlanta	Trainee	11/24/93	$18,500
Coulter	Atlanta	Manager	11/24/93	$100,000
Smith	Atlanta	Account Rep	11/24/93	$65,000
Charles	Boston	Account Rep	3/16/92	$40,000
Manin	Boston	Account Rep	3/16/92	$49,500
Milgrom	Boston	Manager	3/16/92	$57,500
Rubin	Boston	Account Rep	3/16/92	$45,000
Adamson	Chicago	Manager	3/16/92	$52,000
James	Chicago	Account Rep	10/31/89	$42,500
Johnson	Chicago	Account Rep	10/31/90	$47,500
Marder	Chicago	Account Rep	10/31/91	$38,500
Elofson	Miami	Account Rep	10/31/92	$47,500
Gillenson	Miami	Account Rep	10/31/93	$55,000

(a) Employees by Location and Name within Location

Employees Earning Between $40,000 and $60,000

Name	Location	Title	Hire Date	Salary
Milgrom	Boston	Manager	3/16/92	$57,500
Gillenson	Miami	Account Rep	10/31/93	$55,000
Adamson	Chicago	Manager	3/16/92	$52,000
Manin	Boston	Account Rep	3/16/92	$49,500
Johnson	Chicago	Account Rep	10/31/90	$47,500
Elofson	Miami	Account Rep	10/31/92	$47,500
Rubin	Boston	Account Rep	3/16/92	$45,000
James	Chicago	Account Rep	10/31/89	$42,500
Charles	Boston	Account Rep	3/16/92	$40,000

(b) Employees Earning between $40,000 and $60,000

Summary Statistics

Total Salary for Account Reps:	$430,500
Average Salary for Account Reps:	$47,833
Maximum Salary for Account Reps:	$65,000
Minimum Salary for Account Reps:	$38,500
Number of Account Reps:	9

(c) Account Rep Summary Data

FIGURE 5.6 Data versus Information

groups employees according to like values of the primary key (location), then within the primary key, groups the records according to the secondary key (name).

The report in Figure 5.6b displays a subset of the records in the list, which includes only those employees that meet specific criteria. The criteria can be based on any field, or combination of fields; in this case, employees whose salary is between $40,000 and $60,000 (inclusive). The employees are shown in descending order of salary so that the employee with the highest salary is listed first.

The report in Figure 5.6c displays summary statistics for the selected employees—in this example, the salaries for the account reps within the company. Reports of this nature omit the salaries of individual employees (known as detail lines), in order to present an aggregate view of the organization.

CITY, STATE, AND ZIP CODE—ONE FIELD OR THREE?

The answer depends on whether the fields are referenced as a unit or individually. However, given the almost universal need to sort or select on zip code, it is almost invariably defined as a separate field. An individual's last name, first name, and middle initial are defined as individual fields for the same reason.

AutoFilter Command

A *filtered list* displays a subset of records that meet a specific criterion or set of criteria. It is created by the **AutoFilter command** (or the Advanced Filter command discussed in the next section). Both commands temporarily hide those records (rows) that do not meet the criteria. The hidden records are *not* deleted; they are simply not displayed.

Figure 5.7a displays the employee list in alphabetical order. Figure 5.7b displays a filtered version of the list in which only the Atlanta employees (in rows 2, 4, 6, and 15) are visible. The remaining employees are still in the worksheet but are not shown as their rows are hidden.

Execution of the AutoFilter command places drop-down arrows next to each column label (field name). Clicking a drop-down arrow produces a list of the

(a) Unfiltered List

(b) Filtered List (Atlanta employees)

FIGURE 5.7   Filter Command

Click drop-down arrow to further filter the list to Atlanta Managers

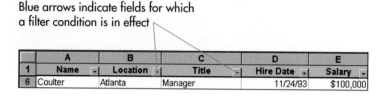

	A	B	C	D	E
1	Name	Location	Title	Hire Date	Salary
2	Adams	Atlanta	(All)	11/24/93	$19,500
4	Brown	Atlanta	(Top 10...)	11/24/93	$18,500
6	Coulter	Atlanta	(Custom...)	11/24/93	$100,000
15	Smith	Atlanta	Account Rep	11/24/93	$65,000
16			Manager		
17			Trainee		
			(Blanks)		
			(NonBlanks)		

(c) Imposing a Second Condition

Blue arrows indicate fields for which a filter condition is in effect

	A	B	C	D	E
1	Name	Location	Title	Hire Date	Salary
6	Coulter	Atlanta	Manager	11/24/93	$100,000

(d) Filtered List (Atlanta managers)

FIGURE 5.7   Filter Command (continued)

unique values for that field, enabling you to establish the criteria for the filtered list. Thus, to display the Atlanta employees, click the drop-down arrow for Location, then click Atlanta.

A filter condition can be imposed on multiple columns as shown in Figure 5.7c. The filtered list in Figure 5.7c contains just the Atlanta employees. Clicking the arrow next to Title, then clicking Manager, will filter the list further to display the employees who work in Atlanta *and* who have Manager as a title. Only one employee meets both conditions, as shown in Figure 5.7d. The drop-down arrows next to Location and Title are displayed in blue to indicate that a filter is in effect for these columns.

The AutoFilter command has additional options as can be seen from the drop-down list box in Figure 5.7c. (All) removes existing criteria in the column and effectively "unfilters" the list. (Custom. . .) enables you to use the relational operators (=, >, <, >=, <=, or <>) within a criterion. (NonBlanks) and (Blanks) select the records that contain, or do not contain, data in the specified field, and are useful in data validation.

Advanced Filter Command

The *Advanced Filter command* extends the capabilities of the AutoFilter command in two important ways. It enables you to develop more complex criteria than are possible with the AutoFilter Command. It also enables you to copy the selected records to a separate area in the worksheet. The Advanced Filter command is illustrated in detail in the hands-on exercise that follows shortly.

Criteria Range

The *criteria range* is used with both the Advanced Filter command and the database functions that are discussed in the next section. It is defined independently of the list on which it operates and exists as a separate area in the worksheet. A criteria range must be at least two rows deep and one column wide as illustrated in Figure 5.8.

First row is field names

Second row is value for filter condition

Name	Location	Title	Hire Date	Salary
	Atlanta			

(a) Employees Who Work in Atlanta

Multiple values in same row

Name	Location	Title	Hire Date	Salary
	Atlanta	Account Rep		

(b) Account Reps Who Work in Atlanta (AND condition)

Multiple values in different rows

Name	Location	Title	Hire Date	Salary
	Atlanta			
		Account Rep		

(c) Employees Who Work in Atlanta or Who Are Account Reps (OR condition)

Relational operators can be used with dates and numeric fields

Name	Location	Title	Hire Date	Salary
			<1/1/93	

(d) Employees Hired before January 1, 1993

Name	Location	Title	Hire Date	Salary
				>$40,000

(e) Employees Who Earn More Than $40,000

Upper boundary

Lower boundary

Name	Location	Title	Hire Date	Salary	Salary
				>$40,000	<$60,000

(f) Employees Who Earn More Than $40,000 but Less Than $60,000

Returns all records with no entry in this field

Name	Location	Title	Hire Date	Salary
	=			

(g) Employees without an Entry in Location

Empty row returns every record in the list

Name	Location	Title	Hire Date	Salary

(h) All Employees (a blank row)

FIGURE 5.8   The Criteria Range

The simplest criteria range consists of two rows and as many columns as there are fields in the list. The first row contains the field names as they appear in the list. The second row holds the value(s) you are looking for. The criteria range in Figure 5.8a selects the employees who work in Atlanta.

Multiple values in the same row are connected by an AND and require that the selected records meet *all* of the specified criteria. The criteria range in Figure 5.8b identifies the account reps in Atlanta; that is, it selects any record in which the Location field is Atlanta *and* the Title field is Account Rep.

Values entered in multiple rows are connected by an OR in which the selected records satisfy *any* of the indicated criteria. The criteria range in Figure 5.8c will identify employees who work in Atlanta *or* whose title is Account Rep.

Relational operators may be used with date or numeric fields to return records within a designated range. The criteria range in Figure 5.8d selects the employees hired before January 1, 1993. The criteria range in Figure 5.8e returns employees whose salary is greater than $40,000.

An upper and lower boundary may be established for the same field by repeating the field within the criteria range. This was done in Figure 5.8f, which returns all records in which the salary is greater than $40,000 but less than $60,000.

The equal and unequal signs select records with empty and nonempty fields, respectively. An equal sign with nothing after it will return all records without an entry in the designated field; for example, the criteria range in Figure 5.8g selects any record that is missing a value for the Location field. An unequal sign (<>) with nothing after it will select all records with an entry in the field.

An empty row in the criteria range returns *every* record in the list, as shown in Figure 5.8h. All criteria are *case insensitive* and return records with any combination of upper- and lowercase letters that match the entry.

THE IMPLIED WILD CARD

Any text entry within a criteria range is treated as though it were followed by the asterisk **wild card;** that is, *New* is the same as *New**. Both entries will return New York and New Jersey. To match a text entry exactly, begin with an equal sign, enter a quotation mark followed by another equal sign, the entry you are looking for, and the closing quotation mark—for example, ="=New" to return only the entries that say New.

Database Functions

The **database functions** DSUM, DAVERAGE, DMAX, DMIN, and DCOUNT operate on *selected* records in a list. These functions parallel the statistical functions presented in Chapter 3 (SUM, AVERAGE, MAX, MIN, and COUNT) except that they affect only records that satisfy the established criteria.

The summary statistics in Figure 5.9 are based on the salaries of the managers in the list, rather than all employees. Each database function includes the criteria range in cells A17:E18 as one of its arguments, and thus limits the employees that are included to managers. The **DAVERAGE function** returns the average salary for just the managers. The **DMAX** and **DMIN functions** display the maximum and minimum salaries for the managers. The **DSUM function** computes the total salary for all the managers. The **DCOUNT function** indicates the number of managers.

	A	B	C	D	E
1	Name	Location	Title	Hire Date	Salary
2	Adams	Atlanta	Trainee	11/24/93	$19,500
3	Adamson	Chicago	Manager	3/16/92	$52,000
4	Brown	Atlanta	Trainee	11/24/93	$18,500
5	Charles	Boston	Account Rep	3/16/92	$40,000
6	Coulter	Atlanta	Manager	11/24/93	$100,000
7	Elofson	Miami	Account Rep	10/31/92	$47,500
8	Gillenson	Miami	Account Rep	10/31/93	$55,000
9	James	Chicago	Account Rep	10/31/89	$42,500
10	Johnson	Chicago	Account Rep	10/31/90	$47,500
11	Manin	Boston	Account Rep	3/16/92	$49,500
12	Marder	Chicago	Account Rep	10/31/91	$38,500
13	Milgrom	Boston	Manager	3/16/92	$57,500
14	Rubin	Boston	Account Rep	3/16/92	$45,000
15	Smith	Atlanta	Account Rep	11/24/93	$65,000
16					
17	Name	Location	Title	Hire Date	Salary
18			Manager		
19					
20					
21			Summary Statistics		
22	Average Salary:				$69,833
23	Maximum Salary:				$100,000
24	Minimum Salary:				$52,000
25	Total Salary:				$209,500
26	Number of Employees:				3

Criteria range is A17:E18 (filters list to Managers)

Summary statistics for Managers

FIGURE 5.9 Database Functions and the Data Extract Command

Each database function has three arguments: the range for the list on which it is to operate, the field to be processed, and the criteria range. Consider, for example, the DAVERAGE function as shown below:

=DAVERAGE(list,"field",criteria)

The criteria range can be entered as a cell range (such as A17:E18) or as a name assigned to a cell range (e.g., Criteria)

The name of the field to be processed is enclosed in quotation marks

The list can be entered as a cell range (such as A1:E15) or as a name assigned to a cell range (e.g., Database).

FORMAT THE DATABASE

Formatting has no effect on the success or failure of database commands, so you can format the entries in a list to any extent you like. Select currency format where appropriate, change fonts, use borders or shading, or any other formatting option. Be sure to format the row containing the column names differently from the rest of the list, so that it can be recognized as the header row in conjunction with the Ascending and Descending Sort buttons on the Standard toolbar.

The entries in the criteria range may be changed at any time, in which case the values of the database functions are automatically recalculated. The other database functions have arguments identical to those used in the DAVERAGE example.

Name Command

The *Name command* in the Insert menu equates a mnemonic name such as *employee_list* to a cell or cell range such as *A1:E15,* then enables you to use that name to reference the cell(s) in all subsequent commands. A name can be up to 255 characters in length, but must begin with a letter or an underscore. It can include upper- or lowercase letters, numbers, periods, and underscore characters.

Once defined, names adjust automatically for insertions and/or deletions within the range. If, in the previous example, you were to delete row 4, the definition of *employee_list* would change to A1:E14. And, in similar fashion, if you were to add a new column between columns B and C, the range would change to A1:F14.

A name can be used in any formula or function instead of a cell address; for example, =SALES−EXPENSES instead of =C1−C10, where Sales and Expenses have been defined as the names for cells C1 and C10, respectively. A name can also be entered into any dialog box where a cell range is required.

THE GO TO COMMAND

Names are frequently used in conjunction with the Go To command. Pull down the Edit menu and click Go To (or click the F5 key) to display a dialog box containing the names that have been defined within the workbook. Double click a name to move directly to the first cell in the associated range and simultaneously select the entire range.   •

HANDS-ON EXERCISE 2

Data versus Information

Objective: To sort a list on multiple keys; to demonstrate the AutoFilter and Advanced Filter commands; to define a named range; to use the DSUM, DAVERAGE, DMAX, DMIN, and DCOUNT functions. Use Figure 5.10 as a guide in the exercise.

STEP 1: Calculate the Years of Service

➤ Start Excel. Reset the TipWizard. Open the **Finished Employee List** workbook created in the previous exercise.

➤ Click the **column heading** in **column D.** Click the **right mouse button** to display a shortcut menu. Click **Insert.** The column of hire dates has been moved to column E.

➤ Click in **cell D1.** Type **Service** and press **enter.**

➤ Click in **cell D2** and enter the formula to compute the years of service **=(Today( )-E2)/365** as shown in Figure 5.10a. Press **enter;** the years of service for the first employee are displayed in cell D2.

➤ Click in **cell D2,** then click the **Decrease Decimal button** on the Formatting toolbar several times to display the length of service with only one decimal place. Reduce the column width as appropriate.

➤ Drag the **fill handle** in cell D2 to the remaining cells in that column (**cells D3** through **D15**) to compute the service for the remaining employees.

Decrease decimal button

Enter field name

Enter =(TODAY( )-E2)/365

Drag fill handle over D3:D15 to copy formula to those cells

	A	B	C	D	E	F	G
1	Name	Location	Title	Service	Hire Date	Salary	
2	Adams	Atlanta	Trainee	1.7	11/24/93	$19,500	
3	Brown	Atlanta	Trainee		11/24/93	$18,500	
4	Coulter	Atlanta	Manager		11/24/93	$100,000	
5	Smith	Atlanta	Account Rep		11/24/93	$65,000	
6	Charles	Boston	Account Rep		3/16/92	$40,000	
7	Manin	Boston	Account Rep		3/16/92	$49,500	
8	Milgrom	Boston	Manager		3/16/92	$57,500	
9	Rubin	Boston	Account Rep		3/16/92	$45,000	
10	Adamson	Chicago	Manager		3/16/92	$52,000	
11	James	Chicago	Account Rep		10/31/89	$42,500	
12	Johnson	Chicago	Account Rep		10/31/90	$47,500	
13	Marder	Chicago	Account Rep		10/31/91	$38,500	
14	Elofson	Miami	Account Rep		10/31/92	$47,500	
15	Gillenson	Miami	Account Rep		10/31/93	$55,000	

(a) Calculate the Years of Service (step 1)

FIGURE 5.10   Hands-on Exercise 2

THE COLUMN HIDE (UNHIDE) COMMAND

The Column Hide command does as its name implies and hides a column from view. Point to the column heading, then click the right mouse button to select the column and display a shortcut menu. Click the Hide command, and the column is no longer visible (although it remains in the worksheet). The column headings will reflect a hidden column in that the letter for the hidden column is not seen. To display (unhide) a hidden column, select (click) the column headings of the adjacent columns on either side, click the right mouse button to display a shortcut menu, then click the Unhide command.

STEP 2: The AutoFilter Command

➤ Click a single cell anywhere within the list. Pull down the **Data menu.** Click the **Filter** command.

➤ Click **AutoFilter** from the resulting cascade menu to display the down arrows to the right of each field name.

➤ Click the **down arrow** next to **Title** to display the list of titles in Figure 5.10b. Click **Account Rep.**

  • The display changes to show only those employees who meet the filter condition.

  • The worksheet is unchanged, but only those rows containing account reps are visible.

  • The row numbers for the visible records are blue.

  • The drop-down arrow for Title is also blue, indicating that it is part of the filter condition.

➤ Click the **down arrow** next to **Location.** Click **Boston** to display only the employees in this city. The combination of the two filter conditions shows only the account reps in Boston.

➤ Click the **down arrow** next to **Location** a second time. Scroll until you can click **All** to remove the filter condition on location. Only the account reps are displayed since the filter on Title is still in effect.

➤ Save the workbook.

Click to display the list of titles

Click a single cell within the list

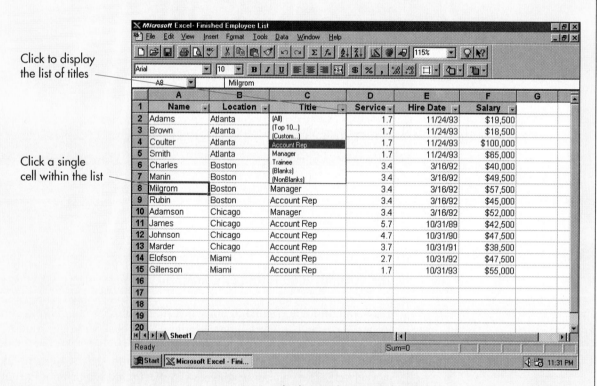

(b) The AutoFilter Command (step 2)

FIGURE 5.10   Hands-on Exercise 2 (continued)

THE TOP 10 AUTOFILTER

To see the records containing the top 10 values in a specific field, turn the AutoFilter condition on, then click the drop-down arrow next to the column heading. Click Top 10 from the list of AutoFilter options, then choose the options you want. You can see any number of the top (or bottom) records by entering the desired values in the Top 10 AutoFilter dialog box. You can also see a desired (top or bottom) percentage rather than a specified number of records. Click the Sort Ascending or Sort Descending button to display the selected records in order.

STEP 3: The Custom AutoFilter Command

➤ Click the **arrow** next to **Salary** to display the list of salaries. Click **Custom** to display the dialog box in Figure 5.10c.

➤ Click the **arrow** in the leftmost drop-down list box for **Salary.** Click the **greater than** sign.

➤ Click in the text box for the salary amount. Type **45000.** Click **OK.**

➤ The list changes to display only those employees whose title is account rep *and* who earn more than $45,000.

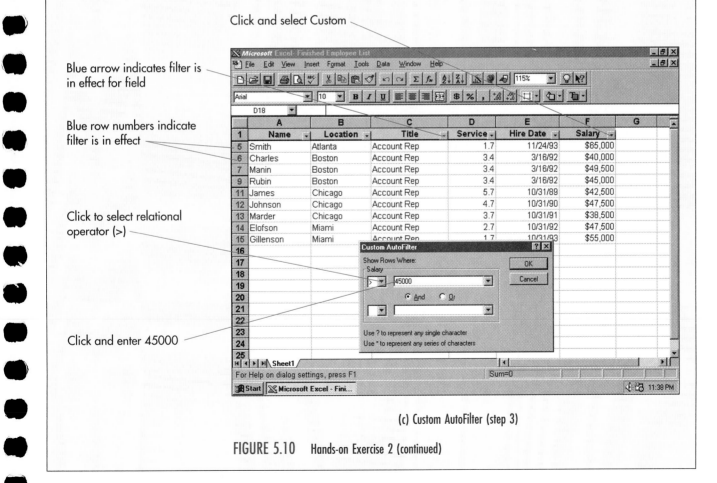

(c) Custom AutoFilter (step 3)

FIGURE 5.10 Hands-on Exercise 2 (continued)

➤ Pull down the **Data menu.** Click **Filter.** Click **AutoFilter** to toggle the Auto-Filter command off, which removes the arrows next to the field names and cancels all filter conditions. All of the records in the list are visible.

WILD CARDS

Excel recognizes the question mark and asterisk as wild cards in the specification of criteria. A question mark stands for a single character in the exact position; for example, B?ll returns Ball, Bill, Bell, and Bull. An asterisk stands for any number of characters; e.g., *son will find Samson, Johnson, and Yohanson.

STEP 4: The Advanced Filter Command

➤ The field names in the criteria range must be spelled exactly the same way as in the associated list. The best way to ensure that the names are identical is to copy the entries from the list to the criteria range.

• Click and drag to select **cells A1** through **F1.**

• Click the **Copy button** on the Standard toolbar. A moving border appears around the selected cells.

• Click in **cell A17.** Click the **Paste button** on the Standard toolbar to complete the copy operation. Press **Esc** to cancel the moving border.

DRAG AND DROP TO NONADJACENT RANGES

You can use the mouse to copy selected cells to a *nonadjacent* range provided the source and destination ranges are the same size and shape. Select the cells to be copied, point to any border of the selected cells (the mouse pointer changes to an arrow), then press and hold the Ctrl key (a plus sign appears) as you drag the selection to its destination. Release the mouse to complete the operation. Follow the same procedure, without pressing the Ctrl key, to move rather than copy the selected cells to a nonadjacent range.

➤ Click in **cell C18.** Enter **Manager.** (Be sure you spell it correctly.)

➤ Click a single cell anywhere within the employee list. Pull down the **Data menu.** Click **Filter.** Click **Advanced Filter** from the resulting cascade menu to display the dialog box in Figure 5.10d. (The range is already entered because you had selected a cell in the list prior to executing the command.)

➤ Click in the **Criteria Range** text box. Click in **cell A17** in the worksheet and drag the mouse to cell F18. Release the mouse. A moving border appears around these cells in the worksheet, and the corresponding cell reference is entered in the dialog box.

➤ Check that the **option button** to Filter the List, in-place is selected. Click **OK.** The display changes to show just the managers; that is, only rows 4, 8, and 10 are visible.

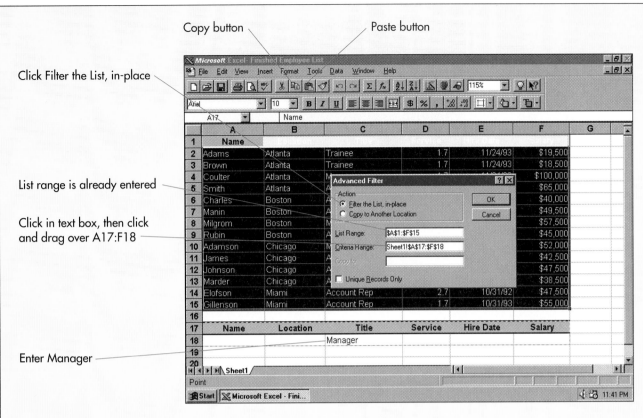

Copy button   Paste button

Click Filter the List, in-place

List range is already entered

Click in text box, then click
and drag over A17:F18

Enter Manager

(d) Advanced Filter Command (step 4)

FIGURE 5.10   Hands-on Exercise 2 (continued)

➤ Click in **cell B18.** Type **Atlanta.** Press **enter.**

➤ Pull down the **Data menu.** Click **Filter.** Click **Advanced Filter.** The Advanced
Filter dialog box already has the cell references for the List and Criteria
ranges (which were the last entries made).

➤ Click **OK.** The display changes to show just the manager in Atlanta; that is,
only row 4 is visible.

➤ Pull down the **Data menu.** Click **Filter.** Click **Show All** to remove the filter
condition. The entire list is visible.

STEP 5: The Insert Name Command

➤ Click and drag to select **cells A1** through **F15** as shown in Figure 5.10e.

➤ Pull down the **Insert menu.** Click **Name.** Click **Define.** Type **Database** in the
Define Name dialog box. Click **OK.**

➤ Pull down the **Edit menu** and click **Go To** (or press the **F5 key**) to display
the Go To dialog box. There are two names in the box: Database, which you
just defined, and Criteria, which was defined automatically when you specified the criteria range in step 4.

➤ Double click **Criteria** to select the criteria range (**cells A17** through **F18**).
Click elsewhere in the worksheet to deselect the cells.

➤ Save the workbook.

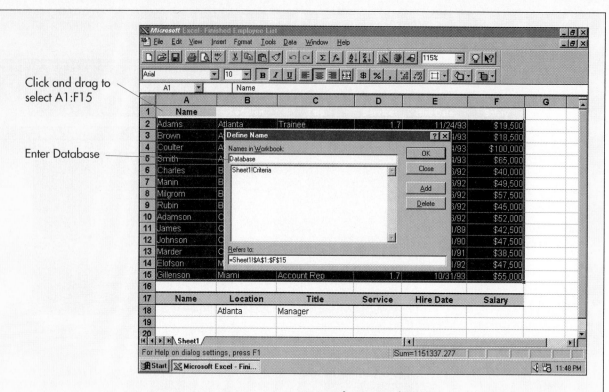

Click and drag to
select A1:F15

Enter Database

(e) Name Define Command (step 5)

FIGURE 5.10   Hands-on Exercise 2 (continued)

THE NAME BOX

Use the *Name box* on the formula bar to select a cell or named range by clicking in the box and then typing the appropriate cell reference or name. You can also click the down arrow next to the Name box to select a named range from a drop-down list. And, finally, you can use the Name box to define a named range, by first selecting the cell(s) in the worksheet to which the name is to apply, clicking in the Name box in order to enter the range name, and then pressing the enter key.

STEP 6: Database Functions (The Function Wizard)

➤ Click in **cell A21.** Type **Summary Statistics.** Select **cells A21** through **F21,** then click the **Center Across Columns** button on the Formatting toolbar to center the heading over the selected cells.

➤ Enter the labels for **cells A22** through **A26** as shown in Figure 5.10f.

➤ Click in **cell B18.** Press the **Del key.** The criteria range is now set to select only managers.

➤ Click in **cell F22.** Click the **Function Wizard button** on the Standard toolbar to display the dialog box in Figure 5.10f.

➤ Select **Database** in the Function Category list box. Select **DAVERAGE** as the function name, then click the **Next command button** to move to step 2 of the Function Wizard.

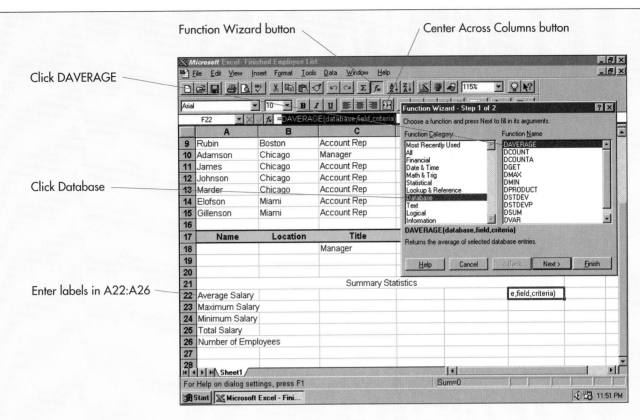

Function Wizard button

Center Across Columns button

Click DAVERAGE

Click Database

Enter labels in A22:A26

(f) Function Wizard (step 6)

FIGURE 5.10   Hands-on Exercise 2 (continued)

DATABASE FUNCTIONS

Database functions should always be placed above or below the list to which they refer, rather than to the left or right. This is done to ensure that (the rows containing) the database functions will always be visible, even when a filter condition is in effect.

STEP 7: The DAVERAGE Function

➤ Click the **database** text box in the Function Wizard dialog box of Figure 5.10g. Type **Database** (the range name defined in step 5), which references the employee list.

➤ Click the **field** text box. Type **Salary,** which is name of the field within the list that you want to average.

➤ Click the **criteria** text box. Type **Criteria** (the range name defined during the Advanced Filter operation). The Function Wizard displays the computed value of 69833.33333.

➤ Click the **Finish command button** to enter the DAVERAGE function into the worksheet.

➤ Save the workbook.

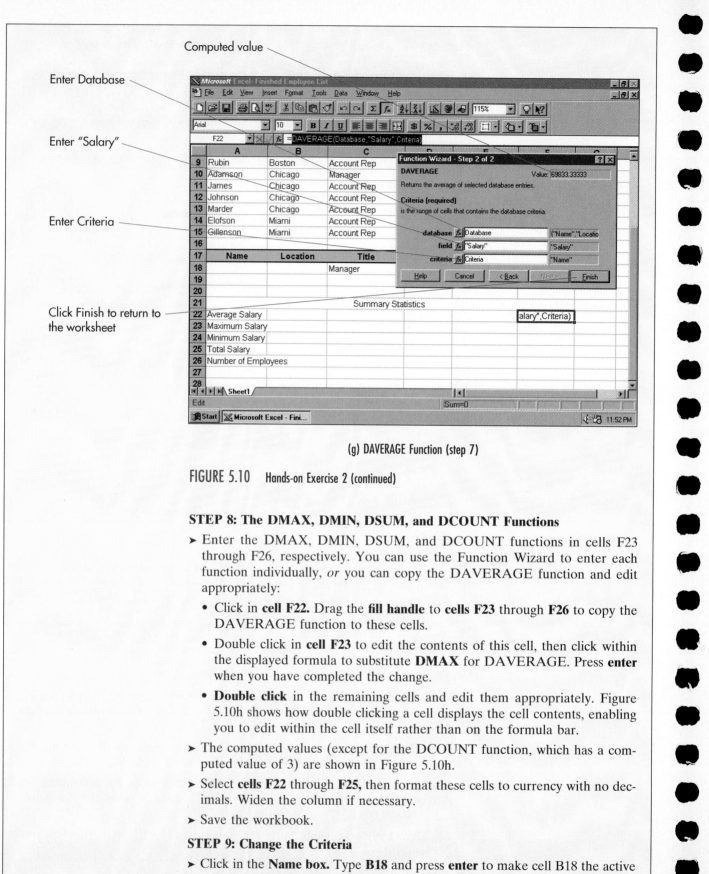

Computed value

Enter Database

Enter "Salary"

Enter Criteria

Click Finish to return to the worksheet

(g) DAVERAGE Function (step 7)

FIGURE 5.10   Hands-on Exercise 2 (continued)

STEP 8: The DMAX, DMIN, DSUM, and DCOUNT Functions

➤ Enter the DMAX, DMIN, DSUM, and DCOUNT functions in cells F23 through F26, respectively. You can use the Function Wizard to enter each function individually, *or* you can copy the DAVERAGE function and edit appropriately:

• Click in **cell F22.** Drag the **fill handle** to **cells F23** through **F26** to copy the DAVERAGE function to these cells.

• Double click in **cell F23** to edit the contents of this cell, then click within the displayed formula to substitute **DMAX** for DAVERAGE. Press **enter** when you have completed the change.

• **Double click** in the remaining cells and edit them appropriately. Figure 5.10h shows how double clicking a cell displays the cell contents, enabling you to edit within the cell itself rather than on the formula bar.

➤ The computed values (except for the DCOUNT function, which has a computed value of 3) are shown in Figure 5.10h.

➤ Select **cells F22** through **F25,** then format these cells to currency with no decimals. Widen the column if necessary.

➤ Save the workbook.

STEP 9: Change the Criteria

➤ Click in the **Name box.** Type **B18** and press **enter** to make cell B18 the active cell. Type **Chicago** to change the criteria to Chicago managers. Press **enter.**

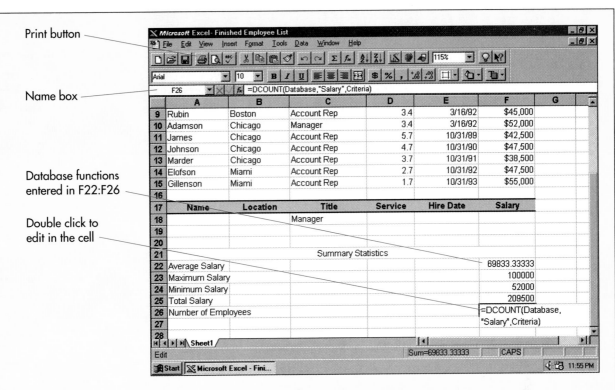

Print button

Name box

Database functions entered in F22:F26

Double click to edit in the cell

(h) DMAX, DMIN, DSUM, and DCOUNT Functions (step 8)

FIGURE 5.10   Hands-on Exercise 2 (continued)

➤ The values displayed by the DAVERAGE, DMIN, DMAX, and DSUM functions change to $52,000, reflecting the one employee (Adamson) who meets the current criteria (a manager in Chicago). The value displayed by the DCOUNT function changes to 1 to indicate one employee.

➤ Click in **cell C18.** Press the **Del key.**

➤ The average salary changes to $45,125, reflecting all employees in Chicago.

➤ Click in **cell B18.** Press the **Del key.**

➤ The criteria range is now empty. The DAVERAGE function displays $48,429, which is the average salary of all employees in the database.

➤ Click in **cell C18.** Type **Manager** and press the **enter key.** The average salary is $69,833, the average salary for all managers.

CLEAR THE CRITERIA RANGE

Clear the existing values within the criteria range before you enter new values, especially when the selection criteria are based on different fields. If, for example, you are changing from managers in any location (Title = Manager) to all employees in Chicago (Location = Chicago), you must clear the title field, or else you will get only employees who are managers and work in Chicago.

SUBTOTALS

The *Subtotals command* in the Data menu computes subtotals based on data groups in a selected field. It also computes a grand total. The totals may be displayed with or without the detail lines as shown in Figure 5.11. Figure 5.11a displays the employee list as well as the totals. Figure 5.11b displays only the totals.

Execution of the Subtotals command inserts a subtotal row into the list whenever the value of the selected field (Location in this example) changes from row to row. In Figure 5.11a the subtotal for the Atlanta employees is inserted into

	A	B	C	D	E	F
1	Name	Location	Title	Service	Hire Date	Salary
2	Adams	Atlanta	Trainee	1.7	11/24/93	$19,500
3	Brown	Atlanta	Trainee	1.7	11/24/93	$18,500
4	Coulter	Atlanta	Manager	1.7	11/24/93	$100,000
5	Smith	Atlanta	Account Rep	1.7	11/24/93	$65,000
6		Atlanta Total				$203,000
7	Charles	Boston	Account Rep	3.4	3/16/92	$40,000
8	Manin	Boston	Account Rep	3.4	3/16/92	$49,500
9	Milgrom	Boston	Manager	3.4	3/16/92	$57,500
10	Rubin	Boston	Account Rep	3.4	3/16/92	$45,000
11		Boston Total				$192,000
12	Adamson	Chicago	Manager	3.4	3/16/92	$52,000
13	James	Chicago	Account Rep	5.7	10/31/89	$42,500
14	Johnson	Chicago	Account Rep	4.7	10/31/90	$47,500
15	Marder	Chicago	Account Rep	3.7	10/31/91	$38,500
16		Chicago Total				$180,500
17	Elofson	Miami	Account Rep	2.7	10/31/92	$47,500
18	Gillenson	Miami	Account Rep	1.7	10/31/93	$55,000
19		Miami Total				$102,500
20		Grand Total				$678,000

Atlanta subtotal — (row 6)
Boston subtotal — (row 11)

(a) Detail Lines

	A	B	C	D	E	F
1	Name	Location	Title	Service	Hire Date	Salary
6		Atlanta Total				$203,000
11		Boston Total				$192,000
16		Chicago Total				$180,500
19		Miami Total				$102,500
20		Grand Total				$678,000

Only totals are displayed

(b) Summary Lines (SUM function)

FIGURE 5.11 The Subtotals Command

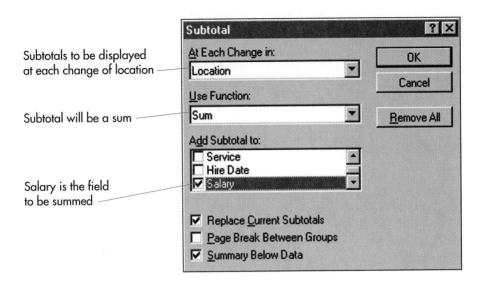

Subtotals to be displayed
at each change of location

Subtotal will be a sum

Salary is the field
to be summed

(c) Subtotals Dialog Box

FIGURE 5.11   The Subtotals Command (continued)

the list as we go from the last employee in Atlanta to the first employee in Boston. In similar fashion, the subtotal for Boston is inserted into the list as we go from the last employee in Boston to the first employee in Chicago. It is critical, therefore, that the list be in sequence according to the field on which the subtotals will be based, *prior* to executing the Subtotals command.

Figure 5.11c displays the Subtotal dialog box set to display the subtotals in Figure 5.11a. The various list boxes within the dialog box show the flexibility within the command. You can specify when the subtotals will be computed (in this example, at each change in the Location field). You can specify the function to use (sum in this example, but average, max, min, and count are also available). Finally, you can specify the field(s) for which the computation is to take place (Salary). Subtotals are removed from a worksheet by re-executing the Subtotals command and clicking the Remove All command button.

PIVOT TABLES

A *pivot table* extends the capability of individual database functions by presenting the data in summary form. It divides the records in a list into categories, then computes summary statistics for those categories. The pivot tables in Figure 5.12, for example, compute statistics based on salary and location.

The pivot table in Figure 5.12a displays the number of employees in each location according to job title. The column labels are the unique values within the list for the Location field. The row labels are the unique values within the list for the Title field. The values in the table show the number of employees in each

Number of Account
Reps in Atlanta

	A	B	C	D	E	F
1	Count of Name	Location				
2	Title	Atlanta	Boston	Chicago	Miami	Grand Total
3	Account Rep	1	3	3	2	9
4	Manager	1	1	1	0	3
5	Trainee	2	0	0	0	2
6	Grand Total	4	4	4	2	14

(a) Number of Employees in Each Job Title at Each Location

FIGURE 5.12   Pivot Tables

Total salaries for Account Reps in Atlanta →

	A	B	C	D	E	F
1	Sum of Salary	Location				
2	Title	Atlanta	Boston	Chicago	Miami	Grand Total
3	Account Rep	$65,000	$134,500	$128,500	$102,500	$430,500
4	Manager	$100,000	$57,500	$52,000	$0	$209,500
5	Trainee	$38,000	$0	$0	$0	$38,000
6	Grand Total	$203,000	$192,000	$180,500	$102,500	$678,000

(b Total Salaries for Each Job Title and at Each Location

FIGURE 5.12   Pivot Tables (continued)

Title–Location combination. Figure 5.12b uses the identical categories (Title and Location) but computes the total salaries instead of the number of employees. Both pivot tables are based on the employee list we have been using throughout the chapter.

A pivot table is created by using the ***PivotTable Wizard,*** which prompts you for the information to develop the pivot table. You indicate the field names for the row and column labels (Title and Location in Figures 5.12a and 5.12b). You also indicate the field on which the computation is to be based and the means of computation (a count of names in Figure 5.12a and a summation of Salary in Figure 5.12b). The PivotTable Wizard does the rest. It creates the pivot table in its own worksheet within the same workbook as the list on which it is based.

Pivot tables provide the utmost in flexibility, in that you can vary the row or column categories and/or the way the statistics are computed. Figure 5.13a illustrates a different pivot table, in which we analyze by gender rather than location. This table computes two statistics rather than one, and displays the number of employees as well as the average salary for each combination of title and gender.

The PivotTable dialog box in Figure 5.13b shows just how easy it is to create a pivot table. The field names within the associated list appear at the right of the dialog box. To create the pivot table, you simply drag a field name(s) to the row, column, or data areas of the table. Click the Next command button to supply the finishing touches to the pivot table, after which the pivot table will appear in its own worksheet.

Once a pivot table has been created, you can easily add or remove categories by dragging the field names on or off the table within the PivotTable Wizard. You can also switch the orientation (pivot the table) by dragging a field to or from the row or column area. And finally, you can modify the worksheet on which the pivot table is based (by adding, editing, or deleting employee records), then refresh the pivot table to reflect the changes made to the worksheet.

Two statistics computed (count and average salary) →

	A	B	C	D	E
1			Gender		
2	Title	Data	F	M	Grand Total
3	Account Rep	Count of Name	5	4	9
4		Average of Salary	$45,600	$50,625	$47,833
5	Manager	Count of Name	1	2	3
6		Average of Salary	$52,000	$78,750	$69,833
7	Trainee	Count of Name	1	1	2
8		Average of Salary	$18,500	$19,500	$19,000
9	Total Count of Name		7	7	14
10	Total Average of Salary		$42,643	$54,214	$48,429

(a) The Pivot Table

FIGURE 5.13   The PivotTable Wizard

Field names within associated list

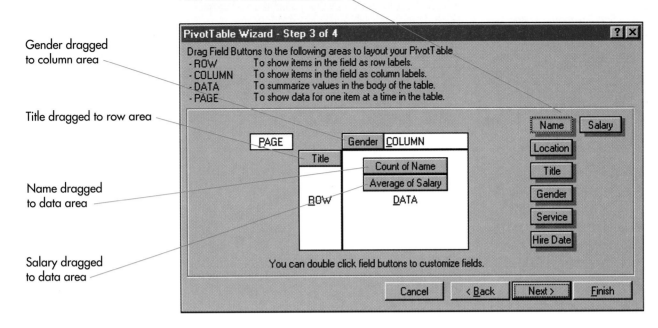

Gender dragged
to column area

Title dragged to row area

Name dragged
to data area

Salary dragged
to data area

(b) The PivotTable Wizard

FIGURE 5.13   The PivotTable Wizard (continued)

HANDS-ON EXERCISE 3

Subtotals and Pivot Tables

Objective: To display and modify subtotals within a list; to use the PivotTable Wizard to create and modify a pivot table. Use Figure 5.14 as a guide in the exercise.

STEP 1: Open the Workbook

➤ Open the **Finished Employee List** workbook from the previous exercise. Clear the criteria range in row 18 so that the summary statistics pertain to all employees.

➤ Click any cell in **column C,** the column containing the employee titles. Click the **Sort Ascending button** on the Standard toolbar. The employees should be arranged according to title within the worksheet, as shown in Figure 5.14a. (This is the field on which the subtotals will be grouped.)

➤ Point to the **column heading** in **column D,** which presently contains the length of service. Press the **right mouse button** to display a shortcut menu. Click **Insert** to insert a new column.

➤ Click in **cell D1.** Type **Gender** (the field name). Press the **down arrow key** to move to **cell D2.** Type **M.**

➤ Add the remaining entries in column D to match those in Figure 5.14a.

➤ Drag the border between the column headings for columns D and E to the left to make column D narrower.

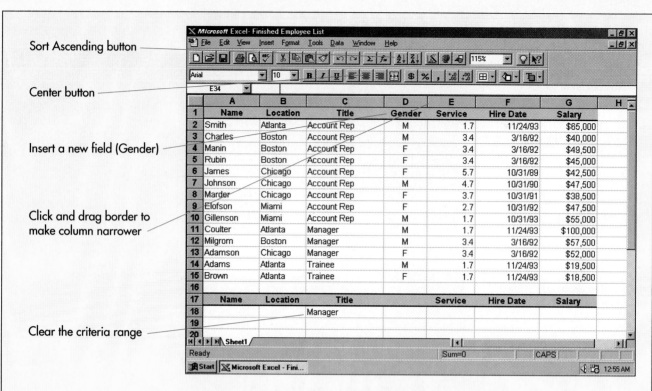

Sort Ascending button

Center button

Insert a new field (Gender)

Click and drag border to
make column narrower

Clear the criteria range

(a) Insert a Field (step 1)

FIGURE 5.14   Hands-on Exercise 3

➤ Click and drag to select **cells D2** through **D15.** Click the **Center button** on
the Formatting toolbar.

➤ Click outside the selected cells to deselect the range. Save the workbook.

THE DOCUMENTS SUBMENU

One of the fastest ways to get to a recently used document, regardless of
the application, is through the Windows 95 Start menu, which includes a
Documents submenu containing the last 15 documents that were opened.
Click the Start button, click (or point to) the Documents submenu, then
click the document you wish to open (e.g., Finished Employee List),
assuming that it appears on the submenu.

STEP 2: Create the Subtotals

➤ Click anywhere in the employee list. Pull down the **Data menu.** Click **Subtotals** to display the Subtotal dialog box in Figure 5.14b.

➤ Click the **arrow** in the At Each Change in list box. Click **Title** to create a
subtotal whenever there is a change in title.

➤ Set the other options to match the dialog box in Figure 5.14b. Click **OK** to
create the subtotals.

Click to select Title, creating a subtotal at each change in title

Click to select Sum as the computation to be performed

Click to select Salary as the field to be summed

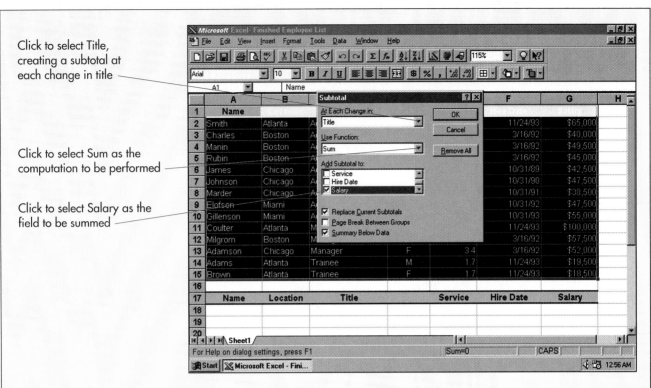

(b) Create the Subtotals (step 2)

FIGURE 5.14   Hands-on Exercise 3 (continued)

STEP 3: Examine the Subtotals

➤ Your worksheet should display subtotals as shown in Figure 5.14c.

➤ Click in **cell G11,** the cell containing the Account Rep subtotal. The formula bar displays =SUBTOTAL(9,G2:G10), which computes the sum for cells G2 through G10. (The number 9 within the argument of the function indicates a sum.)

➤ Click in **cell G15,** the cell containing the Manager subtotal. The formula bar displays =SUBTOTAL(9,G12:G14), which computes the sum for cells G12 through G14.

➤ Click the **level 2 button** (under the Name box) to suppress the detail lines. The list collapses to display the subtotals and grand total.

THE SUBTOTAL FUNCTION

The *SUBTOTAL function* can be entered explicitly into a worksheet or implicitly (and more easily) through the Subtotal command in the Data menu. The function has two arguments: a function number to indicate the type of computation, and the associated cell range. A function number of 9 indicates a sum; thus, the entry =SUBTOTAL(9,E2:E10) computes the sum for cells E2 through E10. Pull down the Help menu and search on the SUBTOTAL function for additional information.

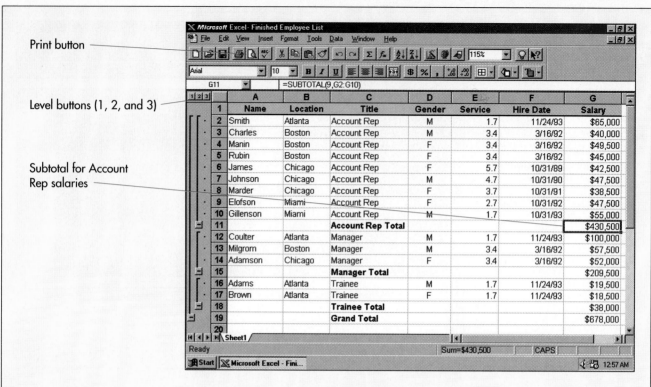

Print button

Level buttons (1, 2, and 3)

Subtotal for Account Rep salaries

	A	B	C	D	E	F	G
1	Name	Location	Title	Gender	Service	Hire Date	Salary
2	Smith	Atlanta	Account Rep	M	1.7	11/24/93	$65,000
3	Charles	Boston	Account Rep	M	3.4	3/16/92	$40,000
4	Manin	Boston	Account Rep	F	3.4	3/16/92	$49,500
5	Rubin	Boston	Account Rep	F	3.4	3/16/92	$45,000
6	James	Chicago	Account Rep	F	5.7	10/31/89	$42,500
7	Johnson	Chicago	Account Rep	M	4.7	10/31/90	$47,500
8	Marder	Chicago	Account Rep	F	3.7	10/31/91	$38,500
9	Elofson	Miami	Account Rep	F	2.7	10/31/92	$47,500
10	Gillenson	Miami	Account Rep	M	1.7	10/31/93	$55,000
11			**Account Rep Total**				$430,500
12	Coulter	Atlanta	Manager	M	1.7	11/24/93	$100,000
13	Milgrom	Boston	Manager	M	3.4	3/16/92	$57,500
14	Adamson	Chicago	Manager	F	3.4	3/16/92	$52,000
15			**Manager Total**				$209,500
16	Adams	Atlanta	Trainee	M	1.7	11/24/93	$19,500
17	Brown	Atlanta	Trainee	F	1.7	11/24/93	$18,500
18			**Trainee Total**				$38,000
19			**Grand Total**				$678,000
20							

(c) Examine the Subtotals (step 3)

FIGURE 5.14 Hands-on Exercise 3 (continued)

➤ Click the **level 1 button** to suppress the subtotals. The list collapses further to display only the grand total.

➤ Click the **level 3 button** to restore the detail lines and subtotals. The list expands to display the employee records, subtotals, and grand total.

➤ Save the workbook. Click the **Print button** on the Standard toolbar if you wish to print the list with the subtotals.

STEP 4: The PivotTable Wizard

➤ The subtotals must be cleared in order to create a pivot table. Click anywhere within the employee list or subtotals. Pull down the **Data menu.** Click **Subtotals.** Click the **Remove All command button.**

➤ Pull down the **Data menu.** Click **PivotTable** to produce step 1 of the PivotTable Wizard. The option button indicates the pivot table will be created from data in a Microsoft Excel List or Database.

➤ Click the **Next command button** to move to step 2 of the PivotTable Wizard. You will see a dialog box where **Database** (the name assigned to the employee list in Hands-on Exercise 2) has already been entered in the Range text box.

➤ Click the **Next command button** to move to step 3 as shown in Figure 5.14d:

• Click the **Title field button** and drag it to the row area.

• Click the **Location field button** and drag it to the column area.

• Click the **Salary field button** and drag it to the data area. (Sum is the default computation for a numeric field, such as Salary. Count is the default computation for a text field, such as Name.)

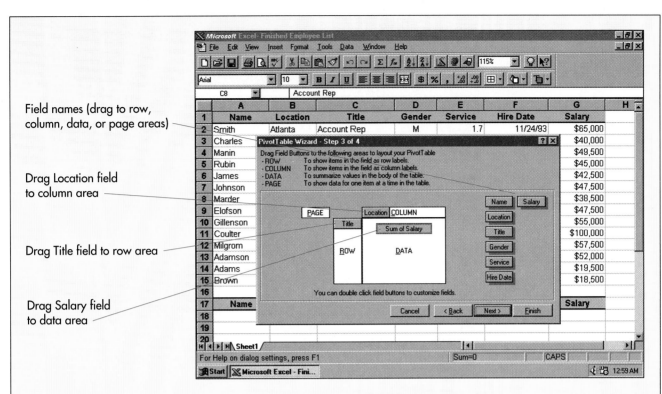

Field names (drag to row, column, data, or page areas)

Drag Location field to column area

Drag Title field to row area

Drag Salary field to data area

(d) The PivotTable Wizard (step 4)

FIGURE 5.14   Hands-on Exercise 3 (continued)

➤ Click the **Next command button** to move to step 4, the final step in the Pivot-Table Wizard:

- The check boxes for all four options should be selected.
- The text box for the PivotTable starting cell should be blank so that the pivot table is created in its own worksheet.

➤ Click the **Finish command button** to create the pivot table and exit the Pivot-Table Wizard. Save the workbook.

FIXED VERSUS FLOATING TOOLBARS

Any toolbar can be docked along the edge of the application window, or it can be displayed as a floating toolbar within the application window. To move a docked toolbar, drag the toolbar background. To move a floating toolbar, drag its title bar. To size a floating toolbar, drag any border in the direction you want to go. Double click the background of any toolbar to toggle between a floating toolbar and a docked (fixed) toolbar.

STEP 5: Modify the Pivot Table

➤ The pivot table is in its own worksheet, and the Query and Pivot toolbar is displayed automatically as shown in Figure 5.14e.

PivotTable Wizard button

Click within the pivot table

Name field button

Drag Gender field
to page area

Drag Name field
to data area

Gender field button

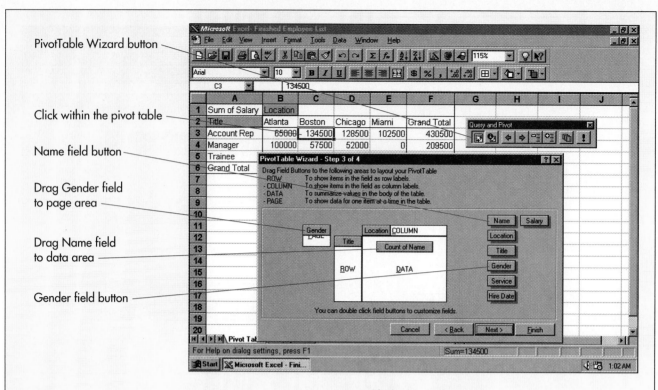

(e) Modify the Pivot Table (step 5)

FIGURE 5.14   Hands-on Exercise 3 (continued)

➤ Rename the worksheets within the workbook:

- Point to the **Sheet2 tab** and click the **right mouse button** to display a short-cut menu. Click **Rename** to display the Rename sheet dialog box. Type **Pivot Table** as the new name of the tab. Click **OK.**

- Point to the **Sheet1 tab** and click the **right mouse button** to display a short-cut menu. Click **Rename** to display the Rename Sheet dialog box. Type **Employee List** as the new name. Click **OK.**

➤ Click the **PivotTable tab** to return to this worksheet, then click anywhere within the pivot table.

➤ Click the **PivotTable Wizard button** on the Query and Pivot toolbar to reopen the PivotTable wizard as shown in Figure 5.14e. (If you are not on step 3 of the PivotTable Wizard, it is because you did not click in the pivot table prior to invoking the Wizard. Click Cancel, click in the pivot table, then click the PivotTable Wizard button.)

- Click and drag the **Name field button** to the data area. The button displays "Count of Name" (the default function for a text field).

- Click and drag the **Gender field** to the page area.

- Click and drag the **Salary field button** out of the data area.

- Click the **Next command button.** Click the **Finish command button.**

➤ The pivot table changes to display the number of employees for each location–title combination. Note that there are two account reps and no managers or trainees in Miami.

THE PAGE FIELD

A page field adds a third dimension to a pivot table. Unlike items in the row and column fields, however, the items in a page field are displayed one at a time. Creating a page field on gender, for example, enables you to view the data for each gender separately, by clicking the drop-down arrow on the page field list box, then clicking the appropriate value of gender. You can see the statistics for all male employees, for all female employees, or for all employees (both male and female).

STEP 6: Modify the Employee List

➤ Click the **Employee List tab** to return to the employee worksheet.

➤ Click in **cell C10.** Type **Manager.** Press **enter** to change Gillenson's title from account rep to manager. Note that Gillenson works in Miami.

➤ Click the **PivotTable tab** to return to the pivot table. There are still two account reps and no managers or trainees in Miami because Gillenson's change in title is not yet reflected in the pivot table.

➤ Click within the pivot table, then click the **Refresh Data button** on the Query and Pivot toolbar to update the pivot table.

➤ Miami now has one manager and one account rep, which reflects the change made to the employee list with respect to Gillenson's change of title. Save the workbook.

REFRESH THE PIVOT TABLE

The data in a pivot table is tied to an underlying list and cannot be edited directly. Thus, to change the data in a pivot table, you must edit the underlying list. Any changes in the list, however, are not reflected in the pivot table until the pivot table is refreshed. Click anywhere in the pivot table, then click the Refresh Data button on the Query and Pivot toolbar to update the pivot table.

STEP 7: Pivot the Table

➤ The pivot table on your monitor should match Figure 5.14f with Gender, Title, and Location as the page, row, and column fields, respectively.

➤ Click and drag the **Gender button** next to the Location button. The page field disappears, and there are now two column fields, Gender and Location.

➤ Click and drag the **Location button** to the previous location of the Gender field to make Location a page field. You have changed the orientation of the table and have a completely different analysis.

STEP 8: The Completed Pivot Table

➤ The pivot table has been modified as shown in Figure 5.14g. Location is now the page field and Gender is the column field. This arrangement of the table

Refresh Data button

Change reflects 1 Account
Rep and 1 Manager
in Miami

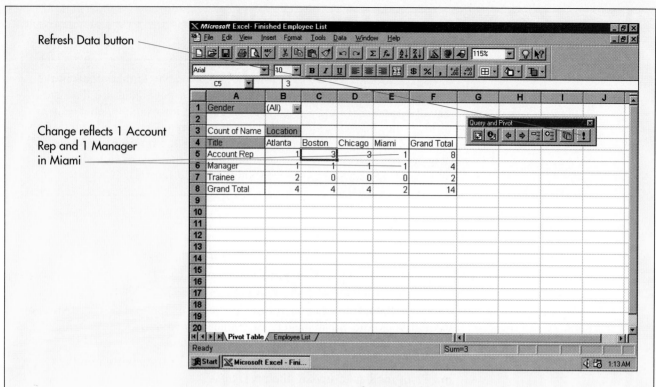

(f) Pivot the Table (step 7)

Drag Location to page area

Drag Gender to column area

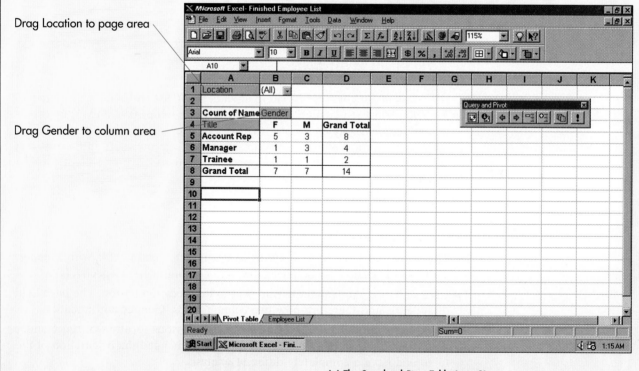

(g) The Completed Pivot Table (step 8)

FIGURE 5.14   Hands-on Exercise 3 (continued)

makes it easy to see the number of male and female employees in each job classification.

➤ Boldface the row and column labels of the pivot table in order to improve its appearance.

➤ Center the column labels. Center all of the values in the pivot table under their respective headings.

➤ Save the workbook. Print the completed workbook and submit it to your instructor. Exit Excel.

SUMMARY

A list is an area in a worksheet that contains rows of similar data. The first row contains the column labels (field names), and each additional row contains a record. A data form provides an easy way to add, edit, and delete records in a list.

Data and information are not synonymous. Data refers to a fact or facts about a specific record, such as an employee's name, title, or salary. Information is data that has been rearranged into a form perceived as useful by the recipient.

A date is stored internally as an integer number corresponding to the number of days in this century. (January 1, 1900 is stored as the number 1.) The number of elapsed days between two dates can be determined by simple subtraction. The TODAY function always returns the current date (the date on which a worksheet is created or retrieved).

A filtered list displays only those records that meet specific criteria. Filtering is implemented through AutoFilter or the Advanced Filter command.

The Sort command arranges a list according to the value of one or more keys. Each key may be in ascending or descending sequence.

The database functions (DSUM, DAVERAGE, DMAX, DMIN, and DCOUNT) have three arguments: the associated list, the field name, and the criteria range. The simplest criteria range consists of two rows and as many fields as there are in the list.

The Subtotals command inserts subtotals (based on a variety of functions) into a list. A list should be sorted prior to execution of the Subtotals command.

A pivot table extends the capability of individual database functions by presenting the data in summary form. It divides the records in a list into categories, then computes summary statistics for those categories. Pivot tables provide the utmost flexibility in that you can vary the row or column categories and/or the way that the statistics are computed.

KEY WORDS AND CONCEPTS

Advanced Filter command	Database functions	DSUM function
Ascending sequence	DAVERAGE function	Field
AutoFilter command	DCOUNT function	Field name
Criteria range	Delete command	File
Data	Descending sequence	Filtered list
Data form	DMAX function	Form command
	DMIN function	Information

Insert Columns command	Name command	Sort command
Insert Rows command	Pivot table	Subtotals command
Key	PivotTable Wizard	SUBTOTAL function
List	Primary key	Tertiary key
Name box	Record	TODAY() function
	Secondary key	Wild card

MULTIPLE CHOICE

1. Which of the following describes the implementation of data management in Excel?
   (a) The rows in a list correspond to records in a file
   (b) The columns in a list correspond to fields in a record
   (c) Both (a) and (b)
   (d) Neither (a) nor (b)

2. Which of the following is suggested for the placement of a list within a worksheet?
   (a) There should be at least one blank row between the list and the other entries in the worksheet
   (b) There should be at least one blank column between the list and the other entries in the worksheet
   (c) Both (a) and (b)
   (d) Neither (a) nor (b)

3. Which of the following is suggested for the placement of database functions within a worksheet?
   (a) Above or below the list with at least one blank row separating the database functions from the list to which they refer
   (b) To the left or right of the list with at least one blank column separating the database functions from the list to which they refer
   (c) Both (a) and (b)
   (d) Neither (a) nor (b)

4. Assume that cells A21:B22 have been defined as the criteria range, that cells A21 and B21 contain the field names City and Title, respectively, and that cells A22 and B22 contain New York and Manager. The selected records will consist of:
   (a) All employees in New York, regardless of title
   (b) All managers, regardless of the city
   (c) Only the managers in New York
   (d) All employees in New York (regardless of title) or all managers (regardless of city)

5. Assume that cells A21:B23 have been defined as the criteria range, that cells A21 and B21 contain the field names City and Title, respectively, and that cells A22 and B23 contain New York and Manager, respectively. The selected records will consist of:
   (a) All employees in New York regardless of title
   (b) All managers regardless of the city

(c) Only the managers in New York

(d) All employees in New York (regardless of title) or all managers (regardless of city)

6. If employees are to be listed so that all employees in the same city appear together in alphabetical order by the employee's last name:

(a) City and last name are both considered to be the primary key

(b) City and last name are both considered to be the secondary key

(c) City is the primary key and last name is the secondary key

(d) Last name is the primary key and city is the secondary key

7. Which of the following can be used to delete a record from a database?

(a) The Edit Delete command

(b) The Data Form command

(c) Both (a) and (b)

(d) Neither (a) nor (b)

8. Which of the following is true about the DAVERAGE function?

(a) It has a single argument

(b) It can be entered into a worksheet using the Function Wizard

(c) Both (a) and (b)

(d) Neither (a) nor (b)

9. The Name box can be used to:

(a) Define a range name

(b) Select the range

(c) Both (a) and (b)

(d) Neither (a) nor (b)

10. Which of the following is recommended to distinguish the first row in a list (the field names) from the remaining entries (the data)?

(a) Insert a blank row between the first row and the remaining rows

(b) Insert a row of dashes between the first row and the remaining rows

(c) Either (a) or (b)

(d) Neither (a) nor (b)

11. The AutoFilter command:

(a) Permanently deletes records from the associated list

(b) Requires the specification of a criteria range elsewhere in the worksheet

(c) Either (a) or (b)

(d) Neither (a) nor (b)

12. Which of the following is true of the Sort command?

(a) The primary key must be in ascending sequence

(b) The secondary key must be in descending sequence

(c) Both (a) and (b)

(d) Neither (a) nor (b)

13. What is the best way to enter January 21, 1996 into a worksheet, given that you create the worksheet on that date, and further, that you always want to display that specific date?

(a) =TODAY()

(b) 1/21/96

(c) Both (b) and (b) are equally acceptable

(d) Neither (a) nor (b)

14. Which of the following best describes the relationship between the Sort and Subtotals commands?

(a) The Sort command should be executed before the Subtotals command

(b) The Subtotals command should be executed before the Sort command

(c) The commands can be executed in either sequence

(d) There is no relationship because the commands have nothing to do with one another

15. Which of the following changes may be implemented in an existing pivot table?

(a) A row field may be added or deleted

(b) A column field may be added or deleted

(c) Both (a) and (b)

(d) Neither (a) nor (b)

ANSWERS

1. c	**6.** c	**11.** d
2. c	**7.** c	**12.** d
3. a	**8.** b	**13.** b
4. c	**9.** c	**14.** a
5. d	**10.** d	**15.** c

EXPLORING EXCEL 7.0

1. Use Figure 5.15 to match each action with its result; a given action may be used more than once or not at all.

Action	Result
a. Click at 3, drag to 2, click at 7	_____ Create a pivot table
	_____ Select a range name
b. Click at 9	_____ Add a record, using a data form
c. Click at 13	_____ Create salary subtotals for each
d. Click at 11	location
e. Click at 4, click at 6	_____ Hide records not meeting the
f. Click at 5 and enter the new data	current criteria
	_____ Sort the list
g. Click at 10	_____ Rename the active worksheet
h. Click at 8	_____ Delete Adamson's record
i. Click at 12	_____ Enter a new city for Manin
j. Click at 1, then click the right mouse button	_____ Assign a name to the criteria range

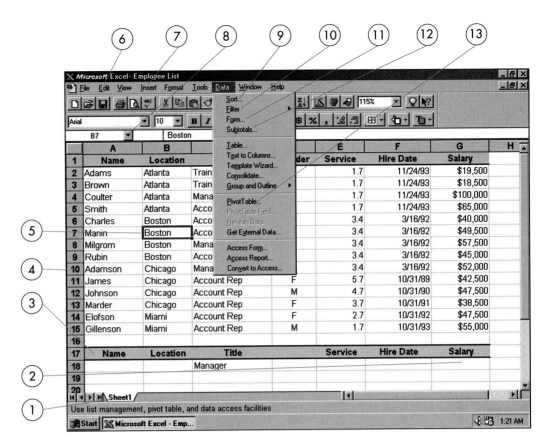

FIGURE 5.15   Screen for Problem 1

2. Careful attention must be given to designing a list, or else the resulting system will not perform as desired. Consider the following:

   a. An individual's age may be calculated from his or her birth date, which in turn can be stored as a field within a record. An alternate technique would be to store age directly in the record and thereby avoid the calculation. Which field—that is, age or birth date—would you use? Why?

   b. Social security number is typically chosen as a record key instead of a person's name. What attribute does the social security number possess that makes it the superior choice?

   c. Zip code is normally stored as a separate field to save money at the post office in connection with a mass mailing. Why?

   d. An individual's name is normally divided into two (or three) fields corresponding to the last name and first name (and middle initial). Why is this done; that is, what would be wrong with using a single field consisting of the first name, middle initial, and last name, in that order?

3. Troubleshooting: The informational messages in Figure 5.16 appeared (or could have appeared) in response to commands that were executed in the various hands-on exercises in the chapter. Indicate the command that was executed prior to each message and the appropriate response.

4. Answer the following with respect to the pivot table in Figure 5.17:

   a. What are the row field(s)? The column field(s)? The page field(s)?

   b. What are the data field(s)? What is the means of computation for each data field?

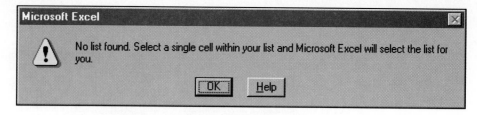

(a) Informational Message 1

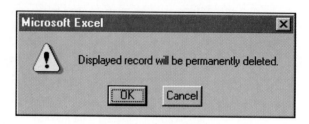

(b) Informational Message 2

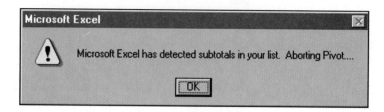

(c) Informational Message 3

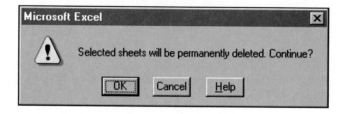

(d) Informational Message 4

FIGURE 5.16   Informational Messages for Problem 3

	A	B	C	D	E
1	Location	Boston			
2					
3			Gender		
4	Title	Data	F	M	Grand Total
5	Account Rep	Count of Name	2	1	3
6		Average of Salary	$47,250	$40,000	$44,833
7	Manager	Count of Name	0	1	1
8		Average of Salary	#DIV/0!	$57,500	$57,500
9	Total Count of Name		2	2	4
10	Total Average of Salary		$47,250	$48,750	$48,000

FIGURE 5.17   Pivot Table for Problem 4

c. Why does the pivot table display data for only four employees when the underlying worksheet contains 14 employees? Would refreshing the pivot table display the data for all 14 employees?

d. What is the significance of the #DIV/0! entry?

e. A second manager, Ms. Henderson, was hired to manage the Boston office at a salary of $62,250. What values will change in the pivot table as a result of the new employee?

Practice with Excel 7.0

1. Figure 5.18 displays the *Chapter 5 Practice 1* workbook as it exists on the data disk. Open the workbook, then implement the following changes:

a. Delete the record for Julie Rubin, who has dropped out of school.

b. Change the data in Rick Fegin's record to show 193 quality points.

c. Use the Data Form command to add a transfer student, Jimmy Flynn, majoring in Engineering. Jimmy has completed 65 credits and has 200 quality points. Use the Tab key to move from one field to the next within the data form; be sure to enter the data in the appropriate text boxes. You cannot enter Jimmy's GPA as it will be computed automatically.

d. Sort the list so that the students are listed in alphabetical order. Specify last name and first name as the primary and secondary keys, respectively.

e. Create the Dean's List by using the Advanced Filter command to copy the qualified students (those with a GPA > 3.20) to cells A22 through A27. Use A19:F20 as the criteria range.

f. Create the list of students on academic probation by using the Advanced Filter command to copy the selected students (those with a GPA < 2.00) to cells A33 through A40. Use A30:F31 as the criteria range for this Advanced Filter command.

g. Add your name as the academic advisor in cell C1. Print the worksheet two ways, with displayed values and cell formulas, and submit both to your instructor.

2. The worksheet in Figure 5.19 is used to determine information about Certificates of Deposit purchased at First National Bank of Miami. A partially completed version of the worksheet can be found in the *Chapter 5 Practice 2* workbook on the data disk. Retrieve the workbook from the data disk, then develop the necessary formulas so that your workbook matches the completed version.

Realize, however, that displayed values on your worksheet will be different from those displayed in the figure in that you are making the calculations on a different day. Thus, when you retrieve the workbook, the entry in cell B1 will reflect the current date, rather than the date in the figure. Other numbers, such as the days to maturity and the indication of whether a CD has matured, will change as well.

Completion of the workbook reviews material from earlier chapters, specifically the use of relative and absolute addressing, and the IF function to determine the maturity status. The determination of whether or not the CD has matured can be made by comparing the Maturity date to the current date; that is, if the Maturity date is greater than the current date, the CD has not yet matured.

	A	B	C	D	E	F
1	Academic Advisor:					
2						
3	Last Name	First Name	Major	Quality Points	Credits	GPA
4	Moldof	Alan	Engineering	60	20	3.00
5	Stutz	Joel	Engineering	180	75	2.40
6	Rubin	Julie	Liberal Arts	140	65	2.15
7	Milgrom	Richard	Liberal Arts	400	117	3.42
8	Grauer	Jessica	Liberal Arts	96	28	3.43
9	Moldof	Adam	Business	160	84	1.90
10	Grauer	Benjamin	Business	190	61	3.11
11	Rudolph	Eleanor	Liberal Arts	185	95	1.95
12	Ford	Judd	Engineering	206	72	2.86
13	Fegin	Rick	Communications	190	64	2.97
14	Flynn	Sean	Business	90	47	1.91
15	Coulter	Maryann	Liberal Arts	135	54	2.50
16						
17						
18	The Dean's List					
19	Last Name	First Name	Major	Quality Points	Credits	GPA
20						
21						
22	Last Name	First Name	Major	Quality Points	Credits	GPA
23						
24						
25						
26						
27						
28						
29	Academic Probation					
30	Last Name	First Name	Major	Quality Points	Credits	GPA
31						
32						
33	Last Name	First Name	Major	Quality Points	Credits	GPA
34						
35						
36						
37						
38						
39						
40						

FIGURE 5.18   Spreadsheet for Practice Exercise 1

	A	B	C	D	E	F
1	Date:	7/30/95				
2						
3			Certificates of Deposit			
4			First National Bank of Miami			
5						
6	Customer	Amount of CD	Date Purchased	Duration	Maturity Date	# Days Remaining Til Mature
7	Harris	$500,000	4/15/95	180	10/12/95	74
8	Bodden	$50,000	1/5/95	180	7/4/95	Mature
9	Dorsey	$25,000	7/18/95	180	1/14/96	168
10	Rosell	$10,000	8/1/94	365	8/1/95	2
11	Klinger	$10,000	5/31/95	365	5/30/96	305

FIGURE 5.19   Spreadsheet for Practice Exercise 2

The workbook on the data disk is unformatted, so you will have to add formatting. Be sure to add your name to the worksheet as a bank officer. Print the worksheet two ways, with displayed values and cell formulas, and submit both to your instructor.

3. Figure 5.20 is a revised version of the employee list that was used throughout the chapter. A field has been added for an employee's previous salary as well as two additional fields for computations based on the previous salary. A partially completed version of this worksheet can be found on the data disk as *Chapter 5 Practice 3*.

	A	B	C	D	E	F	G	Previous H	I	J
	Name	Location	Title	Gender	Service	Hire Date	Salary	Previous Salary	Increase	Percentage
1	Johnson	Chicago	Account Rep	M	4.7	10/31/90	$47,500	$40,000	$7,500	18.75%
2	Rubin	Boston	Account Rep	F	3.4	3/16/92	$45,000	$40,000	$5,000	12.50%
3	Coulter	Atlanta	Manager	M	1.7	11/24/93	$100,000	$90,000	$10,000	11.11%
4	Manin	Boston	Account Rep	F	3.4	3/16/92	$49,500	$45,000	$4,500	10.00%
5	Marder	Chicago	Account Rep	F	3.7	10/31/91	$38,500	$35,000	$3,500	10.00%
6	Elofson	Miami	Account Rep	F	2.7	10/31/92	$47,500	$45,000	$2,500	5.56%
7	Gillenson	Miami	Account Rep	M	1.7	10/31/93	$55,000	$52,500	$2,500	4.76%
8	Milgrom	Boston	Manager	M	3.4	3/16/92	$57,500	$55,000	$2,500	4.55%
9	James	Chicago	Account Rep	F	5.7	10/31/89	$42,500	$41,000	$1,500	3.66%
10	Adams	Atlanta	Trainee	M	1.7	11/24/93	$19,500			
11	Brown	Atlanta	Trainee	F	1.7	11/24/93	$18,500			
12	Smith	Atlanta	Account Rep	M	1.7	11/24/93	$65,000			
13	Charles	Boston	Account Rep	M	3.4	3/16/92	$40,000			
14	Adamson	Chicago	Manager	F	3.4	3/16/92	$52,000			
15										
16	Name	Location	Title	Gender	Service	Hire Date	Salary	Previous Salary	Increase	Percentage
17								>0		
18										
19										
20										
21						Evaluation of Salary Increase				
22						Average Increase		$4,389	8.99%	
23						Maximum Increase		$10,000	18.75%	
24						Minimum Increase		$1,500	3.66%	
25						Number of Employees		9	9	

FIGURE 5.20   Spreadsheet for Practice Exercise 3

The employees in the workbook on the data disk appear in a different sequence from the list in Figure 5.20. Hence, when you open the workbook, you must first determine the proper sequence in which to sort the employees. Note, too, that the recently hired employees do not have a previous salary, and thus the formulas to compute the amount of the salary increase and the associated percent salary increase must first determine if the employee actually had an increase. (You can suppress zero values in a spreadsheet through the View tab in the Options command of the Tools menu.) The summary statistics at the bottom of the worksheet reflect only those employees who actually had an increase.

Complete the workbook on the data disk so that it matches Figure 5.20. Add your name somewhere in the workbook as compensation analyst. Print the cell formulas as well as the displayed values and submit both to your instructor.

4. The compound document in Figure 5.21 consists of a memo created in Microsoft Word and a modified version of the pivot table created in the third hands-on exercise. The document was created in such a way that any change in the worksheet will be automatically reflected in the memo.

The methodology for linking an Excel worksheet to a Word document was presented in Chapter 4 (pages 171–180). Use the same technique to

Soleil Shoes

Italy, London, Madrid

Dear John,

Enclosed please find the salary analysis you requested last Friday. I have broken down the salaries by title and location.

Sum of Salary	Location				
Title	Atlanta	Boston	Chicago	Miami	Grand Total
Account Rep	$65,000	$134,500	$128,500	$47,500	$375,500
Manager	$100,000	$57,500	$52,000	$55,000	$264,500
Trainee	$38,000	$0	$0	$0	$38,000
Grand Total	$203,000	$192,000	$180,500	$102,500	$678,000

I noticed that the manager in Atlanta is paid disproportionately well compared to his counterparts in the other cities. Let me know if you need any other information.

Bob

FIGURE 5.21   Compound Document for Practice Exercise 4

create the compound document in Figure 5.21. Sign your name so that your instructor will know the document came from you.

We want you to create the compound document and submit it to your instructor. You will have to return to the pivot table at the end of the third hands-on exercise in order to modify the table so that it matches Figure 5.21. (Don't forget to format the table.) Then you will have to open Microsoft Word in order to create the memo, and finally you will have to link the worksheet to the memo. *Print this version of the memo and submit it to your instructor.*

Prove to yourself that Object Linking and Embedding really works by returning to the Excel worksheet *after* you have created the document in Figure 5.21. Change Milgrom's salary in cell G12 to $75,000, then refresh (and reformat) the pivot table in the Excel workbook. Switch back to the Word memo, and the pivot table should reflect the adjusted salary (the total of all salaries should be $695,500). Add a postscript to the memo indicating that this reflects Milgrom's revised salary, then print the revised memo and submit it to your instructor with the earlier version.

Case Studies

The United States of America

What is the total population of the United States? What is its area? Can you name the 13 original states or the last five states admitted to the Union? Do you know the 10 states with the highest population or the five largest states in terms of area? Which states have the highest population density (people per square mile)?

The answers to these and other questions are readily available provided you can analyze the data in the *United States* workbook that is available on the data disk. This assignment is completely open-ended and requires only that you print out the extracted data in a report on the United States database. Format the reports so that they are attractive and informative.

The Super Bowl

How many times has the National Football Conference (NFC) won the Super Bowl? When was the last time the American Football Conference (AFC) won? What was the largest margin of victory? What was the closest game? What is the most points scored by two teams in one game? How many times have the Miami Dolphins appeared? How many times did they win? Use the data in the *Super Bowl* workbook to prepare a trivia sheet on the Super Bowl, then incorporate your analysis into a letter addressed to NBC Sports. Convince them you are a super fan and that you merit two tickets to next year's game.

Personnel Management

You have been hired as the Personnel Director for a medium-sized firm (500 employees) and are expected to implement a system to track employee compensation. You want to be able to calculate the age of every employee as well as their length of service. You want to know each employee's most recent performance evaluation. You want to calculate the amount of the most recent salary increase, in dollars as well as a percentage of the previous salary. You also want to know how long the employee had to wait for that increase—that is, how much time elapsed between the present and previous salary.

Design a worksheet capable of providing this information. Enter test data for at least five employees to check the accuracy of your formulas. Format the worksheet so that it is attractive and easy to read.

Equal Employment Opportunity

Are you paying your employees fairly? Is there any difference between the salaries paid to men and women? between minorities and nonminorities? between minorities of one ethnic background versus those of another ethnic background? Use the *Equal Employment* workbook on the data disk to analyze the data for the current employees. Are there any other factors not included in the database that might reasonably be expected to influence an employee's compensation? Write up your findings in the form of a memo to the Vice President for Human Resources.

CONSOLIDATING DATA: 3-D WORKBOOKS AND FILE LINKING

OBJECTIVES

After reading this chapter you will be able to:

1. Distinguish between a cell reference, a worksheet reference, and a 3-D reference; use appropriate references to consolidate data from multiple worksheets within a workbook.

2. Select and group multiple worksheets in order to enter common formulas and/or formats.

3. Explain the advantage of using a function rather than a formula when consolidating data from multiple worksheets.

4. Explain the importance of properly organizing and documenting a workbook.

5. Use the Copy and Paste commands to copy selected data to a second workbook; copy an entire worksheet by dragging its tab from one workbook to another.

6. Distinguish between a source workbook and a dependent workbook; create external references to link workbooks to one another.

OVERVIEW

This chapter considers the problem of combining data from different sources into a summary report. Assume, for example, that you are the marketing manager for a national corporation with offices in several cities. Each branch manager reports to you on a quarterly basis, providing detailed information about each product sold in his or her office. Your job is to consolidate the data from the individual offices into a single report.

The situation is depicted graphically in Figure 6.1. Figures 6.1a, 6.1b, and 6.1c show reports for the Atlanta, Boston, and Chicago

Atlanta Office

	Qtr 1	Qtr 2	Qtr 3	Qtr 4
Product 1	$10	$20	$30	$40
Product 2	$1,100	$1,200	$1,300	$1,400
Product 3	$200	$200	$300	$400

(a)

Boston Office

	Qtr 1	Qtr 2	Qtr 3	Qtr 4
Product 1	$55	$25	$35	$45
Product 2	$150	$250	$350	$450
Product 3	$1,150	$1,250	$1,350	$1,400

(b)

Chicago Office

	Qtr 1	Qtr 2	Qtr 3	Qtr 4
Product 1	$850	$950	$1,050	$1,150
Product 2	$100	$0	$300	$400
Product 3	$75	$150	$100	$200

(c)

Corporate Totals

	Qtr 1	Qtr 2	Qtr 3	Qtr 4
Product 1	$915	$995	$1,115	$1,235
Product 2	$1,350	$1,450	$1,950	$2,250
Product 3	$1,425	$1,600	$1,750	$2,000

(d)

FIGURE 6.1   Consolidating Data

offices, respectively. Figure 6.1d shows the summary report for the corporation as a whole.

You should be able to reconcile the corporate totals with the detail amounts in each office. Consider, for example, the sales of Product 1 in the first quarter. The Atlanta office has sold $10, the Boston office $55, and the Chicago office $850; thus, the corporation as a whole has sold $915 ($10+$55+$850). In similar fashion, the Atlanta, Boston, and Chicago offices have sold $1100, $150, and $100, respectively, of Product 2 in the first quarter, for a corporate total of $1,350.

The chapter presents two different approaches to compute the corporate totals in Figure 6.1. One approach is to use the three-dimensional capability within Excel, in which one workbook contains multiple worksheets. The workbook contains a separate worksheet for each of the three branch offices, and a fourth worksheet to hold the corporate data. An alternate technique is to keep the data for each branch office in its own workbook, then create a summary workbook that uses file linking to reference cells in the other workbooks.

There are advantages and disadvantages to each technique, as will be discussed in the chapter. As always, the hands-on exercises are essential to mastering the conceptual material.

THE THREE-DIMENSIONAL WORKBOOK

An Excel workbook is the electronic equivalent of the three-ring binder. It contains one or more worksheets, each of which is identified by a tab at the bottom of the document window. The workbook in Figure 6.2, for example, contains four worksheets. The title bar displays the name of the workbook (Corporate Sales).

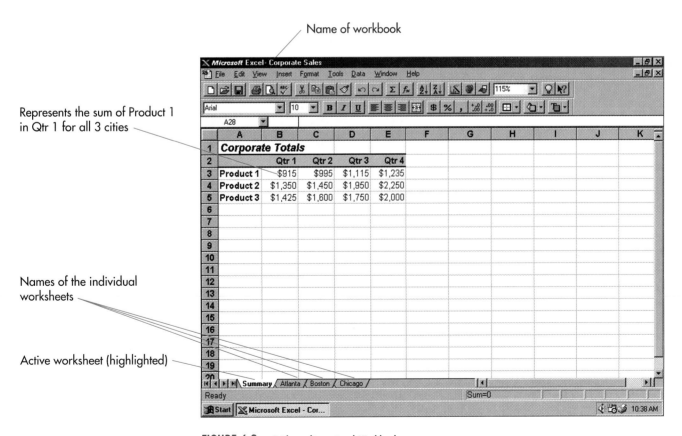

FIGURE 6.2   A Three-dimensional Workbook

The tabs at the bottom of the workbook window display the names of the individual worksheets (Summary, Atlanta, Boston, and Chicago). The highlighted tab indicates the name of the active worksheet (Summary). To display a different worksheet, click on a different tab; for example, click the Atlanta tab to display the Atlanta worksheet.

The Summary worksheet shows the total amount for each product in each quarter. The data in the worksheet reflects the amounts shown earlier in Figure 6.1; that is, each entry in the Summary worksheet represents the sum of the corresponding entries in the worksheets for the individual cities. The amounts in the individual cities, however, are not visible in Figure 6.2. It is convenient, therefore, to open multiple windows in order to view the individual city worksheets at the same time you view the summary sheet.

Figure 6.3 displays the four worksheets in the Corporate Sales workbook, with a different sheet displayed in each window. The individual windows are smaller than the single view in Figure 6.2, but you can see at a glance how the Summary worksheet consolidates the data from the individual worksheets. The *New Window command* (in the Window menu) is used to open each additional window. Once the windows have been opened, the *Arrange command* (in the Window menu) is used to tile or cascade the open windows.

Only one window can be active at a time, and all commands apply to just the active window. In Figure 6.3, for example, the window in the upper left is active, as can be seen by the highlighted title bar. (To activate a different window, just click in that window.)

Copying Worksheets

The workbook in Figure 6.3 summarizes the data in the individual worksheets, but how was the data placed in the workbook? You could, of course, manually type

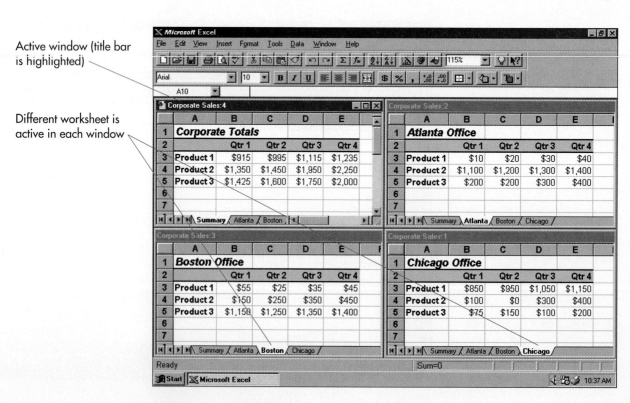

FIGURE 6.3   Multiple Worksheets

in the entries, but there is an easier way, given that each branch manager sends you a workbook with the data for his or her office. All you have to do is copy the data from the individual workbooks into the appropriate worksheets in a new corporate workbook. (The specifics for how this is done are explained in detail in a hands-on exercise.)

Consider now Figure 6.4, which at first glance appears almost identical to Figure 6.3. The two figures are very different, however. Figure 6.3 displayed four different worksheets from the same workbook. Figure 6.4, on the other hand, displays four different workbooks. There is one workbook for each city (Atlanta, Boston, and Chicago) and each of these workbooks contains only a single worksheet. The fourth workbook, Corporate Sales, contains four worksheets (Atlanta, Boston, Chicago, and Summary) and is the workbook displayed in Figure 6.3.

THE HORIZONTAL SCROLL BAR

The horizontal scroll bar contains four **tab scrolling buttons** to scroll through the worksheet tabs in a workbook. (The default workbook has 16 worksheets.) Click ◄ or ► to scroll one tab to the left or right. Click |◄ or ►| to scroll to the first or last tab in the workbook. Once the desired tab is visible, click the tab to select it. The number of tabs that are visible simultaneously depends on the setting of the horizontal scroll bar; that is, you can drag the **tab split box** to change the number of tabs that can be seen at one time.

Atlanta is the open workbook

Corporate Sales is the open (and active) workbook

Chicago is the open workbook

Workbook contains four worksheets

Boston is the open workbook

Workbook contains only one worksheet

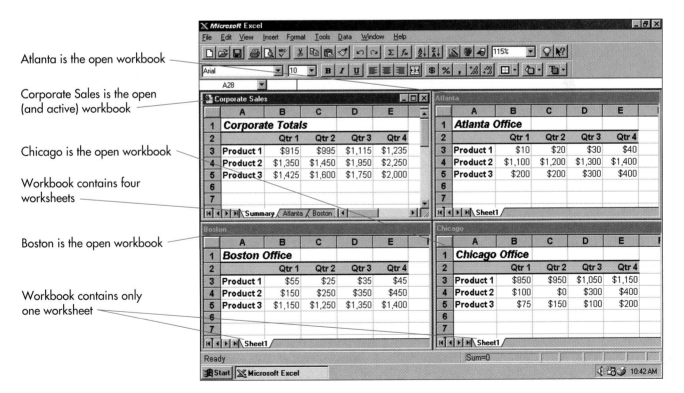

FIGURE 6.4   Multiple Workbooks

Objective: Open multiple workbooks; use the Windows Arrange command to tile the open workbooks; copy a worksheet from one workbook to another. Use Figure 6.5 as a guide in the exercise.

STEP 1: Open a New Workbook

➤ Start Excel. If necessary, click the **New button** on the Standard toolbar to open a new workbook.

➤ Delete all worksheets except for Sheet1:

- Click the tab for **Sheet2.** Press the ▶| **key** to scroll to the last sheet in the workbook (Sheet16).

- Press the **Shift key** as you click the tab for Sheet 16. (Sheets 2 through 16 should be selected and their worksheet tabs appear in white.)

- Point to the tab for **Sheet16** and click the **right mouse button** to display a shortcut menu. Click **Delete.** Click **OK** in response to the warning that the selected sheets will be permanently deleted.

➤ The workbook should contain only Sheet1 as shown in Figure 6.5a. Save the workbook as **Corporate Sales** in the **Exploring Excel folder.**

THE DEFAULT WORKBOOK

A new workbook contains 16 worksheets, but you can change the default value to any number. Pull down the Tools menu, click Options, then click the General tab. Click the up (down) arrow in the Sheets in New Workbook text box to enter a new default value, then click OK to exit the Options dialog box and continue working. The next time you open a new workbook, it will contain the new number of worksheets.

STEP 2: Open the Individual Workbooks

➤ Pull down the **File menu.** Click **Open** to display the Open dialog box as shown in Figure 6.5a.

➤ Click the **Atlanta workbook,** then press and hold the **Ctrl key** as you click the **Boston** and **Chicago workbooks** to select all three workbooks at the same time.

➤ Click **Open** to open the selected workbooks. The workbooks will be opened one after another with a brief message appearing on the status bar as each workbook is opened.

➤ Pull down the **Window menu,** which should indicate the four open workbooks at the bottom of the menu. Only the Chicago workbook is visible at this time.

➤ Click **Arrange** to display the Arrange Windows dialog box. If necessary, select the Tile option, then click **OK.** You should see four open workbooks as shown in Figure 6.5b. (Do not be concerned if your workbooks are arranged differently from ours.)

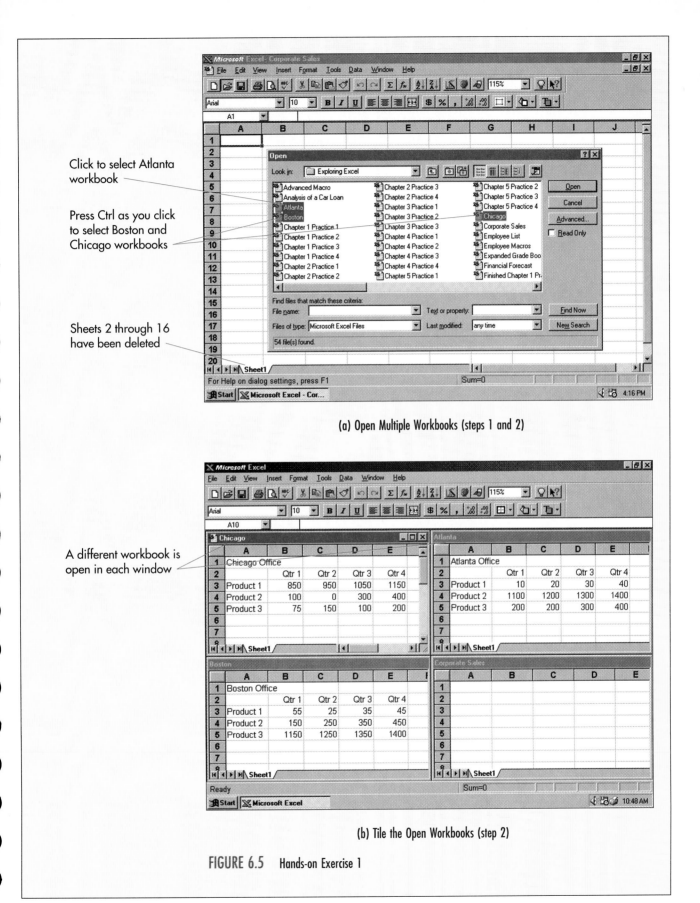

Click to select Atlanta workbook

Press Ctrl as you click to select Boston and Chicago workbooks

Sheets 2 through 16 have been deleted

(a) Open Multiple Workbooks (steps 1 and 2)

A different workbook is open in each window

(b) Tile the Open Workbooks (step 2)

FIGURE 6.5   Hands-on Exercise 1

THE XLS EXTENSION—NOW YOU SEE IT, NOW YOU DON'T

Long-time DOS users will recognize a three-character extension at the end of a filename to indicate the file type. XLS, for example, indicates an Excel workbook. The extension is displayed or hidden in the application's title bar (and in the Open and Save dialog boxes) according to an option in the View menu of My Computer or the Windows Explorer. We suggest you hide the extension if it is currently visible. Open either My Computer or the Explorer, pull down the View menu, click the Options command, click the View tab, then check the box to hide MS-DOS file extensions. Click OK to accept the setting and exit the dialog box. The Excel title bar will display the name of the workbook, but not the XLS extension.

STEP 3: Copy the Atlanta Data

➤ Click in the **Atlanta workbook** to make it the active workbook. Reduce the column widths (if necessary) so that you can see the entire worksheet in the window.

➤ Click and drag to select **cells A1** through **E5** as shown in Figure 6.5c. Pull down the **Edit menu** and click **Copy** (or click the **Copy button** on the Standard toolbar).

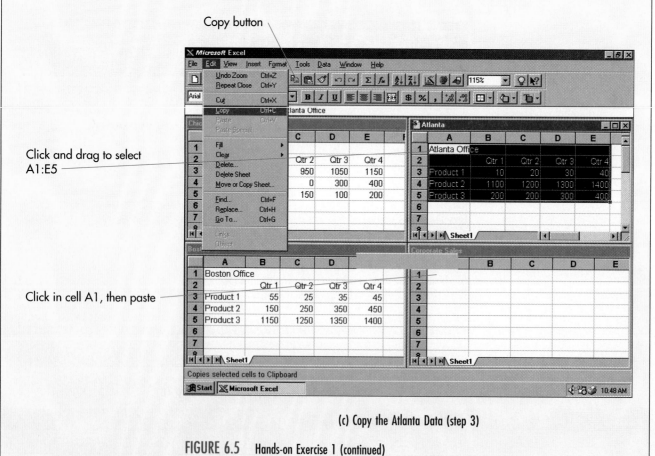

(c) Copy the Atlanta Data (step 3)

FIGURE 6.5   Hands-on Exercise 1 (continued)

➤ Click in **cell A1** of the **Corporate Sales workbook. Click** the **Paste button** on the Standard toolbar to copy the Atlanta data into this workbook.

➤ Point to the **Sheet1 tab** at the bottom of the Corporate Sales worksheet window, then click the **right mouse button** to produce a shortcut menu. Click **Rename.**

➤ Type **Atlanta** in the Rename Sheet dialog box and click **OK.** The worksheet tab has been changed from Sheet1 to Atlanta.

➤ Click the **Save button** to save the active workbook (Corporate Sales).

RENAMING A WORKSHEET

The fastest way to rename a worksheet is to double click the worksheet tab, which automatically displays the Rename Sheet dialog box. Type the new name for the worksheet, then press the enter key.

STEP 4: Copy the Boston and Chicago Data (a Shortcut)

➤ Click in the **Boston workbook** to make it the active workbook as shown in Figure 6.5d.

➤ Click the **Sheet1 tab,** then press and hold the **Ctrl key** as you drag the tab to the right of the Atlanta tab in the Corporate Sales workbook. You will see a tiny spreadsheet with a plus sign as you drag the tab. The plus sign indicates

Click in window to make Boston the active workbook

Click the Sheet1 tab, press Ctrl as you drag the tab to the right of the Atlanta tab in the Corporate Sales workbook

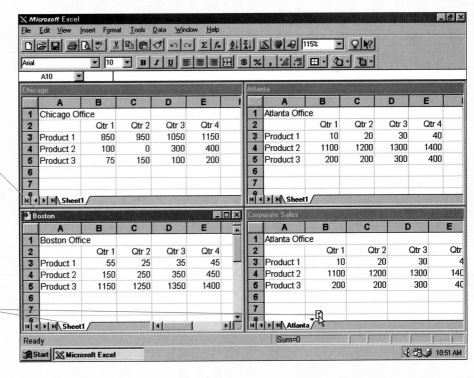

(d) A Shortcut (step 4)

FIGURE 6.5 Hands-on Exercise 1 (continued)

that the worksheet is being copied; the ▼ symbol indicates where the work-sheet will be placed.

➤ Release the mouse, then release the Ctrl key. The worksheet from the Boston workbook should have been copied to the Corporate Sales workbook and appears as Sheet1 in that workbook.

➤ The Boston workbook should still be open; if it isn't, it means that you did not press the Ctrl key as you were dragging the tab to copy the worksheet. If this is the case, pull down the **File menu,** reopen the Boston workbook, and if necessary, tile the open windows.

➤ Double click the **Sheet1 tab** in the Corporate Sales workbook in order to rename the tab. Type **Boston** in the Rename Sheet text box and click **OK.**

➤ The Boston worksheet should appear to the right of the Atlanta worksheet; if the worksheet appears to the left of Atlanta, click and drag the tab to its desired position. (The ▼ symbol indicates where the worksheet will be placed.)

➤ Repeat the previous steps to copy the Chicago data to the Corporate Sales workbook, placing the new sheet to the right of the Boston sheet. Rename the copied worksheet **Chicago.** Remember, you must click in the window containing the Chicago workbook to activate the window before you can copy the worksheet.

➤ Save the Corporate Sales workbook. (The Summary worksheet will be built in the next exercise.)

MOVING AND COPYING WORKSHEETS

You can move or copy a worksheet within a workbook by dragging its tab. To move a worksheet, click its tab, then drag the tab to the new location (a black triangle shows where the new sheet will go). To copy a work-sheet, click its tab, then press and hold the Ctrl key as you drag the tab to its new location. The copied worksheet will have the same name as the original worksheet, followed by a number in parentheses indicating the copy number.

STEP 5: The Corporate Sales Workbook

➤ Check that the Corporate Sales workbook is the active workbook. Click the **Maximize button** so that this workbook takes the entire screen.

➤ The Corporate Sales workbook contains three worksheets. Click the **Atlanta tab** to display the worksheet for Atlanta. Click the **Boston tab** to display the worksheet for Boston. Click the **Chicago tab** to display the worksheet for Chicago.

➤ Pull down the **File menu.** Click **Print.** Click the **Entire Workbook option button** as shown in Figure 6.5e. Click **OK** to print the workbook.

➤ Close the open workbooks, saving changes if requested to do so. Exit Excel if you do not want to continue with the next exercise at this time.

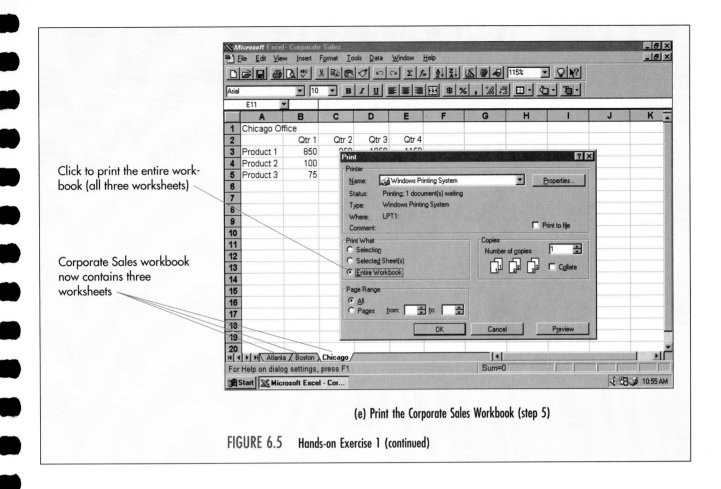

Click to print the entire workbook (all three worksheets)

Corporate Sales workbook now contains three worksheets

(e) Print the Corporate Sales Workbook (step 5)

FIGURE 6.5   Hands-on Exercise 1 (continued)

WORKSHEET REFERENCES

The presence of multiple worksheets in a workbook creates an additional requirement for cell references. You continue to use the same row and column convention when you reference a cell on the current worksheet; that is, cell A1 is still A1. What if, however, you want to reference a cell on another worksheet within the same workbook? It is no longer sufficient to refer to cell A1 because every worksheet has its own cell A1.

To reference a cell (or cell range) in a worksheet other than the current (active) worksheet, you need to preface the cell address with a *worksheet reference;* for example, Atlanta!A1 references cell A1 in the Atlanta worksheet. A worksheet reference may also be used in conjunction with a cell range—for example, Summary!B2:E5 to reference cells B2 through E5 on the Summary worksheet. Omission of the worksheet reference in either example defaults to the cell reference in the active worksheet.

An exclamation point separates the worksheet reference from the cell reference. The worksheet reference (e.g., Atlanta or Summary) is always an absolute reference. The cell reference can be either relative (e.g., Atlanta!A1 or Summary!B2:E5) or absolute (e.g., Atlanta!$A$1 or Summary!$B$2:$E$5).

Consider how worksheet references are used in the Summary worksheet in Figure 6.6. Each entry in the Summary worksheet computes the sum of the corresponding cells in the Atlanta, Boston, and Chicago worksheets. The cell formula in cell B3, for example, would be entered as follows:

Worksheet reference

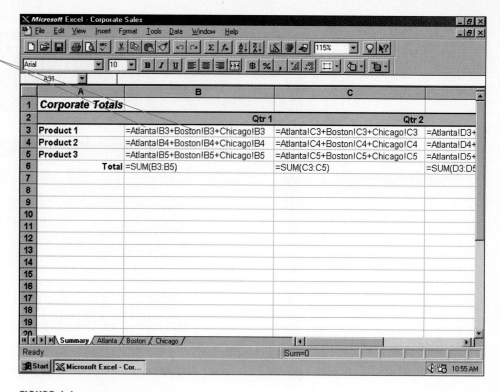

FIGURE 6.6   Worksheet References

=Atlanta!B3+Boston!B3+Chicago!B3

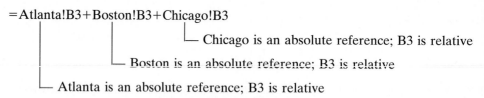

     └ Chicago is an absolute reference; B3 is relative

   └ Boston is an absolute reference; B3 is relative

 └ Atlanta is an absolute reference; B3 is relative

The combination of relative and absolute addresses enables you to enter the formula once (in cell B3), then copy it to the remaining cells in the worksheet. In other words, you enter the formula in cell B3 to compute the total sales for Product 1 in Quarter 1, then you copy that formula to the other cells in row three (C3 through E3) to obtain the totals for Product 1 in Quarters 2, 3, and 4. You then copy the entire row (B3 through E3) to rows four and five (cells B4 through E5) to obtain the totals for Products 2 and 3 in all four quarters.

The proper use of relative and absolute references in the original formula in cell B3 is what makes it possible to copy the cell formulas. Consider, for example, the formula in cell C3 (which was copied from cell B3):

=Atlanta!C3+Boston!C3+Chicago!C3

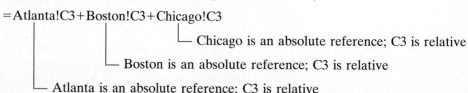

     └ Chicago is an absolute reference; C3 is relative

   └ Boston is an absolute reference; C3 is relative

 └ Atlanta is an absolute reference; C3 is relative

The worksheet references remain absolute (e.g., Atlanta!) while the cell references adjust for the new location of the formula (cell C3). Similar adjustments are made in all of the other copied formulas.

3-D Reference

A *3-D reference* is a range that spans two or more worksheets in a workbook; for example, =SUM(Atlanta:Chicago!B3) to sum cell B3 in the Atlanta, Boston, and Chicago worksheets. The sheet range is specified with a colon between the beginning and ending sheets. An exclamation point follows the ending sheet, followed by the cell reference. The worksheet references are absolute. The cell reference may be relative or absolute.

Three-dimensional references can be used in the Summary worksheet as an alternative way to compute the corporate total for each product–quarter combination. To compute the corporate sales for Product 1 in Quarter 1 (which appears in cell B3 of the Summary worksheet), you would use the function:

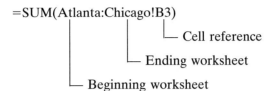

The 3-D reference includes all worksheets between the Atlanta and Chicago worksheets. (Only one additional worksheet, Boston, is present in the example, but the reference would adjust automatically for the insertion of any additional worksheets.) Note, too, that the cell reference is relative and thus the formula can be copied from cell B3 in the Summary worksheet to the remaining cells in row 3 (C3 through E3). Those formulas can then be copied to the appropriate cells in rows 4 and 5.

A 3-D reference can be typed directly into a cell formula, but it is easier to enter the reference by pointing. Click in the cell that is to contain the 3-D reference, then enter an equal sign to begin the formula. To reference a cell in another workbook, click in the window containing that workbook, click the tab for the worksheet you want to reference, then click the cell or cell range you want to include in the formula.

FORMULAS VERSUS FUNCTIONS

Many worksheet calculations, such as an average or a sum, can be performed in one of two ways. You can either enter a formula—for example, =Atlanta!B3+Boston!B3+Chicago!B3—or you can use the equivalent function, =SUM(Atlanta:Chicago!B3). Functions are preferable in that they will adjust automatically for the deletion of existing worksheets or the insertion of new worksheets (within the existing range).

Grouping Worksheets

The worksheets in a workbook are often similar to one another in terms of content and/or formatting. In Figure 6.3, for example, the formatting is identical in all four worksheets of the workbook. You can format the worksheets individually or more easily through grouping.

Excel provides the capability for *grouping worksheets* in order to enter or format data in multiple worksheets at the same time. Once the worksheets are grouped, anything you do in one of the worksheets is automatically done to the other sheets in the group. You could, for example, group all of the worksheets together when you enter row and column labels, when you format data, or when you enter formulas to compute row and column totals. You must, however, ungroup the worksheets when you enter data in a specific worksheet. Grouping and ungrouping is illustrated in the following hands-on exercise.

HANDS-ON EXERCISE 2

3-D References

Objective: Use 3-D references to summarize data from multiple worksheets within a workbook; group worksheets to enter common formatting and formulas; open multiple windows to view several worksheets at the same time. Use Figure 6.7 as a guide in the exercise.

STEP 1: Insert a Worksheet

➤ Start Excel. Open the **Corporate Sales workbook** created in the previous exercise. The workbook contains three worksheets: Atlanta, Boston, and Chicago.

➤ Click the **Atlanta tab** to select this worksheet. Pull down the **Insert menu,** and click the **Worksheet command.** You should see a new worksheet, Sheet1, which is displayed on the screen and whose tab is to the left of the Atlanta tab.

➤ Double click the **tab** of the newly inserted worksheet. Type **Summary** in the Rename Sheet dialog box and press **enter.** The name of the new worksheet has been changed to Summary.

➤ Save the workbook.

SHORTCUT MENUS

Shortcut menus provide an alternate (and generally faster) way to execute common commands. Point to a tab, then click the right mouse button to display a shortcut menu with commands to insert, delete, rename, move, or copy, or select all worksheets. Point to the desired command, then click the left mouse button to execute the command from the shortcut menu. Press the Esc key or click outside the menu to close the menu without executing the command.

STEP 2: The AutoFill Command

➤ Click in **cell A1** of the Summary worksheet. Type **Corporate Totals** as shown in Figure 6.7a.

➤ Click in **cell B2.** Enter **Qtr 1.** Click in **cell B2,** then point to the fill handle in the lower-right corner of cell B2. The mouse pointer changes to a thin crosshair.

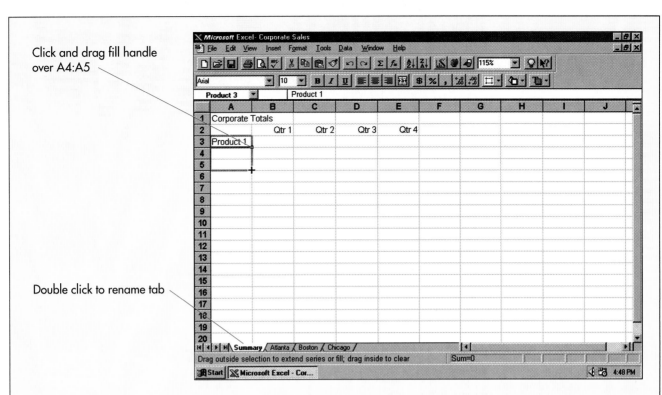

Click and drag fill handle over A4:A5

Double click to rename tab

(a) The AutoFill Command (step 2)

FIGURE 6.7   Hands-on Exercise 2

➤ Drag the fill handle over **cells C2, D2,** and **E2.** A border appears to indicate the destination range. Release the mouse. Cells C2 through E2 contain the labels Qtr 2, Qtr 3, and Qtr 4, respectively. Right align the column labels.

➤ Click in **cell A3.** Enter **Product 1.** Use the AutoFill capability to enter the labels **Product 2** and **Product 3** in cells A4 and A5.

THE AUTOFILL COMMAND

The AutoFill command is the fastest way to enter any type of series in adjacent cells. If, for example, you needed the months of the year in 12 successive cells, you would enter January (or Jan) in the first cell, then drag the fill handle over the next 11 cells in the direction you want to fill. If you need the days of the week, enter Monday (or Mon) and drag over the appropriate number of cells. You can also create a numeric series by entering the first two numbers in that series; for example, to enter the years 1990 through 1999, enter 1990 and 1991 in the first two cells, then select both cells and drag the fill handle.

STEP 3: Sum the Worksheets

➤ Click in **cell B3** of the Summary worksheet as shown in Figure 6.7b. Enter **=SUM(Atlanta:Chicago!B3),** then press the **enter key.** You should see 915

Undo button

Function entered in B3

Click and drag fill handle
over C3:E3 to copy formula

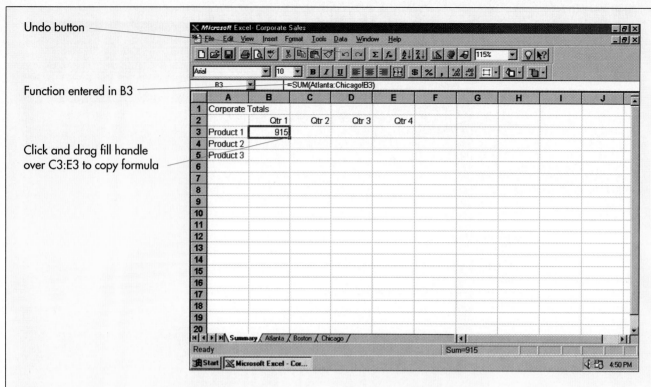

(b) Sum the Worksheets (step 3)

FIGURE 6.7 Hands-on Exercise 2 (continued)

as the sum of the sales for Product 1 in Quarter 1 for the three cities (Atlanta, Boston, and Chicago).

➤ Click the **Undo button** on the Standard toolbar to erase the function so that you can re-enter the function by using pointing:

➤ Check that you are in cell B3 of the Summary worksheet. Enter **=SUM(.**

• Click the **Atlanta tab** to begin the pointing operation.

• Press and hold the **Shift key,** click the **Chicago tab** (scrolling if necessary), then release the Shift key and click **cell B3.** The formula bar should now contain =SUM(Atlanta:Chicago!B3.

• Press the **enter key** to complete the function (which automatically enters the closing right parenthesis) and return to the Summary worksheet.

➤ You should see once again the displayed value of 915 in cell B3 of the Summary worksheet.

➤ If necessary, click in **cell B3,** then drag the fill handle over cells **C3** through **E3** to copy this formula and obtain the total sales for Product 1 in quarters two, three, and four.

➤ Be sure that cells B3 through E3 are still selected, then drag the fill handle to **cell E5.** You should see the total sales for all products in all quarters as shown in Figure 6.7c.

➤ Click **cell E5** to examine the formula in this cell and note that the worksheet references are absolute (i.e., they remained the same), whereas the cell references are relative (they were adjusted). Click in other cells to review their formulas in similar fashion.

➤ Save the workbook.

POINTING TO CELLS IN OTHER WORKSHEETS

A worksheet reference can be typed directly into a cell formula, but it is easier to enter the reference by pointing. Click in the cell that is to contain the reference, then enter an equal sign to begin the formula. To reference a cell in another worksheet, click the tab for the worksheet you want to reference, then click the cell or cell range you want to include in the formula. Complete the formula as usual, continuing to first click the tab whenever you want to reference a cell in another worksheet.

STEP 4: The Arrange Windows Command

➤ Pull down the **Window menu.** The bottom of the menu displays the names of the open windows, with only one window open at this time. (If the list of open windows includes Book1, close that workbook.)

➤ Click **New Window** to open a second window. Note, however, that your display will not change at this time, because the windows are maximized and only one window is displayed at a time.

➤ Pull down the **Window menu** a second time. Click **New Window** to open a third window. Open a fourth window in similar fashion.

➤ Pull down the **Window menu** once again. You should see the names of the four open windows as shown in Figure 6.7c.

➤ Click **Arrange** to display the Arrange Windows dialog box. If necessary, select the **Tile** option, then click **OK.** You should see four tiled windows.

Names of open windows (all four reference the same workbook)

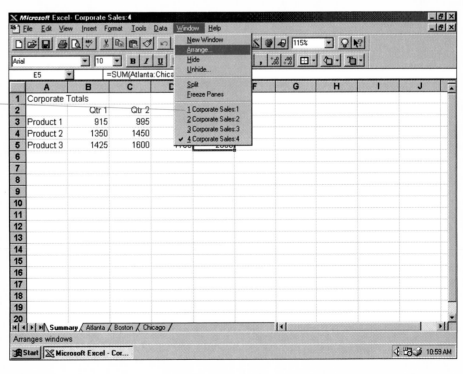

(c) Arrange Windows Command (step 4)

FIGURE 6.7   Hands-on Exercise 2 (continued)

STEP 5: Changing Data

➤ Click in the **upper-right window** in Figure 6.7d. Click the **Atlanta tab** to display the Atlanta worksheet in this window.

➤ Click the **lower-left window.** Click the **Boston tab** to display the Boston worksheet in this window.

➤ Click in the **lower-right window.** Click the **Tab scrolling button** until you can see the Chicago tab, then click the **Chicago tab** to display the Chicago worksheet.

➤ Note that cell B3 in the Summary worksheet displays the value 915, which reflects the total sales for Product 1 in Quarter 1 for Atlanta, Boston, and Chicago (10, 55, and 850, respectively).

➤ Click in **cell B3** of the Chicago worksheet. Enter **250.** Press **enter.** The value of cell B3 in the Summary worksheet changes to 315 to reflect the decreased sales in Chicago.

➤ Click the **Undo button** on the Standard toolbar. The sales for Chicago revert to 850 and the Corporate total is again 915.

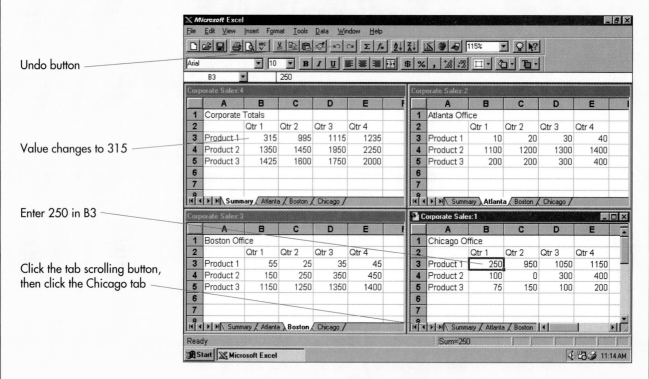

Undo button

Value changes to 315

Enter 250 in B3

Click the tab scrolling button, then click the Chicago tab

(d) Changing the Data (step 5)

FIGURE 6.7 Hands-on Exercise 2 (continued)

STEP 6: Group Editing

➤ Click in the **upper-left window,** which displays the Summary worksheet. Point to the split box separating the tab scrolling buttons from the horizontal scroll bar. (The pointer becomes a two-headed arrow.) Click and drag to the right until you can see all four tabs at the same time.

➤ If necessary, click the **Summary tab.** Press and hold the **Shift key** as you click the tab for the **Chicago worksheet.** All four tabs should be selected (and are displayed in white) as in Figure 6.7e, and you see [Group] in the title bar.

Font Size list box

Click the Summary tab, then
press Shift as you click the
Chicago tab to select all
four tabs

Click and drag to display all
four tabs

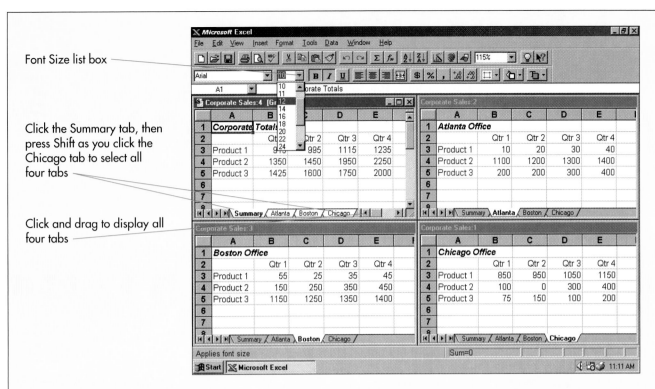

(e) Group Editing (step 6)

FIGURE 6.7   Hands-on Exercise 2 (continued)

➤ Click in **cell A1,** then click the **Bold** and **Italic buttons** to boldface and italicize the title of each worksheet. Click the **drop-down arrow** for the Font Size
list box and change the font to 12.

➤ Boldface the quarterly and product labels. Note that all four sheets are being
formatted simultaneously because of group editing.

➤ Click and drag to select **cells B3** through **E5,** the cells containing the numerical values. Format these cells in currency format with zero decimals. Add
borders and color as desired.

➤ Save the workbook.

SELECTING MULTIPLE SHEETS

You can group (select) multiple worksheets simultaneously, then perform
the same operation on the selected sheets. To select adjacent sheets, select
(click) the first sheet in the range, then press and hold the Shift key as
you click the last sheet in the group. If the worksheets are not adjacent
to one another, click the first tab, then press and hold the Ctrl key as you
click the tab of each additional sheet you want to include in the group.
To select all of the sheets at one time, right click the active tab, then
choose Select All from the shortcut menu. Once multiple sheets have
been selected, Excel indicates that grouping is in effect by appending
[Group] to the workbook name in the title bar. Click any tab within the
selected group to deselect the group.

STEP 7: Sum the Rows and Columns

➤ Be sure that all four tabs are still selected so that group editing is still in effect.

➤ Scroll until you can click in **cell F3** in the Summary worksheet. Enter the function **=SUM(B3:E3).** Copy this formula to **cells F4** through **F6.**

➤ Click in **cell B6** as shown in Figure 6.7f. Enter the function **=SUM(B3:B5).** Copy this formula to **cells C6** through **E6.** Note that the formula is being entered in all four sheets simultaneously since group editing is still in effect.

➤ Enter **Total** in cell F2, then center and boldface the label in the cell. Enter **Total** in cell A6 and boldface it. Boldface the row and column totals.

➤ Save the workbook.

THE AUTOSUM BUTTON

The *AutoSum* button on the Standard toolbar invokes the Sum function over a suggested range of cells. To sum a single row or column, click in the blank cell at the end of the row or column, click the AutoSum button to see the suggested function, then click the button a second time to enter the function into the worksheet. To sum multiple rows or columns, select all of the cells that are to contain the Sum function prior to clicking the AutoSum button.

Function entered in B6

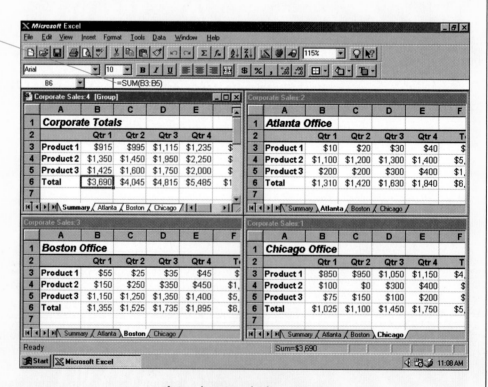

(f) Sum the Rows and Columns (step 7)

FIGURE 6.7   Hands-on Exercise 2 (continued)

STEP 8: Print the Workbook

➤ Pull down the **File menu** and click the **Page Setup command.**

➤ Click the **Margins tab,** then click the check box to center the worksheet horizontally.

➤ Click the **Sheet tab.** Check the boxes to include row and column headings and gridlines.

➤ Click **OK** to exit the Page Setup dialog box.

➤ Pull down the **File menu.** Click **Print** to display the Print dialog box. Click the option button to print the **Entire Workbook.**

➤ Click **OK** to print the workbook, which will print on four separate pages, one worksheet per page.

STEP 9: Exit Excel

➤ Close all four windows, clicking **Yes** to save the workbook as you close the last window.

➤ Exit Excel if you do not want to continue with the next exercise at this time.

THE DOCUMENTATION WORKSHEET

Chapter 2 emphasized the importance of properly designing a worksheet and of isolating the assumptions and initial conditions on which the worksheet is based. A workbook can contain up to 256 worksheets, and it, too, should be well designed so that the purpose of every worksheet is evident. Documenting a workbook, and the various worksheets within the workbook, is important because spreadsheets are frequently used by individuals other than the author. You are familiar with every aspect of your workbook because you created it. Your colleague down the hall (or across the country) is not, however, and that person needs to know at a glance the purpose of the workbook and its underlying structure. Even if you don't share your worksheet with others, you will appreciate the documentation six months from now, when you have forgotten some of the nuances you once knew so well.

One way of documenting a workbook is through the creation of a ***documentation worksheet*** that describes the contents of each worksheet within the workbook as shown in Figure 6.8. The worksheet in Figure 6.8 has been added to the Corporate Sales workbook that was created in the first two exercises. (The Insert menu contains the command to add a worksheet.)

The documentation worksheet shows the author and date the spreadsheet was last modified. It contains a description of the overall workbook, a list of each sheet within the workbook, and the contents of each worksheet. The information in the documentation worksheet may seem obvious to you, but it will be greatly appreciated by someone seeing the workbook for the first time.

The documentation worksheet is attractively formatted and takes advantage of the ability to wrap text within a cell. The description in cell B6, for example, wraps over several lines (just as in a word processor). The worksheet also takes advantage of color and larger fonts to call attention to the title of the worksheet. The grid lines have been suppressed through the View tab in the Options command of the Tools menu. The documentation worksheet is an important addition to any workbook.

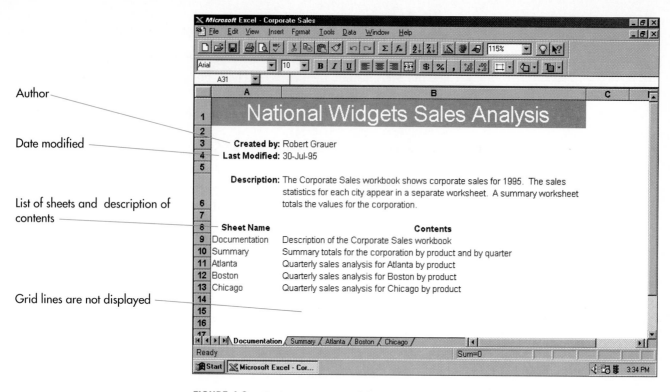

Author —

Date modified —

List of sheets and description of
contents —

Grid lines are not displayed —

FIGURE 6.8   The Documentation Worksheet

HANDS-ON EXERCISE 3

The Documentation Worksheet

Objective: To improve the design of a workbook through the inclusion of a documentation worksheet. To illustrate sophisticated formatting. Use Figure 6.9 as a guide in the exercise.

STEP 1: Insert a Worksheet

➤ Start Excel. Open the **Corporate Sales workbook** created in the previous exercise. The workbook contains four worksheets: Summary, Atlanta, Boston, and Chicago, each in its own window. Close all but one of the windows, then maximize that window.

➤ Click the **Summary tab** to select this worksheet. Pull down the **Insert menu,** and click the **Worksheet command.** You should see a new worksheet, Sheet1, whose tab is to the left of the Summary worksheet. Do not be concerned if the worksheet is other than Sheet1.

➤ Double click the **tab** of the newly inserted worksheet. Enter **Documentation** in the Rename Sheet dialog box and press **enter.** The name of the new worksheet has been changed to Documentation as shown in Figure 6.9a.

➤ Save the workbook.

STEP 2: Enter the Documentation Information

➤ Enter the descriptive entries in cells A3, A4, and A6 as shown in Figure 6.9a.

➤ Click and drag to select **cells A3** through **A6** so that you can format these cells at the same time. Click the **Bold button.** Click the **Align Right button.**

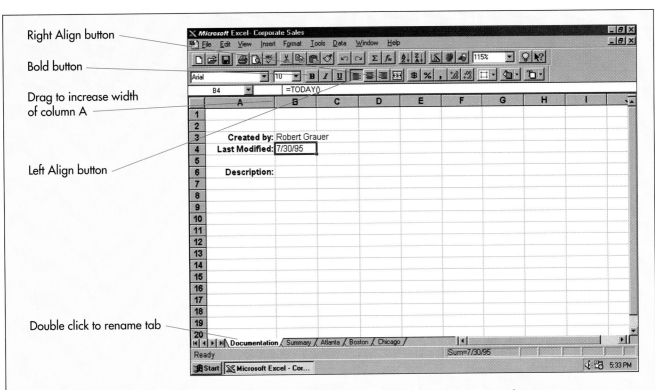

Right Align button

Bold button

Drag to increase width of column A

Left Align button

Double click to rename tab

(a) Add the Documentation Worksheet (steps 1 and 2)

FIGURE 6.9   Hands-on Exercise 3

➤ Increase the width of column A so that the contents of column A are completely visible.

➤ Enter your name in cell B3. Enter **=Today()** in cell B4. Press **enter.** Click the **Left Align button** to align the date as shown in Figure 6.9a.

STEP 3: The Format Cells Command

➤ Increase the width of column B as shown in Figure 6.9b, then click in **cell B6** and enter the descriptive entry shown in the formula bar.

➤ Type the entire entry *without* pressing the enter key as you will be able to wrap the text within the cell. (You are limited to a maximum of 256 characters in the entry.) Do not be concerned if the text in cell B6 appears to spill into the other cells in row six.

➤ Press the **enter key** when you have completed the entry. Click in **cell B6,** then pull down the **Format menu** and click **Cells** (or right click **cell B6** and click **Format Cells**) to display the dialog box in Figure 6.9b.

➤ Click the **Alignment tab.** Click the box to **Wrap Text** as shown in the figure. Click **OK** to close the dialog box. The text in cell B6 wraps to the width of column B. (You can change the width of the column, and the text will wrap automatically.)

➤ Point to **cell A6,** then click the **right mouse button** to display a shortcut menu. Click **Format Cells** to display the Format Cells dialog box. If necessary, click the **Alignment tab,** then click the **Top option button** in the Vertical section of the dialog box.

➤ The entry in cell A6 (the word "Description") now aligns with the top of the description in cell B6.

➤ Save the workbook.

Entry in B6

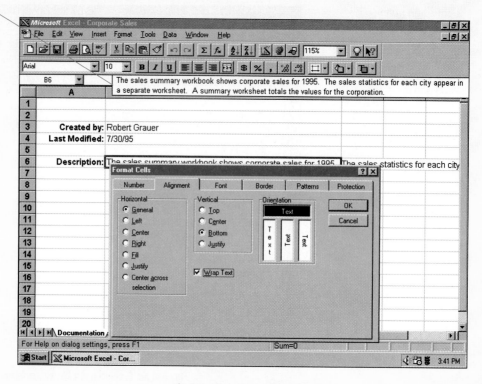

(b) Wrap Text Command (step 3)

FIGURE 6.9   Hands-on Exercise 3 (continued)

EDIT WITHIN A CELL

Double click within the cell whose contents you want to change, then make the changes directly in the cell itself rather than on the formula bar. Use the mouse or arrow keys to position the insertion point at the point of correction. Press the Ins key to toggle between the insertion and over-type modes and/or use the Del key to delete a character. Press the Home and End keys to move to the first and last characters, respectively.

STEP 4: Complete the Descriptive Entries

➤ Complete the text entries in cells A8 through B13 as shown in Figure 6.9c. Click and drag to select cells **A8** and **B8.** Click the **Bold** and **Center buttons** to match the formatting in the figure.

➤ Save the workbook.

STEP 5: Add the Worksheet Title

➤ Click in **cell A1.** Enter **National Widgets Sales Analysis.** Change the font size to **24.**

➤ Click and drag to select **cells A1** and **B1.** Click the **Center Across Columns button** to center the title across cells A1 and B1.

➤ Check that cells A1 and B1 are still selected. Pull down the **Format menu.** Click **Cells** to display the Format Cells dialog box as shown in Figure 6.9d.

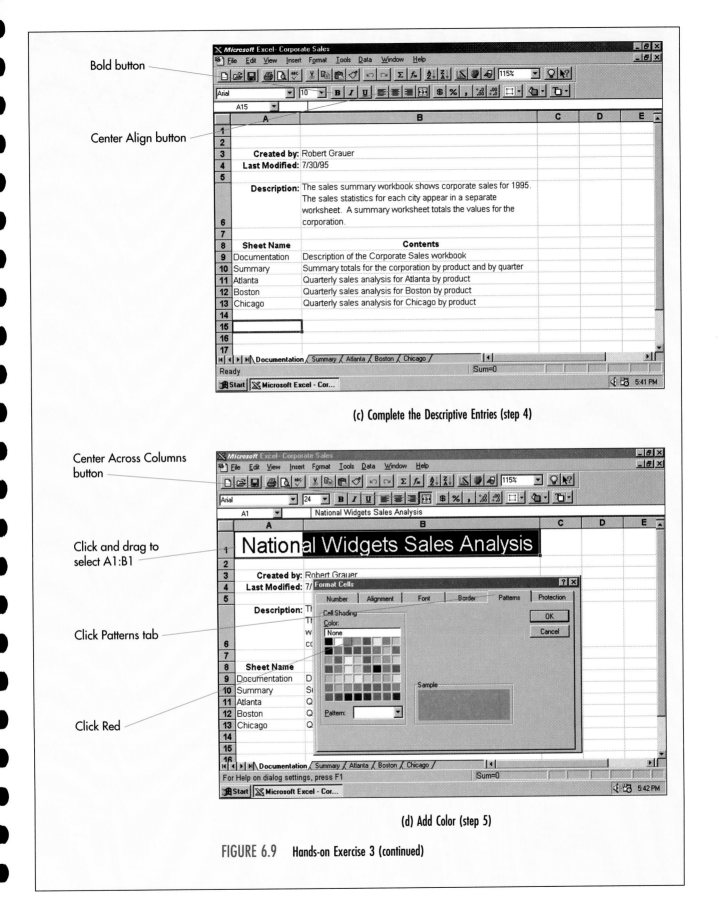

Bold button

Center Align button

(c) Complete the Descriptive Entries (step 4)

Center Across Columns button

Click and drag to select A1:B1

Click Patterns tab

Click Red

(d) Add Color (step 5)

FIGURE 6.9   Hands-on Exercise 3 (continued)

- Click the **Patterns tab.** Click the **Red** color to shade the selected cells.
- Click the **Font tab.** Click the **drop-down arrow** in the Color list box. Click the **White** color.
- Click **OK** to accept the settings and close the Format Cells dialog box.

➤ Click outside the selected cells to see the effects of the formatting change. You should see white letters on a red background.

➤ Remove the gridlines. Pull down the **Tools menu.** Click **Options.** Click the **View tab** and clear the check box for Gridlines in the Window options area.

➤ Save the workbook.

THE FORMATTING TOOLBAR

Use the Color and Font Color buttons on the Formatting toolbar to change the shading (pattern color) and font color, respectively. Select the cell(s) you wish to format, click the down arrow of the appropriate button to display the palette, then click the desired color.

STEP 6: Exit Excel

➤ Click the **Spelling button** on the Standard toolbar to initiate the spell check. Make corrections as necessary.

➤ You have completed the descriptive worksheet shown earlier in Figure 6.8. Exit Excel if you do not want to continue with the next exercise at this time.

THE SPELL CHECK

Anyone familiar with a word processor takes the spell check for granted, but did you know the same capability exists within Excel? Click the Spelling button on the Standard toolbar to initiate the spell check, then implement corrections just as you do in Microsoft Word. All of the applications in Microsoft Office share the same custom dictionary, so that any words you add to the custom dictionary in one application are automatically recognized in other applications.

LINKING WORKBOOKS

As indicated at the beginning of the chapter, there are in essence two different approaches to combining data from multiple sources. You can store all of the data on separate sheets in a single workbook, then create a summary worksheet within that workbook that references values in the other worksheets. Alternatively, you can retain the source data in separate workbooks, and create a summary workbook to reference those workbooks.

The two approaches are equally valid, and the choice depends on where you want to keep the source data. In general, it's easier to keep all of the data in a single workbook as has been done throughout the chapter. Occasionally, however, it may be impractical to keep all of the data in a single workbook, in which case it becomes necessary to link the individual workbooks to one another.

Linking is established through the creation of **external references** that specify a cell (or range of cells) in another workbook. The **dependent workbook** (the Corporate Links workbook in our example) contains the external references and thus reflects (is dependent on) data in the source workbook(s). The **source workbooks** (the Atlanta, Boston, and Chicago workbooks in our example) contain the data referenced by the dependent workbook.

Figure 6.10 illustrates the use of linking within the context of the example we have been using. The figure resembles figures that have appeared earlier in the chapter, but with subtle differences.

Four different workbooks are open, each with one worksheet. The Corporate Links workbook is the dependent workbook and contains external references to obtain the summary totals. The Atlanta, Boston, and Chicago workbooks are the source workbooks.

Cell B3 is the active cell, and its contents are displayed in the formula bar. The corporate sales for Product 1 in the first quarter are calculated by summing the corresponding values in the source workbooks. Note how the workbook names are enclosed in square brackets to indicate the external references to the Atlanta, Boston, and Chicago workbooks. The precise format of an external reference is as follows:

=[ATLANTA.XLS]Sheet1!B3

                                        └─ The cell reference (can be relative or absolute)

                                 └─ The sheet name is followed by an exclamation point

                        └─ The name of the source workbook is enclosed in square brackets

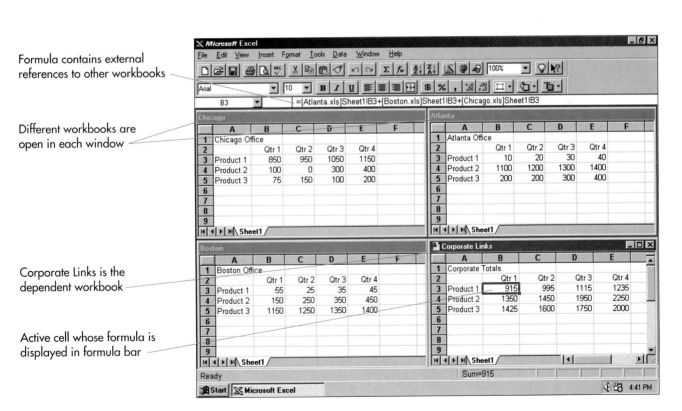

Formula contains external references to other workbooks

Different workbooks are open in each window

Corporate Links is the dependent workbook

Active cell whose formula is displayed in formula bar

FIGURE 6.10   File Linking

The formulas to compute the corporate totals for Product 1 in the second, third, and fourth quarters contain external references similar to those shown in the formula bar of Figure 6.10. The *workbook references* and sheet references are always absolute, whereas the cell reference may be relative (as in this example) or absolute. Once the formula has been entered in cell B3, it may be copied to the remaining cells in this row to compute the totals for Product 1 in the remaining quarters. Cells B3 through E3 may then be copied to rows 4 and 5 to obtain the totals for the other products.

HANDS-ON EXERCISE 4

Linked Workbooks

Objective: Create a dependent workbook with external references to multiple source workbooks; use pointing to create the external reference rather than entering the formula explicitly. Use Figure 6.11 as a guide in the exercise.

STEP 1: Open the Workbooks

➤ Start Excel. If necessary, click the **New Workbook button** on the Standard toolbar to open a new workbook.

➤ Delete all worksheets except for Sheet1 as you did in step 1 of the first hands-on exercise. Save the workbook as **Corporate Links** in the **Exploring Excel folder.**

➤ Pull down the **File menu.** Click **Open** to display the Open dialog box. Click the **Atlanta workbook.** Press and hold the **Ctrl key** as you click the **Boston** and **Chicago workbooks** to select all three workbooks at the same time.

➤ Click **Open** to open the selected workbooks. The workbooks will be opened one after another with a brief message appearing on the status bar as each workbook is opened.

➤ Pull down the **Window menu,** which should indicate four open workbooks at the bottom of the menu. Click **Arrange** to display the Arrange Windows dialog box. If necessary, select the **Tile** option, then click **OK.**

➤ You should see four open workbooks as shown in Figure 6.11a, although the row and column labels have not yet been entered in the Corporate Links workbook. (Do not be concerned if your workbooks are arranged differently.)

STEP 2: The AutoFill Command

➤ Click in **cell A1** in the **Corporate Links workbook** to make this the active cell in the active workbook. Enter **Corporate Totals** as shown in Figure 6.11a.

➤ Click **cell B2.** Enter **Qtr 1.** Click in **cell B2,** then point to the fill handle in the lower-right corner. The mouse pointer changes to a thin crosshair.

➤ Drag the fill handle over **cells C2, D2,** and **E2.** A border appears, to indicate the destination range. Release the mouse. Cells C2 through E2 contain the labels Qtr 2, Qtr 3, and Qtr 4, respectively.

➤ Right-align the entries in **cells B2** through **E2,** then reduce the column widths so that you can see the entire worksheet in the window.

➤ Click **cell A3.** Enter **Product 1.** Use the AutoFill capability to enter the labels **Product 2** and **Product 3** in cells A4 and A5.

New button

Different workbook open
in each window

Complete the text entries in
Corporate Links workbook

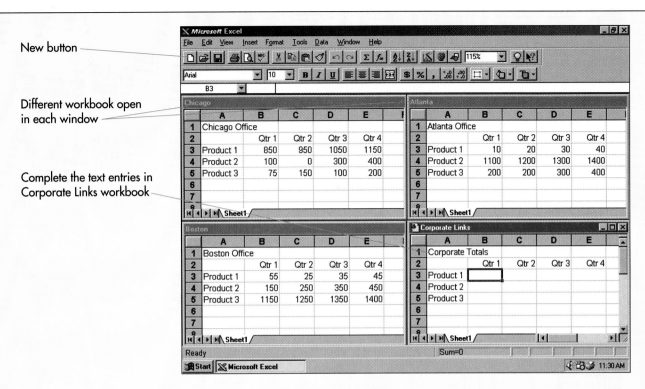

(a) Open the Workbooks (step 2)

FIGURE 6.11   Hands-on Exercise 4

STEP 3: File Linking

➤ Click **cell B3** of the **Corporate Links workbook.** Enter an **equal sign** so that you can create the formula by pointing:

- Click in the window for the **Atlanta workbook.** Click **cell B3.** The formula bar should display =[ATLANTA.XLS]Sheet1!$B$3. Press the **F4 key** continually until the cell reference changes to B3.

- Enter a **plus sign.** Click in the window for the **Boston workbook.** Click **cell B3.** The formula expands to include +[BOSTON.XLS]Sheet1!$B$3. Press the **F4 key** continually until the cell reference changes to B3.

- Enter a **plus sign.** Click in the window for the **Chicago workbook.** Click **cell B3.** The formula expands to include +[CHICAGO.XLS]Sheet1!$B$3. Press the **F4 key** continually until the cell reference changes to B3.

THE F4 KEY

The F4 key cycles through relative, absolute, and mixed addresses. Click on any reference within the formula bar; for example, click on A1 in the formula =A1+A2. Press the F4 key once, and it changes to an absolute reference, $A$1. Press the F4 key a second time, and it becomes a mixed reference, A$1; press it again, and it is a different mixed reference, $A1. Press the F4 key a fourth time, and it returns to the original relative address, A1.

- Press **enter.** The formula is complete, and you should see 915 in cell B3 of the Corporate Links workbook. Click in **cell B3.** The entry on the formula bar should match the entry in Figure 6.11b. Save the workbook.

Formula with external references entered in B3

Click in B3

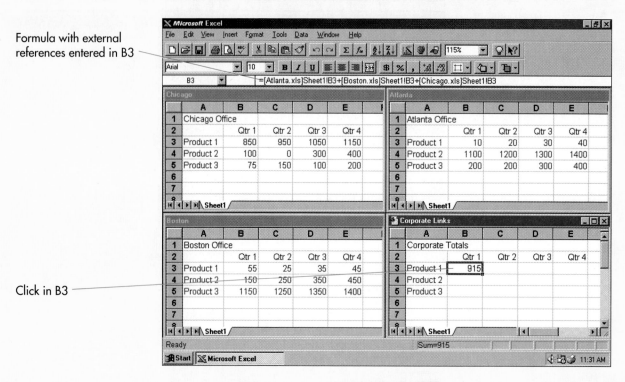

(b) File Linking (step 3)

FIGURE 6.11   Hands-on Exercise 4 (continued)

STEP 4: Copy the Formulas

➤ If necessary, click **cell B3** in the **Corporate Links workbook,** then drag the fill handle over **cells C3** through **E3** to copy this formula to the remaining cells in row 3.

➤ Be sure that cells B3 through E3 are still selected, then drag the fill handle to **cell E5.** You should see the total sales for all products in all quarters as shown in Figure 6.11c.

➤ Click **cell E5** to view the copied formula as shown in the figure. Note that the workbook and sheet references are absolute but that the cell references are relative. Save the workbook.

DRIVE AND FOLDER REFERENCE

An external reference is updated regardless of whether or not the source workbook is open. The reference is displayed differently, however, depending on whether or not the source workbook is open. The references include the path (the drive and folder) if the source workbook is closed; the path is not shown if the source workbook is open.

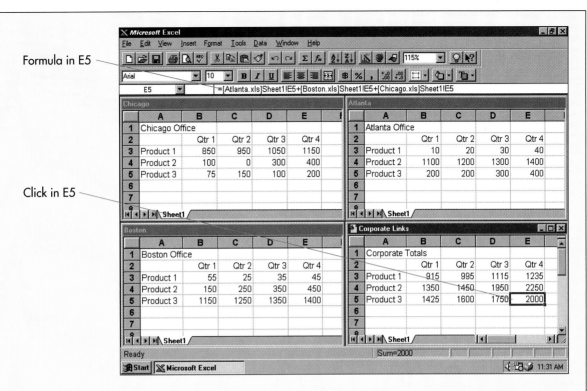

Formula in E5

Click in E5

(c) Copy the Formulas (step 4)

FIGURE 6.11   Hands-on Exercise 4 (continued)

STEP 5: Change the Data

➤ Click **cell B3** to make it the active cell. Note that the value displayed in the cell is 915.

➤ Pull down the **File menu.** Click **Close.** Answer **Yes** if asked whether to save the changes.

➤ Click in the window containing the **Chicago workbook,** click **cell B3,** enter **250,** and press **enter.** Pull down the **File menu.** Click **Close.** Answer **Yes** if asked whether to save the changes. Only two workbooks, Atlanta and Boston, are now open.

➤ Pull down the **File menu** and open the **Corporate Links workbook.** You should see the dialog box in Figure 6.11d, asking whether to re-establish the links. (Note that cell B3 still displays 915). Click **Yes** to re-establish the links.

➤ The value in cell B3 of the Corporate Links workbook changes to 315 to reflect the change in the Chicago workbook, even though the latter is closed.

➤ If necessary, click in **cell B3.** The formula bar displays the contents of this cell, which include the drive and folder reference for the Chicago workbook, because the workbook is closed.

STEP 6: Close the Workbooks

➤ Close the Atlanta and Boston workbooks. Close the Corporate Links workbook. Saving the source workbook(s) before the dependent workbook

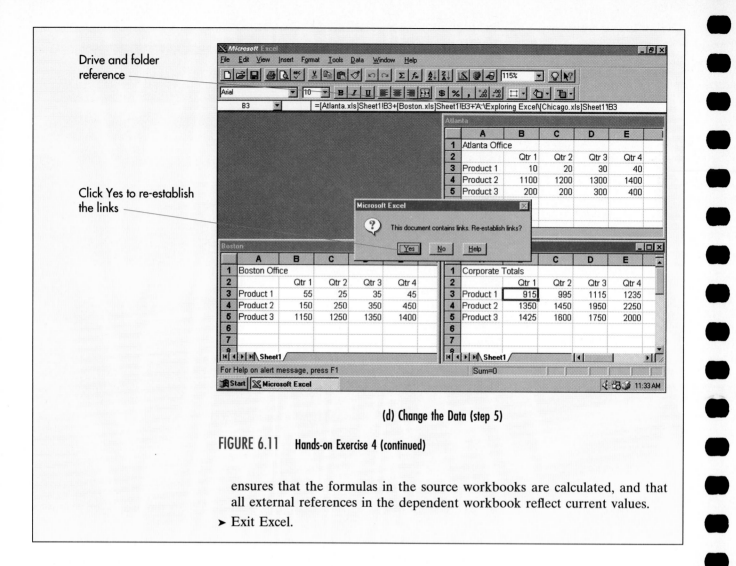

Drive and folder reference

Click Yes to re-establish the links

(d) Change the Data (step 5)

FIGURE 6.11 Hands-on Exercise 4 (continued)

ensures that the formulas in the source workbooks are calculated, and that all external references in the dependent workbook reflect current values.

➤ Exit Excel.

SUMMARY

The chapter showed how to combine data from different sources into a summary report. The example is quite common and applicable to any business scenario requiring both detail and summary reports. One approach is to store all of the data in separate sheets of a single workbook, then summarize the data in a summary worksheet within that workbook. Alternatively, the source data can be kept in separate workbooks and analyzed through linking to a summary workbook. Both approaches are valid, and the choice depends on where you want to keep the source data.

An Excel workbook may contain up to 256 worksheets, each of which is identified by a tab at the bottom of the window. Worksheets may be added, deleted, moved, copied, or renamed through a shortcut menu. The highlighted tab indicates the active worksheet.

A worksheet reference is required to indicate a cell in another worksheet of the same workbook. An exclamation point separates the worksheet reference from the cell reference. The worksheet reference is always absolute. The cell reference may be relative or absolute. A 3-D reference is a range that spans two or more worksheets in a workbook.

A workbook should be clearly organized so that the purpose of every worksheet is evident. One way of documenting a workbook is through the creation of a documentation worksheet that describes the purpose of each worksheet within the workbook.

Linking is used when it is impractical to keep all of the data in the same workbook. Linking is established through an external reference that specifies a cell (or range of cells) in a source workbook. The dependent workbook contains the external references and uses (is dependent on) the data in the source workbook(s).

KEY WORDS AND CONCEPTS

3-D reference	External reference	Source workbook
Arrange command	Grouping worksheets	Tab scrolling buttons
AutoSum	Linking	Tab split box
Dependent workbook	New Window command	Workbook reference
Documentation worksheet	Repeat command	Worksheet reference

MULTIPLE CHOICE

1. Which of the following is true regarding workbooks and worksheets?
   (a) A workbook contains one or more worksheets
   (b) Only one worksheet can be selected at a time within a workbook
   (c) Every workbook contains the same number of worksheets
   (d) All of the above

2. Assume that a workbook contains three worksheets. How many cells are included in the function =SUM(Sheet1:Sheet3!A1)?
   (a) Three
   (b) Four
   (c) Twelve
   (d) Twenty-four

3. Assume that a workbook contains three worksheets. How many cells are included in the function =SUM(Sheet1:Sheet3!A1:B4)?
   (a) Three
   (b) Four
   (c) Twelve
   (d) Twenty-four

4. Which of the following is the preferred way to sum the value of cell A1 from three different worksheets?
   (a) =Sheet1!A1+Sheet2!A1+Sheet3!A1
   (b) =SUM(Sheet1:Sheet3!A1)
   (c) Both (a) and (b) are equally good
   (d) Neither (a) nor (b)

5. The reference CIS120!$A$2:
   (a) Is an absolute reference to cell A2 in the CIS120 workbook
   (b) Is a relative reference to cell A2 in the CIS120 workbook
   (c) Is an absolute reference to cell A2 in the CIS120 worksheet
   (d) Is a relative reference to cell A2 in the CIS120 worksheet

6. Assume that Sheet1 is the active worksheet and that cells A2 through A4 are currently selected. What happens if you press and hold the Shift key as you click the tab for Sheet3, then press the Del key?
   (a) Only Sheet1 will be deleted from the workbook
   (b) Only Sheet3 will be deleted from the workbook
   (c) Sheet1, Sheet2, and Sheet3 will be deleted from the workbook
   (d) The contents of cells A2 through A4 will be erased from Sheet1, Sheet2, and Sheet3

7. Which of the following is true about the reference Sheet1:Sheet3!A1:B2?
   (a) The worksheet reference is relative, the cell reference is absolute
   (b) The worksheet reference is absolute, the cell reference is relative
   (c) The worksheet and cell references are both absolute
   (d) The worksheet and cell references are both relative

8. You are in the Ready mode and are positioned in cell B2 of Sheet1. You enter an equal sign, click the worksheet tab for Sheet2, click cell B1, and press enter.
   (a) The content of cell B2 in Sheet1 is =Sheet2!B1
   (b) The content of cell B1 in Sheet2 is = Sheet1!B2
   (c) Both (a) and (b)
   (d) Neither (a) nor (b)

9. You are in the Ready mode and are positioned in cell A10 of Sheet1. You enter an equal sign, click the worksheet tab for the worksheet called This Year, and click cell C10. You then enter a minus sign, click the worksheet tab for the worksheet called LastYear, click cell C10, and press enter. What are the contents of cell A10?
   (a) =ThisYear:LastYear!C10
   (b) =(ThisYear−LastYear)!C10
   (c) =ThisYear!C10-LastYear!C10
   (d) =ThisYear:C10-LastYear:C10

10. Which of the following can be accessed from a shortcut menu?
    (a) Inserting or deleting a worksheet
    (b) Moving or copying a worksheet
    (c) Renaming a worksheet
    (d) All of the above

11. The Arrange Windows command can display:
    (a) Multiple worksheets from one workbook
    (b) One worksheet from multiple workbooks
    (c) Both (a) and (b)
    (d) Neither (a) nor (b)

12. Pointing can be used to reference a cell in:
    (a) A different worksheet
    (b) A different workbook

(c) Both (a) and (b)

(d) Neither (a) nor (b)

13. The appearance of [Group] within the title bar indicates that:

(a) Multiple workbooks are open and are all active

(b) Multiple worksheets are selected within the same workbook

(c) Both (a) and (b)

(d) Neither (a) nor (b)

14. You are in the Ready mode and are positioned in cell A1 of Sheet1 of Book1. You enter an equal sign, click in the open window for Book2, click the tab for Sheet1, click cell A1, then press the F4 key continually until you have a relative cell reference. What reference appears in the formula bar?

(a) =[BOOK1.XLS]Sheet1!$A$1

(b) =[BOOK1.XLS]Sheet1!A1

(c) =[BOOK2.XLS]Sheet1!$A$1

(d) =[BOOK2.XLS]Sheet1!A1

15. Which of the following is true regarding the example on file linking that was developed in the chapter?

(a) The Atlanta, Boston, and Chicago workbooks were dependent workbooks

(b) The Linked workbook was a source workbook

(c) Both (a) and (b)

(d) Neither (a) nor (b)

ANSWERS

1. a	**6.** d	**11.** c
2. a	**7.** b	**12.** c
3. d	**8.** a	**13.** b
4. b	**9.** c	**14.** d
5. c	**10.** d	**15.** d

EXPLORING EXCEL 7.0

1. Use Figure 6.12 to match each action with its result; a given action may be used more than once or not at all.

Action	Result
a. Click at 2; enter =; click at B3 in the Atlanta sheet; enter +; click at B3 in the Boston sheet; enter +; click at B3 in the Chicago sheet; press enter	_____ Display the Chicago sheet in the lower-right window
	_____ Select all four sheets in upper-left window
	_____ Close the upper-left window
	_____ Change the name of the Sheet1 tab to Corporate Summary
b. Click at 3	_____ Change the size of the selected text in the Summary sheet

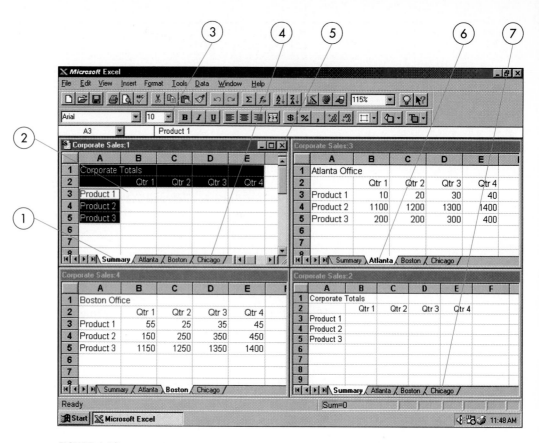

FIGURE 6.12　Screen for Problem 1

Action	Result
c. Click at 1, press the Shift key as you click at 4	_____ Change the size of the selected text in all four sheets
d. Click and drag at 6	_____ Move the Atlanta sheet to the right of the Boston sheet
e. Press the Ctrl key as you click and drag at 6	_____ Copy the Atlanta sheet so that it appears to the right of the Boston sheet
f. Click at 7	
g. Double click at 1	_____ Delete the Summary sheet
h. Click at 5	_____ Enter the formula to determine the total sales for Product 1 in the first Quarter
i. Click at 1, press the Shift key as you click at 4, then click at 3	
j. Point to 1, click the right mouse button, and click Delete	

2. Answer the following with respect to the formula:

=Sheet1!C10+Sheet2!C10+Sheet3!C10

versus the function:

=SUM(Sheet1:Sheet3!C10)

a. Which entry (the formula, function, or both) contains a relative cell reference? An absolute worksheet reference?

b. How many cells are included in the computation for the formula? In the computation for the function?

c. Assume that a new worksheet is inserted between Sheet1 and Sheet3. Will the computed value of the formula change? Will the computed value of the function change?

d. Assume that Sheet2 is deleted. Which entry (the formula, function, or both) will return an error?

3. Figure 6.13 displays a workbook containing worksheets for individual stores as well as a summary worksheet with totals for all stores.

a. What is the name of the workbook displayed in the figure? How many worksheets does it contain?

b. What was the gross profit for the Downtown store in the first quarter? For the Midtown store in the second quarter? For the Uptown store in the third quarter?

c. Assume that the sales in the first quarter for the Downtown store are changed to $109,500. Which other value(s) will change within the Downtown worksheet? Within the All Stores Worksheet?

d. Which worksheet is active? What is the active cell in that worksheet? What are its contents?

e. What formula (function) would you expect to find in cell B10 of the Uptown worksheet? of the Midtown worksheet?

f. What formula (function) would you expect to find in cell B3 in the All Stores worksheet? in cell B4 in the All Stores worksheet? in cell B5 in the All Stores worksheet?

g. Which formula (function) would you expect to find in cell B7 of the All Stores worksheet, given that the formula (function) references only cells within the All Stores worksheet?

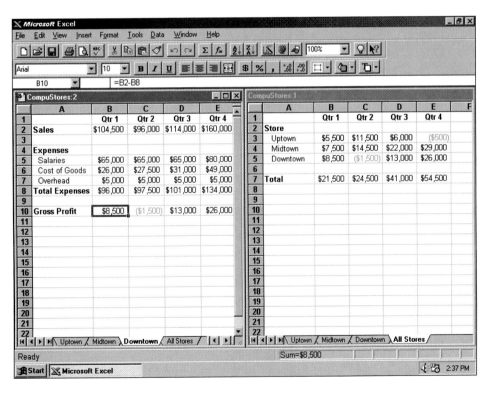

FIGURE 6.13   Screen for Problem 3

4. Answer the following with respect to the workbook(s) shown in Figure 6.14:

a. How many workbooks are open in Figure 6.14?

b. Which workbook is the source workbook? Which workbook is the dependent workbook?

c. Which workbook contains an external reference?

d. What is the active workbook? What is the active worksheet in this workbook? What is the active cell?

e. What are the contents of the formula bar? Why are the drive and folder shown for the San Diego workbook, but not for the Miami workbook?

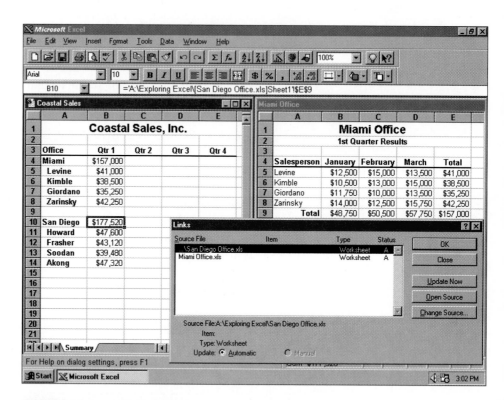

FIGURE 6.14   Screen for Problem 4

PRACTICE WITH EXCEL 7.0

1. A partially completed version of the workbook in Figure 6.15 can be found on the data disk as *Chapter 6 Practice 1*. This workbook contains worksheets for the individual sections but does not contain the summary worksheet.

a. Retrieve the Chapter 6 Practice 1 workbook from the data disk, then open multiple windows so that the display on your monitor matches Figure 6.15.

b. Complete the individual worksheets by adding the appropriate formulas (functions) to compute the class average on each test.

c. Add a summary worksheet that includes the test averages from each of the sections as shown in the figure.

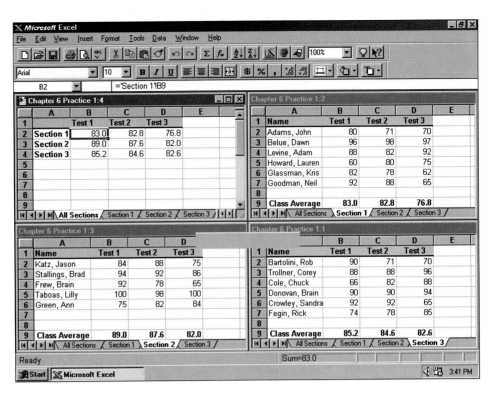

FIGURE 6.15 Screen for Practice Exercise 1

    d. Add a documentation worksheet that includes your name as the grading assistant, the date of modification, and lists all of the worksheets in the workbook.

    e. Print the entire workbook and submit it to your instructor.

2. A partially completed version of the workbook in Figure 6.16 can be found on the data disk as *Chapter 6 Practice 2*. The workbook contains a separate worksheet for each month of the year as well as a summary worksheet for the entire year. Thus far, only the months of January, February, and March are complete. Each monthly worksheet tallies the expenses for five departments in each of four categories to compute a monthly total for each department. The summary worksheet displays the total expense for each department.

    a. Retrieve the Chapter 6 Practice 2 workbook from the data disk, then open multiple windows so that the display on your monitor matches Figure 6.16.

    b. Use the Group Editing feature to select the worksheets for January, February, and March simultaneously. Enter the formula to compute the monthly total for each department in each month.

    c. Use the Group Editing feature to format the worksheets.

    d. Enter the appropriate formulas in the summary worksheet to compute the year-to-date totals for each department.

    e. Add an additional worksheet for the month of April. Assume that department 1 spends $100 in each category, department 2 spends $200 in each category, and so on. Update the summary worksheet to include the expenses for April.

    f. Add a documentation worksheet that includes your name, the date of modification, plus a description of each worksheet within the workbook.

    g. Print the entire workbook (all five worksheets), then print the cell formulas for the summary worksheet only.

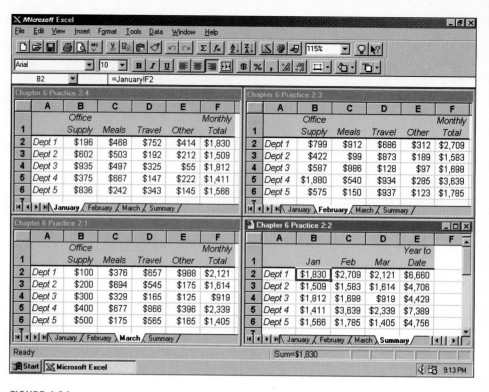

FIGURE 6.16   Screen for Practice Exercise 2

3. Object Linking and Embedding: Create the compound document in Figure 6.17, which consists of a memo, summary worksheet, and three-dimensional chart. The chart is to be created in its own chart sheet within the Corporate Sales workbook, then incorporated into the memo by using the technique described in Chapter 4 (see pages 171–180). Address the memo to your instructor, sign your name, then print the memo as it appears in Figure 6.17.

Prove to yourself that Object Linking and Embedding really works by returning to the Atlanta worksheet *after* you have created the document in Figure 6.17. Change the sales for Product 2 in Quarter 4 to $3,000. Switch back to the Word memo, and the chart should reflect the dramatic increase in the sales for Product 1. Add a postscript to the memo, indicating that the corrected chart reflects the last-minute sale of Product 1 in Atlanta. Print the revised memo and submit it to your instructor with the earlier version.

4. Figure 6.18 on page 292 contains a pivot table that was created from the Corporate Sales workbook used throughout the chapter. The pivot table was created *without* the benefit of a list (as was done in Chapter 5) by specifying multiple consolidation ranges. Do Hands-on Exercises 1, 2, and 3 as they appear in this chapter. Review the material on pivot tables from Chapter 5, then follow the steps below to create the pivot table in its own worksheet within the Corporate Sales workbook.

   a. Pull down the Data menu and click the Pivot Table command. Click the option button to select Multiple Consolidation Ranges in step 1 of the Pivot Table Wizard. Click Next.

   b. Click the option button to create a single-page field for me in step 2. Click Next.

National Widgets, Inc.

Atlanta • Boston • Chicago

To: John Graves, President
       National Widgets, Inc.

From: Susan Powers
       Vice President, Marketing

Subject: Sales Analysis Data

Our overall fourth quarter sales have improved considerably over those in the first quarter. Please note, however, that Product 1, despite a growth in sales, is still trailing the others, and discontinuing its production should be considered. I will await your reply on this matter.

Corporate Totals					
	Qtr 1	Qtr 2	Qtr 3	Qtr 4	Totals
Product 1	$915	$995	$1,115	$1,235	$4,260
Product 2	$1,350	$1,450	$1,950	$2,250	$7,000
Product 3	$1,425	$1,600	$1,750	$2,000	$6,775
Total	$3,690	$4,045	$4,815	$5,485	$18,035

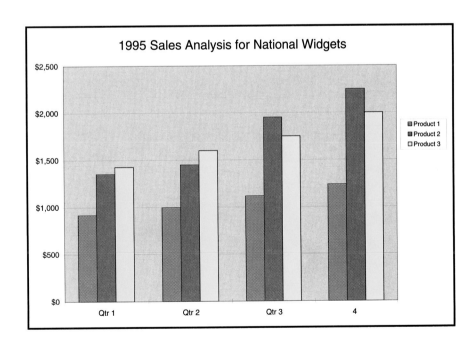

FIGURE 6.17   Memo for Practice Exercise 3

Sum of Amount		Product			
Quarter	City	Product 1	Product 2	Product 3	Grand Total
Qtr 1	Atlanta	$10	$1,100	$200	$1,310
	Boston	$55	$150	$1,150	$1,355
	Chicago	$850	$100	$75	$1,025
Qtr 1 Total		$915	$1,350	$1,425	$3,690
Qtr 2	Atlanta	$20	$1,200	$200	$1,420
	Boston	$25	$250	$1,250	$1,525
	Chicago	$950	$0	$150	$1,100
Qtr 2 Total		$995	$1,450	$1,600	$4,045
Qtr 3	Atlanta	$30	$1,300	$300	$1,630
	Boston	$35	$350	$1,350	$1,735
	Chicago	$1,050	$300	$100	$1,450
Qtr 3 Total		$1,115	$1,950	$1,750	$4,815
Qtr 4	Atlanta	$40	$1,400	$400	$1,840
	Boston	$45	$450	$1,400	$1,895
	Chicago	$1,150	$400	$200	$1,750
Qtr 4 Total		$1,235	$2,250	$2,000	$5,485
Grand Total		$4,260	$7,000	$6,775	$18,035

FIGURE 6.18   Pivot Table for Practice Exercise 4

c. Specify the range in step 3 of the PivotTable wizard through pointing. Click the Sheet tab for Atlanta, select cells A2 through E5, then click the Add command button. You should see Atlanta!$A$2:$E$5 in the Range box. Repeat this step for the other two cities. You should see the same range for Atlanta, Boston, and Chicago.

d. Click the Finish command button to create the pivot table.

e. Edit the pivot table so that it matches Figure 6.18. Click in cell B3 (the field name is Column), then click the formula bar and enter Quarter. Change the entry in cell A4 from Row to Product in similar fashion. Change the entry in cell A1 from Page to City.

f. Click in cell B1, click the drop-down arrow, select Item1, click the formula bar, and enter Atlanta. Click OK when asked to rename Item1 to Atlanta. Repeat these steps to replace Items 2 and 3 with Boston and Chicago, respectively.

g. Pivot the table by dragging Quarter to the row position, Product to the column position, and City to the row position below and to the right of Quarter.

h. Format the pivot table so that it matches Figure 6.18. Save the workbook.

The process seems long, but with practice, it's done rather easily, and the flexibility inherent in the resulting pivot table is worth the effort. Modify the description on the Documentation worksheet to include the pivot table, then print the entire workbook and submit it to your instructor.

CASE STUDIES

Urban Sophisticates

The *Urban Sophisticates* workbook on the data disk is only partially complete as it contains worksheets for individual stores, but does not as yet have a summary worksheet. Your job is to retrieve the workbook and create a summary worksheet, then use the summary worksheet as the basis of a three-dimensional column chart reflecting the sales for the past year. Add a documentation worksheet containing your name as financial analyst, then print the entire workbook and submit it to your instructor.

External References

As marketing manager you are responsible for consolidating the sales information for all of the branch offices within the corporation. Each branch manager creates an identically formatted workbook with the sales information for his or her branch office. Your job is to consolidate the information into a single table, then graph the results appropriately. The branch data is to remain in the individual workbooks; that is, the formulas in your workbook are to contain external references to the *Eastern, Western,* and *Foreign workbooks* on the data disk. Your workbook is to be developed in such a way that any change in the individual workbooks should be automatically reflected in the consolidated workbook.

Pivot Tables

What advantages, if any, does a pivot table have over a conventional worksheet with respect to analyzing and consolidating data from multiple sources? What are the disadvantages? Does the underlying data have to be entered in the form of a list, or can it be taken directly from a worksheet? Use what you learn to extend the analysis of the Atlanta, Boston, and Chicago data that appeared throughout the chapter. (See practice exercise 4 for one example of a pivot table.)

The Spreadsheet Audit

Which tools are found on the Auditing toolbar? What is the difference between precedent and dependent cells? Can the Auditing toolbar detect precedent cells that are located in a different worksheet? In a different workbook? The answers to these and other questions can be found by studying Appendix A (pages 357–368), then experimenting on your own. A spreadsheet audit is an important concept and one with which you should become familiar.

AUTOMATING REPETITIVE TASKS: MACROS AND VISUAL BASIC

OBJECTIVES

After reading this chapter you will be able to:

1. Define a macro; explain how macros facilitate the execution of repetitive tasks.
2. Record and run a macro; view and edit the statements in a simple macro.
3. Use the InputBox statement to obtain input for a macro as it is running.
4. Use a keyboard shortcut and/or a customized toolbar to run a macro; create a custom button to execute a macro.
5. Describe where macros are stored; explain the function of the Personal Macro workbook.
6. Use the Step mode to execute a macro one statement at a time.
7. Use the Copy and Paste commands to duplicate an existing macro; modify the copied macro to create an entirely new macro.
8. Use the Visual Basic If and Do statements to implement decision making and looping within an Excel macro.

OVERVIEW

Have you ever pulled down the same menus and clicked the same sequence of commands over and over? Easy as the commands may be to execute, it is still burdensome to have to continually repeat the same mouse clicks or keystrokes. If you can think of any task that you do repeatedly, whether in one workbook or in a series of workbooks, you are a perfect candidate to use macros.

A **macro** is a set of instructions that tells Excel which commands to execute. It is in essence a program, and its instructions are written in Visual Basic, a programming language. Fortunately, however, you don't have to be a programmer to write macros. Instead, you use the macro recorder within Excel to record your commands, and let Excel write the macros for you.

This chapter introduces you to the power of Excel macros. We begin by creating a simple macro to insert your name, class, and date into a worksheet. We show you how to modify the macro once it has been created and how to execute the macro one statement at a time. We also show you how to store the macro in the Personal Macro workbook, so that it will be available automatically whenever you start Excel.

The second half of the chapter describes how to create more powerful macros that automate commands associated with list management, as presented in Chapter 5. We show you how to copy and edit a macro, and how to create customized buttons with which to execute a macro. We also show you how the power of an Excel macro can be extended through the inclusion of additional Visual Basic statements that implement loops and decision making.

VISUAL BASIC

Visual Basic is a powerful programming language that can be used to develop all types of applications. It may appear intimidating at first, but it is quite easy to learn once you understand its overall structure. We believe the best introduction to Visual Basic is to use the macro recorder in Excel to create simple macros, which are in fact complete programs in Visual Basic. You get results that are immediately usable and can learn a good deal about Visual Basic through observation and intuition.

INTRODUCTION TO MACROS

The *macro recorder* stores Excel commands, in the form of Visual Basic instructions, on a *macro sheet* within a workbook. To use the recorder, you pull down the Tools menu and click the Record Macro command. From that point on (until you stop recording), every command you execute will be stored by the recorder. It doesn't matter whether you execute commands from pull-down menus via the mouse, or whether you use the toolbar or keyboard shortcuts. The macro recorder captures every action you take and stores the equivalent Visual Basic statements in a macro within the workbook.

Once the macro has been created, you can run (execute) the macro at a later time. Sure, you spend time creating the macro, but once this has been accomplished, you have the macro forever, and can run it whenever you need it. The more powerful the macro, the more time it will save you.

Figure 7.1 contains a simple macro to enter your name and class in cells A1 and A2 of the active worksheet. The macro is a *Visual Basic* program and consists of statements that were created through the macro recorder. We don't expect you to be able to write the Visual Basic program yourself, but you don't have to. You just invoke the recorder and let it capture the keystrokes for you. We think it important, however, for you to understand the macro, and so we proceed to explain its statements. As you read our discussion, do not be concerned with the precise syntax of every statement, but try to get an overall appreciation for what the statements do.

The first several statements begin with an apostrophe and are known as *comments.* (Comments appear in green on a color monitor, but it is the apostrophe that is significant rather than the color of the statement.) Comments provide documentation about a macro but do not affect its execution; that is, the results of

Comments begin with
an apostrophe

Sub statement begins the
executable part of the macro
and contains its name

Last macro statement

```
'
' NameAndCourse Macro
' Macro recorded 8/6/95 by Darren Krein
'
' Keyboard Shortcut: Ctrl+n
'
Sub NameAndCourse()
    Range("A1").Select
    ActiveCell.FormulaR1C1 = "Darren Krein"
    Range("A2").Select
    ActiveCell.FormulaR1C1 = "CIS 622"
    Range("A1:A2").Select
    Selection.Font.Bold = True
    Selection.Font.Italic = True
    With Selection.Font
        .Name = "Arial"
        .Size = 12
    End With
    Range("A3").Select
End Sub
```

FIGURE 7.1   A Simple Macro

the macro are the same, whether or not the comments are included. Comments are inserted automatically by the recorder to document the macro name, its author, and shortcut key (if any). You can add additional comments (a comment line must begin with an apostrophe), or delete or modify existing comments, as you see fit.

The executable portion of a macro begins and ends with the Sub and End Sub statements, respectively. The **Sub statement** contains the name of the macro—for example, NameAndCourse in Figure 7.1. (Spaces are not allowed in a macro name.) The **End Sub statement** is physically the last statement and indicates the end of the macro. Sub and End Sub are Visual Basic key words and appear in blue.

Each instruction in a macro is a Visual Basic statement that corresponds to commands in Excel; for example, the statements

```
        Range ("A1").Select
and     ActiveCell.FormulaR1C1 = "Darren Krein"
```

select cell A1 as the active cell, then enter the text "Darren Krein" into the active cell. These statements are equivalent to clicking in cell A1 of a worksheet, typing the indicated entry into the active cell, then pressing the enter key (or an arrow key) to complete the entry. In similar fashion, the statements

```
        Range ("A2").Select
and     ActiveCell.FormulaR1C1 = "CIS622"
```

select cell A2 as the active cell, then enter the text entry "CIS622" into that cell. The concept of select-then-do applies equally well to statements within a macro. Thus, the statements

```
        Range ("A1:A2").Select
        Selection.Font.Bold = True
        Selection.Font.Italic = True
```

select cells A1 through A2, then change the font for the selected cells to bold italic. The **With statement** enables you to perform multiple actions on the same object.

All commands between the With and corresponding **End With statements** are executed collectively; for example, the statements

```
With Selection.Font
    .Name = "Arial"
    .Size = 12
End With
```

change the formatting of the selected cells (A1:A2) to 12 point Arial. The statements are equivalent to selecting cells A1 and A2, selecting Arial as the typeface, then specifying 12 point type. The last statement in the macro, Range ("A3").Select, deselects all other cells, a practice we use throughout the chapter.

As we have already indicated, you are not expected to be able to write the Visual Basic statements from scratch, but you should be able to understand the statements once they have been recorded. Moreover, you can edit the macro (after it has been recorded) to change the selected cells and/or their values. You can also change the typeface, point size, or style, simply by changing the appropriate statement in the macro.

PLAN AHEAD

The macro recorder records everything you do, including entries that are made by mistake or commands that are executed incorrectly. Plan the macro in advance, before you begin recording. Write down what you intend to do, then try out the commands with the recorder off. Be sure you go all the way through the intended sequence of operations prior to turning the macro recorder on.

HANDS-ON EXERCISE 1

Introduction to Macros

Objective: Record, run, view, and edit a simple macro; establish a keyboard shortcut to run a macro. Use Figure 7.2 as a guide in the exercise.

STEP 1: Open a New Workbook

➤ Start Excel. Open a new workbook if one is not already open.

➤ Delete all worksheets except for Sheet1:

• Click the tab for **Sheet2.** Click the ▶| **scrolling button** to scroll to the last worksheet in the workbook (Sheet16 is the default).

• Press the **Shift key** as you click the tab for **Sheet16.** (Sheets 2 through 16 should be selected.)

• Point to the tab for **Sheet16** and click the **right mouse button** to display a shortcut menu. Click **Delete.** Click **OK** in response to the warning that the selected sheets will be permanently deleted.

➤ Your workbook should contain only Sheet1 as shown in Figure 7.2a. Save the workbook as **My Macros** in the **Exploring Excel folder.**

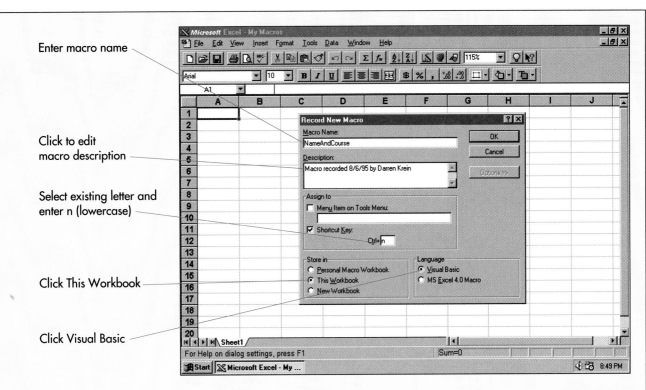

Enter macro name

Click to edit
macro description

Select existing letter and
enter n (lowercase)

Click This Workbook

Click Visual Basic

(a) Set the Macro Options (step 2)

FIGURE 7.2   Hands-on Exercise 1

STEP 2: Set the Macro Options

➤ Pull down the **Tools menu,** click (or point to) the **Record Macro command,** then click **Record New Macro.**

➤ You will see the Record New Macro dialog box in Figure 7.2a. Only the Macro Name and Description text boxes are visible at this time.

➤ Enter **NameAndCourse** as the name of the macro. Do not leave any spaces in the macro name.

➤ The description is entered automatically and contains today's date and the name of the person in whose name this copy of Excel is registered. If necessary, change the description to include your name.

➤ Click the **Options command button** to display additional options within the Record New Macro dialog box as shown in Figure 7.2a:

  • Check the **Shortcut Key check box,** click in the Shortcut key text box, then delete (or select) the existing shortcut (the letter e).

  • Enter a **lowercase n** as shown in Figure 7.2a. Ctrl+n should appear as the shortcut. (If you see Ctrl+Shift+N it means you typed an uppercase "N" rather than a lowercase letter; correct the entry to a lowercase n.)

  • Check that the options buttons for **This Workbook** and **Visual Basic** have been selected.

➤ Click **OK** to begin recording the macro. The Stop Macro button appears on the screen.

➤ Pull down the **Tools menu** a second time and click (or point to) the **Record Macro command:**

- If there is a check next to Use Relative References, click the command to toggle it off. (Relative references are explained on page 309.)
- If Use Relative References does not have a check, click outside the menu to close it.

THE PERSONAL MACRO WORKBOOK

Macros are stored in one of two places: either on a module sheet in the current workbook or in a Personal Macro workbook. The latter is intended for generic macros that you want to use with many workbooks and is discussed in detail, beginning on page 311.

STEP 3: Record the Macro

➤ You should be in Sheet1, ready to record, as shown in Figure 7.2b. A macro sheet (Module1) has been added to the workbook, and the status bar indicates that you are recording the macro:

- Click in **cell A1** even if it is already selected. Enter your name.
- Click in **cell A2.** Enter the course you are taking.
- Click and drag to select **cells A1** through **A2.** Click the **Bold button.** Click the **Italic button.**

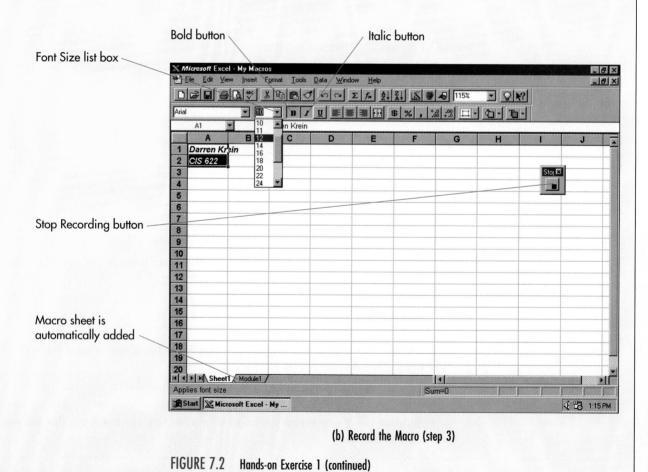

(b) Record the Macro (step 3)

FIGURE 7.2   Hands-on Exercise 1 (continued)

- Click the **arrow** on the **Font Size** list box. Click **12** to change the point size.
- Click in **cell A3** to deselect all other cells prior to ending the macro.

➤ Click the **Stop Recording button** to end the macro. The macro has been recorded on its own worksheet named Module1.

➤ Save the workbook.

THE END RESULT

The macro recorder records only the result of the selection process, with no indication of how the selection was arrived at. It doesn't matter how you get to a particular cell. You can click in the cell directly, use the Go To command in the Edit menu, or use the mouse or arrow keys. The end result is the same, and the macro indicates only the selected cell(s).

STEP 4: Run the Macro

➤ To run (test) the macro, you have to remove the contents and formatting from cells A1 and A2. Click and drag to select **cells A1** through **A2.**

➤ Pull down the **Edit menu.** Click **Clear.** Click **All** from the cascaded menu to erase both the contents and formatting from the selected cells. Cells A1 through A2 are empty as shown in Figure 7.2c.

Click and drag to
select A1:A2

Click to select
NameAndCourse macro

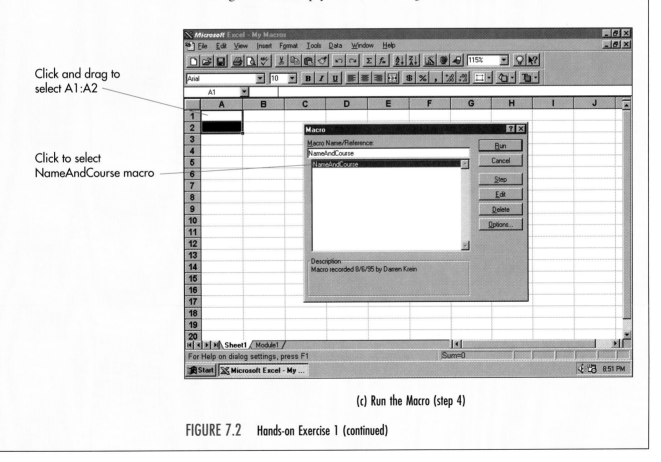

(c) Run the Macro (step 4)

FIGURE 7.2   Hands-on Exercise 1 (continued)

➤ Pull down the **Tools menu.** Click **Macro** to produce the dialog box shown in Figure 7.2c.

➤ Click **NameAndCourse,** which is the macro you just recorded. Click **Run.** Your name and class are entered in cells A1 and A2, then formatted according to the instructions in the macro.

MACRO NAMES

Macro names must begin with a letter and are not allowed to contain spaces or punctuation except for the underscore character. To create a macro name containing more than one word, capitalize the first letter of each word to make the words stand out and/or use the underscore character—for example, NameAndCourse or Name_And_Course.

STEP 5: Simplify the Macro

➤ Click the **Module1 tab** to view the macro you just created. Use the **down (up) arrows** on the vertical scroll bar to display the macro as shown in Figure 7.2d. The commands in your macro may vary slightly from ours if you did not follow the exact instructions in step 3.

➤ Click immediately after the number **12,** then click and drag to select the highlighted statements as shown in Figure 7.2d. Press the **Del key** to delete these

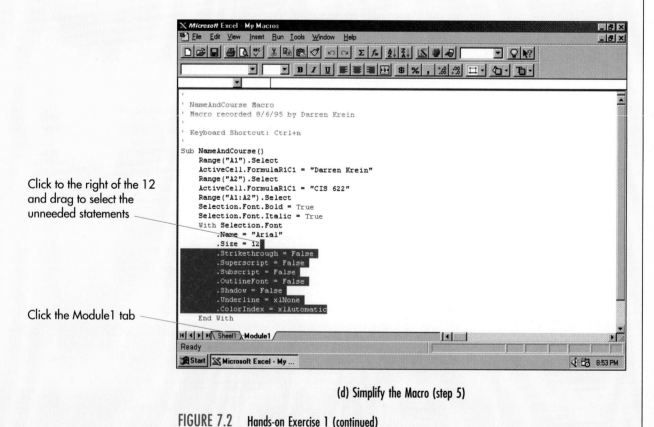

Click to the right of the 12 and drag to select the unneeded statements

Click the Module1 tab

(d) Simplify the Macro (step 5)

FIGURE 7.2   Hands-on Exercise 1 (continued)

statements from the macro. (These statements contain default values and are unnecessary.)

➤ Click the tab for **Sheet1.** Clear the entries and formatting in cells A1 and A2 as you did in step 4, then rerun the **NameAndCourse** macro. Your name and class should once again be entered in cells A1 and A2. (If the macro does not execute correctly, click the Module1 tab and re-edit your macro so that it matches the one in Figure 7.2d.)

➤ Click the **Save button** to save the workbook with the revised macro.

SIMPLIFY THE MACRO

The macro recorder usually sets all possible options for an Excel command or dialog box even if you do not change those options explicitly. We suggest, therefore, that you make a macro easier to read by deleting the unnecessary statements.

STEP 6: Create the Erase Macro

➤ Pull down the **Tools menu.** Click (or point to) the **Record Macro command,** then click **Record New Macro** from the cascaded menu. You will see the Record New Macro dialog box as described earlier.

➤ Enter **EraseNameAndCourse** as the name of the macro. Do not leave any spaces in the macro name. If necessary, change the description to include your name.

➤ Click the **Options command button** to display additional options within the Record New Macro dialog box.

- Check the **Shortcut Key check box,** then (if necessary) delete the current entry and enter a **lowercase e.**

- Check that the options buttons for **This Workbook** and **Visual Basic** have been selected.

➤ Click **OK** to begin recording the macro. The Stop Macro button appears on the screen.

➤ Click and drag to select **cells A1** through **A2** as shown in Figure 7.2e, even if they are already selected.

➤ Pull down the **Edit menu.** Click **Clear.** Click **All** from the cascaded menu to erase both the contents and formatting from the selected cells. Cells A1 through A2 should now be empty.

TO SELECT OR NOT SELECT

If you start recording, then select a cell(s), you limit the macro to the cell(s) you selected from within the macro. If, however, you select the cell(s), then record, the macro is generic and will operate on the selected cells regardless of their location. Both techniques are valid, and the decision on which to choose depends on what you want the macro to do.

Click Edit

Click and drag to
select A1:A2

Click Clear

Click All

Click Stop Recording button

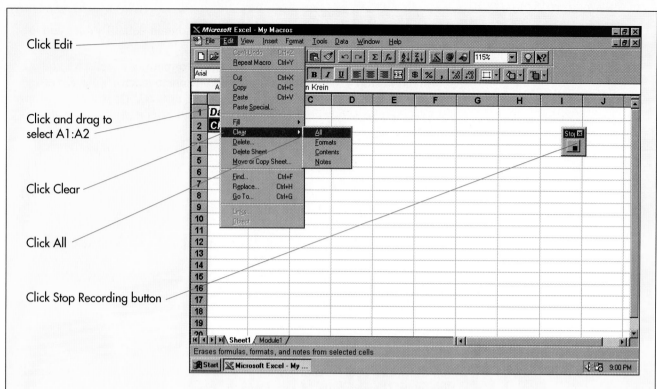

(e) Create the Erase Macro (step 6)

FIGURE 7.2   Hands-on Exercise 1 (continued)

➤ Click in **cell A3** to deselect all other cells prior to ending the macro.

➤ Click the **Stop Recording button** to end the macro. The macro is inserted in
the Module1 worksheet below the NameAndCourse macro created earlier.

STEP 7: Shortcut Keys

➤ Press **Ctrl+n** to execute the NameAndCourse macro. (You need to reenter
your name and course in order to test the newly created EraseNameAnd-
Course macro.)

➤ Your name and course should again appear in cells A1 and A2.

TROUBLESHOOTING

If the shortcut keys do not work, it is probably because they were not
defined properly. Pull down the Tools menu, select the Macro command,
choose the desired macro in the Macro Name/Reference list box, then
click the Options command button. Check the Shortcut Key check box,
then click in the associated text box to enter the shortcut. Enter a *lowercase letter* to create a shortcut with just the Ctrl key; for example, a lowercase "n" establishes Ctrl+n as the shortcut. Enter an *uppercase letter* to
create a shortcut with the Ctrl and Shift keys; e.g., typing an uppercase
"N" establishes Ctrl+Shift+n as the shortcut.

➤ Press **Ctrl+e** to execute the EraseNameAndCourse macro. Cells A1 and A2 should again be empty.

➤ You can press Ctrl+n and Ctrl+e repeatedly, to enter, then erase your name and course. End this step after having erased the data.

STEP 8: Edit the Macro

➤ Click the **Module1 tab** to return to the macros. Click the **down (up) arrow** on the vertical scroll bar to view both macros as shown in Figure 7.2f.

➤ Edit the NameAndCourse macro as follows:

• Change the Font Name to **Times New Roman.**

• Delete the statement **Selection.Font.Bold = True.**

➤ Click the **Sheet1 tab** to test the macro. Press **Ctrl+n** to run the revised Name-AndCourse macro. Your name and course should appear in 12 point Times New Roman Italic.

USE WHAT YOU KNOW

The *Cut, Copy,* and *Paste commands* are the mainstays of editing, regardless of the application. Select the statements to cut or copy to the clipboard, then paste them elsewhere in the macro, as necessary. If the results are different from what you expected or intended, click the Undo command immediately to reverse the effects of the previous command.

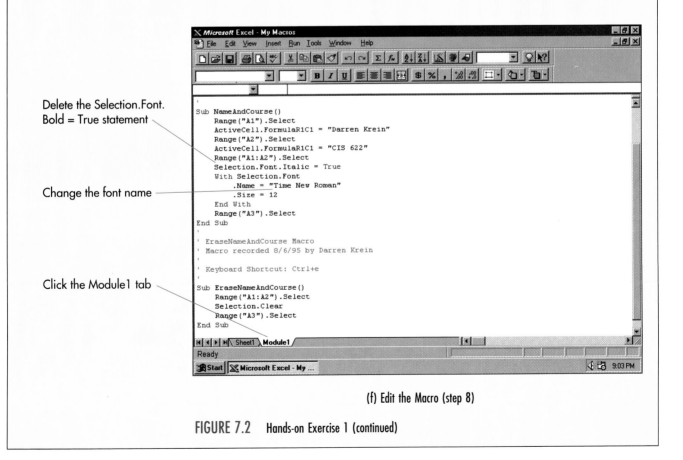

(f) Edit the Macro (step 8)

FIGURE 7.2   Hands-on Exercise 1 (continued)

STEP 9: Step through the Macro

➤ Press **Ctrl+e** to execute the Erase macro and clear the contents and formatting in cells A1 and A2.

➤ Point to any toolbar, then click the **right mouse button** to display a shortcut menu. Check **Visual Basic** to display the Visual Basic toolbar. Dock the toolbar below the Formatting toolbar.

➤ Click the **Run Macro button** on the Visual Basic toolbar. Click the **Name-AndCourse macro** from the list of macros within the workbook, then click the **Step command button.**

➤ You should see a Debug window similar to Figure 7.2g. Drag the left border of the Debug window so that columns A and B of Sheet1 are visible as in Figure 7.2g. There is a rectangle around the Sub statement that begins the macro.

➤ Click and drag the line dividing the two halves of the Debug window to increase the size of the lower window. Click the **Step Into button** on the Visual Basic toolbar to step into the macro.

➤ The first Range statement is selected. Click the **Step Into button** to execute this statement (and select the next statement). Look at the worksheet. Cell A1 is selected as a result of executing the first macro statement.

➤ The ActiveCell statement to enter your name is selected. Click the **Step Into button** to execute this statement (and select the next statement). Look at the worksheet. Your name has been entered into cell A1.

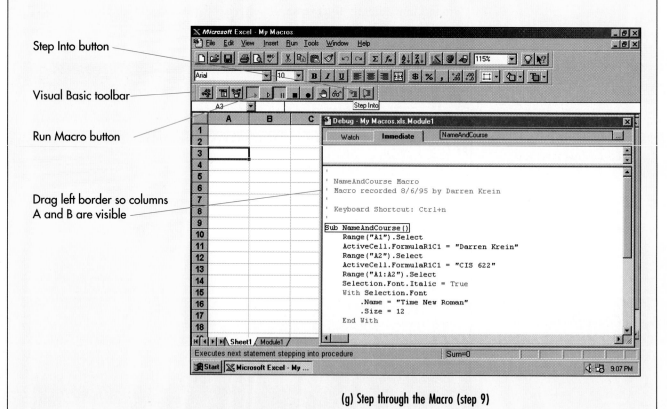

(g) Step through the Macro (step 9)

FIGURE 7.2   Hands-on Exercise 1 (continued)

➤ Continue to click the **Step Into button** until the macro has completed execution, and you again see your name and course in Sheet1, and the Debug window has closed.

THE FIRST BUG

A bug is a mistake in a computer program; hence debugging refers to the process of correcting program errors. According to legend, the first bug was an unlucky moth crushed to death on one of the relays of the electromechanical Mark II computer, bringing the machine's operation to a halt. The cause of the failure was discovered by Grace Hopper, who promptly taped the moth to her logbook, noting, *"First actual case of bug being found."*

STEP 10: Add to the Macro

➤ Click the **Module1 tab.** Click immediately to the left of the Range ("A1:A2").Select statement as shown in Figure 7.2h. This is the position in the macro where you want to insert additional statements.

➤ Pull down the **Tools menu.** Click the **Record Macro command.** Click **Mark Position for Recording** from the cascaded menu as shown in Figure 7.2h.

➤ Click the **Sheet1 tab** and pull down the **Tools menu.** Click the **Record Macro command,** then click **Record at Mark.**

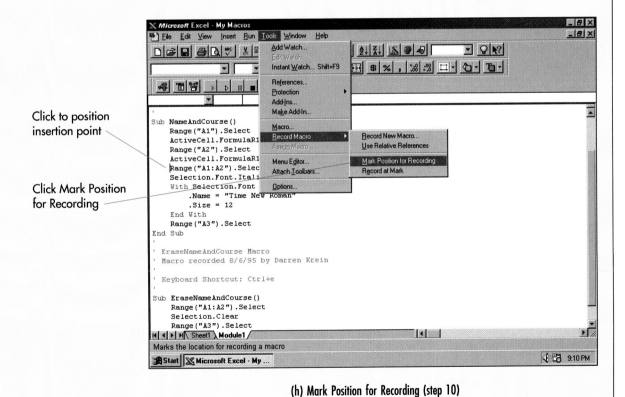

(h) Mark Position for Recording (step 10)

FIGURE 7.2   Hands-on Exercise 1 (continued)

➤ Click **cell A3** (even if it is currently selected), then enter **=TODAY().** Press **enter** to complete the entry in cell A3. Click the **Stop Recording Button** to cease recording.

➤ Click the **Save button** to save the workbook, which includes the revised macro.

MARK THE POSITION

Whenever you close and then reopen a workbook, the macro recorder will record new macros on a new module sheet. You can, however, record a new macro on an existing module sheet by marking the position prior to recording. Click the tab for the macro sheet in which you want the macro recorded, click where you want the new macro to go, pull down the Tools menu, click (or point to) the Record Macro command, then click Mark Position for Recording. Click the worksheet tab, pull down the Tools menu, click Record Macro, click Record New Macro, and proceed as usual.

STEP 11: The Completed Macro

➤ Click the **Module1 tab** to view the revised macro as shown in Figure 7.2i. Three additional statements have been inserted into the macro at the position previously marked for recording.

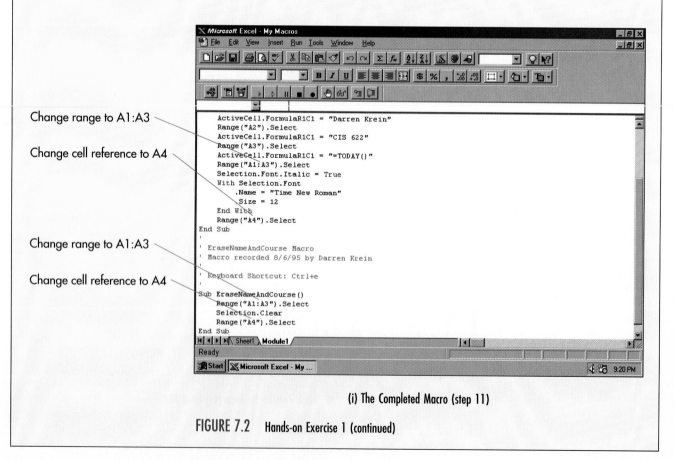

(i) The Completed Macro (step 11)

FIGURE 7.2   Hands-on Exercise 1 (continued)

- Change the Range ("A1:A2").Select statement to reference **cells A1:A3** so that cells A1 through A3 will be formatted.
- Delete the Range ("A4").Select statement, which is unnecessary and was entered because you pressed the enter key after entering the TODAY function in cell A3.
- Change the last statement in the macro to reference **cell A4** (rather than A3).

➤ Edit the Range ("A1:A2").Select statement in the EraseNameAndCourse macro so that it, too, reflects **cells A1** through **A3.** Be sure to change the last statement in this macro to reference **cell A4.**

➤ Click the **Sheet1 tab.** Press **Ctrl+e** to clear the contents of cells A1 through A3.

➤ Press **Ctrl+n** to run the revised NameAndCourse macro.

STEP 12: Print the Macro Sheet

➤ Click the **Module1 tab.**

➤ Pull down the **File menu** and select the **Print command.** If necessary, click the option button to print the **Selected Sheet(s).** Click **OK.**

➤ Save the workbook a final time. Close the workbook. Exit Excel if you do not want to continue with the next exercise at this time.

RELATIVE VERSUS ABSOLUTE REFERENCES

One of the most important options to specify when recording a macro is whether the references are to be relative or absolute. A reference is a cell address. An *absolute reference* is a constant address that always refers to the same cell. A *relative reference* is variable in that the reference will change from one execution of the macro to the next, depending on the location of the active cell when the macro is executed.

To appreciate the difference, consider Figure 7.3, which displays the NameAndCourse macro from the previous exercise with absolute and relative references. Figure 7.3a uses absolute references to place your name, course, and date in cells A1, A2, and A3. The data will always be entered in these cells regardless of which cell is selected when you execute the macro.

Figure 7.3b enters the same data, but with relative references, so that the cells in which the data is entered depend on where you are when the macro is executed. If you happen to be in cell A1, your name, course, and date will be entered in cells A1, A2, and A3. If, however, you are in cell E4 when you execute the macro, then your name, course, and date will be entered in cells E4, E5, and E6.

A relative reference is specified by an *offset* that indicates the number of rows and columns from the active cell. An offset of (1,0) indicates a cell one row below the active cell. An offset of (0,1) indicates a cell one column to the right of the active cell. In similar fashion, an offset of (1,1) indicates a cell one row below and one column to the right of the active cell. Negative offsets are used for cells above or to the left of the current selection.

Relative references may appear confusing at first, but they extend the power of a macro by making it more general. You will appreciate this capability as you learn more about macros. Let us begin by recognizing that the statement:

ActiveCell.Offset (1,0).Range ("A1").Select

Absolute reference
to specified cell

```
' NameAndCourse Macro
' Macro recorded 8/6/95 by Darren Krein
'
' Keyboard Shortcut: Ctrl+n
'
Sub NameAndCourse()
    Range("A1").Select
    ActiveCell.FormulaR1C1 = "Darren Krein"
    Range("A2").Select
    ActiveCell.FormulaR1C1 = "CIS 622"
    Range("A3").Select
    ActiveCell.FormulaR1C1 = "=TODAY()"
    Range("A1:A3").Select
    Selection.Font.Italic = True
    With Selection.Font
        .Name = "Time New Roman"
        .Size = 12
    End With
    Range("A4").Select
End Sub
```

(a) Absolute References

Relative reference to the cell
one row below the active cell

```
' RelativeName Macro
' Macro recorded 8/6/95 by Darren Krein
'
' Keyboard Shortcut: Ctrl+n
'
Sub RelativeName()
    ActiveCell.Select
    ActiveCell.FormulaR1C1 = "Darren Krein"
    ActiveCell.Offset(1, 0).Range("A1").Select
    ActiveCell.FormulaR1C1 = "CIS 662"
    ActiveCell.Offset(1, 0).Range("A1").Select
    ActiveCell.FormulaR1C1 = "=TODAY()"
    ActiveCell.Offset(-2, 0).Range("A1:A3").Select
    Selection.Font.Italic = True
    With Selection.Font
        .Name = "Arial"
        .Size = 12
    End With
    ActiveCell.Offset(3, 0).Range("A1").Select
End Sub
```

Indicates a column of three
cells, not cells A1 to A3

(b) Relative References

FIGURE 7.3 Absolute versus Relative References

means select the cell one row below the active cell. It has nothing to do with cell
A1, and you might wonder why the entry Range ("A1") is included. The answer
is that the offset specifies the location of the new range (one row below the current cell), and the A1 indicates that the size of that range is a single cell (A1).

In similar fashion, the statement:

ActiveCell.Offset (-2,0).Range ("A1:A3").Select

selects a range, starting two rows above the current cell, that is one column by three rows in size. Again, it has nothing to do with cells A1 through A3. The off-set specifies the location of a new range (two rows above the current cell) and the shape of that range (a column of three cells). If you are in cell D11 when the statement is executed, the selected range will be cells D9 through D11. The selection starts with the cell two rows above the active cell (cell D9), then it continues from that point to select a range consisting of one column by three rows (cells D9:D11).

THE PERSONAL MACRO WORKBOOK

The hands-on exercise at the beginning of the chapter created the NameAnd-Course macro in the My Macros workbook, where it is available to that workbook (or to any other workbook that is in memory when the My Macros workbook is open). What if, however, you want the macro to be available at all times, not just when the My Macros workbook is open? This is easily accomplished by selecting the option button to store the macro in the Personal Macro workbook when it is first recorded.

The ***Personal Macro workbook*** is a special workbook that opens automatically whenever Excel is loaded. (The workbook is hidden by default until the ***Unhide command*** in the Window menu is executed.) The macros within the Personal Macro workbook are available to any workbook as long as the Personal Macro workbook is open. The following hands-on exercise modifies the Name-AndCourse macro to include relative references, then stores that macro in the Personal Macro workbook.

NETWORK PRIVILEGES

If you are on a network, as opposed to a stand-alone machine, you will not be able to save the Personal Macro workbook in the startup folder, as only the network supervisor has rights to that folder. Ask your instructor or the network administrator how to establish your own Personal Macro workbook.

HANDS-ON EXERCISE 2

The Personal Macro Workbook

Objective: To create and store a macro in the Personal Macro workbook; to assign a toolbar button to a macro; to use the Visual Basic InputBox statement. Use Figure 7.4 as a guide in the exercise.

STEP 1: Record Relative References
➤ Start Excel and open a new workbook. Delete all worksheets except for Sheet1.
➤ Pull down the **Tools menu.** Click (or point to) the **Record Macro command,** then click **Record New Macro** from the cascaded menu to produce the Record New Macro dialog box.
➤ Enter **NameAndCourse** in the Macro Name text box, then click the **Options command button** to display additional options within the dialog box.

- Check the **Shortcut Key check box,** delete (or select) the existing letter, then enter a **lowercase n** in the appropriate text box. Ctrl+n should appear as the shortcut. (If you see Shift+Ctrl+n, it means you typed an uppercase "N" rather than a lowercase letter.)
- Check the option button for **Personal Macro workbook.** (This is a different option from the one used in the previous exercise.)
- Check the option button for **Visual Basic.**

➤ Click **OK** to begin recording the macro.

➤ Pull down the **Tools menu,** then click (or point to) the **Record Macro command.** If there is no check mark next to **Use Relative References,** click the command to toggle it on, as shown in Figure 7.4a. (The command functions as a toggle switch; click it once and a check appears and relative references are in effect; click the command a second time and the check disappears.)

RELATIVE VERSUS ABSOLUTE REFERENCES

Relative references appear confusing at first, but they extend the power of a macro by making it more general. Macro statements that have been recorded with relative references include an offset to indicate the number of rows and columns the selection is to be from the active cell. An offset of (1,0) indicates a cell one row below the active cell, whereas an offset of (0,1) indicates a cell one column to the right of the active cell. Negative offsets indicate cells above or to the left of the current selection.

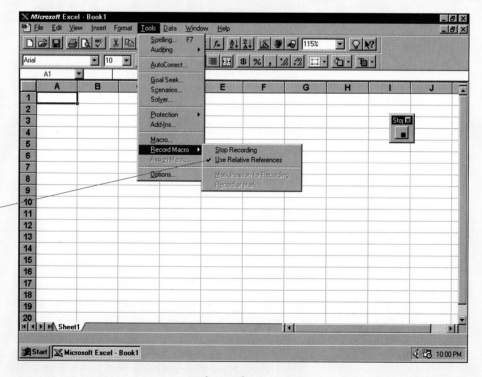

Use Relative References should be toggled on

(a) Relative Reference (step 1)

FIGURE 7.4   Hands-on Exercise 2

STEP 2: Record the Macro

➤ You should be in Sheet1 with cell A1 selected. Enter your name in the active cell.

➤ Press the **down arrow key** to move to the cell immediately underneath the current cell. Enter the course you are taking.

➤ Press the **down arrow key** to move to the next cell. Enter **=TODAY()** to enter today's date.

➤ Click and drag to select the three cells containing the data values you just entered (**cells A1** through **A3** in Figure 7.4b).

• Click the **Bold button.**

• Click the **Italic button.**

• Click the **arrow** on the **Font Size** list box. Click **12** to change the point size.

• Drag the border between the column headings for Columns A and B to increase the width of column A if you see a series of number signs in cell A3. (The latter indicate the column is too narrow to display the date in its current format.)

• Click in **cell A4** to deselect all other cells prior to ending the macro.

➤ Click the **Stop Recording button** to end the macro.

STEP 3: Unhide the Personal Macro workbook

➤ The macro has been recorded but is not yet visible; that is, unlike the previous exercise, there is no Module1 sheet in the current workbook.

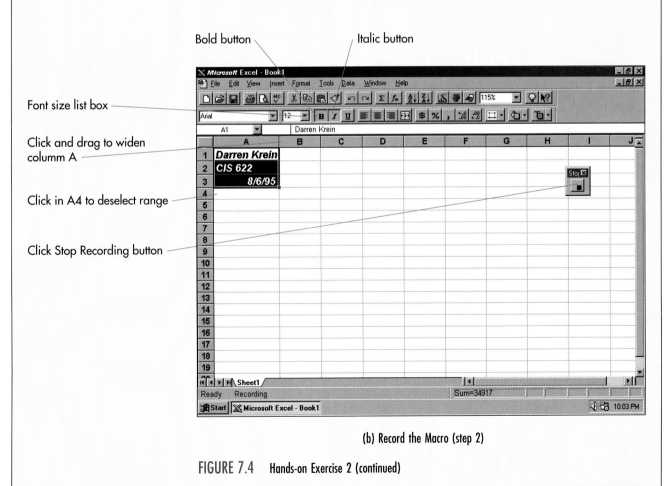

(b) Record the Macro (step 2)

FIGURE 7.4   Hands-on Exercise 2 (continued)

➤ Pull down the **Window menu.** Click **Unhide** to produce the Unhide dialog box. The Personal Macro workbook is already selected. Click **OK** (or press **enter**) to show (unhide) the workbook. If necessary, click the **Maximize button** so that you can edit the macro more easily.

STEP 4: Edit the Macro

➤ The commands in your macro may be slightly different from ours, but they must reflect relative rather than absolute addresses. (You will have to return to the beginning of the exercise and start over if your macro does not contain relative references. Close both workbooks without saving them, then start again, replacing the existing macro when prompted to do so.)

➤ Click immediately after the number **12,** then click and drag to select the highlighted statements in Figure 7.4c. Press the **Del key** to delete the highlighted statements from the macro.

➤ Delete the **Selection.Font.Bold = True** statement, which appears above the With statement.

➤ Change the third statement in the macro (which contains the name of the course) to **ActiveCell.FormulaR1C1 = InputBox("Enter the Course You Are Taking").** Be sure you enter this statement correctly with beginning and ending parentheses, and with beginning and ending quotation marks, as shown.

➤ Click the **Save button** to save the revised workbook.

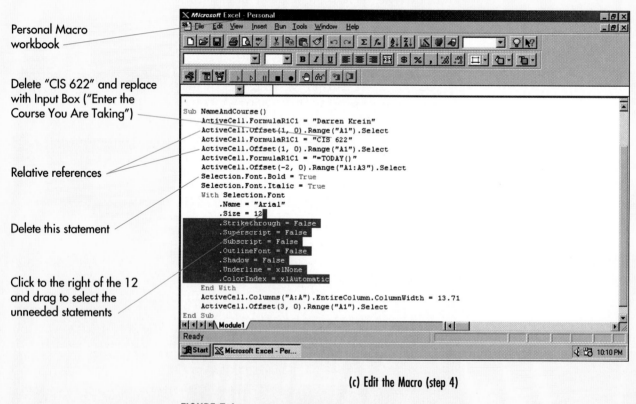

(c) Edit the Macro (step 4)

FIGURE 7.4   Hands-on Exercise 2 (continued)

WHAT DOES RANGE ("A1:A3") REALLY MEAN?

The statement ActiveCell.Offset(−2,0).Range ("A1:A3").Select has nothing to do with cells A1 through A3, so why is the entry Range ("A1:A3") included? The effect of the statement is to select three cells (one cell under the other), starting with the cell two rows above the current cell. The offset (−2,0) specifies the starting point of the selected range (two rows above the current cell). The range ("A1:A3") indicates the size and shape of the selected range (a vertical column of three cells) from the starting cell.

STEP 5: Test the Revised Macro

➤ Pull down the **Window menu.** Click **Book1** to select the window containing the workbook on which you are working. (The Book number is not important, and you may see a different number, depending on how many other workbooks you have opened in this session.)

➤ Click in any cell—for example, **cell C5** as shown in Figure 7.4d. Pull down the **Tools menu.** Click **Macro,** select **PERSONAL.XLS!NameAndCourse,** then click the **Run command button** to run the macro. (Alternatively, you can use the **Ctrl+n** shortcut.)

➤ The macro enters your name in cell C5 (the active cell), then displays the input dialog box in Figure 7.4d. Enter any appropriate course and press the **enter key.** You should see the course you entered followed by the date.

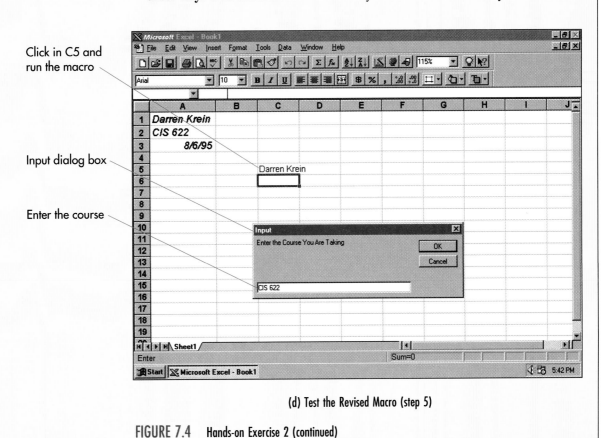

Click in C5 and run the macro

Input dialog box

Enter the course

(d) Test the Revised Macro (step 5)

FIGURE 7.4   Hands-on Exercise 2 (continued)

➤ Click in a different cell (you can click in any cell because the macro uses relative references), then press **Ctrl+n** to rerun the macro. The macro will enter your name, the course you specify, and the date in the selected location.

➤ Be sure you are in Book1 (and not the Personal Macro workbook). Pull down the **File menu.** Click **Close.** Click **No** when prompted to save the changes in Book1, since this workbook is not significant and need not be saved.

➤ The Personal Macro workbook remains open, and its macros can be used in this (or any future) session.

STEP 6: Add a Custom Tool Button

➤ Point to any toolbar, then click the **right mouse button** to display a shortcut menu. Click **Customize** to display the Customize dialog box in Figure 7.4e.

➤ Click the **down arrow** to scroll through the Categories list box until you can select the Custom category.

➤ Click and drag the **Happy Face button** to an available space at the right of the Standard toolbar. Release the mouse. You will see the Assign Macro dialog box. Choose **NameAndCourse** from the open list box and click **OK.** Click **Close** to exit the Custom dialog box.

Click and drag the Happy Face button to the right of the Standard toolbar

Click down arrow to scroll through categories

Click Custom

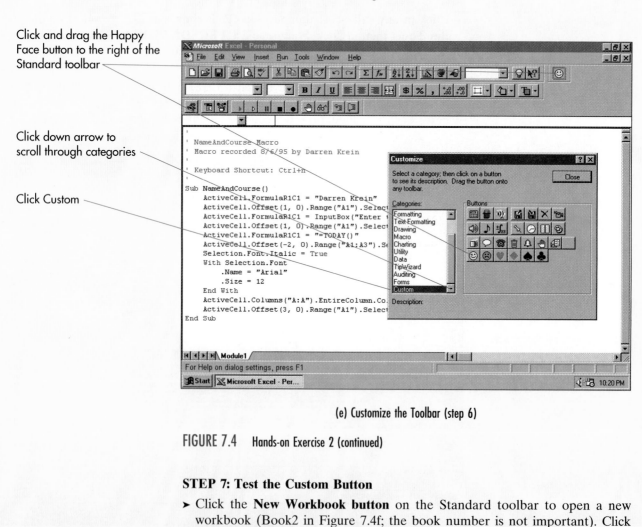

(e) Customize the Toolbar (step 6)

FIGURE 7.4   Hands-on Exercise 2 (continued)

STEP 7: Test the Custom Button

➤ Click the **New Workbook button** on the Standard toolbar to open a new workbook (Book2 in Figure 7.4f; the book number is not important). Click **cell B2** as the active cell from which to execute the macro.

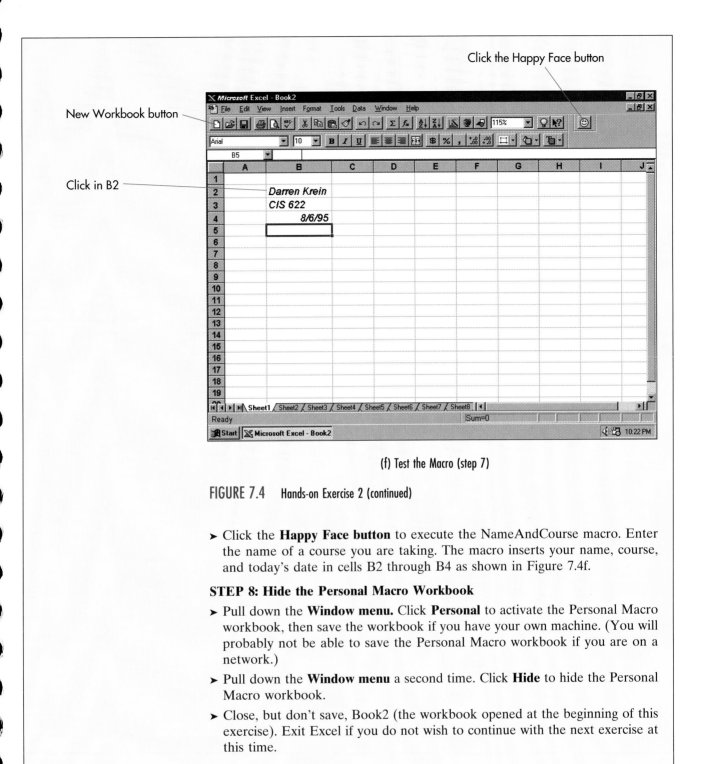

(f) Test the Macro (step 7)

FIGURE 7.4   Hands-on Exercise 2 (continued)

➤ Click the **Happy Face button** to execute the NameAndCourse macro. Enter the name of a course you are taking. The macro inserts your name, course, and today's date in cells B2 through B4 as shown in Figure 7.4f.

STEP 8: Hide the Personal Macro Workbook

➤ Pull down the **Window menu.** Click **Personal** to activate the Personal Macro workbook, then save the workbook if you have your own machine. (You will probably not be able to save the Personal Macro workbook if you are on a network.)

➤ Pull down the **Window menu** a second time. Click **Hide** to hide the Personal Macro workbook.

➤ Close, but don't save, Book2 (the workbook opened at the beginning of this exercise). Exit Excel if you do not wish to continue with the next exercise at this time.

DATA MANAGEMENT MACROS

Thus far we have covered the basics of macros in the context of entering your name, course, and today's date in a worksheet. As you might expect, macros are capable of much more and can be used to automate any repetitive task. The next several pages illustrate the use of macros in conjunction with the list (data) management examples that were presented in Chapter 5.

The worksheet in Figure 7.5a displays an employee list and the associated summary statistics. As you already know, a list is an area in a worksheet that contains rows of similar data. The first row in the list contains the column labels or field names. Each additional row contains a record. Every record contains the same fields in the same order. The list in Figure 7.5a has 14 records. Each record has seven fields: name, location, title, gender, service, hire date, and salary.

A criteria range has been established in cells A17 through G18 for use with the database functions in cells G22 through G26. Criteria values have not been entered in Figure 7.5a, and so the database functions reflect the values of the entire list (all 14 employees).

Field names ——

Data records ——

	A	B	C	D	E	F	G
1	Name	Location	Title	Gender	Service	Hire Date	Salary
2	Adams	Atlanta	Trainee	M	1.8	11/24/93	$19,500
3	Adamson	Chicago	Manager	F	3.5	3/16/92	$52,000
4	Brown	Atlanta	Trainee	F	1.8	11/24/93	$18,500
5	Charles	Boston	Account Rep	M	3.5	3/16/92	$40,000
6	Coulter	Atlanta	Manager	M	1.8	11/24/93	$100,000
7	Elofson	Miami	Account Rep	F	2.9	10/31/92	$47,500
8	Gillenson	Miami	Manager	M	1.9	10/31/93	$55,000
9	James	Chicago	Account Rep	F	5.9	10/31/89	$42,500
10	Johnson	Chicago	Account Rep	M	4.9	10/31/90	$47,500
11	Manin	Boston	Account Rep	F	3.5	3/16/92	$49,500
12	Marder	Chicago	Account Rep	F	3.9	10/31/91	$38,500
13	Milgrom	Boston	Manager	M	3.5	3/16/92	$57,500
14	Rubin	Boston	Account Rep	F	3.5	3/16/92	$45,000
15	Smith	Atlanta	Account Rep	M	1.8	11/24/93	$65,000
16							

Criteria range (A17:G18) ——

	A	B	C	D	E	F	G
17	Name	Location	Title	Gender	Service	Hire Date	Salary
18							
19							
20							
21	Summary Statistics						
22	Average Salary						$48,429
23	Maximum Salary						$100,000
24	Minimum Salary						$18,500
25	Total Salary						$678,000
26	Number of Employees						14

Database functions (G22:G26) compute summary statistics ——

(a) All Employees

List is filtered to employees who work in Chicago ——

	A	B	C	D	E	F	G
1	Name	Location	Title	Gender	Service	Hire Date	Salary
3	Adamson	Chicago	Manager	F	3.5	3/16/92	$52,000
9	James	Chicago	Account Rep	F	5.9	10/31/89	$42,500
10	Johnson	Chicago	Account Rep	M	4.9	10/31/90	$47,500
12	Marder	Chicago	Account Rep	F	3.9	10/31/91	$38,500
16							
17	Name	Location	Title	Gender	Service	Hire Date	Salary
18		Chicago					
19							
20							
21	Summary Statistics						
22	Average Salary						$45,125
23	Maximum Salary						$52,000
24	Minimum Salary						$38,500
25	Total Salary						$180,500
26	Number of Employees						4

Summary statistics reflect only the Chicago employees ——

(b) Chicago Employees

FIGURE 7.5   Data Management Macros

The worksheet in Figure 7.5b displays selected employees, those who work in Chicago. Look carefully at the worksheet and you will see that only rows 3, 9, 10, and 12 are visible. The other rows within the list have been hidden by the Advanced Filter command, which displays only those employees who satisfy the specified criteria. The summary statistics reflect only the Chicago employees; for example, the DCOUNT function in cell G26 shows four employees (as opposed to the 14 employees in Figure 7.5a).

You already know how to execute the list management commands to modify the existing criteria and filter a list accordingly. The process is not difficult, but it does require the execution of several commands. Consider, for example, the steps that would be necessary to modify the worksheet in Figure 7.5b if you wanted to display managers rather than Chicago employees.

You would have to clear the existing criterion (Chicago) in cell B18, then enter the new criterion (Manager) in cell C18. You would then execute the Advanced Filter command, which requires the specification of the list (cells A1 through G15), the location of the criteria range (cells A17 through G18), and the option to filter the list in place.

And what if you wanted to see the Chicago employees after you executed the commands to display the managers? You would have to repeat all of the previous commands to change the criterion back to what it was, then filter the list accordingly. Suffice it to say that the entire process can be simplified through creation of the appropriate macros.

The following exercise develops the macro to select the Chicago employees from the worksheet in Figure 7.5a. A subsequent exercise, beginning on page 328, develops two additional macros, one to select the managers and another to select the managers who work in Chicago.

NAMED RANGES

Use the Name command in the Insert menu to establish a mnemonic name (e.g., Database) for a cell range (e.g., A1:G15). Once defined, names adjust automatically for insertions and/or deletions within the range or a movement of the range within the worksheet. A name can be used in any command or function that requires a cell reference, and its use is highly recommended. This is especially true in macros, both to make the macro easier to read and to make it immune from changes to the worksheet.

HANDS-ON EXERCISE 3

Data Management Macros

Objective: To create a data management macro in conjunction with an employee list; to create a custom button to execute a macro. Use Figure 7.6 as a guide in the exercise.

STEP 1: The Management Functions

➤ Start Excel. Open the **Finished Employee List** workbook that you created in Chapter 5.

➤ Click any cell between A2 and A15, then click the **Ascending Sort button** on the Standard toolbar. The employees should be listed in alphabetical order as shown in Figure 7.6a.

➤ Click in **cell D17.** Type **Gender** to complete the field names in the criteria range. Clear all entries in the range **A18** through **G18.**

➤ Click in **cell G22,** which contains the DAVERAGE function, to compute the average salary of all employees who satisfy the specified criteria. No criteria have been entered, however, so the displayed value of $48,429 represents the average salary of all fourteen employees.

➤ Click **cell B18.** Enter **Chicago.** Press **enter.** The average salary changes to $45,125 to indicate the average salary of the four Chicago employees.

➤ Click **cell C18.** Enter **Manager.** Press **enter.** The average salary changes to $52,000 to indicate the average salary of the one Chicago manager.

PLAN AHEAD

Plan a macro ahead of time by testing its commands prior to turning on the macro recorder. Go through every command to make sure you produce the desired results. Determine the cells you will need to select so that you can assign names to these cells prior to recording the macro.

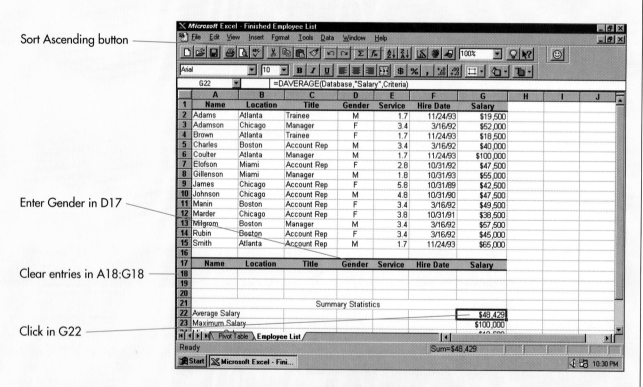

(a) Data Management Functions (step 1)

FIGURE 7.6   Hands-on Exercise 3

STEP 2: The Create Name Command

➤ Click and drag to select **cells A17** through **G18** as shown in Figure 7.6b. Pull down the **Insert menu,** click **Name,** then click **Create** to display the Create Names dialog box.

➤ Check the box to **Create Names in Top Row.** Click **OK.** This command assigns the text in each cell in row 17 to the corresponding cell in row 18; for example, cells B18 and C18 will be assigned the names Location and Title, respectively.

➤ Click and drag to select only **cells A18** through **G18.** (You need to assign a name to these seven cells collectively as you will have to clear the criteria values in row 18 later in the chapter.)

➤ Pull down the **Insert menu.** Click **Name.** Click **Define.** Enter **CriteriaValues** in the Define Name dialog box. Click **OK.**

THE NAME BOX

Use the Name box to define a range by selecting the cell(s) in the worksheet to which the name is to apply, clicking the Name box, then entering the name. For example, to assign the name CriteriaValues to cells A18:G18, select the range, click the Name box, and type CriteriaValues. The Name box can also be used to select a previously defined range by clicking the drop-down arrow next to the box and choosing the desired name from the drop-down list.

Click Top Row to select it

Click in A17 and
drag to G18

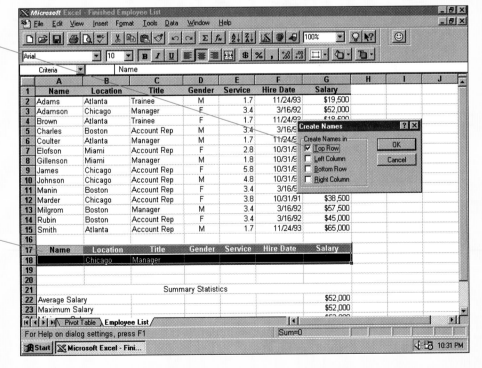

(b) The Create Name Command (step 2)

FIGURE 7.6   Hands-on Exercise 3 (continued)

The Go To Command

➤ Pull down the **Edit menu.** Click **Go To** to produce the Go To dialog box in Figure 7.6c. You should see the names you defined (CriteriaValues, Gender, Hire_Date, Location, Name, Salary, Service, and Title) as well as the two names defined previously by the authors (Criteria and Database).

➤ Click **Database.** Click **OK.** Cells A1 through G5 should be selected, corresponding to cells assigned to the name Database.

➤ Press the **F5 key** (a shortcut for the Edit Go To command), which again produces the Go To dialog box. Click **Criteria.** Click **OK.** Cells A17 through G18 should be selected.

➤ Click the **drop-down arrow** next to the Name box. Click **Location.** Cell B18 should be selected.

➤ You are now ready to record the macro.

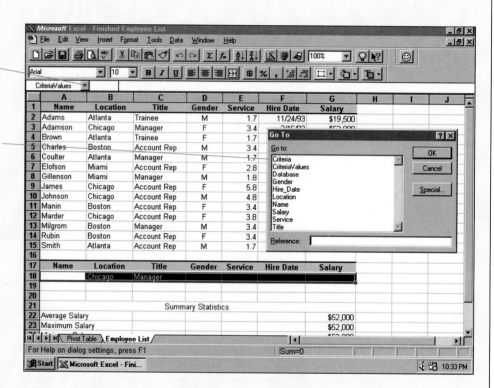

Click to see a list of defined names

List of defined names produced with Edit Go To command or by pressing F5

(c) The Go To Command (step 3)

FIGURE 7.6   Hands-on Exercise 3 (continued)

STEP 4: Set the Macro Options

➤ Pull down the **Tools menu** and click the **Record Macro command.** (Use absolute references; that is, Use Relative References should be toggled off.)

➤ Click **Record New Macro** from the cascaded menu to produce the Record New Macro dialog box. Enter **Chicago** in the Macro Name text box.

➤ Click the **Options command button** to display additional options within the dialog box. If necessary, clear the **Shortcut Key check box.** Check the option button for **This Workbook.** Check the option button for **Visual Basic.**

➤ Click **OK** to begin recording the macro.

STEP 5: Record the Macro (Edit Clear Command)

➤ Pull down the **Edit menu,** click **Go To,** select **CriteriaValues** from the Go To dialog box, and click **OK.** Cells A18 through G18 should be selected as shown in Figure 7.6d. (Alternatively, you can also use the **F5 key** or the Name box to select CriteriaValues.)

➤ Pull down the **Edit menu.** Click **Clear,** then click **All** from the cascaded menu as shown in Figure 7.6d. Cells A18 through G18 should be empty.

Click All to clear entries and formats in selected range (A18:G18)

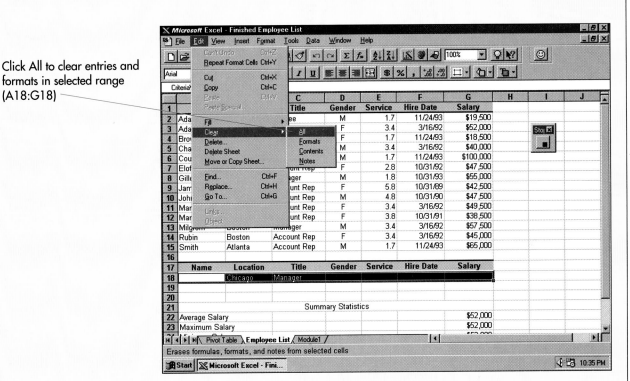

(d) The Edit Clear Command (step 5)

FIGURE 7.6   Hands-on Exercise 3 (continued)

STEP 6: Record the Macro (Advanced Filter Command)

➤ Pull down the **Edit menu,** click **Go To,** select **Location** from the Go To dialog box, and click **OK.**

➤ Cell B18 should be selected. Enter **Chicago** to establish the criterion for both the database functions and the Advanced Filter command.

➤ Click in **cell A2** to position the active cell within the employee list. Pull down the **Data menu.** Click **Filter,** then click **Advanced Filter** from the cascaded menu to display the dialog box in Figure 7.6e.

➤ Enter **Database** as the List Range. Press the **tab key.** Enter **Criteria** as the Criteria Range.

➤ Check that the option to **Filter the List in-place** is checked.

➤ Click **OK.** You should see only those employees who satisfy the current criteria (i.e., Adamson, James, Johnson, and Marder, who are the employees who work in Chicago).

➤ Click the **Stop Record button** to stop recording.

➤ Click the **Save button** to save the workbook with the macro.

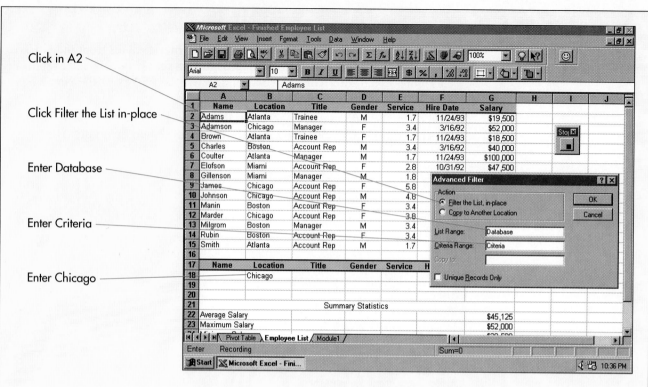

Click in A2

Click Filter the List in-place

Enter Database

Enter Criteria

Enter Chicago

(e) Record the Macro (steps 4 and 5)

FIGURE 7.6   Hands-on Exercise 3 (continued)

STEP 7: View the Macro

➤ Click the **Module1 tab** to display the Chicago macro as shown in Figure 7.6f.

- If you do not see a new tab, it means that the macro was recorded in the Personal Macro workbook because you chose the wrong option in step 4.

- If your macro does not contain references to Database and Criteria within the Advanced Filter function, it means you specified cell ranges rather than defined names.

➤ Correct your macro so that it matches the macro in Figure 7.6f.

- If the correction is minor, it is easiest to edit the macro directly.

- If the changes are significant, delete the macro, then return to step 4 and rerecord the macro from the beginning. (To delete a macro, pull down the **Tools menu,** click **Macro,** select the macro you wish to delete, then click the **Delete button.)**

➤ Click the **Employee List tab** to continue working.

STEP 8: Customize the Toolbar

➤ Pull down the **View menu.** Click **Toolbars.** Click the **Customize command button** to display the Customize dialog box in Figure 7.6g.

➤ Click **Utility** from the Categories list box to display the buttons in the Utility category.

➤ Click the **Macro button** to see its description as shown in Figure 7.6g. Drag the Macro button onto any toolbar or to the gray area to the right of any docked toolbar.

➤ Click the **Close command button** to return to your worksheet.

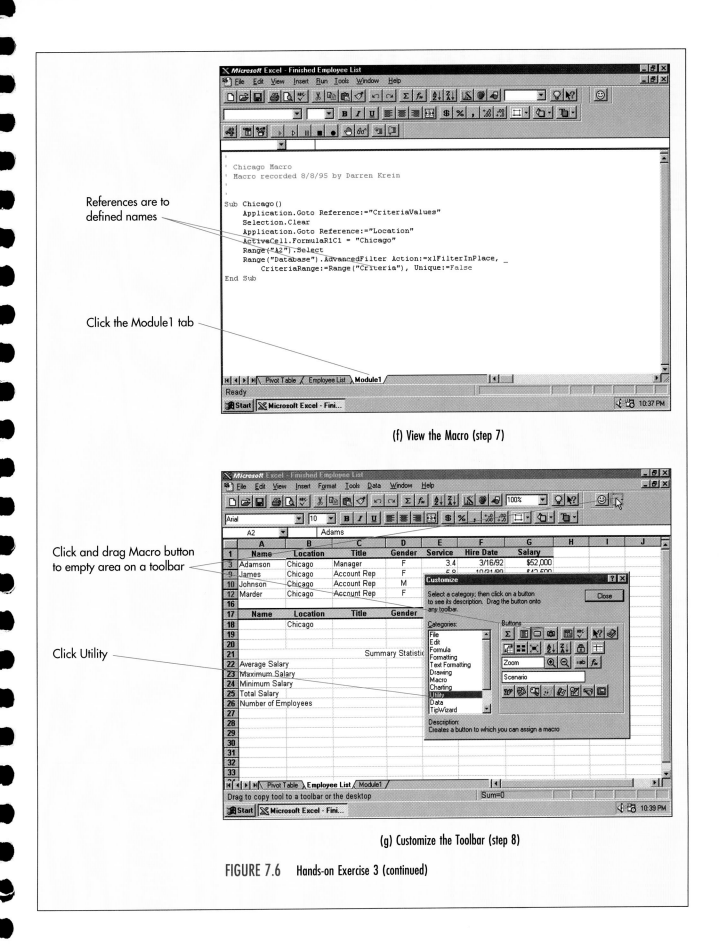

References are to
defined names

Click the Module1 tab

(f) View the Macro (step 7)

Click and drag Macro button
to empty area on a toolbar

Click Utility

(g) Customize the Toolbar (step 8)

FIGURE 7.6   Hands-on Exercise 3 (continued)

STEP 9: Assign the Macro

➤ Click the **Macro button** (the mouse pointer changes to a tiny crosshair). Click and drag in the worksheet as shown in Figure 7.6h to draw a button on the worksheet. Be sure to draw the button *below* the employee list, or the button may be hidden when a subsequent Data Filter command is executed.

➤ Release the mouse, and the Assign Macro dialog box will appear. Choose **Chicago** (the macro you just created) from the list of macro names. Click **OK** to close the Assign Macro dialog box.

➤ The button should still be selected. Click and drag to select the name of the button, **Button 1.**

➤ Type **Chicago** as the new name. Do *not* press the enter key.

➤ Click outside the button to deselect it. You should see a button named Chicago on your worksheet.

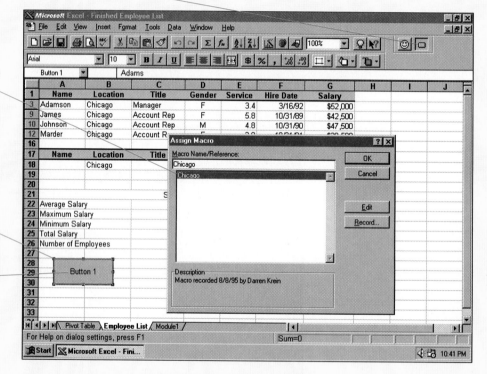

Macro button

Click Chicago to assign it to the selected macro button

Click and drag to draw the button

Click and drag to select Button 1 and enter Chicago as the new name

(h) Assign the Macro (step 9)

FIGURE 7.6 Hands-on Exercise 3 (continued)

STEP 10: Test the Macro

➤ Pull down the **Data menu,** click **Filter,** then click **Show All.**

➤ Click **cell B12.** Enter Miami to change the location for Marder. Press **enter.** The number of employees changes in the summary statistics area, as do the results of the other summary statistics.

➤ Click the **Chicago button** as shown in Figure 7.6i to execute the macro. Marder is *not* listed this time because she is no longer in Chicago.

➤ Pull down the **Data menu.** Click **Filter.** Click **Show All** to display the entire employee list.

➤ Click **cell B12.** Enter **Chicago** to change the location for this employee back to Chicago. Press **enter.** Click the **Chicago button** to execute the macro a second time. Marder is once again displayed with the Chicago employees.

➤ Pull down the **Data menu.** Click **Filter.** Click **Show All.**

➤ Save the workbook. Close the workbook. Exit Excel if you do not want to continue with the next exercise at this time.

SELECTING A BUTTON

The standard Windows convention to select an object is simply to click the object. You cannot, however, select a *Macro button* in this way, because if you click the button, you execute the associated macro. To select a Macro button, press and hold the Ctrl key as you click the left mouse button. (You can also select a button by clicking the right mouse button to produce a shortcut menu.) Once the button has been selected, you can edit its name, and/or move or size the button just as you can any other Windows object.

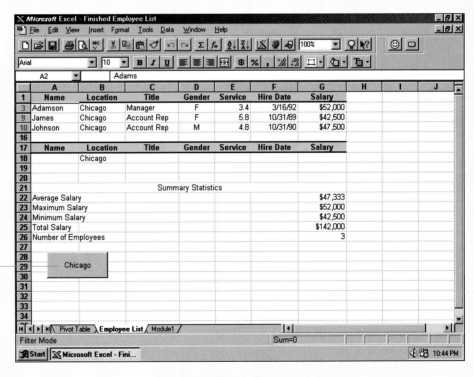

Click to execute the Chicago macro

(i) Test the Macro (step 10)

FIGURE 7.6   Hands-on Exercise 3 (continued)

The macro to filter the Chicago employees is only one of several macros that could be developed in conjunction with the employee list with which we have been working. It's reasonable to assume that you might want additional macros to select other groups of employees, such as employees in another city or employees with a particular job title.

You could develop the additional macros by recording them from scratch as you did the Chicago macro. Alternatively, you could copy the Chicago macro, give it a different name, then edit the copied macro so that it performs the desired function. This is the approach we follow in the next hands-on exercise.

Visual Basic statements are edited the same way text is edited in a word processing program. Thus, you toggle back and forth between the insertion or overtype modes to insert or type over text. You can also use the Cut, Copy, and Paste commands just as you would with a word processor. Text (Visual Basic commands) is cut or copied from one location to the clipboard, from where it can be pasted to another location.

THE FIND AND REPLACE COMMANDS

Anyone familiar with a word processor takes the Find and Replace commands for granted, but did you know the same capabilities exist in Excel? Pull down the Edit menu and choose either command. You have the same options as in the parallel command in Word, such as a case-sensitive (or insensitive) search or a limitation to a whole word search.

HANDS-ON EXERCISE 4

Creating Additional Macros

Objective: Use the Copy and Paste commands to duplicate an existing macro, then modify the copied macro to create an entirely new macro. Use Figure 7.7 as a guide in the exercise.

STEP 1: Copy the Chicago Macro

➤ Start Excel. Open the **Finished Employee List** workbook from the previous exercise.

➤ Click the **Module1 tab** to make it active. Click at the beginning of the **Chicago** macro, then click and drag to select the entire macro as shown in Figure 7.7a.

➤ Pull down the **Edit menu** and click **Copy** (or click the **Copy button** on the Standard toolbar).

➤ Click below the End Sub statement to deselect the macro and simultaneously establish the position of the insertion point. Press **enter** to insert a blank line below the End Sub statement.

➤ Pull down the **Edit menu** and click **Paste** (or click the **Paste button** on the Standard toolbar). The Chicago macro has been copied and now appears twice in Module1.

Copy button

Click and drag to select the macro statements

Click the Module1 tab

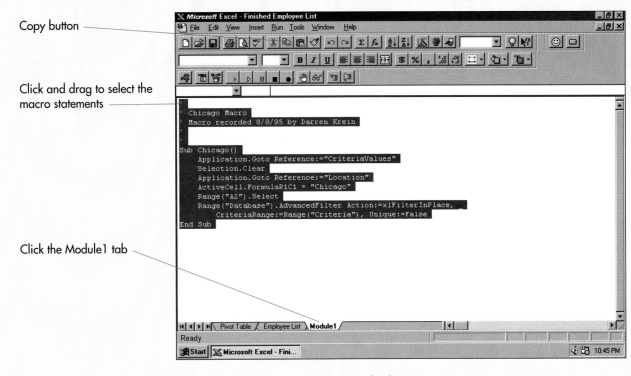

(a) Copy the Chicago Macro (step 1)

FIGURE 7.7   Hands-on Exercise 4

THE SHIFT KEY

You can select text for editing (or replacement) with the mouse, or alternatively, you can select by using the cursor keys on the keyboard. Set the insertion point where you want the selection to begin, then press and hold the Shift key as you use the cursor keys to move the insertion point to the end of the selection.

STEP 2: Create the Manager Macro

➤ Click in front of the second Chicago macro to set the insertion point. Pull down the **Edit menu.** Click **Replace** to display the Replace dialog box as shown in Figure 7.7b.

➤ Enter **Chicago** in the Find What text box. Press the **tab key.** Enter **Manager** in the Replace with text box. Click the **Find Next command button.**

➤ Excel searches for the first occurrence of Chicago, which should be in the comment statement of the copied macro. (If this is not the case, click the **Find Next command button** until your screen matches Figure 7.7b.)

➤ Click the **Replace command button.** Excel substitutes Manager for Chicago, then looks for the next occurrence of Chicago. Click **Replace.** Click **Replace** a third time to make another substitution. You are now positioned at the top of the sheet (at the beginning of the Chicago macro), where you *don't* want to make the substitution. Click the **Close command button.**

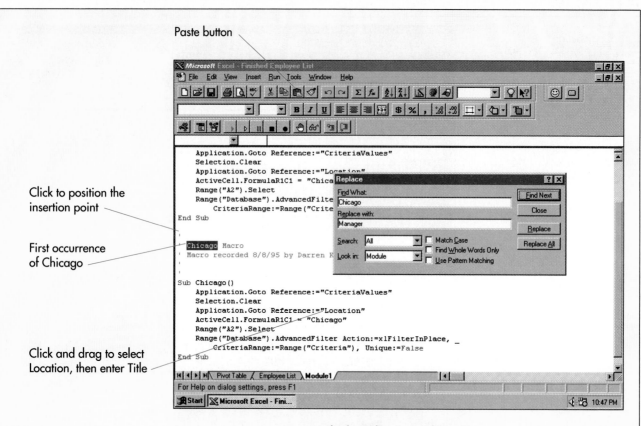

Paste button

Click to position the insertion point

First occurrence of Chicago

Click and drag to select Location, then enter Title

(b) The Replace Command (step 2)

FIGURE 7.7   Hands-on Exercise 4 (continued)

➤ Click and drag to select **Location** within the Application.Goto.Reference statement in the Manager macro. Enter **Title.** (The criteria within the macro have been changed from employees who work in Chicago to those whose title is Manager.)

➤ Save the workbook.

STEP 3: Run the Manager Macro

➤ Click the **Employee List tab** to return to the worksheet. Pull down the **Tools menu.** Click **Macro** to display the Macro dialog box as shown in Figure 7.7c.

➤ You should see two macros: Chicago, which was created in the previous exercise, and Manager, which you just created. (If the Manager macro does not appear, click the **Module1 tab** and correct the appropriate Sub statement to include Manager() as the name of the macro.)

➤ Select the **Manager macro,** then click **Run** to run the macro, after which you should see four employees (Adamson, Coulter, Gillenson, and Milgrom). If the macro does not execute correctly, click the **Module1 tab** to make the necessary corrections, then rerun the macro.

STEP 4: Assign a Button

➤ Click the **Macro button** on the toolbar (the mouse pointer changes to a tiny crosshair), then click and drag in the worksheet to draw a button on the worksheet. Release the mouse.

➤ Choose **Manager** (the macro you just created) from the list of macro names as shown in Figure 7.7d. Click **OK** to close the Assign Macro dialog box.

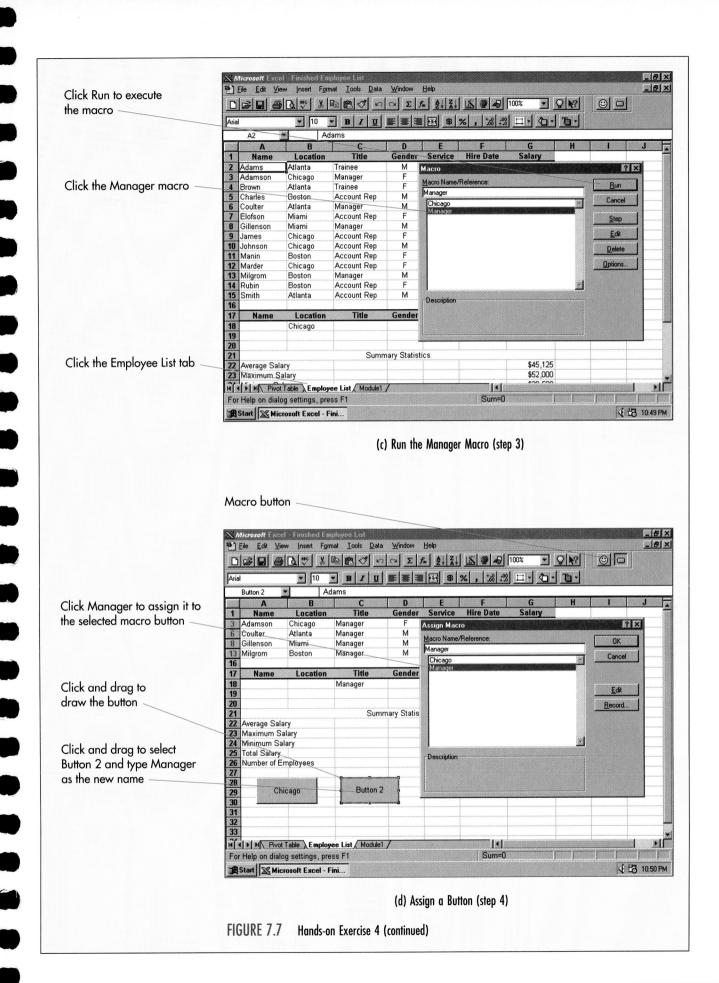

Click Run to execute the macro

Click the Manager macro

Click the Employee List tab

(c) Run the Manager Macro (step 3)

Macro button

Click Manager to assign it to the selected macro button

Click and drag to draw the button

Click and drag to select Button 2 and type Manager as the new name

(d) Assign a Button (step 4)

FIGURE 7.7   Hands-on Exercise 4 (continued)

➤ The button should still be selected. Click and drag to select the name of the button, **Button 2,** then type **Manager** as the new name. Do *not* press the enter key. Click outside the button to deselect it.

➤ There should be two buttons on your worksheet, one each for the Chicago and Manager macros.

➤ Click the **Chicago button** to execute the Chicago macro. You should see four employees with an average salary of $45,125.

➤ Click the **Manager button** to execute the Manager macro. You should see four employees with an average salary of $66,125.

THE STEP INTO COMMAND

The Step Into command helps to debug a macro, as it executes the statements one at a time. Pull down the Tools menu, click Macro, select the macro to debug, then click the Step command button. Move and/or size the Debug window so that you can see both the worksheet and the macro. Click the *Step Into button* on the Visual Basic toolbar to move into the macro, then click the Step Into button again to execute the first statement in the macro and view its results. Continue to click the Step Into button to execute the statements one at a time until the macro has completed execution.

STEP 5: Create the Chicago Manager Macro

➤ Click the **Module1 tab.** Press **Ctrl+Home** to move to the beginning of Module 1. Click and drag to select the entire Chicago macro. Be sure to include the End Sub statement in your selection.

➤ Click the **Copy button** on the Standard toolbar to copy the selected macro to the clipboard.

➤ Press **Ctrl+End** to move to the end of the module sheet. Click the **Paste button** on the Standard toolbar to complete the copy operation.

➤ Change **Chicago** to **ChicagoManager** in both the comment statement and the Sub statement as shown in Figure 7.7e.

➤ Click at the end of the line ActiveCell.FormulaR1C1 = "Chicago". Press **enter** to begin a new line, then enter the two statements to include managers as part of the criteria:

• Click and drag to select the two statements in the **Manager macro** as shown in Figure 7.7e.

• Click the **Copy button** to copy these statements to the clipboard.

• Click in the **ChicagoManager macro** where you want the statements to go.

• Click the **Paste button** to complete the copy operation.

• Delete any unnecessary blank lines or spaces that may remain.

➤ Save the workbook.

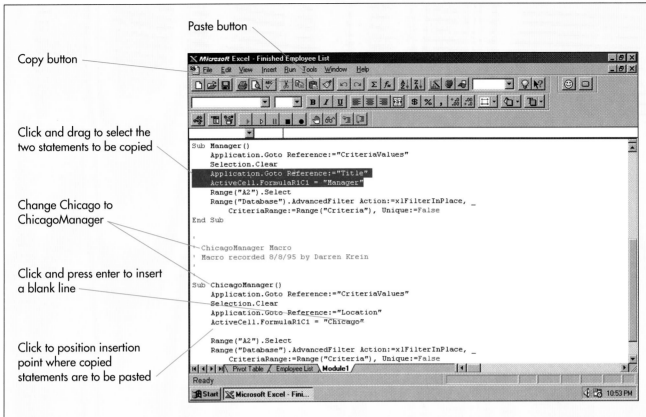

Copy button

Paste button

Click and drag to select the two statements to be copied

Change Chicago to ChicagoManager

Click and press enter to insert a blank line

Click to position insertion point where copied statements are to be pasted

(e) Create the ChicagoManager Macro (step 5)

FIGURE 7.7   Hands-on Exercise 4 (continued)

THE INPUT BOX STATEMENT

The Visual Basic InputBox adds flexibility to a macro by obtaining input from the user when the macro is executed. You can generalize the ChicagoManager macro to select employees with any title from any location by using the InputBox statement instead of specifying the specific selection criteria. See practice exercise 1 at the end of the chapter.

STEP 6: Assign a Button

➤ Click the **Employee List tab.** Click the Macro button on the toolbar, then click and drag to draw a new button on the worksheet. Assign the **Chicago-Manager macro** to this button. Click and drag to select the name of the Button, **Button 3.** Enter **Chicago Manager** as the new name. Do not press enter.

➤ Click outside the button to deselect it. Point to the **ChicagoManager button,** then press and hold the **Ctrl key** as you click the mouse to select the button. Drag a sizing handle to size it appropriately. Click outside the button to deselect it.

➤ Click the **ChicagoManager button** to execute the macro. You should see one employee, Adamson, who is the only Chicago manager.

➤ Click the **Chicago button** to execute the Chicago macro. You should see an average salary of $45,125.

➤ Click the **Manager button** to execute the Manager macro. You should see an average salary of $66,125.

CREATE UNIFORM BUTTONS

The easiest way to make all buttons the same size is to create the first button, then copy that button to create the others. To copy a button, press the Ctrl key as you select (click) the button, then click the Copy button on the Standard toolbar. Click in the worksheet where you want the new button to appear, then click the Paste button. Click and drag over the name of the button and enter a new name. Right click the new button, then click Assign Macro from the shortcut menu. Select the name of the new macro, then click OK.

STEP 7: Object Properties

➤ Point to the **ChicagoManager button,** then press and hold the **Ctrl key** to select this button.

➤ Press the **Ctrl key,** then press and hold the **Shift key** as you click the **Chicago button.** The ChicagoManager and Chicago buttons are both selected.

➤ Press and hold both the **Shift** and **Ctrl keys** as you click the **Manager button** to add it to the selection.

➤ All three buttons should be selected as shown in Figure 7.7f. Point to any of the buttons and click the **right mouse button** to display a shortcut menu. Click **Format Object.**

➤ Click the **Properties tab** in the Format Object dialog box:

- Check the **Print Object box** so that the macro buttons are included on the printed output.

- Click the **Move but Don't Size with Cells** option button.

- Click **OK** to exit the dialog box and return to the worksheet.

➤ Click anywhere in the worksheet to deselect the buttons.

➤ Click the **Print button** on the Standard toolbar to print the worksheet.

➤ Click the **Module1 tab.** Click the **Print button** to print the macros.

➤ Save the workbook a final time. Close the workbook. Exit Excel if you don't want to continue with the next exercise at this time.

OBJECT PROPERTIES

The size and/or position of a macro button changes in accordance with the cell(s) on which it is positioned. To prevent this from happening, select the macro button, click the right mouse button to display a short-cut menu, then click the Format Object command. Click the Properties tab, choose the appropriate Object Positioning option button, then click OK to close the Format Object dialog box.

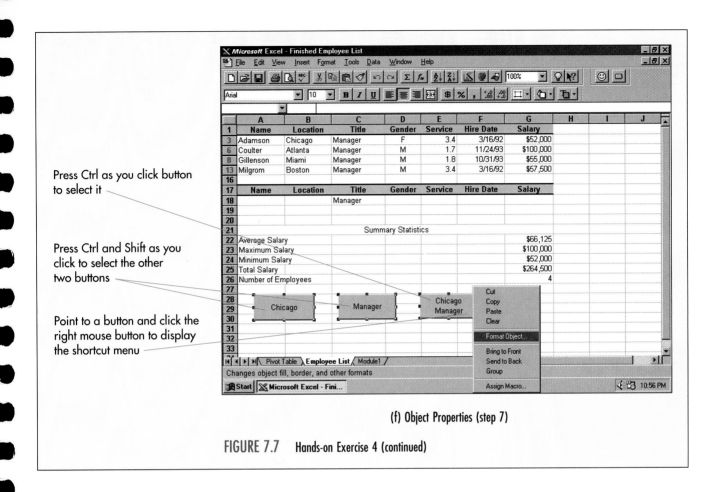

Press Ctrl as you click button to select it

Press Ctrl and Shift as you click to select the other two buttons

Point to a button and click the right mouse button to display the shortcut menu

(f) Object Properties (step 7)

FIGURE 7.7   Hands-on Exercise 4 (continued)

LOOPS AND DECISION MAKING

Thus far, all of the macros in the chapter have consisted entirely of Excel commands that were captured by the macro recorder as they were executed. Excel macros can be made significantly more powerful by incorporating additional Visual Basic statements that enable true programming. These include the If statement for decision making, and the Do statement to implement a *loop* (one or more commands that are executed repeatedly until a condition is met).

Consider, for example, the worksheet and associated macro in Figure 7.8. The worksheet is similar to those used in the preceding exercises, except that the font color of the data for managers is red. Think for a minute how you would do this manually. You would look at the first employee in the list, examine the employee's title to determine if that employee is a manager, and if so, change the font color for that employee. You would then repeat these steps for all of the other employees on the list. It sounds tedious, but that is exactly what you would do if asked to change the font color for the managers.

Now ask yourself whether you could implement the entire process with the macro recorder. You could use the recorder to capture the commands to select a specific row within the list and change the font color. You could not, however, use the recorder to determine whether or not to select a particular row (i.e., whether the employee is a manager) because you make that decision by comparing the cell contents to a specific criterion. Nor is there a way to tell the recorder to repeat the process for every employee. In other words, you need to go beyond merely capturing Excel commands. You need to include additional Visual Basic statements to enable true programming.

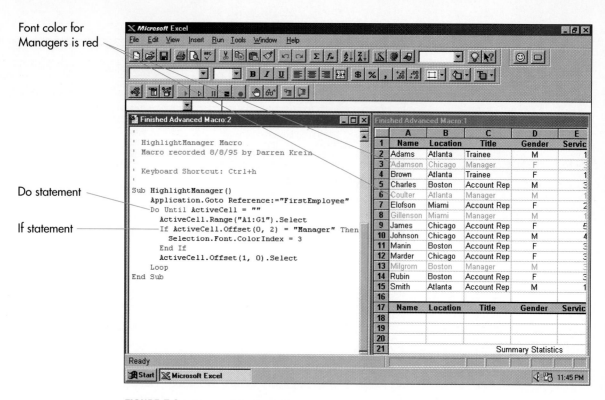

Font color for
Managers is red

Do statement

If statement

FIGURE 7.8 Loops and Decision Making

The HighlightManager macro in Figure 7.8 uses the If statement to implement a decision (to determine whether the selected employee is a manager) and the Do statement to implement a loop (to repeat the commands until all employees in the list have been processed). To understand how the macro works, you need to know the basic syntax of each statement.

If Statement

The **If statement** conditionally executes a statement (or group of statements), depending on the value of an expression (condition). The If statement determines whether an expression is true, and if so, executes the commands between the If and End If. For example:

```
If ActiveCell.Offset(0, 2) = "Manager" Then
    Selection.Font.ColorIndex = 3
End If
```

IF-THEN-ELSE

The If statement includes an optional Else clause whose statements are executed if the condition is false. Consider:

> If condition Then statements [Else statements] End If

The condition is evaluated as either true or false. If the condition is true, the statements following Then are executed; otherwise the statements following Else are executed. Either way, execution continues with the statement following End If. Use the Help command for additional information and examples.

This If statement determines whether the cell two columns to the right of the active cell (the offset indicates a relative reference) contains the text "Manager", and if so, changes the font color of the (previously) selected text. The number three corresponds to the color red. No action is taken if the condition is false. Either way, execution continues with the command below the End If.

Do Statement

The *Do statement* repeats a block of statements until a condition becomes true. For example:

```
Do Until ActiveCell = ""
    ActiveCell.Range("A1:G1").Select
    If ActiveCell.Offset(0, 2) = "Manager" Then
        Selection.Font.ColorIndex = 3
    End If
    ActiveCell.Offset(1, 0).Select
Loop
```

The statements within the loop are executed repeatedly until the active cell is empty (i.e., ActiveCell = ""). The first statement in the loop selects the cells in columns A through G of the current row. (Relative references are used, and you may want to refer to the earlier discussion on page 309, which indicated that A1:G1 specifies the shape of a range rather than a specific cell address.) The If statement determines whether the current employee is a manager and, if so, changes the font color for the selected cells. The last statement selects the cell one row below the active cell to process the next employee. (Omission of this statement would process the same row indefinitely, creating what is known as an infinite loop.)

The macro in Figure 7.8 is a nontrivial macro that illustrates the potential of Visual Basic. Try to gain a conceptual understanding of how the macro works, but do not be concerned if you are confused initially. Do the hands-on exercise, and you'll be pleased at how much clearer it will be when you have created the macro yourself.

A SENSE OF FAMILIARITY

Visual Basic has the basic capabilities found in any other programming language. If you have programmed before, whether in Pascal, C, or even COBOL, you will find all of the logic structures you are used to. These include the Do While and Do Until statements, the If-Then-Else statement for decision making, nested If statements, a Case statement, and/or calls to subprograms.

HANDS-ON EXERCISE 5

Loops and Decision Making

Objective: To implement loops and decision making in a macro through the Do Until and If statements. Use Figure 7.9 as a guide in doing the exercise.

STEP 1: The ClearColor Macro

➤ Open the **Advanced Macro workbook** in the **Exploring Excel folder,** then save the workbook as **Finished Advanced Macro** workbook. The data for the employees in rows 3, 6, 8, and 13 appears in red to indicate these employees are managers.

➤ Pull down the **Tools menu.** Click the **Macro** command to produce the dialog box in Figure 7.9a.

➤ Select **ClearColor,** then click **Run** to execute this macro and clear the red color from the managerial employees. It is important to know that the Clear-Color macro works, as you will use it throughout the exercise.

Click Run to execute the macro

Click to select ClearColor macro

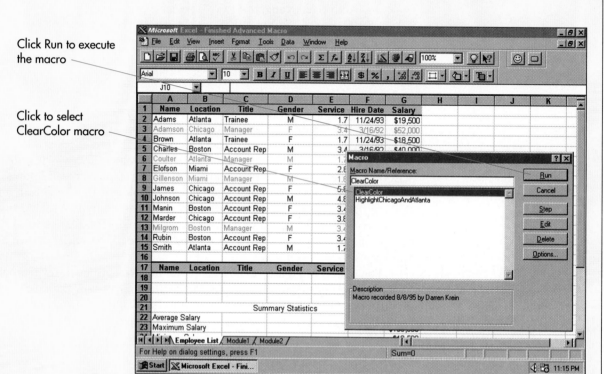

(a) The ClearColor Macro (step 1)

FIGURE 7.9   Hands-on Exercise 5

STEP 2: Mark the Position for Recording

➤ Click the tab for **Module1.** Press **Ctrl+End** to move the insertion point to the end of the ClearColor macro. Press **enter** to insert a blank line.

➤ Pull down the **Tools menu,** then click (or point to) the **Record Macro command.** Click **Mark Position for Recording** (so that the new macro will be inserted on the existing macro sheet instead of on a new sheet).

➤ Click the **Employee List tab** to return to the worksheet and begin recording the macro.

STEP 3: Record the Macro

➤ You must choose the active cell before recording the macro. Click **cell A3,** the cell containing the name of the first manager.

➤ Pull down the **Tools menu,** then click the **Record Macro** command.

- If **Use Relative References** is already checked, click **Record New Macro** from the cascaded menu to produce the Record New Macro dialog box.
- If **Use Relative References** is not checked, click the command on, then pull down the **Tools menu** and click (or point to) the **Record Macro command** a second time. Click **Record New Macro** from the cascaded menu to produce the Record New Macro dialog box.

➤ Enter **HighlightManager** in the Macro Name text box.

➤ Click the **Options command button** to display additional options within the dialog box. Check the **Shortcut Key check box,** delete the existing letter (e), and replace the existing shortcut with a **lowercase h.** (Ctrl+h should appear as the shortcut.)

➤ Check the option button for **This Workbook.** Check the option button for **Visual Basic.** Click **OK** to begin recording the macro.

➤ Click and drag to select **cells A3** through **G3** as shown in Figure 7.9b. Click the **drop-down arrow** in the **Font color** list box. Click **Red.** Click the **Stop Recording button.**

➤ Click anywhere in the worksheet to deselect cells A3 through G3 so you can see the effect of the macro; cells A3 through G3 should be displayed in red.

➤ Save the workbook.

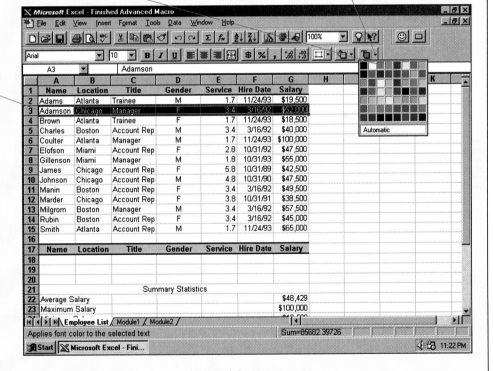

(b) Record the Macro (step 3)

FIGURE 7.9   Hands-on Exercise 5 (continued)

STEP 4: View and Test the Macro

➤ Pull down the **Window menu** (and close Book1 if it is open). Click **New Window** to open a second window as shown in Figure 7.9c.

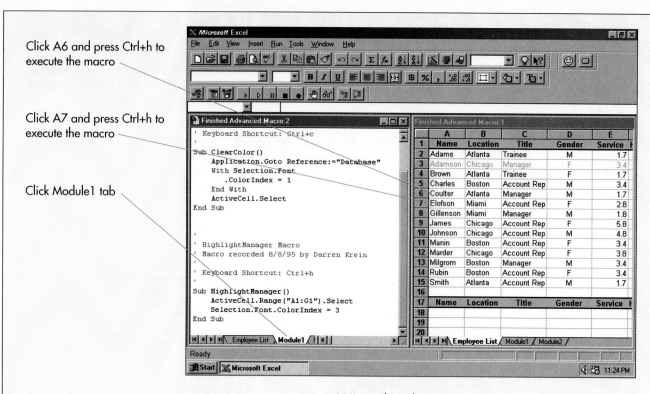

Click A6 and press Ctrl+h to execute the macro

Click A7 and press Ctrl+h to execute the macro

Click Module1 tab

(c) View and Test the Macro (step 4)

FIGURE 7.9   Hands-on Exercise 5 (continued)

➤ Pull down the **Window menu** a second time. Click **Arrange.** Chose the **Tiled option button,** then click **OK** to display the open windows side by side.

➤ Click in the window on the left. Click the **Module1 tab** to view the newly created macro in this window. Your screen should match Figure 7.9c.

➤ Click in the window on the right. Click **cell A6** (the cell containing the name of the next manager). Press **Ctrl+h** to execute the HighlightManager macro. The font in cells A6 through G6 changes to red.

➤ Click **cell A7.** Press **Ctrl+h** to execute the HighlightManager macro. The font for this employee is also red, although the employee is *not* a manager.

STEP 5: Add the If Statement

➤ Press **Ctrl+c** to execute the ClearColor macro. The data for all employees is again displayed in black.

➤ Click in the window containing the **HighlightManager** macro. Add the **If** and **End If** statements exactly as they are shown in Figure 7.9d. Use the **Tab key** (or press the **space bar**) to indent the Selection statement within the If and End If statements.

➤ Click in the window containing the worksheet, then click **cell A3.** Press **Ctrl+h** to execute the modified HighlightManager macro. Cells A3 through G3 are highlighted since this employee is a manager.

➤ Click **cell A4.** Press **Ctrl+h.** The row is selected, but the color of the font remains unchanged. The If statement prevents these cells from being highlighted because the employee is not a manager. Press **Ctrl+c** to remove all highlighting.

➤ Save the workbook.

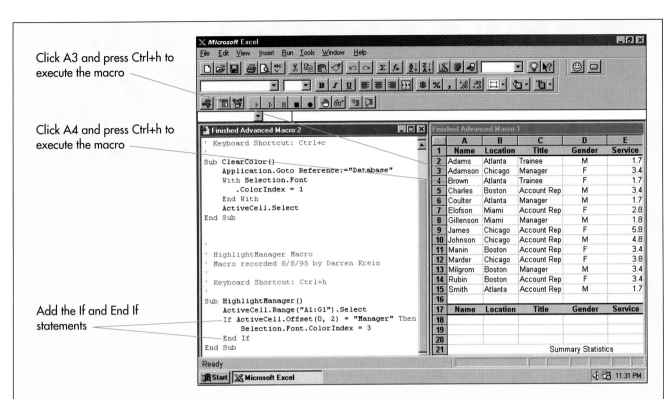

Click A3 and press Ctrl+h to execute the macro

Click A4 and press Ctrl+h to execute the macro

Add the If and End If statements

(d) Add the IF Statement (step 5)

FIGURE 7.9   Hands-on Exercise 5 (continued)

INDENT

Indentation does not affect the execution of a macro. It, does, however, make the macro easier to read, and we suggest you follow common conventions in developing your macros. Indent the conditional statements associated with an If statement by a consistent amount. Place the End If statement on a line by itself, directly under the associated If.

STEP 6: An Endless Loop

➤ Click in the window containing the **HighlightManager** macro. Add the **Do Until** and **Loop** statements exactly as they appear in Figure 7.9e. Indent the other statements as shown in the figure.

➤ Click **cell A3** of the worksheet. Press **Ctrl+h** to execute the macro. Cells A3 through G3 will be displayed in red, but the macro continues to execute indefinitely as it applies color to the same record over and over. The macro is in an infinite loop (as can be seen by the hourglass that remains on your monitor).

➤ Press **Ctrl+Break** to cease execution of the macro. You will see the dialog box in Figure 7.9e, indicating that an error has been encountered during the execution of the macro.

➤ Click the **Debug command button** to debug the macro, then continue as described in step 7.

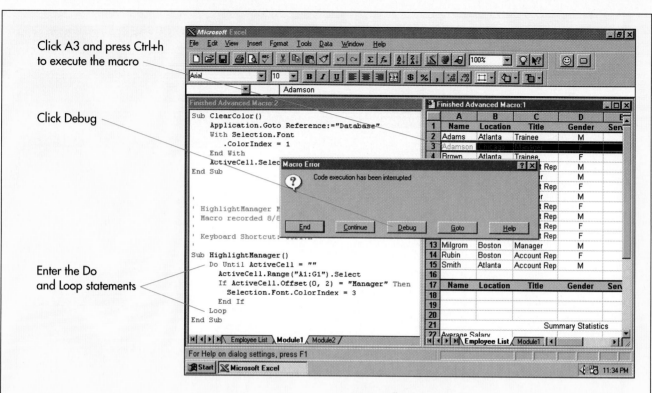

Click A3 and press Ctrl+h to execute the macro

Click Debug

Enter the Do and Loop statements

(e) An Endless Loop (step 6)

FIGURE 7.9   Hands-on Exercise 5 (continued)

AN ENDLESS LOOP

The glossary in the Programmer's Guide for a popular database contains the following definitions:

> Endless loop—See loop, endless
> Loop, endless—See endless loop

We don't know whether these entries were deliberate or not, but the point is made either way. Endless loops are a common and frustrating bug. Press Ctrl+Break to halt execution, then click the Debug command button to step through the macro and locate the source of the error.

STEP 7: Debug the Macro

➤ Click and drag the **Debug window** so that its position approximates that of Figure 7.9f.

➤ Click the **Step Into button** on the Visual Basic toolbar several times to view the execution of the next several steps in the macro. You will see that the macro is stuck in a loop as the If statement is executed indefinitely.

➤ Close the Debug window.

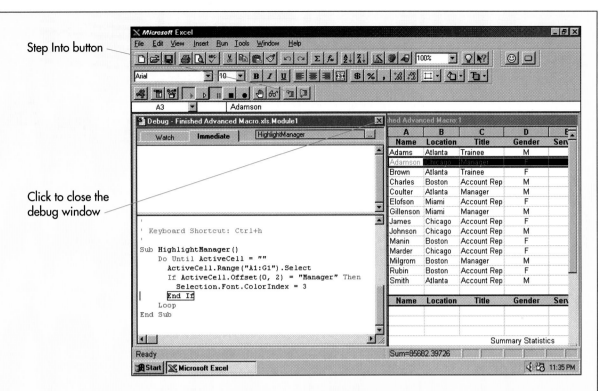

Step Into button

Click to close the debug window

(f) Debug the Macro (step 7)

FIGURE 7.9 Hands-on Exercise 5 (continued)

RED, GREEN, AND BLUE

Visual Basic automatically assigns different colors to different types of statements (or a portion of those statements). Any statement containing a syntactical error appears in red. Comments appear in green. Key words such as Sub, End Sub, If, End If, Do Until, and Loop appear in blue.

STEP 8: Complete the Macro

➤ Click in **cell A2** of the worksheet. Click in the **Name Box.** Enter **FirstEmployee** to name this cell. Press **enter.**

➤ Click in the window containing the macro. Click at the end of the Sub statement and press **enter** to insert a blank line. Add the statement to select the cell named FirstEmployee as shown in Figure 7.9g. This ensures that the macro always begins in row two by selecting the cell named FirstEmployee.

➤ Click immediately after the End If statement. Press **enter.** Add the statement containing the offset (1,0) as shown in Figure 7.9g, which selects the cell one row below the current row.

➤ Click anywhere in the worksheet except cell A2. Press **Ctrl+c** to clear the color. Press **Ctrl+h** to execute the HighlightManager macro.

➤ The macro begins by selecting cell A2, then proceeds to highlight all managers in red. Save the workbook a final time. Exit Excel.

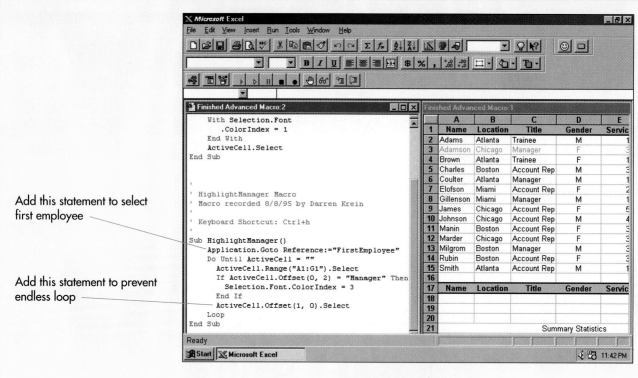

Add this statement to select first employee

Add this statement to prevent endless loop

(g) The Completed Macro (step 8)

FIGURE 7.9 Hands-on Exercise 5 (continued)

HELP FOR VISUAL BASIC

Click within any Visual Basic key word, then press the F1 key for context-sensitive help. You will see a help screen containing a description of the statement, its syntax, key elements, and several examples. You can print the help screen by clicking the Options command button and selecting Print Topic. (If you do not see the help screens, ask your instructor to install Visual Basic Help.)

SUMMARY

A macro is a set of instructions that automates a repetitive task. It is, in essence, a program, and its instructions are written in Visual Basic, a programming language. The macro recorder in Excel records your commands and writes the macro for you. Once a macro has been created, it can be edited by manually inserting, deleting, or changing its statements.

Macros are stored in one of two places, either in the current workbook or in a Personal Macro workbook. Macros that are specific to a particular workbook should be stored in that workbook. Generic macros that can be used with any workbook should be stored in the Personal Macro workbook.

A macro is run (executed) by pulling down the Tools menu and selecting the Run Macro command. A macro can also be executed through a keyboard short-cut, by placing a button on the worksheet, or by customizing a toolbar to include an additional button to run the macro.

A comment is a nonexecutable statement that begins with an apostrophe. Comments are inserted automatically at the beginning of a macro by the macro recorder to remind you of what the macro does. Comments may be added, deleted, or modified, just as any other statement.

A macro begins and ends with the Sub and End Sub statements, respectively. The Sub statement contains the name of the macro.

The With statement enables you to perform multiple actions on the same object. All commands between the With and corresponding End With statements are executed collectively.

A macro records either absolute or relative references. An absolute reference is constant; that is, Excel keeps track of the exact cell address and selects that specific cell. A relative reference depends on the previously selected cell, and is entered as an offset, or number of rows and columns from the current cell.

An Excel macro can be made more powerful through inclusion of Visual Basic statements that enable true programming. These include the If statement to implement decision making and the Do statement to implement a loop.

KEY WORDS AND CONCEPTS

Absolute reference	Keyboard shortcut	Paste command
Comment statement	Loop	Personal Macro
Copy command	Macro	workbook
Cut command	Macro button	Relative reference
Debugging	Macro recorder	Replace command
Do Statement	Macro sheet	Shortcut key
End If statement	Mark Position for	Step Into button
End Sub statement	Recording	Sub statement
End With statement	Name	Unhide command
Find command	Name box	Visual Basic
If statement	Offset	With statement

MULTIPLE CHOICE

1. Which of the following best describes the recording and execution of a macro?
   (a) A macro is recorded once and executed once
   (b) A macro is recorded once and executed many times
   (c) A macro is recorded many times and executed once
   (d) A macro is recorded many times and executed many times

2. Which of the following can be used to execute a macro?
   (a) A keyboard shortcut
   (b) A customized toolbar button

(c) Both (a) and (b)

(d) Neither (a) nor (b)

3. A macro is stored in a:

(a) Separate sheet within the current workbook

(b) Personal Macro workbook

(c) Both (a) and (b)

(d) Neither (a) nor (b)

4. Which of the following is true regarding comments in Visual Basic?

(a) A comment is executable; that is, its inclusion or omission affects the outcome of a macro

(b) A comment begins with an apostrophe

(c) Both (a) and (b)

(d) Neither (a) nor (b)

5. Which statement must contain the name of the macro?

(a) The Sub statement at the beginning of the macro

(b) The first comment statement

(c) Both (a) and (b)

(d) Neither (a) nor (b)

6. Which commands(s) are necessary to record additional statements within an existing macro?

(a) Mark the position for recording

(b) Record at the marked position

(c) Both (a) and (b)

(d) Neither (a) nor (b)

7. The statement Selection.Offset (1,0).Range ("A1").Select will select the cell:

(a) In the same column as the active cell but one row below

(b) In the same row as the active cell but one column to the right

(c) In the same column as the active cell but one row above

(d) In the same row as the active cell but one column to the left

8. The statement Selection.Offset (1,1).Range ("A1").Select will select the cell:

(a) One cell below and one cell to the left of the active cell

(b) One cell below and one cell to the right of the active cell

(c) One cell above and one cell to the right of the active cell

(d) One cell above and one cell to the left of the active cell

9. The statement Selection.Offset (1,1).Range ("A1:A2").Select will select:

(a) Cell A1

(b) Cell A2

(c) Both (a) and (b)

(d) Neither (a) nor (b)

10. Which commands are used to duplicate an existing macro so that it can become the basis of a new macro?

(a) Copy command

(b) Paste command

(c) Both (a) and (b)

(d) Neither (a) nor (b)

11. Which of the following is used to protect a macro from the subsequent insertion or deletion of rows or columns in the associated worksheet?
    (a) Range names
    (b) Absolute references
    (c) Both (a) and (b)
    (d) Neither (a) nor (b)

12. Which of the following is true regarding a customized button that has been inserted as an object onto a worksheet and assigned to an Excel macro?
    (a) Point to the customized button, then click the left mouse button to execute the associated macro
    (b) Point to the customized button, then click the right mouse button to select the macro button and simultaneously display a shortcut menu
    (c) Point to the customized button, then press and hold the Ctrl key as you click the left mouse to select the button
    (d) All of the above

13. You want to create a macro to enter your name in a specific cell. The best way to do this is to:
    (a) Select the cell for your name, turn on the macro recorder with absolute references, then type your name
    (b) Turn on the macro recorder with absolute references, select the cell for your name, then type your name
    (c) Either (a) or (b)
    (d) Neither (a) nor (b)

14. You want to create a macro to enter your name in the active cell (which will vary whenever the macro is used) and the course you are taking in the cell immediately below. The best way to do this is to:
    (a) Select the cell for your name, turn on the macro recorder with absolute references, type your name, press the down arrow, and type the course
    (b) Turn on the macro recorder with absolute references, select the cell for your name, type your name, press the down arrow, and type the course
    (c) Select the cell for your name, turn on the macro recorder with relative references, type your name, press the down arrow, and type the course
    (d) Turn on the macro recorder with relative references, select the cell for your name, type your name, press the down arrow, and type the course

15. The InputBox statement:
    (a) Displays a message (prompt) requesting input from the user
    (b) Stores the user's response in a designated cell
    (c) Both (a) and (b)
    (d) Neither (a) nor (b)

ANSWERS

1. b	6. c	11. a
2. c	7. a	12. d
3. c	8. b	13. b
4. b	9. d	14. c
5. a	10. c	15. c

EXPLORING EXCEL 7.0

1. Use Figure 7.10 to match each action with its result; a given action may be used more than once or not at all.

Action

a. Click at 13
b. Click at 11
c. Click at 14, then click at 5
d. Click at 10
e. Click at 3, then click at 8 to mark the position for recording
f. Click the right mouse button at 1
g. Click at 8
h. Click at 12

Result

_____ Step through the macro one statement at a time

_____ Unhide the Personal Macro workbook

_____ Record a new macro

_____ Run the Chicago macro

_____ Create a button for the Manager macro

_____ Copy the Chicago macro

_____ Run the Manager macro

_____ Add additional steps within the Chicago macro

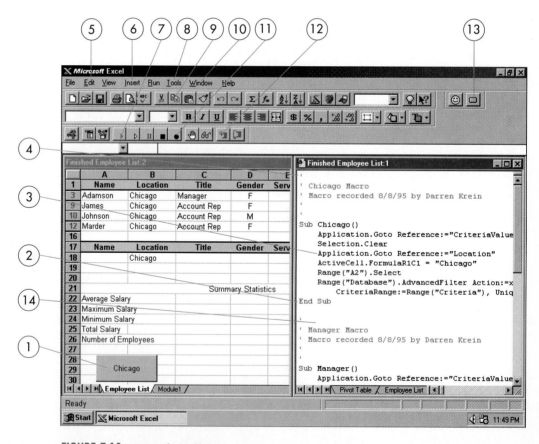

FIGURE 7.10   Screen for Problem 1

Action	Result
i. Click at 4 and drag to 2, then click at 9	_____ Change the Manager macro to an Account Rep macro by changing all occurrences of Manager to Account Rep
j. Click the left mouse button at 1	_____ Change the properties of the Chicago button so that it will print with the worksheet

2. Each of the messages in Figure 7.11 appeared (or could have appeared) in conjunction with the exercises in the chapter. Explain the meaning of each message and indicate what (if any) corrective action is required.

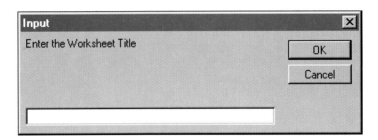

(a) Message 1

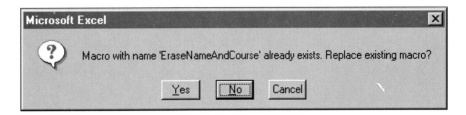

(b) Message 2

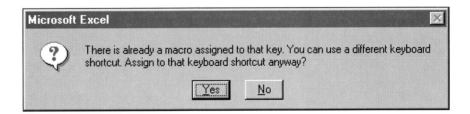

(c) Message 3

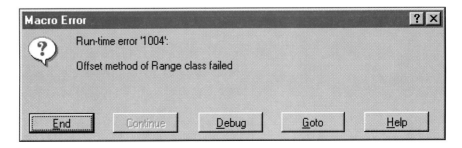

(d) Message 4

FIGURE 7.11   Messages for Problem 2

3. Answer the following with respect to the macros in Figure 7.12, both of which enter a student's name, class, and today's date in a worksheet:

   a. In which cells does Macro1 enter the data?

   b. In which cells does Macro2 enter the data?

   c. Which macro was recorded with absolute references? With relative references?

   d. Which macro was created by selecting the active cell, then turning on the macro recorder? Which macro was created by turning on the macro recorder, then selecting the active cell within the macro?

   e. Assume that the first statement of Macro1 is deleted. In which cells will the data appear after the macro has been modified?

   f. Assume that the first statement of (the original) Macro1 is entered as the first statement in Macro2. In which cells will the data appear after the statement is added to Macro2?

   g. Where should the macros be stored if they are to be accessible from any workbook?

```
'  Macro1 Macro
'
'  Keyboard Shortcut: Ctrl+e
'
Sub Macro1()
    Range("D5").Select
    ActiveCell.FormulaR1C1 = "John Smith"
    Range("D6").Select
    ActiveCell.FormulaR1C1 = "CIS 622"
    Range("D7").Select
    ActiveCell.FormulaR1C1 = "=TODAY()"
End Sub
'
'  Macro2 Macro
'
'  Keyboard Shortcut: Ctrl+f
'
Sub Macro2()
    ActiveCell.FormulaR1C1 = "John Smith"
    ActiveCell.Offset(1, 0).Range("A1").Select
    ActiveCell.FormulaR1C1 = "CIS 622"
    ActiveCell.Offset(1, 0).Range("A1").Select
    ActiveCell.FormulaR1C1 = "=TODAY()"
End Sub
```

FIGURE 7.12 Macros for Problem 3

4. Answer the following with respect to the screen displayed in Figure 7.13.

   a. How many workbooks are open in the figure? Which workbook is active?

   b. How many sheets are there in the active workbook? Which sheet is active?

   c. What is the name of the visible macro? What shortcut key (if any) has been established for that macro?

   d. Which macro statements are comments?

   e. Does the macro use relative or absolute references?

   f. What does the macro do?

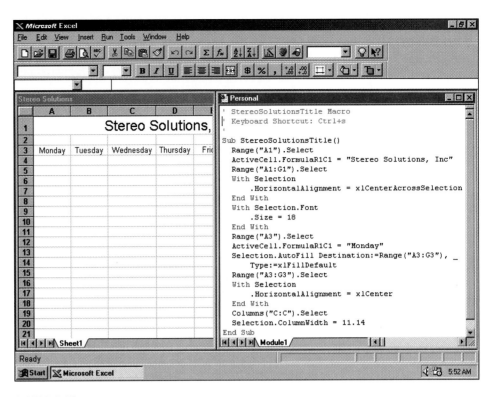

FIGURE 7.13   Screen for Problem 4

PRACTICE WITH EXCEL 7.0

1. Figure 7.14 displays a modified version of the Finished Employee List workbook that was developed in Hands-on Exercises 3 and 4. The worksheet contains the three command buttons (Chicago, Manager, and Chicago/Manager) that correspond to the macros that were developed in the chapter. It also contains a fourth command button that is the focus of this problem.

   a. Do Hands-on Exercises 3 and 4 as they are described in the chapter in order to create the first three macros and associated command buttons.

   b. Create a fourth macro that prompts the user to enter a city, prompts the user a second time to enter a title, then displays all employees with that city–title combination.

   c. Create a command button corresponding to the macro in part b as shown in the figure.

   d. Add a documentation worksheet (see pages 271–276) that describes all of the macros in the workbook. Be sure your name and date are on this worksheet.

   e. Submit a disk containing the completed workbook to your instructor.

2. Figure 7.15 displays a partially completed macro that can be found on the Module2 sheet in the Finished Advanced Macro workbook described in the fifth hands-on exercise. The macro is intended to highlight the Chicago employees in red and the Atlanta employees in blue.

   a. Do Hands-on Exercise 5 as it is described in the chapter, which introduced loops and decision making within a macro.

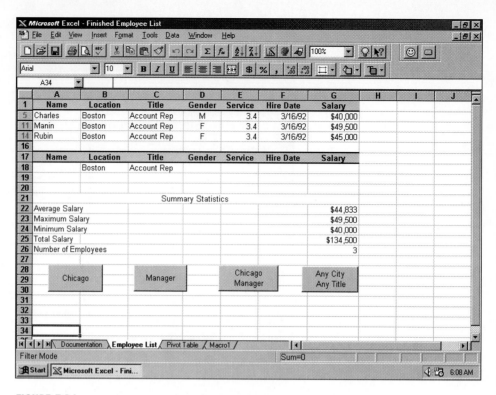

FIGURE 7.14   Data Management Macros for Practice Exercise 1

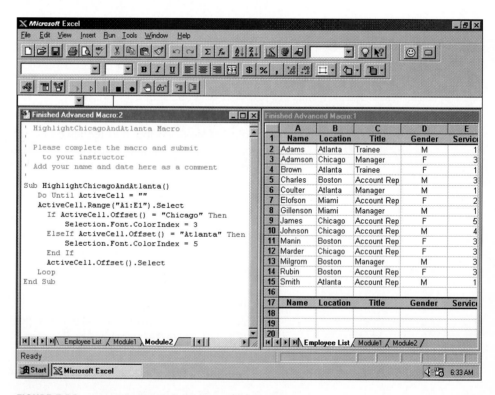

FIGURE 7.15   Advanced Macro for Practice Exercise 2

b. Complete the HighlightChicagoAndAtlanta macro by entering the appropriate offsets in three different statements within the macro. Completion of the macro also requires you to enter a statement at the beginning of the macro that positions you at the first employee within the list.

c. Test the completed macro to be sure that it works properly. You can use the existing ClearColor macro within the workbook (press Ctrl+c as a shortcut) to clear the color within the employee list.

d. Assign Ctrl+a as the shortcut for the macro. The workbook should now have three shortcuts. Ctrl+c and Ctrl+h to clear color and highlight the managers are shortcuts for the ClearColor and HighlightManager macros from the existing hands-on exercise.

e. Add a documentation worksheet that describes all of the macros in the workbook. Be sure your name and date are on this worksheet.

f. Submit a disk containing the completed workbook to your instructor.

3. The workbook in Figure 7.16 is based on the three-dimensional example from Chapter 6. Open the *Chapter 7 Practice 3* workbook as it exists on the data disk and save it as *Finished Chapter 7 Practice 3*. Do the following:

a. Run Macro1, Macro2, and Macro3 in succession. What does each of these macros do?

b. Run the StartOver macro. What does this macro do?

c. Run Macro4. What does it do? How many statements does the macro contain? Explain why the macro is so powerful even though it contains a limited number of statements.

d. A branch office has been opened in a fourth city, and its sales are found in the New York workbook. Determine which macro(s) have to be modified so that the sales of the New York office are included in the corporate totals, then modify those macros appropriately.

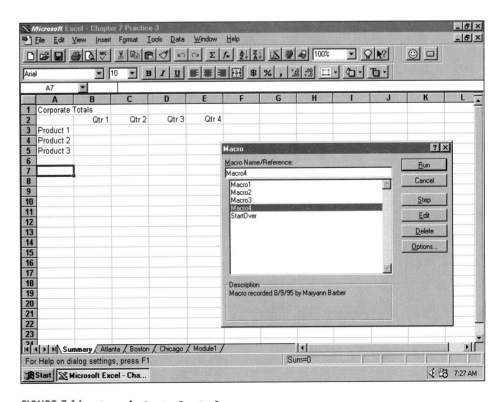

FIGURE 7.16   Screen for Practice Exercise 3

e. Modify Macro4 and the StartOver macro so that they can be run with the keyboard shortcuts Ctrl+a and Ctrl+b, respectively.

f. Submit a disk containing the finished workbook to your instructor. (The disk should also contain the Atlanta, Boston, Chicago, and New York workbooks.)

4. Microsoft Excel includes several templates to help run a business or plan your personal finances. A template is a partially completed workbook that contains formatting, text, formulas, and macros, and it is the macros that make the template so valuable. One of those templates, the Loan Manager, is the basis of the workbook in Figure 7.17. The workbook contains four worksheets and several macros, which Microsoft has chosen to hide. The macros execute automatically, however, as you enter data in the workbook and move from one worksheet to another.

To create the workbook in Figure 7.17, pull down the File menu, click New, click the Spreadsheet Solutions tab, open the Loan Manager template, then save it as *Chapter 7 Practice 4*. Click the Customize Your Loan Manager tab and enter your personal information. Enter the parameters for a real (or imaginary) loan, then explore the workbook by examining its worksheets. Enter a beginning date at least two years prior to today's date so that the workbook will record several loan payments. Print the Loan Data, Loan Amortization Table, and Summary worksheets, then submit all three pages as proof that you did the exercise.

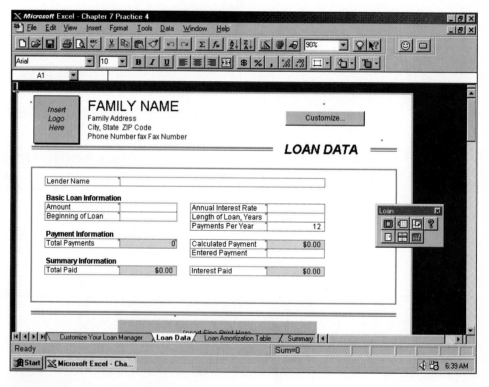

FIGURE 7.17   Screen for Practice Exercise 4

CASE STUDIES

Spreadsheet Solutions

The Loan Manager is one of several templates that are supplied with Microsoft Excel. The other templates include a Sales Invoice, Purchase Order, Expense Statement, Business Planner, and Personal Budget. Choose any template that seems of interest to you, then enter real or hypothetical data. Print one or more worksheets from the workbook and submit the output to your instructor.

Microsoft Word

Do you use Microsoft Word on a regular basis? Are there certain tasks that you do repeatedly, whether in the same document or in a series of different documents? If so, you would do well to explore the macro capabilities within Microsoft Word. How are these capabilities similar to Excel's? How do they differ?

Starting Up

Your instructor is very impressed with the Excel workbook and associated macros that you have created. He would like you to take the automation process one step further and simplify the way in which Excel is started and the workbook is loaded. Use your knowledge of Windows 95 to implement your instructor's request. The problem is open ended, and there are many different approaches. You might, for example, create a shortcut on the desktop to open the workbook. You might also explore the use of the Startup folder.

Dade County Metro Zoo

The Dade County Metro Zoo workbook is similar in concept to the Employee List workbook that was used throughout the chapter. Open the workbook and run the three existing macros. Create two additional macros of your own that you think are appropriate, then submit a disk containing the completed workbook to your instructor.

APPENDIX A: THE SPREADSHEET AUDIT

OVERVIEW

In one of the most celebrated spreadsheet errors of all time, the comptroller of James A. Cummings, Inc, a Florida construction company, used a spreadsheet to develop a bid on a multi-million dollar office complex. At the last minute, he realized that he had forgotten to include $254,000 for overhead, and so he inserted this number at the top of a column of numbers. Unfortunately for both the comptroller and the company, the $254,000 was not included in the final total, and the contract was underbid by that amount. The company was awarded the contract and forced to make good on its unrealistically low estimate.

Seeking to recover its losses, the construction company brought suit against the spreadsheet vendor, claiming that a latent defect within the spreadsheet failed to add the entry in question. The vendor contended that the mistake was in fact a *user error* and the court agreed, citing the vendor's licensing agreement:

". . . Because software is inherently complex and may not be completely free of errors, you are advised to verify your work. In no event will the vendor be liable for direct, indirect, special, incidental, or consequential damages arising out of the use of or inability to use the software or documentation, even if advised of the possibility of such damages. In particular, said vendor is not responsible for any costs including, but not limited to, those incurred as a result of lost profits or revenue."

The purpose of this appendix is to remind you that the spreadsheet is only a tool, and like all other tools it must be used properly, or there can be serious consequences. Think, for a moment, how business has become totally dependent on the spreadsheet, and how little validity checking is actually done. Ask yourself if any of your spreadsheets contained an error, and if so, what the consequences would have been if those spreadsheets represented real applications rather than academic exercises.

USE FUNCTIONS RATHER THAN FORMULAS

The entries =A1+A2+A3+A4 and =SUM(A1:A4) may appear equivalent, but the function is inherently superior and should be used whenever possible. A function adjusts automatically for the insertion (deletion) of rows within the designated range, whereas a formula does not. Including a blank row at the beginning and end of the function's range ensures that any value added to the top or bottom of a column of numbers will automatically be included in the sum. Had this technique been followed by the James A. Cummings company, the error would not have occurred.

A WORD OF CAUTION

The formatting capabilities within Excel make it all too easy to get caught up in the appearance of a worksheet without paying attention to its accuracy. Consider, for example, the grade book in Figure A.1, which is used by a hypothetical professor to assign final grades in a class. The grade book is nicely formatted, *but its calculations are wrong*, and no amount of fancy formatting can compensate for the erroneous results. Consider:

- Baker should have received an A rather than a B. He has an 87 average on his quizzes, he received an 87 on the final exam, and with two bonus points for each of his two homeworks, he should have had an overall final average of 91.

- Charles should have received a B rather than a C. True, he did not do any homework and he did do poorly on the final, but, with the semester quizzes and final exam counting equally, his semester average should have been 80.

1	Name	HW 1	HW 2	HW 3	Quiz 1	Quiz 2	Quiz 3	Quiz Average	Final Exam	HW Bonus	Semester Average	Grade
2	Baker		OK	OK	77	89	95	87	87	2	89	B
3	Charles				84	76	86	82	78	0	79	C
4	Goodman	OK	OK			95	94	63	95	4	89	B
5	Johnson	OK	OK		90	86	70	82	90	4	92	A
6	Jones		OK	OK	75	85	71	77	86	2	85	B
7	Irving	OK		OK	65	85	75	75	78	2	79	C
8	Lang				84	88	83	85	94	0	91	A
9	London		OK		72	69	75	72	82	2	81	B
10	Milgrom	OK	OK		100	65	90	85	100	4	100	A
11	Mills	OK	OK		75	85	80	80	65	4	74	C
12	Nelson	OK	OK		65	60	61	62	60	4	65	D
13												
14		Grading Criteria									Grading Scale	
15		Bonus for each homework					2				Average	Grade
16		Weight of semester quizzes					50%				0	F
17		Weight of final exam					50%				60	D
18											70	C
19											80	B
20											90	A

Baker should have received an A

Charles should have received a B

Goodman should have received an A

FIGURE A.1   *The Professor's Grade Book*

- Goodman should have received an A rather than a B. She aced both quizzes (she was excused from the first quiz) as well as the final, and in addition, she received a four-point bonus for homework.

The errors in our example are contrived, but they could occur. Consider:

- At the class's urging, the professor decided at the last minute to assign a third homework but neglected to modify the formulas to include the additional column containing the extra homework.
- The professor changed the grading scheme at the last minute and decided to count the semester quizzes and final exam evenly. (The original weights were 30% and 70%, respectively.) Unfortunately, however, the formulas to compute each student's semester average specify constants (.30 and .70) rather than absolute references to the cells containing the exam weights. Hence the new grading scheme is not reflected in the student averages.
- The professor forgot that he had excused Goodman from the first quiz and hence did not adjust the formula to compute Goodman's average on the basis of two quizzes rather than three.

Our professor is only human, but he would have done well to print the cell formulas in order to audit the mechanics of the worksheet and double check its calculations. Suffice it to say that the accuracy of a worksheet is far more important than its appearance, and you are well advised to remember this thought as you create and/or use a spreadsheet.

THE SPREADSHEET AUDIT

The *Auditing toolbar* helps you understand the relationships between the various cells in a worksheet. It enables you to trace the *precedents* for a formula and identify the cells in the worksheet that are referenced by that formula. It also enables you to trace the *dependents* of a cell and identify the formulas in the worksheet that reference that cell.

The identification of precedent and/or dependent cells is done graphically by displaying tracers on the worksheet. You simply click in the cell for which you want the information, then you click the appropriate button on the Auditing toolbar. The blue arrows (tracers) appear on the worksheet, and will remain on the worksheet until you click the appropriate removal button. The tracers always point forward, from the precedent cells to the dependent formula.

To see how valuable the tracers can be, consider Figure A.2, which contrasts the professor's original worksheet (Figure A.2a) with the corrected worksheet (Figure A.2b). Consider first the precedents for cell J2, which contains the formula to compute Baker's homework bonus. The tracers (the blue lines) in the invalid worksheet identify homeworks 1 and 2 (note the box around cells B2 and C2) as precedents. The corrected worksheet, however, shows that all three homeworks (cells B2, C2, and D2) are used in the determination of the bonus. (Both worksheets show that cell G15, which contains the homework bonus, is also a precedent for cell J2.)

The analysis of dependent cells is equally telling. There are no dependent cells for cell G16 in the invalid spreadsheet because the formulas to compute the students' semester averages do not reference this cell. The valid worksheet, however, corrects the error, and hence each cell in column K is dependent on cell G16.

The Auditing toolbar is displayed through the View menu and is shown in both Figures A.2a and A.2b. You can point to any button on the Auditing toolbar to display a ToolTip to indicate the purpose of that button.

Tracer identifies B2:C2 as precedents

Tracer identifies G15 as a precedent

G16 has no dependent cells

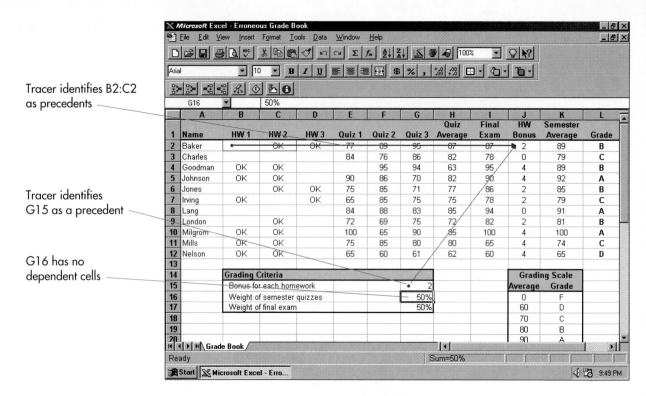

(a) The Invalid Worksheet

Tracer identifies B2:D2 as precedents

Tracer identifies G15 as a precedent

Tracers show dependent cells (i.e., G16 is a precedent for K2:K12)

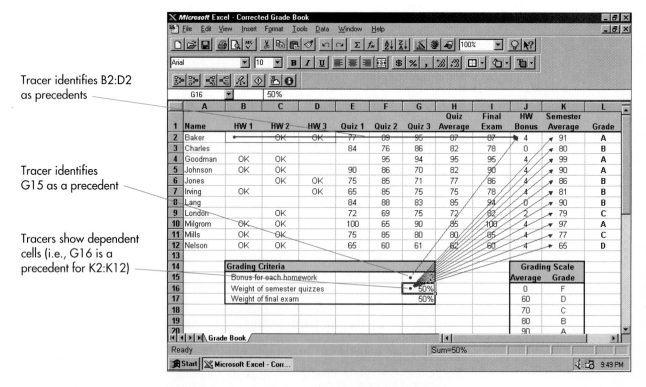

(b) The Corrected Worksheet

FIGURE A.2   The Spreadsheet Audit

ANNOTATE YOUR SPREADSHEETS

The Attach Note button on the Auditing Toolbar enables you to create the equivalent of your own ToolTip for any cell in a spreadsheet. It is an excellent way to annotate a spreadsheet and attach an explanation to any cell containing a complex formula. See step 5 in the hands-on exercise for details on attaching a note.

A SECOND EXAMPLE

Financial planning and budgeting is one of the most common business applications of spreadsheets. Figure A.3 contains a revised (and invalid) version of the financial forecast that was developed in Chapter 2 (see pages 69–75). As in the professor's grade book, the spreadsheet is nicely formatted, but its calculations are wrong, as will be explained shortly. Any decisions based on the spreadsheet will also be in error.

How do you know when a spreadsheet displays invalid results? One way is to "eyeball" the spreadsheet and try to approximate its results. Look for any calculations that are obviously incorrect. Look at the financial forecast, for example, and see whether all the values are growing at the projected rates of change. The number of units sold and the unit price increase every year as expected, but the cost of the production facility remains constant after 1997. This is an obvious error because the production facility is supposed to increase at eight percent annually, according to the assumptions at the bottom of the spreadsheet. The consequence of this error is that the production costs (after 1997) are too low and hence the projected earnings are too high. The error was easy to find, even without the use of a calculator.

Cost of the production facility is not increasing as expected after 1977

Earnings should be 0 ($225,000 – $225,000)

	A	B	C	D	E	F
1	Get Rich Quick - Financial Forecast					
2		1996	1997	1998	1999	2000
3	Income					
4	Units sold	100,000	110,000	121,000	133,100	146,410
5	Unit price	$2.25	$2.36	$2.48	$2.60	$2.73
6	Gross revenue	$225,000	$259,875	$300,156	$346,680	$400,415
7						
8	Fixed costs					
9	Production facility	$50,000	$54,000	$54,000	$54,000	$54,000
10	Administration	$25,000	$26,250	$27,563	$28,941	$30,388
11	Variable cost					
12	Unit mfg cost	$1.50	$1.65	$1.82	$2.00	$2.20
13	Variable mft cost	$150,000	$181,500	$219,615	$265,734	$321,538
14						
15	Earnings before taxes	$25,000	$24,375	$26,541	$26,946	$24,877
16						
17	Initial conditions			Annual increase		
18	First year sales	100,000		10%		
19	Selling price	$2.25		5%		
20	Unit mfg cost	$1.50		10%		
21	Production facility	$50,000		8%		
22	Administration	$25,000		5%		
23	First year of forecast	1996				

FIGURE A.3   The Erroneous Financial Forecast

A more subtle error occurs in the computation of the earnings before taxes. Look at the numbers for 1996. The gross revenue is $225,000. The total cost is also $225,000 ($50,000 for the production facility, $25,000 for administration, and $150,000 for the manufacturing cost). The projected earnings should be zero, but are shown incorrectly as $25,000, because the administration cost was not subtracted from the gross revenue in determining the profit.

The errors in the financial forecast are easy to discover if only you take the time to look. Unfortunately, however, too many people are prone to accept the results of a spreadsheet, simply because it is nicely formatted on a laser printer. We urge you, therefore, to "eyeball" every spreadsheet for obvious errors, and if a mistake is found, a spreadsheet audit is called for.

TEST WITH SIMPLE AND PREDICTABLE DATA

Test a spreadsheet initially with simple and predictable data that you create yourself so that you can manually verify the spreadsheet is performing as expected. Once you are confident the spreadsheet works with data you can control, test it again with real data to further check its validity. Adequate testing is time consuming, but it can save you from embarrassing, not to mention costly, mistakes.

HANDS-ON EXERCISE 1

The Auditing Toolbar

Objective: To illustrate the tools on the Auditing toolbar; to trace errors in spreadsheet formulas; to identify precedent and dependent cells; to attach a note to a cell. Use Figure A.4 as a guide in the exercise.

STEP 1: Display the Auditing Toolbar

➤ Load Excel. Open the **Erroneous Financial Forecast** workbook in the **Exploring Excel folder** as shown in Figure A.4a. Save the workbook as **Finished Erroneous Financial Forecast.**

➤ Point to any toolbar, click the **right mouse button** to display the shortcut menu in Figure A.4a, then click **Auditing** to display the Auditing toolbar.

➤ If necessary, click and drag the title bar of the Auditing toolbar to dock the toolbar under the Formatting toolbar.

FIXED VERSUS FLOATING TOOLBARS

Any toolbar can be docked along the edge of the application window, or it can be displayed as a floating toolbar within the application window. To move a docked toolbar, drag the toolbar background. To move a floating toolbar, drag its title bar. To size a floating toolbar, drag any border in the direction you want to go. Double click the background of any toolbar to toggle between a floating toolbar and a docked (fixed) toolbar.

Point to a toolbar and click right mouse button to display shortcut menu

Select (click) the Auditing toolbar

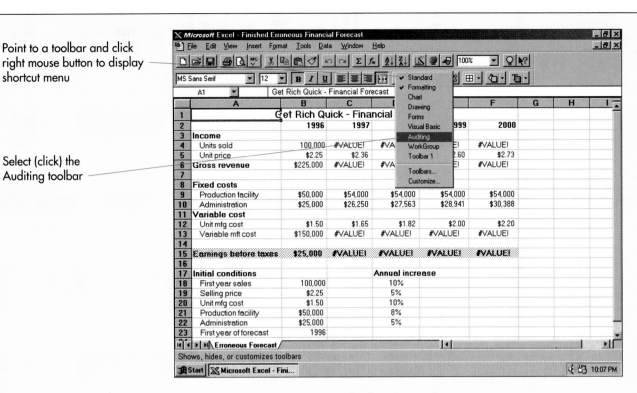

(a) Display the Auditing Toolbar (step 1)

FIGURE A.4   Hands-on Exercise 1

STEP 2: The Trace Error Command

➤ Click in **cell C4**, the first cell that displays the #VALUE error. Click the **Trace Error button** on the Auditing toolbar to display the tracers shown in Figure A.4b.

➤ The tracers identify the error in graphic fashion and show that cell C4 is dependent on cells A4 and D18 (i.e., cells A4 and D18 are precedents of cell C4). Cell A4 contains a text entry and is obviously incorrect.

➤ Click in the formula bar to edit the formula for cell C4 so that it references cell B4 rather than cell A4. (The correct formula is =B4+B4*$D$18). Press **enter** when you have corrected the formula.

➤ The tracer arrows disappear (they disappear automatically whenever you edit a formula to which they refer). The #VALUE errors are also gone because the formula has been corrected and all dependent formulas have been automatically recalculated.

THE #VALUE ERROR

The #VALUE error occurs when the wrong type of entry is used in a formula or as an argument in a function. It typically occurs when a formula references a text rather than a numeric entry. The easiest way to resolve the error is to display the Auditing toolbar, select the cell in question, then click the Trace Error button.

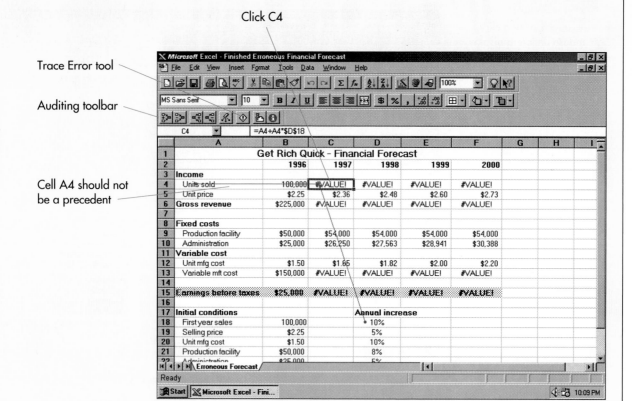

Click C4

Trace Error tool

Auditing toolbar

Cell A4 should not
be a precedent

(b) The Trace Error Command (step 2)

FIGURE A.4   Hands-on Exercise 1 (continued)

STEP 3: Trace Dependents

➤ The worksheet is in error because the production costs do not increase after 1997. Click in **cell D21** (the cell containing the projected increase in the cost of the production facility).

➤ Click the **Trace Dependents button** to display the dependent cells as shown in Figure A.4c. Only one dependent cell (cell C9) is shown. This is clearly an error because cells D9 through F9 should also depend on cell D1.

➤ Click in **cell C9** to examine its formula (=B9+B9*D21). The production costs for the second year are based on the first-year costs (cell B9) and the rate of increase (cell D21). The latter, however, was entered as a relative rather than an absolute address.

➤ Change the formula in cell C9 to include an absolute reference to cell D21 (i.e., the correct formula is =B9+B9*$D$21). The tracer arrow disappears due to the correction.

➤ Drag the fill handle in **cell C9** to copy the corrected formula to **cells D9, E9, and F9.** (The displayed value for cell F9 should be $68,024.)

➤ Click in **cell D21.** Click the **Trace Dependents button,** and this time it points to the production costs for years 2 through 5 in the forecast. Click the **Remove Dependents button** to remove the arrows.

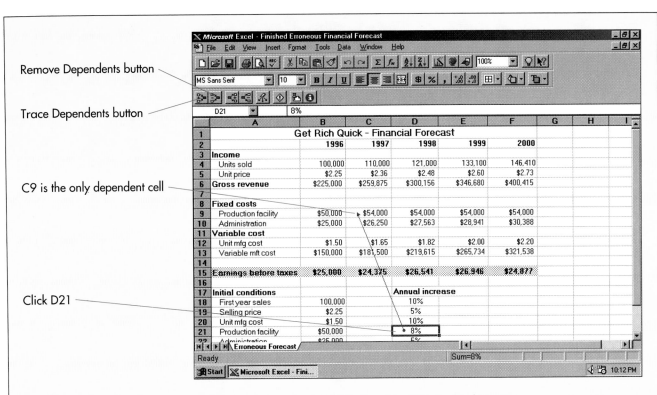

Remove Dependents button

Trace Dependents button

C9 is the only dependent cell

Click D21

(c) The Trace Dependents Command (step 3)

FIGURE A.4   Hands-on Exercise 1 (continued)

ISOLATE ASSUMPTIONS AND INITIAL CONDITIONS

A spreadsheet is first and foremost a tool for decision making, and as such, the subject of continual what-if speculation. It is critical, therefore, that the input and assumptions be isolated and clearly visible, and further that all formulas in the spreadsheet accurately reflect the cells containing these values.

STEP 4: Trace Precedents

➤ The earnings before taxes in cell B15 should be zero. (The gross revenue is $225,000, as are the total expenses, which consist of production, administration, and manufacturing costs of $50,000, $25,000, and $150,000, respectively.) Click in **cell B15.**

➤ Click the **Trace Precedents button** to display the precedent cells as shown in Figure A.4d. The projected earnings depend on the revenue (cell B6) and various expenses (cells B9 and B13). The problem is that the administration expense (cell B10) is omitted, and hence the earnings are too high.

➤ Change the formula in cell B15 to **=B6−(B9+B10+B13)** so that the administration expense is included in the expenses that are deducted from the gross revenue. The tracer arrow disappears.

➤ Drag the fill handle in **cell B15** to copy the corrected formula to **cells C15** through **F15.** (The displayed value in cell F15 is a *negative* $19,535.)

Click in formula bar to edit the formula

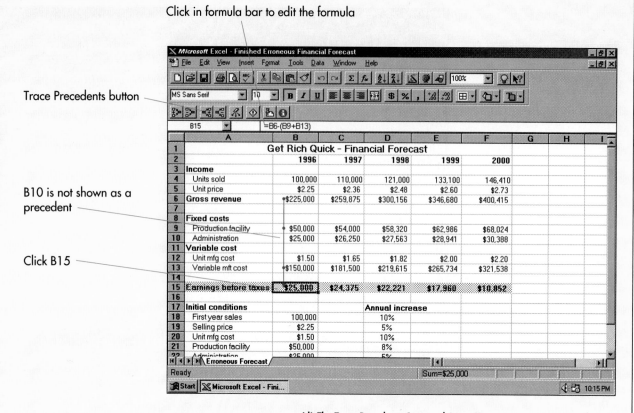

Trace Precedents button

B10 is not shown as a precedent

Click B15

(d) The Trace Precedents Command (step 4)

FIGURE A.4   Hands-on Exercise 1 (continued)

STEP 5: Attach a Note

➤ Click in **cell B19** (the cell containing the selling price for the first year). Click the **Attach Note button** to display the Cell Note dialog box as shown in Figure A.4e.

➤ Type the text of the note you want attached to cell B19. Click **OK** to close the dialog box and return to the worksheet.

➤ Click outside cell B19 to deselect this cell. Look carefully at cell B19 in Figure A.4f. You should see a red dot in the upper-right corner of the cell, indicating that a note has been attached.

➤ Point to cell B19, and the text of the note you just created appears over the spreadsheet in the form of a ToolTip. Point to a different cell, and the note disappears from view.

➤ Save the workbook.

THE EDIT CLEAR COMMAND

The Clear command in the Edit menu erases the contents, format, and/or notes within a cell. Select the cell(s), pull down the Edit menu, click (or point to) the Clear command, then select the desired option (All, Format, Contents, or Notes) from the resulting submenu.

Type text of note

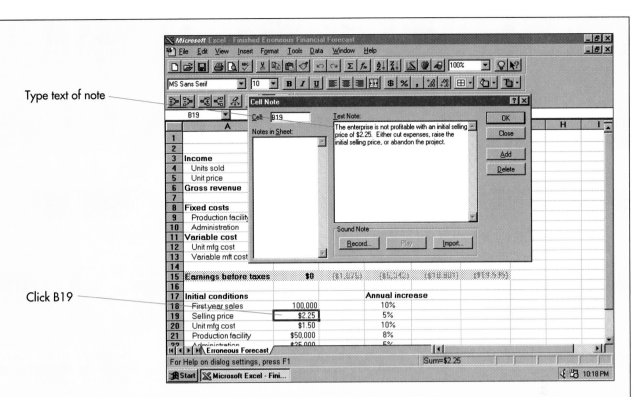

(e) Attach a Note (step 5)

Attach Note tool

Red dot indicates
attached note

Click B19

Tooltip displays note
when you point to B19

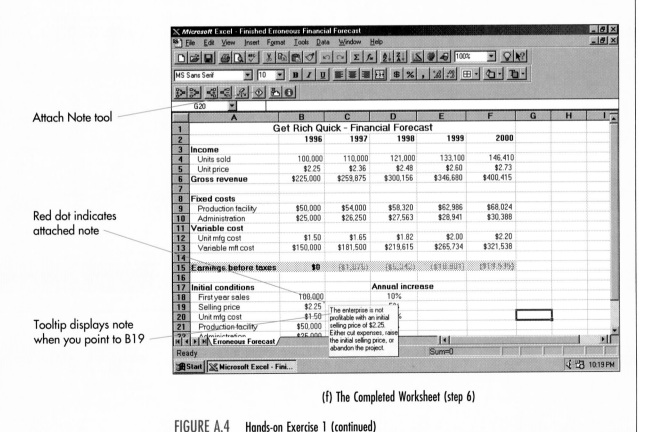

(f) The Completed Worksheet (step 6)

FIGURE A.4   Hands-on Exercise 1 (continued)

STEP 6: Conduct Your Own Audit

➤ The erroneous grade book is on the data disk so that you can continue to practice. Open the **Erroneous Gradebook** workbook in the **Exploring Excel folder.**

➤ You should see the professor's grade book that was described at the beginning of the appendix. Conduct your own audit of the grade book, using the techniques in the exercise.

➤ Exit Excel when you have completed the exercise.

SUMMARY

A spreadsheet is only a tool, and like all other tools, it must be used properly, or else there can be serious consequences. The essential point in the grade book and financial forecast examples is that the potential for spreadsheet error does exist, and that you cannot blindly accept the results of a spreadsheet. Every spreadsheet should be checked for obvious errors, and if any are found, a spreadsheet audit is called for.

The Auditing toolbar helps you understand the relationships between the various cells in a worksheet. It enables you to trace the precedents for a formula and identify the cells in the worksheet that are referenced by that formula. It also enables you to trace the dependents of a cell and identify the formulas in the worksheet that reference that cell.

KEY WORDS AND CONCEPTS

Audit	Auditing toolbar	Precedents
Attach Note command	Dependents	Trace Error command

APPENDIX B: SOLVER

OVERVIEW

The use of a spreadsheet in decision making has been emphasized throughout the text. We showed you how to design a spreadsheet based on a set of initial conditions and assumptions, then see at a glance the effect of changing one or more of those values. We introduced the Scenario Manager to store sets of assumptions so that they could be easily recalled and reevaluated. We discussed the Goal Seek command, which enables you to set the value of a target cell, then determine the input needed to arrive at that target value. The Goal Seek command, useful as it is, however, is limited to a *single* input variable. This appendix discusses *Solver,* a powerful add-in that is designed for problems involving *multiple* variables.

Solver is an optimization and resource allocation tool that helps you achieve a desired goal. You specify a goal, such as maximizing profit or minimizing cost. You indicate the constraints (conditions) that must be satisfied for the solution to be valid, and you specify the cells whose values can change in order to reach that goal. Solver will then determine the values for the changing cells (i.e., it will tell you how to allocate your resources) in order to reach the desired goal.

This appendix provides an introduction to Solver through two different examples. The first example shows how to maximize profit. The second example minimizes cost. Both examples are accompanied by a hands-on exercise.

EXAMPLE 1—MAXIMIZE PROFIT

Assume that you are the production manager for a company that manufactures computers. Your company divides its product line into two basic categories, desktop computers and laptops. Each product is sold under two different labels, a discount line and a premium line. As production manager you are to determine how many computers of each type, and of each product line, to make each week.

Your decision is subject to various constraints that must be satisfied during the production process. Each computer requires a specified number of hours for assembly. Discount and premium-brand desktops require two and three hours, respectively. Discount and premium-brand laptops use three and five hours, respectively. The factory is working at full capacity, and you have only 4,500 hours of labor to allocate among the different products.

Your production decision is also constrained by demand. The marketing department has determined that you cannot sell more than 800 desktop units, nor more than 900 laptops, per week. The total demand for the discount and premium lines is 700 and 1,000 computers, respectively, per week.

Your goal (objective) is to maximize the total profit, which is based on a different profit margin for each type of computer. A desktop and a laptop computer from the discount line have unit profits of $600 and $800, respectively. The premium desktop and laptop computers have unit profits of $1,000 and $1,300, respectively. How many computers of each type do you manufacture each week in order to maximize the total profit?

This is a complex problem, but one which can be easily solved provided you can design the spreadsheet to display all of the information. Figure B.1 illustrates one way to set up the problem. In essence, you need to determine the values of cells B2 through B5, which represent the quantity of each computer to produce. You might be able to solve the problem manually through trial and error, by substituting different values and seeing the impact on profit. That is exactly what Solver will do for you, only it will do it much more quickly. (Solver uses various optimization techniques that are beyond the scope of this discussion.)

Once Solver arrives at a solution, assuming that it can find a solution, it creates a report such as the one shown in Figure B.2. The solution shows the value of the target cell (the profit in this example), based on the values of the adjustable cells (the quantity of each type of computer). The solution that will maximize profit is to manufacture 700 discount laptops and 800 premium desktops for a profit of $1,270,000.

The report in Figure B.2 also examines each constraint and determines whether it is binding or not binding. A ***binding constraint*** is one in which the resource is fully utilized (i.e., the slack is zero). The number of available hours, for example, is a binding constraint because every available hour is used, and hence the value of the target cell (profit) is limited by the amount of this resource (the number of hours). Or stated another way, any increase in the number of available hours (above 4,500) will also increase the profit.

A ***nonbinding constraint*** is just the opposite. It has a nonzero slack (i.e., the resource is not fully utilized), and hence it does not limit the value of the target cell. The laptop demand, for example, is not binding because a total of only 700 laptops were produced, yet the allowable demand was 900 (the value in cell E13). In other words, there is a slack value of 200 for this constraint, and increasing the allowable demand will have no effect on the profit. (The demand could actually be decreased by up to 200 units with no effect on profit.)

SOLVER

The information required by Solver is entered through the ***Solver Parameters dialog box*** as shown in Figure B.3. The dialog box is divided into three sections: the target cell, the changing cells, and the constraints. The dialog box in Figure B.3 corresponds to the spreadsheet shown earlier in Figure B.1.

Need to determine the values of cells B2:B5

	A	B	C	D	E
1		Quantity	Hours	Unit Profit	
2	Discount desktop		2	$600	
3	Discount laptop		3	$800	
4	Premium desktop		3	$1,000	
5	Premium laptop		5	$1,300	
6					
7	Constraints				
8	Total number of hours used				
9	Labor hours available				4,500
10	Number of desktops produced				
11	Total demand for desktop computers				800
12	Number of laptops produced				
13	Total demand for laptop computers				900
14	Number of discount computers produced				
15	Total demand for discount computers				700
16	Number of premium computers produced				
17	Total demand for premium computers				1,000
18	Hourly cost of labor				$20
19	Profit				

FIGURE B.1   The Initial Worksheet

Value of target cell (profit)

Quantity of each type of computer to be produced

Indicates whether constraint is binding or nonbinding

Target Cell (Max)

Cell	Name	Original Value	Final Value
$E$19	Profit	$0	$1,270,000

Adjustable Cells

Cell	Name	Original Value	Final Value
$B$2	Discount desktop Quantity	0	0
$B$3	Discount laptop Quantity	0	700
$B$4	Premium desktop Quantity	0	800
$B$5	Premium laptop Quantity	0	0

Constraints

Cell	Name	Cell Value	Formula	Status	Slack
$E$8	Total number of hours used	4500	$E$8<=$E$9	Binding	0
$E$10	Number of desktops produced	800	$E$10<=$E$11	Binding	0
$E$12	Number of laptops produced	700	$E$12<=$E$13	Not Binding	200
$E$14	Number of discount computers produced	700	$E$14<=$E$15	Binding	0
$E$16	Number of premium computers produced	800	$E$16<=$E$17	Not Binding	200
$B$2	Discount desktop Quantity	0	$B$2>=0	Binding	0
$B$3	Discount laptop Quantity	700	$B$3>=0	Not Binding	700
$B$4	Premium desktop Quantity	800	$B$4>=0	Not Binding	800
$B$5	Premium laptop Quantity	0	$B$5>=0	Binding	0

FIGURE B.2   The Solution

The *target cell* identifies the goal (or objective function)—that is, the cell whose value you want to maximize, minimize, or set to a specific value. Our problem seeks to maximize profit, the formula for which is found in cell E19 (the target cell) of the underlying spreadsheet.

The *changing cells* (or decision variables) are the cells whose values are adjusted until the constraints are satisfied and the target cell reaches its optimum value. The changing cells in this example contain the quantity of each computer to be produced and are found in cells B2 through B5.

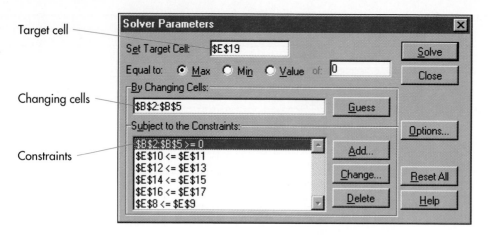

Target cell

Changing cells

Constraints

FIGURE B.3 Solver Parameters Dialog Box

The ***constraints*** specify the restrictions. Each constraint consists of a cell or cell range on the left, a relational operator, and a numeric value or cell reference on the right. (The constraints can be entered in any order, but they always appear in alphabetical order.) The first constraint references a cell range, cells B2 through B5, and indicates that each of these cells must be greater than or equal to zero. The remaining constraints reference a single cell rather than a cell range.

The functions of the various command buttons are apparent from their names. The Add, Change, and Delete buttons, are used to add, change, or delete a constraint. The Options button enables you to set various parameters that determine how Solver attempts to find a solution. The Reset All button clears all settings and resets all options to their defaults. The Solve button begins the search for a solution.

THE GREATER-THAN-ZERO CONSTRAINT

One constraint that is often overlooked is the requirement that the value of each changing cell be greater than or equal to zero. Physically, it makes no sense to produce a negative number of computers in any category. Mathematically, however, a negative value in a changing cell may produce a higher value for the target cell. Hence the nonnegativity (greater than or equal to zero) constraint should always be included for the changing cells.

HANDS-ON EXERCISE 1

Maximize Profit

Objective: Use Solver to maximize profit; create a report containing binding and nonbinding constraints. Use Figure B.4 as a guide in the exercise.

STEP 1: Enter the Cell Formulas

➤ Start Excel. Open the **Optimization** workbook in the **Exploring Excel folder.** Save the workbook as **Finished Optimization** so that you can return to the original workbook if necessary.

➤ If necessary, click the tab for the **Production Mix** worksheet, then click **cell E8** as shown in Figure B.4a. Enter the formula shown in Figure B.4a to compute the total number of hours used in production.

➤ Enter the remaining cell formulas as shown below:

- Cell E10 (Number of desktops produced) **=B2+B4**
- Cell E12 (Number of laptops produced) **=B3+B5**
- Cell E14 (Number of discount computers produced) **=B2+B3**
- Cell E16 (Number of premium computers produced) **=B4+B5**
- Cell E19 (Profit) **=B2*D2+B3*D3+B4*D4+B5*D5−E18*E8**

➤ Save the workbook.

USE POINTING TO ENTER CELL FORMULAS

A cell reference can be typed directly into a formula, or it can be entered more easily through pointing. The latter is also more accurate as you use the mouse or arrow keys to reference cells directly. To use pointing, select (click) the cell to contain the formula, type an equal sign to begin entering the formula, then click (or move to) the cell containing the reference. Type any arithmetic operator to place the cell reference in the formula, then continue pointing to additional cells. Press the enter key (instead of typing an arithmetic operator) to complete the formula.

Click E8 and enter formula to compute total hours used

Click Production Mix tab

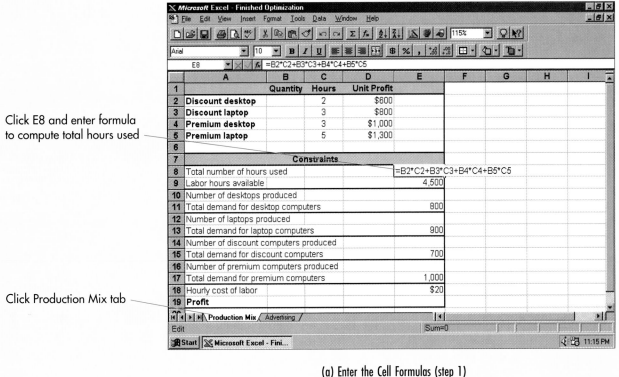

(a) Enter the Cell Formulas (step 1)

FIGURE B.4   Hands-on Exercise 1

STEP 2: Set the Objective and Variable Cells

➤ Check that the formula in cell E19 is entered correctly as shown in Figure B.4b. Pull down the **Tools menu.** Click **Solver** to display the Solver Parameters dialog box shown in Figure B.4b.

➤ The target cell is already set to **cell E19** (since this was the active cell when you started Solver). The **Max option button** is selected by default.

➤ Click in the **By Changing Cells** text box. Click and drag **cells B2** through **B5** in the worksheet to select these cells.

➤ Click the **Add command button** to add the first constraint as described in step 3.

MISSING SOLVER

Solver is an optional component of Excel and hence may not be loaded or installed on your system. Pull down the Tools menu and click Add-ins, then check the box next to Solver to load it. If Solver does not appear, you need to install it. Click the Windows 95 Start button, click Settings, then click Control Panel. Double click the icon to Add/Remove programs, click the Install/Uninstall tab, click Microsoft Office application, then click the Add/Remove command button and follow the instructions.

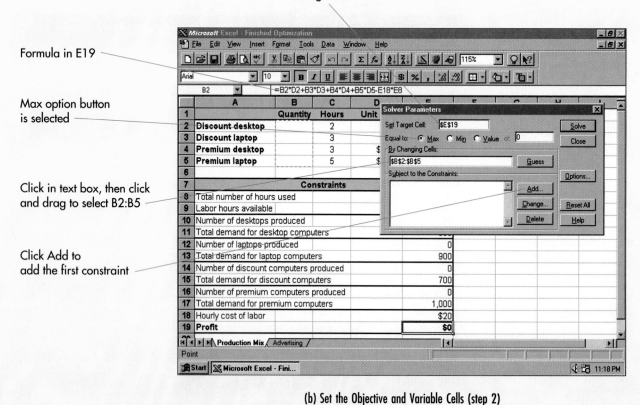

(b) Set the Objective and Variable Cells (step 2)

FIGURE B.4   Hands-on Exercise 1 (continued)

STEP 3: Add the Constraints

➤ You should see the Add Constraint dialog box in Figure B.4c with the insertion point (a flashing vertical line) in the Cell Reference text box.

- Click in **cell E8** (the cell containing the formula to compute the total number of hours used).
- The <= constraint is selected by default.
- Click in the text box to contain the value of the constraint, then click **cell E9** in the worksheet to enter the cell reference.
- Click **Add** to complete this constraint and add another.

➤ You will see a new (empty) Add Constraint dialog box, which enables you to enter additional constraints. Use pointing to enter each of the constraints shown below. (Solver automatically converts each reference to an absolute reference.):

- Enter the constraint **E10<=E11.** Click **Add.**
- Enter the constraint **E12<=E13.** Click **Add.**
- Enter the constraint **E14<=E15.** Click **Add.**
- Enter the constraint **E16<=E17.** Click **Add.**

➤ Add the last constraint. Click and drag to select **cells B2** through **B5.** Click the >= operator in the Add Constraint dialog box. Type **0** in the text box to indicate that the production quantities for all computers must be greater than zero. Click **OK** to return to the Solver Parameters dialog box.

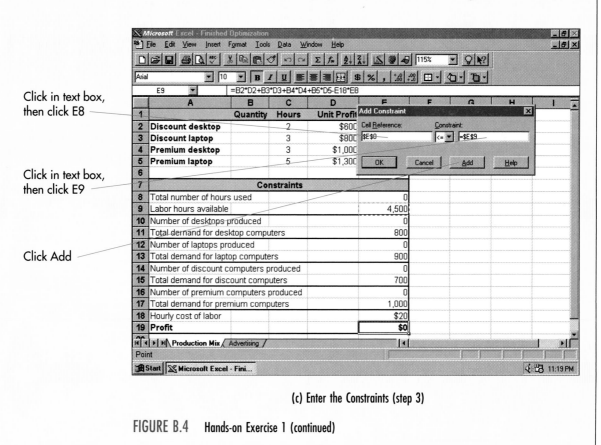

(c) Enter the Constraints (step 3)

FIGURE B.4 Hands-on Exercise 1 (continued)

STEP 4: Solve the Problem

➤ Check that the contents of the Solver Parameters dialog box match those of Figure B.4d. (The constraints appear in alphabetical order rather than the order in which they were entered.)

- To change the Target cell, click the **Set Target Cell** text box, then click the appropriate target cell in the worksheet.

- To change (edit) a constraint, select the constraint, then click the **Change button.**

- To delete a constraint, select the constraint and click the **Delete button.**

➤ Click the **Solve button** to solve the problem.

Click Solve button

Constraints are in alphabetical order

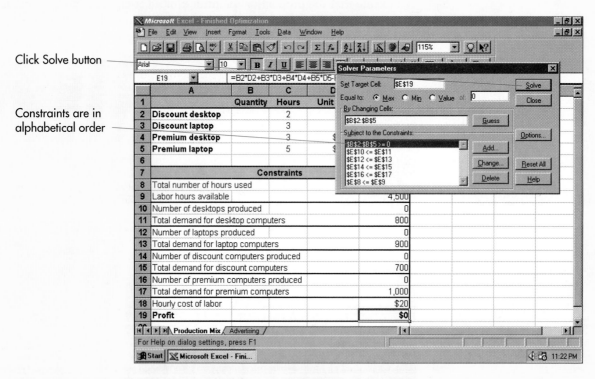

(d) Solve the Problem (step 4)

FIGURE B.4   Hands-on Exercise 1 (continued)

STEP 5: Create the Report

➤ You should see the Solver Results dialog box in Figure B.4e, indicating that Solver has found a solution. The option button to Keep Solver Solution is selected by default.

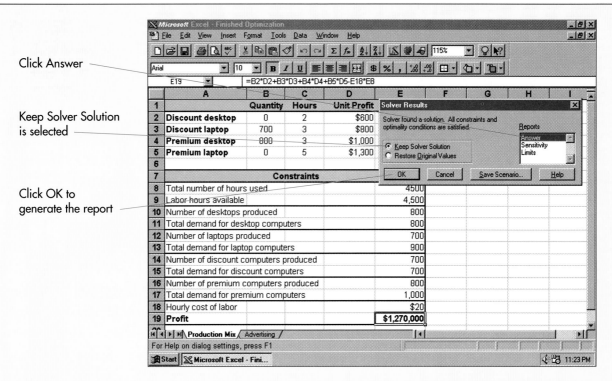

Click Answer

Keep Solver Solution
is selected

Click OK to
generate the report

(e) Create the Report (step 5)

FIGURE B.4   Hands-on Exercise 1 (continued)

➤ Click **Answer** in the Reports list box, then click **OK** to generate the report. You will see the report being generated, after which the Solver Results dialog box closes automatically.

➤ Save the workbook.

STEP 6: View the Report

➤ Click the **Answer Report 1 worksheet tab** to view the report as shown in Figure B.4f. Click in **cell A4,** the cell immediately under the entry showing the date and time the report was created. (The gridlines and row and column headings are suppressed by default for this worksheet.)

➤ Enter your name in boldface as shown in the figure, then press **enter** to complete the entry. Print the answer sheet and submit it to your instructor as proof you did the exercise.

➤ Exit Excel if you do not wish to continue with the next exercise at this time.

VIEW OPTIONS

Any worksheet used to create a spreadsheet model will display gridlines and row and column headers by default. Worksheets containing reports, however, especially worksheets generated by Excel, often suppress these elements to make the reports easier and more appealing to read. To suppress (display) these elements, pull down the Tools menu, click Options, click the View tab, then clear (check) the appropriate check boxes under Window options.

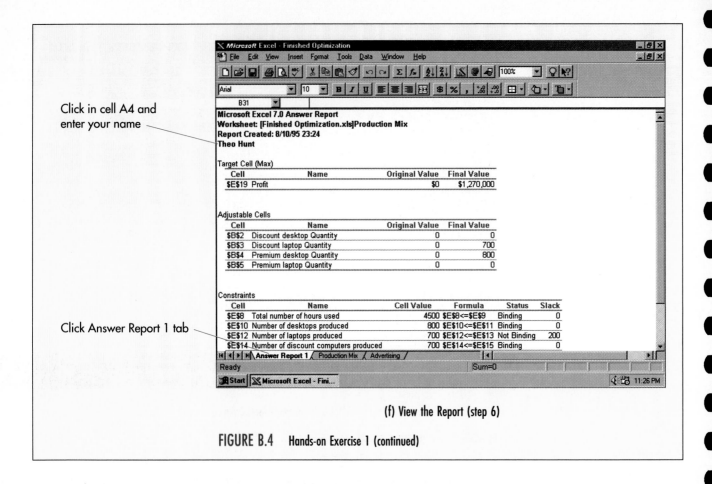

Click in cell A4 and enter your name

Click Answer Report 1 tab

(f) View the Report (step 6)

FIGURE B.4   Hands-on Exercise 1 (continued)

EXAMPLE 2—MINIMIZE COST

The example just concluded introduced you to the basics of Solver. We continue now with a second hands-on exercise, to provide additional practice, and to discuss various subtleties that can occur. This time we present a minimization problem in which we seek to minimize cost subject to a series of constraints. The problem will focus on the advertising campaign that will be conducted to sell the computers that you have produced.

The director of marketing has allocated a total of $125,000 in his weekly advertising budget. He wants to establish a presence in both magazines and radio, and requires a minimum of four magazine ads and ten radio ads each week. Each magazine ad costs $10,000 and is seen by one million readers. Each radio commercial costs $5,000 and is heard by 250,000 listeners. How many ads of each type should be placed in order to reach at least 10 million customers at minimum cost?

All of the necessary information is contained within the previous paragraph. You must, however, display that information in a worksheet before you can ask Solver to find a solution. Accordingly, reread the previous paragraph, then try to set up a worksheet from which you can call Solver. (Our worksheet appears in step 1 of the following hands-on exercise. Try, however, to set up your own worksheet before you look at ours.)

FINER POINTS OF SOLVER

Figure B.5 displays the **Solver Options dialog box** that enables you to specify how Solver will approach the solution. The Max Time and Iterations entries determine

Settings determine how long Solver will work on finding a solution

Setting determines how close the computed value will come to the specified value

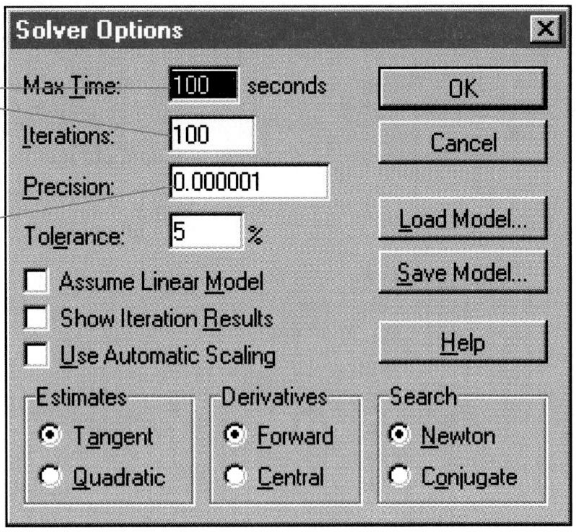

Solver Options
Max Time:
100
seconds
OK
Iterations:
100
Cancel
Precision:
0.000001
Load Model...
Tolerance:
5
%
Save Model...
Assume Linear Model
Show Iteration Results
Use Automatic Scaling
Help
Estimates
Tangent
Quadratic
Derivatives
Forward
Central
Search
Newton
Conjugate

FIGURE B.5 Options Dialog Box

how long Solver will work on finding the solution. If either limit is reached before a solution is found, Solver will ask whether you want to continue. The default settings of 100 seconds and 100 iterations are sufficient for simpler problems, but may fall short for complex problems with multiple constraints.

The Precision setting determines how close the computed values in the constraint cells come to the specified value of the resource. The smaller the precision, the longer Solver will take in arriving at a solution. The default setting of .0000001 is adequate for most problems and should not be decreased. The remaining options are beyond the scope of our discussion.

HANDS-ON EXERCISE 2

Minimize Cost

Objective: Use Solver to minimize cost; impose an integer constraint and examine its effect on the optimal solution; relax a constraint in order to find a feasible solution. Use Figure B.6 as a guide in the exercise.

STEP 1: Enter the Cell Formulas

- Open the **Finished Optimization** workbook from the previous exercise.
- Click the tab for the **Advertising** worksheet, then click in **cell E6.** Enter the formula **=B2*C2+B3*C3** as shown in Figure B.6a.
- Click in **cell E10.** Enter the formula **=B2*D2+B3*D3** to compute the size of the audience. Save the workbook.

THE ANSWER WIZARD

The Answer Wizard lets you ask questions in your own words. Pull down the Help menu, click Answer Wizard, type the question "What is Solver?", then press the enter key. The Answer Wizard will return a list of available help topics pertaining to Solver.

Click E6 and enter
the formula

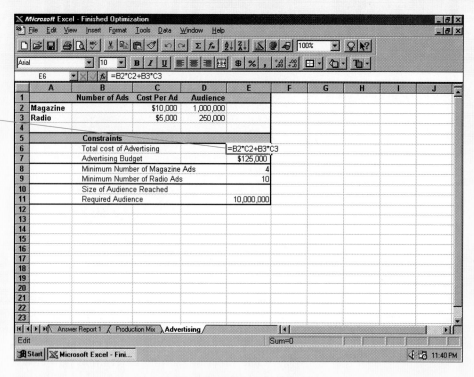

(a) Enter the Cell Formulas (step 1)

FIGURE B.6   Hands-on Exercise 2

STEP 2: Set the Objective and Variable Cells

➤ Pull down the **Tools menu.** Click **Solver** to display the Solver Parameters dialog box shown in Figure B.6b.

➤ Set the target cell to **cell E6.** Click the **Min (Minimize) option button.** Click in the **By Changing Cells** text box.

➤ Click and drag **cells B2** and **B3** in the worksheet to select these cells as shown in Figure B.6b.

➤ Click the **Add command button** to add the first constraint as described in step 3.

STEP 3: Add the Constraints

➤ You should see the Add Constraint dialog box in Figure B.6c with the insertion point (a flashing vertical line) in the Cell Reference text box.

• Click in **cell E6** (the cell containing the formula to compute the total cost of advertising).

• The <= constraint is selected by default.

• Click in the text box to contain the value of the constraint, then click **cell E7** in the worksheet to enter the cell reference in the Add Constraint dialog box.

• Click **Add** to complete this constraint and add another.

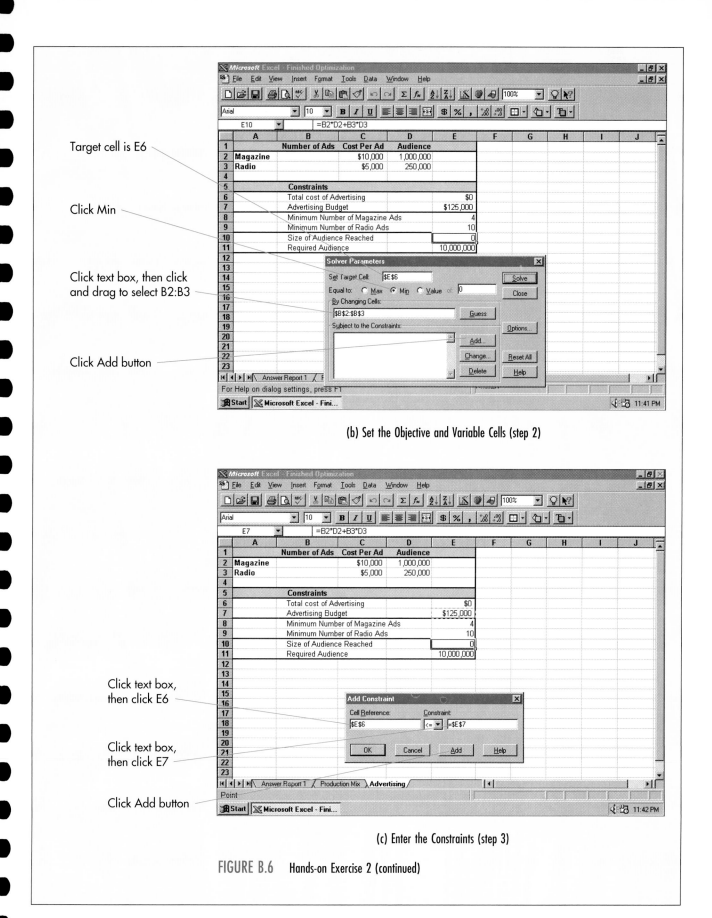

Target cell is E6

Click Min

Click text box, then click and drag to select B2:B3

Click Add button

(b) Set the Objective and Variable Cells (step 2)

Click text box, then click E6

Click text box, then click E7

Click Add button

(c) Enter the Constraints (step 3)

FIGURE B.6   Hands-on Exercise 2 (continued)

➤ You will see a new (empty) Add Constraint dialog box, which enables you to enter additional constraints. Use pointing to enter each of the constraints shown below. (Solver automatically converts each reference to an absolute reference.)

- Enter the constraint **E10>=E11.** Click **Add.**
- Enter the constraint **B2>=E8.** Click **Add.**
- Enter the constraint **B3>=E9.** Click **OK** since this is the last constraint.

SHOW ITERATION RESULTS

Solver uses an iterative (repetitive) approach in which each iteration (trial solution) is one step closer to the optimal solution. It may be interesting, therefore, to examine the intermediate solutions, especially if you have a knowledge of optimization techniques, such as linear programming. Click the Options command button in the Solver Parameters dialog box, check the Show Iterations Results box, click OK to close the Solver Options dialog box, then click the Solve command button in the usual fashion. A Show Trial Solutions dialog box will appear as each intermediate solution is displayed in the worksheet. Click Continue to move from one iteration to the next until the optimal solution is reached.

STEP 4: Solve the Problem

➤ Check that the contents of the Solver Parameters dialog box match those in Figure B.6d. (The constraints appear in alphabetical order rather than the order in which they were entered.)

➤ Click the **Solve button** to solve the problem. The Solver Results dialog box appears and indicates that Solver has arrived at a solution.

➤ The option button to Keep Solver Solution is selected by default. Click **OK** to close the Solver Results dialog box and display the solution.

STEP 5: Impose an Integer Constraint

➤ The number of magazine ads in the solution is 7.5 as shown in Figure B.6e. This is a noninteger number, which is reasonable in the context of Solver but not in the "real world" as one cannot place half an ad.

➤ Pull down the **Tools menu.** Click **Solver** to once again display the Solver Parameters dialog box. Click the **Add button** to display the Add Constraint dialog box in Figure B.6e.

➤ The insertion point is already positioned in the Cell Reference text box. Click and drag to select **cells B2** through **B3.** Click the **drop-down arrow** in the Constraint list box and click **int** (for integer).

➤ Click **OK** to accept the constraint and close the Add Constraint dialog box.

➤ The Solver Parameters dialog box appears on your monitor with the integer constraint added. Click **Solve** to solve the problem.

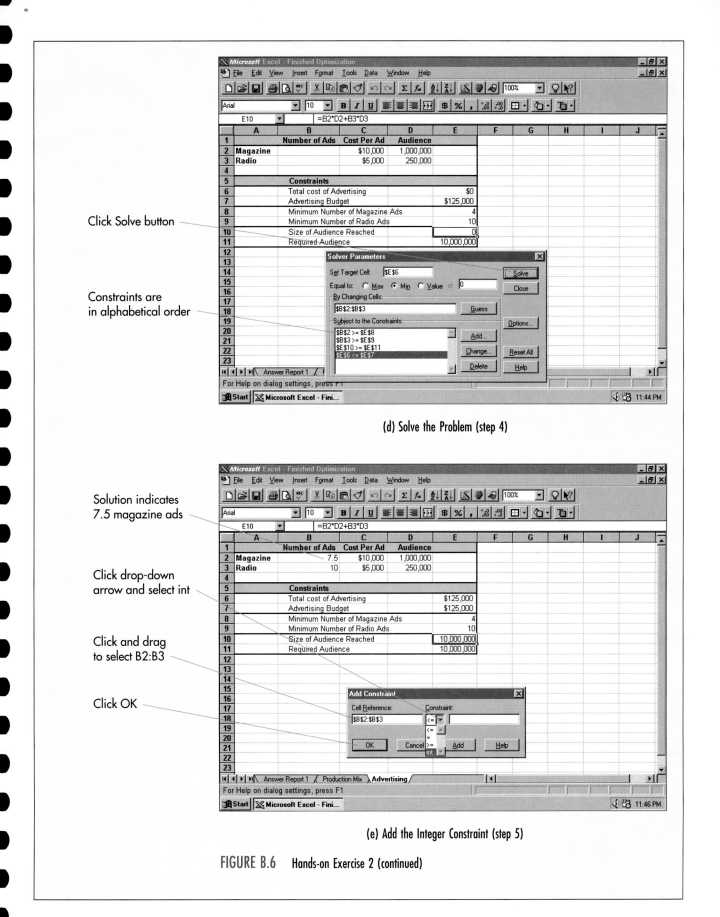

Click Solve button

Constraints are in alphabetical order

(d) Solve the Problem (step 4)

Solution indicates 7.5 magazine ads

Click drop-down arrow and select int

Click and drag to select B2:B3

Click OK

(e) Add the Integer Constraint (step 5)

FIGURE B.6   Hands-on Exercise 2 (continued)

DO YOU REALLY NEED AN INTEGER SOLUTION?

It seems like such a small change, but specifying an integer constraint can significantly increase the amount of time required for Solver to reach a solution. The examples in this chapter are relatively simple and did not take an inordinate amount of time to solve. Imposing an integer constraint on a more complex problem, however, especially on a slower microprocessor, may challenge your patience as Solver struggles to reach a solution.

STEP 6: The Infeasible Solution

➤ You should see the dialog box in Figure B.6f, indicating that Solver could *not* find a solution that satisfied the existing constraints. This is because the imposition of the integer constraint raised the number of magazine ads from 7.5 to 8, which increased the total cost of advertising to $130,000, which exceeded the budget of $125,000.

➤ The desired audience can still be reached but only by relaxing one of the binding constraints. You can, for example, retain the requisite number of magazine and radio ads by increasing the budget. Alternatively, the budget can be held at $125,000, while still reaching the audience by decreasing the required number of radio ads.

➤ Click **Cancel** to exit the dialog box and return to the worksheet.

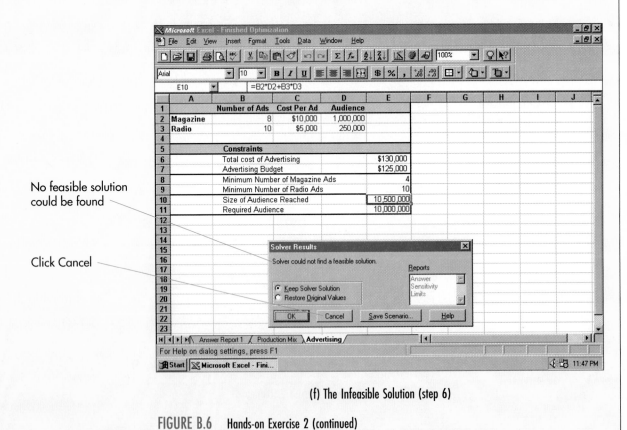

No feasible solution could be found

Click Cancel

(f) The Infeasible Solution (step 6)

FIGURE B.6   Hands-on Exercise 2 (continued)

UNABLE TO FIND A SOLUTION

Solver is a powerful tool, but it cannot do the impossible. Some problems simply do not have a solution because the constraints may conflict with one another, and/or because the constraints exceed the available resources. Should this occur, and it will, check your constraints to make sure they were entered correctly. If Solver is still unable to reach a solution, it will be necessary to relax one or more constraints.

STEP 7: Relax a Constraint

➤ Click in **cell E9** (the cell containing the minimum number of radio ads). Enter **9** and press **enter.**

➤ Pull down the **Tools menu.** Click **Solver** to display the Solver Parameters dialog box. Click **Solve.** This time Solver finds a solution as shown in Figure B.6g.

➤ Click **Answer** in the Reports list box, then click **OK** to generate the report. You will see the report being generated, after which the Solver Results dialog box closes automatically.

➤ Click the **Answer Report 2 worksheet tab** to view the report. Add your name to the report, boldface your name, print the answer report, and submit it to your instructor.

➤ Save the workbook a final time. Exit Excel.

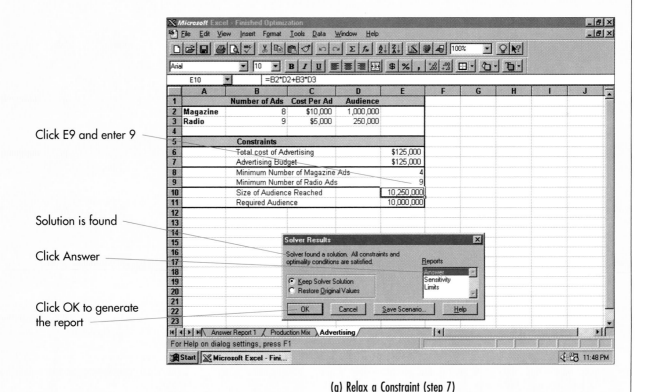

(g) Relax a Constraint (step 7)

FIGURE B.6 Hands-on Exercise 2 (continued)

Solver is an optimization and resource allocation tool that helps you achieve a desired goal, such as maximizing profit or minimizing cost. The information required by Solver is entered through the Solver Parameters dialog box, which is divided into three sections: the target cell, the changing cells, and the constraints.

The target cell identifies the goal (or objective function), which is the cell whose value you want to maximize, minimize, or set to a specific value. The changing cells are the cells whose values are adjusted until the constraints are satisfied and the target cell reaches its optimum value. The constraints specify the restrictions. Each constraint consists of a comparison, containing a cell or cell range on the left, a relational operator, and a numeric value or cell reference on the right.

The Solver Options dialog box lets you specify how Solver will attempt to find a solution. The Max Time and Iterations entries determine how long Solver will work on finding a solution. If either limit is reached before a solution is found, Solver will ask whether you want to continue. The default settings of 100 seconds and 100 iterations are sufficient for simpler problems, but may fall short for complex problems with multiple constraints.

KEY WORDS AND CONCEPTS

Adjustable cells
Answer Report
Binding constraint
Changing cells
Constraint
Feasible solution

Integer constraint
Iteration
Nonbinding constraint
Nonnegativity
   constraint
Precision

Solver Options dialog
   box
Solver Parameters
   dialog box
Target cell

APPENDIX C: DATA MAPPING

OVERVIEW

"A picture is worth 1,000 words." It is a well-documented fact that a chart can convey information more effectively than the corresponding table of numbers. Chapter 4 explored the use of conventional charts (pie charts, column charts, line charts, and so on) as an effective way to represent the information in a worksheet. This appendix extends that discussion to the use of maps, a capability that is built into Microsoft Office.

Consider, for example, the worksheet and associated maps in Figure C.1, which display the results of the 1992 presidential election as well as a strategy for 1996. The worksheet in Figure C.1a contains the statistical data on which the maps are based. It lists the states in alphabetical order, and for each state, the number of electoral votes and the candidate who received those votes. The worksheet also shows the number of popular votes received by each candidate, although that information is not conveyed in either map. (The District of Columbia is not shown in the worksheet, but its three electoral votes are included in Mr. Clinton's total.)

The maps in Figures C.1b and C.1c display (some of the) information that is contained within the worksheet, but in a form that is more quickly grasped by the reader. Figure C.1b shows at a glance which candidate won which state by assigning different colors to each candidate. Figure C.1c groups the states according to the number of electoral votes in order to develop a strategy for the 1996 election.

This appendix shows you how to use the Data Mapping application in Microsoft Office to create the maps in Figure C.1. The appendix also introduces you to the Mapstats workbook that contains demographic information for the United States as well as several foreign countries, and enables you to create a variety of additional maps.

1	State	Electoral Votes	Winner	Bush	Clinton	Perot
2	Alabama	9	Bush	804,283	690,080	183,109
3	Alaska	3	Bush	102,000	78,294	73,481
4	Arizona	8	Bush	572,086	543,050	253,741
5	Arkansas	6	Clinton	337,324	505,823	99,132
6	California	54	Clinton	3,630,574	5,121,325	2,296,006
7	Colorado	8	Clinton	562,850	629,681	366,010
8	Connecticut	8	Clinton	578,313	682,318	348,771
9	Delaware	3	Clinton	102,313	126,055	59,213
10	Florida	25	Bush	2,173,310	2,072,798	1,053,067
11	Georgia	13	Clinton	995,252	1,008,966	309,657
12	Hawaii	4	Clinton	136,822	179,310	53,003
13	Idaho	4	Bush	202,645	137,013	130,395
14	Illinois	22	Clinton	1,734,096	2,453,350	840,515
15	Indiana	12	Bush	989,375	848,420	455,934
16	Iowa	7	Clinton	504,891	586,353	253,468
17	Kansas	6	Bush	449,951	390,434	312,358
18	Kentucky	8	Clinton	617,178	665,104	203,944
19	Louisiana	9	Clinton	733,386	815,971	211,478
20	Maine	4	Clinton	206,504	263,420	206,820
21	Maryland	10	Clinton	707,094	988,571	281,414
22	Massachusetts	12	Clinton	805,039	1,318,639	630,731
23	Michigan	18	Clinton	1,554,940	1,871,182	824,813
24	Minnesota	10	Clinton	747,841	1,020,997	562,506
25	Mississippi	7	Bush	487,793	400,258	85,626
26	Missouri	11	Clinton	811,159	1,053,873	518,741
27	Montana	3	Clinton	144,207	154,507	107,225
28	Nebraska	5	Bush	344,346	217,344	174,687
29	Nevada	4	Clinton	175,828	189,148	132,580
30	New Hampshire	4	Clinton	202,484	209,040	121,337
31	New Jersey	15	Clinton	1,356,865	1,436,206	521,829
32	New Mexico	5	Clinton	212,824	261,617	91,895
33	New York	33	Clinton	2,346,649	3,444,450	1,090,721
34	North Carolina	14	Bush	1,134,661	1,114,042	357,864
35	North Dakota	3	Bush	136,244	99,168	71,084
36	Ohio	21	Clinton	1,894,310	1,984,942	1,036,426
37	Oklahoma	8	Bush	592,929	473,066	319,878
38	Oregon	7	Clinton	475,757	621,314	354,091
39	Pennsylvania	23	Clinton	1,791,841	2,239,164	902,667
40	Rhode Island	4	Clinton	131,605	213,302	105,051
41	South Carolina	8	Bush	577,507	479,514	138,872
42	South Dakota	3	Bush	136,718	124,888	73,295
43	Tennessee	11	Clinton	841,300	933,521	199,968
44	Texas	32	Bush	2,496,071	2,281,815	1,354,781
45	Utah	5	Bush	322,632	183,429	203,400
46	Vermont	3	Clinton	88,122	133,592	65,991
47	Virginia	13	Bush	1,150,517	1,038,650	348,639
48	Washington	11	Clinton	731,235	993,039	541,801
49	West Virginia	5	Clinton	241,974	331,001	108,829
50	Wisconsin	11	Clinton	930,855	1,041,066	544,479
51	Wyoming	3	Bush	79,347	68,160	51,263
52						
53	Total	535		39,083,847	44,717,270	19,632,586
54						
55	Electoral Vote totals					
56	Clinton	370				
57	Bush	168				

(a) Worksheet Data

FIGURE C.1   Data Mapping

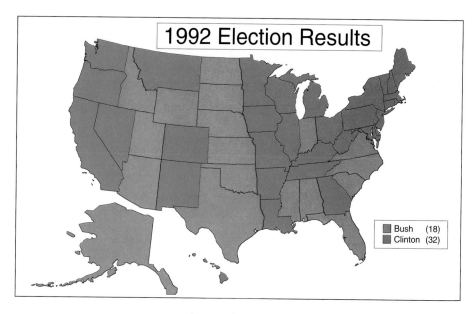

(b) 1992 Election Results

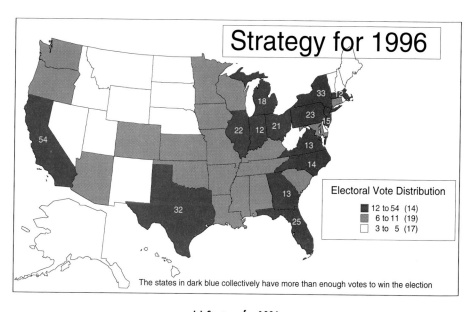

(c) Strategy for 1996

FIGURE C.1   Data Mapping (continued)

CREATING A MAP

The exercise that follows shortly illustrates the basic commands in the Data Mapping application and gives you an appreciation for its overall capability. Creating a map is easy provided you have a basic proficiency with Microsoft Excel. In essence, you do the following:

1. Select the cell range(s) containing the data for the map. (At least one column of the data must be recognizable as geographic names that are present in one of the available maps.)

2. Click the Map button on the Standard toolbar, then click and drag in the worksheet where you want the map to go.

3. Determine the type of map you want to create by selecting one of several formatting options. (The formatting options are specified in the Data Map Control dialog box, which is described in greater detail on page 397.)

4. Add the finishing touches by changing the title, legend, or other features.

Each step displays a dialog box in which you specify the options you want. The best way to learn is to create a map. Let's begin.

HANDS-ON EXERCISE 1

Introduction to Data Mapping

Objective: Illustrate basic features of the Data Mapping application to create a map showing the winning candidate in each state in the 1992 presidential election. Use Figure C.2 as a guide in the exercise.

STEP 1: Insert a Cell Note

➤ Start Excel. Open the **Presidential Election** workbook in the **Exploring Excel folder.** Save the workbook as **Finished Presidential Election** so that you can return to the original workbook if necessary.

➤ Press **Ctrl+End** to move to the end of the worksheet as shown in Figure C.2a. You can see the number of popular votes received by each candidate as well as the number of electoral votes.

➤ Click in **cell B56.** Pull down the **Insert menu.** Click **Note** to display the dialog box in Figure C.2a. Enter the cell note shown in the figure, then click **OK** to insert the note.

➤ There should be a tiny red dot in the upper-right corner of cell B56. Point to cell B56 and you will see a ToolTip that displays the note you just added. (To remove a note, select the cell, pull down the **Edit menu,** click **Clear,** then click **Notes.**)

RESOLVE UNKNOWN GEOGRAPHIC DATA

The Data Mapping application uses its own version of a spell check to ensure that the selected data matches predefined geographic data. The states must be spelled correctly, for example, or else mapping is not possible. Any unrecognized entry is flagged as unknown geographic data. You may be offered suggestions for a simple misspelling, in which case you can accept the suggestion. A more serious error, however, such as including an extraneous row (e.g., totals) in the data range, requires you to discard the entry.

STEP 2: Draw the Map

➤ Press **Ctrl+Home** to move to the beginning of the worksheet. Click in **cell A1,** then click and drag to select **cells A1** through **C51.** The AutoCalculate

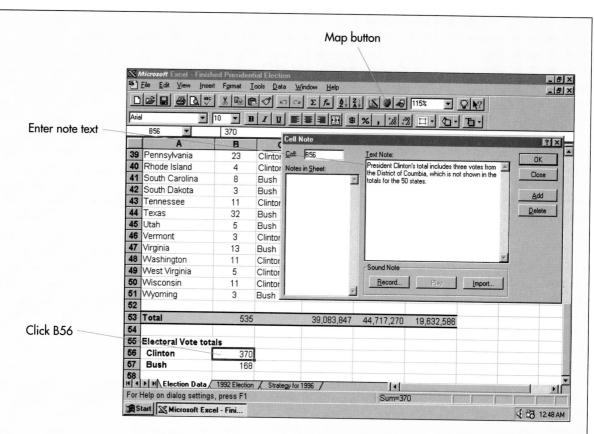

Map button

Enter note text

Click B56

(a) Insert a Note (step 1)

FIGURE C.2   Hands-on Exercise 1

indicator on the status bar (see boxed tip) should display 535 as the total number of electoral votes in the selected range.

➤ Click the **Map button** on the Standard toolbar. Click the **down scroll arrow** until cell A59 comes into view. Click in **cell A59,** then click and drag as shown in Figure C.2b. (Excel requires that the map be created on the same sheet as the data. You can, however, move the map to a different sheet after it has been created to facilitate printing.) Release the mouse.

➤ A dialog box will appear on the screen with the message, "Retrieving current selection", followed by a second message, "Matching Data". You should then see the dialog box in Figure C.2b, indicating that multiple maps are available.

THE AUTOCALCULATE FEATURE

The AutoCalculate feature lets you check a total without having to use a calculator or enter a temporary formula in a worksheet. You can use the feature to check that you have selected all 50 states prior to drawing the map. Just select the range, and the status bar displays the result. You can change the AutoCalculate function (to display the count, average, maximum, or minimum value) by right clicking the AutoCalculate area of the status bar, then selecting the desired function.

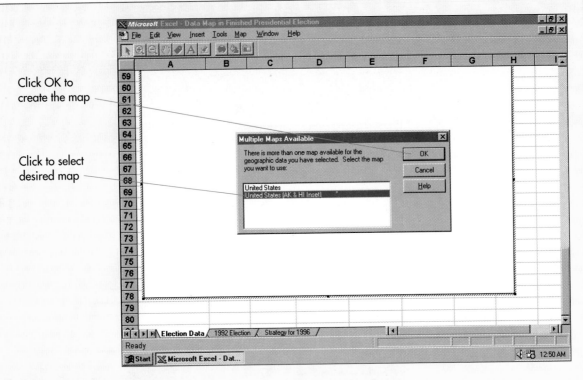

Click OK to
create the map

Click to select
desired map

(b) Draw a Map (step 2)

FIGURE C.2   Hands-on Exercise 1 (continued)

➤ The program recognizes the state names in Column A and presents two options for U.S. maps. Click **United States (AK & HI Inset),** then click **OK** to create the map.

STEP 3: Data Map Control

➤ You should see the Data Map Control dialog box in Figure C.2c. Excel has (by default) plotted the number of electoral votes, rather than the candidate who won the votes.

➤ Click and drag the **Electoral Votes button** out of the Data Map Control dialog box work area until you see a recycle bin. Release the mouse. The data disappears from the map, and all of the states appear in light green.

CHANGE THE CATEGORY COLORS

You can change the category colors by double clicking the column heading button within the Data Map Control box. To change the color for President Clinton, for example, double click the Winner button within the work area of the Data Map Control box to display the Category Shading Options dialog box. Select the category (e.g., Clinton), then click the down arrow in the color list box to choose a different color. Click OK to accept the color change and close the Category Shading Options dialog box.

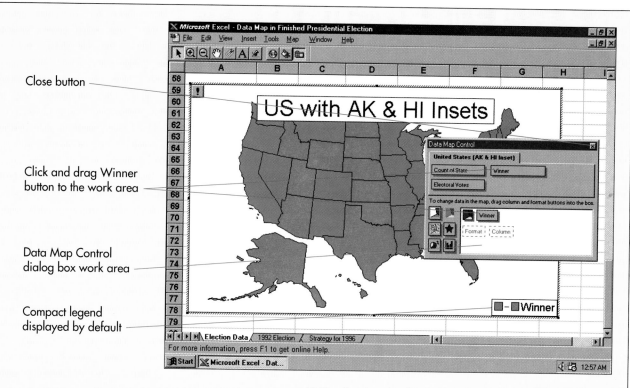

Close button

Click and drag Winner
button to the work area

Data Map Control
dialog box work area

Compact legend
displayed by default

(c) Data Map Control Dialog Box (step 3)

FIGURE C.2   Hands-on Exercise 1 (continued)

➤ Click and drag the **Winner button** (the name of the button corresponds to
the column heading in the worksheet) to the work area in the dialog box.
Release the mouse.

➤ A map is created with the various states shaded in red or green according to
the winning candidate in each state. The significance of the different colors
is determined from the legend as explained in step 4.

➤ Click the **Close button** to close the Data Map Control dialog box.

STEP 4: Edit the Legend

➤ To determine the meaning of the shadings, you need to display the complete
(not the compact) legend.

• Pull down the **View menu.** Click **All Legends** if you do not see a legend.

• Point to the legend (it may appear differently from the legend in Figure
C.2d), then click the **right mouse button** to display a shortcut menu.

• Click **Edit** to display the Edit Legend dialog box in Figure C.2d. If necessary, clear the Use Compact Legend check box.

➤ Click and drag to select the contents of the legend Title text box. Press the
Del key. Clear the contents of the Subtitle text box in similar fashion.

➤ Click **OK** to accept the changes and close the dialog box. The legend should
consist of two lines, Bush and Clinton, with the numbers 18 and 32, respectively, indicating the number of states each candidate carried.

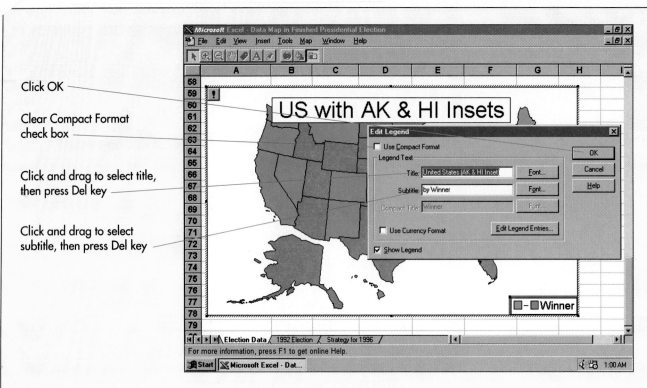

Click OK

Clear Compact Format
check box

Click and drag to select title,
then press Del key

Click and drag to select
subtitle, then press Del key

(d) Edit the Legend (step 4)

FIGURE C.2   Hands-on Exercise 1 (continued)

➤ Click inside the legend to select it. A shaded border appears around the legend. If necessary, click and drag the legend to position it within the map frame.

IN-PLACE EDITING

In-place editing enables you to edit an embedded object by using the toolbar and pull-down menus of the server application. Thus, when editing a map that has been embedded into an Excel worksheet, the title bar is that of the client application (Microsoft Excel), but the toolbars and pull-down menus reflect the server application (the Data Map application within Microsoft Office). There are, however, two exceptions; the File and Window menus are those of the client application (Excel). The File menu enables you to save the worksheet. The Window menu enables you to view (and edit) multiple workbooks in different windows.

STEP 5: The Finishing Touches

➤ Double click immediately in front of the "U" in "US with AK and HI Insets" in order to edit the title. A flashing vertical line (the insertion point) will appear at the place where you double clicked.

➤ Click and drag to select the entire title, then type **1992 Election Results** as the new title. Press **enter** to complete the title.

➤ Point to the title, then click the **right mouse button** to display the shortcut menu shown in Figure C.2e.

➤ Click **Format Font** to display the Format Font dialog box. Change the font size to **20 points.** Change the other parameters (e.g., font color) as you see fit, then close the Format Font dialog box.

➤ You can position the title, legend, and map independently within the frame:

   • Click and drag the **title** to move the title anywhere within the frame.

   • Click and drag the **legend** to move the legend anywhere within the frame.

   • Click the **Grabber button** (a hand) on the Data Map toolbar to select it. Point to the map (the mouse pointer changes to a hand), then click and drag the **map** to move it within the frame.

   • Pull down the **File menu.** Click **Save** to save the worksheet.

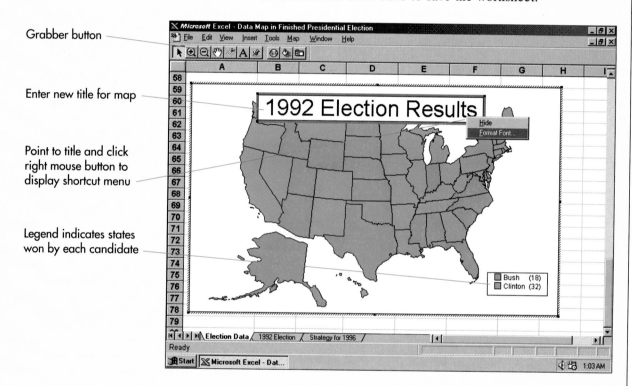

(e) The Finishing Touches (step 5)

FIGURE C.2   Hands-on Exercise 1 (continued)

TO CLICK OR DOUBLE CLICK

Clicking a map selects the map and displays the sizing handles that are used to move or size the frame containing the map. Double clicking the map loads the underlying Data Mapping application that created the map and enables you to edit the map.

STEP 6: Place the Map in Its Own Worksheet

➤ Click outside the map to exit the Data Mapping application, then click anywhere on the map to select the map as an Excel object.

➤ Click the **Cut button.** The map is placed in the clipboard and disappears from the worksheet.

➤ Click the **1992 Election tab.** Click in **cell A1.** Click the **Paste button** to paste the map onto this worksheet.

STEP 7: The Print Preview Command

➤ Pull down the **File menu.** Click **Page Setup** to display the Page Setup dialog box.

- Click the **Page tab.** Click the **Landscape orientation button.**
- Click the option button to adjust **Scaling to 120%** of size.
- Click the **Margins tab.** Check the box to center the worksheet **Horizontally.**
- Click the **Sheet tab.** Clear the boxes to include Row and Column Headings and Gridlines.

➤ Click the **Print Preview button** to preview the map before printing as shown in Figure C.2f.

- If you are satisfied with the appearance of the worksheet, click the **Print button** within the Preview window, then click **OK** to print the worksheet.
- If you are not satisfied with the appearance of the map, click the **Setup button** within the Preview window to make the necessary changes, after which you can print the worksheet.

➤ Pull down the **File menu.** Click **Close.** Click **Yes** if prompted to save changes.

➤ Exit Excel if you do not want to continue with the next exercise at this time.

Click Print button ———

(f) Print Preview Command (step 7)

FIGURE C.2   Hands-on Exercise 1 (continued)

DATA MAP CONTROL

We trust you completed the hands-on exercise without difficulty. The exercise introduced you to the basic features in the Data Mapping application and enabled you to create a map showing the winning candidate in each state. The format of the map was chosen automatically according to the nature of the data. The exercise had you plot a qualitative variable, which had one of two values (Bush or Clinton). The mapping program automatically selected *category shading* and assigned a different color to each value of a category, green to Mr. Clinton and red to Mr. Bush.

The next exercise directs you to plot a quantitative variable (the number of electoral votes in each state), then has you experiment with different formats for the resulting map. The selection is made in the ***Data Map Control dialog box*** as shown in Figure C.3. Six different formats are available, but not every format is suitable for every type of data. Figure C.3 illustrates three types of formatting.

Figure C.3a displays the Data Map Control dialog box, which appears automatically as the map is created. The top half of the dialog box indicates the columns that have been selected from the associated worksheet. The bottom half of the dialog box (the work area) shows the data that is to be plotted and the type of formatting in effect.

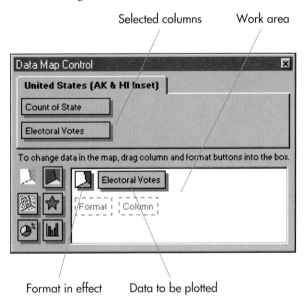

(a) Data Control Dialog Box

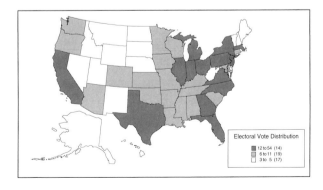

(b) Value Shading

FIGURE C.3   Data Map Control

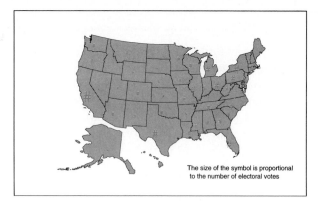

The size of the symbol is proportional
to the number of electoral votes

(c) Graduated Symbol

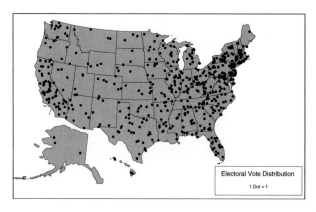

Electoral Vote Distribution

1 Dot = 1

(d) Dot Density

FIGURE C.3   Data Map Control (continued)

The maps in Figure C.3 plot the identical data (the number of electoral votes in each state), but in three different formats. Figure C.3b uses *value shading* to divide the states into groups and assign a different shade to each group. Figure C.3c uses the ***graduated symbol*** format to convey the same information. (The size of the symbol corresponds to the number of electoral votes.) Figure C.3d uses the ***dot density*** format to enable the user to see the actual number of electoral votes in each state. (Each dot corresponds to one electoral vote.) The choice between these maps is one of personal preference as will be seen in the next exercise.

HANDS-ON EXERCISE 2

Data Map Control

Objective: To create a map showing the distribution of electoral votes in the United States; to experiment with different formatting options in the Data Map Control dialog box. Use Figure C.4 as a guide in the exercise.

STEP 1: Draw the Map

➤ Start Excel. Open the **Finished Presidential Election** workbook from the previous exercise. Click the **Election Data tab.**

➤ Click in **cell A1,** then click and drag to select **cells A1** through **B51.** (The AutoCalculate indicator on the status bar should display 535 as the total number of electoral votes in the selected range.)

➤ Click the **Map button** on the Standard toolbar. Click the **down scroll arrow** until cell A59 comes into view. Click in **cell A59,** then click and drag to draw the frame that will contain the map. Release the mouse.

➤ A dialog box will appear on the screen with the message, "Retrieving current selection", followed by a second message, "Matching Data".

➤ The program recognizes the state names in Column A and presents two options. Click **United States (AK & HI Inset),** then click **OK** to create the map as shown in Figure C.4a.

➤ Close the Data Map Control box. Pull down the **File menu.** Click **Save** to save the worksheet.

Click A59 and drag to draw frame to contain the map

Click to close the Data Map Control dialog box

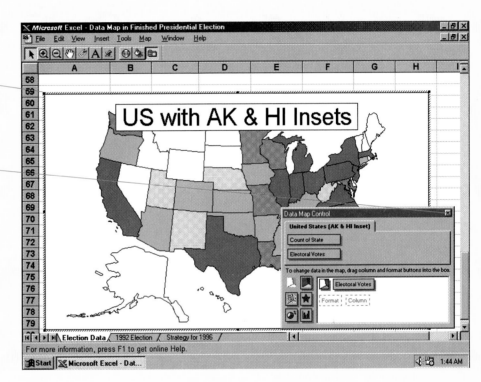

(a) Create the Map (step 1)

FIGURE C.4   Hands-on Exercise 2

STEP 2: Edit the Legend

➤ The various states are shaded according to the number of electoral votes in each state. To determine the meaning of the shadings, you need to display the complete (not the compact) legend.

- Pull down the **View menu** and click **All Legends** if you do not see a legend.

- Point to the legend (it may appear differently from the legend in Figure C.4b), then click the **right mouse button** to display a shortcut menu.

- Click **Edit** to display the Edit Legend dialog box. If necessary, clear the Use Compact Legend check box so that your legend will match the one in the figure.

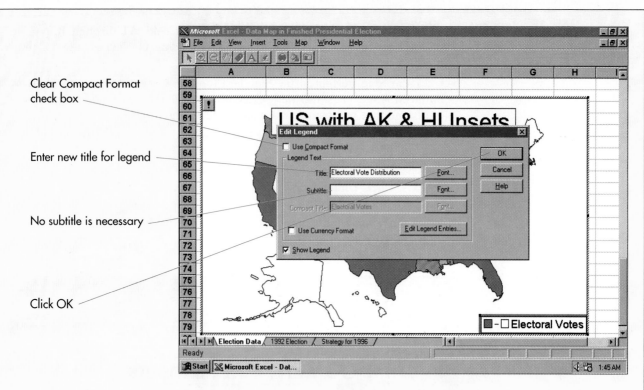

Clear Compact Format
check box

Enter new title for legend

No subtitle is necessary

Click OK

(b) Change the Legend (step 2)

FIGURE C.4   Hands-on Exercise 2 (continued)

➤ Click and drag to select the contents of the Title text box. Type **Electoral Vote Distribution** to replace the selected text. Clear the contents of the Subtitle text box as shown in Figure C.4b.

➤ Click **OK** to accept the changes and close the dialog box.

➤ Pull down the **File menu** and click the **Save command.**

STEP 3: Data Map Control

➤ Click the **Show/Hide Data Map Control button** to open the Data Map Control box as shown in Figure C.4c. Click **OK** if asked to refresh the map.

• Click and drag the **Dot Density button** to a position next to the Electoral Votes button as shown in Figure C.4c. The shading on the map changes so that each state contains a number of dots proportional to its electoral votes.

• Click and drag the **Graduated Symbol button** to a position next to the Electoral Votes button. The map changes to place a graduated symbol (the same symbol in different sizes) in each state according to its number of electoral votes.

• Click and drag the **Category Shading button** to a position next to the Electoral Votes button. The states are displayed in a variety of colors, which is totally *inappropriate* for this map. (Category shading is used only when the number of distinct values is small; e.g., to indicate the winning candidate in each state as in the earlier map.)

• Click and drag the **Value Shading button** to a position next to the Electoral Votes button.

➤ Close the Data Map Control box. Pull down the **File menu.** Click **Save** to save the worksheet.

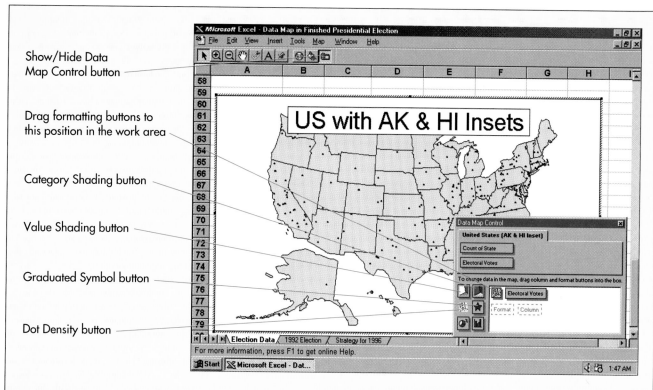

Show/Hide Data
Map Control button

Drag formatting buttons to
this position in the work area

Category Shading button

Value Shading button

Graduated Symbol button

Dot Density button

(c) Data Map Control (step 3)

FIGURE C.4   Hands-on Exercise 2 (continued)

CATEGORY SHADING VERSUS VALUE SHADING

Category shading is used with a nonquantitative variable (such as a candidate's name) and assigns a different color to each value of the category—for example, green to Mr. Clinton and red to Mr. Bush as was done in the map in exercise 1. Value shading is used with a quantitative variable (such as the number of electoral votes in each state) and is necessary when there are a large number of distinct values. Value shading divides the states into groups with a different shade assigned to each group.

STEP 4: Value Shading Options

➤ Pull down the **Map menu.** Click **Value Shading Options** to display the dialog box in Figure C.4d. (Click **OK** if asked to refresh the map.)

➤ Click the **drop-down arrow** to change the number of value ranges to **three.** Click the **drop-down arrow** in the **color** list box to change the color of the shading to **blue.**

➤ Click the option button for an equal number of items in each range of values. Click **OK** to close the Value Shading Options dialog box.

➤ The number of groups changes to three. The legend shows 14 states with 12 to 54 votes, 19 states with 6 to 12 votes, and 17 states with 3 to 6 votes. The legend uses *inclusive* ranges and needs to be modified.

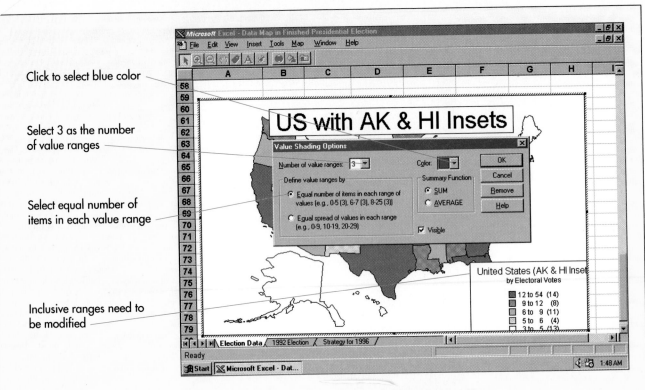

Click to select blue color

Select 3 as the number of value ranges

Select equal number of items in each value range

Inclusive ranges need to be modified

(d) Value Shading Options (step 4)

FIGURE C.4   Hands-on Exercise 2 (continued)

➤ Point to the legend, click the **right mouse button** to display a shortcut menu, then click **Edit** to display the Edit Legend dialog box.

➤ Click the command button to **Edit Legend Entries,** then change the text for the latter two groups to read **6 to 11** and **3 to 5.** Click **OK** to close the Edit Legend Entries dialog box. Click **OK** to close the Edit Legend dialog box.

MISLEADING LEGEND

The legend created by the data mapping program incorrectly uses inclusive values, which need to be adjusted manually if the legend is to make sense. In creating groups for the electoral vote distribution, the number 12 is used as a break point in that there is a group of states with 12 to 54 electoral votes and a second group with 6 to 12 electoral votes. In actuality, the latter group consists of states with 6 to 11 electoral votes (i.e., the upper bound is less than 12).

STEP 5: Map Labels

➤ Click the **Map Labels button** to display the Map Labels dialog box. Click the option button to **Create labels from Values from Electoral Votes** (the only option in the drop-down list). Click **OK** to close the Map Labels dialog box.

➤ Point to a state (the mouse pointer changes to a crosshair), and you see the corresponding number of electoral votes. Point to California, for example, and you see 54. Point to Texas and you see 32.

➤ Point to a state, such as California, then **click the mouse** to create a label containing the number of electoral votes. The number 54 is entered on the map and surrounded in sizing handles to indicate that the label is currently selected.

➤ Click the **Select Objects button** (the arrow) on the Data Map toolbar to turn off the labeling feature so that we can change the color of the label and make it easier to read. Point to the number 54 and click the **right mouse button** to display a shortcut menu.

➤ Click **Format Font** to display the Font dialog box in Figure C.4e:

• Click the **drop-down arrow** on the **Color** list box. Click **aqua** as the color of the text.

• If necessary, change the type size to **8** points.

• Click **OK** to accept the color change and close the Font dialog box.

➤ Click the **Map Labels button,** click **OK** to close the Map Labels dialog box, then label all of the other states in the category with the highest numbers of electoral votes. When you are finished, click the **Select Objects button** (the arrow) on the Data Map toolbar to turn off the labeling feature.

➤ Pull down the **File menu** and click the **Save command.**

Map Labels button

Select Objects button

Point to a state, click the mouse to create a label

Point to the label and click right mouse button to display shortcut menu

(e) Map Labels (step 5)

FIGURE C.4   Hands-on Exercise 2 (continued)

STEP 6: Complete the Map

➤ Click the **Text tool,** click at the bottom of the map as shown in Figure C.4f, then start to type the text shown in the figure. The text appears in aqua.

➤ Click the **right mouse button,** click **Format Font,** and change the color back to black. Click **OK** to close the Font dialog box, then finish entering the text.

➤ Click the title to select it. Click before the first character in the title, drag to select the entire title, then enter **Strategy for 1996** as shown in Figure C.4f.

> You can position the title, legend, and map independently within the frame:
> - Click and drag the **title** to move the title anywhere within the frame.
> - Click and drag the **legend** to move the legend anywhere within the frame.
> - Click the **Grabber button** on the Data Map toolbar to select it, then click and drag the **map** (the mouse pointer changes to a hand) to move it within the frame.
> Pull down the **File menu** and click the **Save command.**

STEP 7: Place the Map in Its Own Worksheet

> Click outside the map to exit the Data Mapping application, then click anywhere on the map to select it as an Excel object.
> Click the **Cut button.** The map is placed in the clipboard and disappears from the worksheet.
> Click the **Strategy for 1996 tab.** Click in **cell A1.** Click the **Paste button** to paste the map onto this worksheet.
> Print the worksheet and map. Save the workbook a final time. Exit Excel.

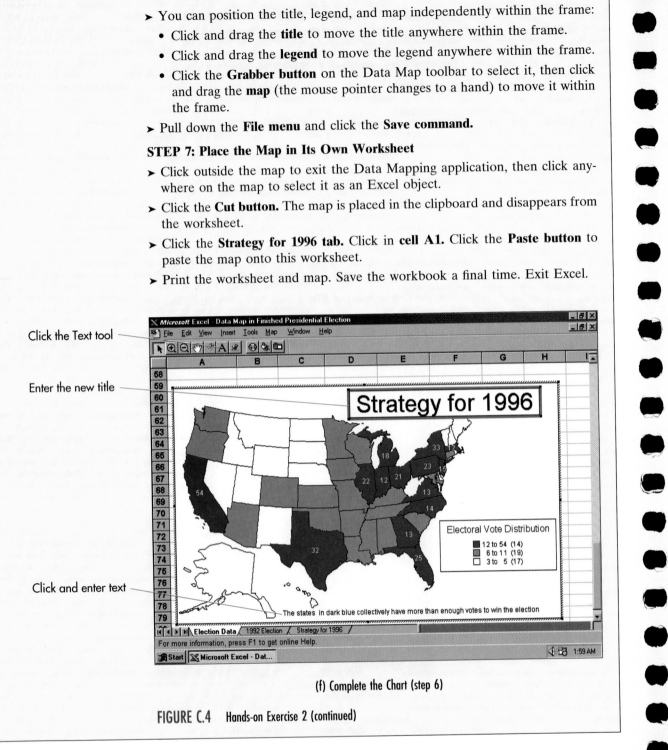

Click the Text tool

Enter the new title

Click and enter text

(f) Complete the Chart (step 6)

FIGURE C.4 Hands-on Exercise 2 (continued)

THE MAPSTATS WORKBOOK

Microsoft Excel comes with an assortment of maps, together with demographic data for each map. The demographic data is contained in the *Mapstats workbook* as shown in Figure C.5. The Table of Contents worksheet in Figure C.5a shows the countries for which a map and demographic data are supplied. Figure C.5b displays (some of) the demographic data for the United States.

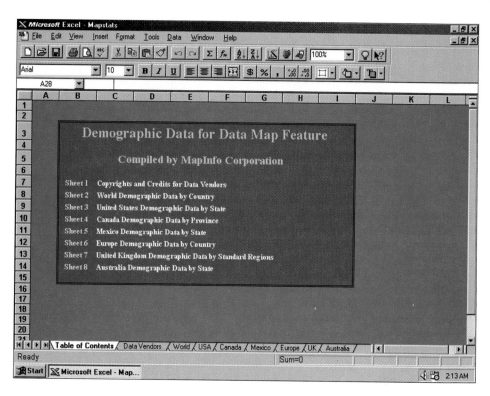

(a) Table of Contents Page

Map tool

Notes exist for all
column headings

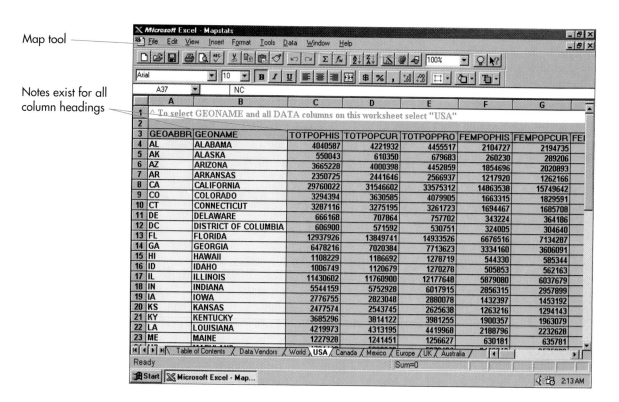

(b) USA Data Worksheet

FIGURE C.5   The Mapstats Workbook

The column headings in Figure C.5b are abbreviated, and hence the precise nature of the data is not immediately apparent. The cells containing the column headings are annotated, however (note the red dot in each cell), so that you can point to any heading and display the cell tip that fully describes the data. There are more than 30 categories of demographic data available for the United States. Similar, but not necessarily identical, data is available for the other countries in the workbook.

You can create a map based on any column of demographic data by following the steps in the hands-on exercise. Just select the data, click the Map button on the Standard toolbar, then click in the worksheet where you want the map to go. Choose the type of map you want, add the finishing touches as was done in the exercises, and you will be able to create a variety of useful and attractive maps. Cartography has never been so easy.

FINDING THE MAPSTATS WORKBOOK

The easiest way to open the Mapstats workbook is through the Windows 95 Find command. Click the Start button, click (or point to) the Find command, then click Files or Folders to display the Find dialog box. Enter Mapstats in the Named text box and My Computer in the Look In box. Click Find Now. Double click the icon next to the Mapstats workbook to start Excel and open the workbook. Save the workbook under a different name so that you can return to the original workbook should it become necessary.

SUMMARY

Computer mapping enables you to visualize quantitative data and is made possible through the Data Mapping application included with Microsoft Office 95. Creation of a map is straightforward and consists of four general steps. You select the data to be mapped, indicate where the map is to go, choose the type of map, then apply the finishing touches.

The Data Map Control dialog box determines the type of formatting in effect. Category shading is always used with a nonquantitative variable and assigns a different color to each value of a category. Value shading is one of several different formats that can be used with a quantitative variable and is used when many different outcomes are possible. The outcomes are divided into groups with a different shade assigned to each group. Dot density and graduated symbol are other formats that can be used with a quantitative variable.

The mapping application includes an assortment of maps together with demographic data for each map. The demographic data is contained in the Mapstats workbook (which can be located through the Windows 95 Find command). Maps are available for the United States, Mexico, Canada, Australia, the United Kingdom, and the world.

KEY WORDS AND CONCEPTS

AutoCalculate	Graduated symbol	Legend
Category shading	In-place editing	Mapstats workbook
Data Map Control	Label	Value shading
Dot density		

APPENDIX D: TOOLBARS

OVERVIEW

Microsoft Excel has thirteen predefined toolbars to provide access to commonly used commands. The toolbars are displayed in Figure D.1 and are listed here for convenience. They are: the Auditing, Chart, Drawing, Formatting, Forms, Full Screen, Microsoft, Query and Pivot, Standard, Stop Recording, TipWizard, Visual Basic, and WorkGroup toolbars. The Standard and Formatting toolbars are displayed by default and appear immediately below the menu bar. The other toolbars can be displayed as needed or, in some cases, may appear automatically when you access their corresponding feature (e.g., the Chart toolbar and the Query and Pivot toolbar).

The buttons on the toolbars are intended to be indicative of their function. Clicking the Printer button (the fourth button from the left on the Standard toolbar), for example, executes the Print command. If you are unsure of the purpose of any toolbar button, point to it, and a ToolTip will appear that displays its name.

You can display multiple toolbars at one time, move them to new locations on the screen, customize their appearance, or suppress their display.

- To display or hide a toolbar, pull down the View menu and click the Toolbars command. Select (deselect) the toolbar(s) that you want to display (hide). The selected toolbar(s) will be displayed in the same position as when last displayed. You may also point to any toolbar and click with the right mouse button to bring up a shortcut menu, after which you can select the toolbar to be displayed (hidden).
- To change the size of the buttons, display them in monochrome rather than color, or suppress the display of the ToolTips, pull down the View menu, click Toolbars, and then select (deselect) the appropriate check box. Alternatively, you can click on any

toolbar with the right mouse button, select Toolbars, and then select (deselect) the appropriate check box.

- Toolbars may be either docked (along the edge of the window) or left floating (in their own window). A toolbar moved to the edge of the window will dock along that edge. A toolbar moved anywhere else in the window will float in its own window. Docked toolbars are one tool wide (high), whereas floating toolbars can be resized by clicking and dragging a border or corner as you would with any window.
  - To move a docked toolbar, click anywhere in the gray background area and drag the toolbar to its new location.
  - To move a floating toolbar, drag its title bar to its new location.
- To customize one or more toolbars, display the toolbar(s) on the screen, pull down the View menu, click Toolbars, and then click the Customize command button. Alternatively, you can click on any toolbar with the right mouse button and select Customize from the shortcut menu.
  - To move a button, drag the button to its new location on that toolbar or any other displayed toolbar.
  - To copy a button, press the Ctrl key as you drag the button to its new location on that toolbar or any other displayed toolbar.
  - To delete a button, drag the button off the toolbar and release the mouse button.
  - To add a button, select the category from the Categories list box and then drag the button to the desired location on the toolbar. (To see a description of a tool's function prior to adding it to a toolbar, click the tool in the Customize dialog box and read the displayed description.)
  - To restore a predefined toolbar to its default appearance, pull down the View menu, click Toolbars, select (highlight) the desired toolbar, and click the Reset command button.
- The Borders, Color, and Font Color buttons on the Formatting toolbar, the Chart Type button on the Chart toolbar, and the Pattern button on the Drawing toolbar also function as movable tear-off palettes. Display the desired palette by clicking the associated down arrow, then drag the palette onto the worksheet in order to make it more accessible as you work. Click the Close button to close the palette.
- To create your own toolbar, pull down the View menu and click Toolbars. Alternatively, you can click on any toolbar with the right mouse button and select Toolbars from the shortcut menu.
  - Enter a name for the toolbar in the Toolbar Name text box. The name can be any length and can contain spaces.
  - Click the New command button.
  - The new toolbar will appear at the top left of the screen. Initially, it will be big enough to hold only one button. Add, move, and delete buttons following the same procedures as outlined above. The toolbar will automatically size itself as new buttons are added and deleted.
- To delete a custom toolbar, pull down the View menu, click Toolbars, and make sure that the custom toolbar to be deleted is the only one selected (highlighted). Click the Delete command button. Click OK to confirm the deletion. (Note that a predefined toolbar cannot be deleted.)

MICROSOFT EXCEL 7.0 TOOLBARS

Auditing Toolbar

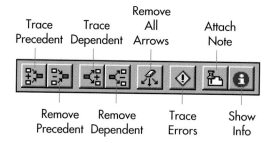

Chart Toolbar

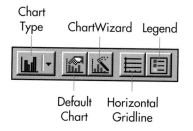

Drawing Toolbar

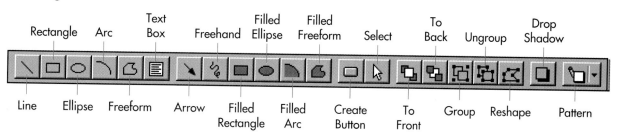

Formatting Toolbar

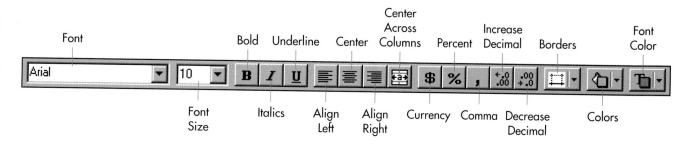

FIGURE D.1   Toolbars

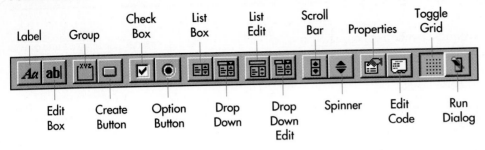

Full Screen Toolbar

Full Screen

Microsoft Toolbar

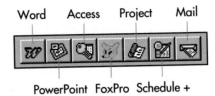

Query and Pivot Toolbar

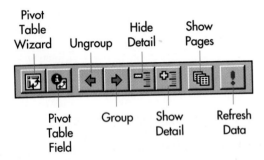

Standard Toolbar

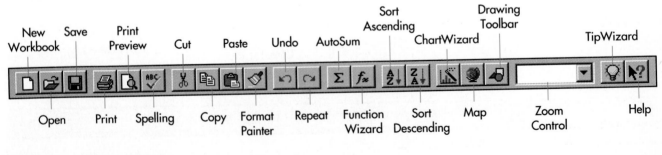

FIGURE D.1   Toolbars (continued)

Stop Recording Toolbar

Stop
Macro

TipWizard Toolbar

TipWizard Box

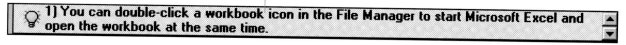

Visual Basic Toolbar

Insert   Object   Step   Stop   Toggle   Step
Module   Browser   Macro   Recording   Break   Into

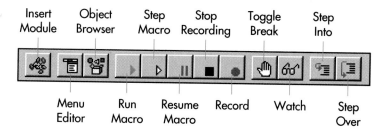

Menu   Run   Resume   Record   Watch   Step
Editor   Macro   Macro   Over

WorkGroup Toolbar

Find   Send   Toggle
File   Mail   Status

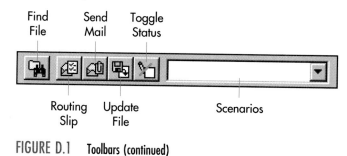

Routing   Update   Scenarios
Slip   File

FIGURE D.1   Toolbars (continued)

PREREQUISITES: ESSENTIALS OF WINDOWS 95®

OBJECTIVES

After reading this appendix you will be able to:

1. Describe the objects on the Windows desktop; use the Start button to access the online help.
2. Explain the function of the minimize, maximize, restore, and close buttons; move and size a window.
3. Discuss the function of a dialog box; describe the different types of dialog boxes and the various ways in which information is supplied.
4. Format a floppy disk.
5. Use My Computer to locate a specific file or folder; describe the different views available for My Computer.
6. Describe how folders are used to organize a disk; create a new folder; copy and/or move a file from one folder to another.
7. Delete a file, then recover the deleted file from the Recycle Bin.
8. Describe the document orientation of Windows 95; use the New command to create a document without explicitly opening the associated application.
9. Explain the differences in browsing with My Computer versus browsing with the Windows Explorer.

OVERVIEW

Windows 95 is a computer program (actually many programs) that controls the operation of your computer and its peripherals. One of the most significant benefits of the Windows environment is the common user interface and consistent command structure that are imposed on every Windows application. Once you learn the basic concepts and techniques, you can apply that knowledge to every Windows application. This appendix teaches you those concepts so that you will be able to work productively in the Windows environment. It is written for you, the computer novice, and assumes no previous knowledge about a computer or about Windows. Our goal is to get you "up and running" as quickly as possible so that you can do the work you want to do.

We begin with an introduction to the Windows desktop, the graphical user interface that lets you work in intuitive fashion by pointing at icons and clicking the mouse. We show you how to use the online help facility to look up information when you need it. We identify the basic components of a window and describe how to execute commands and supply information through various types of dialog boxes.

The appendix also shows you how to manage the hundreds (indeed, thousands) of files that are stored on the typical system. We describe the use of My Computer to search the drives on your computer for a specific file or folder. (All files in Windows 95 are stored in folders, which are the electronic equivalent of manila folders in a filing cabinet.) We show you how to create a new folder and how to move or copy a file from one folder to another. We show you how to rename a file, how to delete a file, and how to recover a deleted file from the Recycle Bin.

All file operations are done through My Computer or through the more powerful Windows Explorer. My Computer is intuitive and geared for the novice, as it opens a new window for each folder you open. Explorer, on the other hand, is more sophisticated and provides a hierarchical view of the entire system in a single window. A beginner will prefer My Computer, whereas a more experienced user will most likely opt for the Explorer. This is the same sequence in which we present the material. We start with My Computer, then show you how to accomplish the same result more quickly through the Explorer.

THE DESKTOP

Windows 95 creates a working environment for your computer that parallels the working environment at home or in an office. You work at a desk. Windows operations take place on the *desktop.*

There are physical objects on a desk such as folders, a dictionary, a calculator, or a phone. The computer equivalent of those objects appear as *icons* (pictorial symbols) on the desktop. Each object on a real desk has attributes (properties) such as size, weight, and color. In similar fashion, Windows assigns properties to every object on its desktop. And just as you can move the objects on a real desk, you can rearrange the objects on the Windows desktop.

Figure 1a displays the desktop when Windows is first installed on a new computer. This desktop has only a few objects and is similar to the desk in a new office, just after you move in. Figure 1b displays a different desktop, one with three open windows, and is similar to a desk during the middle of a working day. Do not be concerned if your Windows desktop is different from ours. Your real desk is arranged differently from those of your friends, and so your Windows desktop will also be different.

The simplicity of the desktop in Figure 1a helps you to focus on what's important. The *Start button,* as its name suggests, is where you begin. Click the Start button (mouse operations are explained in the next section) and you see a menu that provides access to any program (e.g., Microsoft Word or Microsoft Excel) on your computer. The Start button also gives you access to an online help facility that provides information about every aspect of Windows.

In addition to the Start button, the desktop in Figure 1a contains three objects, each of which has a special purpose. *My Computer* enables you to browse the disk drives (and optional CD-ROM drive) that are attached to your computer.

Double click to
browse disk drives

Double click to access
network drives

Double click to
recover deleted files

Click here to begin

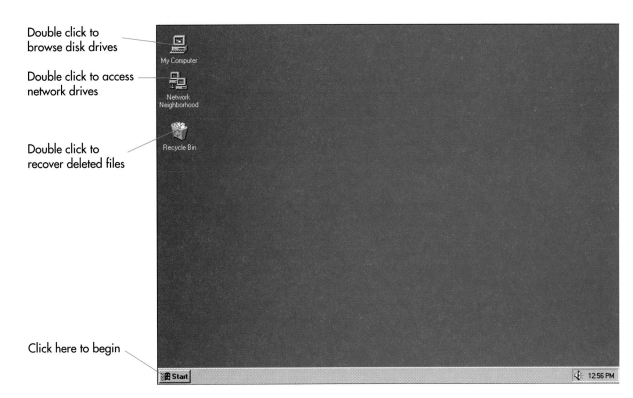

(a) New Desktop

Microsoft Word is in
memory

Microsoft Excel is in
memory

My Computer shows disk
drives and folders

Menu produced by
clicking the Start button

Task bar shows all
programs currently running

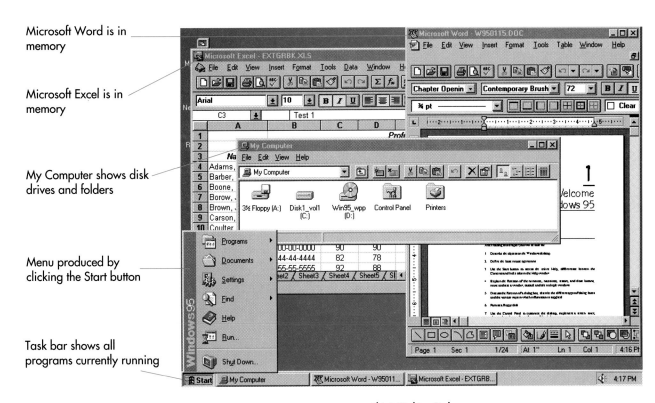

(b) A Working Desk

FIGURE 1   The Windows Desktop

Network Neighborhood extends your view of the computer to include the accessible drives on the network to which your machine is attached, if indeed it is part of a network. (You will not see this icon if you are not connected to a network.) The *Recycle Bin* lets you recover a file that was previously deleted and is illustrated in a hands-on exercise later in the appendix (see page 40).

Each object in Figure 1a contains additional objects that are displayed when you open (double click) the object. Double click My Computer in Figure 1a, for example, and you see the objects contained in the My Computer window of Figure 1b. Double click Network Neighborhood, and you will see all of the drives available on your network.

Two additional windows are open on the desktop in Figure 1b and correspond to programs that are currently in use. Each window has a title bar that displays the name of the program and the associated document. (The Start button was used to open each program, Microsoft Word and Microsoft Excel, in Figure 1b.) You can work in any window as long as you want, then switch to a different window. *Multitasking,* the ability to run several programs at the same time, is one of the major benefits of the Windows environment. It lets you run a word processor in one window, a spreadsheet in a second window, communicate online in a third window, run a game in a fourth window, and so on.

The *taskbar* at the bottom of the desktop shows all of the programs that are currently running (open in memory). It contains a button for each open program and lets you switch back and forth between those programs, by clicking the appropriate button. The taskbar in Figure 1a does not contain any buttons (other than the Start button) since there are no open applications. The taskbar in Figure 1b, however, contains three additional buttons, one for each open window.

ANATOMY OF A WINDOW

Figure 2 displays a typical window and labels its essential elements. Every window has the same components as every other window, which include a title bar, a Minimize button, a Maximize or Restore button, and a Close button. Other elements, that may or may not be present, include a horizontal and/or vertical scroll bar, a menu bar, a status bar, and a toolbar. Every window also contains additional objects (icons) that pertain specifically to the programs(s) or data associated with that window.

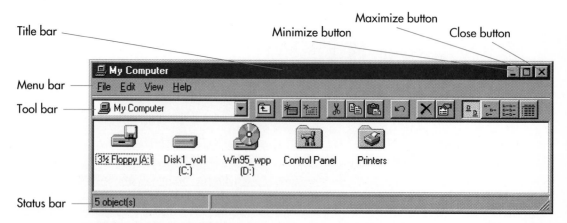

FIGURE 2 Anatomy of a Window

The *title bar* appears at the top of the window and displays the name of the window—for example, My Computer in Figure 2. The icon at the extreme left of the title bar provides access to a control menu that lets you select operations relevant to the window. The *Minimize button* shrinks the window to a button on the taskbar. The *Maximize button* enlarges the window so that it takes up the entire desktop. The *Restore button* (which is not shown in Figure 2) appears instead of the Maximize button after a window has been maximized, and restores the window to its previous size. The *Close button* closes the window and removes it from the desktop.

The *menu bar* appears immediately below the title bar and provides access to pull-down menus as discussed in the next section. A *toolbar* appears below the menu bar and lets you execute a command by clicking an icon, as opposed to pulling down a menu. The *status bar* is found at the bottom of the window and displays information about the window as a whole or about a selected object within a window.

A *vertical (horizontal) scroll bar* appears at the right (bottom) border of a window when its contents are not completely visible and provides access to the unseen areas. Scroll bars do not appear in Figure 2 since all five objects in the window are visible.

MY COMPUTER

My Computer lets you browse the disk drives (and CD-ROM) on your system. It is present on every desktop, but the contents depend on the specific configuration. Our system, for example, has one floppy drive, one hard disk, and a CD-ROM, each of which is represented by an icon within the My Computer window. My Computer is discussed in greater detail later in this appendix, beginning on page 19.

Moving and Sizing a Window

Any window can be sized or moved on the desktop through appropriate actions with the mouse. To *size a window,* point to any border (the mouse pointer changes to a double arrow), then drag the border in the direction you want to go: inward to shrink the window or outward to enlarge it. You can also drag a corner (instead of a border) to change both dimensions at the same time. To *move a window* while retaining its current size, click and drag the title bar to a new position on the desktop.

Pull-down Menus

The menu bar provides access to *pull-down menus* that enable you to execute commands within an application (program). A pull-down menu is accessed by clicking the menu name or by pressing the Alt key plus the underlined letter in the menu name; for example, press Alt+V to pull down the View menu. Three pull-down menus associated with My Computer are shown in Figure 3.

The commands within a menu are executed by clicking the command once the menu has been pulled down, or by typing the underlined letter (for example, C to execute the Close command in the File menu). Alternatively, you can bypass the menu entirely if you know the equivalent keystrokes shown to the right of the command in the menu (e.g., Ctrl+X, Ctrl+C, or Ctrl+V to cut, copy, or paste as

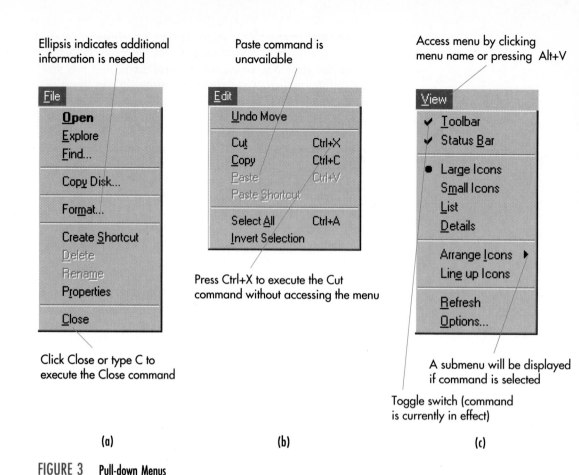

Ellipsis indicates additional information is needed

Paste command is unavailable

Access menu by clicking menu name or pressing Alt+V

Click Close or type C to execute the Close command

Press Ctrl+X to execute the Cut command without accessing the menu

A submenu will be displayed if command is selected

Toggle switch (command is currently in effect)

(a)   (b)   (c)

FIGURE 3   Pull-down Menus

shown within the Edit menu). A ***dimmed command*** (e.g., the Paste command in the Edit menu) means the command is not currently executable, and that some additional action has to be taken for the command to become available.

An ***ellipsis*** (...) following a command indicates that additional information is required to execute the command; for example, selection of the Format command in the File menu requires the user to specify additional information about the formatting process. This information is entered into a dialog box (discussed in the next section), which appears immediately after the command has been selected.

A check next to a command indicates a toggle switch, whereby the command is either on or off. There is a check next to the Toolbar command in the View menu of Figure 3, which means the command is in effect (and thus the toolbar will be displayed). Click the Toolbar command and the check disappears, which suppresses the display of the toolbar. Click the command a second time, the check reappears, as does the toolbar in the associated window.

An arrowhead after a command (e.g., the Arrange Icons command in the View menu) indicates a ***submenu*** will follow with additional menu options.

Dialog Boxes

A ***dialog box*** appears when additional information is needed to execute a command. The Format command, for example, requires information about which drive to format and the type of formatting desired.

Option (radio) buttons indicate mutually exclusive choices, one of which must be chosen; for example, one of three Format Type options in Figure 4a. Click a button to select an option, which automatically deselects the previously selected option.

Click here to see other options

Drop-down list box shows
current selection only

Option buttons indicate
mutually exclusive choices

Text box is used to enter
descriptive information

Check boxes indicate choices
that are not mutually exclusive

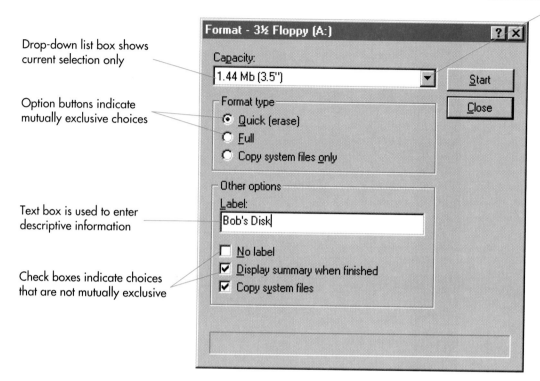

(a) Option Boxes and Check Boxes

Command buttons

Open list box displays
multiple options

Scroll bar indicates that
not all options are visible

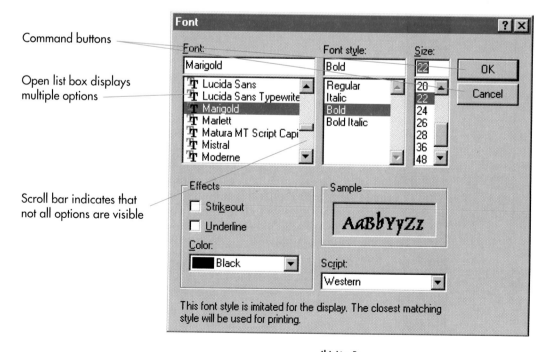

(b) List Boxes

FIGURE 4   Dialog Boxes

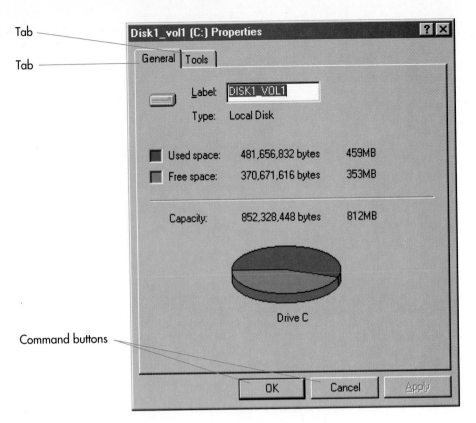

Tab

Tab

Command buttons

(c) Tabbed Dialog Box

FIGURE 4   Dialog Boxes (continued)

Check boxes are used instead of option buttons if the choices are not mutually exclusive or if an option is not required. Multiple boxes can be checked as in Figure 4a, or no boxes may be checked as in Figure 4b. Individual options are selected (cleared) by clicking on the appropriate check box.

A *text box* is used to enter descriptive information, such as Bob's Disk in Figure 4a. A flashing vertical bar (an I-beam) appears within the text box (when the text box is active) to mark the insertion point for the text you will enter.

A *list box* displays some or all of the available choices, any one of which is selected by clicking the desired item. A *drop-down list box,* such as the Capacity list box in Figure 4a, conserves space by showing only the current selection. Click the arrow of a drop-down list box to produce a list of available options. An *open list box,* such as those in Figure 4b, displays the choices without having to click a down arrow. (A scroll bar appears within an open list box if not all of the choices are visible at one time and provides access to the hidden choices.)

A *tabbed dialog box* provides multiple sets of options. The dialog box in Figure 4c, for example, has two tabs, each with its own set of options. Click either tab (the General tab is currently selected) to display the associated options.

All dialog boxes have a title bar, which contains a What's This button (in the form of a question mark) and a Close button. The *What's This button* provides help for any item in the dialog box; click the button, then click the item in the dialog box for which you want additional information. The Close button at the right of the title bar closes the dialog box.

All dialog boxes also contain one or more *command buttons,* the function of which is generally apparent from the button's name. The Start button, in Figure 4a, for example, initiates the formatting process. The OK Command button in

Figure 4b accepts the settings and closes the dialog box. The Cancel button does just the opposite, and ignores (cancels) the settings, then closes the dialog box without further action.

ONLINE HELP

Windows 95 has an extensive *online help* facility that contains information about virtually every topic in Windows. We believe that the best time to learn about help is as you begin your study of Windows. Help is available at any time, and is accessed most easily by clicking the *Help command* in the Start menu, which produces the help window in Figure 5.

The *Contents tab* in Figure 5a is similar to the table of contents in an ordinary book. The major topics are represented by books, each of which can be opened to display additional topics. Each open book will eventually display one or more specific topics, which may be viewed and/or printed to provide the indicated information.

The *Index tab* in Figure 5b is analogous to the index of an ordinary book. Type the first several letters of the topic to look up, click the topic when it appears in the window, then click the Display button to view the descriptive information as shown in Figure 5c. The help information is task-specific and describes how to accomplish the desired task.

You can print the contents of the Help windows in Figures 5a and 5b by clicking the Print command button at the bottom of a window. You can also print the contents of the display window in Figure 5c by right clicking in the window, then clicking the Print topic command from the shortcut menu.

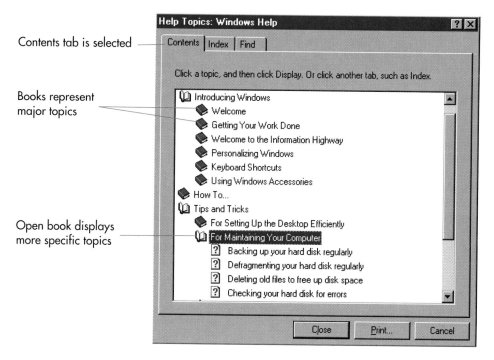

(a) Contents Tab

FIGURE 5   Online Help

Index tab is selected ————

Type first letters of topic ————

Click desired topic ————

Click Display button ————

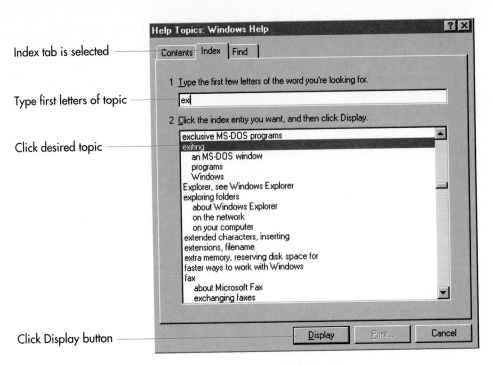

(b) Index Tab

Descriptive Information describes
how to accomplish the task ————

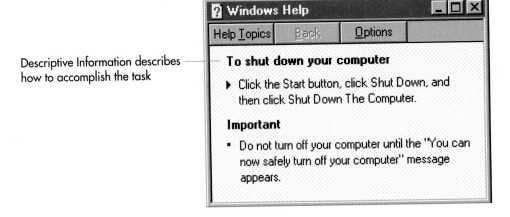

(c) Help Display

FIGURE 5   Online Help (continued)

THE MOUSE

The mouse is indispensable to Windows and is referenced continually in the hands-on exercises throughout the text. There are four basic operations with which you must become familiar:

- To **point** to an object, move the mouse pointer onto the object.
- To **click** an object, point to it, then press and release the left mouse button; to **right click** an object, point to the object, then press and release the right mouse button.

- To **double click** an object, point to it, then quickly click the left button twice in succession.
- To **drag** an object, move the pointer to the object, then press and hold the left button while you move the mouse to a new position.

The mouse is a pointing device—move the mouse on your desk and the **mouse pointer,** typically a small arrowhead, moves on the monitor. The mouse pointer assumes different shapes according to the location of the pointer or the nature of the current action—for example, a double arrow when you change the size of a window, an I-beam to insert text, a hand to jump from one help topic to the next, or a circle with a line through it to indicate that an attempted action is invalid.

The mouse pointer will also change to an hourglass to indicate that Windows is processing your last command, and that no further commands may be issued until the action is completed. The more powerful your computer, the less frequently the hourglass will appear; and conversely, the less powerful your system, the more you see the hourglass.

The Mouse versus the Keyboard

Almost every command in Windows can be executed in different ways, using either the mouse or the keyboard. Most people start with the mouse but add keyboard shortcuts as they become more proficient. There is no right or wrong technique, just different techniques, and the one you choose depends entirely on personal preference in a specific situation. If, for example, your hands are already on the keyboard, it is faster to use the keyboard equivalent. Other times, your hand will be on the mouse and that will be the fastest way. Toolbars provide still other ways to execute common commands.

In the beginning you may wonder why there are so many different ways to do the same thing, but you will eventually recognize the many options as part of Windows' charm. It is not necessary to memorize anything, nor should you even try; just be flexible and willing to experiment. The more you practice, the faster all of this will become second nature to you.

FORMATTING A DISK

All disks have to be formatted before they can hold data. The formatting process divides a disk into concentric circles called tracks, then further divides each track into sectors. You don't have to worry about formatting a hard disk, as that is done at the factory prior to the machine being sold. You do, however, have to format a floppy disk in order for Windows to read from and write to the disk. The procedure to format a floppy disk is described in step 6 of the following exercise.

FORMATTING A DISK

You must format a floppy disk at its rated capacity or else you may be unable to read the disk. There are two types of 3½-inch disks, double-density (720KB) and high-density (1.44MB). The easiest way to determine the type of disk is to look at the disk itself for the labels DD or HD, for double- and high-density, respectively. You can also check the number of square holes in the disk; a double-density disk has one, a high-density has two.

Learning is best accomplished by doing, and so we come to the first of four exercises in this appendix. The exercises enable you to apply the concepts you have learned, then extend those concepts to further exploration on your own.

Our first exercise welcomes you to Windows 95, shows you how to open, move, and size a window on the desktop, and how to format a floppy disk.

HANDS-ON EXERCISE 1

Welcome to Windows 95

Objective: To turn on the computer and start Windows 95; to use the help facility and explore the topic "Ten Minutes to Using Windows"; to open, move, and size a window; to format a floppy disk. Use Figure 6 as a guide in the exercise.

STEP 1: Turn the Computer On

➤ The floppy drive should be empty prior to starting your machine. This ensures that the system starts by reading files from the hard disk (which contains the Windows files), as opposed to a floppy disk (which does not).

➤ The number and location of the on/off switches depend on the nature and manufacturer of the devices connected to the computer. The easiest possible setup is when all components of the system are plugged into a surge protector, in which case only a single switch has to be turned on. In any event:

- Turn on the monitor if it has a separate switch.
- Turn on the printer if it has a separate switch.
- Turn on the power switch of the system unit.

➤ Your system will take a minute or so to get started, after which you should see the desktop in Figure 6a (the Start menu is *not* yet visible). Do not be concerned if the appearance of your desktop is different from ours.

➤ You may (or may not) see the Welcome message in Figure 6a. All of the command buttons are interesting and merit further exploration, which we will do at a later time. But for now, we ask that you click the **Close button** if you see the Welcome message.

➤ Click the **Start button** to display the Start menu. Again, do not be concerned if your start menu is different from ours, or if your icons are smaller (or larger) than ours.

➤ Click the **Help command** as shown in Figure 6a.

> ### MASTER THE MOUSE
>
> Moving the mouse pointer is easy, but it takes practice to move it to an exact position on the screen. If you're having trouble, be sure the mouse is perpendicular to the system unit. Move the mouse to the left or right, and the mouse pointer moves left or right on the screen. Move the mouse forward or back, and the pointer moves up or down.

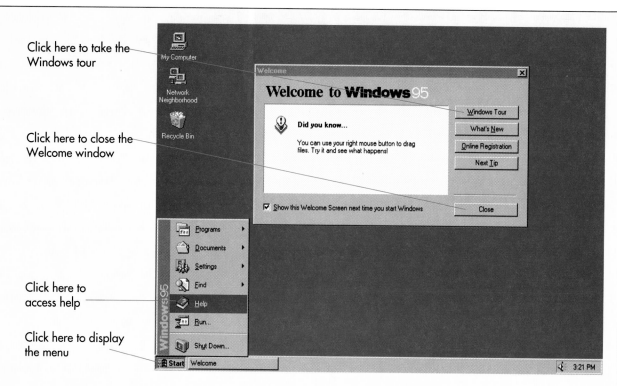

Click here to take the Windows tour

Click here to close the Welcome window

Click here to access help

Click here to display the menu

(a) Welcome to Windows 95 (step 1)

FIGURE 6   Hands-on Exercise 1

STEP 2: Ten Minutes to Windows

➤ If necessary, click the **Contents tab** in the Help Topics dialog box. All of the books on your screen will be closed.

➤ Click the topic **Ten Minutes to Using Windows,** then click the **Display button** to begin the Windows tour. (You can double click the topic to avoid having to click the Display button.)

➤ You should see the menu in Figure 6b. Click the **Book icon** next to Using Help to learn about the help facility.

➤ Follow the instructions provided by Windows until you complete the session on help. Click the **Exit button** at the upper right of the screen, then click the **Exit Tour button** to return to the desktop and continue with the exercise.

DOUBLE CLICKING FOR BEGINNERS

If you are having trouble double clicking, it is because you are not clicking quickly enough, or more likely, because you are moving the mouse (however slightly) between clicks. Relax, hold the mouse firmly on your desk, and try again.

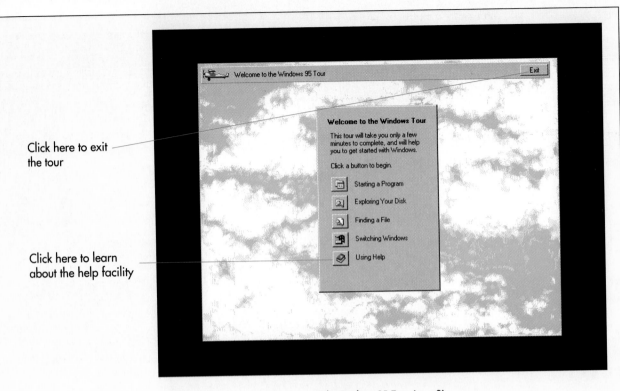

Click here to exit the tour

Click here to learn about the help facility

(b) Windows 95 Tour (step 2)

FIGURE 6 Hands-on Exercise 1 (continued)

STEP 3: Open My Computer

➤ Point to the **My Computer icon,** click the **right mouse button,** then click the **Open command** from the shortcut menu. (Alternatively, you can double click the **icon** to open it directly.)

➤ My Computer will open into a window as shown in Figure 6c. (The menus are not yet visible.) Do not be concerned if the contents of your window or its size and position on the desktop are different from ours.

➤ Pull down the **View menu** (point to the menu and click) as shown in Figure 6c. Make or verify the following selections. (You have to pull down the menu each time you choose a different command.)

- The **Toolbar command** should be checked. The Toolbar command functions as a toggle switch. Click the command and the toolbar is displayed; click the command a second time and the toolbar disappears.)

- The **Status Bar command** should be checked. The Status Bar command also functions as a toggle switch.

- **Large Icons** should be selected.

➤ Pull down the **View menu** a final time. Click the **Arrange Icons command** and (if necessary) click the **AutoArrange command** so that a check appears. Click outside the menu (or press the **Esc key**) if the command is already checked.

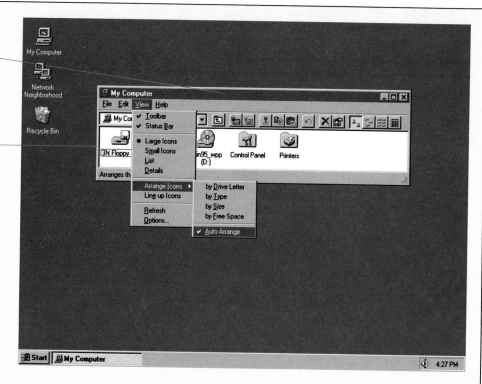

Drag the title bar to move the window (when menu is closed)

Click and drag a border to size the window (when menu is closed)

(c) My Computer (step 3)

FIGURE 6   Hands-on Exercise 1 (continued)

TOOLTIPS

Point to any button on the toolbar, and Windows displays the name of the button, which is indicative of its function. Point to the clock at the extreme right of the taskbar, and you will see a ToolTip with today's date. Point to the Start button, and you will see a ToolTip telling you to click here to begin.

STEP 4: Move and Size the Window

➤ Move and size the My Computer window on your desk to match the display in Figure 6c. (Press **Esc** to close the open menus.)

- Click the **Restore button** (which appears only if the window has been maximized) or else you will not be able to move and size the window.

- To change the width or height of the window, click and drag a border (the mouse pointer changes to a double arrow) in the direction you want to go; drag the border inward to shrink the window or outward to enlarge it.

- To change the width and height at the same time, click and drag a corner rather than a border.

- To change the position of the window, click and drag the title bar.

➤ Click the **Maximize button** so that the window expands to fill the entire screen. Click the **Restore button** (which replaces the Maximize button and is not shown in Figure 6c) to return the window to its previous size.

➤ Click the **Minimize button** to shrink the My Computer window to a button on the taskbar. My Computer is still open and remains active in memory.

➤ Click the **My Computer button** on the taskbar to reopen the window.

STEP 5: Scrolling

➤ Pull down the **View menu** and click **Details** (or click the **Details button** on the toolbar). You are now in the Details view as shown in Figure 6d.

➤ Click and drag the bottom border of the window inward so that you see the vertical scroll bar in Figure 6d. The scroll bar indicates that the contents of the window are not completely visible.

• Click the **down arrow** on the scroll bar. The top line (for drive A) disappears from view, and a new line containing the Control Panel comes into view.

• Click the **down arrow** a second time, which brings the Printers folder into view at the bottom of the window as the icon for drive C scrolls off the screen.

➤ Click the **Small Icons button** on the toolbar. Size the window so that the scroll bar disappears when the contents of the window become completely visible.

➤ Click the **Details button** on the toolbar. The scroll bar returns because you can no longer see the complete contents. Move and/or size the window to your personal preference.

(d) Scrolling (step 5)

FIGURE 6   Hands-on Exercise 1 (continued)

THE DETAILS VIEW

The Details view provides information about each object in a folder—for example, the capacity (total size) and amount of free space on a disk. To switch to the Details view, pull down the View menu and click Details. You can also click the Details button on the toolbar, provided the toolbar is displayed.

STEP 6: Format a Floppy Disk

➤ Click the **icon** for **drive A.** Pull down the **File menu** and click **Format.**

➤ You will see the dialog box in Figure 6e. Move the dialog box by clicking and dragging its **title bar** so that your screen matches ours.

➤ Click the **What's This button** (the mouse pointer changes to a question mark). Click the **Full option button** (under Format type) for an explanation. Click anywhere in the dialog box to close the popup window.

➤ Set the formatting parameters as shown in Figure 6e:

  • Set the **Capacity** to match the floppy disk you purchased (see boxed tip on page 11).

  • Click the **Full option button** to choose a full format. This option is well worth the extra time as it ensures the integrity of your disk.

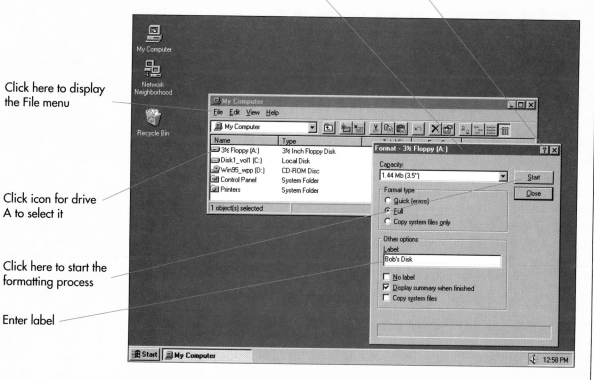

(e) Format a Floppy Disk (step 6)

FIGURE 6   Hands-on Exercise 1 (continued)

- Click the **Label text box** if it's empty, or click and drag over the existing label if there is an entry. Enter a new label such as **Bob's Disk** as shown in Figure 6e.
➤ Click the **Start command button** to begin the formatting operation. This will take about a minute, and you can see the progress of the formatting process at the bottom of the dialog box.
➤ After the formatting process is complete, you will see an informational dialog box with the results of the formatting operation. Read the information, then click the **Close command button** to close the informational dialog box.
➤ Click the **Close button** to close the Format dialog box.

WHAT'S THIS?

The What's This button (a question mark) appears in the title bar of almost every dialog box. Click the question mark, then click the item you want information about, which then appears in a popup window. To print the contents of the popup window, click the right mouse button inside the window, and click Print Topic. Click outside the popup window to close the window and continue working.

STEP 7: Disk Properties

➤ Click the **drive A icon** in the My Computer window, click the **right mouse button** to display a shortcut menu, then click the **Properties command.**
➤ You should see the Properties dialog box in Figure 6f although you may have to move and size the window to match our figure. The pie chart displays the percentage of free and unused space.
➤ Click **OK** to close the Properties dialog box. Click the **Close button** to close My Computer.

PROPERTIES EVERYWHERE

Windows assigns *properties* to every object on the desktop and stores those properties with the object itself. Point to any object on the desktop, including the desktop itself, then click the right mouse button to display the property sheet for that object.

STEP 8: Exit Windows

➤ Click the **Start button,** then click the **Shut Down command.** You will see a dialog box asking whether you're sure that you want to shut down the computer. (The option button to shut down the computer is already selected.)
➤ Click the **Yes command button,** then wait as Windows gets ready to shut down your system. Wait until you see another screen indicating that it is OK to turn off the computer.

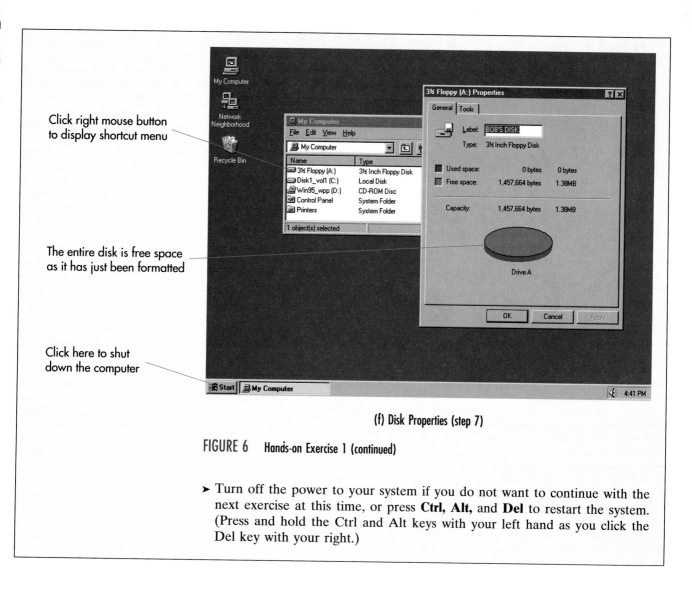

Click right mouse button to display shortcut menu

The entire disk is free space as it has just been formatted

Click here to shut down the computer

(f) Disk Properties (step 7)

FIGURE 6   Hands-on Exercise 1 (continued)

➤ Turn off the power to your system if you do not want to continue with the next exercise at this time, or press **Ctrl, Alt,** and **Del** to restart the system. (Press and hold the Ctrl and Alt keys with your left hand as you click the Del key with your right.)

MY COMPUTER

My Computer enables you to browse all of the drives (floppy disks, hard disks, and CD-ROM drive) that are attached to your computer. It is present on every desktop, but its contents will vary, depending on the specific configuration. Our system, for example, has one floppy drive, one hard disk, and a CD-ROM as shown in Figure 7. Each drive is represented by an icon and is assigned a letter.

The first (often only) floppy drive is designated as drive A, regardless of whether it is a 3½-inch drive or the older, and now nearly obsolete, 5¼-inch drive. A second floppy drive, if it exists, is drive B. Our system contains a single 3½ floppy drive (note the icon in Figure 7a) and is typical of systems purchased in today's environment.

The first (often only) hard disk on a system is always drive C, whether or not there are one or two floppy drives. A system with one floppy drive and one hard disk (today's most common configuration) will contain icons for drive A and drive C. Additional hard drives (if any) and/or the CD-ROM are labeled from D on.

In addition to an icon for each drive on your system, My Computer contains two other folders. (Folders are discussed in the next section.) The *Control Panel* enables you to configure (set up) all of the devices (mouse, sound, and so on) on your system. The ***Printers folder*** lets you add a new printer and/or view the progress of a printed document.

The contents of My Computer can be displayed in different views (Large Icons, Small Icons, Details, and List) according to your preference or need. You can switch from one view to the next by choosing the appropriate command from the View menu or by clicking the corresponding button on the toolbar.

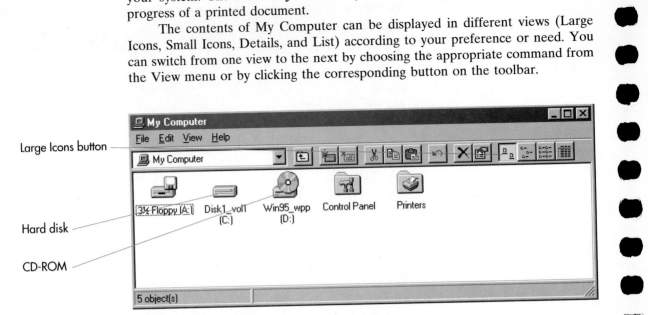

(a) Large Icons

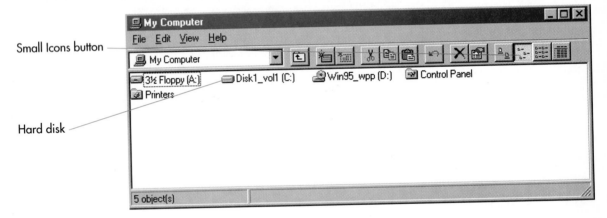

(b) Small Icons

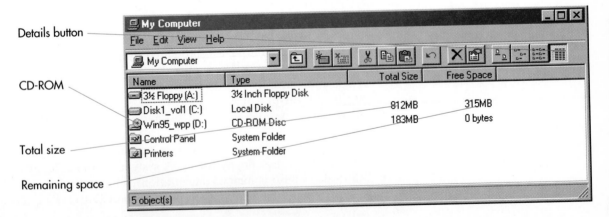

(c) Details View

FIGURE 7   My Computer

The **Large Icons view** and **Small Icons view** in Figures 7a and 7b, respectively, display each object as a large or small icon. The choice between the two depends on your personal preference. You might, for example, choose large icons if there are only a few objects in the window. Small icons would be preferable if there were many objects and you wanted to see them all. The **Details view** in Figure 7c displays additional information about each object. You see the type of object, the total size of the disk, and the remaining space on the disk. (A List view is also available and displays the objects with small icons but without the file details.)

FILES AND FOLDERS

A **file** is any data or set of instructions that have been given a name and stored on disk. There are, in general, two types of files, program files and data files. Microsoft Word and Microsoft Excel are program files. The documents and spreadsheets created by these programs are data files. A **program file** is executable because it contains instructions that tell the computer what to do. A **data file** is not executable and can be used only in conjunction with a specific program.

A file must have a name by which it can be identified. The file name can contain up to 255 characters and may include spaces and other punctuation. (This is very different from the rules that existed under MS-DOS that limited file names to eight characters followed by an optional three-character extension.) Long file names permit descriptive entries such as, *Term Paper for Western Civilization* (as opposed to a more cryptic *TPWCIV* that would be required under MS-DOS).

Files are stored in **folders** to better organize the hundreds (often thousands) of files on a hard disk. A Windows folder is similar in concept to a manila folder in a filing cabinet and contains one or more documents (files) that are somehow related to each other. An office worker stores his or her documents in manila folders. In Windows, you store your data files (documents) in electronic folders on disk.

Folders are the key to the Windows storage system. You can create any number of folders to hold your work just as you can place any number of manila folders into a filing cabinet. You can create one folder for your word processing documents and a different folder for your spreadsheets. Alternatively, you can create a folder to hold all of your work for a specific class, which may contain a combination of word processing documents and spreadsheets. The choice is entirely up to you, and you can use any system that makes sense to you. Anything at all can go into a folder—program files, data files, even other folders.

Figure 8 displays two different views of a folder containing six documents. The name of the folder (Homework) appears in the title bar next to the icon of an open folder. The Minimize, Maximize, and Close buttons appear at the right of the title bar. A toolbar appears below the menu bar in each view.

The Details view in Figure 8a displays the name of each file in the folder (note the descriptive file name), the file size, the type of file, and the date and time the file was last modified. Figure 8b shows the Large Icons view, which displays only the file name and an icon representing the application that created the file. The choice between views depends on your personal preference. (A Small Icons view and List view are also available.)

File Type

Every data file has a specific **file type** that is determined by the application that created the file initially. One way to recognize the file type is to examine the Type column in the Details view as shown in Figure 8a. The History Term Paper, for

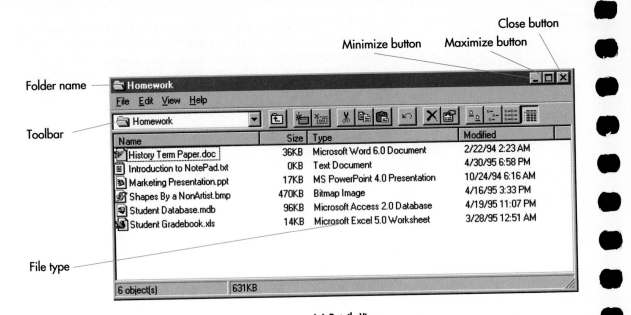

(a) Details View

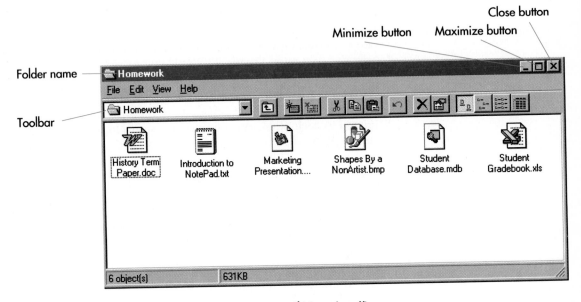

(b) Large Icons View

FIGURE 8   The Homework Folder

example, is a Microsoft Word 6.0 document, and the Student Gradebook is an Excel 5.0 workbook.

You can also determine the file type (or associated application) from any view (not just the Details view) by examining the application icon displayed next to the file name. Look carefully at the icon next to the History Term Paper in Figure 8a, for example, and you will recognize the icon for Microsoft Word. The application icon is recognized more easily in the Large Icons view in Figure 8b.

Still another way to determine the file type is through the three-character extension displayed after the file name. (A period separates the file name from the extension.) Each application has a specific extension, which is automatically assigned to the file name when the file is created. DOC and XLS, for example, are the extensions for Microsoft Word and Excel, respectively. The extension may be suppressed or displayed according to an option in the View menu of My Computer. See step 2 of the hands-on exercise on page 25.

Browsing My Computer

You need to be able to locate a folder and/or its documents quickly so that you can retrieve the documents and go to work. There are several ways to do this, the easiest of which is to browse My Computer. Assume, for example, that you are looking for the Homework folder in Figure 9 in order to work on your term paper for history. Figure 9 shows how easy it is to locate the Homework folder.

You would start by double clicking the My Computer icon on the desktop. This opens the My Computer window and displays all of the drives on your system. Next you would double click the icon for drive C because this is the drive that contains the folder you are looking for. This opens a second window, which displays all of the folders on drive C. And finally you would double click the icon for the Homework folder to open a third window containing the documents in the Homework folder. Once you are in the Homework folder, you would double click the icon of any existing document (which starts the associated application and opens the document), enabling you to begin work.

LEARNING BY DOING

The following exercise has you create a new folder on drive C, then create various files in that folder. The files are created using Notepad and Paint, two accessories that are included in Windows 95. We chose to create the files using these

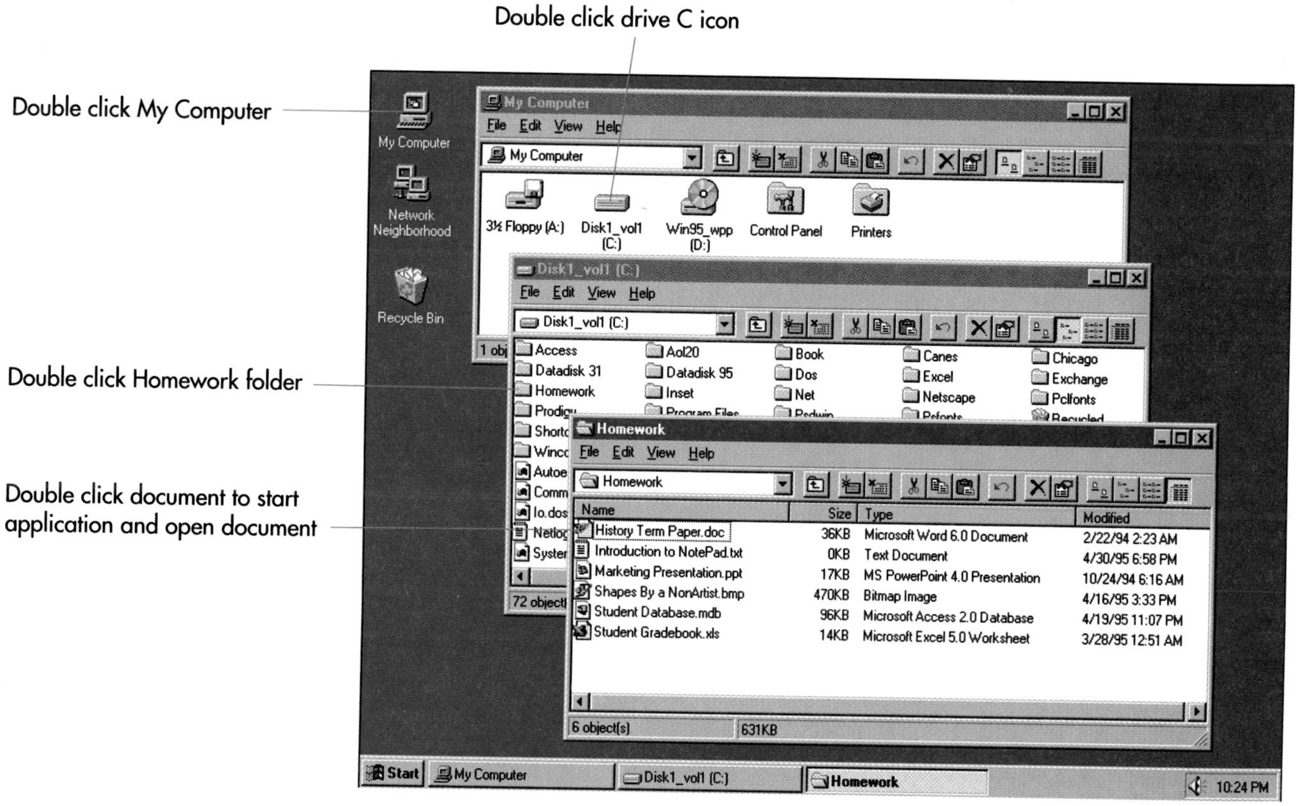

Double click drive C icon

Double click My Computer

Double click Homework folder

Double click document to start application and open document

FIGURE 9   Browsing My Computer

simple accessories, rather than more powerful applications such as Word or Excel, because we wanted to create the files quickly and easily. We also wanted to avoid reliance on specific applications that are not part of Windows 95. The emphasis throughout this appendix is the ability to manipulate files within the Windows environment after they have been created.

The exercise also illustrates the document orientation of Windows 95, which enables you to think in terms of the document rather than the application that created it. You simply point to an open folder, click the right mouse button to display a shortcut menu, then select the *New command.* You will be presented with a list of objects (file types) that are recognized by Windows 95 because the associated applications have been previously installed. Choose the file type that you want, and the associated application will be opened automatically. (See step 4 in the following hands-on exercise.)

THE NOTEPAD ACCESSORY

The Notepad accessory is ideal to create "quick and dirty" files that require no formatting and that are smaller than 64K. Notepad opens and saves files in ASCII (text) format only. Use a different editor, e.g., the WordPad accessory or a full-fledged word processor such as Microsoft Word, to create larger files or files that require formatting.

HANDS-ON EXERCISE 2

My Computer

Objective: Open My Computer and create a new folder on drive C. Use the New command to create a Notepad document and a Paint drawing. Use Figure 10 as a guide in the exercise.

STEP 1: Create a Folder

➤ Double click the **My Computer icon** to open My Computer. Double click the **icon** for **drive C** to open a second window as shown in Figure 10a. The size and/or position of your windows will be different from ours.

➤ Make or verify the following selections in each window. (You have to pull down the View menu each time you choose a different command.)

- The **Toolbar command** should be checked.
- The **Status Bar command** should be checked.
- **Large Icons** should be selected.

➤ If necessary, click anywhere within the window for drive C to make it the active window. (The title bar reflects the internal label of your disk, which was assigned when the disk was formatted. Your label will be different from ours.)

➤ Pull down the **File menu,** click (or point to) **New** to display the submenu, then click **Folder** as shown in Figure 10a.

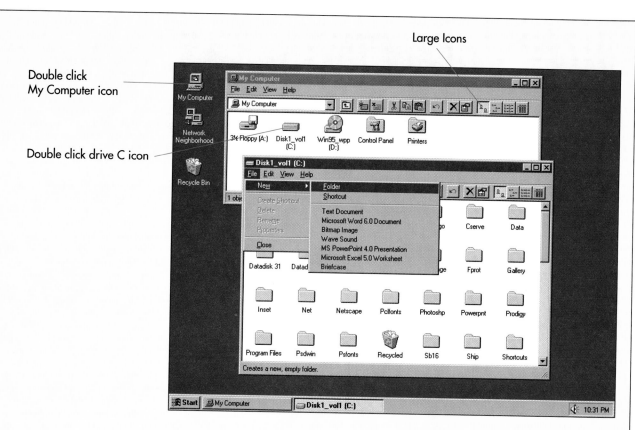

Double click
My Computer icon

Large Icons

Double click drive C icon

(a) Create a Folder (step 1)

FIGURE 10   Hands-on Exercise 2

ONE WINDOW OR MANY

If opening a window for drive C causes the My Computer window to disappear (and its button to vanish from the taskbar), you need to set an option to open each folder in a separate window. Pull down the View menu, click Options, click the Folder tab, then click the option button to use a separate window for each folder. Click the OK command button to accept this setting and return to the desktop

STEP 2: The View Menu

➤ A new folder has been created within the window for drive C with the name of the folder (New Folder) highlighted. Type **Homework** to change the name of the folder as shown in Figure 10b. Press **enter.**

➤ Pull down the **View menu** and click the **Arrange Icons command.** Click **By Name** to arrange the folders alphabetically within the window for drive C.

➤ Pull down the **View menu** a second time. Click **Options,** then click the **View tab** in the Options dialog box. Check the box (if necessary) to **Hide MS-DOS file extensions.** Click **OK.**

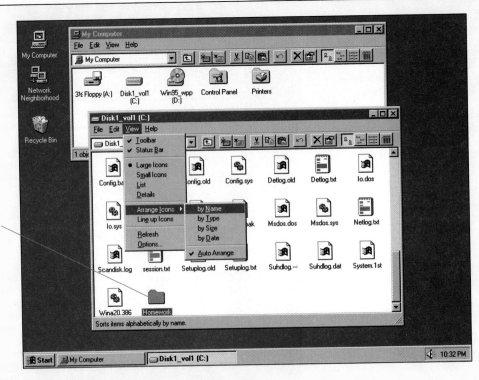

New folder

(b) View Menu (step 2)

FIGURE 10   Hands-on Exercise 2 (continued)

RENAME COMMAND

Point to a file or a folder, then click the right mouse button to display a menu with commands pertaining to the object. Click the Rename command. The name of the file or folder will be highlighted with the insertion point (a flashing vertical line) positioned at the end of the name. Type a new name—for example, Homework—to replace the selected name, or click anywhere within the name to change the insertion point and edit the name.

STEP 3: Open the Homework Folder

➤ Click the **Homework folder** to select it. Pull down the **File menu** and click **Open** (or double click the **folder** without pulling down the menu) to open the Homework folder.

➤ The Homework folder opens into a window as shown in Figure 10c. The window is empty because the folder does not contain any documents. If necessary, pull down the **View menu** and check the **Toolbar command** to display the toolbar.

➤ **Right click** a blank position on the taskbar to display the menu in Figure 10c. Click **Tile Vertically** to tile the three open windows.

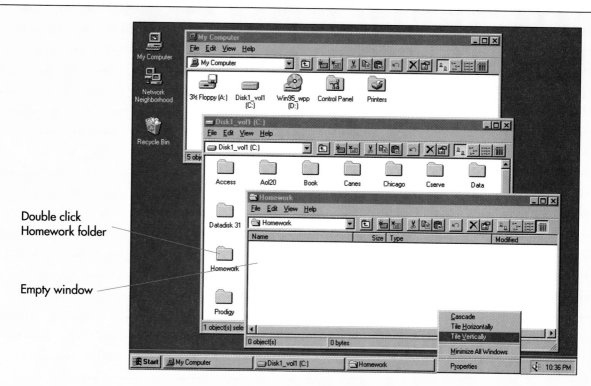

Double click
Homework folder

Empty window

(c) Open the Homework Folder (step 3)

FIGURE 10   Hands-on Exercise 2 (continued)

THE RIGHT MOUSE BUTTON

The right mouse button is the fastest way to change the properties of any object on the desktop or even the desktop itself. Point to a blank area on the desktop, click the right mouse button, then click Properties in the shortcut menu to display the dialog box (property sheet) for the desktop. In similar fashion, you can right click the taskbar to change its properties. You can also right click any icon on the desktop or any icon in a window.

STEP 4: The New Command

➤ The windows on your desktop should be tiled vertically as shown in Figure 10d. Click in the **Homework window.** The title bar for the Homework window should be highlighted, indicating that this is the active window.

➤ Pull down the **File menu** (or point to an empty area in the window and click the right mouse button).

➤ Click (or point to) the **New command** to display a submenu. The document types depend on the installed applications:

• You may (or may not) see Microsoft Word Document or Microsoft Excel Worksheet, depending on whether or not you have installed these applications.

- You will see Text Document and Bitmap Image, corresponding to the Notepad and Paint accessories that are installed with Windows 95.
➤ Select (click) **Text Document** as the type of file to create as shown below in Figure 10d. The icon for a new document will appear with the name of the document, New Text Document, highlighted.
➤ Type **Files and Folders** to change the name of the document. Press the **enter** key.

THE DOCUMENT, NOT THE APPLICATION

Windows 95 enables you to create a document without first starting the associated application. Select the folder that is to contain the document, pull down the File menu, and click New (or right click an empty space within a folder), then choose the type of document you want to create. Once the document has been created, double click its icon to load the associated application and begin editing the document. In other words, you can think about the document and not the application.

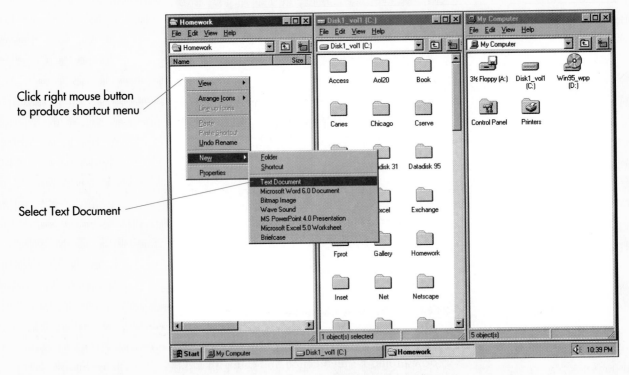

Click right mouse button to produce shortcut menu

Select Text Document

(d) The New Command (step 4)

FIGURE 10   Hands-on Exercise 2 (continued)

STEP 5: Create the Document

➤ If necessary, pull down the **View menu** and change to the **Large Icons view** so that the view in your Homework folder matches the view in Figure 10e.

➤ Select (click) the **Files and Folders document.** Pull down the **File menu.** Click **Open** (or double click the **Files and Folders icon** without pulling down the File menu) to load Notepad and open a Notepad window. The window is empty because the text of the document has not yet been entered.

➤ Pull down the **Edit menu:**

- If there is no check mark next to Word Wrap, click the **Word Wrap** command to enable this feature.
- If there is a check mark next to Word Wrap, click outside the menu to close the menu without changing any settings.

➤ Type the text of the document as shown in Figure 10e. Type just as you would on a regular typewriter with one exception—press the enter key only at the end of a paragraph, not at the end of every line. Since word wrap is in effect, Notepad will automatically start a new line when the word you are typing does not fit at the end of the current line.

➤ Pull down the **File menu** and click **Save** to save the document when you are finished.

➤ Click the **Close button** to close the Notepad accessory.

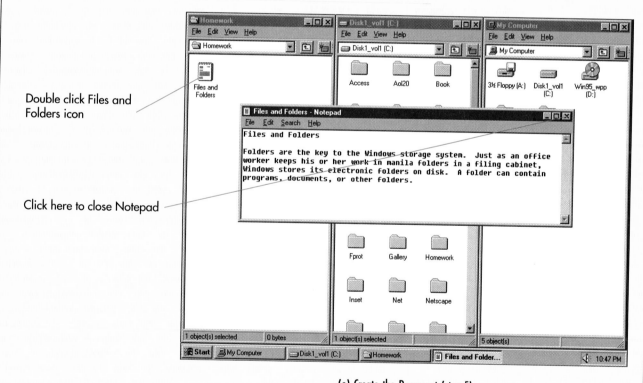

Double click Files and Folders icon

Click here to close Notepad

(e) Create the Document (step 5)

FIGURE 10   Hands-on Exercise 2 (continued)

STEP 6: Create a Drawing

➤ **Right click** within the Homework folder, click the **New command,** then click **Bitmap Image** as the type of file to create. The icon for a new drawing will appear with the name of the drawing (New Bitmap Image) highlighted.

➤ Type **Rectangles** to change the name of the drawing. Press **enter.**

➤ Pull down the **File menu** and click **Open** (or double click the **Rectangles icon** without pulling down the menu) to open a Paint window. The window is empty because the drawing has not yet been created.

➤ Click the **Maximize button** (if necessary) so that the window takes the entire desktop. Create a drawing of various rectangles as shown in Figure 10f.

➤ To draw a rectangle:

• Select (click) the rectangle tool.

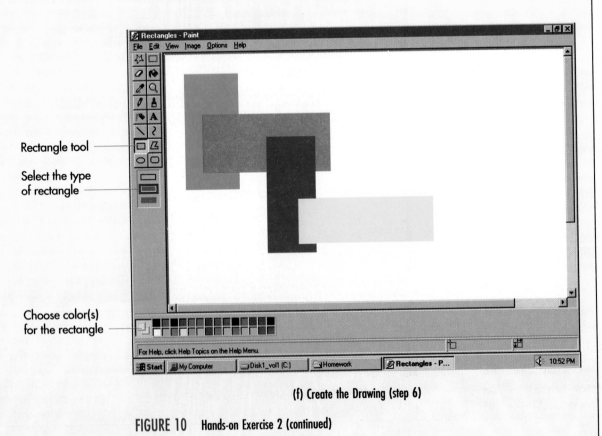

(f) Create the Drawing (step 6)

FIGURE 10   Hands-on Exercise 2 (continued)

- Select (click) the type of rectangle you want (a border only, a filled rectangle with a border, or a filled rectangle with no border).
- Select (click) the colors for the border and fill using the left and right mouse button, respectively.
- Click in the drawing area, then click and drag to create the rectangle.

➤ Pull down the **File menu** and click **Save As** to produce the Save As dialog box. Change the file type to **16-Color Bitmap** (from the default 256-color bitmap) to create a smaller file and conserve space on the floppy disk.

➤ Click **Save.** Click **Yes** to replace the file.

➤ Click the **Close button** to close Paint when you have finished the drawing.

THE PAINT ACCESSORY

The Paint accessory enables you to create simple or (depending on your ability) elaborate drawings. There is a sense of familiarity to the application since it follows the common user interface and consistent command structure common to all Windows applications. The Open, Save, and Print commands, for example, are found in the File menu. The Cut, Copy, Paste, and Undo commands are in the Edit menu. There is also a Help menu, which explains the various Paint commands and which functions identically to the Help menu in all Windows applications.

STEP 7: Edit the Document

➤ Double click the **Files and Folders icon** to reopen the document in a Notepad window. Pull down the **Edit menu** and toggle **Word Wrap on.** Press **Ctrl+End** to move to the end of the document.

➤ Add the additional text as shown in Figure 10g. Do *not* save the document at this time.

➤ Click the **Close button** to exit Notepad. You will see the informational message in Figure 10g, which indicates you have forgotten to save the changes. Click **Yes** to save the changes and exit.

DOS NOTATION

The visually oriented storage system within Windows 95 makes it easy to identify folders and the documents within those folders. DOS, however, was not so simple and used a text-based notation to indicate the drive, folder, and file. For example, C:\HOMEWORK\FILES AND FOLDERS specifies the file FILES AND FOLDERS, in the HOMEWORK folder, on drive C.

STEP 8: Change the View

➤ Right click an empty space on the taskbar, then click the **Tile Horizontally command** to tile the windows as shown in Figure 10h. (The order of your windows may be different from ours.)

Double click Files and
Folders icon

Add new text

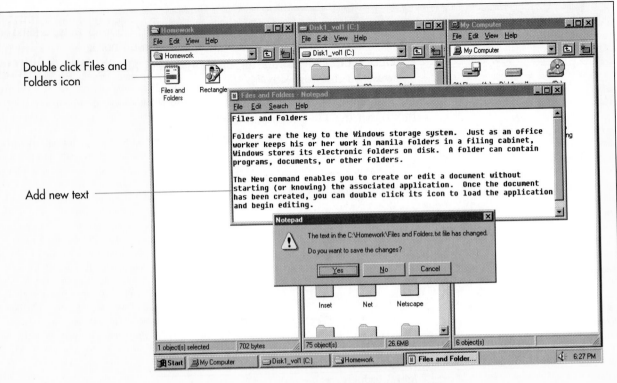

(g) Edit the Document (step 7)

Details button

Small Icons button

Right click empty space
on taskbar to produce
shortcut menu

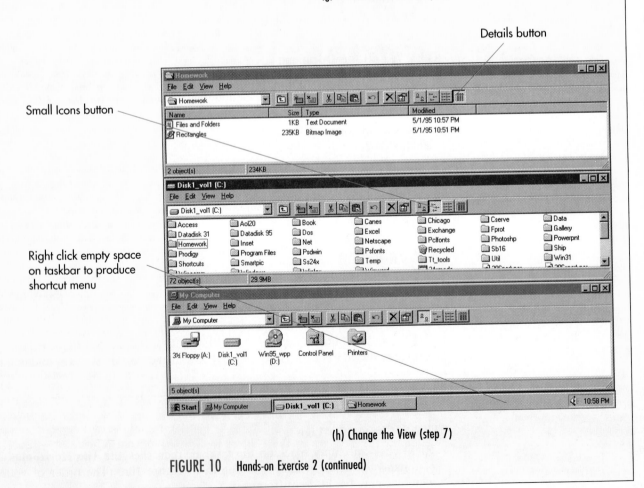

(h) Change the View (step 7)

FIGURE 10   Hands-on Exercise 2 (continued)

> ➤ Click in the window for the **Homework folder,** then click the **Details button** on the toolbar to display the details view.

> ➤ Press the **F5 key** to refresh the window and update the file properties (the file size, type, and the date and time of the last modification).

> ➤ Click in the window for drive C, then click the **List view** or **Small Icons button** on the toolbar to display small icons as shown in Figure 10h.

STEP 9: Exit Windows

> ➤ Click the **Close button** in each of the three open windows (My Computer, drive C, and Homework) to close each window.

> ➤ Exit Windows if you do not want to continue with the next exercise at this time.

FILE OPERATIONS

The exercise just completed had you create a folder and place documents in that folder. As you continue to work on the computer, you will create additional folders, as well as files within those folders. Learning how to manage those files is one of the most important skills you can acquire. This section describes the different types of file operations that you will perform on a daily basis.

Moving and Copying a File

There are two basic ways to move or copy a file from one location to another. You can use the *Cut, Copy,* and *Paste commands,* or you can simply drag and drop the files from one location to the other. Both techniques require you to open the disk or folder containing the source file (the file you are moving or copying) in order to select the file you will move or copy. This is typically done by opening successive windows through My Computer.

Assume, for example, that you want to copy a file from the Homework folder on drive C to a floppy disk in drive A. You would begin by double clicking the My Computer icon to open the My Computer window. Then you would double click the icon for drive C because that is the drive containing the file you want to copy. And then you would double click the icon for the Homework folder (opening a third window) because that is the folder containing the file to be copied.

To copy the file (after the Homework folder has been opened), select the file by clicking its icon, then drag the icon to the drive A icon in the My Computer window. (Alternatively, you could select the file, pull down the Edit menu, and click the Copy command, then click the icon for drive A, pull down the Edit menu, and click the Paste command.) It sounds complicated, but it's not and you will get a chance to practice in the hands-on exercise.

Backup

It's not a question of if it will happen, but when—hard disks die, files are lost, or viruses may infect a system. It has happened to us and it will happen to you, but you can prepare for the inevitable by creating adequate *backup* before the problem occurs. The essence of a backup strategy is to decide which files to back up, how often to do the backup, and where to keep the backup. Once you decide on a strategy, follow it, and follow it faithfully!

Our strategy is very simple—back up what you can't afford to lose, do so on a daily basis, and store the backup away from your computer. You need not copy every file, every day. Instead copy just the files that changed during the current session. Realize, too, that it is much more important to back up your data files, rather than your program files. You can always reinstall the application from the original disks, or if necessary, go to the vendor for another copy of an application. You, however, are the only one who has a copy of the term paper that is due tomorrow.

Deleting Files

The *Delete command* deletes (removes) a file from a disk. If, however, the file was deleted from a hard disk, it is not really gone, but moved instead to the Recycle Bin from where it can be subsequently recovered.

The *Recycle Bin* is a special folder that contains all of the files that were previously deleted from any hard disk on your system. Think of the Recycle Bin as similar to the wastebasket in your room. You throw out (delete) a report by tossing it into a wastebasket. The report is gone (deleted) from your desk, but you can still get it back by taking it out of the wastebasket as long as the basket wasn't emptied. The Recycle Bin works the same way. Files are not deleted from the hard disk per se, but are moved instead to the Recycle Bin from where they can be recovered. The Recycle Bin should be emptied periodically, however, or else you will run out of space on the disk. Once a file is removed from the Recycle Bin, it can no longer be recovered.

WRITE-PROTECT YOUR BACKUP DISKS

You can write-protect a floppy disk to ensure that its contents are not accidentally altered or erased. A 3½-inch disk is write-protected by sliding the built-in tab so that the write-protect notch is open. The disk is write-enabled when the notch is covered. The procedure is reversed for a 5¼-inch disk; that is, the disk is write-protected when the notch is covered and write-enabled when the notch is open.

HANDS-ON EXERCISE 3

File Operations

Objective: Copy a file from drive C to drive A, and from drive A back to drive C. Delete a file from drive C, then restore the file using the Recycle Bin. Demonstrate the effects of write-protecting a disk. Use Figure 11 as a guide in the exercise.

STEP 1: Open the Homework Folder

➤ Double click the **icon** for **My Computer** to open My Computer. Double click the **icon** for **drive C** to open a second window showing the contents of drive C. Double click the **Homework folder** to open a third window showing the contents of the Homework folder.

➤ Right click the taskbar to tile the windows vertically as shown in Figure 11a. Your windows may appear in a different order from those in the figure.

➤ Make or verify the following selections in each window. (You have to pull down the View menu each time you choose a different command.)

- The **Toolbar command** should be checked.
- The **Status Bar command** should be checked.
- Choose the **Details view** in the Homework window and the **Large Icons view** in the other windows.

➤ Pull down the **View menu** in any open window. Click **Options,** then click the **View tab** in the Options dialog box. Check the box (if necessary) to **Hide MS-DOS file extensions.** Click **OK** to exit the dialog box.

QUICK VIEW

If you forget what is in a particular document, you can use the Quick View command to preview the document without having to open it. Select (click) the file you want to preview, then pull down the File menu and click Quick View (or right click the file and select the Quick View command) to display the file in a preview window. If you decide to edit the file, pull down the File menu and click Open File for Editing; otherwise click the Close button to close the preview window.

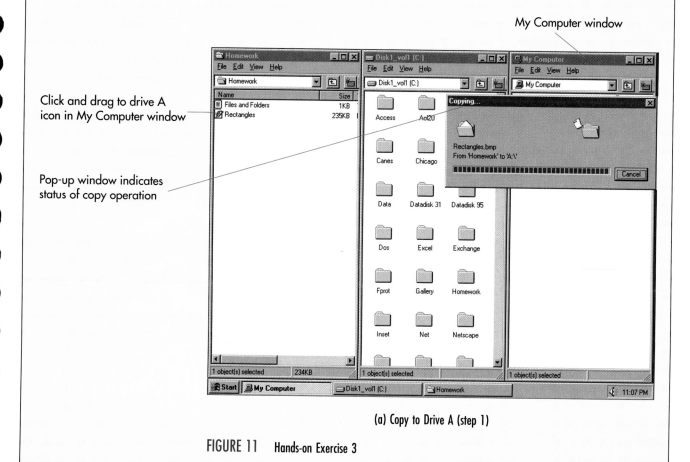

My Computer window

Click and drag to drive A icon in My Computer window

Pop-up window indicates status of copy operation

(a) Copy to Drive A (step 1)

FIGURE 11   Hands-on Exercise 3

STEP 2: Backup the Homework Folder

➤ Place a freshly formatted disk in drive A. Be sure that the disk is not write-protected or else you will not be able to copy files to the disk.

➤ Click and drag the icon for the **Rectangles file** from the Homework folder to the icon for **drive A** in the My Computer window.

- You will see the ⊘ symbol as you drag the file until you reach a suitable destination (e.g., until you point to the icon for drive A). The ⊘ symbol will change to a plus sign when the icon for drive A is highlighted, indicating that the file can be copied successfully.

- Release the mouse to complete the copy operation. You will see a popup window as shown in Figure 11a, indicating the progress of the copy operation. This takes several seconds since Rectangles is a large file (235KB).

➤ Click and drag the icon for the **Files and Folders file** from the Homework folder to the icon for drive A. You may or may not see a popup window showing the copy operation since the file is small (1KB) and copies quickly.

USE THE RIGHT MOUSE BUTTON TO MOVE OR COPY A FILE

The result of dragging a file with the left mouse button depends on whether the source and destination folders are on the same or different drives. Dragging a file to a folder on a different drive copies the file. Dragging the file to a folder on the same drive moves the file. If you find this hard to remember, and most people do, click and drag with the right mouse button to produce a shortcut menu asking whether you want to copy or move the file. This simple tip can save you from making a careless (and potentially serious) error. Use it!

STEP 3: View the Contents of Drive A

➤ Double click the **icon** for **drive A** in the My Computer window to open a fourth window.

➤ Right click a blank area on the taskbar. Tile the windows vertically or horizontally (it doesn't matter which) to display the windows as in Figure 11b.

➤ Click in the window for drive A. If necessary, pull down the **View menu,** display the toolbar, and change to the **Details view.**

➤ Compare the file details for each file in the Homework folder and drive A; the details are identical, reflecting the fact that the files have been copied.

CHANGE THE COLUMN WIDTH

Drag the right border of a column heading to the right (left) to increase (decrease) the width of the column in order to see more (less) information in that column. Double click the right border of a column heading to automatically adjust the column width to accommodate the widest entry in that column.

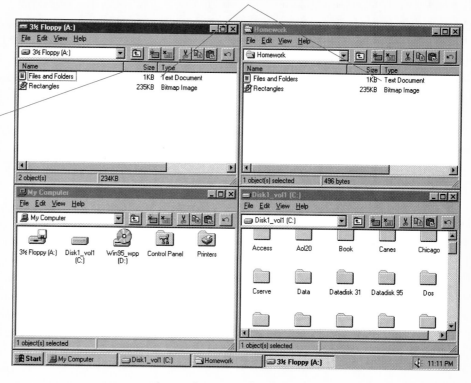

File details are identical

Drag border to increase column width

(b) View the Contents of Drive A (step 3)

FIGURE 11   Hands-on Exercise 3 (continued)

STEP 4: Delete a File

➤ Select (click) the **Files and Folders icon** in the Homework folder. Pull down the **File menu.** Click **Delete.**

➤ You will see the dialog box in Figure 11c, asking whether you want to delete the file. Click **Yes** to delete the file.

➤ Right click the **Rectangles icon** in the Homework folder to display a shortcut menu. Click **Delete.**

➤ Click **Yes** when asked whether to delete the Rectangles file. The Homework folder is now empty.

THE UNDO COMMAND

The Undo command pertains not just to application programs such as Notepad or Paint, but to file operations as well. It will, for example, undelete a file if it is executed immediately after the Delete command. Pull down the Edit menu and click Undo to reverse (undo) the last command. Some operations cannot be undone (in which case the command will be dimmed out), but Undo is always worth a try.

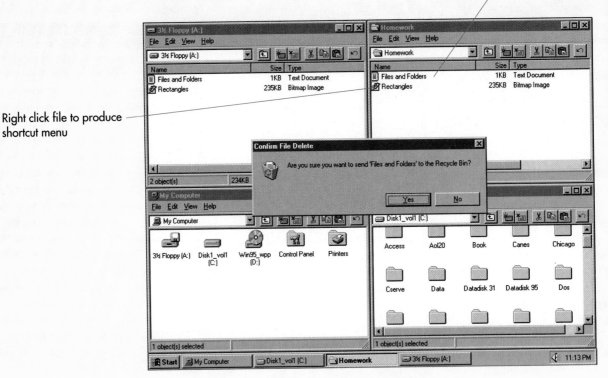

Right click file to produce shortcut menu

Click file and press delete key

(c) Delete a File (step 4)

FIGURE 11   Hands-on Exercise 3 (continued)

STEP 5: Copy from Drive A to Drive C

➤ The backup you did in step 2 enables you to copy (restore) the Files and Folders file from drive A to drive C. You can do this in one of two ways:

- Select (click) the **Files and Folders icon** in the window for drive A. Pull down the **Edit menu.** Click **Copy.** Click in the **Homework folder.** Pull down the **Edit menu.** Click **Paste** as shown in Figure 11d.
- Click and drag the **icon** for the **Files and Folders file** from drive A to the Homework folder.

➤ Either way, you will see a popup window showing the Files and Folders file being copied from drive A to drive C.

➤ Use whichever technique you prefer to copy the Rectangles file from drive A to drive C.

BACK UP IMPORTANT FILES

We cannot overemphasize the importance of adequate backup and urge you to copy your data files to floppy disks and store those disks away from your computer. It takes only a few minutes, but you will thank us, when (not if) you lose an important file and wish you had another copy.

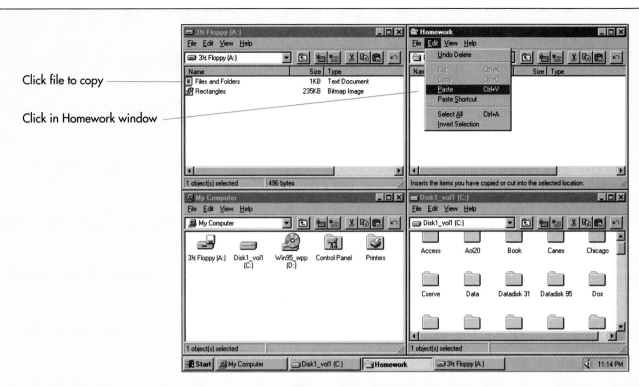

Click file to copy

Click in Homework window

(d) Copy to Drive C (step 5)

FIGURE 11   Hands-on Exercise 3 (continued)

STEP 6: Modify a File

➤ Double click the **Files and Folders icon** in the Homework folder to reopen the file as shown in Figure 11e. Pull down the **Edit menu** and toggle **Word Wrap on.**

➤ Press **Ctrl+End** to move to the end of the document. Add the paragraph shown in Figure 11e.

➤ Pull down the **File menu** and click **Save** to save the modified file. Click the **Close button** to close the file.

➤ The Files and Folders document has been modified and should once again be backed up to drive A. Click and drag the **icon** for **Files and Folders** from the Homework folder to the drive A window.

➤ You will see a message indicating that the folder (drive A) already contains a file called Files and Folders (which was previously copied in step 2) and asking whether you want to replace the existing file with the new file. Click **Yes.**

THE SEND TO COMMAND

The Send To command is an alternative way to copy a file to a floppy disk and has the advantage that the floppy disk icon need not be visible. Select (click) the file to copy, then pull down the File menu (or simply right click the file). Click the Send To command, then select the appropriate floppy drive from the resulting submenu.

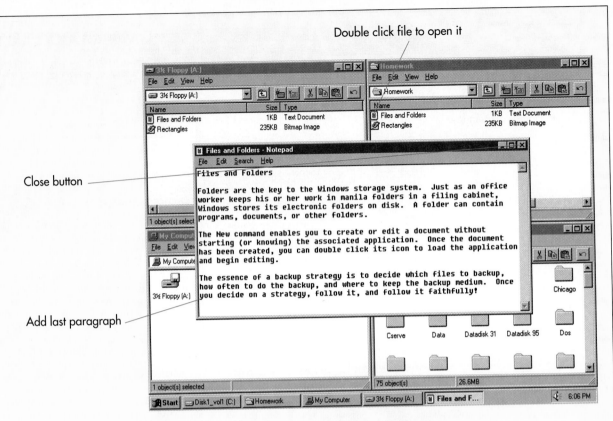

Double click file to open it

Close button

Add last paragraph

(e) Modify the File (step 6)

FIGURE 11   Hands-on Exercise 3 (continued)

STEP 7: Write-protect a Disk

➤ You can write-protect a floppy disk so that its contents cannot be changed; that is, existing files cannot be modified or erased nor can new files be added.

➤ Remove the floppy disk from drive A and follow the appropriate procedure:

- To write-protect a 3½ disk, move the built-in tab so that the write-protect notch is open.
- To write-protect a 5¼ disk, cover the write-protect notch with a piece of opaque tape.

➤ Return the write-protected disk to the floppy drive.

➤ Click the **icon** for the **Rectangles file** on drive A, then press the **Del key** to delete the file.

➤ You will see a warning message asking whether you are sure you want to delete the file. Click **Yes.**

➤ You will see the error message in Figure 11f, indicating that the file cannot be deleted because the disk is write-protected. Click **OK.**

➤ Remove the write-protection by reversing the procedure you followed earlier. Select the **Rectangles file** a second time and delete the file. Click **Yes** in response to the confirmation message, after which the file will be deleted from drive A.

➤ You have just deleted the Rectangles file, but we want it back on drive A for the next exercise. Accordingly, click and drag the **Rectangles icon** in the Homework folder to the icon for **drive A** in the My Computer window.

Click file to delete, press —— Del key

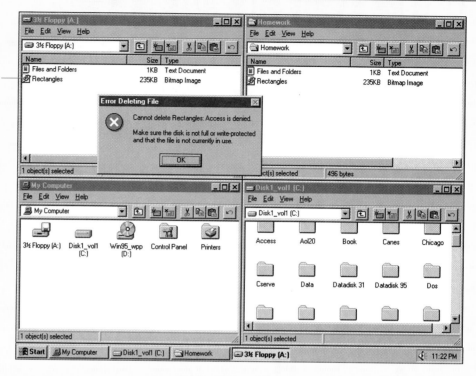

(f) Write-Protect a Disk (step 7)

FIGURE 11   Hands-on Exercise 3 (continued)

➤ Click the **Close button** in the window for drive A.

STEP 8: The Recycle Bin

➤ Select (click) the **Files and Folders icon** in the Homework folder. Pull down the **File menu** and click **Delete.** Click **Yes** in the dialog box asking whether you want to delete the file.

➤ To restore a file, you need to open the Recycle Bin:
- Double click the **Recycle Bin icon** if you can see the icon on the desktop *or*
- Double click the **Recycled icon** within the window for drive C. (You may have to scroll in order to see the icon.)

➤ Right click a blank area on the taskbar, then tile the open windows as shown in Figure 11g. The position of your windows may be different from ours. The view in the Recycle Bin may also be different.

➤ Your Recycle Bin contains all files that have been previously deleted from drive C, and hence you may see a different number of files than those displayed in Figure 11g.

➤ Scroll until you can select the (most recent) **Files and Folders icon.** Pull down the **File menu** and click the **Restore command.** The Files and Folders file is returned to the Homework folder.

EMPTY THE RECYCLE BIN

All files that are deleted from a hard drive are automatically moved to the Recycle Bin. This enables you to restore (undelete) a file, but it also prevents you from recovering the space taken up by those files. Accordingly, you should periodically delete files from the Recycle Bin or otherwise you will find yourself running out of space on your hard disk. Be careful, though, because once you delete a file from the Recycle Bin, it is gone for good!

Recycle Bin

Select file to restore

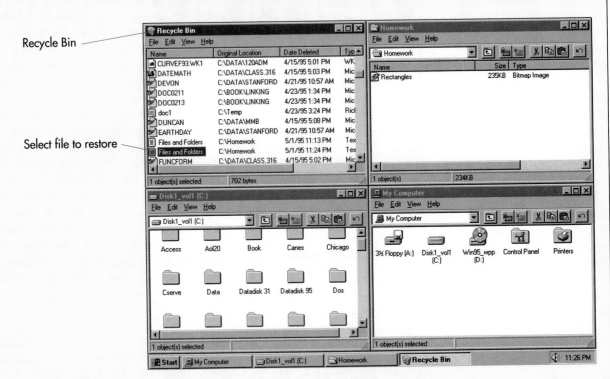

(g) The Recycle Bin (step 8)

FIGURE 11   Hands-on Exercise 3 (continued)

STEP 9: Exit Windows

➤ Click the **Close button** in each of the four open windows (the Recycle Bin, My Computer, drive C, and Homework) to close each window.

➤ Exit Windows if you do not want to continue with the next exercise.

WINDOWS EXPLORER

The *Windows Explorer* enables you to browse through all of the drives, folders, and files on your system. It does not do anything that could not be accomplished through successive windows via My Computer. The Explorer does, however, let you perform a given task more quickly, and for that reason is preferred by more experienced users.

Assume, for example, that you are taking five classes this semester, and that you are using the computer in each course. You've created a separate folder to hold the work for each class and have stored the contents of all five folders on a single floppy disk. Assume further that you need to retrieve your third English assignment so that you can modify the assignment.

You can use My Computer to browse the system as shown in Figure 12a. You would start by opening My Computer, double clicking the icon for drive A to open a second window, then double clicking the icon for the English folder to display its documents. The process is intuitive, but it can quickly lead to a desktop cluttered with open windows. And what if you next needed to work on a paper for Art History? That would require you to open the Art History folder, which produces yet another open window on the desktop.

The Explorer window in Figure 12b offers a more sophisticated way to browse the system as it shows the hierarchy of folders as well as the contents of the selected folder. The Explorer window is divided into two panes. The left pane contains a tree diagram of the entire system, showing all drives and optionally the folders in each drive. One (and only one) object is always selected in the left pane, and its contents are displayed automatically in the right pane.

Look carefully at the tree diagram in Figure 12b and note that the English folder is currently selected. The icon for the selected folder is an open folder to differentiate it from the other folders, which are closed and are not currently selected. The right pane displays the contents of the selected folder (English in Figure 12b) and is seen to contain three documents, Assignments 1, 2, and 3. The right pane is displayed in the Details view, but could just as easily have been displayed in another view (e.g., Large or Small Icons) by clicking the appropriate button on the toolbar.

As indicated, only one folder can be selected (open) at a time in the left pane, and its contents are displayed in the right pane. To see the contents of a different folder (e.g., Accounting), you would select (click) the Accounting folder, which will automatically close the English folder.

The tree diagram in the left pane displays the drives and their folders in hierarchical fashion. The desktop is always at the top of the hierarchy and contains My Computer, which in turn contains various drives, each of which contains folders, which in turn contain documents and/or additional folders. Each object may be expanded or collapsed to display or hide its subordinates.

Look again at the icon next to My Computer in Figure 12b, and you see a minus sign indicating that My Computer has been expanded to show the various drives on the system. There is also a minus sign next to the icon for drive A to indicate that it too has been expanded to show the folders on the disk. Note, however, the plus sign next to drives C and D, indicating that these parts of the tree are currently collapsed and thus their subordinates are not visible.

A folder may contain additional folders, and thus individual folders may also be expanded or collapsed. The minus sign to the left of the Finance folder in Figure 12b, for example, shows that the folder has been expanded and contains two additional folders, for Assignments and Spreadsheets, respectively. The plus sign next to the Accounting folder, however, indicates the opposite; that is, the folder is collapsed and its folders are not currently visible. A folder with neither a plus or minus sign, such as Art History or Marketing, means that the folder does not contain additional folders and cannot be expanded or collapsed.

The advantage of the Windows Explorer over My Computer is the uncluttered screen and ease with which you switch from one folder to the next. If, for example, you wanted to see the contents of the Art History folder, all you would do would be to click its icon in the left pane, which automatically changes the right pane to show the documents in Art History. The Explorer also makes it easy to move or copy a file from one folder or drive to another as you will see in the hands-on exercise that follows shortly.

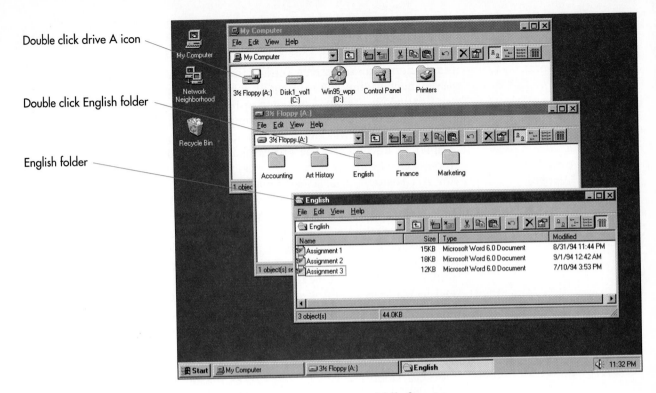

Double click drive A icon

Double click English folder

English folder

(a) My Computer

Tree diagram

Contents of selected folder

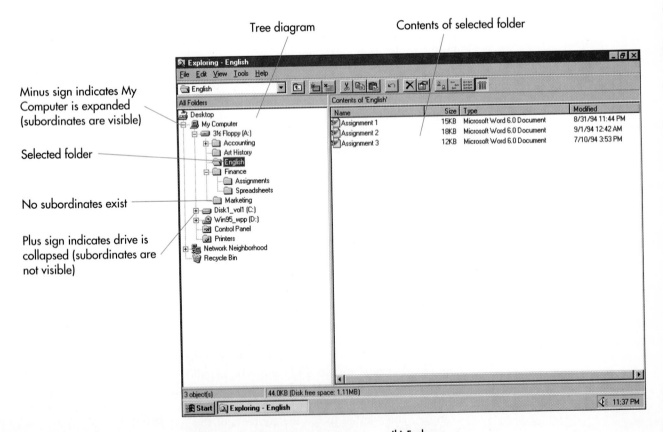

Minus sign indicates My Computer is expanded (subordinates are visible)

Selected folder

No subordinates exist

Plus sign indicates drive is collapsed (subordinates are not visible)

(b) Explorer

FIGURE 12   Browsing a System

LEARN BY DOING

The Explorer is especially useful for moving or copying files from one folder or drive to another. You simply open the folder that contains the file, use the scroll bar in the left pane (if necessary) so that the destination folder is visible, then drag the file from the right pane to the destination folder. The Explorer is a powerful tool, but it takes practice to master.

The next exercise illustrates the procedure for moving and copying files and uses the floppy disk from the previous exercise. The disk already contains two files—one Notepad document and one Paint drawing. The exercise has you create an additional document of each type so that there are a total of four files on the floppy disk. You then create two folders on the floppy disk, one for drawings and one for documents, and move the respective files into each folder. And finally, you copy the contents of each folder from drive A to a different folder on drive C. By the end of the exercise you will have had considerable practice in both moving and copying files.

HANDS-ON EXERCISE 4

Windows Explorer

Objective: Use the Windows Explorer to copy and move a file from one folder to another. Use Figure 13 as a guide in the exercise.

STEP 1: Open the Windows Explorer

➤ Click the **Start button.** Click (or point to) the **Programs command** to display the Programs menu. Click **Windows Explorer.**

➤ Click the **Maximize button** so that the Explorer takes the entire desktop as shown in Figure 13a. Do not be concerned if your screen is different from ours.

➤ Make or verify the following selections using the **View menu.** (You have to pull down the View menu each time you choose a different command.)

- The **Toolbar command** should be checked.
- The **Status Bar command** should be checked.
- The **Details view** should be selected.

➤ Pull down the **View menu** a second time. Click **Options,** then click the **View tab** in the Options dialog box. Check the box (if necessary) to **Hide MS-DOS file extensions.** Click **OK.**

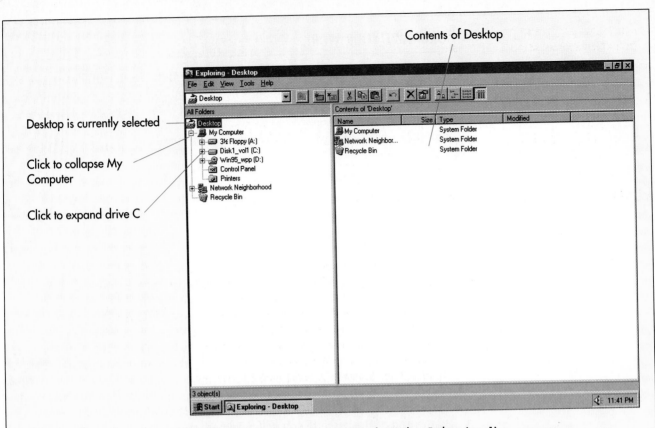

Contents of Desktop

Desktop is currently selected

Click to collapse My Computer

Click to expand drive C

(a) Open the Windows Explorer (step 1)

FIGURE 13   Hands-on Exercise 4

STEP 2: Collapse and Expand My Computer

➤ Click (select) the **Desktop icon** in the left pane to display the contents of the desktop in the right pane. Our desktop contains only the icons for My Computer, Network Neighborhood, and the Recycle Bin. Your desktop may have different icons.

➤ Toggle back and forth between expanding and collapsing My Computer by clicking the plus or minus sign that appears next to the icon for My Computer. Clicking the plus sign expands My Computer, after which a minus sign is displayed. Clicking the minus sign collapses My Computer and changes to a plus sign. End with My Computer expanded and the **minus sign** displayed as shown in Figure 13a.

➤ Place the disk from the previous exercise in drive A. Expand and collapse each drive within My Computer. (Drive A does not have any folders at this time, and hence will have neither a plus nor a minus sign.)

➤ End with a **plus sign** next to drive C so that the hard drive is collapsed as shown in Figure 13a. (The contents of My Computer will depend on your particular configuration.)

STEP 3: Create a Notepad Document

➤ Click the **icon** for **drive A** in the left pane to view the contents of the disk in the right pane. You should see the Files and Folders and Rectangles files that were created in the previous exercise.

➤ Pull down the **File menu.** Click (or point to) **New** to display the submenu. Click **Text Document** as the type of file to create.

➤ The icon for a new document will appear with the name of the document (New Text Document) highlighted. Type **About   Explorer** to change the name of the document. Press **enter.** Double click the **file icon** to open the Notepad accessory and create the document.

➤ Move and/or size the Notepad window to your preference. You can also maximize the window so that you have more room in which to work.

➤ Pull down the **Edit menu** and toggle **Word Wrap** on. Enter the text of the document as shown in Figure 13b.

➤ Pull down the **File menu** and click **Save** to save the document when you are finished. Click the **Close button** to close Notepad and return to the Explorer.

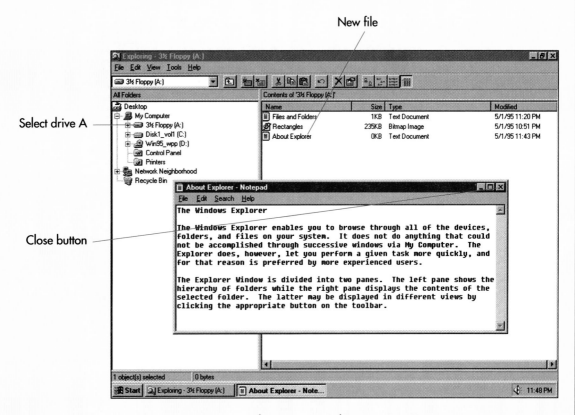

(b) Create a NotePad Document (step 3)

FIGURE 13   Hands-on Exercise 4 (continued)

STEP 4: Create a Paint Drawing

➤ Click the **icon** for **drive A** in the Explorer window, then pull down the **File menu.** (Alternatively, you can click the **right mouse button** in the right pane of the Explorer window when drive A is selected in the left pane.)

➤ Click (or point to) the **New command** to display the submenu. Click **Bitmap Image** as the type of file to create.

➤ The icon for a new drawing will appear with the name of the file (New Bitmap Image) highlighted. Type **Circles** to change the name of the file. Press **enter.** Double click the **file icon** to open the Paint accessory and create the drawing.

➤ Move and/or size the Paint window to your preference. You can also maximize the window so that you have more room in which to work.

➤ Create a simple drawing consisting of various circles and ellipses as shown in Figure 13c.

➤ Pull down the **File menu.** Click **Save As** to produce the Save As dialog box. Change the file type to **16-Color Bitmap** (from the default 256-color bitmap) to create a smaller file and conserve space on the floppy disk. Click **Save.** Click **Yes** to replace the file.

➤ Click the **Close button** to close Paint and return to the Explorer.

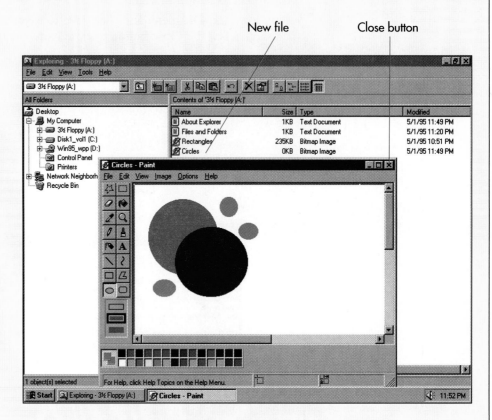

(c) Create a Drawing (step 4)

FIGURE 13 Hands-on Exercise 4 (continued)

STEP 5: Create the Folders

➤ If necessary, click the **icon** for **drive A** in the left pane of the Explorer window. Drive A should contain four files as shown in Figure 13d (the folders have not yet been created).

➤ Pull down the **File menu,** click (or point to) the **New command,** then click **Folder** as the type of object to create.

➤ The icon for a new folder will appear with the name of the folder (New Folder) highlighted. Type **Documents** to change the name of the folder. Press **enter.**

➤ Click the **icon** for **drive A** in the left pane. Pull down the **File menu.** Click (or point to) the **New command.** Click **Folder** as the type of object to create.

➤ The icon for a new folder will appear with the name of the folder (New Folder) highlighted. Type **Drawings** to change the name of the folder. Press **enter.** The right pane should now contain four documents and two folders.

➤ Pull down the **View menu.** Click (or point to) the **Arrange Icons command** to display a submenu, then click the **By Name command.**

➤ Click the **plus sign** next to drive A to expand the drive. Your screen should match Figure 13d:

- The left pane shows the subordinate folders on drive A.
- The right pane displays the contents of drive A (the selected object in the left pane). The folders are shown first and appear in alphabetical order. The document names are displayed after the folders and are also in alphabetical order.

Contents of drive A

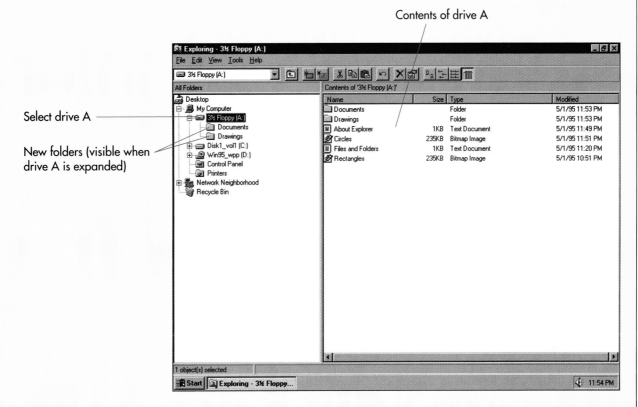

(d) Create the Folders (step 5)

FIGURE 13   Hands-on Exercise 4 (continued)

STEP 6: Move the Files

➤ This step has you move the Notepad documents and Paint drawings to the Documents and Drawings folders, respectively.

➤ To move the About Explorer document:

- Point to the **icon** for **About Explorer** in the right pane. Use the **right mouse button** to click and drag the icon to the Documents folder in the left pane.
- Release the mouse to display the menu shown in Figure 13e. Click **Move Here** to move the file. A popup window will appear briefly as the file is being moved.

Right click and drag About Explorer to Documents folder

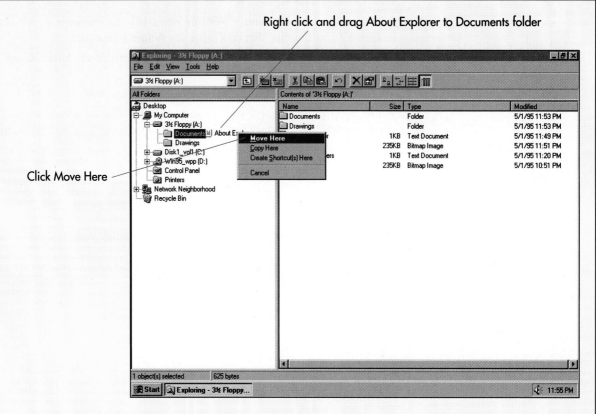

Click Move Here

(e) Move the Files (step 6)

FIGURE 13   Hands-on Exercise 4 (continued)

➤ To prove that the file has been moved, you can view the contents of the Documents folder:

 • Click the **Documents folder** in the left pane to select the folder. The icon for the Documents folder changes to an open folder and its contents (About Explorer) are displayed in the right pane.

➤ Move the Files and Folders document to the Documents folder:

 • Click the **icon** for **drive A** to select the drive and display its contents.

 • Point to the **icon** for **Files and Folders.** Use the **right mouse button** to click and drag the icon to the Documents folder in the left pane.

 • Release the mouse to display a menu. Click **Move Here** to move the file.

➤ Use the **right mouse button** to move the Circles and Rectangles files to the Drawings folder.

STEP 7: Copy the Contents of the Documents Folder

➤ This step has you copy the contents of the Documents folder on drive A to the Homework folder on drive C. Click (select) the **Documents folder** on drive A to open the folder and display its contents as shown in Figure 13f.

➤ Click the **plus sign** next to the icon for drive C to expand the drive and display its folders. You should see the Homework folder that was created in the first exercise. Do *not* click the folder on drive C as the Documents folder on drive A is to remain open.

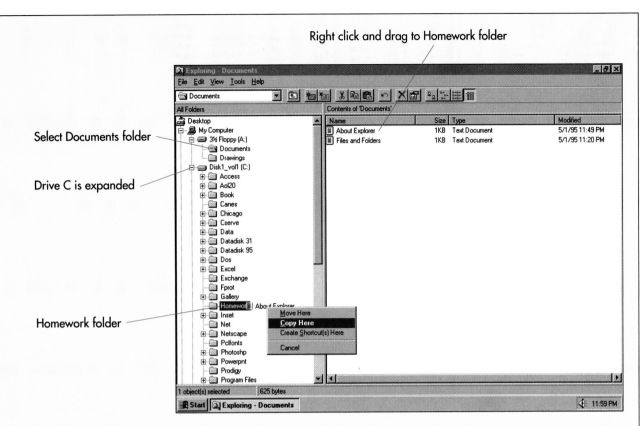

Right click and drag to Homework folder

Select Documents folder

Drive C is expanded

Homework folder

(f) Copy to Drive C (step 7)

FIGURE 13   Hands-on Exercise 4 (continued)

➤ Point to the **About Explorer file** (in the Documents folder on drive A). Use the **right mouse button** to click and drag the icon to the Homework folder on drive C. Release the mouse. Click **Copy Here** to copy the file to the Homework folder.

➤ Point to the **Files and Folders file** (in the Documents folder on drive A). Use the **right mouse button** to click and drag the icon to the Homework folder on drive C. Release the mouse. Click **Copy Here.**

➤ You will see a dialog box asking whether you want to replace the Files and Folders file that is already in the Homework folder (from the previous hands-on exercise). Click **No** since the files are the same.

OPEN FOLDERS QUICKLY

Click in the left pane of the Explorer window, then type any letter to select (open) the first folder whose name begins with that letter. If you type two letters in quick succession—for example, W and O—you will open the first folder beginning with the letters W and O. Pausing between the letters—that is, typing W, then leisurely typing O—will open a folder beginning with W, then open a second folder (while closing the first) whose name begins with O.

STEP 8: Copy the Contents of the Drawings Folder

➤ This step has you copy the contents of the Drawings folder on drive A to the Homework folder on drive C. Click (select) the **Drawings folder** on drive A to open the folder and display its contents. You should see the Circles and Rectangles files that were moved to this folder in the previous step.

➤ Click the **icon** for the **Circles file,** then press and hold the **Ctrl key** as you click the **icon** for the **Rectangles file** to select both files.

➤ Point to either of the selected files, then click the **right mouse button** as you drag both files to the Homework folder on drive C. Release the mouse. Click **Copy Here** to copy the files to the Homework folder.

➤ Explorer will begin to copy both files. You will, however, see a dialog box asking whether you want to replace the Rectangles file that is already in the Homework folder (from the previous hands-on exercise). Click **No** since the files are the same.

SELECT MULTIPLE FILES

You can perform the same operation on multiple files at the same time by selecting the files prior to executing the command. Press and hold the Ctrl key as you click the icon of each additional file you want to select. If the files are adjacent to one another, click the icon of the first file, then press and hold the Shift key as you click the icon of the last file.

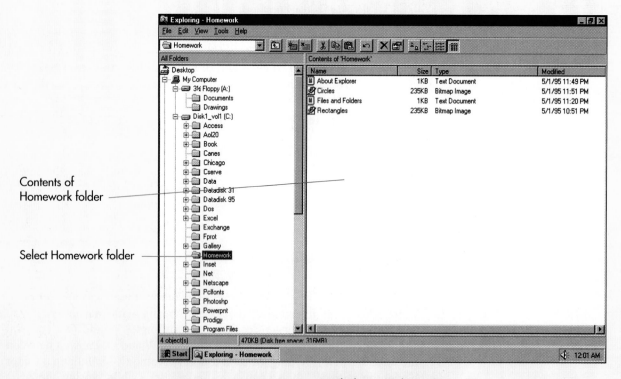

Contents of Homework folder

Select Homework folder

(g) Check Your Work (step 9)

FIGURE 13   Hands-on Exercise 4 (continued)

> STEP 9: Check Your Work

> ➤ Select (click) the **Homework folder** on drive C to display its contents.

> ➤ The icon changes to an open folder, and you should see the four files in Figure 13g.

> ➤ Click the **Close button** to close Explorer. Click the **Start button.** Click the **Shut Down** command to exit Windows.

SUMMARY

All Windows operations take place on the desktop. The Start button, as its name suggests, is where you begin. Online help is accessed by clicking the Help command from the Start button. The mouse is essential to Windows and has four basic actions: pointing, clicking (with the left or right button), double clicking, and dragging. The mouse pointer assumes different shapes according to the nature of the current action.

Every window contains the same basic elements, which include a title bar, a Minimize button, a Maximize or Restore button, and a Close button. Other elements that may be present include a menu bar, vertical and/or horizontal scroll bars, a status bar, and a toolbar. All windows may be moved and sized.

A dialog box supplies information needed to execute a command. Option buttons indicate mutually exclusive choices, one of which must be chosen. Check boxes are used if the choices are not mutually exclusive or if an option is not required. A text box supplies descriptive information. A (drop-down or open) list box displays multiple choices, any of which may be selected. A tabbed dialog box provides access to multiple sets of options.

The first (often only) floppy drive on a system is designated as drive A. The first (often only) hard disk is drive C regardless of whether there are one or two floppy drives. Additional hard drives and/or the CD-ROM drive are labeled from D on.

A file name can contain up to 255 characters in length and may include spaces and other punctuation. Files are stored in folders to better organize the hundreds (or thousands) of files on a disk. A folder may contain program files, data files, and/or other folders.

The most basic way to locate a specific file or folder is to use My Computer, which opens a new window for each successive folder. The Windows Explorer is a more sophisticated tool that displays a hierarchical view of the entire system in a single window.

The Delete command deletes (removes) a file from a disk. If, however, the file was deleted from a hard disk, it is not really gone, but moved instead to the Recycle Bin from where it can be subsequently recovered.

The result of dragging a file icon from one folder to another depends on whether the folders are on the same or different drives. Dragging the file to a folder on the same drive moves the file. Dragging the file to a folder on a different drive copies the file. It's easier, therefore, to click and drag with the right mouse button to produce a menu from which you can select the operation.

KEY WORDS AND CONCEPTS

Backup	Click	Command button
Check box	Close button	Contents tab

Control Panel

Copy command

Cut command

Data file

Delete command

Desktop

Details view

Dialog box

Dimmed command

Double click

Drag

Drop-down list box

Ellipsis

File

File type

Folder

Help command

Horizontal scroll bar

Icons

Index tab

Large Icons view

List box

Maximize button

Menu bar

Minimize button

Mouse pointer

Move a window

My Computer

Network Neighborhood

New command

Online help

Open list box

Option buttons

Paste command

Point

Printers folder

Program file

Properties

Pull-down menu

Recycle Bin

Rename command

Restore button

Right click

Size a window

Small Icons View

Start button

Status bar

Submenu

Tabbed dialog box

Taskbar

Text box

Title bar

Toolbar

Vertical scroll bar

What's This button

Windows Explorer

Windows 95

INDEX